Administrative Procedures
for the **Canadian Office**

Tenth Edition

Administrative Procedures
for the **Canadian Office**

Tenth Edition

Lauralee Kilgour
Northern Alberta Institute of
Technology

Edward Kilgour
Management Support
& Services (MSS)

Marie Rutherford
Georgian College

Sharon C. Burton
Brookhaven College

Nelda J. Shelton
Tarrant County College

 Pearson

Pearson Canada Inc., 26 Prince Andrew Place, North York, Ontario M3C 2H4.

9780133951646

1   20

Library and Archives Canada Cataloguing in Publication

Kilgour, Lauralee, 1953-, author
   Administrative procedures for the Canadian office / Lauralee Kilgour
[and four others].—Tenth edition.
Includes bibliographical references.
ISBN 978-0-13-395164-6 (softcover)

   1. Office practice—Textbooks. 2. Office procedures—Textbooks.
3. Textbooks. I. Title.

HF5547.5.K54 2018   651.3'74   C2018-904271-0

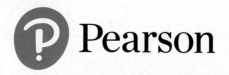

To all my students, past and present, for providing the inspiration to undertake this endeavour for a second time. A special thanks to my husband, Ray, my mother, Maureen, and my son, Christopher, for your encouragement and patience.
Finally, thanks to my colleague Janette O'Neill-Scott for providing a remarkable scope of insight driven for continual improvement.

— Marie Rutherford

Brief Contents

PART I   The Working Environment   1

Introduction A Career as an Office Professional   1

Chapter 1   Human Relations   12

Chapter 2   Diversity and International Business Relations   33

Chapter 3   Management of Work, Time, and Resources   48

Chapter 4   Research and Reference Sources   71

Chapter 5   Organization Structure and Office Layout   85

PART II   Office Services   99

Chapter 6   Front-Line Reception   99

Chapter 7   Office Technology   127

Chapter 8   Web Tools and Security   145

Chapter 9   Incoming and Outgoing Mail   158

Chapter 10 Project Management   191

Chapter 11 Information Management   203

Chapter 12 Travel Arrangements   235

Chapter 13 Meetings, Events, and Conferences   253

Chapter 14 Business Communication   278

Chapter 15 Office Commerce and Record Keeping   314

PART III   The Future of the Administrative Professional   334

Chapter 16 Employment Strategies   334

Chapter 17 Professional Development   373

Appendix   385
Glossary   387
Index   393

Contents

Preface *xvii*

Acknowledgements *xix*

PART I The Working Environment 1

Introduction A Career as an Office Professional 1

LEARNING OUTCOMES 1

Introduction 2

Workplace Trends 2

   COMPANY PROFILE Fidelity Investments Canada 3

Multidimensional Communication 4

Employability 5

Employment Profiles 6

   Administrative Assistant (AA) 6

   Executive Assistant (EA) 6

   Personal Assistant (PA) 7

   Legal and Medical Assistants 7

Digital Age 7

Employment Outlook 7

Next Step 7

What You Will Learn 7

Questions for Study and Review 8

Key Terms 8

Everyday Ethics 8

Problem Solving 8

Special Reports 9

Production Challenges 9

Weblinks 10

References 11

1 Human Relations 12

LEARNING OUTCOMES 12

Overview of Human Resources Management (HRM) 13

Business Organization Types 14

Skills for Relationship Building 14

   GRADUATE PROFILE Stephanie Pilon 15

Developing Interpersonal Skills 16

   Be a Team Player 16

   Avoid Nonproductive Team Behaviours 18

   Recognize Individual Differences 18

   Manage People and Personalities 18

   Teach Others 19

   Offer Exceptional Customer Service 20

   Exercise Leadership 20

   Negotiate Effectively 20

   Embrace Constructive Criticism 20

   Keep Confidential Information Confidential 21

   Be Considerate 21

   Be Sociable 22

Developing Personal Qualities 22

   Be Responsible 22

   Be Dependable 22

   Be a Self-Starter 22

   Develop Positive Self-Esteem 23

   Exhibit Self-Management 23

   Display Integrity/Honesty 23

   Remember to Always Project a Professional Image 23

Office Politics 24

   Recognize Office Politics 24

   Good or Bad? 24

Workplace Ethics 25

   Ethical Practice 25

   Work, Time, and Resources 25

Change in the Workplace 26

   Change Is Constant 26

   Adapt to New Management 26

Managing Stress 27

   Wellness in the Workplace 27

   What Causes Stress in the Office? 27

   Stress Management 27

Social Skills 28

   Keep Personal Relationships Private 28

   Let's Do Lunch! 29

Questions for Study and Review 30

Key Terms 30

Everyday Ethics 31

Problem Solving 31

Special Reports 31

Production Challenges 32

Weblinks 32

References 32

2 Diversity and International Business Relations 33

LEARNING OUTCOMES 33

Diversity and Equity 34

   Diversity in the Workplace 34

   COMPANY PROFILE SaskPower Corporation Regina Saskatchewan 36

   Understanding the Benefits of Diversity 36

Human Rights and Equity Standards 37

Discriminatory Workplace Protections and Employer Obligations 38

Developing Diversity Consciousness 38

Cultural Competence and Awareness 38

Cross-Cultural Competence 39

Developing Cultural Awareness 39

Guidelines for Cross-Cultural Encounters 39

Diversity in the Global Business Environment 40

Time Management Perception 40

Interpersonal Communication in the Global Market 40

Managing International Client Relations 41

Working on International Teams 42

Working in a Foreign Country 42

Hosting International Visitors 43

Questions for Study and Review 44

Key Terms 45

Everyday Ethics 45

Problem Solving 45

Special Reports 46

Production Challenges 46

Weblinks 46

References 47

3 Management of Work, Time, and Resources 48

LEARNING OUTCOMES 48

COMPANY PROFILE Fluid Life 49

Leadership and Management 49

Management Process and Theories 50

Total Quality of Management 50

Management by Objectives 52

Effectiveness and Efficiency 52

Time Management 52

Establish Efficient Work Habits 52

Take Charge of Your Time 53

Learn the Job 53

Take Time to Think 54

Assign Priorities 54

Adopt a Flexible Plan 56

Manage Details 57

Work at One Task at a Time 58

Start the Day with a Difficult Task 58

Group Similar Tasks 58

Avoid Procrastination 59

Build Relaxation into Your Schedule 59

Do It Right the First Time 60

Prepare in Advance 60

Complete a Task 61

Managing Interruptions 61

Excuse Me! 62

Make a Daily Plan 62

Operate within Easy Reach 63

Office Organization 63

Organize the Office Supplies 63

Organize the Workstation 64

Nontraditional Work Arrangements 65

Flextime 65

Job Sharing 65

Remote Office 65

Environmental Management 66

Environmentally Sustainable Office 66

Questions for Study and Review 67

Key Terms 67

Everyday Ethics 67

Problem Solving 68

Special Reports 68

Production Challenges 69

Weblinks 70

4 Research and Reference Sources 71

LEARNING OUTCOMES 71

Research and Development (R&D) 72

COMPANY PROFILE Bombardier Aerospace and Rail Transportations 72

Sources of Information 73

Common Types of Business Research 73

Business Research Methods 73

Libraries Support and Assistance 74

Selecting a Reference Database 75

Search Engines 75

Evaluating Website Content 76

Quick Sources of References 76

Books in Print 76

Almanacs and Yearbooks 76

Dictionaries, Encyclopedias, and Atlases 76

Biographical Information 77

Financial Information 77

Etiquette Books and Quotation Sources 77

Periodical and Newspaper Indexes 78

Canadian Government Publications 78

Directories 79

Plagiarism 79

Recognition and Avoidance 79

Referencing Styles 80

Office Manuals 81

Questions for Study and Review 82

Key Terms 82

Everyday Ethics 82

Problem Solving 83

Production Challenges 83

Weblinks 84

5 Organization Structure and Office Layout 85

LEARNING OUTCOMES 85

Organization Structures 86
Building Blocks of Organizational Structures 87
Classifications of Authority 87
COMPANY PROFILE MNP 88
Management Styles 89
Organization Charts 90
Organizational Linkages and Value 90
Informal Organizations 90

Office Plan 91
Closed Office Layout 91
Arrangement of the Open Office 91
Decor 92
High-Tech Office and Workstation Design 92

Ergonomics 92
Furniture 93
Lighting 93
Acoustics 93
Position and Posture 94

Questions for Study and Review 95
Key Terms 96
Everyday Ethics 96
Problem Solving 96
Special Reports 97
Production Challenges 97
Weblinks 98

PART II Office Services 99

6 Front-Line Reception 99

LEARNING OUTCOMES 99

Reception Design and Layout 100
GRADUATE PROFILE Devika Bala 101

Virtual Receptionists 101
Digital Assistants 102
Who Uses a VR? 102

Visitor Management Systems 102

Additional Reception Tools 103
Telecommunications 103
Phone Communication Skills 103
Using Voice Mail 104
Using Phone Directories 109
Placing Local Calls 109
Placing Domestic Long-Distance Calls 109
Placing International Calls 112
Phone Equipment 112

Appointment Management 112
Scheduling Appointments 113
Using Electronic Calendars 114
Using Paper Calendars 115
Making Entries in Calendars 115
Changing Appointments 116

Greeting Visitors 116
Immediate Attention 116
Preparing for Visitors 117
Introductions 117
Terminating a Meeting 118
Refusing Appointments 118

Handling Difficult Customers 119
Difficult Callers 119
Unwanted Visitors 119
Complaining Customers 119
Abusive Customers 120
Tips for Success 120

Managing Diverse Situations 120
Visitors and Language Barriers 120
Visitors with Special Needs 121

Ethics and Visitors 122

Questions for Study and Review 122
Key Terms 123
Everyday Ethics 123
Problem Solving 123
Special Reports 124
Production Challenges 124
Weblinks 126

7 Office Technology 127

LEARNING OUTCOMES 127

Computer Resources and Digital Devices 128
Types of Computers 128
COMPANY PROFILE Google 128
Computer Basic Functions 130
Networking Computers 131

Computers in the Office 132
The Versatile Computer 132
Artificial Intelligence (AI) 132
Artificial Intelligence Apps 132
Augmented Reality (AR) 133
Computer Troubleshooting 133
Accuracy of Input Information 134
Using Computer Storage 134

Application Programs 135
Word Processing 135
Spreadsheets 136
Desktop Publishing 136
Presentation Software 137
Integrating Application Software 137
Increasing Your Productivity 137

Phone Technology 138
Interconnect Equipment 138
Wireless Phones 138
Phone Messages 139

The Web 139
  Internet Networking 139
  Uses for the Internet 139
Using Reprographics 140
  Copiers 140
  How to Select a Copier 141

Questions for Study and Review 142
Key Terms 142
Everyday Ethics 143
Problem Solving 143
Special Reports 143
Production Challenges 144
Weblinks 144

8 Web Tools and Security 145

LEARNING OUTCOMES 145
Benefits of Web Presence 146
Content Management Systems 146
  Capabilities of Content Management Systems 146
  Getting Connected 146
  COMPANY PROFILE Herjavec Group 147
  Methods of Connectivity 148
  Types of Networks 148
  Search Engines 148
Web Applications 149
  Web 1.0, 2.0, and 3.0 149
  Examples of Web Tools 150
  Web and Video Conferencing 150
  Webcasting 151
  Podcasting 151
  Webinars 151
  Web Usage in a Professional Setting 151
Data Security 152
  General Data Security Risks 152
  Methods of Cybersecurity Threats 153
  Maintaining Internet Security 154

Questions for Study and Review 155
Key Terms 156
Everyday Ethics 156
Problem Solving 156
Special Reports 157
Production Challenges 157
Weblinks 157

9 Incoming and Outgoing Mail 158

LEARNING OUTCOMES 158
Overview of Business Services Available from Canada Post 159
  GRADUATE PROFILE Vanessa McInnis 160
Handling Office Technology 160

Automated Mail Services—Email 160
Email Alternatives—Integrated Business Messaging Platforms 162
Facsimiles 162
Sending Money Electronically 163
Electronic Services 163
Electronic Post Office 165
Voice Mail 165
Handling Incoming Mail 165
  Sorting Mail 166
  Opening Mail 166
  Inspecting the Contents 166
  Date-Time Stamping Mail 166
  Reading and Annotating Mail 167
  Presenting Mail 168
Handling Packages, Publications Mail, and Advertising by Mail 168
  Distributing Mail 169
  Answering Mail in the Manager's Absence 171
Handling Outgoing Mail 172
  Types of Domestic Mail 172
  Supplemental Services 174
  Dangerous Goods 175
  U.S. and International Mail 175
  Other Delivery Options 176
  Proper Addressing 176
  Metered Mail 185
Exceptions 185
  Changing an Address 185
  Returning Undelivered Mail 186
  Refusing Mail 186
Ethical Issues Regarding Email 186
  International Holidays and Mail Service 187

Questions for Study and Review 187
Key Terms 188
Everyday Ethics 188
Problem Solving 188
Special Reports 189
Production Challenges 189
Weblinks 190

10 Project Management 191

LEARNING OUTCOMES 191
What Is Project Management? 192
Phases of Project Management 192
  COMPANY PROFILE Fusion Projects 193
The Project Team 194
  The Project Manager 194
  Administrative Professionals Duties and Core Skills 195
  Building the Project Team 196
  Certifications and Credentials 196

Project Management Tools   198
Tool Categories   198
Project Management Software and Apps   198
Problem Solving and Decision-Making Techniques   199

Questions for Study and Review   200
Key Terms   200
Everyday Ethics   200
Problem Solving   201
Special Reports   201
Production Challenges   201
Weblinks   202
References   202

11 Information Management   203

LEARNING OUTCOMES   203

Protecting Information   204
GRADUATE PROFILE Tracy Staunton   204
Privacy Legislation   205
Access to Information Guidelines   205
Personal Information   205
Canada's Anti-Spam Legislation (CASL)   205
Organizing Information   206
Preparation for Visible Filing   206
Techniques for Assembling Papers   209
Charge-Out Methods   209
Organization of Electronic Files   210
Benefits and Drawbacks of Electronic Filing   211
Ordering Supplies Online   211
Supplies for Visible Filing   211
Supplies for Electronic Filing   213
Storing Information   213
Storing Visible Documents   213
Storing Electronic Media   214
Storing Business Contact Information   214
Electronic Databases   214
Retaining and Transferring Records   215
Life Cycle of a Record   215
Paper Records Retention   215
Record Classification for Retention   216
Paper Records Transfer   216
Electronic Records Retention   217
Maintaining Records in Medical and Legal Offices   217
Disposing of Records   217
Alphabetic Filing Procedures   218
Primary Guides   218
Individual Name Folders   218
Miscellaneous Folders   218
Special Guides   218
Colour Coding   218
Alphabetic Filing Rules   219
Order of Filing Units   219
Rule 1—Basic Names   220
Rule 2—Symbols and Minor Words   220

Rule 3—Punctuation   221
Rule 4—Abbreviations and Single Letters   221
Rule 5—Titles and Suffixes   222
Rule 6—Prefixes   223
Rule 7—Numbers   223
Rule 8—Organizations and Institutions   224
Rule 9—Identical Names for People or Businesses   224
Rule 10—Government Names   225
Variations in Alphabetic Filing Rules   225
Other Filing Systems   226
Subject Filing   226
Geographic Filing   227
Numeric Filing   227
Ethical Issues in Records Management   229
International Standards in Records Management   229

Questions for Study and Review   229
Key Terms   230
Everyday Ethics   230
Problem Solving   230
Special Reports   231
Production Challenges   231
Weblinks   233

12 Travel Arrangements   235

LEARNING OUTCOMES   235

Planning the Trip   236
COMPANY PROFILE Travel Masters   236
Digital Travel Services   237
Travel Consultants and Agencies   237
Trip Information Needed   237
Arranging Travel   238
Air Travel   238
Car Rental Services   241
Hotel Reservations   241
Passports and Passport Substitutes   242
Visas   242
Immunization Requirements   243
Carry-On Luggage   243
Security   243
Following Through   244
Prior to the Trip   244
During the Manager's Absence   246
After the Manager Returns   247
Ethical Issues in Reporting Travel Expenses   247
Culture and International Travel   247

Questions for Study and Review   248
Key Terms   248
Everyday Ethics   249
Problem Solving   249
Special Reports   250
Production Challenges   250
Weblinks   252

13 Meetings, Events, and Conferences 253

LEARNING OUTCOMES 253

Conferences 254
    Defining and Branding the Conference 254
    Setting the Budget 254
    Gathering Request for Proposals 254
    Reviewing Room Setup and Seating Plans 255
    Organizing Food and Beverage 255
    Engaging Speakers and Entertainment 255
    Managing Technology 255
    Arranging Accommodations and Travel 255

Business Meetings 256
    Creating an Action Checklist 256
    COMPANY PROFILE Canadian Society of Professional Event
    Planners (CanSPEP) 256
    Arranging the Date and Time 257
    Reserving the Meeting Room 257
    Sending Notices 258
    Preparing the Agenda 258
    Planning for Supplies, Equipment, and Software 260
    Planning Refreshments and Food 260
    Assembling Materials 261
    Recording the Meeting 261
    Following Up 262
    Preparing Minutes 262

Team Meetings 265
    Preparation for the Meeting 265
    Roles of the Participants 266
    Off to a Good Start 267
    Brainstorming 268
    Nominal Group Technique 268
    Discussion and Solution 269
    Closure 269

Meeting Dynamics 270
    Poor Body Language 270
    Tardiness 270
    Being Unprepared 271
    Not Participating 271
    Being Rude 271
    Creating Solutions 271

Virtual Meetings 272
    Teleconferences 272
    Web Conferences 272
    Videoconferences 272

Ethical Behaviour in Meetings 273

International Conferencing 274

Questions for Study and Review 274
Key Terms 275
Everyday Ethics 275
Problem Solving 276
Special Reports 276
Production Challenges 276
Weblinks 277

14 Business Communication 278

LEARNING OUTCOMES 278

Interpersonal Communication 279
Verbal Communication 279
    COMPANY PROFILE Alectra Utilities 279
Nonverbal Communication 280
    Image 280
    Personal Space 281
    Eye Contact 281
    Posture 281
    Facial Expressions 281

Listening and Providing Feedback 282
    Active Listening 282
    Constructive Feedback 282

Public Speaking 283
    Be at Ease in the Spotlight 283
    Avoid Anxiety 284

Ethics in Public Speaking 285
Written Communication 285
Business Letters 285
    Communication Effectively 285
    Know Your Purpose 286
    Focus on the Reader 286
    Convey a Meaningful Message 286
    Establish an Appropriate Tone 288
    Develop a Natural Style 288

Types of Business Letters 289
    Favourable Letters 290
    Letters of Disappointment 291
    Persuasive Letters 292
    Correspondence for the Manager's Signature 293
    Correspondence for the Administrative Professional's
    Signature 293

Formats of Business Letters 296
    Organizational Document Style Guide 296
    Component of a Letter 296
    Full-Block Letter Style 297
    Modified-Block Letter Style 298

Classification of Reports 298
Informal Reports 299
    Letter Reports 299
    Short Internal Reports 300
    Email Reports 300

Formal Reports 301
    Guidelines for Formatting 301
    Preliminary Sections 305
    Supplementary Sections 305
    Guidelines for Composing the Report 307

Ethics in Writing 310
International Correspondence 310
    Addressing Envelopes 310
    Writing Letters 310

Questions for Study and Review   311
Key Terms   311
Everyday Ethics   312
Problem Solving   312
Special Reports   312
Production Challenges   313
Weblinks   313

15 Office Commerce and Record Keeping   314

LEARNING OUTCOMES   314

COMPANY PROFILE KPMG   315

ECommerce   316

Concerns with ECommerce   316
Web-Banking   317
Mobile Banking   317
Automated Teller Machines   317
Direct Payroll Deposit   317
Preauthorized Payment   317

Nonelectronic Transfers   318

Certified Cheque   318
Bank Draft   319
Money Order   319

Writing Cheques   319

Chequebooks and Cheque Forms   319
Rules for Writing Cheques   319
Stop-Payment Notification   320
Cash Withdrawals   321
Endorsing Cheques   321
Restrictive Endorsement   321
Blank Endorsement   321
Full Endorsement   321

Deposits   321

Preparing Deposits   322
Preparing the Deposit Slip   322
Depositing after Hours   322

Reconciling the Bank Statement with the Chequebook Balance   323

Adopt a Consistent Method   324
Prepare the Reconciliation Statement   324
Search for Errors   324
File Cancelled Cheques   325

Keeping Records   325

Petty Cash Fund   325
Payroll Processing   327
Office Supplies on Hand   328

Budget Preparation   328

Ethics in Accounting Procedures   330

International Currency Exchange   330

Questions for Study and Review   330
Key Terms   331
Everyday Ethics   331

Problem Solving   331
Special Reports   331
Production Challenges   332
Weblinks   333

PART III   The Future of the Administrative Professional   334

16 Employment Strategies   334

LEARNING OUTCOMES   334

Employability Skills   335

COMPANY PROFILE Office Team   335
Ready for Work   336
The Conference Board of Canada   336

Sources for Job Prospects   336

Networking   336
College Placement Office   338
Employment Fairs   338
Direct Application   338
Federal Government   339
Staffing Agencies   339
Job Search Boards and Search Engines   339
Prospects in Another Geographic Area   339

The Rebound: Bouncing Back   340

Becoming Eligible for Employment   340
Applying for Jobs   341

Résumés   341

Rules for Writing a Résumé   341
Competitive Résumés   342
The Education Section   342
Work Experience   343
Optional Sections   343
Skill Statements   343
Questions to Help Generate Your Accomplishments   344
Résumé Styles   344
Top Five Dos and Don'ts for Résumés   344
References   350
Appearance of the Résumé   350
Emailed Résumés   352
Electronically Submitted Résumés   352
Electronically Scanned Résumés   352
Résumé Reminders   352

Application/Cover Letters   354

The Prospecting Letter   354
The Solicited Letter   354
Appearance of the Application Letter   357
Application/Cover Letter Guidelines   357
Application Forms   357

Job Interviews   358

Preparing before the Job Interview   358
Preparing Portfolios   360

Preparing to Go to the Interview   360
Conducting Yourself During the Interview   362
Preparing for the Second Interview   364
Following Up after the Interview   364
Ethical Issues in the Job Search   366
International Employment   367

Questions for Study and Review   369
Key Terms   369
Everyday Ethics   370
Problem Solving   370
Special Reports   370
Production Challenges   371
Weblinks   372

17 Professional Development   373
LEARNING OUTCOMES   373
Challenge Traditional Stereotypes   374
Develop a Professional Image   374
Prepare for Advancement and Demonstrate Value   374
Learn from a Mentor   374
GRADUATE PROFILE Daryan Coryat   375

Advance by Education   376
Join a Professional Association   377
Increase Technical Certification   378
Cross-Train   378
Become a Supervisor   378
Know What It Takes   378
Prepare to Be an Office Manager   379
Continue to Develop Professionally   380
Contemporary Office Professional   380
Get Started on Your Career Path   380
Commit to Your Values and Ethics   381
Create an Ethical Climate   382

Questions for Study and Review   382
Key Terms   382
Everyday Ethics   382
Problem Solving   383
Special Reports   383
Weblinks   384

Appendix   385
Glossary   387
Index   393

Preface

Welcome to the tenth edition of *Administrative Procedures for the Canadian Office*!

Administrative professionals are valued for their diverse technological, interpersonal, and process-driven skills. Organizations appreciate the wealth of these skills at a higher rate than ever seen before in the industry. An essential component of working in today's Canadian office is the ability to make critical business decisions, as the administrative professional is positioned as the eyes and ears of an organization. Excellent soft skills and a positive attitude are essential for career success in a diverse and global environment.

Revisions that appear in the tenth edition are reflective of developments in technology and the constantly evolving role of the administrative professional. The text expands its focus on emerging technologies and explores varied employability requirements. Introduced in this edition are human resource functions, equity standards, and management and leadership concepts. A greater emphasis is placed on diversity understanding, and the concepts surrounding organizational structure climate, and culture. Working in a global economy makes it essential for administrative professionals to develop knowledge of broad business practice. These additions facilitate greater competency and equip graduates to meet forthcoming challenges.

NEW FOR THIS EDITION

To keep up with new trends in business, new developments in technology, and new ways of looking at the world, the contemporary office is constantly changing. Specific chapters have changed order for improved flow and conceptual learning. To showcase Canadian office settings, this edition includes company profiles of various organizations across the country. The tenth edition includes the addition and/or expansion of numerous topics. The major changes are listed as follows:

- Workplace trends and employability of core competencies (Introduction)
- Human resource concepts highlight organizational culture, climate, and behaviour (Chapter 1)
- The chapter has been renamed "Diversity and International Business Relations" and includes coverage related to age, gender, race, ethnic, and sexual orientation (Chapter 2)

- Management and leadership concepts (Chapter 3)
- The chapter has been renamed "Research and Reference Sources"; it includes research and development concepts (Chapter 4)
- Highlighted organizational linkage and value chain concepts (Chapter 5)
- "Front-Line Reception" has been moved to begin Part II for improved flow (Chapter 6)
- Artificial intelligence and augmented reality technology (Chapter 7)
- Web content management systems (Chapter 8)
- Project management roles and responsibilities (Chapter 10)
- Record life cycle (Chapter 11)
- Canada's Anti-Spam Legislation (CASL) (Chapter 11)
- Travel for business best practices (Chapter 12)
- Conference planning; requests for proposals, budgets, and branding an event (Chapter 13)
- Organizational style guide format and concepts (Chapter 14)
- Expanded ecommerce learning and detailed payroll tables and requirements (Chapter 15)
- Exploring job search engines and enhanced job search documentation composition (Chapter 16)
- Updated professional development suggestions (Chapter 17)
- Updated chapter-specific, content-relevant material on the issue of ethics throughout the text
- Updated chapter-specific, content-relevant material on international business issues are included throughout the text
- Revised targeted learning objectives and end-of-chapter questions are in all chapters
- New Profile boxes include 13 Company Profiles and 5 Graduate Profiles
- List of key terms have been added to the end of each chapter
- Updated and new weblinks are at the end of each chapter

New to the Companion Website

- Video series for specific chapters in support of content exercises
- Interactive flash cards per chapter
- Gamification option for students of strategies to play to assist in understanding the chapter learning outcomes
- Opportunities to test yourself option at the end of each chapter
- Online course supplement of weblinks and relative online tools or resources to benefit students
- Working Papers for each chapter that students can apply what they have learned into exercises and discussion questions.

New to the Instructor's Manual

- Suggested teaching resources and strategies section for instructors that includes best practices for lecture delivery, exercises, or activities
- Suggested online tools to aid in teaching and student learning

New to the Test Bank

- New multiple choice, fill-in-the-blanks, matching, and short answer questions
- Essay style/capstone style alternative assessment, which is essential in theory-based practice

FEATURES

Administrative Procedures for the Canadian Office has many features to inspire students and help them learn, as well as support the instructor.

- Each chapter opens with a Profile box that focuses on a successful organization (Company Profile) or a graduate (Graduate Profile).
- The boxed **pro-Link** features professional tips on specific topics.
- **Self-Check** questions appear after short segments of text throughout the chapters, allowing students to evaluate their knowledge at appropriate intervals.
- **Questions for Study and Review** help students review the chapter's content.
- **Everyday Ethics** cases found in each chapter are excellent for class discussion and give students an opportunity to evaluate their personal and professional moral codes of conduct. The cases explore ethical and moral judgments and pose light problem-solving questions to help students improve their decision-making skills.
- **Problem Solving** cases encourage students to think critically and develop their problem-solving and decision-making skills.
- **Special Reports** provide the opportunity for more in-depth research into particular topics.
- The practical exercises provided in the **Production Challenges** encourage students to apply the knowledge they have gained. Many Challenges refer to **Working Papers**; these are provided on the redeveloped and enhanced companion website.
- A list of updated and expanded **weblinks** at the end of each chapter leads students to further explore the ideas presented within the text and to learn independently.
- Throughout the text, **key terms** are highlighted in boldface. These boldfaced terms are included at the end of each chapter and in the **Glossary** at the back of the book.
- The Appendix introduces students to a list of **Common Proofreaders' Marks**.

Acknowledgements

The publisher and authors would like to thank Devika Bala, Daryan Coryat, Vanessa McInnis, Stephanie Pilon, and Tracey Staunton for contributing to the new Graduate Profiles featured in this edition.

Special thanks to my colleagues who provided their feedback, expertise, and guidance through the development of this edition:

Janette O'Neill-Scott
Professor
Georgian College

Pat Roberts
Career Consultant
Co-operative Education and Career Success
Georgian College

Sheila Musgrove
Calgary, Alberta

Thanks are also due to the following reviewers who provided valuable feedback that helped shape the tenth edition:

Jim Benedek
Fanshawe College

Nancy Breen
Nova Scotia Community College

Rhonda Burns
Niagara College

Janet Chee
Vancouver Community College

Cathy Goodwin

Kellie Hayward
Sheridan Institute of Technology and Advanced Learning

Doug McLean
Vancouver Island University

Amy Peltonen
Sault College

Brenda Ridgeley-Ketchell
Okanagan College

Melinda Vanzanten
St. Lawrence College

Sheree Wright

Introduction
A Career as an Office Professional

G-stockstudio/ShutterStock

LEARNING OUTCOMES

After completion of this chapter, the student will be able to:

1 Describe workplace trends influencing the administrative professional's role.

2 Explain what employability encompasses.

3 Differentiate between three employability skill groups as categorized by the Conference Board of Canada.

4 Recite core competencies of administrative professionals.

5 Explore channels of communication and communication protocol.

6 Explain how the Digital Age has affected the role of the office professional.

7 Summarize the employment outlook for the administrative office professional.

8 Review the textbook to locate pertinent information for learning.

INTRODUCTION

The office of today is constantly evolving. Businesses offer their services to clients around the world as well as to the online global marketplace. With core competencies such as software expertise, office administrators provide foundational structure to ensure tasks are managed effectively and efficiently. The administrative office professional's role routinely involves understanding and implementing management's priorities. The variable nature of the office environment means that an administrative professional needs to be prepared and flexible to adapt to organizational changes. Many employment opportunities require an advanced skill set in specific areas such as technology, human resources, and business processes. Knowledge of business principles, superior interpersonal skills, and an intuitive understanding of organizational needs provide an industry related human element. The proactive approach of the administrative professional often sets the tone and culture of an organization.

Employers seek well-rounded administrative professionals. They require professionals who have initiative and can keep pace with the ever-shifting demands and increasing workflow of the contemporary workplace.

WORKPLACE TRENDS

Here is a description of current workplace trends influencing the office professional's role:

1. **Automated office tasks.** Technology enables offices to automate many tasks and procedures. The level of skill and responsibility is consistently evolving. Administrative professionals use sophisticated office management software to coordinate a myriad of tasks. They manage people as deftly as they handle technology. The gap between management functions and administrative responsibilities is narrowing due to the broad skill capability, automated processes, and the enhanced knowledge base of the office professional.

2. **Data analytics (DA).** Business offices rely on data to understand customer needs and interactions. Data analytics (DA) is the process of examining data sets in order to draw conclusions about the information they contain—increasingly, this is achieved with the aid of specialized systems and software. Social media and websites are fundamental platforms for businesses to interact with customers. Analytics gained from such interactions help businesses decide how to improve marketing and customer service; this is referred to as **business intelligence (BI)**. Data literacy will become an essential skill moving forward. Administrative professionals often source the analytics used in this capacity.

3. **Immersive technology.** This technology distorts the line between the physical world and digital or simulated world, thereby creating a sense of immersion. Technological advancements allow personnel located in other parts of the world to attend the same meeting and conferences virtually, which has changed the face of business. This technology is often referred to as **augmented reality**. Augmented reality has the capability to transform global business initiatives.

4. **Online tools mobilization.** Businesses use intranets, apps, emails, and video-enabled calls to communicate with employees and clients across departments and locations. For example, internal and external business announcements are often made through social media, as the organization's personnel are readily accessible using mobile and smart devices. The ever-increasing use of mobile devices provides an opportunity for many online communication solutions. Many businesses are already taking advantage of online technologies because of easy implementation and reduced cost. Real-time communication provides an enhanced business communication solution as compared to on-site systems. The administrative professional is often responsible for maintaining and updating these communication vessels as well as promoting business-related activities. It often involves handling customer/client feedback—a crucial task, since responding effectively can help to preserve a company's positive reputation.

5. **Cross-functional teamwork.** This is best described as a group of people within an organization with different functional expertise working towards a common goal. It may include administrative personnel from Finance, Marketing, Operations, and Human Resource departments. Typically, it includes employees from all levels of an organization. Administrative office professionals are team members whose skills are categorically essential to the operation of the business. The role of an administrative professional is moving from a generalist role to a specialized one, so advanced technical training and human relations competencies are paramount. The administrative professional is a contributing team member who makes valuable business and leadership decisions within the realm of their authority.

6. **Flexible work scheduling.** Work hours have converted to a flexible approach. The concept of working 9 a.m. to 5 p.m. Monday to Friday is disappearing. With remote access and globalization, many office professionals perform some of their responsibilities from their home base.

Fidelity Investments Canada

Ken Wolter/Shutterstock

Fidelity Investments Canada is a multinational portfolio management company first established in Canada in 1987 with major hiring locations in Toronto, Montreal, Calgary, and Vancouver.

Fidelity Canada is focused on helping their employees strike a balance between their work and private lives. It offers a number of alternative work arrangements, including flexible hours, telecommuting, a shortened workweek option, and reduced summer hours. The company also participates in the Partners for Mental Health's "Not Myself Today" awareness campaign. This campaign promotes protecting the mental health of employees as critically important. Fidelity Canada recognizes that a mentally healthy workforce is good for business as it can enhance performance and lower costs associated with disability and absenteeism. Fidelity Canada recently increased its support for employees who are new mothers and fathers (including adoptive parents), offering maternity and parental leave top-up payments of up to 100% of salary for up to 25 weeks (an increase from 17 weeks)—and provides the option to extend their leave into an unpaid leave of absence.

Workplace atmosphere features in the Toronto office include an employee lounge with various amenities such as comfortable seating, music, television, board games, and table tennis. Vending machines have healthy options. Healthy alternative snacks and meals are provided when employees are required to work through lunch or overtime. An on-site fitness facility is a shared use facility with subsidized membership, treadmills, stationary bikes, and instructor-led fitness classes.

Fidelity Canada invites employees to share in the company's success with profit sharing and offers a full array of additional financial benefits, including signing bonuses and year-end bonuses.

This organization is also recognized for investing in employee career growth and development, as Fidelity Canada prides itself on fostering a culture of continuous learning and continuous improvement. The company provides professional development by investing in employee training and through mentorship, project work, and networking. Fidelity also has a Mentor Match program. In addition to traditional mentoring, where a senior manager advises a junior employee, Fidelity's program includes reverse mentoring, where younger employees mentor executives.

Fidelity has a number of employee resource groups, which speaks to its commitment to diversity and inclusion. These groups include Pride for LGBTQ staff, Aspire for Black and Latino, a women's leadership group, and, most recently, Enable for recognition of varying abilities. These initiatives are employee-driven communities for sharing ideas and diverse experiences. For instance, the Aspire group partners with Junior Achievement to teach financial literacy to elementary children. Fidelity values the cross-organization networking it makes possible.

In recent times, Fidelity was selected as one of Canada's Top 100 Employers for 2018 based on its employee and family focus as announced by MediaCorp Inc. on November 7, 2017, the full listing is found at http://www.canadastop100. com/national/.

Flexible time work schedules often fit well for parents who want to shift their working day to meet family needs. The mode of working from home and having flexible hours means that employees have become managers of their own time. Self-discipline for these office professionals is an essential skill.

7. **Creative collaboration.** Companies increasingly recognize the importance of collaboration. Organizations look for ways to foster it utilizing their cross-departmental teams and administrative professionals play a significant role in efforts to boost collaboration. Creative collaboration begins with welcoming input, sharing ideas, and valuing the diversity that everyone has something special to bring to the table.

8. **Entrepreneurial and short-term work focus.** Entrepreneurship is the mindset to see opportunity everywhere. It could be a business idea and the ability to see the bigger picture. Office professionals have the opportunity

to be entrepreneurial in their approach. Settling into long-term employment with benefits and eventual retirement used to be a standard employment staple, but now more short-term contracts exist. According to CBC News Business, "contract work has surged. With the number of Canadians aged 25 to 54 in temporary work growing nearly six times faster than overall employment" (CBC NEWS, 2016). In order to thrive, the administrative professionals must be constantly ready for change, in search of new assignments, and ready to upgrade technical expertise. Fortunately, the skills of an administrative professional lend themselves to an entrepreneurial approach, in terms of opening their own businesses that offer office support to individuals or corporations.

9. **Employee engagement.** This is not the same as employee satisfaction. Engagement is the extent to which employees feel passionate about their jobs and are committed to the organization. It is a place where people want to work. Employers seek to build a constituency of engaged employees by promoting a top-down transparency, providing updates, being consistent, and demonstrating the value of the employee simply by saying thank you. In a recent Robert Half study, surveying 12,000 professionals in North America, research revealed that, on a scale of one to five, admins ranked four in their level of happiness (Half, 2017).

10. **Corporate social responsibility (CSR).** Social and environmental issues are continuing to gain greater focus. Companies are examining their business practices and looking for ways to give back to their communities and to protect the environment. Involvement in community projects, fundraisers, and green-based initiatives is now critical for promoting a strong corporate image. Employees want to engage in CSR initiatives at the office and sophisticated initiatives and experiences beyond a one-day service or matching donation. Employees want to be immersed into the experiences and find personal meaning from these activities (Triple Pundit, 2016).

11. **Work–life balance.** Businesses are encouraging employees to achieve a better balance between work and life. Businesses no longer reward those that put in the extra time to get projects done. Instead, there is an emphasis on leaving work when you are supposed to at the end of the day and taking enough breaks as well as using up your vacation time. Some companies provide employees with portable wireless tools, giving them greater control over their work schedules. This, in turn, enables employees to balance and prioritize work and personal commitments. The lines between work and life are more integrated because professionals can perform many tasks at home during what can be considered personal time.

The future is bright, and the opportunities are infinite. Office professionals should always be looking for new opportunities, responsibilities, and possibilities.

MULTIDIMENSIONAL COMMUNICATION

Workplace communication is critical to an organization's ability to be productive and operate effectively. Communication channels, which are the various methods an organization elects to use to facilitate and maintain information flow. In an organization, several considerations related to the various channels is key to ensure messages are transmitted as well as understood. Communication strategies within an organization can prove challenging with multi-layered levels and multiple issues. When all components of an organization communicate easily, it will benefit with improved workflow and, by extension, the organization can build a stronger enterprise with greater resilience. An administrative professional's role involves interaction with employers, staff, and clients. Most administrative positions involve written communications involving letter, report, and memo writing, preparing material for the company website, or communicating via email. The ability to write clearly, accurately, and professionally is constant.

The following are examples of communication channels:

1. Face-to-face or personal communication is one of the preeminent channels of communication used within an organization. Physical presence, the tone of the speaker's voice, and facial expressions help recipients of a message interpret a message as the speaker intends. This is the best channel to use for complex messages because it permits for interaction between speaker and recipients to clarify uncertainty. The narrator can appraise whether a listener has received the message as planned and ask or answer follow-up questions.

2. Electronic communication channels include email, internet, intranet, and social media platforms. This channel is used for one-on-one, group, or mass communication. It is a less personal method of communication but more efficient. When using this channel, care is considered to compose messages with clarity and to avoid ambiguity.

3. Mobile communication channels are used when a private or intricate message is conveyed to an individual or small group. These communications methodologies can include online and video conferencing

modalities. A mobile channel allows for an interactive exchange. Some may well elect to use this channel versus a face-to-face channel to save on the time and effort it takes to organize face-to-face gatherings.

4. Written communication is suitable when a message does not require interaction while necessitating communication to an employee or group. Procedures, letters, memos, manuals, notices, and announcements are all message examples that work well for this channel. Recipients may follow up through an electronic or face-to-face channel if questions arise.

5. Various media channels are utilized to reach a wide audience range and to deliver a broad scope of information to people within and outside the organization.

The following are examples of strategic communication benefits:

1. **Relationships.** Solid communication is crucial to building relationships between all levels of employees, both on a professional and social level. An environment of open communication makes it welcoming for employees to express their concepts and concerns. Communication averts employees from feeling secluded, builds teamwork, and creates a more collegial atmosphere in the office. When relationships are strong, employees are better able to trust one another and work together more effectively.

2. **Trust.** Open and clear communication can create a sense of transparency in an organization. Keeping employees in the dark can result in resentments, tension, and a feeling of compromised job security. Strong communication can help employees feel valued and trusted.

3. **Clarity.** In organizations, uncertainty can create a tense environment. Ensure roles and responsibilities are clear to employees and the information needed to get tasks done is provided. Communication reduces misunderstandings and cuts the costs related with mistakes.

4. **Globalization.** The ability and know-how to communicate with international corporate entities is essential for success. The understanding of how locations throughout the world communicate is crucial to supporting global initiatives.

5. **Workplace diversification.** A concrete awareness of diversity existing globally and within an organization reduces the likelihood of misunderstandings from a gender, cultural, and generation perspective. Figure In-1 demonstrates the importance of the communication relationship in the workplace.

FIGURE IN-1 The administrative assistant provides the communication link between people and technology.

Hongqi Zhang/123RF

EMPLOYABILITY

Employability refers to a person's capability for gaining and maintaining employment. Acquiring and developing technical, personal, and social skills is essential for employability success. Administrative work is a broad category of employment and, as such, the roles and titles of office professionals transform continually. Some of these titles, administrative assistant and office coordinator, for instance, refer to jobs with very similar duties. Specialized roles, rather than general expertise, are reflected in the many new titles now assigned to administrative office professionals. Entry-level and middle management positions are popular among job seekers looking for administrative office work.

To eliminate confusion, the term administrative professional is used throughout this text to designate all classifications of office professionals.

The Conference Board of Canada, a not-for-profit organization, is involved in researching and analyzing Canadian employability trends related to the skills you need to enter, stay in, and progress in the world of work (Conference Board of Canada, 2017). Three key areas of vocational skills categorized from an employability standpoint include fundamental, personal management, and teamwork skills.

Fundamental skills are needed as a basis for further development. The skills included within these abilities are communication, information management, numerical thinking, and problem-solving skills.

Personal management skills cover the scope of attitudes and behaviours, which encourages opportunity for personal growth and development. These capabilities include the demonstration of responsibility, positive attitude, adaptability, learn continuously, and work safely.

Teamwork skills are attributes needed to contribute productively with a view to add value to team outcomes.

The elements of teamwork performance identified include work with others and participation in tasks and projects.

EMPLOYMENT PROFILES

Annually, Workopolis compiles statistics surrounding the top 12 jobs in demand in Canada; the role of administrative professionals consistently makes this list. Typically, most jobs take about 45 days to fill, while administrative professional positions experience a short posting duration of 36 days on average (Workopolis, 2017).

To better quantify the administrative employment umbrella, here are commonly recognized job titles, roles, and core competencies.

Administrative Assistant (AA)

An effective administrative assistant is worth a substantial measure to an organization especially when their ability reflects the capacity to be self-regulating, possess

FIGURE IN-2 Technology has automated procedures at all levels of the office.

Cathy Yeulet/123RF

both reliability and consistency, able to learn and problem solve well, and have exceptional organizational skills. Acting as the point of contact for both internal and external clients, the administrative professional handles requests from these stakeholders using their knowledge of office management systems and procedures. An ideal candidate should have excellent oral and written communication skills and be able to organize their work using tools, such as spreadsheets and office equipment. Advanced information technology enables office professionals to perform their jobs better and faster than ever before. Figure In-2 depicts an administrative professional in a technology driven workplace.

Executive Assistant (EA)

The executive assistant is responsible for a wide variety of administrative duties in support of senior management within an organization. They are responsible for planning and overseeing all administrative support and office services for the company. Duties include, but are not limited to, meeting minute-taking and distribution, scheduling appointments and drafting both internal and external correspondence, coordinating and communicating office activities, shipping and receiving, contract management, supplies, human resources, and general troubleshooting. This higher-level functioning role requires the ability to maintain confidentiality and professionally interact with employees, management and the clients, and meeting the requirements of the organization. EAs often conduct research and prepare reports that influence company policy. These responsibilities mean that EAs must thoroughly understand their employer's work. This position is the new power job and generally remuneration is at the top end of the office professional pay scale.

Personal Assistant (PA)

The personal assistant role is somewhat different. It too is well respected, and remuneration for it is at the top end of the office professional pay scale. However, the responsibilities of a PA often extend to personal work as well. A busy executive may need an efficient and capable office professional who, in addition to handling office-related work, also assists with the executive's personal life. This could mean making travel arrangements for a family vacation, handling the executive's personal banking, or even organizing social functions that don't relate to the office.

Legal and Medical Assistants

Legal and medical administrative professionals perform vastly specialized work requiring knowledge of technical terminology and procedures.

Legal administrative professionals will possess knowledge related to business organizational practices, governmental legal procedures, legal research analysis, and writing. Foundational tasks or duties to the role includes preparing correspondence and specific legal documents such as summonses, complaints, motions, responses, and subpoenas.

Medical administrative professionals are employed in a variety of healthcare facilities. They often keep both the business and clinical needs of the facility on track. The role also involves preparing correspondence, appointment scheduling, and assisting the healthcare team or medical scientists with reports, speeches, articles, and conference proceedings. Most medical assistants need to be accustomed with billing practices as well as hospital, clinical, and laboratory procedures.

DIGITAL AGE

Modern technology has led the way for the evolution known as the Digital Age, in which there is an abundant and rapid flow of data available for decision making. Material is often digitally or computer aide developed and electronically distributed. Heavy hitter social platforms like Facebook or Twitter have changed the way communication exists with internal and external clients. The administrative professional provides the critical human element in the rapid and unceasing flow of information in today's business world. Clearly, communication is an important part of every administrative professionals' role.

The Digital Age has made the administrative assistant's profession one that is exciting and challenging, and one that requires fine-tuned technical, administrative, and human relations skills. Administrative professionals are the lifeblood of an organization. They are information and people managers, and few companies could be successful without them.

EMPLOYMENT OUTLOOK

Historically, there has always been employment for skilled office professionals. Today is no exception. The service-based economic landscape of Canada relies on skill expertise of administrative professionals, the broad skill base of an office professional is portable, flexible, transferable, and in demand. About 10% of people employed in Canada are administrative professionals, equalling approximately 1.8 people, and this provides a strong talent pool to draw from. To place this into context, there are 30,700 active office job listings. The competition for these jobs is fierce, with an average of 67 applicants per job.

Every organization needs personnel who can effectively manage technology, administrative objectives, and people. If you live in a community where employment is scarce, don't be discouraged. Remember, your skills are portable to source employment opportunity just about anywhere in the world. This gives you choices and opportunities. Upgrade your skills as you evolve throughout your career and have an entrepreneurial spirit. This will be the winning formula for continuous employment.

NEXT STEP

By now, you have an understanding of the responsibilities of an administrative professional and the possibilities for future employment. Are you still interested in pursuing this exciting career? If you are, then take the next step—work through the chapters in this textbook.

WHAT YOU WILL LEARN

The information, exercises, and challenges in this book will help you to learn:

1. organizational structure, human resource function, diversity in the workplace, ethics, and human rights standards
2. organizing work, managing time, maintaining desirable attitudes, and setting priorities
3. research techniques and sources
4. managing electronic office tools, travel, and meeting arrangements
5. access information related to Canada's privacy laws impacting confidential issues
6. employability skills as defined by the Conference Board of Canada

7. business communication—transcribing, composing letters, processing incoming and outgoing mail, and preparing reports

8. front-line reception, guidelines for dealing with people—locally and internationally—and appointment setting

9. office equipment—computers, copiers, fax machines, telephones—for effective job performance

10. information management—filing procedures, rules, systems, supplies, equipment, retention, storage, and retrieval

11. project management, web-based tools and security matters

12. office commerce and record keeping

13. employment search strategies

14. professional development

QUESTIONS FOR STUDY AND REVIEW

1. Discuss six trends found in the contemporary workplace.

2. List three skills a typical organization would seek from an administrative profession.

3. Recite key objectives as defined by the Conference Board of Canada from an employability perspective.

4. Differentiate between the role of an executive assistant and a personal assistant.

5. Discuss how the Digital Age has affected the administrative professional's role.

6. Describe how legal and medical administrative professionals have specialized roles.

7. What is a communication channel, and what relevance does it have relative to the role of the administrative office professional?

8. Provide two benefits of face-to-face communication from an organizational perspective.

9. Identify reasons you have chosen this direction for your career.

Key Terms

business intelligence 2
augmented reality 2

Digital Age 7

EVERYDAY ETHICS

With each end-of-chapter activity in this textbook, an ethical dilemma is presented and explored. To ensure we have an understanding of ethical concepts, consider the following: An ethical code is a document outlining the mission statement and values of the organization. Often, it identifies how professionals are to approach situations. The ideologies are based mainly on the organization's core values and the standards to which all personnel within the organization are held.

Research three organizations and review their code of ethics. After reviewing these companies, decide which of the three align predominantly with your core values. Prepare an overview of the code and indicate how it supports your core values.

Problem Solving

1. The organization you recently started working with has invited a consultant to hold a seminar for administrative professionals on "Inspiring Superior Performance." You read the first announcement and wanted to attend, but you did not apply because you were new to this role and felt you might take valuable time away from the office. Today another announcement arrived, stating there is room for three more to attend. You have decided to inform your manager of your interest in attending the seminar. Write the statements you will use when you make the request.

2. You work in a law office. More than 35% of the material you review and edit is presented by voice-activated digital recording. You review the computer-generated documentation. You notice a number of errors consistently as you review the documents. To edit the documents accurately, you decide to replay the recordings.

You immediately notice you have difficulty understanding recordings from one team member. This recorder often has many distractions interrupting the recordings—crumpling paper, music playing, etc. Because of the difficulty experienced, your production is very slow. What should you do?

3. You worked as an administrative professional with your first job for four years before the organization merged with another organization. At that time, you were offered a job as a document specialist. You accepted it and have now been on the job for one year, but you strongly dislike the work. On a daily basis, you find yourself in a cycle of repeating the same three tasks; you are not getting the growth experience you had hoped. You have met with a Human Resources representative two times requesting an enhanced diverse opportunity similar to the one you had before the two organizations merged, but this type of position is not available. What are your alternatives?

Special Reports

1. Visit the website for the Association of Administrative Professionals (www.aaa.ca). Review the membership information and prepare a one-page summary related to the purpose of the association as well as how it benefits an administrative professional to secure and maintain membership within this association. Research and locate another administrative association that interests you and mention it in your summary.

2. Locate two recent career postings for an administrative office professional in your geographical area. List key skills mentioned in each posting. Note the educational requirements for each posting. Based on the postings, would either position interest you? Why or why not?

PRODUCTION CHALLENGES

Production Challenges will appear at the end of each chapter. In each Production Challenge, consider that you are an administrative professional with

> Progressive Digital Innovations Inc. (PDI)
> 3431 Bloor Street
> Toronto, ON M8X 1G4

Progressive Digital Innovations Inc., also known as PDI Inc., is an organization offering a broad range of products from cybersecurity to website optimization tools. Businesses utilizing PDI see a 5% to 15% increase in website traffic within the first year. In 2017, PDI made the list for the World's Top 75 Innovation-Based Companies.

You work for Noah Wilson, Vice-President of Marketing (email nwilson@PDI.ca), and his four assistant vice-presidents:

> Alexander R. Rush
> Assistant Vice-President of Marketing
> Eastern Region
> Extension 534
> arush@PDI.ca

> Emma Yee
> Assistant Vice-President of Marketing
> Midwestern Region
> Extension 535
> eyee@PDI.ca

> Jacob Levine
> Assistant Vice-President of Marketing
> Northwestern Region
> Extension 536
> jlevine@PDI.ca

> Olivia Azam
> Assistant Vice-President of Marketing
> Western Region
> Extension 537
> oazam@PDI.ca

Most of your communications are with the following managers of the four regional sales offices:

> Abigail Hansen
> Manager, Sales Office
> Eastern Region
> 197 Queen Street
> Fredericton, NB E3B 1A6
> ahansen@PDI.ca

> Jonathan Reddin
> Manager, Sales Office
> Midwestern Region
> 3436 College Avenue
> Regina, SK S4T 1W4
> jreddin@PDI.ca

> Mia Karlovsky
> Manager, Sales Office
> Northwestern Region
> 9129 Jasper Avenue
> Edmonton, AB T5H 3T2
> mkarlovsky@PDI.ca

FIGURE IN-3 Organization chart for the marketing division of PDI.

Karuna Singe
Manager, Sales Office
Western Region
3152 West 45th Avenue
Vancouver, BC V6N 3M1
ksinge@PDI.ca

Please refer to Figure In-3 to view the regional organization chart for the Marketing Division of PDI Inc.

In-A Searching for Information

Supplies needed:

- *Plain paper*
- *This textbook*

PDI employs 24 administrative office professionals. Noah Wilson proposes additional resource materials to assist with a variety of common organizational tasks and objectives. He hands you this textbook and asks you to search the book to see if it contains information on the following topics. He suggests that you create a table showing the topic and the exact page number where that topic is discussed in the book. Add three additional topics covered in the textbook not listed here (on the right side) that, in your opinion, have significant relevance to the administrative role:

- dealing with difficult customers
- human resource function
- diversity
- organizational structure
- dealing with customer abuse
- immersive technology
- coping with stress
- setting up a wellness program for employees
- acting ethically in the office
- office politics
- ergonomics
- project management
- organizing office supplies
- reading an organizational chart
- business correspondence
- setting up a video conference
- hosting international guests
- arranging flight tickets through the internet
- choosing the most efficient mail services
- preparing minutes of meetings
- effective presentations
- online banking
- getting professional certification for administrative assistants
- accessing information on Canada's privacy laws

Weblinks

IAAP
http://www.iaap-hq.org/
This is the home page of the International Association of Administrative Professionals®. It is a registered not-for-profit professional association for administrative professionals. IAAP strives to ensure individuals working in office and administrative professions have the opportunity to connect, learn, lead, and excel. Its magazine, *OfficePro*, is a benefit of membership and discusses issues that administrative professionals often face.

Association of Administrative Professionals®
https://aaa.ca/
A Canadian chartered nonprofit professional organization that was founded in April 1951. The Association is proactive in encouraging its members to further their education and enhance their career opportunities by continuously upgrading their skills and professionalism.

The Conference Board of Canada
http://www.conferenceboard.ca
A not-for-profit think tank dedicated to researching and analyzing economic trends, as well as organizational performance and public policy issues.

Business Ethics
http://www.businessethics.ca/
Business Ethics presents various ethical dilemmas and provides suggestions to equip business professionals with effective decision making.

Deskdemon
http://us.deskdemon.com
Resources, articles, and information for administrative professionals of all types are available. Also offered is a free monthly e-magazine.

Gaebler Resources for Entrepreneurs
http://www.gaebler.com
Tips and advice on how to run a small business office are abundant on this site. Topics include how to write a mission statement, how to set up a conference call, how to run a meeting, common administrative assistant complaints, and hiring an office administrator.

References

CBC News. (2016, January 01). *The future of work: mobile offices, flexibility, but temporary jobs*. Retrieved from http://www.cbc.ca/news/business/workplace-trends-office-1.3386128.

Half, R. (2017, January 3). *No one wants to face an unhappy admin: engagement strategies that can help*. Retrieved from https://www.roberthalf.com/blog/management-tips/no-one-wants-to-face-an-unhappy-admin-engagement-strategies-that-can-help.

Triple Pundit. (2016, December 27). *A year in CSR: The TOP 10 TRENDS of 2016*. Retrieved from https://www.triplepundit.com/2016/12/year-csr-top-10-trends-2016/.

Conference Board of Canada. (n.d.). *Employability skills*. Retrieved on 2017, November 16. http://www.conferenceboard.ca/spse/employability-skills.aspx.

Workopolis. (2017, April 10). *The 12 most in demand jobs in Canada*. Retrieved from https://careers.workopolis.com/advice/the-12-most-in-demand-jobs-in-canada-and-what-they-pay/.

Chapter 1
Human Relations

G-stockstudio/Shutterstock

LEARNING OUTCOMES

After completion of this chapter, the student will be able to:

1 Understand the importance of human relations within an organization.

2 Discuss organizational culture, climate, and citizenship as it relates to industry.

3 Identify four functions of human resources management.

4 Understand the different types of business organizations.

5 Discuss interpersonal skills that professionals practice in the workplace.

6 Describe teamwork best practices and highlight nonproductive behaviours within a team.

7 Understand the importance of confidentiality.

8 Recognize office politics behaviours and identify unethical practice.

9 Explain the significance of change and health and wellness in the workplace.

Human relations in the workplace are a major part of what makes a business work. A happy, inspired employee tends to be a productive employee. Additionally, relationships between employees and management are of substantial value in any workplace. Organizations, no matter what the size, are beginning to recognize that their greatest asset is people or human capital. **Human capital** is the knowledge, skills, and abilities possessed by people or groups of people within an organization. The utilization of this capital can help to make or break an organization. The evolving Canadian business landscape is beginning to enable companies to view assets beyond financial capital and see the economic value of their people as a competitive advantage. A **competitive advantage** implies that the company does something better than other organizations, and it may or may not be sustained over time; in some cases, an organization can secure an advantage with designed recruitment, selection, and performance management structure. It is no coincidence that effective management of the human resources within an organization has a direct impact on organizational success. **Human resources management (HRM)** is the term used to describe formal systems devised for the management of people within an organization.

This chapter is interconnected to The Conference Board of Canada's categories of employability of Personal Management Skills with special emphasis on interacting with people, problems, and situations with honesty, integrity, and personal ethics.

OVERVIEW OF HUMAN RESOURCES MANAGEMENT (HRM)

Every company has its own distinctive personality, as people do. This uniqueness of an organization is referred to as its culture. In groups working together, **organizational culture** is both a visible and invisible powerful entity that influences the behaviour of the members of that group. It is the underlying values and beliefs of an organization and can be expressed in members' self-image with those inside and outside of the company. **Organizational climate** defines how the members of an organization experience their work and workplace on a daily basis. It is described as the feeling or atmosphere within the organization. A toxic or negative climate can eventually affect organizational culture. Job satisfaction fosters organizational citizenship; this is what is witnessed when employees strive continually to improve their skill set and personal performance. Many factors influence business achievement and a result-orientated organizational culture often helps to support a high-performance environment. It includes beliefs, traditions, routines, and values within the organization. Specific descriptive words come to mind with high-performance organizations such as team-orientated, respectful, and fair.

The human resources (HR) department in organizations is essential for a productive employee-focused workplace where employees feel motivated and inspired. HR objectives often reflect a balance of the main goals of HRM and the demands of industry that is to maintain or increase performance of organizations. The HR functions encompassing HRM are multidimensional and linked to various outcomes. To better appreciate this concept and how this fits into human relations, consider the following functions of a human resource department:

1. **Recruitment, selection, and performance management.** Based on job design and analysis, an organization can determine the employees needed to position itself for success. Recruitment is the process an organization undertakes to seek and attract employees. Selection is the process to determine the candidates who have the matching knowledge, skills, and abilities for the job opportunity. Performance management is an unending process of communication between a manager and an employee that occurs continually and supports accomplishing the strategic objectives of the organization. Retention of selected employees is an aspect of this function as well. Employee retention refers to policies and practices that companies use to prevent valuable employees from leaving their jobs. High turnover rates are costly to an organization; they are disruptive to a positive organizational culture and productively.

2. **Orientation, training, and development.** An employee orientation program is intended to help acquaint new employees with the ins and outs of how the company operates and the people they will be working with. The amount of investment an employer devotes to employee orientation can be directly correlated with reduced turnover, job satisfaction, and employee retention. The training and development function is interconnected as a focused organizational activity designed to enhance the job performance of individuals and groups in organizational settings. Developing an employee is an investment in the future of the organization and the employee. Indirectly, it can lend to succession planning and employee retirements.

3. **Compensation and benefits.** When determining methodologies in terms of compensating employees, organizations should strive to develop a consistent and fair approach to attract and retain the right people. It is equally important to make your employees feel that their compensation is fair in connection to their co-workers and industry standards. Many organizations arrange employee rights based on equal pay for equal work and also provide other protections that address fairness concerns. Compensation ranges from earnings

to everything that has a positive effect on the overall happiness of employees. Nonmonetary compensation can come in several forms and could be custom-made to the inclinations of the employee; some examples include recognition, extra time off, participation in decision making, work–life balance, and additional benefits packages. Statutory benefits are fixed benefits mandated by a government statute that includes Canada Pension Plan (CPP) and Employment Insurance (EI). Optional benefits can take the form of health and dental plans or disability plans.

4. **Employee and labour relations.** Every individual shares a certain relationship with his or her colleagues at the workplace—whether positive or negative, it has an impact on the organization. **Organizational behaviour (OB)** is the study of both group and individual performance and activity within an organization. From this extension, OB examines matters such as leadership, motivation, attitudes, and productivity. Labour relations is the study of how employers and employees work together to create a fair workplace. Labour relations matters could include conflict resolution, hours and wage issues, and adequate safety in the workplace.

It is important to mention that in smaller organizations the administrative office professional may perform some or all of these HR functions within their role. Awareness of these key functions and how they fit within the scope of an organization is beneficial for the office professional and enhances career potential.

BUSINESS ORGANIZATION TYPES

Organizational structure is a system used to outline order within an organization. It identifies job roles, functions, and reporting hierarchy within the organization. This configuration is established to determine how an organization operates and assists an organization in obtaining its goals and for future growth. Often, the structure is shown using an organizational chart (see Chapter 5 for further information regarding organizational structures).

There are three main types of business organizations:

1. **Sole proprietorship.** This is the simplest form of a business entity. Usually, an individual owner is responsible for all the debt and obligations. A sole proprietor can hire employees; there is no limit on the number it can hire. This type of business is easier to register, and direct decision making is streamlined.

2. **Partnership.** A partnership is a relationship between two or more persons carrying on a business with a purpose of making a profit. The organization is usually more complex than that of a sole proprietorship, and there is more than one owner to share in the profit and/or losses. It is beneficial because startup costs are shared and management is also shared.

3. **Corporation.** A corporation can be done at the provincial or federal level. It usually has several shareholders. Shareholders are usually individuals of the corporation, but an institution can also be a shareholder. Shareholders are not held personally liable for debts of the corporation. A corporation can transfer ownership to others easily and can maintain a continuous existence.

SKILLS FOR RELATIONSHIP BUILDING

Businesses typically sustain interconnectivity to virtually the entire world by technological systems. Administrative professionals understand the unpredictability they sometimes encounter in relationship management. Whatever the situation, they are called upon to respond in a manner that will keep, or make, positive gains for their organization. This is a critical part of relationship building. See the Wordle shown in Figure 1-1, which includes key relationship-building words.

Administrative professionals spend abundant time either directly in contact with people or producing and channelling information that will affect people. They collect, analyze, transmit, and store information. However they manage their work, administrative professionals are always connecting with internal or external clients.

As discussed in the introductory chapter an effective administrative professional requires attributes regarded as hard skills. **Hard skills**, or technical skills, include working with a variety of technological systems and core

FIGURE 1-1 Wordle depicting relational-building components.

Iqoncept/123RF

Stephanie Pilon

Stephanie Pilon
Barrie Family Healthcare Team
Human Resources
Graduation Year 2001
Office Administration

"I especially enjoy mentoring recent graduates."

Stephanie Pilon has been working as a human resources coordinator with the Barrie and Community Family Health Team since 2011. When Stephanie graduated from the Office Administration—Medical program at Georgian College 10 years earlier, she didn't anticipate this would be the path her career would take her, but she couldn't be happier that it did!

Shortly after graduation, she began working as an administrative assistant with a busy physiotherapy and massage therapy clinic. She was thrilled to be applying all the skills she had learned in school, including transcription, which she enjoyed. This motivated her to start her own part-time business providing medical transcription services, and she successfully carried this on for nearly a decade while also working full-time.

Meanwhile, within five years at the physiotherapy clinic, she was promoted to office manager. Her responsibilities expanded to include overseeing the administrative team, hiring new staff, and providing the necessary on-the-job training. "I especially enjoyed mentoring recent graduates from the Office Administration program."

While she appreciated the growth she had experienced with the new role and responsibilities, she knew it was as far as she could go within that company. A few years later, she began looking for new opportunities to further her career. This was at a time when Family Health Teams were being implemented across Ontario. The concept of multidisciplinary primary healthcare intrigued her, and in 2008 she pursued employment with the Barrie and Community Family Health Team (BCFHT) as an administrative assistant within one of their clinical programs.

As the BCFHT grew, opportunities for advancement began developing. When a position within the Human Resources department became available, Stephanie jumped at the opportunity. With her previous experience as an office manager she felt this would be a very fitting progression in her career. Her employer was very supportive in her professional development as she pursued part-time human resources studies, and this further allowed her to grow within her new role. "Employers often recognize the importance of investing in their employees' professional development. When you prove yourself to be a valuable and dedicated member of the team, they will take notice."

Since directing her career to the human resources field, Stephanie has found that her responsibilities have continually expanded as the organization has grown. As a human resources coordinator, her responsibilities include collaborating with hiring managers in the recruitment process for all positions within the organization. This consists of assisting with the development of job postings, managing incoming applications, coordinating interviews, and completing reference checks. "One of the things I find most rewarding about my role is getting to personally connect with each new employee from the time they start with the organization." On an employee's very first day on the job, she welcomes them by providing a full day of orientation to help them get started on the right foot.

Building those relationships from the start enables employees to come to her whenever they have questions at any time during their employment. "I certainly don't have all the answers myself, but being able to provide direction to the answer is often half the battle—and that's a skill I've developed through my longstanding history with the organization."

"I continue to be challenged in my role, and I don't see that changing any time soon. In a day and age where many people stay with an employer five years or less, I consider myself quite fortunate to have been with my current employer for a decade, and still look forward to many more fulfilling years!"

administrative tasks to produce and manage information, and troubleshooting problems as they arise.

More importantly, though, employers place substantial emphasis on the **soft skills** that are necessary for success on the job. Success in gaining employment may be relatively easy, but the likelihood of your continued employment with the company might well depend on your highly developed soft skills.

Human relations or people skills include **personal qualities** such as having a positive attitude, being dependable and responsible, having a positive self-image, being a self-starter, displaying integrity and honesty, and projecting a professional image. In addition to valued personal qualities, soft skills that employers seek include well-developed **interpersonal skills**, or the ability to interact effectively with others. Examples of interpersonal skills include working as part of a team, teaching others, interacting with customers, having effective conflict resolution and negotiating skills, and respecting diversity.

Employees can learn hard or technical skills with time and practice, but development of soft skills requires a genuine desire on the part of the employee to develop a positive attitude and to leave a favourable impression with interactions. Sociologists refer to soft skills as translating directly to the EQ or emotional intelligence of the individual. The five key aspects of emotional intelligence include self-awareness, self-regulation, motivation, empathy, and social skills. Possessing excellent human relations skills, both personal and interpersonal, will position you to be recognized as a professional and as a valuable asset to your company.

DEVELOPING INTERPERSONAL SKILLS

Effective administrative professionals are aware of people they encounter, whether a client or co-worker. Individuals form an image of the organization, your manager, and you based on the impression made, and the administrative professional is often the first point of contact. You rely on your business personality to communicate effectively with everyone you meet in your business activities.

You cannot entirely depend on knowledge, skills, and abilities alone for success in your job. Your performance as an office professional and your happiness on the job will be closely linked to your ability to communicate and to get along with people. This, in turn, will depend on understanding the importance of interpersonal skills. Consider what happened to an administrative professional, Isabella.

Isabella was one of several administrative professionals at an open office space company. The manager and assistant manager were discussing which of the administrative professionals should be promoted to office manager to replace the present office manager, who has been promoted to events and marketing consultant after she received her certification in event management. The manager mentioned that Isabella should be selected for the office manager position. He stated that she had less experience than the other four administrative professionals had and had adequate technical skills, but that she would make a great office manager. The assistant manager said he thought that Emily would make a better office manager. Emily knew more about the computer system being used and had several years of experience. The first manager said, "I agree that Emily has better technical

skills and more experience, but I have personally seen Isabella resolve several difficult problems. Isabella has refined people skills and works effectively with our client base as well as the rest of the office staff." Based on several variables they decided to promote Isabella and agreed to develop Emily for future career growth potential.

Situations like this occur routinely in the workplace. Often a person is promoted simply because he or she has remarkable interpersonal skills combined with adequate technical skills. You should strive to display solid interpersonal skills at all times. Do not depend solely on your technical skills and knowledge, even if they are superior skills.

Interpersonal skills are not just about getting along with people. When you promote an atmosphere that encourages idea sharing and that recognizes experiences and individual differences, your interpersonal skills are further enhanced. Your intrinsic reward is personal satisfaction, the respect of others, and your co-workers' recognition of you as a professional.

Figure 1-2 details how you can improve your interpersonal skills by working on one skill at a time. Here are some of the interpersonal skills to help you succeed in the workplace.

Be a Team Player

Teamwork has replaced individual work as the basic building block of organizations. Teamwork is viewed as an effective and efficient way to accomplish work, to build harmony, to increase individual and group knowledge, and to strengthen the organization. In fact, employers value team skills so highly that they search for new employees who can contribute to

FIGURE 1-2 Improving your interpersonal skills one step at a time can help you to achieve a professional image.

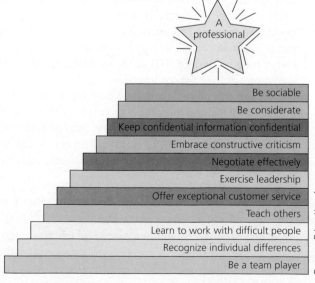

the corporate team just as much as they can contribute independently. A team that works well together understands the strengths and weaknesses of each team member.

As you contribute effectively to team efforts, your membership on other teams will become a desirable commodity. The more teams to which you contribute, the more opportunities you will have to expand your knowledge, responsibilities, and career opportunities.

Setting ground rules is an essential part of ensuring a productive and effective work team. (Refer to the section "Team Meetings" in Chapter 13 for examples of ground rules.)

Here are some of the many team best practices leading to productivity and serving as a basis for ground rules:

- treating every member with respect
- basing decisions on data and fact rather than opinion
- communicating clearly and honestly
- balancing participation among all team members at meetings
- staying on topic and not allowing digressions during meetings
- seeking creative ways to solve problems through brainstorming
- summarizing decisions at the end of team meetings
- committing to do equal work
- believing that every member has talents that will contribute to the team's work
- not personalizing criticism of the project; remember, it's a team effort

Become a role model by displaying these positive team behaviours. In return, you will earn the respect of your team members. Figure 1-3 shows a team working effectively and cooperatively.

As an administrative professional, take opportunities to work in a team. This will increase your knowledge, job

FIGURE 1-3 Good teamwork consists of clear and full communication.

Konstantin Chagin/Shutterstock

satisfaction, and value to the company. Take full responsibility for your part of the workload and for any problems that arise within the team. If you think in terms of what you can contribute rather than of what you can get, you will earn greater acceptance by the office team and a greater sense of self-satisfaction. Strive for excellence and be enthusiastic about your team responsibilities. When the team is successful, every individual has the opportunity to be successful.

The benefits of teamwork are numerous.

- An effective group can accomplish more work than an effective individual.
- Teams provide social interaction. Knowledge spillover occurs during interactions among team members where input and collaboration are encouraged.
- During stressful periods of work, the team will provide emotional support for its members.
- As team members share information, the knowledge and experience of the team members grow.
- The company values employees who contribute to the organization's goals and decision making through teamwork.

Good teamwork consists of clear and full communication as well as trust. A successful team will be one that displays transparency with all its members in collaboration with management. A high level of disclosure leads to trust and relationship building by removing communication barriers between team members and management. Trust is essential if the team members and the team as a whole are to be **empowered** and capable.

Avoid Nonproductive Team Behaviours

No matter how well-intentioned your team is, nonproductive behaviours might still exist, conflicts might arise, and hard conversations might need to take place. The following are descriptions of five nonproductive behaviours encountered in many teams. Also provided are some suggested remedies.

1. **Dominant or reluctant team members.** When one or more members of a team monopolize discussions, or when you have a member who is reluctant to discuss the team's issues for whatever reason, you need to work at balancing the participation. While treating all members with courtesy and respect, you should point out the ground rules where you agreed to balance and share the team discussions. As a team leader, you could encourage a balanced discussion by interjecting with comments such as, "Sophia, thanks for sharing that information. Rima, we haven't heard from you. What are your thoughts on the . . . ?"

2. **Lack of direction.** When team members lack direction, members do not know how to get started or what the next step should be. If the team establishes an action plan in the early stages of the process, the members will find it easier to stay on track.

3. **Digressing.** Not staying on topic is a common team problem. When the conversation starts to drift, tactfully make the team aware of it and ask the members to focus on the topic at hand. For example, you might say, "Getting back to the agenda item we were discussing . . ." or "Mark, getting back to the point you were making on . . ." or simply, "Getting back to Item #3. . . ." This should be enough to bring the team back to the topic being discussed.

4. **Quarrelling.** When two or more team members begin to argue, the other team members are left feeling uncomfortable and frustrated by the team's lack of productivity. If this should occur, act as the mediator. Mediation may take the form of speaking privately to the members involved. However, you might simply compare their behaviour to the ground rule discouraging such behaviour and remind them that their actions are unproductive.

5. **Discounting.** People sometimes discount the work and opinions of others through their unkind criticism, lack of attention, poor body language, and so on. Every person deserves respect and attention. If you sense that someone on your team is being discounted, support that person. Comments that show consideration and attention are not difficult to make.

Recognize Individual Differences

To manage human relations in the workplace, it is necessary to recognize that people have individual differences—different capabilities, needs, and interests. The purpose of learning and understanding about individual differences in personality types is to help you build better working relationships and establish rapport with others.

Manage People and Personalities

Before exploring challenging workplace personalities and how to strategically handle them, it is important to understand personality. **Personality** is the sum of characteristics and traits that define a person's typical thoughts, emotions, and behaviours over time. Even if you are congenial, cooperative, and a strong team player, you will encounter people with whom it is difficult to interact effectively. Many types of difficult people have been identified. Here are a few common types and some suggestions on how to cope with them.

The Bully   The bully uses intimidation to gain control by making others angry or afraid. The bully tries to push all your buttons by yelling, name-calling, sarcasm, mocking, putting down, belittling, embarrassing, or negativity to cause these reactions in others. Not all forms of bullying are directly obvious, as some are more subtle such as remarks or statements that intimidate and present as a threat. In recent years, cyber-bullying has become a method of choice for bully related infractions. Cyber-bullying involves using social media or other technologies to intimidate or present a threat online.

Coping:

- Think only about the positive attributes of the bully— what you like about her when they are not in bullying mode.

- Look them directly in the eye. Using a calm, normal voice and "I" and not "you" words, say exactly what you don't like about their behaviour. For instance, you might say, "I do not like it when people raise their voices at me. I feel as if I am being treated like a child. I am not a child. I am an adult and want to be treated as such."

- Report to your supervisor situations whereby you feel intimidated or threatened by a bullying colleague.

The Gossip   The gossip goes from person to person spreading negative rumours about others, whether true or not, and trying to set one person against the other. They look for people who will listen and agree with them. They feel open to use anyone's name who listens to them; they say such things as, "I just talked to Jo and she told me. . . ." It makes them feel powerful.

Coping:

- When the gossip begins telling the rumour, break into the conversation and say something positive about the person or situation.

- Each time the gossip resumes by saying, "Yes, but . . . ," break in again and give a positive statement about the person or situation. Gossips dislike talking to people who always find the good in others or in situations.

- If you refuse to listen, sooner or later the gossip will get the message.

The Know-It-All   Know-it-alls believe they are the expert. Know-it-alls have opinions about everything, but when found to be wrong, they become defensive.

Coping:

- Manage a know-it-all on a one-on-one basis, not in a group setting.

- Check the facts, be sure they are correct, and then state your facts.

- Do not put down the know-it-all.

- Give the person a way to save face.

The Backstabber   The backstabber will attempt to get you to discuss a problem or situation in which you are involved. Backstabbers might appear to befriend you and encourage you to talk freely. Later, they go to the person or supervisor with whom they know and can cause the most damage to you and then repeat what you said, often embellishing the information. They ultimately want to discredit you to others.

Coping:

- Do not retaliate by talking about the backstabber. It may appear as if you are the backstabber.

- Always think before you speak. Don't say anything to anyone in the office you wouldn't want repeated.

- Keep an accurate record of what happens. If the backstabber is your boss, you need verification of what was said—date, time, conversation, and anyone else who heard it.

The Blamer   The blamer never solves or takes responsibility for problems. When faced with a problem, a blamer thinks someone else caused it—the supervisor, a group member, or you.

Coping:

- Attempt to get the blamer to answer the question, "Whose responsibility was it for (whatever the problem is)?"

Answering that question gets to the heart of the problem.

- Difficult people tend to bring out the worst in us. Many know how to "push our buttons" to cause us to react emotionally, to cause us distress, or simply to create tension. Here is a plan to follow to help you deal with these difficult situations:

1. Do not react emotionally; stand back and take a look at the situation. If you do not have to respond immediately, take time to write down everything in as much detail as possible.

2. Analyze the behaviour of the difficult person. Identify exactly what was said that caused you to feel threatened or upset. What do you believe motivated the person to make the statement or to create the situation?

3. Analyze your behaviour and emotional response (e.g., anger, frustration, disappointment).

4. Decide exactly what behaviour—all or part—you believe you must acknowledge and respond to and why.

5. Define all the ways you might respond.

6. Decide on a plan: What will you say (making sure you form the statements using "I" and not "you"), where will you say it, and when will you say it?

7. Imagine how the person might respond.

The more experience you gain in dealing with difficult people, the easier it will be to maintain a positive attitude throughout adverse experiences.

Teach Others

Often the opportunity will arise on the job for you to help others learn new techniques, processes, software, equipment, or other new skills. Seize every opportunity to volunteer when the need arises to help others learn. In addition to creating an environment of cooperation, your actions will highlight you as a highly skilled and valuable employee with potential for leading others. Helpful hints to successfully teach others include the following:

- Do not give the impression that you think you "know it all," which could lead to resentment from the co-worker whom you are helping.

- Be patient; not everyone learns at the same rate.

- Recognize that some learn by doing rather than by just being told.

- Don't view others' learning as a threat to your job.

- Recognize that in the process of teaching others, you often learn from them as well. Let your co-workers know that you have learned through teaching them.

Offer Exceptional Customer Service

Exceptional customer service is helping customers, clients, or co-workers with a willingness to put their needs first in order to resolve their complications. Some of these skills are:

- Know what your customer expects.
- Follow up on positive or negative feedback.
- Offer to help before asked.
- If you can't help, locate someone who can.
- If the person is upset, let him or her vent frustration; then show empathy and understanding.
- Go the extra step beyond what would normally be expected of you.
- Continuously look for ways to improve the customer experience.

These highly desirable skills will promote your professional image and the customers-first image of your company. Customer service does not mean just offering excellent service to those customers outside your business; it also means you see each person within your organization as a customer as well and treat them as such.

Exercise Leadership

Exercising leadership means communicating your position on certain matters clearly and effectively, persuading or convincing others, and responsibly challenging existing procedures and policies when necessary. A good leader displays self-confidence and intelligence, follows the rules, stands behind his or her word, is trustworthy, and has a good sense of humour.

It has been said that good leaders are made, not born. If you have the desire and the willingness to become a leader, your chances of attaining that goal will improve by developing leadership skills. Good leaders develop through a never-ending process of self-study, education, training, and experience. Remember, power does not make you a good leader; power just means you are the boss. A good leader influences employees to want to do a good job by leading rather than just bossing people around.

Negotiate Effectively

Negotiating is the process of exchanging ideas, information, and opinions with others to work towards agreements; consequently, policies and programs are formulated, and decisions, conclusions, or solutions are the result of a joint effort. Here are some tactics of a good negotiator:

- Think before you begin. Do your homework so you will know the other's side, and then develop a plan and write

it down. Know the minimum and maximum for which you are willing to settle.

- Be ready to compromise. Identify the benefits of your offer. Even getting a little of what you want makes you a winner.
- Display excellent people skills. You must observe other people and be ready to adjust to their personality.
- Be a good listener. Develop the habit of summarizing what other people say to make sure you understand their intent.

Embrace Constructive Criticism

Constructive criticism is the process of offering one's opinion about the work of another. The criticism includes both positive and constructive comments, and the comments are offered in a friendly manner rather than a confrontational one. Some people tend to take criticism negatively. However, you should welcome it because it can help you to develop professionally.

When giving constructive criticism:

1. Be genuine. Criticism is only constructive if the person giving it truly means to help the person receiving it and feels it is important.
2. Always give criticism in private.
3. Don't sound threatening. Avoid statements that start with, "I think you should . . ." or, "You have to . . ." or "You had better . . . ." It would be better to say, "Let's take a look at what has been happening and see if, between the two of us, we can work out a solution. What do you think?"
4. Focus on the problem, not the person.

When receiving constructive criticism:

1. Welcome the criticism. See it as a way for you to improve.
2. Listen carefully to the criticism; restate the criticism when necessary.
3. Focus on the problem, not the person giving it.
4. Understand that this dialogue can help improve the interpersonal relationship between you and the person giving the criticism.

Positive vs. Negative Criticism Processing criticism positively is an important life skill. At some point in your career, you will face criticism. Sometimes it will be difficult to accept, but others will notice your reaction and will judge whether you handle criticism well. Assess if the criticism is constructive or rude. Consider the following contrasting examples of helpful and unhelpful forms of criticism.

Negative

You have just completed work on a complex proposal and submitted it to the management team. A day after the submission, your immediate supervisor sends you an email stating the work you completed on the project was boring and mind numbing so she had to stay late and fix all your errors.

Positive

Using the same scenario, your supervisor thanks you for the work you completed on the proposal and offers suggestions for improvement. She offers to set up a meeting with you to talk further about your proposal.

Everyone wants to experience success. Positive criticism—feedback that explores positives as opposed to focusing on negatives—is consistently a best practice.

Keep Confidential Information Confidential

In today's increasingly litigious, technology-intensive, and variable workplace, confidentiality is important for many reasons. Failure to secure and protect confidential business and personal information can lead to the loss of business and or clients. Depending on industry, a company will develop policy regarding confidentiality. Additionally, depending on the industry, various privacy laws form a key component of the company's identity and compliance is required along with a reporting structure. Whatever management system you work in, you will always have to practice discretion when it comes to confidential information.

Refrain from repeating the opinions of your management. In fact, most activities that take place in your office should be kept confidential. To gain the trust of your organization, manager, and co-workers, never discuss company business outside the office.

If there is an upcoming company announcement and you are aware of it, keep it confidential. Reporting structure is observed and only authorized personnel make company announcements.

Be careful not to give away confidential information to your colleagues or to your company's competitors. Sometimes just one isolated fact obtained from you is all the information that a competitor needs. Confidential information is often given away without intent. For example, you are proud of where you work and the decisions that management is making. As a result, you discuss this information with new acquaintances at a social event. When this happens, however, you never know where the information will end up and how it will be used. Always use good judgment and discretion when sharing company information.

Be Considerate

"Good morning" is viewed by some people as only a necessary, routine greeting. But a pleasant and cheerful greeting is appreciated when it is sincere and optimistic. Take the high road! Speak first and call other people by name. Be pleasant and respectful of everyone, from the cleaning staff to the owner of the company. Make an effort to get acquainted with as many co-workers as possible. People prefer to work with upbeat people. Be one of them.

Other people will see you as approachable if you are pleasant, courteous, and responsive. Listen attentively when someone is talking with you. Be responsive to what is going on around you. Avoid being condescending when giving instructions. Suggest rather than command. Request rather than demand.

Be considerate of others by doing the following:

1. Stop at the administrative professional's desk when you go in to see his or her manager.

2. Wait your turn to use the office copier.

3. When you must interrupt someone, time your interruption so it will have the least impact on the people being interrupted.

4. Remember that everyone has personal interests and pursuits. These might include family, education, and leisure activities. Inquiring about these nonbusiness topics shows diplomacy.

Knowing what *not* to say is as important as knowing what to say. Be very careful when discussing sensitive subjects such as religion, money, morals, or politics; you don't want to offend a co-worker. These tips will help you to gain others' trust:

- Keep general criticism to yourself.
- Treat others as you wish to be treated.
- Talk positively about colleagues.
- Do not make negative remarks about co-workers.
- Do not pry into others' personal affairs.
- Do not criticize your employer, colleagues, or management at any time.
- Think and then speak; otherwise, your statements may come out wrong and place you in an embarrassing position.
- Be cooperative and do more than is expected of you.

Create a pleasant, businesslike atmosphere by establishing good rapport with employees and customers at all levels. Besides creating a pleasant atmosphere in which to work, your thoughtfulness will help you enjoy your relationships with others.

Be Sociable

Sociable people demonstrate understanding, friendliness, adaptability, empathy, and politeness in group settings. Some employees develop social bonds with certain co-workers. You may find others with whom you work who have interests similar to your own, and because of these similar interests, you will become closer to them. You should, however, strive to be friendly towards each person in your work group. A pleasant smile and an acknowledgment of each individual will continually show others that you are a friendly, pleasant co-worker.

Always take part in office get-togethers such as birthday celebrations, lunches, or holiday celebrations. Your attendance and participation will demonstrate that you belong to the office group and will show your desire to support your co-workers.

Self-Check

1. List five important interpersonal skills.
2. What are three benefits of teamwork?
3. What are five nonproductive team behaviours?
4. What is meant by individual differences?
5. How would you manage a backstabber?
6. List any interpersonal skills you plan to improve.

DEVELOPING PERSONAL QUALITIES

When you accept a position with a company, management expects you to do the best job you can and to get along with everyone to the best of your ability. Remember that your contribution is essential to a smooth-running, productive, and efficient office. By upholding a high standard of personal qualities, you will demonstrate excellent human relations skills to those around you, and your role will become a central one on the office team. Figure 1-4 illustrates personal qualities for industry success.

Be Responsible

Responsibility means accepting the assignment of duties. When you accept a position, you are being entrusted with and assigned numerous tasks. You are counted on to perform these duties in a professional manner following prescribed processes and protocol. To be responsible, you must answer to someone for your actions, and in this capacity, it often means your supervisor. Displaying responsibility is one of the key elements human relations.

FIGURE 1-4 Personal qualities needed to project a professional image.

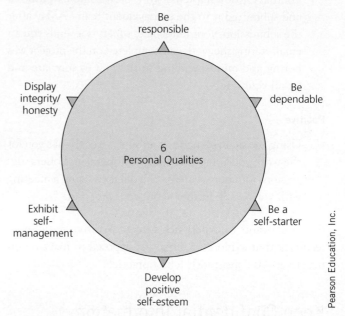

6 Personal Qualities

Be responsible
Be dependable
Be a self-starter
Develop positive self-esteem
Exhibit self-management
Display integrity/honesty

Pearson Education, Inc.

Be Dependable

Dependability means being consistent and reliable in your behaviour. For instance, you would display dependability by having an excellent attendance record and by being prompt in arriving at work each morning and in returning on time to your workstation after each break and lunch. Dependability helps create a desirable office atmosphere.

Each employee in your office depends on every person being there. When someone is absent, no matter the reason, or is late returning from lunch or a break, someone in the office must cover for that person. When someone is covering for another individual, that person is not getting his or her own work completed. Hostile feelings can grow quickly towards any people who do not carry their workloads and are not dependable.

Be a Self-Starter

Self-starters take the initiative to begin tasks for which they are responsible. Don't wait for your manager to ask you to do something—be observant and anticipate what you are expected to do without requiring constant direction or reminders.

When you finish your work, assist someone else if practical. Everyone feels overworked and underpaid, and when someone sits idly by while others are swamped, a negative attitude builds towards the person who is not busy. You can't just say, "It isn't my job," because it is your job to help anyone at any time you are not busy. You are paid to work a full day's work, and you should project the image of always wanting to help when help is needed.

Develop Positive Self-Esteem

Self-esteem is the opinion you have of yourself. As you perform a task or handle a situation well, you gain confidence that you can do it well again. With practice and success, your confidence will grow. Once you have gained self-confidence, you will rely on your competence and the strength of your own judgment.

The following list identifies some of the concepts that affect your self-esteem:

- the value you place on yourself as a person
- the opinion you believe others hold of you
- your strengths and weaknesses
- your social status and how you relate to others
- your ability to be independent

Low self-esteem is when you view one or more of these items negatively, which results in a poor self-image. High self-esteem is just the opposite and causes you to be confident and believe in your ability to succeed. Having positive self-esteem is critical to your living a happy life both at home and in the workplace. People who are self-confident rely on the correctness of their own judgment and competence in spite of the discouragement and influence of others.

Confident people can maintain **composure** even under pressure. Composure is a sense of calmness or tranquility. Confident people also exhibit **poise**, which denotes ease and dignity of manner. Keep the following tips in mind:

1. Believe in your abilities and remain in control of your reactions. Be consistent in maintaining your composure. There is no place in the professional world for a temperamental person. If your colleagues cannot rely on you to be cooperative and pleasant, they will avoid working with you. A temperamental attitude is a serious barrier to effectiveness and cooperation in the office.

2. You cannot control all the circumstances that surround your work. Most of the daily happenings in the office—new problems, minor changes, major changes, new situations, emergencies—are beyond your control. However, how you react to them is within your control. Don't overreact. Turn challenges into opportunities for growth.

3. When you feel impatient, don't show it! Be patient, take time to distinguish fact from fiction, and withhold judgment until you have all the facts.

Exhibit Self-Management

Self-management means that you set personal goals, monitor your progress, assess yourself accurately, and exhibit self-control. Your goals may be for self-improvement in certain areas, attempting something new, or working on a personal problem.

When you are faced with difficult situations in the workplace, you should always exhibit self-control. You know yourself better than anyone else; therefore, if this is an area you need to work on, set self-management goals to develop the ability to react as you should in stressful situations. When you are in a tense situation, stop and think before you speak. Give yourself time to analyze the reactions of others to what you might say. This time can allow you to organize your thoughts and response, help you develop the desired attitude, and help you avoid reacting inappropriately.

You should seek to cultivate attitudes and traits that will contribute to your success. When you succeed in displaying an appropriate attitude or trait in a difficult situation, you will be able to apply that experience in coping with the next difficult situation.

Display Integrity/Honesty

Integrity and honesty both involve being sincere and trustworthy. No one wants to work with someone who does not possess these characteristics. The lack of these characteristics can lead to disruptive terms of employment. Just as you set these standards for yourself, you should expect the same standards from everyone with whom you work. Integrity encompasses sound moral or ethical principles, fairness, honesty, sincerity, and the courage to stand up for these moral precepts. Strength of character, the behaviour that demonstrates you live by your values, and integrity are among the most important traits a person can possess.

You will be respected if your dealings with others are fair, honest, and sincere. Not all aspects of business are as ethical as they should be. When you face a serious ethical situation, rely on your strength of character to make your decision. Your only alternative may be to change employment. Whatever your decision, never cover for another person's transgression. You must be accountable for your actions.

Remember to Always Project a Professional Image

What is professionalism? **Professionalism** is aspiring to meet the highest possible standards of your profession rather than a set of minimum requirements. Embrace these opportunities rather than shying away from them.

First impressions are everything, and the first impression you want to make is by projecting a positive professional image. A professional image reflects:

- an educated and skilled employee
- a team player who contributes valuable ideas
- a polished individual with a neat, groomed appearance and a clear, concise communication style

- a person who can solve problems and integrate ideas
- a person who takes pride in each piece of work he or she produces
- an employee who works for the betterment of the organization and is not self-serving
- a person who takes pride in his or her career and who has aspirations for the future
- an employee who manages assignments by applying quality standards
- an employee who is willing to work hard and accept new and more challenging responsibilities
- an employee who is willing to learn and grow professionally
- one who seeks to learn about professional organizations such as the International Association of Administrative Professionals (IAAP; see Chapter 17)

Sir Walter Scott said, "Success or failure is caused more by mental attitude than by mental capacity." You should approach life and your job with a positive attitude. Periodically take inventory of your needs and your accomplishments. Set new goals and keep reaching. Your rewards will be many, including physical vitality, an alert mind, and an optimistic attitude towards life.

> **Self-Check**
>
> 1. Describe two strategies for projecting a professional image.
> 2. List any personal qualities you plan to improve.

OFFICE POLITICS

Office politics can be defined simply as actions taken by office employees to influence others for personal reasons. Depending on how you react to office politics, it can work either to your advantage or your disadvantage. In industry, a hierarchy is considered necessary to streamline tasks and ensure the right people stay informed when important decisions are being made. When office politics are transferred from person to person, sometimes-petty competitions and one-upmanship problems emerge (Randstad, 2017).

Recognize Office Politics

These attempts to influence others are often exhibited in some of the following ways:

- **Withholding or selectively sharing information.** If an employee chooses to pass along damaging information, it can seriously affect the careers of other employees. The same is true when accurate information is withheld.

- **Creating political networks.** When a person cultivates a relationship with someone for the purpose of getting advancement in the office, gaining information, getting approval on a project, or reaching other personal objectives, it is referred to as political networking. If you are excluded from the office social network, you may become quite powerless.

- **Accusing other people.** Sometimes one employee will repeatedly place blame on a particular employee. This action might be to target a person who is in a desirable position. Eventually management may be convinced that the employee being blamed is detrimental to the staff. In this case, the accused person may lose his/her job, leaving the job open for the accuser.

- **Forming groups.** How often have we heard the expression "strength in numbers"? When two or more people with a common purpose join together to force a change in the office, they are acting politically. This group may attempt to change office procedures or even to change management decisions.

Being able to recognize office politics is important. But for many people, this skill is acquired only with some first-hand experience.

Good or Bad?

We acknowledge that office politics exists, but is it a good thing or is it a bad thing for the office?

If you become politically involved in your company for the good of others, especially your co-workers or subordinates, you will be favourably recognized. An example would be creating a political network that allows you to grow close to management personnel. Your association with management may get your department an increase in budget. Subsequently, that budget increase might create some new work in your department, providing opportunity for yourself and or co-workers. On the other hand, the people who lose at the game of office politics or are the victim of another person's political gain will view office politics as unfavourable.

Whether you approve of office politics or not, it does exist. The best policy is to stay away from politics that will adversely affect others. However, some healthy political manoeuvres that bring success to your team and are not at the expense of other people are characteristic of good leadership.

> **Self-Check**
>
> 1. Give three examples of positive results of office politics.
> 2. Give three examples of negative office politics.

WORKPLACE ETHICS

The concept of ethics is difficult to understand. Cultures have wrestled with it for millennia without developing a set of rules describing what is good and what is bad. Whether you act ethically or unethically at work will depend on several factors, including the way you were raised, your individual values, personality, and experience. It will also have a lot to do with the organization's culture and the issue in question. In fact, ethics and behaviour are just as critical for companies as performance. It encompasses elements such as behaviour, integrity, accountability, and commitment.

Ethical Practice

Many common practices are questionable in the workplace. They are often associated with irresponsible work practice and the theft of time and resources.

Examples of questionable behaviour are:

- doing something unethical based on a request by your manager—for example, shredding documents to hide the fact that they ever existed

- not paying an employee a final payment or not paying for all the earned hours

- theft of company property or time

- cyberslacking, using company time and resources to surf websites for personal interests

- altering information on documents to falsify information

- not reporting incidents, such as accidents, in a manufacturing company

Along with these common practices comes the rationalization: the devil made me do it, they don't pay me enough, I put so much time in here anyway, and I write reports at home . . . I think "they" should supply the paper! But employees, regardless of their roles, are ethically obliged to follow the ethical policies at work just as they are legally obliged to follow civil law. Obviously, we should not steal, lie, or harass others in the workplace. We should treat others with respect and expect the same consideration in return.

Employees are obliged to fulfill the terms of their contract. If they are hired to work eight hours a day, they should work that amount of time. They should work conscientiously according to the terms of their contract. We are obliged to consider the interests of the organization for which we work. These obligations are sometimes spelled out in employment contracts and job descriptions.

Without rules, good ethical practice becomes **ambiguous**. Codes of ethical practice are an increasingly popular tool for reducing that ambiguity. A **code of ethics** is a formal document developed by your organization that states the organization's primary values and ethical rules of conduct. The best ones are specific and not only guide employees in what they are supposed to do but also allow employees the freedom to exercise judgment in their decisions.

Decisions, especially ambiguous ones, can be tested by asking yourself questions such as:

- What benefit and what harm will my decision produce?

- What rights do the other people have that are involved in my decision, and what can I do to respect those rights?

- Which decision treats everyone the same and does not show favouritism or discrimination?

- Does my decision benefit most people in the organization or just me?

- Does my decision consider my ideas of honesty, compassion, integrity, fairness, and good sense?

Adopting a code of corporate ethics is a necessary entity for contemporary organizations. If a code of ethics exists at the organization where you work, read it and commit to its principles. If used well, the code will guide you through those ambiguous decisions. Included in the ethical code would be clear directions surrounding company values, guiding principles, personal responsibility, and management support. Codes of ethics can be effective depending on whether the organization supports them and the consequences when a breach of conduct is experienced when code is broken. In the end, as an employee you have the responsibility to do the right thing based on your own judgment, personal principles, and the company values.

Work, Time, and Resources

Good judgment and discretion are much more than keeping information confidential. Their foundation lies in sound ethical conduct, which has a far-reaching effect in the contemporary business office. Let's review ethical responsibilities as they relate to the office. If you find yourself considering any of the following activities, recognize that your organization's policies and trust are likely to be compromised.

With Regard to Work

- plagiarizing
- harassing co-workers
- exaggerating on your résumé
- pretending to be ill
- spreading untrue information
- endangering others
- deceiving others
- acting unreasonably
- speaking negatively in public about the organization

With Regard to Time

- taking extended breaks
- arriving late
- leaving early
- wasting time
- talking at length on personal telephone calls
- checking your personal email during company time

With Regard to Resources

- exaggerating on expense claims
- playing games on the company computer
- downloading software for personal use
- conducting personal research on the internet
- taking supplies for personal use at home
- using the photocopier for personal documents

Consider your company's code of ethics as well as your own standards of loyalty, fairness, and truthfulness. Then ask yourself if you would be comfortable if your actions were published on the front page of the office newsletter. After this simple test, you'll know whether or not you have compromised any codes or standards.

Self-Check

1. List two additional examples of unethical situations.

CHANGE IN THE WORKPLACE
Change Is Constant

In today's workplace, the organization you work for is likely to experience consistent change due to competitive pressures and technological developments. Organizations today compared to a few years ago tend to be:

- leaner and more responsive
- less hierarchical in structure
- focused on identifying customer needs
- competitive requirements and strategy
- periodically reorganizing to maintain or gain competitive edge

Change has become the expectation in the office. Change, both organizational and technological, is an important part of doing business and cannot be avoided. **Change management** seeks to steer organizational results and outcomes by engaging employees and inspiring their adoption of a new way of working. Changes come about rapidly because evolving corporate landscape dictates it, competition between companies, and the restructuring of organizations to become more efficient. Newer technology is enabling administrative professionals to produce more with greater speed and ease than in the past. Organizations need to replace outdated equipment and systems with modernized equipment, so accept the fact that the equipment and software you learn to operate today will be replaced by new technology tomorrow.

The pressure of competition has increased because of international trade. Telecommunications and the internet have made competing in the **global marketplace** common practice.

Another major change has been the restructuring of organizations. Companies are constantly striving to outdo their competition, a process that involves combining or eliminating functions, increased staff training, and equipment investments that will improve their operations. All of these advances result in operational and procedural change.

As well, company **mergers** and **buyouts** occur, resulting in a duplication of jobs and positions that must be addressed. In a merger, the two companies agree on the restructuring. In a buyout, one company buys out the other, and there may be less agreement on restructuring.

Regardless of where you work, change is inevitable. Anticipate it and realize that change is a constant element. Expect yourself to abruptly transition to new equipment and new software, to be assigned an entirely new role within your organization, or to be looking for employment with another organization. Instead of wasting energy over changes you cannot avoid, direct your energy towards getting in step with new arrangements. If an opportunity to use new equipment or software presents itself, or a chance to participate in further training or new responsibilities arises, grasp the opportunity. You should always welcome new possibilities for growth, since professional development prepares you for steady employment and improves your prospects for career advancement.

Adapt to New Management

You can expect to have more than one change in management as well as a variety of roles and possibly a variety of careers in your lifetime. Your challenge is to prove yourself in all situations. Never expect a new management team to be like the last one. No two managers are exactly alike. The best advice to handle changes in management is to be flexible, adaptable, and tolerant (FAT). Show tolerance to different ideas and beliefs expressed by the new management team.

Management can change rapidly, but successful managers do share some of the same qualities. For example, all good managers have a capacity for smart work practices and are dedicated to the organizational objectives and support their team. They are never satisfied with the status quo; they can't afford to be.

Respect your manager's position. A managerial job involves continual challenges that are not always easy to troubleshoot. You can contribute by listening and offering solutions instead of layering problems. Whenever you need to address an issue with the manager, always be prepared to offer viable solutions.

You should be as dependable and accountable to the new management as to the previous management. At all levels of management, loyalty is rated as one of the most desirable traits an employee can possess. Being loyal means supporting the organization's policies and actions. Being loyal can be difficult when you believe management is not working in the best interests of the organization. If you find yourself in this situation, don't jump to conclusions. Not all managers are good managers, and many lose their positions because of poor management skills. Working for a manager who does not perform the job well will be difficult. However, by being loyal to the company, diplomatic, and tolerant, you should be able to preserve a stake in the organization if you choose to remain in place.

A promotion for you could mean working for new management. Be flexible. Be willing to accept change and to adjust to new situations. View change as the opportunity for new and exciting challenges. The more you demonstrate your ability to accept the challenges of your new assignments, the more professional opportunities will come your way.

MANAGING STRESS

Anyone who has ever held a job has felt the pressure of work-related stress. Any job can have stressful elements, even if you love what you do. Jobs in contemporary offices can be stressful. Some people seem to thrive on **stress** while others crumble under it. The difference is that those who cope well with stress have control over their jobs. This control enables them to meet their own deadlines, as well as deadlines set for them by others. There are often aspects or parts of jobs where control is not possible, so it is helpful to create strategies to manage elements beyond the span of control. Having a positive attitude towards work helps people to deal with stress.

Wellness in the Workplace

Although the workplace may seem to be safe, hazards abound. Ergonomic illnesses such as repetitive stress injuries, neck strain, eye stress, and muscle strain are just the beginning. The most common workplace illness in the professional environment is mental stress.

Companies are well aware of the effect that stress has on employees. They are equally aware of the cost to the company when workers are away from their jobs either through physical illness or mental stress leaves. It is in the company's best interest to take good care of its employees. That's why programs for prevention of workplace illness are in place at many organizations. Some of the common programs include:

- free access to wellness counsellors, social workers, and psychologists
- company-sponsored memberships for health clubs
- health seminars held at lunchtime
- health videos, CDs, and books available in the company library
- company-paid massage therapy
- company-sponsored healthcare and dental plans
- health food in the company cafeteria
- fitness programs offered at the company's own gym or courts

What Causes Stress in the Office?

What makes office work stressful? This question is difficult to answer, since what causes negative stress for one person is stimulating and positive to the next worker. The following is a list of reported sources of work-related stress for many office professionals:

- Select office professionals are hired to complete temporary assignments. In these cases, there is very little long-term employment security.
- Technology improves rapidly, requiring constant retraining.
- Management styles and organizational structures continue to change. Companies have flattened their management and downsized their staff, causing insecurity for workers. In these cases, employees work under the constant threat of losing their jobs.
- The responsibilities of office professionals have broadened and intensified.
- Dealing with challenging managers or co-workers, employees often leave positions not based on the company but based on personnel issues.
- Workloads have become heavier as companies cut back their budgets and expect to do more with fewer resources.
- In order to keep up with the workload, many office professionals work through the day without taking time for lunch, refreshments, or even washroom breaks.

Stress Management

People often blame the company or their jobs for causing their high levels of stress. In fact, stress leave is a common request for people who believe they need relief from their work.

FIGURE 1-5 Recognize when your co-workers are under stress.

Dmitry Melnikov/Shutterstock

However, work is not the only source of negative stress. People who carry a lot of responsibility outside their employment often suffer from stress because they are trying to do too much—balancing the responsibilities for family and home, community work, continued education and training, and so on. Figure 1-5 shows an office worker experiencing stress in her job.

To cope with stress, analyze what is happening to you. Often it is not the situation that causes stress but how you react to it and what you do about it.

A certain amount of stress helps us to be alert, efficient, and creative. Here are some suggestions for handling stress that becomes *too* great:

1. Recognize what your body is telling you, and recognize that anger and frustration are energy wasters. Keep notes on what is happening and the cause.

2. Organize your work and your time for the entire day. Assign priorities to your work; don't plan more than is possible to do in a day.

3. When faced with an overload of work, analyze it and discuss it with your supervisor. Offer solutions. By facing a situation, you will relieve stress and ensure that you don't become overwhelmed.

4. Don't be overly critical of your own work and don't expect impossible levels of work from others. Strive for excellence, but at times be pleased with an acceptable performance.

5. Slow down! This is good advice for office professionals who race around doing their work at turbo speeds. You will accomplish more and also eliminate stress by working at a comfortable pace—one that enables you to keep mistakes to a minimum, to relate well with others, and to avoid backtracking and revising.

6. Avoid taking on too much. Learn to say "no" tactfully. Don't hesitate to refuse outside organizations that ask you to do volunteer work. Consider hiring help for home and family responsibilities.

7. Talk out your stressful problems. Find someone in whom you can confide—someone away from the job, someone who is a good listener. Simply talking out your problem can be helpful.

8. Eat nourishing food regularly and in moderate amounts.

9. Program relaxation into your schedule. Use lunch and coffee breaks to relax. Don't use these breaks to rush around on personal errands. During your breaks, be quiet, and practise relaxation techniques until you feel yourself relaxing. Use waiting time to relax. Allow yourself a quiet hour at home. Schedule some time for a hobby.

10. Get regular exercise. Exercise is one of the best ways to shed stress.

11. Escape to a movie, to your favourite TV program, to spend time with others, or to do something for someone in need.

Self-Check

1. Suggest two ways to navigate and manage stress.

SOCIAL SKILLS

For the office professional, it's not enough to just be technically competent, an excellent office administrator, and a tactful communicator in the office. The responsibilities of many business professionals extend outside the walls of the office. Many administrative professionals find themselves entertaining customers of the company, and most administrative professionals socialize with company personnel or customers outside the office. These social situations require a special set of skills. It may be difficult in some social situations to retain your professionalism and ethical correctness. A common ethical dilemma is office romance.

Keep Personal Relationships Private

The professional office is an obvious place to meet new friends and to establish romantic relationships. Many professionals with fast-paced jobs spend more time at work than they do away from work. Work brings people with common goals and interests into the same environment, an environment where people look their best, perform at their best, work cohesively together, and show respect for each other. This environment makes the office an appealing place to find a partner for a romantic relationship.

However, in general, organizations do not condone romantic relationships in the working environment.

Romantic relationships are seen as getting in the way of work goals and productivity.

So before you enter a romantic relationship with a colleague, ask yourself if the positives outweigh the negatives. Whatever you perceive to be the advantages, consider the following questions:

- How will this relationship affect your professionalism and productivity on the job?
- How will the romance affect your working relationships with other colleagues?
- Will you be able to refrain from sharing confidential work-related issues with your partner?
- Do you share interests outside of work, or will your social conversation be restricted to only work topics?
- If your partner is dismissed from work, how will this affect the security of your job or your desire to continue with the same company?
- If your romantic relationship ends, will you be able to continue working together professionally?

The best advice for people involved romantically with a colleague is to keep the personal relationship private. If it becomes common knowledge that you are partners, don't deny it, but beyond that, avoid sharing information about your social activities, your future plans, and personal information about your partner. Once your colleagues learn that you have no intention to share this kind of private information, they will stop asking for it and will respect you for your confidentiality.

Let's Do Lunch!

Knowing how to care for a guest and displaying good manners at a business lunch are desirable social skills for any office professional. Management may expect you to take new employees or customers for lunch, you might attend a business lunch for an association you belong to, or you might be attending a luncheon at a conference or business meeting. Whatever the occasion, you will want to make the right impression.

Entire books have been devoted to the subject of using proper manners and business etiquette in social circumstances. This short section is not meant to be a detailed guide; rather, the intent here is to help you avoid making embarrassing mistakes. The following are some simple but important guidelines for business dining:

1. When escorted by the restaurant host to a table, your guest should walk ahead of you and behind the host.

2. If you take a guest to a restaurant that has open seating, lead the way to an appropriate table.

3. Unless you intend to negotiate with your guest during lunch, offer your guest the best seat at the table;

remember, your objective is to make your guest feel comfortable. Often the best seat is the one facing the main eating area. Never seat guests so they are facing the exit doors, or the kitchen or washroom doors.

4. Place your napkin on your lap only *after* everyone has arrived and is seated; once the meal begins, the napkin should not be placed on the table until the meal is finished.

5. Guests will get an idea of acceptable price range from the meal you suggest or order. Having your guest order first is a courteous gesture; but, unless your guest knows what you plan to eat, you may be placing your guest in an awkward position.

6. When the server takes your order, refer to the other party as your guest ("I will let my guest order first," or "My guest would like to order . . ." or similar). This is a clue to the server that you would like the bill brought to you.

7. Let hot food cool naturally; do not blow on your food, stir soup or coffee that is too hot, or fan your food. These activities are distracting and considered rude and unbusinesslike behaviour.

8. Begin eating only after everyone has been served. Often meals will arrive at the table a few minutes apart. It is considered rude to begin eating while someone is left sitting without a meal.

9. If you reach for something, such as a condiment or breadbasket, offer the item to your guest before you serve yourself.

10. Table settings are often confusing and leave a person wondering which glass or fork to use. The general rule for utensils is *outside in*. If there is a series of forks or spoons, simply begin by using the one on the outer edge of your table setting and work inward towards your plate. Your glass will be at the top of your knife on the right side of your plate; your bread and butter plate will be to your left.

11. Never chew with your mouth open or talk with food in your mouth. It's wise to take only small bites so that you can carry on a conversation.

12. If the need arises to remove something undesirable from your mouth (such as a seed, bone, pit, or partially chewed food), you should use a utensil rather than your fingers to catch the food. Lift your napkin to your mouth at the same time to conceal the unwanted food.

13. The proper way to eat any form of bread is to break it off as needed, into bite-sized pieces.

14. When you are finished eating, never remove or stack dishes for the server. You want to maintain a professional business image.

15. Never primp at the table. If you wish to apply cosmetics, comb your hair, straighten your clothing or—worst of all—blow your nose, do so in the washroom.

Following these general guidelines will increase your confidence and pleasure at any business lunch.

Self-Check

1. What are two rules of etiquette when hosting a business lunch? Can you think of one more?

QUESTIONS FOR STUDY AND REVIEW

1. Describe the administrative professional's role in forming the image of the organization.

2. What is human resources, and why is it relevant to human relations?

3. Provide a description for organizational culture, climate, and citizenship.

4. State the impact for an organization of effective teamwork.

5. Provide an example of a team-building guideline that supports an effective team.

6. Describe a nonproductive team behaviour and explain how you, as a team member, might influence a positive change in this behaviour.

7. Explain how human resource management supports and contributes to organizational success.

8. Would a career in human resource management interest you? Why or why not?

9. Describe what it means to create political networks.

10. Consider two possible reasons why a person might withhold or selectively share information in an office.

11. List three unethical behaviours commonly found in office environments.

12. Could the term "strength in numbers" be interpreted as office politics? Why or why not?

13. Give examples of healthy office politics that could bring success to your office team.

14. What is a code of ethics?

15. State two guidelines for maintaining the confidentiality of work-related information.

16. State three unethical practices that relate to each of the following: work, time, and resources. Include an additional unethical practice not included in the chapter.

17. Discuss two examples of actions you can take to develop respectful relationships in the office

18. If an office professional has integrity, what traits might they display?

19. Why is change constant in the office and suggest how you can prepare for change?

20. Why would being flexible, adaptable, and tolerant with new management be beneficial?

21. If you believe that management is not working in the best interests of the organization, what should you do?

22. Discuss progressive steps a company could take to reduce stress in the workplace.

23. State reasons why the work of an office professional may be stressful.

24. Suggest eight strategies you might employ to reduce stress.

25. Why do companies discourage personal relationships between employees?

26. Suggest five guidelines you might follow when taking a guest for a business lunch.

Key Terms

ambiguous 25

buyouts 26

change management 26

code of ethics 25

competitive advantage 13

composure 23

empowered 18

global marketplace 26

hard skills 14

human capital 13

human resources management (HRM) 13

interpersonal skills 16

merger 26

negotiating 20

office politics 24

organizational behaviour (OB) 14

organizational climate 13

organizational culture 13

organizational structure 14

personal qualities 15

personality 18

poise 23

professionalism 23

soft skills 15

stress 27

EVERYDAY ETHICS

Dating the Boss

Alex has been Patti's supervisor for the last three years. They started dating over a year ago and agreed to keep their relationship confidential and quite separate from their professional lives. It's worked well so far because Patti is working as a senior administrative professional in another department quite separate from Alex.

However, a great, new executive assistant opportunity has occurred—working directly for Alex! The problem is that Neela, the only other competitor for the new position, has seen Patti and Alex together socially.

Not surprisingly, Neela has spread the rumour that Patti is dating the boss and that she, Patti, will obviously have an unfair advantage when interviews begin.

- Do you see any *potential* harm in this scenario?
- What should Patti do in this situation?

Problem Solving

1. You work for Dynamic Systems as an executive assistant. The longer you work for this organization, the more often you have to make decisions about whether the behaviour of you and your colleagues is ethical or unethical. What will you do when the following situations occur?

   a. As a part of your professional responsibilities, you make many long-distance calls from the telephone in your office. These calls are not tracked. You would like to use your office telephone to make a personal call long distance to your mother.

   b. Your company policy states that it deducts wages for people who come to work late or leave early. One of your assistant's works very hard, accomplishes a great deal, and is essential to your success at work. Her only method of transportation is the public bus service. To make her transportation convenient, she arrives 15 minutes late every day. It's your responsibility to deduct her salary.

   c. You are responsible for hiring a new receptionist. Your friend really needs the job but is not the most qualified person who applied.

   d. During a sales meeting with a client, the sales representative presents false information about a company product. This information leads to the signing of a contract during that meeting.

2. You are an administrative professional in the purchasing department. The other administrative professional, Janice McCall, is getting married on November 18. The purchasing department employs 12 office workers. According to a rumour, Janice is not coming back to work after the wedding, and two of the office workers want to apply for her position. They have come to you to find out if the rumour is true. You have not seen an official announcement about Janice's employment plans after she gets married. However, Janice did tell you that she does not plan to come back to work after the wedding. What should you say to your two co-workers?

3. You and Chris met at work three years ago, and you have now been married for one year. Your main social group is made up of your office colleagues. The company is going through a reorganization, and, unfortunately, Chris has been given notice that his position will be eliminated at the end of next month. Chris is bitter about the company's decision, and, as a result, he has been outspoken and critical about company policy and management. How should you react to this?

Special Reports

1. Think of someone whose personality you admire. Make a list of this person's personality traits that you like and then select the most outstanding traits and describe them in detail. Try to decide why these traits appeal to you. Do you think they would appeal to others? Share your ideas by writing an email with your comments to your instructor.

2. Select two organizations where you vision yourself working. Research their code of ethics or code of conduct and hiring practices. Do any policies concern you? Do any codes or hiring practices affect your desire to work for either of these organizations? Why or why not?

PRODUCTION CHALLENGES

1-A Exercising Ethics

Supplies needed:

- *Personal Values, Form 1-A, Companion Website*

To develop professionally, everyone needs to develop a personal framework of ethics. To do this, consider what you value the most and what you value the least. Refer to Form 1-A in your Working Papers, where you will rank 15 different values by placing the number 1 next to the item you value the most and the number 15 next to the item you value the least. You must give each item a number. Do not repeat any of the numbers. This is a difficult exercise. There are no right or wrong answers. This will simply encourage you to think about your own values.

1-B Challenging Personalities

Supplies needed:

- *Difficult Personalities, Form 1-B, Companion Website*

3. If you were seeking employment today, what steps do you think you could take to research a company's organizational culture? Prepare a list of steps to share with your class.

Noah Wilson has asked you to attend a workshop to learn more about challenging personalities and the conflicts that may arise within teams because of the challenges.

The workshop is held at your local college. When you arrive, your instructor puts you into small groups and asks you to discuss specific personality types and to come up with possible coping strategies. Refer to Form 1-B in your Working Papers, and in small groups (consisting of your classmates) discuss personality behaviours.

When you return to your office, Noah Wilson advises that he is looking forward to learning about the insights you have gained from this workshop. He asks you to prepare a report on what you have discovered about challenging personalities and to include a copy of the form you have completed.

Weblinks

Business Ethics
www.businessethics.ca
This site offers access to a wide variety of Canadian resources for business ethics including articles, case studies, and more.

Human Resource Management Canada
https://www.canada.ca/en/services/business/hire/humanresourcesmanagement.html
A government of Canada website populated with information for business surrounding human resources, requirements and best practices.

Publications for Corporate Wellness
www.personalbest.com
The topics on this site are devoted to corporate wellness. It advertises self-help publications for organizations.

Office Politics
www.managementhelp.org
Here you will find various perspectives on many topics from interpersonal skills to evaluations to personal development.

Stress Management
http://www.helpguide.org/mental/stress_management_relief_coping.htm
Topics dealing with how to reduce prevent, and cope with stress are featured on this site along with links to many other valuable resources on the topic.

Protocol and Etiquette
www.charlestonschoolofprotocol.com
Here's a site that provides online professional etiquette information.

References

Randstad. (2017). How to avoid office drama and engaging in office politics. Retrieved from https://www.randstad.ca/job-seeker/job-tips/archives/how-to-avoid-office-drama-and-politics_549/

Chapter 2
Diversity and International Business Relations

G-stockstudio/Shutterstock

LEARNING OUTCOMES

After completion of this chapter, the student will be able to:

1 Understand the components of diversity.

2 Comprehend the importance and benefits of organizational diversity management.

3 Identify human rights, equity standards, protections, and employer obligations influencing the Canadian workplace.

4 Describe methods for developing cross-cultural awareness.

5 Identify ways for improving international communication.

6 Discuss the importance of international business relations.

7 State important considerations when travelling to foreign countries and hosting international visitors.

DIVERSITY AND EQUITY

Diversity encompasses acceptance and respect for others, as well as an understanding that each individual is unique. It involves recognizing individual differences, including culture, race, ethnicity, gender, sexual orientation, socioeconomic status, age, physical abilities, and religious beliefs. It entails moving beyond simple tolerance to embracing and celebrating the dimensions of diversity found within each individual.

Successful businesses embrace and encourage diversity in the workplace. The concept of workplace diversity incorporates awareness of, and respect for, differences in the way people communicate, approach tasks, and interact. To be effective in industry an administrative professional takes steps to develop an awareness and understanding of a diversified workplace. Building connections with individuals, groups, and industry stakeholders is usually essential to the success of an organization, based on a foundation of mutual respect. In your role, you will frequently cultivate and sustain successful business relations. Oftentimes the administrative professional is the first point of contact within an organization, making it imperative to ensure all visitors and callers receive courteous and respectful treatment.

Diversity adds a special richness to the workplace, but it brings rise to some direct and indirect challenges. Several of these direct challenges are addressed as protections under specific Canadian statutes. Canada is committed to ensuring equitable and fair treatment of all citizens in and outside of the workplace. Two federal acts, the *Canadian Charter of Rights and Freedoms* as well as the *Canadian Human Rights Act,* express these protections.

Organizations have adopted diversity management programs to ensure charter rights are upheld along with enhancing workforce diversity. A diversity management program can position organizations for success in today's competitive global market.

Diversity in the Workplace

Diversity has gained increasing attention in recent years due to the changing demographics in the Canadian workplace. **Demographics** refers to a structure of populations. By 2020, the demographic of the Canadian workforce will be more culturally diverse, older, and more female than ever before. With these factors in mind, consider the following related to workplace diversity.

Age/Generational Diversity According to Statistics Canada, approximately 48% of the population is 25–64 years of age. The highest groups, in terms of numbers, are represented by both ends of the spectrum;

25–35 and 50–59. This is an interesting contrast from the perspective that generational work and life experiences of both groups could be drastically different. Relational communicational dynamics are affected when generational differences come into play. The current generations identified in the Canadian workforce include the baby boomers born 1945–1965, generation X born 1966–1980, millennials born 1981–1996, and generation Z born after 1996. Each generation tends to have its preferred method of communication—for instance, studies show baby boomers tend to like phone calls and emails for communication, while millennials prefer the instant communication style of texting. If these differences are not well understood by both employees and management, the potential for conflict is high. Organizational leadership with this heightened awareness sets clear ground rules in order to differentiate what is acceptable and what is not. Coming from different generations means that people will have diverse perspectives, core values, and methodologies. Another component that each generation sometimes brings forth is their stereotypes of other generations. Elder workers may perceive younger ones as entitled or lazy. In contrast, younger workers may think their older counterparts as unwilling to adapt and thus set in their ways. Employees across generational groups are encouraged to understand each other's individual differences; from an enhancement perspective, think of the cross-generation integration and the mentorship opportunities. Mature workers can provide guidance and support the development of younger workers. The younger work force may bring an enhanced technological medium skill set or new procedures to streamline specific tasks or processes. High-functioning organizations know to address age diversity and its impact, negative or positive.

Cultural Diversity Cultural diversity is the integration and acceptance of multiple cultures in a specific place or demographic location. In Canada, our society is made up of people and groups with various traditions and racial origins. With the arrival of the *Canadian Multiculturalism Act* in 1971, Canada became the first country in the world to declare multiculturalism an official state policy. This bold step charted the path to a vibrant and changing cultural mosaic built on mutual respect for Canadians of all backgrounds and ancestry.

The roots of multiculturalism in Canada can be seen in the country's origins, as three founding cultures—Indigenous, British, and French—were soon joined by many others from around the world. Today, multiculturalism is a key element of Canadian national identity. In fact, individuals who have neither French nor British heritage now make up the largest part of Canadian society. Policies and standards are in place in Canada that encourages cultural integration in the workplace and in society.

Culture diversity within the workplace creates differing views surrounding, beliefs, communication, formality, hierarchy, time perception, priorities, value, and uniqueness. To provide additional context, in North America there tends to be a directness in communication style, while in other cultures a more indirect approach is customary; however, it may be perceived as being misleading or deceptive, depending on the cultural background of the recipient regarding communication styles. In terms of formality, cultures differ greatly in greetings, manners, and etiquette. Again, formality is more valued in several cultures and is an essential sign of respect, while in other cultures it does not hold significant importance. Diverse cultural perspectives can drive innovation and inspire creativity. In Canada, workplace diversity is the new normal.

Race and Ethnic Diversity

Race is the word used to describe the physical characteristics of a person. These characteristics can include everything from skin color to eye color and facial structure to hair color. **Ethnicity** is the word used to describe the cultural identity of a person. These identities can include language, religion, nationality, ancestry, dress, and customs. One example of the difference between these two terms is by examining people who share the same ethnicity. Two people can identify their ethnicity as American, yet their races may be black and white. Additionally, a person born of Asian descent who grew up in Germany may identify racially as Asian and ethnically as German.

Religious Diversity

Religion in Canada encompasses a wide range of groups and beliefs. Christianity is the largest religion in Canada, with Roman Catholics having the most identified affiliation. However, Canada has no official religion, and support for religious pluralism and freedom of religion is an important part of Canada's culture. According to Statistics Canada, over 22.1 million people, two-thirds of Canada's population, reported that they were affiliated with a Christian religion. Roman Catholics at 12,728,900 were by far the largest Christian group, with the United Church the second largest group of about 2,007,600. Additionally, over 1 million individuals identified themselves as Muslim, representing 3.2% of Canada's total population. Hindus represented 1.5%, Sikhs 1.4%, Buddhists 1.1%, and Jews 1.0%. Finally, about 7.8 million people, nearly one-quarter of the population (23.9%) had no religious affiliation (Statistics Canada, 2017).

With effective diversity management, employers understand accommodations will need to be made on the basis of religious observances. This entails changing a schedule to accommodate holy days, time off for prayers, or providing breaks. It is important to remember that we don't leave our identities at home when we come to work, and for some, spirituality is an essential part of who they are as individuals.

Sexual Orientation and Gender Identity

Sexual orientation is an inherent or absolute continuing emotional, romantic, or sexual attraction to other people. Sexual orientation covers lesbian, gay, bisexual, transgender, queer (LGBTQ) and heterosexual, as well as people perceived to fall into one or identify within one of these groups. The acronym LGBTQ is sometimes shown as LGBTQX with the X representing additional groups. In 1996, the *Canadian Human Rights Act* was amended to specifically include sexual orientation as one of the prohibited grounds of discrimination.

Discrimination is an action or a decision that results in the unfair or negative treatment of a person or group because of differences such as race, age, religion, sex, etc. Most forms of discrimination are considered illegal under federal and provincial human rights laws. Provinces and territories have included sexual orientation in their human rights legislation as prohibited grounds of discrimination. In recent years, a group of individuals formed Pride at Work Canada to improve the climate of inclusiveness for lesbian, gay, bisexual, and transgender identified (LGBTQ) employees in Canadian workplaces (Ellard-Gray, 2015).

Gender identity and gender expression is one's innermost concept of self as male, female, a blend of both, or neither—how individuals perceive themselves and what they call themselves. One's gender identity can be the same or different from their sex assigned at birth. Expression refers to the gender an individual presents themselves as in public.

For individuals who identify as part of the LGBTQ community, disclosure at work is a concern due to real or perceived stigma. Within the framework of a diversity management plan, employers examine their organizational culture to ensure an inclusive and welcoming workplace exists. Business leaders put this belief into practice. The vast majority of Canadian workplaces are representative of the communities in which they operate, and have a diversity committee.

Physical Ability and Disability

References to definitions surrounding ability and disability constantly evolve. According to the United Nations Convention on the Rights of Persons with Disabilities, persons with disabilities include those who have long-term physical, mental, intellectual, or sensory impairments, which interaction with various barriers may hinder their full and effective participation in society on an equal basis with others. Recent studies have revealed that

SaskPower Corporation Regina Saskatchewan

Michael Bell/The Canadian Press/AP Images

SaskPower Hydroelectric power generation located in Regina, Saskatchewan, employs over 3,000 and proudly maintains a diversity department. This department is responsible for the implementation and development of a diverse employee base. Its managers believe their workforce should be as diverse as the customers they serve. Building a diverse labour force benefits all and reflects a fair and equitable workplace. This extends to and is foundational to the SaskPower Corporation strategic plan for 2017–2020.

The inclusive nature includes race, ethnicity, gender, age, religion, disability, and sexual orientation and extends to include professional characteristics such as work habits, behaviours, and communication style. The goal is to create an organizational culture that encourages all employees to reach their full potential every day.

SaskPower has established six affinity groups that include an aboriginal employee network, network of employees for disabilities, and visible minority network, all with a goal of maintaining a diverse and inclusive workspace. Additionally, SaskPower has a partnership with the Canadian Centre for Diversity and Inclusion (CCDI) and an equity agreement with the Saskatchewan Human Rights Committee (SHRC).

Additional initiatives include mentorship through the Women's Resource Group (WRG), participation by employees in their communities Pride events, and opportunities to engage in networking events such as the Visible Minorities Network (VMN), which invites immigrants to socialize and share information.

The SaskPower Diversity and the affinity groups provide substantial leadership in helping to ensure the power corporation attains its diversity and inclusive goals. This group generally represents all employees by providing a voice to make a difference in securing a share vision of both diversity and inclusion. Values such as safety, openness, collaboration, and equitable opportunity building on each employee's strength promotes respect and engagement with customers, communities, and SaskPower shareholders.

hiring people with disabilities improves both organizational culture and financial sustainability. The more commonly people within an organization consider their workplace wonderful, the further the organization increases its competitive edge compared to its rivals in areas that include growth and retention.

For more consideration and as an example, the Ontario Human Rights Commission OHRC hosts a website containing a tab called Education & Outreach where case studies outlining some violations of rights are profiled for academic purposes. There are some variances between provincial and territorial HRC's websites; however, most provide case ruling examples.

Understanding the Benefits of Diversity

At no other time has there been a more complex array of diverse individuals within the Canadian workplace. In Canada, we have many cultures living and working together. There are significant advantages to diversity in the workplace. By integrating workers from diverse backgrounds into the workforce, organizations become much stronger. This strengthening can be achieved through increased recruiting opportunities, open-minded learning, and enhanced completive advantages. Diversity needs to be seen as an integral part of the business plan, essential to successful operation of the organization. This is especially true in today's global marketplace as companies interact with different cultures and clients.

By embracing diversity initiatives, a company can show that it recognizes and celebrates the differences associated with different backgrounds. By recognizing the value of each individual, a company can encourage employees to make worthy contributions to the organization. Indeed, when a company actively works towards achieving diversity in the workplace, it can increase productivity and overall morale.

The benefits of workplace diversity are numerous:

■ Fairness and equality can be achieved by having open lines of communication where each contribution is appreciated and respected. No one is favoured over another.

■ Hiring and promotional policies are based on qualifications and performance. This ensures that the most qualified individuals are recognized for what they have to offer.

■ New ideas and varying perspectives are shared. When we encourage an atmosphere where all team members are involved in the creative process, individuals will be comfortable in sharing ideas.

■ Utilization of the strengths and talents of team members can be realized, since people from diverse backgrounds often have assorted skills and abilities.

■ Differences can be harnessed and made to work for the organization in positive ways.

HUMAN RIGHTS AND EQUITY STANDARDS

The *Canadian Human Rights Act* is a statute passed by the Parliament of Canada in 1977. The goal of this act is to ensure equal opportunity to individuals who may be disadvantaged due to discrimination based on set prohibited grounds such as gender, disability, or religion. The *Canadian Human Rights Act* outlines the creation of the Canadian Human Rights Commission (CHRC), which investigates claims of discrimination. The protections offered by this legislation extend into the workplace: in the Canadian workplace, we have the right to be treated fairly, free from discriminatory practices. A discriminatory practice might involve not hiring someone for a job based on age, gender, race, physical abilities, or religious beliefs. The Canadian Centre for Diversity and Inclusion is a national organization with the objective to assist individuals and organizations they work with to be inclusive and free of prejudice and discrimination. Additionally, their purpose serves to generate awareness, encourage discussion, and promote action for people to recognize diversity as an asset and not a barrier. See Figure 2-1 detailing the elements of the *Canadian Human Rights Act* that prohibit grounds of discrimination.

Discrimination in the workplace can also stem from stereotyping. **Stereotypes** are standardized and simplified conceptions of groups based on prior assumptions. We could consider stereotyping as a type of bias we form based either on preconceptions or on personal experience. Stereotyping can turn into discrimination if acted upon in a negative manner. Take, for example, a situation in which two equally qualified individuals are applying for the same job. One candidate is a mother with two children, and the other candidate is childless. If the employer treats these two candidates differently, or assumes that the mother will miss a lot of time at work or be preoccupied with her children, this would be a case of negative stereotyping.

In order to ensure equity in the Canadian workplace, a variety of protective standards have been established under the *Employment Equity Act (EEA)*. A key element of this law is the duty to accommodate; this provision refers to the obligation of an employer to take measures to eliminate disadvantages to employees and prospective employees that result (or may result) from a rule, practice, or physical barrier. The employer must make reasonable accommodations so that individuals with differing needs can work to the best of their ability. Differences that must be accommodated include gender, ethnic or cultural origin, physical ability, or religious affiliation. For example, a violation could involve an employer prohibiting an employee from wearing an item of clothing required by his or her religious practices, or otherwise not respecting this need.

FIGURE 2-1 *Canadian Human Rights Act* protected rights.

Race	Disability	Gender Identity	Gender Expression
Citizenship	Colour	Ethnic Origin	Ancestry
Sexual Orientation	Gender	Age	Family or Marital Status

DISCRIMINATORY WORKPLACE PROTECTIONS AND EMPLOYER OBLIGATIONS

The *Canadian Human Rights Act (CHRA)* functions alongside the *Employment Equity Act (EEA)*. Hours of work, minimum wages, sick days, vacation provisions, and many more related items are stipulated as employment standards. These are the minimum standards established by law that define and guarantee rights in the workplace. The employment laws of provinces or territories protect most workers in Canada. Provinces and territories have their own employment standards legislation. The major difference between the two is that the CHRA prohibits discrimination in general, whereas the EEA requires employers to use measures that improve employment opportunities for all. If you are the target of discrimination under the EEA, you can file a complaint with the CHRC. An employee must file a valid complaint with CHRC within 12 months of the incident. Missing the 12-month requirement results in the potential refusal of the complaint. As a practice, employees would first address their concerns with their manager and their human resources department before moving to the CHRC. A recent ruling by the Supreme Court of Canada said a British Columbia employee could not only open a case against the employer or supervisor for perceived violations but could also file a human rights complaint against people from other companies.

Under the CHRA, an employer or organization has the obligation to create and maintain a safe and healthy workplace. This will ensure a work environment that attracts and retains employees. An organization can ensure that it meets standards by following a proactive leadership initiative whereby policies and practices are reviewed from the perspective of direct or indirect discriminatory violations. An indirect discriminatory violation occurs when a practice, policy, or rule applies to everyone in the same way, but it has a harmful effect on some people more than others, such as a dress code that would prevent an individual from wearing a religious symbol. A direct discriminatory violation occurs when an individual is treated differently and worse than someone else for specific reasons, such as gender or age. Importantly, it is best practice for organizations to provide human rights training within each organizational level, inclusive of managers and employees. Ensuring the awareness of rights, responsibilities, and potential human rights prohibitions can prevent discriminatory practices.

The Canada Research Chairs Program (CRCP) is a national strategy providing recommendations to industry surrounding equity, diversity, and inclusion best practices for recruitment, hiring, and retention. The best practices are reviewed and updated annually.

DEVELOPING DIVERSITY CONSCIOUSNESS

Diversity consciousness is the basic recognition that workplaces in Canada are diverse. By being aware of the impact of diversity, you and your organization are prepared to take advantage of diversity benefits and enable countermeasures if potential conflicts erupt when diverse people come together. Canada's best companies recognize that in the global business atmosphere, it is critical to build a more diverse workforce encompassing different perspectives, experiences, insights, and multicultural complements in order to enhance organizational competitiveness and effectiveness. Successful organizations invest in diversity and sensitivity training to equip their workforce with the knowledge base to reach these goals. A diverse workforce can maximize aptitude and resourcefulness and foster innovation, ultimately leading to an increased positive public image.

Cultural Competence and Awareness

A key component of diversity in Canada is cultural competence and awareness. Immigrants represent approximately 23% of the Canadian population; these numbers are expected to grow by 300,000 each year for the next several years. One would expect many cultures to make up the immigration landscape.

Advances in modern technology have brought the world much closer. Today's working environment often spans numerous cultures. Businesses can expand their operations globally, and administrative professionals will find themselves communicating remotely or face to face with individuals from diverse regions or cultural backgrounds. Understanding one's own culture and the impact of culture on the actions of others is essential for effective business human relations.

As a reminder, **culture** refers to a system of shared values, beliefs, morals, and social standards embraced by a group of people. This system is usually passed from one generation to another. Cultural systems encompass features such as languages, religious practices, and social interactions. Something as simple as social distance varies greatly among cultures. For example, in North America we generally like to have a distance of 18 inches in a social situation, while in Japan the ideal distance is 36 inches. Communication can immediately break down if we don't make a considerable effort to be aware of subtle differences.

Developing an understanding of cultural differences will enable you to be a productive and contributing member of your organization. As an administrative professional, take the opportunity to develop knowledge of cultural practices.

Cross-Cultural Competence

Cross-cultural competence involves the ability to interact effectively with people from a variety of different cultural backgrounds. Good communication skills are the cornerstone of all business interactions, and this is particularly true when working collaboratively with individuals from differing cultures. Cross-cultural communication skills are best developed through practice and experience. Moreover, cross-cultural competence involves more than merely obtaining cultural information; we must understand how to apply this knowledge effectively. This level of understanding is not something we are naturally born with. It is developed over time with considerable effort. Adapting to different cultural beliefs and practices requires flexibility and a respect for others' viewpoints.

The need for cross-cultural competence in today's business environment has never been greater. Not only has the workplace become more diverse, but business is increasingly conducted on an international scale. The stronger your cross-cultural competence, the less likely it is that you will fall victim to cross-cultural misunderstandings or make unfortunate blunders.

By putting aside our own cultural mindsets and assumptions, we remove barriers to cross-cultural communication in the workplace. It is especially important to avoid cultural stereotyping, or treating others on the basis of a preconceived belief about their culture, which can prevent us from relationship building. By the same token, setting aside these stereotypes will allow us to work more effectively with individuals from a wide range of backgrounds. Although it may not be easy to give up some of our own cultural assumptions, doing so will enable us to have more successful and productive business relationships. In fact, you may eventually be selected for international assignments because of your well-honed skills in cross-cultural communication.

Cultural competence can be developed at both the professional and social levels. One way to develop cultural competence is to participate in activities that expose you to other cultures. Choose to become involved in community activities that may expose you to a network of people with diverse cultural backgrounds. You may also want to be involved with meetings that involve international business relations. Cross-cultural competence requires us to investigate new cultures by keeping an open mind and removing some of our personal prejudices. When interacting with a new culture, we need to avoid judging it—and its values—by comparing it to our own. Instead, we need to bridge our own cultural insights with new ones; this skill is at the heart of all cross-cultural competency.

However, there is no one recipe for cultural competency. Developing cultural competence is an ongoing process, as we continually adapt and re-evaluate our practices, assumptions, and outlook.

Developing Cultural Awareness

Workplace cross-cultural awareness has become an increasingly important aspect of business. The term *cross-cultural awareness* refers to the development of an understanding of and sensitivity to other cultures. We are raised with a set of beliefs and practices, and as a result, sometimes we don't view beliefs that are different from ours as acceptable. It is important to remember, however, that we usually have more similarities than differences.

The first step in developing cross-cultural awareness or cultural competence is to be aware of and examine your own beliefs through self-discovery. Consider some of these suggestions for developing cross-cultural and diversity awareness:

- **Become more self-aware.** Don't think that your way is the only way. Have an open mind when presented with new opportunities to explore diverse ways of doing things.

- **Avoid stereotyping.** Your expectations of another person's behaviour may be based on a stereotype that simply is not true.

- **Don't generalize.** Everybody is unique.

- **Ask questions.** By keeping these questions professional, you will minimize misunderstandings and keep lines of communication open.

- **Be positive and enthusiastic.** Your willingness to work together will be apparent, and your co-workers will appreciate your cooperative approach.

Guidelines for Cross-Cultural Encounters

Following some basic principles will greatly limit the potential for misunderstandings. Here are some tips to follow in cross-cultural encounters:

- **Greeting.** It is critical that you acknowledge the other person. In some cultures, you may need to make direct eye contact, shake hands, and exchange a few words. In general, no matter what the culture, it is rude not to acknowledge the other person. Ask how to address the other person. In some cultures the use of nicknames is

---

Self-Check

1. What are two goals of the *Canadian Human Rights Act*?
2. State why it is important to be aware of diversity.
3. What is cross-cultural competence?

---

an acceptable practice, while in others it might be considered impolite. Be upfront and ask.

- **Responsiveness.** Show the person you want to get to know them. This attitude is critical in cross-cultural communication, as it shows a willingness to understand why someone does something perhaps a little differently from what you are used to.

- **Clarity.** Be transparent in your communication with others. You can avoid misunderstandings by giving as much detail as possible.

- **Create a connection.** Be friendly. Show that you really want to connect with the other person by asking questions that initiate interaction.

- **Flexibility.** You may need to send a message using a variety of methods of communication, including appropriate use of body language.

DIVERSITY IN THE GLOBAL BUSINESS ENVIRONMENT

Diversity can be a challenge in any business environment. With the massive growth of the global marketplace, understanding how business is conducted internationally is critical to organizational success. In order to be productive on a global scale, we must explore the business culture of those countries or regions where we wish to conduct business. Business culture is a model or style of business operations. The business culture determines how staff members interact with each other and how employees deal with clients.

The leadership role—and how members of an organization perceive that role—is a critical element of organizational culture. Depending on our background, we may have certain expectations of the leader that may or may not be shared by all members within an organization. In countries such as Canada, Germany, and Russia, for example, there is a tendency to elevate the role of the leader almost to a glorified status. By contrast, in the Netherlands the position of the leader is often regarded with skepticism; indeed, if someone is employed as a manager, he or she typically will not brag about it. Given the globalization of the working environment, it is essential to understand cultural leadership differences. What may be acceptable in one culture may not be in another. This creates a substantial challenge for the office of today. Being aware of the perceptions we have in relation to leadership may help to foster a harmonious working environment.

Contract negotiations may also need to be approached differently when performed on a global scale. We can't assume because of our traditions and beliefs that others will

judge, behave, perceive, and reason as we do. Managers cannot negotiate successfully if they neglect other countries' cultures, beliefs, and rituals. Therefore, managers need to learn how cultures and traditions differ in the countries where their company operates so that they can efficiently and effectively negotiate and be able to manage across cultures and borders.

Time Management Perception

The essence of time management—organizing and sequencing tasks—may be perceived by cultures in different ways. For example, imagine you are a local employee in the home office in Dubai, and a Canadian employee from the Burnaby, British Columbia, office comes by for her 2 p.m. appointment. She arrives promptly, and as you greet and begin to help her, you also handle a telephone call, answer a co-worker's question, and send a fax to someone else. From your point of view and in keeping with your perception of time management, you consider that you are very efficient; you are, after all, accomplishing several other tasks in addition to dealing with the visitor. However, from your visitor's point of view, your activity may appear unfocused and inefficient. Your visitor may perceive your multitasking while meeting with her as an indication that you regard her visit as unimportant or as a disruption to your routine; she may even feel that it has not been given the appropriate attention. In Canada, business success is often judged on the ability to balance time efficiently while still meeting the needs of clients. For instance, if a project is not completed on time as promised, the organization will lose profits and its reputation may suffer.

To understand how the perception of time can differ in various parts of the world, consider the following examples: in India and Japan, people tend to favour coordinating work on related tasks rather than tackling them consecutively. In France, two-hour lunches are considered normal. In Japan, Saturday is considered a standard workday, while in Muslim countries the workweek ends on Thursday evening and Sunday is a workday. Holiday time standards vary among countries throughout the world. See Figure 2-2 reflecting the importance of meeting timelines in business.

Interpersonal Communication in the Global Market

When conducting business globally, we may encounter language barriers that will require us to make some adjustments in our communication methods. Even if someone speaks your language, it does not mean that person has the same understanding of the verbal message that you are sending. Sometimes language barriers result because we apply mental

FIGURE 2-2 Clock—The importance of time in the workplace.

Super Crimson/Shutterstock

filters to the messages others send to us. The term *mental filter* describes our capacity to accept some facts and ideas and to screen out others—perhaps those that are unfamiliar or that are different from our own. The mental filters we use are closely related to the unique way each of us views the world. When faced with some of these barriers, we should practice the following basic guidelines:

- **Learn common greetings and responses.** For example, "hello" in French is spelled "bonjour" and is pronounced "bone-zhoor"; "thank you" in Spanish is spelled "gracias" and is pronounced "gRAH-see-ahs."

- **Use simple English.** It has been said that English is one of the most difficult languages to learn. Use simple words in short sentences. For example, use *little* rather than *petite*, *like* rather than *resemble*. Avoid using puns, slang, jargon, and sports or military references.

- **Speak slowly and enunciate.** If you are speaking in a rushed tone, many words may be lost in your message. By taking the time to clearly pronounce words, you will ensure your message is heard and better understood.

- **Watch for blank stares.** A blank stare or a glazed expression tells you the listener may not comprehend your message.

- **Ask the listener to paraphrase.** When the listener can repeat your message, there is a better chance it is being understood. Giving your listener the opportunity to paraphrase what you've said will also allow you to correct any misunderstandings.

- **Accept blame for misunderstanding.** Accepting blame will make the listener feel less embarrassed about not understanding your message. Doing so will also allow him or her to "save face."

- **Listen without interrupting.** Don't help the speaker finish his or her sentences. Finishing sentences only points

out what a poor command the speaker has of the language; it also indicates impatience on the part of the listener.

- **Follow up in writing when negotiating.** A follow-up message that summarizes an agreement will confirm the results of your negotiation and minimize misunderstandings. A person with limited English-speaking skills may have very good reading comprehension. In some countries, people are taught how to read and write English but often have limited opportunities to practise speaking it.

- **Observe nonverbal messages.** Examples of nonverbal messages are the use of personal space and eye contact, as discussed earlier in this chapter. Watch your gestures: some gestures may seem harmless in Canada but can have a very different interpretation elsewhere. Take, for instance, the symbol commonly used to mean "okay" in North America, the thumb and index finger forming a circle and the other fingers raised. In France this gesture means "zero," it is a symbol for money in Japan, and it carries a vulgar connotation in Brazil.

Managing International Client Relations

Recent innovations in communication technology have allowed employees to work more closely with international clients and teams than ever before. Being separated by location and often culture, however, can present some unique challenges. **Customer relationship management (CRM)** is a strategy for understanding your customers and their needs in order to optimize your interactions with them.

Simple things like time difference can make communication a lot trickier, depending on what areas of the world and nationalities you are dealing with. You will need to pay attention to time zones so you just don't pick up the phone to call your client in Paris, for example, and wake him up in the middle of a good night's sleep. Keep track of your customers' time zones by checking an online tool like the World Clock (http://www.timeanddate.com/worldclock/), which tells you the current time in countries around the world. Prearrange a time that works for both of you.

Pay attention to cultural differences. Before working with an international client, do some research on the client's local customs and etiquette. You may find that in some locations in the world, talking about pricing upfront is not appreciated, so you might need to customize the way you discuss your estimate for a project. Take extra care when interpreting emails and other communications. Whether or not your client is from an English-speaking country, you're likely to notice differences in language and local slang. If you're not certain exactly what your client is telling you or asking for, be sure to ask for further clarification via email, stating what you think the client is saying, and then asking whether your interpretation is correct.

Working on International Teams

Working with teams across continents can be exciting and rewarding, but it also presents some challenges. Research suggests that some of these challenges include differences in culture, language, business practices, and attitudes. Face-to-face communication is highly valued in European countries, while in Canada there is a greater acceptance of virtual communication. It may be wise to plan for an initial face-to-face meeting when first working together. If that is not practical, perhaps a videoconference can be arranged to allow people to visit team members virtually so they can associate faces with names. Most companies have access to web tools that help to facilitate this initial meeting. You also may want to consider rotating communication times to be considerate of time differences between countries. Team leaders of international virtual teams must be aware and sensitive to differences and take appropriate action to ensure optimal performance and results.

Working in a Foreign Country

Every year, thousands of Canadians relocate to foreign countries to work and acquire new skills. Many companies are "going global," and this may mean that you will need to relocate to another country for an extended period of time. You will require special permission from the Canadian government to work abroad. Permission must be granted by the country you wish to work in as well. Find out the requirements well in advance of deciding to relocate.

Working abroad can enhance and diversify your administrative skills. A wide variety of international work opportunities exist around the world. A helpful publication from the Canadian government called *Living Abroad—A Canadian's guide to working, studying, volunteering or retiring in a foreign country*—offers a breadth of information for those considering international work.

You will need a passport before working abroad. A work visa or special permission in the form of a work permit will be required. If you are planning to go for a long time you may also require a residency permit. Additionally, some countries may require a medical certificate as an entry requirement. Another consideration may be obtaining an international driver's license.

Before You Go   The Department of Foreign Affairs, Trade and Development is committed to providing services throughout the world to Canadians working and travelling abroad. There are more than 260 offices worldwide, and it would be wise to find a list of where these offices are located prior to your departure. This department can also provide information on documentation needed, as well as travel reports and warnings.

Look to employment agencies, the internet, newspapers, and magazines to find international opportunities. If you are offered a job overseas, it is important to evaluate it carefully before you accept it. Find out as much as you can about the organization by visiting the company website. Talk to others who you know may have worked for the business, or ask to speak to someone who is currently working for the company.

International Workplace Challenges   Relocating to live and work in a foreign country can be an exciting experience. Many times, however, we may not be as prepared for the extent of dissimilarity we encounter. This phenomenon is referred to culture shock. In order to be successful, we need to adapt to the new culture. When relocating, we often go through stages prior to reaching the point of adaptation.

Initially we go through a short stage after arriving in our new country where the excitement and newness of our environment is a delight. Normally, these feelings wear off after some time. Then feelings of culture shock begin to set in. Culture shock can best be described as the emotional and sometimes physical reaction experienced while settling into a new culture. Homesickness, irritability, and depression are some of the symptoms people may experience as they adapt to their new environment. These are normal reactions to relocation, and in most cases these feelings pass. As you psychologically adapt to the new environment, which involves participating in the local surroundings and learning the language, you should begin to enjoy your new life.

Taking the following steps will help you to adapt to your host country:

1. **Work etiquette.** Learn your host country's workplace etiquette. This involves knowing how to introduce yourself and how to address others. Find out if religion plays a role in daily work. Determine if there are items of clothing considered appropriate or inappropriate.

2. **Work environment.** Learn about expectations in terms of work commitment. Are you expected to work extra hours? Will you need to take work home? What are the cultural views about social engagement in and outside of the workplace?

3. **Importance of time.** Learn about how time is handled in the host country. Is punctuality important? How are lunch and breaks handled? What days of the week are considered workdays?

4. **Laws.** Learn about workplace legislation. What rights do you have as a worker? How are rights enforced?

5. **Pay.** Learn how you will be paid. Determine if you will need to open up a bank account. Find out what deductions are made and what benefits are provided to you.

6. **Language.** Learn the language in which business is normally conducted in your host country. Be aware that certain phrases may be considered offensive.

7. **Women in the workplace.** Learn the view of women in the workplace. Depending on the host country, views of women in the workplace can differ greatly.

8. **Supervisory.** Learn the host country's view towards authority. In some countries, criticism of your supervisor is unacceptable and is grounds for dismissal.

HOSTING INTERNATIONAL VISITORS

If your manager travels to meet international clients, it's very possible that those clients will also visit your office. Being able to build positive relationships with international clients is highly desirable and worth achieving. Your office may also host international employees, and they may want to tour your office or city.

Here are some tips for your success when hosting international visitors:

1. Take the time to learn a few courteous words in your visitor's language if different from your own. Expressions like "good morning," "welcome," "please," and "thank you" spoken in the visitor's language will be interpreted as a gesture of goodwill and will set a positive tone for the visit. See Figure 2-3 depicting a professional greeting.

2. Locate the client's nearest consulate's office. As a courtesy to your international clients, have handy the nearest consulate's location, phone number, and ambassador's name for reference should you need them.

3. Research what cultural attitudes exist about time management. As you learned earlier, different cultures treat time differently. Time does not have the same priority in all cultures. Some have a much more relaxed view of time. In fact, in some cultures people do not work in the afternoon and prefer to have only morning and evening meetings. This can create the need to make some

FIGURE 2-3 Professional greeting.

Michaeljung/Shutterstock

adjustments in terms of scheduling meetings, completing projects, and closing deals. Keep this in mind when scheduling meetings, and be as flexible as possible.

4. Learn the preferred eating habits of the country. Although many international visitors are open to experimenting with new foods, many are not. For example, in some cultures people do not eat pork. In this case, it would be a gross error to arrange a meal where pork is on the menu. Be certain coffee and lunch breaks include food and beverages the international clients will enjoy.

5. Consider international differences in customs when greeting visitors. Greetings in North America are initiated with a firm handshake, whereas in many other cultures bowing and kissing are the norms. In some cultures, men and women do not touch. Although women and men in these cultures do not shake hands, members of the same gender may deliver a very warm and physical greeting.

6. Be aware of body language. A friendly hand gesture in one country can be obscene in the next and even illegal in another. Be sure to pay close attention to how others use certain gestures (movements of the hands, arms, legs, or head) to convey a message.

7. Learn to pronounce names correctly. In some cultures, such as China and Korea, the family's surname is stated first and then the given name. Show your respect by using names correctly. Learn the titles of respect that go with names and when it is appropriate to use them.

8. Take the time to research national holidays and important events in the visitor's country of origin. Be respectful of those occasions and avoid scheduling meetings or activities at times that would give the impression of disrespect or disregard for the visitor's culture. Acknowledging your understanding of the importance of those

occasions in your visitor's culture will, in turn, gain respect for your organization.

9. Determine if physical space is of importance. When receiving visitors from outside your culture, pay attention to what is considered an appropriate distance between you and the visitor when talking. With some visitors, standing too far away may be interpreted as being unconcerned, too formal, or too distant. On the other hand, if you stand too close to a visitor, it may be interpreted as being too casual or too informal. Learn how to use space or distance to your advantage so as not to offend visitors.

10. Recognize that your international visitor may not be familiar with your city and will likely want to do some sightseeing. Prepare a portfolio that includes maps of the area, recommended restaurants, special-interest sites, and special events. Ask if there are any attractions the visitor would like to explore, and offer to arrange for a tour guide.

The bottom line is that you want your international visitor to have a pleasant, positive visit to Canada, a visit that produces a profitable yet cordial relationship. With more and more international trade between Canadian and foreign companies, developing your skills in this area will be viewed favourably by your manager and increase your value as a knowledgeable employee.

pro-Link
Avoiding Diversity Blunders

In your busy working day you are bound to meet and greet many people from diverse cultural backgrounds. Planning in advance how to handle these situations will help you to eliminate diversity blunders. Of course, you can't avoid all blunders, but the way you manage yourself will go far to reduce their occurrence and impact.

- Accept the fact that you will make some blunders, so if you make a mistake don't focus on it; focus on what you can do differently in the future.
- Stay focused on communication. Note what is said, how it is said, and what is not said.
- Watch for gestures that may convey a message and will help you correct your blunder. You can tell by a facial reaction that demonstrates surprise that you may have asked or answered a question incorrectly.
- Avoid questions on age, marital status, and income.
- Don't ignore hierarchy in the workplace. Buy gifts according to rank and seniority.

Remember that you want your guests to feel comfortable and welcome in your place of business. By avoiding cultural blunders, you will help to ensure the success of their visit.

QUESTIONS FOR STUDY AND REVIEW

1. Describe what diversity encompasses.
2. Suggest how a diverse workplace benefits an organization.
3. What is the difference between race and ethnicity?
4. When did Canada officially adopt the *Multicultural Act?*
5. Define the term *culture*.
6. Explain why an administrative professional should have an understanding of cultural diversity.
7. Distinguish between cultural and workplace diversity.
8. Suggest four ways you could develop more cross-cultural awareness.
9. Explain how people may have different expectations of a leader depending on their cultural background.
10. List four suggestions for improving international communication.

11. Suggest how gestures can impact the communication process when involving international relations.
12. State three important considerations when thinking about working in another country.
13. Discuss how the perception of time management varies depending on cultural standards.
14. List four suggestions for hosting international visitors.
15. Suggest additional steps you could take to ensure your international visitor has a pleasant experience.
16. State three factors to consider if you or your manager is travelling for business.
17. State the importance of becoming familiar with the social norms and acceptable practices of your international visitor's home country.
18. What is culture shock? What can someone do to adapt to a new work culture?

Key Terms

culture 38

customer relationship management (CRM) 41

demographics 34

discrimination 35

diversity 34

ethnicity 35

race 35

stereotype 37

Gender identity 35

EVERYDAY ETHICS

Gender Matters

You have been working as an executive assistant to Ms. Simmons, the CEO of a prominent marketing company in Canada. Recently, Ms. Simmons has decided to do business with a Saudi Arabian firm. You have been in contact with administrative counterparts at the Saudi firm, exchanging information on the services your marketing firm can provide. Things have been progressing well until a meeting was set up between Ms. Simmons and Mr. al-Ghamdi, the owner of the Saudi business. This meeting will involve Ms. Simmons travelling to Saudi Arabia to meet directly with Mr. al-Ghamdi and his management team. When Mr. al-Ghamdi discovers the CEO of your firm is female, he refuses to meet with her for the negotiation process and insists on meeting with a man from your organization. Women are not often found in leadership roles in Saudi Arabia, and this situation creates a conflict with Mr. al-Ghamdi's cultural values.

Your company does not want to lose this contract, and a solution must be found.

■ What can be done to resolve this situation?

■ Is there something that could have been done in advance to prevent this situation from arising?

Gift Giving

Your company has strict rules on gift giving. The company practice reflects the belief that gift giving can be perceived as a form of bribery, and your company wants to ensure this perception is never invited. Your supervisor is travelling to Italy on business, where gift giving is expected and is often considered necessary for establishing and building a trusting relationship. Your supervisor has asked you to order a nice pen with the recipient's name and your company logo engraved on it. You will need to submit this purchase to accounting, and questions will be raised about it.

■ What should you do?

■ How can this matter be handled in a mutually satisfying manner?

Problem Solving

1. Your work group successfully completed a project well before the required deadline. The team leader decides to invite everyone on the team to a celebration after work on Friday. Most of the team are happy with the exception of one person, Mandy, who is of Orthodox Jewish faith. Instead of making an issue about it, Mandy does not show up to the Friday event since it is considered the Sabbath. Mandy assumed team leader would not understand her religious observance, or even worse, did not care. However, when Mandy didn't attend, the team concluded that she wasn't a team player. What steps could have prevented this misunderstanding from occurring?

2. Your telecommunications company has spent a significant amount of time trying to attract new international clients. Finally, Mr. Chang has agreed to make the trip from China to tour your office and meet extensively with your supervisor, Alan Jacobs. As the administrative assistant, you have responsibility for coordinating the schedule of events for Mr. Chang's visit. You have also arranged an interpreter for Mr. Chang, as he speaks a limited amount

of English. The day before Mr. Chang is due to arrive in Canada, the interpreter has a family emergency and will need to travel out of the country, which means that he can no longer help you with Mr. Chang's visit. What can you do on such limited notice to ensure Mr. Chang has a good visit?

3. Your company is hosting three business associates from India for one week. Your manager has purchased a bottle of wine for each of the visitors. As you are preparing for their arrival, you realize that one of your visitors is Hindu. Because you have researched beliefs and cultural values surrounding the Hindu culture, you realize that alcohol is not an appropriate gift. What should you do?

4. Adam was working in the accounting department of your organizations, and he began the transition from female to male. You noticed he started receiving comments from his supervisor and co-workers, which he considered offensive, related to his transition. He came to you to share his concerns about the unfair treatment he felt he was experiencing. What would you recommend he do?

Special Reports

1. Interview an office professional to determine how workplace diversity is handled and promoted in their organization. Report your findings to the class or to the instructor.

2. Research three countries to determine how business gift giving and receiving is handled in these cultures. Prepare a memo for your instructor detailing your findings.

3. Search online for two international employment opportunities that may be suitable for you to apply to. Provide a brief report detailing the job location, qualifications, and method for applying for this position. Present your findings to your instructor.

4. Using the information you obtained by completing Question 3, research four business culture practices of one of the international employment opportunities you have discovered, and prepare a memo for your instructor detailing your findings.

5. Liam met with an employment recruiter this week. The recruiter told him many of their requests are for a recent college graduate because they haven't developed bad habits yet. He told you he felt it was unfair remark just because he is older than most recent college graduates are. He is feeling defeated. In a paragraph, form a response to Liam to counter his current mindset.

6. Research a recent case heard by the Human Rights Commission local to your province or territory and prepare a one-page summary of the case for discussion in class.

PRODUCTION CHALLENGES

2-A Cultural Self-Awareness

Supplies needed:

- *Exploring Your Own Cultural Background, Form 2-A, Companion Website*

One of the first steps in developing cultural awareness is to learn about your own cultural beliefs and values. This exercise will help you understand how your own personal cultural exposures have an impact on how you react to and view other cultures. Share your findings with your classmates.

2-B Cultural Understanding

Supplies needed:

- *Plain paper*

Develop an interactive activity that can be used with a group of people in your class that will explore and celebrate the rich diversity of backgrounds of the people in your classroom.

1. Plan this activity to last for approximately 10 to 15 minutes.

2. Carefully consider all aspects of the activity to ensure it is fun and engaging, but be sure not to include anything that might make a person feel embarrassed.

2-C Celebrations (Cultural Awareness)

Supplies needed:

- *Plain paper*

Respond to the following questions, drawing on your personal background. Answering these questions will help you to appreciate the importance of being aware of your own cultural practices and will thus help you to understand the importance of traditions in all cultures.

1. Describe your favourite family tradition.
2. How did this tradition begin?
3. Why is this tradition important to you?
4. Write down a traditional celebration you are aware of that another culture in your community practices.
5. Do you know why this practice is important to this culture?

Weblinks

Canadian Business
www.canadianbusiness.com
This Canadian site provides useful information on conducting business in a global marketplace.

Citizenship and Immigration Canada
www.cic.gc.ca
This Canadian site provides multicultural information. It addresses a variety of subjects, including multicultural programs, and it provides links to select publications.

Diversity in the Workplace
www.diversityintheworkplace.ca/
This is an online publication dealing with diversity in the workplace. The site publishes monthly newsletters and also sponsors webinars that explore issues surrounding workplace diversity.

Centre for Diversity and Inclusion
www.ccdi.ca
The Canadian Centre for Diversity and Inclusion (CCDI) this website help employers, diversity and inclusion/human rights/equity-interested parties, and human resources practitioners effectively address inclusion and diversity in the workplace.

Canada's International Gateway

www.canadainternational.gc.ca

This site offers information about culture, travel, and doing business in Canada.

Newspapers and Magazines

www.ipl.org/div/news

This site provides links to newspapers and magazines around the world. This is beneficial for an international job search.

Passport Canada

www.passportcanada.gc.ca

This is a Government of Canada website providing information about acquiring a passport as well as locations of local passport offices.

Centre for Intercultural Learning

www.intercultures.gc.ca

This is a Government of Canada website that provides information about countries around the world. The site provides geographical statistics about the country, language spoken, religion, and ethnicity.

References

Ellard-Gray. (2015) LGBT-In-and-Out-Diverging-Perspectives-on-LGBT-Inclusion-in-the-Workplace. Canadian Centre for Diversity and Inclusion. Canada.

Statistics Canada. Immigration and Ethnocultural Diversity in Canada. Retrieved from http://www12.statcan.gc.ca/nhs-enm/2011/as-sa/99-010-x/99-010-x2011001-eng.cfm

Chapter 3
Management of Work, Time, and Resources

G-stockstudio/Shutterstock

LEARNING OUTCOMES

After completion of this chapter, the student will be able to:

1 Identify leadership and management concepts.

2 Discuss management process, function, and operational theories.

3 Outline the key concepts of total quality management.

4 Explain differences between working efficiently and working effectively.

5 Outline methods for setting and tracking organizational priorities.

6 Describe procedures supporting accuracy of documentation.

7 Discuss strategies for managing interruptions.

8 Understand the importance of planning and managing resources.

9 Identify administrative tools to support time and task management.

10 Explain environmental sustainability.

Rawpixel.com/Shutterstock

Fluid Life

Edmonton, Alberta
*One Canada's 25 Best Managed
Companies 2018*

As a leading provider of asset management solutions, Fluid Life based out of Edmonton, Alberta, has over 35 years under its belt. Its focus is on helping industrial clients keep their equipment operational utilizing such methodologies as innovative testing technologies and training services.

Recently, the organization matured beyond its current space leading to the building of an innovative laboratory populated with several amenities to enhance the working environment for employees.

Several years ago, Fluid Life underwent a strategic metamorphosis instead of staying on a trajectory, which amounted to a race to the bottom competing solely on lower pricing, the focus shifted to a consultative model where it provided insight and recommendations on everything from staffing services to data management. Fluid Life invested in a new engineering department. Educating their client based with their transformation was key to the success of the new focus. The president and the leadership team formulated a strategic goal to achieve by 2025 a total savings of $250 million for their clients. To ensure this goal is always prevalent in the mind of personnel, information screens are placed throughout the organization with a crawl of text appearing at the bottom of the screen recognizing when Fluid Life has saved a client $100,000 or more. This accomplishment recognition involves everyone in the organization, not just the leadership team.

The organization charges ahead in a responsible fashion, by controlling spending during productive times and continuously improving their processes. They invest heavily in their people with a bold and courageous outlook setting high expectations for success. The company president with over 20 years of experience has done everything from answering the phones to overseeing operations. The recent office design was deployed to have everyone in the company thinking big and fundamentally understanding what they are working towards a common vision and shared goals.

The support provided by an administrative professional is vital to an organization's ability to achieve its goals and meet objectives. Most senior managers expect administrative office professionals to possess leadership and managerial skills in order to set administrative priorities. Administrative professionals work with a constant and rapid flow of information and superior organizational skills are required to process the flow. Office professionals not only manage their time and organize their work, but they also evaluate their own effectiveness and efficiency to continuously improve their contributions to the organization.

Systematic methods of organizing work, managing time, and managing resources provide indicators with which to measure your accomplishments each day, regardless of your long-term goals. This chapter identifies management concepts, tools, and techniques to facilitate development of your competency as an effective administrative office professional.

LEADERSHIP AND MANAGEMENT

The main difference between leaders and managers is that leaders have people follow them while managers have people who work for them. A successful business entity needs strong leadership in their managers to motivate their team to follow their vision of success. Leadership is about inspiring people to ensure they understand and believe in a unified vision and to work with you to achieve these goals while managing is more about administering the day-to-day tasks to ensure they are accomplished as required. From a simplistic perspective, a primary way an administrative professional can practice leadership is when presented with an unexpected challenge instead of stating the problem or complaining about it, you as a leader look for ways to resolve the challenge.

MANAGEMENT PROCESS AND THEORIES

As we examine the management of time and resources in this chapter, it is helpful to understand a variety of managerial concepts as it relates to the administrative professional's role and development of knowledge based competencies. **Management process** is the series of steps taken in partnership with basic management functions. These functions include establishing goals, planning, controlling, organizing, and the execution of any type of activity, such as a project. Figure 3-1 shows the five functions of management. **Management theory** encompasses how managers and leaders relate to their organizations in the knowledge of organizational objectives; it is also the implementation of effective methods to meet objectives along with how to motivate employees to perform to a high standard. Management theories are initiated to increase organizational productivity and quality. Most managers use several theories or concepts when implementing strategies in the workplace: The use of a combination of theories is dependent on the workplace and purpose. Contingency theory, Theory X, Theory Y, and Systems theory are popular management

theories. Contingency theory is an organizational theory that asserts there is no single best way to organize or lead an organization. The best course of action is contingent or dependent upon the situation. Theory X is based on the assumption that the typical worker lacks motivation. The manager believes a hands-on approach is best to ensure motivation. In contrast, Theory Y of management believes workers are naturally internally motivated and are driven individually to achieve high-quality performance. Systems theory is founded in the belief of broadly applicable concepts and principles, as opposed to concepts and principles applicable to only one area of knowledge.

Total Quality Management

Total quality management (TQM) is a strategic management approach that aims to improve business as a whole and add value for customers. TQM uses interventions and other techniques to help identify and eliminate mistakes, reduce waste, and improve productivity, leading to continuous improvement of organizational processes and products, while enhancing the efficiency of employees. This management approach is intended for long-term success through customer satisfaction. In TQM, all members of an organization are immersed in improving processes, products, services, and organizational culture. To stay competitive in this global marketplace, many businesses have adopted TQM as an effective approach for achieving success. This

FIGURE 3-1 Five functions of management.

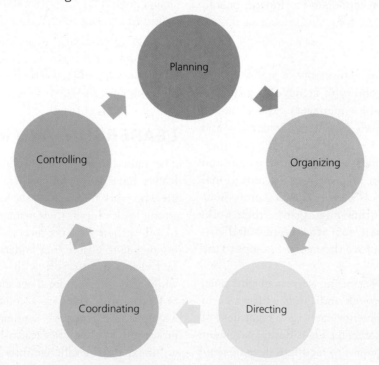

fundamental business methodology is practiced through four basic principles:

1. Customer focus
2. Continuous improvement and learning
3. Strategic planning and leadership
4. Teamwork

The TQM approach recognizes the customer as the real judge of the quality of a company's products or services. Companies that adopt TQM not only plan for strategic business improvement but also encourage learning and new leadership ideas from their employees. As an administrative professional in a company that embraces this approach to business, you are likely to become a member of a problem-solving team or a team working to improve a business process somewhere in the organization. Most certainly you will be empowered to make broader decisions within your sphere of work and span of control.

In the office, TQM means that each employee is participating in teamwork and focused on customer satisfaction. Employees at every level are encouraged to find new and innovative ways of doing their jobs more effectively and to be flexible enough to assist others. You may be empowered—that is, given more autonomy and broader responsibilities—with the goal of simplifying office operations. You will be assigned responsibility for making decisions that will have an impact on your own effectiveness and performance.

You will be assessed on your team contribution and on your innovation: If the filing system does not correspond to the operation—change it! If your colleague is having difficulty completing a project—help out! If a customer has a complaint—resolve it!

As an example, the administrative professional may be invited to become part of a team that reviews the problem of products that are not being delivered to the customer on time. The team would consist of employees who are directly involved in the delivery process under review. In this case, all members of the team would have equal responsibility and an equal voice in identifying all the steps and problems involved in the delivery cycle.

Refer to the section "Team Meetings" in Chapter 13 for details of how to participate in a team meeting. The problem must be clearly understood and stated in written form. All the issues that team members consider important are recorded. Team members then prioritize (by vote) the stated problems. The problem that is deemed the most significant is the first one the team deals with.

This first-priority problem is then thoroughly examined. Each step of the current procedure is analyzed for its effectiveness and necessity. The process of examining the entire procedure will inspire improvements. Additionally, each member will feel that he or she has contributed to a solution for improving customer satisfaction.

This team problem-solving approach is typical of process-improvement activities that organizations conduct as part of their quality approach. Let's review a sequence of events that might occur as a cross-functional team is formed to address a late delivery problem:

1. A team of employees who are directly involved in the order and delivery process is formed. This team may include the administrative professional.
2. A team leader is selected to chair the meeting.
3. All input is documented by a designated recorder.
4. A facilitator may be involved to organize the team members' input.
5. The general problem is clearly defined during the first team meeting.
6. Each team member has an equal opportunity to state what he or she believes to be the contributing factors to the general problem. This step, which allows the employees the freedom of open suggestion without criticism, is known as **brainstorming**. In this case, examples of contributing factors to the general problem may be:
    a. The person who places the orders is often away from work.
    b. When the orders are placed, the suppliers do not have ready stock; they must get stock from foreign markets.
    c. When suppliers deliver stock, it is sometimes in damaged condition and therefore must be reordered.
7. The team members now vote on what they believe to be the most important specific problems (contributing factors). In this case, the most significant factor may be that the stock is often received in poor condition and must be reordered.
8. Next, each team member helps outline the exact steps that take place in the process. In the case of goods arriving in damaged condition, it may be discovered that the foreign suppliers are not packing the goods carefully enough.
9. As the process is completely identified, team members provide input about possible changes until an improved process is developed. In this case, employees might suggest that proper packaging and careful handling of goods would expedite the delivery of the product to the customer.
10. The team will now make a recommendation to management for improving the delivery process.

Management by Objectives

Management by objectives (MBO) is a management and operational strategy designed to improve performance; employees and management come together to identify common goals, form action plans to secure participation, and foster commitment with employees. Management systems are developed to measure accomplishment in comparison to key objectives. In contrast, TQM solves problems based on external customer satisfaction. MBO solves problems based on internal goals and targets. Transitioning further is a shift to blend customer focus with an employee-minded business model, where the necessity to treat employees in a fair manner is viewed as having significant organizational benefit.

EFFECTIVENESS AND EFFICIENCY

For the administrative professional, being effective and being efficient are equally important. However, these two qualities are often confused with each other. These terms, while interrelated, are separate and distinct. Effectiveness is often defined as *doing the right things*; efficiency as *doing things right*.

Effectiveness means producing a definite or desired result. **Efficiency** means producing the desired result with a minimum of effort, expense, and waste. While it is possible to be effective without being efficient, the cost of inefficiency is usually too great for profit-making organizations; they must couple efficiency with effectiveness.

Whether administrative professionals work for one manager or for more than one, they must always do the following three things to organize their work so that they can perform efficiently:

1. Divide large projects into manageable segments of work.

2. Group related isolated tasks to reduce the time consumed in changing from one unrelated task to another.

3. Match the work to the time frames in which it must be performed, by classifying it as work that must be done today, work that must be done this week, or work that has no specific deadline.

TIME MANAGEMENT

Ask any administrative professional what their greatest challenge is in the workplace and typically somewhere on that list will be not enough time to get things done. It can sometimes lead to frustration during the workday. **Time management** involves developing work habits that result in maximum efficiency; acquiring knowledge, skills, and equipment to extend performance beyond present capabilities; controlling attitudes and emotions that tend to steal time; and developing an effective reminder method for following through on each task at the appropriate time. There will always be something critical demanding time. The key is to know how to prioritize work and complete work within an appropriate time frame.

Establish Efficient Work Habits

You can boost your own morale by increasing your organizational skills and by managing your time and working efficiently.

Be a self-starter; that is, take the initiative to begin a task for which you are responsible. Don't wait for your supervisor to prompt you. You also need to be a finisher. If you have many tasks started and none finished, your workload will seem heavier than it actually is. As you face a load of unfinished tasks, you may become less efficient. If you fall behind in your work and you can't catch up during regular hours, re-examine your methodologies and assess for continual improvement. As you lighten your load by completing unfinished tasks, you will feel more relaxed and find it easier to cope and be effective.

---

pro-Link
Stop Wasting Time

Do time-wasters plague you? Here are a few time-wasters that can make you very ineffective, as well as some sure-fire solutions to get you back on track:

■ Defocusing from your work every time the phone rings?

Solution—When you are doing work that requires focus, forward your telephone calls to your voice mail.

■ Colleagues socializing at your desk?

Solution—Change the direction that your desk faces, remove the chairs near your desk, acknowledge your colleagues but keep working when they come to socialize, and most important, let your colleagues know you are busy but you are looking forward to socializing with them at lunch.

■ So much work that you can't complete anything?

Solution—Set up a priority list and get at it!

■ Afraid to delegate?

Solution—Take time to give another person clear details of how to complete the work. Now live with the results! Remember that you are not the only person who can do the job well!

It's much easier to complete your work if you have an exemplary attendance record, arrive on time each day, keep focused while at work, and put in the full expected hours.

An administrative professional often works under the pressure of juggling priorities. One of the most difficult parts of your job will be learning how to judge these priorities. Prioritizing your workload is more about managing your tasks and projects than actually doing them. It is about setting your own deadlines for individual items in your workload. It is about time usage, too.

As an administrative professional, you have no shortage of tasks and projects, and along with this you have several interruptions that interfere or prevent you from completing them. Additionally, you have to account for the interruptions when prioritizing your workload simply because these interruptions are not going to suddenly stop. You will have to learn what degree of importance to place on each task and when to shift quickly to another task and apply extra effort.

Timing is an important factor in efficiency; a job must be performed not only well but also at the right time. To make time for urgent priorities and to feel that you are in control of your job, work willingly and with enthusiasm.

Self-Check

1. How are leadership and management different?
2. What does "effectiveness" mean?
3. What does "efficiency" mean?
4. Describe a time management concept.

Take Charge of Your Time

There is no single "right way" for managing time on the job. The rules are often job-specific and change from organization to organization. Exactly what constitutes successful time management is difficult to define without reference to specific examples from the workplace. There is no doubt that effective employees establish recognizable work *patterns*, but no two employees necessarily follow the *same* pattern. Nevertheless, the ideas presented in this chapter can be used as a guide to establish your own work habits and time-management techniques. It is important to remember, though, that this is only a guide. You will have to work hard and think about how best to adapt these rules and suggestions to your own situation.

For example, balancing family responsibilities and work responsibilities is a significant challenge for many administrative professionals. Some organizations have developed employee-friendly policies and support systems that provide

flexible work schedules and permit more work-at-home and remote communication options.

In a type of schedule design known as **flextime**, employees work a set number of hours each day but vary the starting and ending times. Flextime allows management to relax some of the traditional "time clock" control of employees' time. Similarly, working from home and telecommuting present an extraordinary opportunity to take charge of your own time.

Learn the Job

The organization expresses its objectives—the tasks to be accomplished—in terms of short-range, intermediate, and long-range goals. Management focuses its attention on achieving organizational objectives by accomplishing those goals. In any given week, your manager will devote time to both dealing with the work at hand and also addressing longer-range goals. As you join this dynamic environment, be as flexible, adaptable, and tolerant as you can in order to provide real value-added assistance.

In a new job, you will want to know how your manager works. Streamline your day's work so that it dovetails with that of your manager; do not expect your manager to adjust to your work schedule. At first:

1. Concentrate on learning.
2. Be cautious about taking initiative until you understand what is expected of you.

Typically, your role and expectations will be defined. Take full advantage of an **orientation** as provided. You should listen, take notes, and ask questions that will increase your understanding of your new job. Try to remember the names of people you meet and what their roles are in the organization.

In addition to learning new procedures to follow, it may be prudent to inquire about:

1. supporting information
2. location of supplies
3. priority items
4. your manager's preferences

Every day, make an effort to learn more about your job and how your manager and team prefers in terms of work approach and task completion. Learn the job not just for the current week and the next but for three months to a year in advance. Become familiar with the information in your office. For example:

1. Carefully study all the instructions left for you by the previous administrative professional.

2. Locate organizational style guides in place stipulating the protocol for reports and various documentation representing the organization.

3. Read all communications provided.

4. Study the office manual, if provided.

5. Find out what is in the active files.

6. Refer to the directory of the organization to learn the names of the executives and other employees and their titles.

When you report to work, the former administrative professional may not be there to train you. Perhaps there will not be an office manual describing your responsibilities. In this situation your manager will direct you. You will have to rely heavily on your own resourcefulness and use good judgment in seeking and finding answers. Keep in mind that you may not be fully effective until you understand the scope and responsibilities of your new job.

Take Time to Think

After working overtime the evening before, you arrive at work early the next morning to try to get a head start on some of your priorities. Instead, you find an urgent request left on the seat of your chair and several messages. Your phone message light is blinking, and before you can remove your coat, your telephone is ringing. The day is young and already you feel stressed!

With this level of pressure, responsibility, and expectations, how can administrative professionals find the time and the right environment to think clearly? We often underestimate the importance of taking time to think; but, without clear thinking, office professionals cannot improve procedures, streamline office policies, or provide creative solutions to problems. Improving procedures, streamlining policies, and being creative about solving problems are as much the responsibility of the administrative professional as they are of the executive.

Many office professionals find it challenging and exhausting just keeping up with the daily demands of the office and so leave strategic thinking to their managers. Get involved! You may be in a role where you are supervising and mentoring a team of professionals. You need to contribute by putting improvements and solutions forward. Your recommendations for improving office procedures will add to the big picture of the organization. As well, they let your organization know that you are counted on for your institutional knowledge. Your contribution counts.

Finding the Time   So just how do you find the time for creative thinking and planning? You could ask yourself the same question about where you will find the time to manage the phone or reply to emails. Solving problems and making improvements should be as much a part of your job as answering the telephone. So schedule thinking time into your working day.

Creating the Environment   Solving problems and developing better procedures are often done best as a team. When you have a definite problem or procedure that needs attention, call an informal brainstorming session with people who are involved in the concern identified. If you need to think through a problem or procedure on your own, put the phone on hold, shut the door, and ask a co-worker to cover your desk for the next half hour while you move to a place void of interruption. If this is impossible, do your creative thinking on a scheduled break or early before others arrive. It's your job to think.

Thoughts on Thinking   Where do you do your best thinking? When do you do your best thinking? How do you do your best thinking? Doodling on paper? Staring at a wall? Listening to music? Sitting in complete silence? Drinking a cup of coffee? Discussing ideas with others?

Experts say that the most creative thought happens differently for individuals. While one person gets his best inspiration in the shower, the next person does her best thinking while listening to music, and yet another while sitting in complete silence. Studies indicate that most students study better in a quiet environment with no interruptions. However, this solitude won't work for everyone. The environment most conducive for your thinking could be very distracting to the next person.

Assign Priorities

Setting **priorities** could be the most challenging part of organizing your work and assigning your time.

Although you are guided by general policies about priorities, you will need to make judgments concerning performing the work in the most beneficial way for others and for the organization. Performing the work in the order in which it is submitted to you will not always be feasible; some tasks will have more pressing deadlines than others. An example of a low-priority item is a memorandum written only as a matter of record. It can be keyed and filed at any time.

The demands of managers will be the overriding factor in how you divide your time. When you are working for two executives, one may have a lot of work for you and the other very little. When you work for a group, it may be made up of managers who are out of the office much of the time. Each one may have very little work for you, but each one will expect you to do it on the day he or she returns to the office. Under this arrangement, prepare a schedule a week in advance showing who will be in the office on which days of the week. This information may not be easy to obtain, but it will be helpful when it comes to answering the telephone and anticipating your own workload.

Eventually you will learn how much time you will need to perform work. For your own use, keep a record of how you spend your time. Several software applications are helpful to visualize and assess your time distribution in a graphical representation. Using a time distribution record as a metric is beneficial to track the overall effectiveness of your methodologies. A **metric** is a system or standard of measurement. A simplistic **time distribution chart** is shown in Figure 3-2. The time distribution chart is designed to show the distribution of work and time for several workers performing related office tasks; however, with minor changes it can be used to show the distribution of time and duties performed by one worker for several others. At the top of the columns, write the names of those for whom you perform work. Enter the time used and a brief description of the task performed in the columns below the names.

After keeping the charts for several weeks, total the time used on behalf of each person and compute percentages and covert it to a graphical chart. Your analysis will give you some estimate of how much work to expect

from each person, and it will reflect what you are doing that could be channelled elsewhere. When you have so much work to be done that some of it must be reassigned, your charts will be especially helpful to you and your manager in deciding which duties can be handled by someone else.

Historically, administrative professionals who work for groups comprising employees of different ranks award highest priority to the work of the top manager in their group, second priority to the manager next in rank, and so on. This ranking system will largely depend on the organizational structure. This arrangement may ensure a good relationship with your manager, but it may also create problems, particularly if some employees in junior-level positions feel that they can never get their work done on time or at all. Eventually they will express concerns. Avoid this problem by learning how to assess the urgency of the work of the senior managers in the group. Ask facilitating questions when necessary to help you assess the importance and timeline of the work involved. You will discover that some of their work can wait. Make your own judgment without discussing it with anyone and

FIGURE 3-2 Time distribution chart.

MAJOR ACTIVITIES	Napoli	hrs.	Carson	hrs.	Jones	hrs.	Parker	hrs.	Ramos	hrs.	For Group	hrs.	TOTAL
Mail											Open and distribute	1 1/2	1 1/2
Research	Internet	1 1/2			Internet	1/2							2
Keying	Letters	1/2	Report	1/2			Letters	1/4	Memos	1/4			1 1/2
Setting Appointments	By electronic calendar	1/2					Telephone and in person	1/2					1
Payroll											Time sheets, distribute cheques	1/2	1/2
Misc.											Handle calls	1/2	1/2
TOTAL		2 1/2		1/2		1/2		3/4		1/4		2 1/2	7

Dorothy Auvigne   TIME DISTRIBUTION CHART   *Week of: 20— 03 23*

Pearson Education, Inc.

proceed with performing the tasks. However, when your work is backed up to the extent that it must be discussed formally, the most senior manager has the responsibility of assessing the total workload and determining the need for extra help.

Some people, in an effort to gain priority for their requests, will label all requests RUSH. In each case you will have to judge what is a rush item and what is not. When you sense that these employees are under a lot of pressure, you might occasionally prevent a disruption by giving priority to their work; however, this practice must not become the norm. By giving priority to managers who mark all items RUSH, you are encouraging this behaviour at the expense of other managers' work. Those managers who decrease the stress in the office by practising effective time management should not be penalized. Deal with this issue in a diplomatic way. The best advice is to collect facts before you approach the problem. How many rush items are you receiving? Which managers are giving you the rush items? What are the rush items? Exactly what dates are you being given the rush items, and when are the deadlines? The time distribution chart will assist with collection of these data.

You can maintain more control over your work schedule by relying on your own judgment about the order in which work should be done, instead of trying to follow rigid rules. Your judgment must be good, and you should be as concerned about your rapport with the members of the group as you are about the quality of the work you perform.

Some administrative professionals aspire to work for only one manager. There are advantages and disadvantages to such a situation.

Advantages of Working with Only One Manager

1. You are often viewed as having more status within the company.

2. You do not have to adjust to conflicting management styles.

3. Your manager has a clearer idea of your time constraints. Where several managers share the same assistant, the managers often are not aware of pressures being placed on you by their colleagues.

Disadvantages of Working with Only One Manager

1. Your responsibilities may be more routine. Where an assistant works for more than one manager, the assistant often receives a greater variety of projects to complete. Remember—the more experience you receive, the more marketable you become.

2. An assistant who works for only one manager gains business contacts from only that source. If you work for a number of managers, your chances of networking are improved; this, of course, could improve your future employment opportunities.

Working for only one manager may not allow you to practise your organizational skills to the same degree that working for multiple managers would. The preference is a personal one. Both positions may offer equal challenges. If the challenges do not present themselves, find them!

Adopt a Flexible Plan

There's an adage that advises, "Plan your work, then work your plan." This is good advice for the overtaxed administrative professional.

You must plan for the ideal distribution of your time, but your plan must be flexible. Use your plan as an overall guide, but do not become discouraged if you cannot follow it closely. Your reputation of being flexible, adaptable, and tolerant with your plan will serve you well for the rest of your career.

One of your major responsibilities is to save your manager's time. To accomplish this, decrease interruptions or at least schedule them, and assist your manager by collecting and verifying facts and assembling materials that he or she will need to accomplish the task. To enable both you and your manager to perform with maximum efficiency, tackle the most pressing or important job first and keep adjusting your plan so that you can meet the corresponding deadlines.

There are three ways that you may learn the order of priority:

1. Ask questions of those involved in the process.

2. Listen to your manager's requests to determine a "pattern."

3. Keep a record of how work flows in and out of the office.

For example, know when routine reports are due and how much in advance to request work from service departments, learn mail pickup and transportation schedules, and be cognizant of the most convenient times to reach executives by telephone.

You must recognize that your work schedule is not truly your own. Your work schedule is governed not only by your manager's objectives and deadlines but also by the organization's schedule and need for information. For example:

■ You may plan to devote the morning hours to starting a lengthy assignment only to discover that your manager wants you to process a new expense summary in order to meet a scheduled payroll run.

- A telephone call from corporate head office requesting critical information may take precedence over everything else.

- The deadline for sending the department's weekly and monthly revenue report is based on a routine and defined schedule.

- Whenever an associated department with which your work is interrelated changes its schedule, you must adjust your schedule to accommodate the department.

Manage Details

You, like every other administrative professional, will be faced with the problem of keeping up with a myriad of details. In fact, you will be driven to devise methods for managing them. Not only is it good practice to record them immediately, but you should put them in a form that will enable you to locate and use these details later.

To capture detail and build institutional knowledge, develop systems to record key details and provide yourself with an opportunity to reflect on the recorded information. Using an electronic notebook or form to record information is an example of how to log important details. A daily to-do list is an excellent record to trigger reminders for yourself of actions to take. Refer to Figure 3-3 to examine a sample to-do list.

A computer, tablet, and smartphone are excellent tools to manage details and reminders. Add to that, forms and simple templates are readily available in software applications enabling administrative professionals to store the recorded detail in electronic format. Refer to the electronic task list in Figure 3-4.

The advantage of an electronic format is that the detail is easily changed or modified and its distribution to other staff is simple.

To decrease the time you spend recording certain kinds of information, design a form in which you key and duplicate the constant information and leave space to write in the variable information. Forms bring related information together in one place and prompt the user to record all the essential facts.

FIGURE 3-3 To-do list.

Tom Davison/Shutterstock

Recording facts as soon as they become available to you is an important aspect of capturing details. You will discover that the practice of "do it now" is in conflict with the concept of grouping tasks to save time and energy; nevertheless, you need to capture details at the precise moment they arise in order to keep up with them.

Actually, the means you devise for keeping up with details can vary from task to task according to the work involved and your personal preferences. That being said, recognize in all your work:

- the importance of having some method for capturing details

- the need to be consistent in following your method

You can use check marks, initials, codes, and symbols to indicate the status of each detail that you want to capture. For instance:

1. The date stamp you place on a piece of incoming mail will tell you that you have already seen it.

2. The check mark by the enclosure notation on the file copy of a letter will remind you that you did include the enclosure.

3. The electronic date and time attached to a computer file will indicate when the file was last updated.

FIGURE 3-4 Electronic task list.

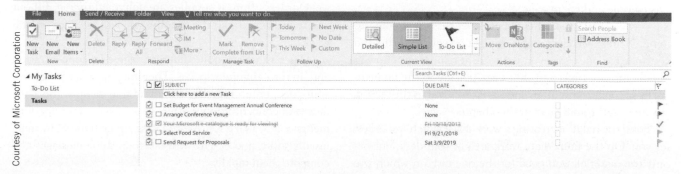

Courtesy of Microsoft Corporation

In addition, be consistent in using each type of notation to convey its respective meaning. The absence of an appropriate notation will alert you to give attention to that particular item.

When you encounter a new task, spend a little time deciding how you are going to manage the details, and then be consistent in doing so.

Details arranged in the chronological order in which they were originally recorded usually are not in their most usable form. Details must be arranged so that they can be located quickly. The arrangement can range from simple indexing on cards to computer information search tools.

Organizing the details you need to keep—such as the names of new contacts, phone numbers, changes of address, and schedule changes—can be done with great efficiency with a computer, as you only need to record them once. Not everything you jot down needs to be transferred; this is especially true of reminders of things to do or other temporary items. Cross out the reminders as you complete the tasks, but go over your list carefully and transfer the reminders of tasks yet to be done to your to-do list for the following day.

Self-Check

1. List four ways to become familiar with the information in your office.
2. Why is setting priorities one of the most challenging parts of organizing your work and assigning your time?
3. What are two advantages of working with only one manager? Two disadvantages?
4. What is a to-do list?

Work at One Task at a Time

Schedule your work so that you can stay with one task until you finish it. Jumping from one task to another is confusing. Furthermore, reviewing work to figure out where to begin and recalling what has and has not been done results in wasted time and energy.

As you work, thoughts about other tasks will come to mind. Write down each usable thought on your to-do list and continue to concentrate on the work at hand. Learn how to handle interruptions and shift back quickly to the immediate task; coping with interruptions is discussed in the section "Excuse Me!" found later in this chapter.

Form the habit of creating a work space which works best for you. On the immediate work area of your desk, put out only the materials you need for the one task on which you

are working. Since you can give attention to only one main task at a time, put the other work aside, carefully organized and labelled.

Start the Day with a Difficult Task

Begin your day in an unhurried way so that you will not need the first 30 minutes at the office to "pull yourself together." If you commute and often find yourself worrying about your transportation being late, try to improve your day by taking earlier transportation. If you drive to work, allow yourself an extra 5 or 10 minutes to get a head start on the morning rush hour. Arrive early, go over your plans for the day (which you prepared the day before), and then tackle a task that requires concentration and effort on your part. Tackle either a task that is difficult or one that you dislike. It will seem easier when you have energy and your mind is clear.

Make the first hour one of accomplishment, not one in which you simply get ready to work. Perhaps your first tasks will be to listen to your voice mail, to take down messages, or to read your email. As soon as you finish these regular responsibilities, start a challenging task. Of course, there will be times when you use the first hour to complete unfinished work from the day before.

Some office workers claim that they perform best early in the day; others, in the afternoon; and still others claim that they concentrate best very late in the day. In fact, psychologists have confirmed that every person has her or his own preferred work cycle. If you consider yourself an afternoon performer, use your afternoon hours for your most creative and challenging work, but force yourself to make the first hour a brisk one. Workers who waste time getting started are only putting themselves under unnecessary pressure to accomplish their work in what remains of the day. At any rate, do not use the beginning of the day to perform those easy tasks that can provide relaxation at intervals during the day.

Group Similar Tasks

You can save time and energy by not shifting from one task to another. For example, replenish your supplies once a week or less often. If supplies are delivered to you, fill out one requisition for all the supplies you will need for several weeks.

Different tasks require different degrees of concentration and, in turn, different speeds. Therefore, in order to control your pace, group together the tasks that require the same degree of concentration. Letters or emails to grant appointments and to make routine requests are favourable in tone, usually short, and easy to write. Group these messages and compose them rapidly.

In addition, group tasks to increase effectiveness. For example, making a telephone call should not be a routine task to be sandwiched between other work in an offhand way. A telephone call conveys an impression of the organization to the receiver. By grouping your telephone calls, you can give them your complete attention and project your personality in a thoughtful, business-like way.

Avoid Procrastination

Procrastination is an unproductive behaviour pattern that causes you to delay working on your most important assignments and to focus on tasks that aren't priorities. We all procrastinate to some degree at certain times, but to some people it is a habit. To break the habit of procrastination, you must first gain an understanding of your behaviour and then work to overcome it. You can gain a better understanding of this behaviour by taking three steps:

1. Admit that you are procrastinating.

2. Ask yourself what types of projects cause you to procrastinate. Some office workers might see a major project as a horrendous task, while others might find the daily routine tasks too much to face.

3. Ask yourself why you avoid these projects or tasks. Are you bored with the routine or afraid of the challenge? Are you avoiding interaction with certain office workers or authority figures? Do you fear failing at greater responsibility?

After answering these questions, you will be better prepared to overcome this unproductive behaviour. The following tips will help you avoid procrastination and become more productive:

1. Ask yourself what is the worst thing that can happen while you perform this task. Once you think it through, you will find that the risk created by the project is not that great; in fact, the benefits of completing the project will far outweigh the difficulties.

2. If the project is large, divide it into smaller sections. Several small tasks always appear to be easier to accomplish than one large task.

3. Reward yourself often. Allow yourself a break or a more pleasant task once you have completed a portion of the work. Small and frequent rewards work better for procrastinators than one large reward after completion of a very strenuous task.

4. Ask yourself what is the downside of not completing the task on time—or worse, not completing the task at all. Does not doing the project mean the loss of your job, a demotion, or the loss of respect from your peers and managers? This alone may encourage you to get started.

5. If you are a perfectionist, you may be avoiding a simple task because of your working style. Remember that not all work must be flawless. Working *smarter*, instead of *harder*, means recognizing the difference between work that must be perfect and work that can contain minor flaws, and acting on it.

Build Relaxation into Your Schedule

Most organizations provide a lunch hour and short morning and afternoon breaks during a regular workday. With these exceptions, employees are expected to perform efficiently throughout the day.

To maintain your best performance throughout the day and the week, experiment with alternating difficult and easy tasks to establish the best combination for conserving your energy. Observe which tasks consume a great deal of energy and which ones seem to require little energy. Rotate tasks that require a great deal of concentration and effort with tasks that require less thought and energy. Whether a task is difficult or easy for you to perform will depend on your ability, your experience in performing the given task, and your attitude towards it.

Performing an undesirable task requires an extra expenditure of energy. Repetitive tasks are often disliked. Here the dislike arises from the repetition rather than from the work itself. Fortunately, new computer technology and software have introduced interesting and productive methods of accomplishing tasks.

Once you discover which tasks are easy for you, save them to perform between difficult tasks. Use them to provide relaxation as you work. Start your day with a difficult task and work at a vigorous pace. Keep at one task for at least two hours or until you reach a stopping place. Throughout the day, alternate difficult tasks with easy ones. When possible, also alternate sitting with standing tasks. When you cannot change the task, change your pace. After lunch and after your morning and afternoon breaks, tackle difficult tasks.

Save easy tasks for late in the day. When you are estimating the time needed for performing a long, complicated task, allow for a decrease in production as you continue working. You cannot expect to perform at your maximum rate for six or seven hours. Your productivity will be highest when you can keep fatigue to a minimum. Discover and maintain a pace that will make it possible for you to do your best work.

Because of the pressure of work, you may forgo your morning or afternoon break and shorten your lunch hour.

You will possibly stick to the difficult task and postpone other work. You may be asked to work overtime, and others in the office may be asked to assist you. You may feel that you have no control over your work schedule. When you face these situations, evaluate your working plan. Establish the duration of the peak load, how often it will occur, and what you can do about it. Determine what preparation you can make in advance to lessen the peak load. If there is no letup in the work, either you are not approaching your job in the right way or you need assistance. Discuss the situation with your manager, but be prepared to offer viable solutions.

Do It Right the First Time

To produce acceptable work on the first try, plan each task before you begin, focus on the exactness of the details as you perform, and then check each finished task for correctness and completeness before you release it. When possible, seek recommendations for best practices from colleagues.

Remember that waste results when work that could have been completed correctly on the first try must be redone.

Before you start performing a task, make sure you understand the instructions; then review the facts, visualize the work in its finished form, and make a plan. Spend sufficient time determining exactly what you are expected to do: do not guess. You will discover that the extra minutes needed to perform the task correctly the first time are fewer than you would spend redoing the task. Work at a pace that will result in the most productivity for you.

The speed with which business information flows places a premium on accuracy. An error that has been released is difficult to retrieve. Problems created by errors that are released into the channels of information are not only time-consuming to correct, but can also result in losses to the organization. So check your work carefully. Be sure that every detail is correct and that each item is complete before you transmit it. On the job, you will discover ways to check the various tasks you perform to ensure their correctness. Develop your own checkpoints and guidelines for each task. Here are a few guidelines that should be observed for checking printed work:

1. Edit the copy for meaning. At the same time, watch for typographical, spelling, and punctuation errors. Do this while the copy is still on the screen so that making corrections will be easy.

2. Go over the copy a second time, scanning it for figures such as dates and amounts of money. Then check their accuracy.

3. Use a calculator to check a long list of keyed figures that have been totalled.

4. When a long series appears, count the items and compare the number with the list in the original.

5. When you must proofread a document that you have copied from keyed material, follow the original line by line, using a ruler to keep your place.

6. Always proofread the two-letter provincial abbreviations and the postal codes in addresses. One wrong stroke at the keyboard, if not caught, can mean a delayed letter.

Prepare in Advance

With the exception of routine tasks, office work requires planning. The amount of planning time needed depends on how complicated the job is, the length of it, and whether or not the person doing the work has ever performed similar tasks.

Executives in successful organizations plan three to five years in advance. Managers at all levels plan at least one year in advance. Observe how your manager and others in your organization think ahead, and then apply some of their techniques to your own assignments. The time you spend thinking through what needs to be done will save you minutes and hours of redoing work.

Take time to study a job until you can visualize it to its completion regardless of how complicated or lengthy it is. People who work aimlessly seldom reach the goals towards which they should have been working. Ask yourself what the expected outcome and purpose of the specific assignment is. When an assignment is new and you find it difficult to visualize it through to completion, ask your team manager for guidance.

The most critical parts of an assignment are the ones that require other people either to supply information or to actually perform certain tasks. Begin your preparation with the segments of the work that involve others.

During the last decade, the rise of the administrative professional as the *knowledge worker* has emerged. Working in diverse teams assigned to projects that are valued more by quality rather than quantity. Rarely do administrative professionals work on a single project for three months or more. They will have several ongoing projects, which they constantly need to manage. By extension, this has spun off the development of the specialized area of project management. Figure 3-5 illustrates a Gantt chart, which is a basic form of project management. This chart is an excellent tool for comparing your planned work schedule against the actual time that is required to complete a task.

FIGURE 3-5 Gantt chart.

GANTT CHART

NAME OF PROJECT: Keying Analysis   NAME OF TEAM LEADER: Ilka Stiles

ESSENTIAL TASKS		CRITICAL DATES												
		May 01	May 03	May 05	May 07	May 09	May 11	May 13	May 15	May 17	May 19	May 21	May 23	May 25
1. Design a questionnaire to examine the keying equipment used in offices.	S	■												
	A	■												
2. Make appointments with admin. assistants to collect answers for questionnaires.	S		■	■										
	A		■											
3. Prepare and mail confirmation letters with attached questionnaires to admin. assistants.	S				■									
	A					■								
4. Interview admin. assistants to collect info. and questionnaires.	S							■	■					
	A							■						
5. Send each admin. assistant a thank-you letter for his/her contribution.	S								■					
	A													
6. Collate, calculate, and analyze the results of the questionnaires.	S								■					
	A									■				
7. Prepare graphs to indicate results of information collected on questionnaires.	S									■				
	A										■			
8. Compose and edit report to describe the findings of the data.	S											■	■	
	A												■	
9. Key, assemble, and bind report.	S											■		
	A												■	
10. Submit report to general manager.	S												■	
	A												■	
	S													
	A													

S = Scheduled Time   A = Actual Time

Complete a Task

You will be doubly rewarded when you stay with a task until it is complete:

1. You will feel satisfaction at having finished the task.
2. You will experience the emotion of accomplishment.

Always think more about what you have accomplished than about what you still must get done. Enjoy the satisfaction that one naturally experiences from completing an assignment or reaching a goal. When you are working on a lengthy project that seems endless, break the assignment into segments that you can complete in a morning or an afternoon, or into even smaller parts that you can complete in an hour or two. Plan on stopping occasionally to measure your accomplishment by the number of segments completed. Don't get sidetracked. If you stay focused on one task there is less likelihood of errors occurring. If you must put work aside unfinished, make detailed notes of what still needs to be done. Make your notes carefully so that you can rely on them.

Managing Interruptions

Every challenging position that demands a variety of responsibilities will be punctuated by interruptions. There are ways of avoiding some interruptions.

1. Practise avoidance by organizing your work area so that it is less accessible to co-workers who wish to socialize during work hours. Try moving extra chairs away from your desk or moving or angling your desk so that it cannot easily be seen by passers-by.
2. Interruptions are often caused by noise. You can avoid this type of interruption by having noisy equipment relocated away from your desk.
3. When you are working on a project that requires your full attention, ask another administrative professional to handle your telephone calls; explain the urgency of your task to co-workers, and then move to a location away from your desk.

Excuse Me!

Your success in coping with interruptions will depend on your attitude towards them and your ability to handle them and then resume work quickly.

You know that interruptions cannot always be prevented—the telephone will ring, a visitor will walk in, a co-worker will ask you a question, your manager will need assistance. What you do not know is the precise moment when the interruption will occur. Recognize that interruptions are a part of the job, and allow time for them in your planning.

Don't resent interruptions. Keep calm; do not allow yourself to become upset. You will feel less frustrated if you know how much time you will need to perform each of your normal tasks. For example, keep a record of how long it takes to key a two-page letter, to compose a one-page memo, to develop a 12-page formal report, and to process the daily general communications. This is useful information for future planning and scheduling. If you discover that you are running out of time to meet a deadline, decide for yourself which work can be postponed. Use your time for the priority item.

Give adequate time to handling each interruption. Do not appear to be rushed. Be courteous, but do not waste time because of an interruption. To reduce the time used for each interruption, proceed in the following way:

1. Mark your place as soon as you are interrupted—a light, erasable check mark in the margin with a soft lead pencil will suffice.

2. Once you are interrupted, handle the interruption immediately if it can be dealt with in only a few minutes. If a co-worker asks for information, look it up and supply the information while the co-worker is at your desk. In response to a telephone call you can handle, follow through on the caller's request, even looking up information if you can do so without keeping the caller waiting a noticeable length of time. However, if the interruption requires prolonged attention, you may have to postpone action on it. Realize, however, that each time you must postpone following through on a request, you are creating a new item for your to-do list.

3. Quickly resume work where you left off at the time of the interruption. Do not encourage co-workers to linger in your office. Be courteous, but do not continue a telephone conversation beyond the time actually necessary to handle the call.

4. Avoid interrupting yourself because of lack of planning.

5. Keep a pencil in your hand, or keep your hands on the keyboard. These actions inform the visitor that you are eager to continue your work.

6. Do not get involved in office gossip. Small talk creates big interruptions.

7. When a co-worker drops into your office for a visit, stay standing. Often a person feels invited to sit if you are sitting.

8. When possible, hold meetings in another person's office. This allows you to leave as soon as the business is complete. Meeting with visitors in reception areas or conference rooms helps to keep the meeting short, since these areas often do not provide the privacy of an office.

When you must interrupt others, be considerate. Wait until the other person is at a break in her or his work. Direct your questions to the correct person, and do not interrupt others unnecessarily. Do not ask others to answer questions if you can find the answers yourself by looking them up. Accumulate the questions you must ask your manager; then ask several at one time to cut down on interrupting her or him. A concise memo or electronic message enumerating your questions is an excellent way to avoid a direct interruption and to obtain a quick response.

Make a Daily Plan

At the end of the day, review the work you must do the following day. Estimate the time each of your tasks will take and fit them one by one into time slots. Go through the same steps daily, and then leave your office with the satisfaction of knowing that your work is well organized for the following day. To prepare a systematic daily plan, you could proceed as follows:

1. Verify that everything you have entered into the computer during the day has been saved.

2. If you use an **electronic calendar** or a desk calendar, make sure the appointment entries in your manager's calendar and yours are identical.

3. Go over your to-do list. If something on the list must be carried out the following day, enter it in your daily calendar. As you are planning your work, you will think of other tasks that must be done some time during the day. Put notes about these on your to-do list.

4. Manage your supervisors' activities for the following day. Include all appointments, showing with whom, the purpose, the time, and where (if it is not in your manager's office). At the bottom of the sheet, add reminders of work your manager must complete during the day.

5. Locate reports, correspondence, and other items to which you know your manager will need to refer during conferences, or before he or she places a telephone call, writes a report, or carries out other responsibilities. Flag these so that you can retrieve them quickly the following day. Likewise, locate the information you will need in order to proceed with your own work. Also, create electronic files containing important information readily available to you and your manager.

6. Clear your desk, putting everything in place.

By using this system, you will be well prepared to start your work immediately. You will enjoy the satisfaction of having a plan for your tasks and priorities.

Operate within Easy Reach

Normal and maximum working areas at a desk have been established through time and motion studies. Materials and tools should be positioned within the normal working area if the worker is to attain maximum efficiency.

You can determine the *normal* working area of the desk for either the right or the left hand by swinging the extended hand and forearm across the desk. You can determine the *maximum* working area for either the right or the left hand by swinging the extended hand and the entire arm across the desk.

Before you begin a task at a desk or a table, place the equipment, supplies, and tools you will need in the normal working area.

Use the space in your desk to store supplies, stationery, and work in progress. Materials should pass across the top of your desk but should not be stored on it. Keep a minimum of items on top of your desk.

File all your work in progress together in one drawer, unless your manager is working on a project that generates so much paperwork that the materials must be subdivided into several folders. Allocate separate space in a vertical file drawer for a project of this magnitude. Never put a single folder of pending material in an unusual place—relocation of this material can lead to confusion and wasted time.

In case you might be absent, let your manager know where you keep the correspondence folder and other work in progress. If the work in progress is highly confidential, you may have to lock it up in special file cabinets, especially at night.

If you have a drawer that is not deep enough to hold file folders in vertical positions, keep it empty. Use it as a temporary storage when you want to clear your desk to store the papers on which you are currently working—for instance, while you sort the mail or go to lunch.

OFFICE ORGANIZATION

By organizing office supplies and the workstation, an administrative professional can save a great deal of time, as well as save the company money. Following are some suggestions for getting the office supplies and workstation organized.

Organize the Office Supplies

1. Label the shelves where supplies are kept. This way staff members know where to look without interrupting you. This procedure also helps you keep track of supplies on hand.

2. Make sure that one person is responsible for controlling inventory and ordering supplies. This is a task that a senior administrative professional will often delegate.

3. Develop your own requisition form. Keep these forms in the supply room. Staff will be expected to complete the form if they notice a product is running low. Be sure the form has room for a full description. Encourage the staff to fill in as much information as possible (descriptions, quantities, colours, sizes, unit numbers, and so on). This will simplify your work when it comes to completing the requisition for ordering.

4. Compose a list of all items you use on a regular basis. Include the item unit numbers, unit prices, descriptions, colours available, and so on. Post this list in the supply room along with a stack of the requisition forms you have developed. This is necessary if you expect staff members to partially complete the requisition forms.

5. Discourage staff members from placing verbal orders with you. This type of interruption can be very time-consuming: you must stop your work, listen to the request, write down the information, check the supplies, and perhaps get back to the staff members for further clarification. Insist that all orders be completed on requisition forms.

6. When staff members have rush orders, request that they fill in a requisition, mark it RUSH, and bring it to your desk.

7. Take inventory on a regular basis. Taking inventory once or twice a month on a designated day works well for most offices.

8. Before placing an order, compare prices between the office supply catalogues and advertisements sent to you. The office supply market is a competitive one, and you may be able to order your items on sale.

9. Ordering items in standard package sizes may save you money. Ordering items one at a time is short-sighted and expensive.

10. Do not over-order supplies, unless you are ordering supplies in standard-size packages. Too many supplies will cause confusion. Because space is often at a premium, excess supplies tend to create a storage problem. As well, some supplies have a shelf life: if not used before a certain date, they become less useful.

11. When you place an order, be prepared with all the required information. Having requisition forms returned or needing to make a follow-up telephone call to clarify an order will delay delivery.

Organize the Workstation

A cluttered desk gives clients, co-workers, and managers the impression that you are disorganized. A cluttered desk is not necessarily a sign that you are busy; in fact, a cluttered desk simply adds to your workload. It is essential that you purge any extraneous materials and then organize the materials you intend to keep.

Purge Unnecessary Items   One of the first steps to take in organizing your desk is to eliminate all that you don't need. Each time you pick up a document from your desk and wonder where to file it, ask yourself whether there's a law that says you must keep it. If not, consider the recycling box or the garbage bin.

If any of the following applies to a document, you have just cause to purge yourself of paper:

1. An electronic copy is available.

2. You will not really use the information; it is just *nice* to have.

3. The document is a duplicate. Once you get organized, one copy is all you need of any document or a scanned electronic copy may be sufficient.

4. The document is out of date.

5. Chances are, you will never find the time to read the information.

Organize Necessary Items   Ridding your workstation of excess paper is only the first step in getting organized.

The importance of a highly organized workstation cannot be emphasized enough.

One of the most frustrating time-wasters is searching for information that has been filed incorrectly or has simply disappeared. Of course, employing the correct ARMA filing rules is imperative; these rules are discussed in Chapter 11. However, there is much more to organizing your workstation. When your workstation is organized, you save valuable time.

The following are some suggestions to help you get started:

1. If your workstation is currently in a cluttered condition, plan several uninterrupted hours you can use to attack the problem.

2. If your office does not have a paper shredder, approach your manager about purchasing one. Employees are often reluctant to discard confidential material, so they let it accumulate in what eventually becomes a very thick folder tucked into a corner of the desk. Compact shredders can be placed on top of wastebaskets.

3. A basket placed in your workstation to hold work that is pending often becomes a storage bin. If you do not intend to work on a document immediately, file it in its appropriate labelled folder.

4. Use one calendar for all your appointments. If you keep your personal appointments separate from your business appointments, you will constantly be referring to two calendars. This is a time-waster and will result in disorganization. Ensure you have access to your calendar at every meeting and seminar you attend.

5. Wherever you store information—electronically or in drawers, cabinets, folders, baskets, and so on—develop a systemic and appropriate naming convention that describes the type of information that should be stored in this location.

6. Attempt to follow this rule: *Never handle a piece of paper more than once.* At times this rule may be unrealistic, but it will force you to make a decision rather than procrastinate, then rehandle and reread a document.

7. Never use the surface of your desk as storage space. Your desk is a work area; you need all of it available to remain organized while you conduct your work.

8. Keep your computer reference information current. If names, addresses, and telephone numbers are indexed on your computer system, consider it a priority to update the system as often as possible. You cannot enjoy the efficiency of using a computer system unless it provides correct information.

9. Continually organize, purge, and alphabetize your filing system. When you discover a document out of place or out of date, take action immediately. Your filing

cabinet is a work area you should take pride in. Refer to Chapter 10 for filing strategies.

10. Create a reference database for frequently used phone and contact information.

11. Place reference sources (books, portable media storage devices) at an arm's length from your work area. These references should include a dictionary, a thesaurus, and administrative professional's reference manuals.

12. Your files should contain no paper clips. When you want to avoid pages being separated, staple them.

13. Do you really know what is in your desk and cabinets? Schedule 15 minutes every month to purge your current bookshelves, desk drawers, and cabinets. You must keep current with the contents of your workstation. Keep the wastebasket and recycling box handy; you should constantly purge your workstation of unwanted materials.

14. If there is a bulletin board in your workstation, be sure the information is current and well organized. If the bulletin board is not easy to use, it is just occupying space and adding to the office clutter.

15. Keep the equipment you rely upon the most within easy reach; you should be able to slide your chair easily between the telephone, the computer, fax machine, and so on.

16. Your workstation will require drawer space for office supplies. Store only a limited supply at your desk; store larger amounts away from your workstation in a supply cabinet. The small supplies you keep at your desk (stapler, tape, pens, clips, adhesive notes, and the like) can be stored with drawer organizers, which are sold at stationery stores. Letterhead, envelopes, forms, and other major paper supplies should be placed in drawer trays, not left out in visible stacks.

17. Your personal items need a place, too; but do not crowd your desk surface with family photos. Leave the desk surface as clear as possible and place the photos on top of your **credenza** or filing cabinet. Coats and spare shoes should be stored in the coatroom. Lunches and tea bags belong in the lunchroom. Awards belong on the walls. If your office contains plants, place small ones on the window ledge, credenza, and so on, and large ones on the floor. Keep personal items to a minimum. The workstation is professional space, not personal space.

Self-Check

1. What does "purge" mean?
2. List three suggestions that you will adopt to help you organize your workstation.

NONTRADITIONAL WORK ARRANGEMENTS

Why do we believe that working in an office means working 9 a.m. to 5 p.m., with two refreshment breaks and one lunch hour? Many organizations offer flexible working arrangements for administrative professionals such as flexible working hours, job sharing, and using remote offices—working from home.

Good managers know that allowing employees to have working arrangements that better suit their lifestyles means happier and more productive employees.

Flextime

For administrative professionals with front-line reception responsibilities, working face to face with other employees and with clients is a priority. In this case, it is essential to have standardized working hours that match those of the organization's business hours.

However, where there is more than one administrative professional with similar responsibilities, there is an opportunity for flexible hours. A cooperative working arrangement between administrative professionals will mean that there is always at least one person available to handle clients and employees and generally cover administrative work while another assistant is enjoying the benefits of flextime. Managers often approve an arrangement in which employees have extended working hours for nine days and then are given the tenth day as a holiday. Flexible hour arrangements thus offer an excellent opportunity for frequent long weekends. Another advantage of flextime is that one can avoid rush-hour traffic by starting work early or finishing late.

Job Sharing

An office with a cooperative team environment lends itself to job sharing. Where employees have a good understanding of what must be accomplished and the procedures for handling the work, it is possible for two or more people to share one job. Many office professionals have a lifestyle that suits a part-time working arrangement. In this case, job sharing is an excellent option.

Remote Office

For administrative professionals whose work involves a concentration of tasks such as document production, travel arrangements, or project and event management, it is not necessary for these employees to perform all their work at the office.

It is so convenient and effective to communicate using data sharing platforms, email, voice mail, and other forms of instant messaging. Without question, smartphones allow people to stay in touch more effectively than stationary desk phones. Laptop and tablet computers offer easy mobile technology usage, which allows work to be accessed almost anywhere and anytime. So with the cooperation of management, office professionals with the appropriate tools may be able to maximize their performance by working away from the office.

> **Self-Check**
>
> 1. List three nontraditional work arrangements.
> 2. Give an example of each nontraditional arrangement.

ENVIRONMENTAL MANAGEMENT

Administrative professionals can take the lead in making the office an environmentally conscious workplace. Consider the opportunities for recycling, reusing, and reducing that present themselves each workday.

Many organizations take their environmental responsibilities so seriously that it is often written into their vision, mission, and values statements. Individual offices are similarly taking a more responsible approach to managing resources. Most companies make a serious effort to recycle and reuse materials, reduce waste, and purchase products that have been recycled.

Environmentally Sustainable Offices

If your office has not yet committed itself to environmental sustainability, you can help to initiate this change. **Environmental sustainability** is a state in which the demands placed on the environment are met without draining resources and its capacity to allow all people to live well. For reference, see Figure 3-6 showing common symbols for recycling or recyclable materials. Here are suggestions for environmental sustainability at work:

1. **Waste**. Look for opportunities for reducing, reusing, and recycling. This could include a paper, supplies, and food waste protocol. You could lead a campaign to bring awareness of these initiatives to the attention of all employees. Post notices reminding staff of these suggestions. Have paper-recycling bins available.
2. **Electricity**. Place energy reminders to turn off lights and equipment when not in use.

FIGURE 3-6 Signs depicting recycled or recyclable materials.

Pearson Education, Inc.

Recycled   Recyclable

3. **Heating**. Conduct checks by walking to identify areas in the office that are being heated unnecessarily and take action to save energy as required.
4. **Material procurement**. Look into how some of the supplies used in your office are made. You could source how office supplies are made and purchase those made with recycled materials.

Canadian manufacturers are expected to publish the percentage of recycled material in the product along with the recycled logo (see Figure 3-7). If you cannot buy recycled products, buy those that are recyclable. Your office colleagues will have more ideas about responsible resource management that might pertain to your office. Continue to explore these options. Welcome their ideas and publish them in a monthly newsletter. Of course, the newsletter can be distributed electronically as an environmentally sustainable approach.

FIGURE 3-7 Sample of product displaying percentage of recycled material.

This envelope is made of
100% recycled paper
and is recyclable

*Cette enveloppe est
fabriquée de papier
100% recyclé et est
recyclable*

Pearson Education, Inc.

QUESTIONS FOR STUDY AND REVIEW

1. What is the key difference between leadership and management?
2. Briefly explain a management theory presented in this chapter.
3. List the five management functions.
4. Distinguish between effectiveness and efficiency. Provide an example of effective practice and an example of efficient practice.
5. What effect will a manager's work preferences have on the way the administrative professional's daily work is organized?
6. Who should establish an understanding of priorities with all the members of the office team? Explain why.
7. Suggest ways that an administrative professional can take initiative in learning a new job.
8. Explain how you can justify taking time at your desk for creative thinking.
9. Suggest four ways you can create an environment that is conducive to creative thinking while you are located at your workstation.
10. Should all segments of the working day be structured? Why or why not? Explain.
11. Why should details be recorded immediately?
12. What are the advantages of keeping the work you have in progress carefully organized?
13. Provide an example of how similar tasks can be grouped.
14. What do you believe the phrase "work smarter, not harder" means?
15. In order to get work right the first time, what should you do before actually performing the task?
16. What is the primary advantage of focusing on a task until it is finished?
17. Suggest three ways to avoid interruptions before they occur.
18. Suggest three ways to deal successfully with interruptions once they have occurred.
19. Why should you discourage staff members from verbally placing supply requests?
20. State two things you could do to make a quiet environment if you wanted time to think and be creative.
21. Suggest three ways to support environmental sustainability in your office.

Key Terms

brainstorming 51

credenza 65

effectiveness 52

efficiency 52

electronic calendar 62

environmental sustainability 66

flextime 53

management by objectives (MBO) 52

management process 50

management theory 50

metric 55

orientation 53

priorities 54

procrastination 59

time distribution chart 55

time management 52

total quality management (TQM) 50

EVERYDAY ETHICS

Smoking Supervisor

You are the office supervisor for a respected consulting firm in Saskatoon. You supervise four administrative professionals. The office hours are from 8:00 a.m. until 4:30 p.m. five days a week. All your employees respect the established office hours and the allotted time for lunch. In addition to lunch, everyone is allowed two 30-minute refreshment breaks.

One of the people you supervise, Kylie, is a good friend, and you see each other socially outside the office. You and Kylie are the only smokers on staff. Because your office is a nonsmoking environment, you take an average of four additional breaks per day, each break taking about 10 minutes.

Do the math! You and Kylie are taking 40 extra minutes on breaks every day. By the end of every working week, you and Kylie have each spent more than three and a half hours away from work. By the end of the month, you each have spent almost two extra days on breaks.

Your three nonsmoking employees come to you with this issue of Kylie's time. They say that Kylie is working fewer hours than they are working. They report that the other administrative professionals handle the clients and managers that come to Kylie's desk while she is on smoking breaks. They have spoken to Kylie several times about the issue, and Kylie's response has always been, "See my supervisor." The nonsmoking administrative professionals recommend that they too be given equivalent time away from their desks.

■ What is your approach to manage this situation effectively?

Problem Solving

1. Instant messaging (IM) *can* be a useful tool within the office. It is generally informal by its nature and can also reduce productivity. How often has a discussion about something work-related quickly turned into a half-hour gossip session? You have a colleague who seems to have less work to do than you do, who is always tempting you into a chat session. How can you manage this effectively without compromising the relationship between you and your colleague?

2. You are in the middle of something when you get an urgent email. You reply, only to receive a phone call shortly after. You finish the call; only have another email that demands a response. This goes on and on for most of the day. Before you know it, it is 3 p.m., and you still have not made headway in what you had tried to start in the morning. All administrative professional can relate to this. You have two hours before your day ends at 5 p.m. How can you salvage the rest of the day to get some planned tasks done?

3. You have a colleague who uses speakerphone to discuss everything from meetings with clients to dinner plans with his partner. You find this distracting. What are the solutions to this problem? What can you do to relieve your frustration?

4. Five weeks ago, you were promoted to a senior administrative professional for the sales department. There are 25 salespeople in the department, and you are having difficulty prioritizing your work. This morning, one of the salespeople shouted, "You never get my work done by the time I need it. You are always doing work for Kristien and Adam." Kristien and Adam do give you more work than the other salespeople, and you are aware that you've spent much of your time doing their work. What can you do to ensure that you allocate a fair portion of your time to the other salespeople?

Special Reports

1. Interview an office professional who works for more than one person—several executives, everyone within a department, or everyone within a division. Request an interview in order to ask questions about how the office professional organizes and handles the work. Phrase your questions in advance. Develop your questions carefully. As you formulate your questions, be sure to inquire about priorities for completing work, standards of acceptability, phone and data management responsibilities, problems encountered, and suggestions that might be helpful to you on the job. Do not limit your questions to the ideas given here. Report your findings to the class or to the instructor.

2. How many unfinished projects do you have? Are you burdened with the thought that "everything is started and nothing is finished"? Make a list of your unfinished projects and tasks. Select the one you can finish in the least amount of time and complete it. Select another task that you can complete in a few minutes and then complete it. Notice how you lighten your load by finishing tasks. Use what you have discovered to remind yourself to finish tasks as soon as possible, thus leaving your mind free to tackle new assignments. Write a memorandum to your instructor about what you learned.

3. Are you using your time effectively? To find out, keep a record. Begin by keeping a list of minor tasks that you perform between major tasks. Leave space to the right of each item on your list. As you complete each minor task, jot down the date, the time, and the number of minutes used. For example, did you pay unplanned attention to the postage? Did you package up literature for transfer to another branch office? Did you search for stationery that was not found in the appropriate location? At the end of one week, analyze your list for similar tasks, for redundant tasks, and for those tasks that were the result of interruptions. Add the time spent for each category and then multiply the time by 52 for an estimate of the time spent in a year. Write a brief report for your instructor that summarizes your findings and suggests methods to manage your minor-task time more effectively.

PRODUCTION CHALLENGES

3-A Setting Priorities

Supplies needed:

- *Daily Plan Chart, Form 3-A, Companion Website*

The time is 9 a.m., Monday, June 2, and you have enough work to keep you busy for one week. Mr. Wilson is leaving on a business trip at noon today. At 8 a.m., Mr. Wilson used speech recognition software to dictate three letters and discussed with you work to be done in his absence.

Here are the notes you took during your conference with Mr. Wilson:

1. Send copies of the combined sales report for the week of May 19 to the four regional managers. (You will use a copier to make copies of the sales summary from a computer printout.)

2. Call A. R. Rush, assistant vice-president of marketing, eastern region, extension 534, and ask him to see Dave Romphf, an out-of-town supplier, who had an appointment with Mr. Wilson on Wednesday, June 4, at 10 a.m.

3. Review, edit, and mail the letter to Allen Fitzgerald that Mr. Wilson dictated earlier. Mr. Wilson stressed that it must be mailed today. The letters to Nancy Evans and Robert Berger may be mailed tomorrow.

4. Make a daily digest of the incoming mail. Hold all mail for Mr. Wilson to answer. Call Mr. Wilson if something is urgent.

5. Key a letter to Nancy Cromwell, Regina, advising her that Mr. Wilson will accept her invitation to speak at the National Sales Conference in Regina on November 28 at 2:30 p.m.

6. Rekey the last two pages of the talk that Mr. Wilson gave at the local chamber of commerce and send a copy of the talk to Art Winfield so that he will receive it by Friday afternoon. (Art Winfield has a local address.)

7. Call Jacob Levine, assistant vice-president of marketing, northwestern region, extension 536, to remind him that Mr. Wilson will be out of town for the week. Mr. Wilson counts on Mr. Levine to represent him when Mr. Wilson cannot attend weekly executive committee meetings, held every Wednesday at 10 a.m.

8. Make copies of an article on time management and distribute them to the four assistant vice-presidents of marketing.

9. Call Creighton's Restaurant at 555-0611 to set up a luncheon meeting on Monday, June 9, at 12:30 p.m. for 12 members of the planning committee for the November sales seminar.

10. Call Air Canada at 555-1414 to cancel Mr. Wilson's reservation to Vancouver on Wednesday, June 4.

The assistant vice-presidents have left the following work in your in-basket:

A. A six-page report written by Emma Yee to be keyed in final form by Wednesday afternoon.

B. A note from A. R. Rush asking you to obtain online the sales figures for the four regions for the week of May 26. He wrote, "Please key the figures on cards so that I may refer to them in a staff meeting at 10 a.m. on Tuesday."

C. A note from Jacob Levine asking you to copy the figures he has circled in red on the computer printout. He wrote, "I need this information by 2 p.m. today (Monday). Just key them on a couple of cards."

D. A revised 12-page report written by Olivia Azam. She needs to receive the completed report on Friday to review it before she presents it to Mr. Wilson on Monday, June 9. (You stored the first draft of this report on a flash drive. You will need to key the revisions.)

Before you begin working on these tasks, take a Daily Plan Chart, Form 3-A, from your desk, write down the work to be done, and assign priorities to the items.

3-B Correcting Letters

Supplies needed:

- *Plain paper*

Correct the spelling and capitalization errors in the following two letters. List the incorrect words, correctly spelled, on a separate sheet of paper. Key the two letters in an acceptable letter style.

(Current date) Mrs. M. M. Freedman, Financial Manager, Super Stove Store, 4909–50 Avenue, Red Deer, AB, T4N 4A7. Each year Progressive Digital Innovations Inc, provides you with a complete annual statement of the debits and credits made with our company. However, the statement we are curenntly enclosing includes all tranactions that occured during this past year, with the exception of those for the month of September and October. (P) You will recall that during those months, we offered our retail customers a 30% discount on all colored appliances. Unfortunately, however, we neglected to include this discount on our new computerized accounting system. Therefore, your statement does not reflect this discount; when this oversite is corrected, we will forward an updated statement to you. We expect to have your corected statement in the mail within the next too weeks. Please except our apologies for any inconvenience this may cause. (P) If you have any additional conserns about the statement, please call our office. We look forward to your continued business in the year a head. Sincerely, Noah Wilson, Vice President of Marketing.

(Current date) Lori Anderson, 630 Beach Blvd., Hamilton, ON, L8H 6Y4. Thank you for submiting your oficial transcript and resume as applicant for the position of administrative assistent. (P) This year their have been many well qualified canidates expressing intrest in employment at Millennium Appliances, Inc. We have not fill all the positions for administrative assistents. Because of the definate promise you education and experience reflect, we know you have much to offer and employer. (P) In the mean time we shall keep your credantials on active file for six months in case another opening ocurrs for which you qualify. You interest in applying for employment with our organization and your cooperation in submitting the neccesary information requested of you is appreciated. Sincerely, Noah Wilson, Vice-President of Marketing.

3-C Distribution of Time

Supplies needed:

- *Time Distribution Chart, Form 3-C-1, Companion Website*
- Locate *Notes on time spent during week of May 19–23, Form 3-C-2, Companion Website*
- *Plain paper*

You know you can plan your work more efficiently if you keep a record of the demands on your time. You want to know how much time you spend working for some of your managers.

Your notes on the time spent are in Form 3-C-2. You have already prepared the Time Distribution Chart, Form 3-C-1. Under the heading Major Activities, use broad categories such as processing mail and word processing.

Processing the postal mail, handling telephone calls, and filing is done for the entire group. The email and voice mail you handle is your own.

Summarize the information given in Form 3-C-2. Enter the categories of tasks performed in the Major Activities column of the distribution chart. Enter the total time spent working for each person.

Optional—Create your own distribution chart that will summarize the amount of time spent on each activity.

3-D Requisitioning Supplies

Supplies needed:

- *Progressive Digital Innovations Inc. Requisition for Supplies, Forms 3-D-1 and 3-D-2, Companion Website*

You had a note from Alexander Rush saying, "Please get me six ruled office pads, 21.5 cm × 28 cm, white."

You decided to check the supplies you had on hand and to requisition what you needed. The following supplies were low: ruled office pads, letterhead, self-stick notepads, index cards, and ballpoint pens.

All the employees at Progressive Digital Innovations Inc. requisition office supplies from the Stationery and Supplies Department. You have the authority to sign your own requisitions for office supplies. Your location is office 216, on the second floor. The requisition number is 21.

Here is what you requested: six ruled office pads, 21.5 cm × 28 cm, white; one ream of letterhead; five packages of removable self-stick notepads, yellow, 76 mm × 127 mm; four packages of index cards, 7.5 cm × 12.5 cm, white; six ballpoint pens, black, fine point.

Prepare the requisition.

Weblinks

Tools of the Trade
www.mindtools.com
Mind Tools' extensive information base includes articles on time management, stress management, creativity tools, tips on effective management, techniques for effective decision making, and more.

Time Management Ninja
https://timemanagementninja.com/
This site provides useful tips for managing your time personally and professionally. Use the Tabulator link to compare how you are spending your time with how you would like to spend your time and how others in your category spend theirs.

Management Help
https://managementhelp.org/
This is a free online and reference library covering a variety of management and leadership related topics.

World Organization
www.world.org/weo/recycling
The World Organization's website provides links to other environmentally conscious sites including Earth's 911 and Canadian Centre for Pollution Prevention.

Chapter 4
Research and Reference Sources

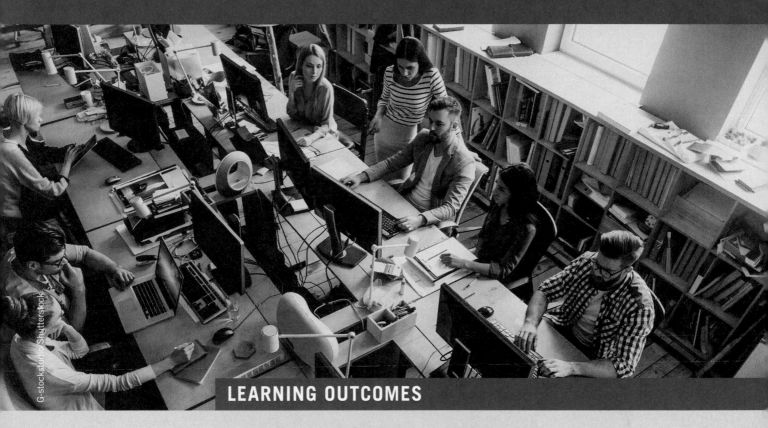

G-stockstudio/Shutterstock

LEARNING OUTCOMES

After completion of this chapter, the student will be able to:

1 Recognize the significance of research and development in the business environment.

2 Explore and understand source types, including research databases and common research methodologies.

3 State services provided by organizational, public, private, and specialty libraries.

4 Identify the purpose of various reference directories.

5 Explain the benefits of internet-based information and guidelines to evaluate credible online reference sources.

6 Identify and avoid plagiarism.

7 Understand the parameters for referencing sources utilizing APA, MLA, and Chicago referencing styles.

8 Describe the components of an office procedure manual.

All levels within an organization require accurate and timely information for decision making. Whether the decisions made are at the technical or strategic levels precise and timely information consistently leads to enhanced decision capability. Gathering information through research processes is a best practice for organizations. Research is enabled as a systemic attempt to study a problem for a general or specific purpose. Each year, organizations invest significant amounts of their resources into research and development in order to maintain their competitive edge. Accurate information obtained through research adds benefits leading to enhanced organizational performance. As an example, research collected provides information concerning markets, competitors, trends, opportunities, and internal and external clients. Research conducted by the administrative professional assists in identifying optimal business practices. Client-based research often determines loyalty, satisfaction, and preferences.

RESEARCH AND DEVELOPMENT (R&D)

Research and development (R&D) in the workplace is frequently directed towards innovation, introduction, and improvement of products and processes. R&D plays a significant role in the success of a business and contributes to the sustainability of the organization as an entity. The R&D function

---

Company Profile

Paul Chiasson/Canadian Press/AP Images

Bombardier Aerospace and Rail Transportations

Montreal, Quebec
Canada's number 1 company for R&D expenditure

Bombardier is a globally based organization headquartered in Montreal, Quebec, with a network that stretches into 28 countries. It prides itself on maintaining excellent performance related to innovation and contribution to the knowledge-based economy. Words such as *creativity* and *industry leading* come to mind when describing Bombardier. Its aerospace transportations programs involve both commercial and business development. Bombardier Commercial Aircraft forecasts 12,550 deliveries in the 60- to 150-seat segment over the 2017–2036 period. Additionally, Bombardier is a leader in rail transportation.

In Canada, Bombardier is recognized for the investment it continually makes in research and development (R&D). In fact, currently, Bombardier is Canada's number 1 business for R&D expenditure. It leads all manufacturers in R&D, quantifying as one-third of all R&D activity in Canada's manufacturing segment. Since 2010, Bombardier has over 160 original inventions patented and has spent over C$7 billion on R&D in the 10-year period from 2007–2017. A strategic core value includes

the drive for continuous improvement and sustainability for transportation.

In recent years, Bombardier has been listed on Forbes Canada's Best 25 employers. Bombardier believes its success is made possible by the talent pool of 69,500 employees worldwide, with approximately 21,000 employed in Canada. Employee annual compensation is 1.7 the national average. Actively enlisting, engaging, and developing its workforce talent contributes to the overall success. It utilizes employee feedback in sustaining growth while supporting a diverse labour force. Bombardier practices various methodologies to achieve this success, including providing opportunities for employees to enhance their skills in training programs, eLearning, and courses especially designed to develop recognized leaders.

Additionally, Bombardier boasts that for every job it creates with Bombardier, it creates an additional 1.9 jobs among its Tier 1 and Tier 2 suppliers. Bombardier has over 1000 suppliers with more than C$2 billion in spending in direct support of the Canadian economy, contributing over C$12 billion to Canada's gross domestic product (GDP). As an organization, Bombardier consider itself a Canadian ambassador, with over C$21 billion in revenue worldwide.

Bombardier as an organization continues to respond to challenges while developing innovative technologies to position its current and future success.

provides a platform for creativity and innovation to flourish in an organization. It is important to remember that R&D is not limited to developing new products or services. Its purpose is to evaluate and diversify current products and services.

As mentioned, organizational research is deployed to find answers to practical questions. This differs comparatively to academic research undertaken to answer a scholarly question. Workplace research focuses on improving conditions for the organization. Research also forms the first step in a successful program for retention and development to learn what every member of the team thinks, feels, knows, and wants. This particular research input influences behaviour, helping personnel see the big picture. Accurate and complete information enhances planning, decision making, and buy-in within the entire organization.

SOURCES OF INFORMATION

In their day-to-day responsibilities, administrative office professionals use information that comes from many sources. Most information comes from sources within the organization; some comes from external sources, but all should be current and accurate. In order to locate such information, administrative professionals should develop an understanding of the various research sources and methods available for locating such information.

Primary sources are direct, firsthand accounts of a subject, from people who had an immediate connection with it. Primary sources include original documents, newspaper reports, letters, interviews, datasets (collections of data), surveys, statistical information, and video or audio that captures a specific event. Primary sourcing is frequently used in business-related research.

Secondary sources are one step removed from primary sources, although they often quote or otherwise use primary sources. They can cover the same topic, but add a layer of interpretation and analysis. Secondary sources can include books about a topic, analysis or interpretation of data, and scholarly or other articles about a topic, especially by people not directly involved.

Common Types of Business Research

1. **Applied research.** The study and research that seeks to solve practical problems and helps in developing innovative technologies. Examples of applied research include:
   - a study into the methods for improving the levels of customer retention
   - an investigation into methods of improving employee motivation
   - development of strategies to introduce change in supply-chain management with a goal of cost reduction

2. **Qualitative research.** This is mainly exploratory research. It is used to gain an understanding of underlying reasons, opinions, and motivations. It provides insights into the problem or helps to develop ideas for potential quantitative research. A sample size of population can be a small group or even an individual. Examples of qualitative research include:
   - data collection involving interviews, observations, and focus groups
   - interpretation based on a combination of researcher perspective and data collected

3. **Quantitative research.** Quantification of a problem by way of generating numerical data or data that are transformed into usable statistics. It helps to quantify attitudes, opinions, behaviours, and other defined variables as well as to generalize results from a larger sample population. Examples of quantitative research include:
   - data collected through polls, questionnaires, and surveys, or by manipulating pre-existing statistical data
   - descriptive questioning aimed to describe variables to be measured. Think of research questions that start with words such as *how much*, *how often*, or *what percentage*.

Business Research Methods

Data Collection   Information is gathered from a range of sources. There are a variety of techniques to use when gathering primary or firsthand data:

1. **Surveys.** A survey can be one of the more inexpensive research options, especially if conducted online. There are even free options, such as Survey Monkey. Whether a survey is based on employee engagement or consumer satisfaction, it is more likely to be completed if its design is concise. Additionally, surveys can be linked to your own website or a social media post to provide smooth data collection methodology. Completion incentives sometimes offer a greater rate of return.

2. **Interviews.** Defined as a qualitative research technique, which can be structured or unstructured, individual interviews involve a small number of respondents to explore their perspectives on a particular idea, program or situation.

3. **Web tools.** In addition to developing an online survey and placing it on the organization's website, you can also harness traffic data from your website to effectively spot trends in page views and keyword use. Analysis of who is visiting your site can make you aware of consumer demographics that you have not yet targeted. There are also research website resources that can help you focus on what the competition is doing.

4. **Case studies.** The case study method aims, through real-life examples, to generate open discussion among participants by providing a realistic illustration from the business world. Nothing can give you more quality and in-depth insight than talking to people who use your product.

At a correspondingly rapid rate, technology is providing us with faster and broader opportunities to search for information than previously possible. Virtual reference libraries and other textual databases have enabled the administrative professional to become a virtual researcher.

LIBRARIES SUPPORT AND ASSISTANCE

Tracking down information is time-consuming. Effective research depends on your knowledge of reliable resources and how to use them efficiently. Traditional sources of information such as books and periodicals are still available at most libraries throughout Canada. However, the same material is often committed to more technologically based media and supplements traditional sources. As mentioned, the web provides the easiest and, perhaps, first access to find your information. To be sure of the most current reference resource, you should consult with a skilled reference librarian.

Libraries provide access to a host of statistics and information that can otherwise be difficult or expensive to obtain. Many library systems subscribe to a detailed array of databases to be used for research initiatives. A **database** is a collection of information organized so that it can be easily accessed, managed, and updated. Information searched within the database is based on a set criteria or use of keywords. **Subscription databases** consist of published journals, magazines, reports, documents, newspapers, books, image collections, encyclopedias, government documents, statistical data, and specific groups of books. Subscription databases are not freely available to the public, but libraries contract with database vendors or providers, such as EBSCO, ProQuest, and others, to provide journals that meet specific collection criteria. These subscription databases offer basic search and advanced search options. Many of these subscription databases are available through online e-resources with specific access granted through a library, corporation, or direct membership subscription. When you search for articles in a subscription database, articles that appear in full text may also appear in printed format. Additionally, numerous free research databases exist online requiring no subscription to access the resources. See Figure 4-1 for a brief listing of commonly used databases for research.

Librarians at reference desks can suggest databases to search based on a specific topic. Also, some librarians specialize in particular subject areas, and they can provide expertise in searching those specialized databases. Librarians have created research guides on broad topical discipline areas such as business, sociology, and medicine. As an initial starting point, many researchers start by searching through multitopic databases as a way to help refine their topic before utilizing a specialized database.

FIGURE 4-1 Sample research databases.

DATABASE	TYPE	DESCRIPTION
Business Premium Collection	Full text	Provides full-text access and/or indexing to thousands of business sources, including scholarly journals, magazines, trade publications, newspapers, books, reports, videos, and more
Business Source Complete	Citations and full text	Contains citations and full-text articles from over 11,000 sources, including academic journals, magazines, and trade publications; also includes business videos, worldwide company, and country and industry reports
Conference Board of Canada e-Library	Full text	Full-text database containing research publications and recorded conferences and webinars on economic trends, public policy issues, and organizational performance; subscription access is available for annual purchase; also offers customized research through on-staff dedicated researchers
Factiva	Full text	Provides full-text access to current and archived international news as well as corporate and financial data
Web of Science	Indexing	Indexes and abstracts articles from over 12,000 international scholarly journals in a variety of subject areas including business; searchable by topic, cited works, and more

Selecting a Research Database

The key to finding the right database is to know what a specific database contains. The choice in database will influence the kind of analysis enabled. Finding the right database to search for your topic is a learning process. Do not get frustrated by wasting time in the wrong database. There are a variety of database types, such as full text, citation, and bibliographic. A full-text database, also known as a complete-text database, is a database that contains the complete text of books, journals, magazines, newspapers, or other kinds of textual documents. Citation databases are developed to evaluate publications. The citation database enables a researcher to count citations and to determine the most cited articles or journals. A bibliographic database is a database that contains descriptive records of books, periodical articles, conference proceedings, and audio-visual collections. It may be a database containing information about books and other materials held in a library.

Thousands of Canadian business organizations maintain their own libraries, which are staffed with professionally trained librarians. If you work for one of these organizations, direct your search for facts to your organization's librarians. If they do not have the information in their library, they will contact other libraries to obtain it.

You may also use the public library. Every library maintains a catalogue of what is housed in the library; this is a ready reference for users. Most catalogues are available at the library on the library computer or online through the internet.

All libraries have reference books and many other valuable reference sources that you can use by request. The internet will provide access to virtual libraries, which will allow you to identify titles that are in the library system and, occasionally, will allow you to download selected information to your desktop computer.

Whether you visit the reference library in person or via the internet, library staff are helpful. When you are unsure of your request, ask the librarian what you are looking for or researching; you can depend on the librarian to suggest an appropriate approach.

Many private and specialty libraries are located in cities and towns throughout Canada. The government of Canada publishes the *Canadian Library Gateway*, a comprehensive directory of Canadian libraries that may be searched by province. This directory lists federal, university, and specialty libraries. Private and some specialty libraries are not open to the public. However, it is possible to make special arrangements to borrow materials from them and to get help from their librarians.

Great cooperation exists among public and private libraries. Public libraries, college and university libraries, libraries in business organizations, and private libraries in a given community participate actively in interlibrary loans. They also borrow from libraries in other communities.

Through interlibrary loans, you can obtain books and copies of articles that your organization's library or the public library does not have. This service is provided for a small charge; some libraries charge only for the photocopying involved. If the organization for which you work does not have a library, make your request through the public library.

Private libraries in your community might include the following:

- a law library in a federal court building or at a college of law
- an industrial library at the local chamber of commerce
- a Canadian commerce library, if your city has a regional office of Industry Canada
- a specialized library at an art or historical museum
- a medical library at a hospital or a college of medicine
- a technical library maintained by a professional society
- an international business library at a local or regional International Trade Organization centre

To start a broad search, visit www.worldcat.org first. WorldCat is a large, comprehensive catalogue database maintained by over 9000 libraries and institutions, and contains millions of online records for books, ebooks, journals, magazines, newspapers, sheet music, DVDs, and more. Given some information about the item you are searching for together with your postal code, WorldCat will find a public library in your vicinity where the item may be located.

Search Engines

The internet provides an important in-house alternative to the organization's library. If you are aware of effective internet search engines to enhance research, a broader, less time-consuming search for information can be achieved.

Search engines are complex software tools that send out probes called bots into the internet to find, analyze, and index webpages and other forms of content, constantly growing their database of information. Using intuitive intelligence, they sift the content gathered by various criteria and organize the information in a relevant and useful fashion. Search engines present the results in an ordered format that tries to list the most valuable material highest so that their users can find them quickly and conveniently. In a sense, search engines try to create organization out of the chaotic forms of information and data on the internet. Keywords are what a searcher types into an engine. Some common search engines used include Google, Bing, and Yahoo. Some lesser known but powerful search engines also include several options. Google Scholar is a special version of Google. Google Scholar focuses on scientific and hard-research academic material that has been subjected to scrutiny by scientists and scholars. DuckDuckGo at first looks like other search engines; however, there are many slick features, such as all your answers are found on the first results page. It does not track your searches, and very little spam is found with this search engine. Yippy is a deep web engine that searches other search engines for information matching your search.

Evaluating Website Content

It can be challenging to determine whether a website you are using is reliable. Here are five key identifiers to look for when evaluating web content:

1. **Investigate author.** Information on the internet with a listed author is one indication of a credible site. Do a search on the author's name to investigate further and obtain some perspective on the author's background.

2. **Date.** The date of research information is beneficial. By including a date, the website allows readers to make decisions about whether that information is recent enough for their purposes.

3. **Sources.** Credible websites, like books and scholarly articles, should cite the source of the information presented.

4. **Domain.** Specific domains such as .com, .org, and .net can be purchased and used by any individual. The domain .edu is reserved for colleges and universities, while .gc denotes a Canadian government website. These two are usually credible sources for information. A word of caution with domain .org because .org is usually used by nonprofit organizations, which may have an agenda of persuasion rather than education.

5. **Writing style.** Spelling and grammar errors indicate that the site might not be credible. To make the information presented easy to understand, credible sites monitor writing style for consistency and accuracy.

Self-Check

1. What are the three types of common business research?
2. List examples of private libraries that might be found in your area.

QUICK SOURCES OF REFERENCE

Office professionals often consult references such as almanacs, yearbooks, dictionaries, encyclopedias, atlases, biographical publications, and financial directories. You will find the titles referred to in this chapter in most large public libraries.

Some reference sources discussed are available from two different sources: online and hard copy. However, there is a publishing industry trend to move away from the hard-copy form to the more cost-effective and environmentally friendlier media of online. This technology adds a completely new dimension to reference resources; it precludes many of the traditional, laborious methods of research.

Books in Print

All libraries and many bookstores have up-to-date sources about books that are available from publishers. These sources give all the information needed for ordering publications, including the date and the price. Since these sources are used for ordering, they are kept in the catalogue section of the library. Sources to look for include the following:

- University of Toronto Press. This is a standard library reference that can also be found online.
- *Whitaker's Books in Print* (J. Whitaker & Sons). An authoritative source of information about books available in print from the United Kingdom.
- *Quill & Quire* (Key Publishers). Reviews new Canadian books.

Almanacs and Yearbooks

Almanacs and yearbooks contain the latest statistics and facts on all types of human activity. They are updated annually. Most of them are available in both hardcover and paperback, and may be purchased at many local bookstores. Consider these sources:

- *The World Almanac and Book of Facts 2018* (This title is published annually and is an excellent source of recent facts.)
- *Canadian Almanac and Directory* (Micromedia)
- *Whitaker's Almanack* (J. Whitaker & Sons)

Dictionaries, Encyclopedias, and Atlases

Dictionaries   For your own desk, choose the latest edition of an **abridged** or **unabridged** dictionary:

- *Canadian Oxford Dictionary*
- *Webster's New Collegiate Dictionary*
- *Random House Dictionary of the English Language* (College Edition)

Abridged dictionaries will fit easily on your desk and are easy to use. Some of these resources are also available online through a business or institutional subscription. You will require a login to use these resources.

Encyclopedias   Encyclopedias are useful for researching a variety of general and unrelated facts. Available in practically every library is the *Encyclopaedia Britannica* (Encyclopaedia Britannica, Inc.), an internationally acclaimed source of dependable facts. The last print edition of the *Encyclopaedia Britannica* was published in 2010; it is now available in digital format. Also popular are:

- *The Canadian Encyclopedia*, from Historica, is an online encyclopedia promoting Canadian history education. Available online at www.thecanadianencyclopedia.ca/en/

- *The Columbia Encyclopedia* is offered as one of the online references from Bartleby (www.bartleby.com), which provides a compendium of encyclopedic data.

Atlases   As with most published reference material, atlases are readily available online. If your geographic search includes dynamic facts such as migration, climate, or territorial borders, reference to a good online atlas database may provide more current information. The most comprehensive atlas for Canadians is the *Atlas of Canada*, published by Natural Resources Canada, which features maps of climate, population, income, forestry, industries, transportation, and trade. A **gazetteer** (an index of geographical names) may also be helpful.

Biographical Information

Many sources have been compiled to provide biographical information about notable people and other individuals who have made contributions in their respective fields.

Consult the following:

- *The Canadian Who's Who* (University of Toronto Press). This contains comprehensive biographies on leading and influential Canadians.

- *The Blue Book of Canadian Business* (Morris and Mackenzie, Inc.), which contains biographies of the chief executive officers of 2500 prominent Canadian firms. This book ranks major Canadian companies by their net worth. This book is also available as an online resource.

Financial Information

There are many sources of financial data. The four best-known publishers of financial information are:

- Dun & Bradstreet
- The Financial Post Data Group

- Moody's Investors Service
- Standard & Poor's

Dun & Bradstreet is widely known for its credit ratings. In addition to credit and capital ratings, this book gives type of business, address, and a brief history for each listing.

The Financial Post Data Group deals with Canadian companies whose securities are actively traded on the stock market.

Moody's services to investors are numerous. Among them are *Moody's Manual of Investment, American and Foreign*. Bound annually, it is divided into separate manuals covering the following fields:

- industrial
- transportation
- utilities
- banks, insurance, real estate, and investment trusts
- government and municipal bonds

These manuals include financial statements, descriptions of plants and products, officers, history, and other pertinent information. These publications cover foreign companies, including Canadian companies, listed on U.S. stock exchanges.

Among the publications offered by Standard & Poor's is *Standard and Poor's Register of Corporations, Directors, and Executives*, listing approximately 34 000 leading U.S. and Canadian corporations.

Due to the nature of corporate and financial information, there is a vast range of literature available.

Etiquette Books and Quotation Sources

Other sources of information that an administrative professional will find useful are books on **etiquette**. If your responsibilities include helping to prepare speeches, oral presentations, or articles, books of quotations will also be useful.

The etiquette books are helpful in all areas of gracious living, but they are especially helpful to the administrative professional in search of suggestions for writing: formal invitations, acceptances, and regrets; thank-you letters; and letters of congratulations and condolence. Among the available books are:

- *The Simple Art of Business Etiquette: How to Rise to the Top by Playing Nice* Paperback by Jeffrey Seglin (TYCO Press, 2016)

- *Emily Post's The Etiquette Advantage in Business: Personal Skills for Professional Success* 3rd ed. by Peter Post, Anna Post, Lizzie Post et al. (William Morrow, 2014)

When your manager wants to support his or her ideas with well-known quotations or to add a clever statement, look to a book of quotations. Many such books are available.

In a business environment, the application of the guidelines found in *Robert's Rules of Order* is to assist a meeting to accomplish, in the most orderly way, the purpose of the meeting. To do this, it is often necessary to curb individuals or groups from "hijacking" the meeting and, in the end, defeating its purpose. On the other hand, contributions even from the most boisterous participant should not be totally eliminated; they too may be valuable. Proceedings may be controlled in an orderly fashion based on respected methods of organization, meetings, and rules. *Robert's Rules of Order* is one of the most popular procedural guides for business, club, and organizational meetings. Familiarization with these procedures could be very helpful to the administrative professional who is called upon to take minutes of formal or informal meetings. *Robert's Rules of Order* us available in hard-copy, online and downloadable PDF formats.

Self-Check

1. What information can be found in *Robert's Rules of Order*?
2. What information would you find in *The Canadian Encyclopedia*? *The Canadian Who's Who*?
3. Suggest two reasons why an administrative professional might consult a book of etiquette.

Periodical and Newspaper Indexes

Your organization may subscribe to several professional journals. An effective approach to keeping up with the array of publications will be either to develop and maintain an office library or to develop a systematic disposal system for the journals after a prescribed period of time. The latter should include an effective recycling process.

Check if the professional journals are available at the local reference library and if the office staff refers to back issues infrequently. If either is the case, it may not be necessary to subscribe to these journals.

You may want to save and file the annual indexes to the magazines you dispose of. With many periodicals, once a year one issue contains an index to all the articles it published during the previous year. In addition, before you dispose of technical or specialized magazines, find out if your organization's library or another local library needs extra copies of the magazines you have on hand.

The most efficient way to search for magazine and newspaper articles is to consult an index in the reference section of a library. The *Canadian Periodical Index* (Thomson Gale) is a widely used periodical, newspaper, and business index available in online format.

Periodical Indexes   Administrative professionals who prepare speeches and articles for publication need to know how to locate articles that have been published on a given subject. The fastest way to locate a magazine or journal article is to consult the general or specialized index. When doing research, consult both types, for articles on popular technical topics appear in general periodicals as well as in specialized journals and periodicals.

Many libraries now have online periodical indexes. For example:

- *Canadian Business and Current Affairs* (CBCA) (Thomson Gale) carries listings for periodical and newspaper articles.
- *Ulrich's International Periodicals Directory* (Ovid) can be used to locate business and general periodicals published in other parts of the world.

Consult specialized indexes to locate articles of a technical or specialized nature. For example, the H.W. Wilson Company publishes the *Readers' Guide*, which provides a guide to more than 300 periodicals and abstracts.

Newspaper Indexes   Generally, newspaper indexes can be found on the Library Database Network as part of the comprehensive CBCA index. CBCA is an excellent broad information source; other sources provide direct and local information.

One means of quickly locating information through news events is through www.onlinenewspapers.com. This site indexes more than 300 major Canadian newspapers.

Libraries in major Canadian cities may have an index solely for the city's own newspaper, or they may have a publicly available facility for searching newspaper articles online. Most major newspapers provide online information free of charge.

Similarly, the full texts of Southam newspapers are available through CanWest Interactive (the electronic publishing arm of Southam newspapers). The following short list identifies some of those available:

- *Edmonton Journal*
- *Calgary Herald*
- *Vancouver Sun*
- *National Post*
- *Ottawa Citizen*
- *The Gazette* (Montreal)
- *Windsor Star*

Canadian Government Publications

The Canadian government is one of the largest publishers in the country. Many of its publications, which cover nearly all subject areas, are available for a nominal price. All libraries except specialized libraries keep some government publications on file. Some libraries are depository libraries for government publications; that is, they are designated by law to receive all material published by the government in certain broad categories.

The official publisher of the Government of Canada is Canadian Government Publishing (CGP), a division of Communications Canada, which provides a wide range of topics in various formats. It not only maintains a central ordering and distribution source but, through its associated network of bookstores and retailers across Canada and abroad, it ensures that publications are easily and readily available. CGP can be contacted through http://publications.gc.ca; or 1-800-635-7943.

Directories

Hundreds of business directories are published in Canada each year. Administrative professionals should not overlook these directories:

- local and out-of-town telephone directories, including Canadian Yellow Pages Directory
- *Canadian Almanac and Directory* (Micromedia) available in print and online
- Canada's Postal Code Directory (Canada Post)
- directories of chambers of commerce

Also useful to you might be *Scott's Directories* (Southam). These directories list manufacturers in four Canadian geographic areas. As well, see the "Weblinks" section at the end.

Telephone directories list the names, addresses, and telephone numbers of subscribers. Because telephone directories are usually published annually, they are useful for verifying addresses. You will find them to be an excellent source for locating a street address when the address you have is incomplete. Alternatively, there are many free internet services that provide international directories for both White and Yellow Pages. Canada 411 is an example of an internet directory service. See "Weblinks" for the address.

City Directories   City directories may include links to the following:

- a buyer's guide and classified directory
- an alphabetical street directory of householders and businesses (street numbers are listed in consecutive order with the occupant's name and telephone number)
- a numerical telephone directory, which gives the name of the person at each telephone number listed

Canadian Parliamentary Guide   *The Canadian Parliamentary Guide*, published and maintained by Desmarais Library, Laurentian University, lists the members of the Senate and the House of Commons, of the provincial governments, and of the Supreme Court, as well as other high-ranking public officials. It also contains some biographical material. It is available in hardcover, ebook versions, and downloadable PDF.

Chamber of Commerce Directories   Most towns of any size in Canada have an active chamber of commerce. Each local chamber of commerce publishes a list of its members. If your manager is chairing a convention or coordinating a regional sales meeting in another city, the chamber of commerce directory for that city is helpful for locating business personnel who take a special interest in the community. If you wish to obtain information from a chamber of commerce in another city, contact your local chamber of commerce, which will supply the telephone number and address for the chamber of commerce you are requesting.

Self-Check

1. List three directories that are very useful to an administrative professional.
2. What information is contained in a city directory?
3. How might you find contact information for a chamber of commerce in another city?

PLAGIARISM
Recognition and Avoidance

Both in business and in an academic setting, we continually absorb information and ideas from other people: we discuss them at meetings, research them on the internet, or read about them in books and magazines. Often, we use the information or idea as our own and incorporate it in our writing. However, using information and ideas from others without giving them credit for their work is a serious offence and is known as **plagiarism**. Plagiarism occurs when you fail to credit the original source for:

1. information that is not common knowledge
2. drawings, statistics, or graphs that you did not develop
3. direct quotations of spoken or written words
4. texts that you paraphrase rather than quote
5. viewpoints or theories of other people, or ideas that gave you inspiration

When consciously writing to avoid plagiarism, one of the more difficult tasks is to determine which information is common knowledge. Common knowledge is generally found in many places and is known by many people but is mostly limited to historical facts and geographical data. So, for example, while most Canadians know Wayne Gretzky is a hockey player, we must cite the source from where we learn the number of career goals he scored.

There are a few general rules to keep us safe from plagiarism:

1. Use your own words and credit all sources. Try to:
    a. Cite information and ideas that are new to you.
    b. Paraphrase instead of copying word for word.
    c. Take notes as you are reading material, including title, author, and date of publication.
2. Give credit for adopted, paraphrased, and copied work.
    a. Do *not* make minor cosmetic changes without citing.
    b. Do *not* assume everything is common knowledge.
3. Learn to cite properly.
    a. Be clear when you are using a direct quotation.
    b. Write a full list of references and a bibliography when you are developing lengthy documents.

One method of successfully paraphrasing is to read the information you want to include in your work, taking notes in the margin or on notepaper as you progress. When your reading is complete, cover up the original text and summarize the margin notes in good grammatical form. Now check this paraphrased version against the original text to make sure you have not used the same words or phrases. Don't forget to reference the original author's work.

Providing a reference to others' information and ideas will allow readers to refer back to the original source for further study. It also provides credibility to your work by suggesting that your information is based on integrity and thorough research. Schools and colleges are particularly sensitive to the issue of plagiarism because rampant plagiarism not only damages the reputation of the school but also devalues the diploma that students work so hard to achieve.

Your college may publish guidelines and responsibilities for students in its Plagiarism Policy; take note, as the penalty for plagiarism is often severe and can lead to expulsion. **Copyright** violation is the business equivalent of plagiarism. Companies or individuals may not use original material or products of others without permission. The law deals with copyright violations.

Referencing Styles

There are many referencing styles used at colleges—your instructor will tell you the style that your college prefers to use. Referencing styles attempt to standardize the format of a reference. Three of the most widely used styles are:

- APA—The American Psychological Association, www.apastyle.org/
- MLA—Modern Language Association, www.mla.org/
- Chicago—Chicago Manual of Style, www.chicagomanualofstyle.org/

Following are examples of a single book with two authors and an edition number as a reference and will illustrate the differences of each style:

APA Style Format   Author(s). (Year of Publication). *Title of book* (Edition [if needed]). Place of Publication: Publisher.
Example:
Strunk, W., Jr., & White, E. B. (2000). *The elements of style* (4th ed.). New York: Allyn and Bacon.

MLA Style Format   Author(s). *Title of Book.* Edition [if needed], Publisher, Year of Publication.
Example:
Strunk, William, Jr., and E. B. White. *The Elements of Style.* 4th ed., Allyn and Bacon, 2000.

Chicago Style Format   Author(s). *Title of Book.* Edition [if needed]. Place of Publication: Publisher, Year of Publication.
Example:
Strunk, William, Jr., and E. B. White. *The Elements of Style.* 4th ed. New York: Allyn and Bacon, 2000.

All styles of reference require:

1. name of author(s)
2. full title of the publication
3. date of publication
4. publisher
5. place of publication

When referencing business reports, you should also include as many of the following details as possible:

1. title of report
2. report number (if it has one)
3. name of organization issuing the report
4. province or city headquarters of the issuing organization
5. report date

Most of these details will be available with any credible publication. At a minimum, you should include these details in your references and be consistent in your style.

Remember, if you are unsure, it is better to reference a source than to risk any suggestion of plagiarism.

FIGURE 4-2 Sample of procedure manual.

PROCEDURE MANUAL OUTLINE	
DOCUMENT OR RESOURCE	**DESCRIPTION**
Chapter 1 Company Overview	
1.A Mission Statement	Our goals and objectives
1.B Letter from the President	Letter of welcome
1.C Organizational Chart	Description of roles
Chapter 2 HR Policies	
2.A Employment Process	Hiring process for candidates
2.B Interview Process	Description of the interview process
2.C Vacation Policy	Request for vacation process
Chapter 3 Document Preparation	
3.A Letter Style Guide	Letter format
3.B Memorandum	Memo preparation
3.C Report Style Guide	Report preparation
3.D Branding and Marketing Policy	Trademarks and marketing
Chapter 4 Purchasing Policy	
4.A Supplies ordering	Process for ordering supplies
4.B Suppliers	Approved list of suppliers
4.C Purchase Order Form	Form to be completed for orders

OFFICE MANUALS

A critical resource for any office is an office manual. If the manual is current, well-organized, and easy to follow, it will assist office staff in performing work correctly and efficiently. Although creating an office manual can seem tedious, it is a great guideline and framework for a business. Over the years, organizations have learned to create an office manual that documents important recurring business tasks. Otherwise they find themselves reinventing the wheel with every new employee. When it comes to training, you really only have two decisions to make: either provide training using an instruction manual or leave the new employees to figure out their job on their own. Refer to Figure 4-2.

Often it is the responsibility of an administrative professional to prepare, update, and maintain this reference resource. The purpose of an office manual is not only to provide succession planning and to help co-workers who cover temporary absences, but also to provide consistent procedures for everyone in the office. The office manual provides guidance for everyone who might need to know those procedures. If you develop a manual, here are some key items to include:

- a process map or description of the process you use
- key inputs, process steps, and outputs
- references to standards, laws, and regulations that must be achieved
- references to forms, tools, software, or reporting systems required

Most organizations support their own intranet and will upload an electronic version of the procedure manual. This helps to ensure that the information is easily accessible and up to date. Many businesses host procedure manual content once populated using an online platform available to employees within the organization and secured from public viewing. The list of administrative procedures that may be included in an office manual is endless. It may be useful to include some of the following:

- reception duties
- receiving and sending messages
- preparing correspondence
- processing incoming and outgoing mail
- appointment scheduling
- conference and event management
- preparing travel expenses
- order supply management

This is a very brief list; the choice of tasks to be included in an office manual will depend on the range of responsibilities held by the administrative professional.

QUESTIONS FOR STUDY AND REVIEW

1. Describe the importance of workplace research and how it supports organizational goals and objectives.
2. Discuss and provide an example of a primary source.
3. In what ways does applied research benefit an organization?
4. What is a database, and how does it foster enhanced research capability?
5. How does a search engine assist in streamlining the research process?
6. List four examples of private libraries.
7. When starting a research initiative, why would you consult with a librarian or visit a public library?
8. What useful information could an almanac provide?
9. What useful information could a bibliographical source provide?
10. Name two sources where you would locate financial data such as stock market trends and credit ratings of businesses.
11. From what local directory source can an administrative professional locate all the businesses in the local vicinity and contact information?
12. What is plagiarism? Discuss five common causes.
13. Discuss three methods to avoiding plagiarism.
14. What information would you expect to be contained in an office procedures manual?

Key Terms

abridged 76

almanacs 76

copyright 80

database 74

etiquette 77

gazetteer 77

plagiarism 79

primary sources 73

search engine 75

secondary sources 73

subscription database 74

unabridged 76

EVERYDAY ETHICS

The "Cover Letter"

Jeanie knew it would happen one day. Her manager, Cynthia Bell, asked her to write a 40-second speech for delivery the following day. Cynthia planned to read the speech to a selection committee as part of a proposal. "It should be something like reading a cover letter," Cynthia explained.

Fortunately, Jeanie didn't despair—she had learned to research in her Office Administration course—she was sure she could come up with something! Next day, just before the selection committee meeting, Jeanie gave the speech to Cynthia for presentation. It read as follows:

Ladies and Gentlemen of the Proposal Committee, I'm just preparing my impromptu remarks and fear that the length of this document defends it well against the risk of its being read. However, the proposal that I put before you today not only is revolutionary in design but also marks another improvement in the way we do things; an improvement to the processes that are not serving us well today.

To improve is to change; to be perfect is to change often. So, I suggest to you that this is not the end. It is not even the beginning of the end. But it is, perhaps, the end of the beginning.

While Cynthia was pleased with the writing style and the composition, the committee failed to be impressed. Even though the concept and timing were perfect, something else bothered them. What do you think that was?

- Do some research on the words and phrases found in Jeanie's composition. (Just enter phrases and quotes into a search engine to get results.)
- Why was the committee uncomfortable with Cynthia's presentation?
- What do you think the consequences of the committee's discomfort could be?
- How might Jeanie have avoided the problem?

Problem Solving

1. Today, your manager asked you to provide information on three of the most common business services provided by the local public library. She has advised you that she needs this information by tomorrow. How will you source this information?

2. Your manager has been asked to give a 15-minute presentation on ethical behaviour in the workplace to a group of management trainees. He has asked you to research this topic and find three sources he could reference in his presentation. Where would you start?

3. Your manager has asked you to locate and provide two business directories used in the United States. He would like you to evaluate these directories and provide some reasons as to why he might find each of them useful. How will you begin?

4. The speech that Jeanie wrote in this chapter's Everyday Ethics feature was given to you to correctly reference. Rewrite the speech giving proper credit, where appropriate, to Sir Winston Churchill.

PRODUCTION CHALLENGES

4-A Selecting Quotations

Supplies needed:

- *Access to the internet or a library*

Your supervisor is giving the keynote address at Career Day for graduating high school students. He asked you to find two quotations that will impress on students the importance of continuing their education. Use quotation sources from the library or internet to select your quotations. Key each quotation verbatim.

4-B Finding Information

Supplies needed:

- *Access to the internet*

For each of the following internet activities, reference the source of your information using the appropriate APA format.

1. Reference the Government of Canada's report on *Achieving a Sustainable Future: A Federal Sustainable Development Strategy for Canada 2016–2019* and rekey the government's section on what is the Federal Sustainable Development Strategy. Be sure to reference the source correctly.

2. What was Otto Eduard Leopold von Bismarck otherwise known as? For what was he most famous?

3. Conduct an internet search for the article *Workplace Bullying Stories* on www.Balance.com. Paraphrase the section on types of bullying and submit to for evaluation or discuss as a class.

4. Conduct biographical research on a Canadian whose name is often in the national news. Write three interesting facts about this person.

4-C Developing an Office Manual

Using the information presented in this chapter, develop a bulleted list that will go into an office manual for your company, covering procedures for conducting effective research both in print and online. You will prepare a document that lists a minimum of five steps necessary for effective research and that specifies an acceptable citation style your company will use when referencing material.

4-D Team Research (Collaborative Exercise)

Supplies needed:

- *Email template, Form 4-D, Companion Website*
- *Access to the internet or a library*

For this exercise, form a team with three of your classmates. Each team member should find an online reference that will help you to identify and avoid plagiarism. Each of you will then prepare an email to your other team members recommending the resource you have found and describing why it would be beneficial to use. Use the email template provided.

Weblinks

Ebsco
www.ebsco.com
Provider of research databases, e-journals, magazine subscriptions, ebooks, and discovery service for the academic, medical, corporate, school, library, and government fields

Canada Library Gateway
http://www.collectionscanada.gc.ca/
Service providing access to information about Canadian library catalogues, websites, interlibrary lending policies, and special collections.

Canadian Who's Who
https://canadianwhoswho.ca/
Canadian biography, listing prominent Canadians selected on merit alone.

Dun & Bradstreet
www.dnb.com/
Offers information on commercial credit as well as reports on businesses.

My Virtual Reference Desk
www.refdesk.com
This is a comprehensive source for facts on the internet.

Canada 411
www.Canada411.ca
Here you may locate a person or business in Canada from over 12 million listings.

Newspapers and Magazines of the World
http://www.world-newspapers.com
This site lists all online English-language media—newspapers, magazines, television stations, colleges, visitor bureaus, governmental agencies, and more.

Canadian Federal Government Site
www.canada.gc.ca
The Government of Canada's primary site, available in both English and French, contains links to a government overview, federal organizations, programs and services, a search engine, and other services.

H.W. Wilson
www.hwwilson.com
This site provides several search tools that allow subscribers to retrieve records of interest in Wilson databases. They include full text, catalogues, abstracts, and indexes. Free trial offered.

Virtual Library
www.virtualreferencelibrary.ca
Toronto Public Library's website has excellent links to many other Canadian reference sites. Offerings include access to librarian-selected websites; online magazine, journal, and newspaper articles; and self-guided research support. Special focus is placed on Canadian and Ontario information.

World Catalogue Mobile App
www.worldcat.org/mobile

Chapter 5
Organization Structure and Office Layout

G-stockstudio/Shutterstock

LEARNING OUTCOMES

After completion of this chapter, the student will be able to:

1 Understand key elements of organizational structure.

2 Discuss the building blocks of organizational structure.

3 Explore management styles and classifications of authority.

4 Review and interpret an organization chart.

5 Describe the physical features of an open and closed office layout.

6 Describe how office ergonomics involve furniture, lighting, acoustics, and position of equipment.

All organizations have three things in common: goals, people, and structure. Organizational goals are those goals developed by senior management to provide direction for people working in the organization. Organizational structure is a systematic way of subdividing tasks and allocating resources to best accomplish the organizational goals. Contemporary organizations are designed to manage and anticipate that their people are both effective and flexible in their activities. Organizational structure provides effective and efficient framework for organizations to operate and ensure tasks are accomplished.

ORGANIZATION STRUCTURES

An organization structure outlines by what method tasks are formally distributed, clustered, and coordinated. It specifies the ability to learn authority, responsibilities, and the flow of information through an organization. Planning the organization structure forms the company operational blueprint. Each element influences employee interaction with each other to accomplish goals and objectives.

Traditional organizational structures are designed for managers and supervisors to organize workers within a chain of command, where each lower level of the organization is controlled by a higher one. The person with the most formal authority occupies the topmost position in the organization with lower layers of management responsible to that person. Many organizations are structured in this way, where each worker is assigned tasks from a supervisor and is expected to perform the task and report to the supervisor. In such organizations, the subdivision of work is based on job specialization and departments where people use their specialized skills and knowledge to contribute towards the organizational goals. Responsibilities and duties of people within the organization are clearly defined and respected.

Contemporary organizational structures, on the other hand, are more logically formed and come together as a result of naturally interrelated functions. They are more adaptable and work well in less bureaucratic environments. In these organizations, workers are expected to be flexible and adaptable in order to enable the organization's success. Individual workers may find themselves reporting to more than one supervisor at the same time when called for by the organization; for example, a worker might normally work in one department but report to someone else while serving on a cross-functional team to complete a special project Here are the typical organizational structures in business today:

1. **Functional**. This structure sometimes referred to as bureaucratic defines tasks divided into separate parts in an organization grouped in similar roles. Work specialization, also known as division of labour, is foundational to separate divisions based on similar job tasks. For instance, all accounting personnel work together in one division, or all sales and marketing employees are grouped together. Advantages include the ability to make decisions quickly, reduce confusion through clearly defined roles, and learn from each other based on similar interests. Segregation can be a disadvantage of this structure, as it lends to a reduced interaction with other areas within the organization.

2. **Divisional**. Divisional structure clusters organizational functions into product or regional divisions. Each division within this structure can align with each other concerning products or geographical location. Each division contains the resources and functions within it to support the product or geography. This leverages the focus of the division on one aspect of organizational objectives and enhances the culture of the division with a group unified for a common goal. Disadvantages could involve a set-up where one division is pitted against another division or one division may undermine another.

3. **Matrix**. A matrix organizational structure is a structure in which the reporting relationships are set up as a grid, or matrix, rather than in the traditional hierarchy. A hierarchy refers to the levels of management and reporting structure in any business, from highest to lowest. The matrix structure divides authority both by functional area and by project. Each employee answers to two immediate supervisors: a project and functional supervisor. Typically, team members have more autonomy and take direct responsibility for their work. Matrix structures maintain an organization's functional structure, allowing for the creation of efficient project structures that utilize several personnel within the organization. The disadvantages are that reporting to two supervisors could lead to conflict and the reporting structure tends to increase organizational complexity.

4. **Flat.** Management is decentralized, sometimes referred to as a horizontal structure. Employees supervise themselves and are responsible for managerial decisions. It removes perceived excess levels of management. This organization structure sees reduced salary expenses. Open collaboration is encouraged, as is innovation. Disadvantages of flat organizational structures include confusion in terms of leadership, lack of a formal structure, and lack of motivation for employees. Some of the most common organizational structures are shown in Figure 5-1.

FIGURE 5-1 Typical organizational structures.

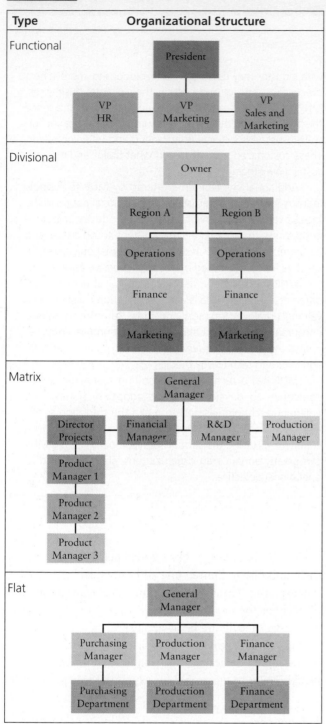

Type	Organizational Structure
Functional	President; VP HR, VP Marketing, VP Sales and Marketing
Divisional	Owner; Region A, Region B; Operations, Operations; Finance, Finance; Marketing, Marketing
Matrix	General Manager; Director Projects, Financial Manager, R&D Manager, Production Manager; Product Manager 1; Product Manager 2; Product Manager 3
Flat	General Manager; Purchasing Manager, Production Manager, Finance Manager; Purchasing Department, Production Department, Finance Department

Building Blocks of Organizational Structures

Businesses need to formulate a plan and structure to know how to organize people. These are considered the building blocks of organizational structure.

Work Specialization This is known as **division of labour**. Tasks in an organization are divided into individual jobs in this manner. While division of labour fuels efficiency, it also creates a challenge. Having a sound organizational structure reduces the challenges. Specialization can offer benefits for an organization, as employees become highly skilled in their assigned skill base, leading to an increase in productivity. Without specialization, flexibility exists for employees to learn a variety of skill set.

Chain of Command The basic element of an organizational structure is the chain of command: an uninterrupted line of authority that extends from the top of the organization down to the bottom. **Chain of command** specifies who reports to whom within the organization.

Span of Control Span of control references a scope of personnel a supervisor manages. The more employees, the wider the span of control under a particular supervisor.

Centralization **Centralization** refers to who makes the decisions in an organization. If decision-making power is concentrated at a sole level, the organizational structure is considered centralized. If decision-making power is spread out, the structure is viewed as decentralized. A decentralized structure encourages a democratic decision-making process; it can also slow down the decision-making process, making it harder for organizations to operate efficiently.

Classifications of Authority

Regardless of the structural approach used, authority and responsibility within the organization must be established. Three main types of authority are found within a typical organization. These types of authority exist to enable managers to perform their duties effectively and traditionally are classified as:

1. line authority
2. staff authority
3. functional authority

Line managers are those who contribute directly to the organization's goals. They are said to have *line authority*, which is an authority that follows an organization's direct chain of command. In a **line organization**, staff managers provide advice and expertise in support of the line managers. They are considered to be contributing indirectly to achieving the organization's goals. Staff managers have *staff authority*.

Staff managers usually advise and assist line managers and make recommendations based on their areas of expertise: marketing research, human resources, and legal counselling, for example. However, line managers usually have the final say in accepting or rejecting the recommendations

MNP

Artur Widak/NurPhoto/Getty Images

Celebrated as one of Canada's largest full-service charted accountancy firms with over 4 000 employees and offices throughout Canada, MNP has been recognized as a platinum level best employer for over eight consecutive years by AON Hewitt. MNP provides a collaborative approach, supporting its business clients by offering personalized strategies to help organizations succeed.

Consultative services available to their clients range from organizational strategy and planning, performance improvement, organization and people, technology, training and economic research. Its consultants are experts in key aspects of organizational management. Working closely with industry, they devise practical solutions to improve best practices to attract and sustain their clients' businesses. MNP understands how management practices influence the business from the human resources perspective. Action plans assist MNP's clients in attracting and retaining talent. These customized plans focus on what builds and makes a sustainable organization.

Additional key elements offered by MNP to support industry include its expertise in organizational design in the face of various economic challenges in industry and competitiveness that pressure organizations to do better and be better. MNP believes it offers an external objective perspective for clients, based on a comprehensive assessment.

MNP takes pride in its organizational structure being different. This difference is achieved through collaboration, valuing employee opinion and ideas, promoting talent, encouraging work–life balance, and fostering an entrepreneurial approach. MNP services a variety of industries from agriculture to technology media.

MNP has a technology consulting team that assists companies to develop strategic adoption of new and emerging technologies and to make the transition seamless. It enables organizations to make these decisions with confidence. Having the support of a company such as MNP can greatly enhance an organization's ability to reach its operational objectives.

---

of staff managers, as their authority flows in a straight *line* from the president of the organization to the supervisor. The most frequently established formal structure in larger organizations provides a combination of these management roles in a **line-and-staff organization**. The line-and-staff organization is effective because the staff managers are specialists in their areas and are available to support the line managers throughout the organization.

Functional authority allows staff managers to broaden their authority to limited line authority relating directly to staff expertise. The authority of functional managers reaches throughout the organization to wherever their specialized knowledge or skills are being applied.

Figure 5-2 identifies where typical line-and-staff functions interact and provides typical examples of functional authority. Also refer to Figure 5-3, in which the vice president of

FIGURE 5-2 Functional authority: Examples of line-and-staff functions.

LINE FUNCTION	STAFF FUNCTION	FUNCTIONAL AUTHORITY
Production	Human Resources	Vice president of human resources has functional authority over human resource personnel in departments.
Customer Service	Corporate Accounting	Corporate accounting reviews departmental budgets.
Marketing	Legal	Legal counsel endorses contracts between suppliers of services and departments.

FIGURE 5-3 Organization chart.

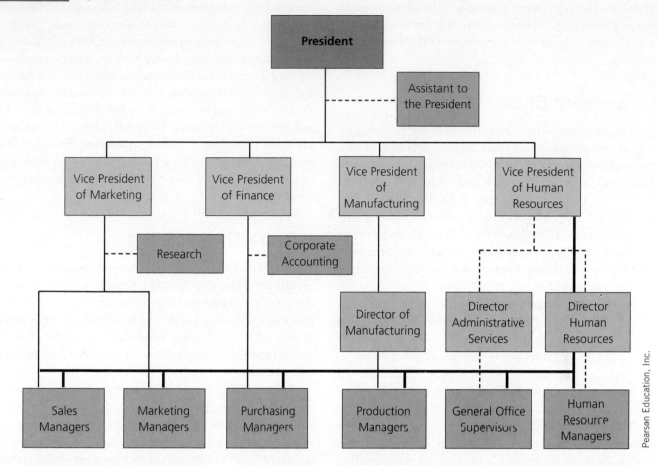

Pearson Education, Inc.

human resources is shown as having functional authority over human resources personnel as well as other functional divisions of the organization.

The ability to wisely use the authority and empowerment entrusted within your scope will be a measure of your maturity and professionalism. Prepare yourself by first studying your company's organization chart to determine where the formal authority lies. Be observant, adaptable, and tolerant of your ever-changing environment.

Management Styles

Management styles refer to the way a manager makes decisions relating to subordinates. Management styles are largely reflective of the corporate culture. The concept of **authoritarian management** style has existed for a long time and relates to managers who provide vision for their employees by providing clear direction. Employees refer to this style as firm but fair. It is most effective when the manager is credible, consistent, and motivating. It is least effective when employees are underdeveloped and the leader is not viewed as credible.

Participatory management, or democratic style, has the objective of building commitment and accord among employees. This manager encourages participation from everyone on the team. It works best when personnel are working effectively together in a steady work environment. It is least effective during pressure-filled times that lack the opportunity for consultation and employees must be coordinated under direct leadership.

Administrative management is a type of management style in which a leader displays **conscientiousness**, especially related to orderliness. The prime focus is *on rules and processes over individual* **personal preference**. It is a successful, proven style, as processes typically guide work and flow. However, its prime weakness is that it relies on human application of work, and errors in processes will ultimately occur.

Organizations today, in an effort to increase productivity and be competitive, are focusing more on the customer. Employees working in smaller units or teams within the larger organization are encouraged to communicate freely with different levels of management. Employees are asked for input about their areas of responsibility and often are brought together in management conferences to discuss and offer solutions to organizational issues. In this environment, managers share the decision making with the teams; however, the managers still maintain final authority.

Organization Charts

Most organizations draw charts that describe the relationship of people and their tasks in the organization. An **organization chart** graphically describes who reports to whom and often describes their responsibility through the position on the chart (see Figure 5-3). To understand an organization chart, look for lines of authority, existing divisions of work, and the relationship of the work groups to one another. If an office manual exists, descriptions of the work divisions and of the positions shown on the organization chart will be provided.

As an administrative professional, you may be asked to update or draw an organization chart. Begin by preparing an outline showing those functions of work that are on the same management level and those that are subordinate. To save time, get the outline and draft of the chart approved by the proper executive before you print the chart in final form.

The titles shown in an organization chart may be expressed as either functions or positions, but the form chosen should be used consistently throughout. Functions that occupy the same level of management should be shown on the same horizontal line, as illustrated by the vice presidential positions in Figure 5-3.

For illustration purposes, solid lines indicate line authority, broken lines indicate staff authority, and the thick line shows the functional authority of the vice president of human resources. A crowded organization chart is difficult to read. You may have to prepare one chart to show the main functions and then provide supporting charts to indicate subordinate functions under each main function.

Organizational Linkages and Value

An organizational **linkage** is the connection and interactions between tasks, functions, departments promoting information flow, and productivity. Both horizontal and vertical linkages exist within most organizations, influencing productivity. A horizontal linkage is a relationship between two equals in an organization—it could be co-workers or departments. With this linkage, resources are pooled to accomplish common organizational goals. A vertical linkage within an organization means the up-and-down production chain for a particular product.

How does an organization create value? Michael Porter discussed this in his influential book *Competitive Advantage*. Porter introduced the concept of a **value chain**, which is a set of activities that an organization carries out to create value for its customers. A **supply chain** is the connection between a company and its suppliers to produce and distribute its products. Producers compete with each other only through their supply chains. The key difference between supply and value chains is the supply chain is the process involved in meeting customer satisfaction through filling an order or request while a value chain is a set of related processes a company uses to create its own competitive advantage.

Informal Organizations

An **informal organization** is a natural grouping of individuals according to personality, preferences, and interests. An informal organization, or grouping, is not created; it exists in every situation in which individuals are relating to one another. Members of workgroups or departments that get together occasionally would constitute an informal organization.

Informal organization satisfies certain social needs; it also can become a channel of communication, referred to as the **grapevine**. The grapevine is used extensively where the official channels are not meeting the informal organization's communication needs, such as with rumours or the premature release of information.

An informal leader usually exists within every informal organization. This leader is not designated—she or he becomes the leader as a natural outgrowth of the needs of the group. The group looks to the leader for guidance, and the leader is its spokesperson.

Managers in the formal structure need the support of the informal organization and often use it as a supplementary means for carrying out the objectives of the organization or for propagating information.

Managers have the ability to change the formal organization because they created it. However, they cannot change the informal organization or make it go away. Wise managers will be aware of the natural groupings of individuals. They should also be aware of the influence these groupings have on one another and of the influence they have in furthering or impeding the objectives of the organization.

> ### Self-Check
> 1. Describe two classifications of authority found within a typical organization.
> 2. Define *linkage* within an organization.

Recognize that managers need the support of the informal organization, but beware of your own involvement. Many office professionals are privy to confidential information that should not find its way to the grapevine. Unauthorized distribution of such information will be seen as a serious violation of trust and professional responsibilities and may result in dismissal.

OFFICE PLAN

Many factors contribute to how personnel feel about their job; the office space design contributes to satisfaction or dissatisfaction affecting mood and productivity. Different workstations work well for different tasks. In recent years, the popular office layout has been the open office, designed without conventional walls, corridors, or floor-to-ceiling partitions. Figure 5-4 shows a typical open office layout style. The open office referred to as a landscaped office, when it has a layout that has been designed effectively. An open office can be a huge time saver. Email traffic seems to decrease because most of your co-workers are in easy range. Decision making appears to accelerate because team members are formally able to meet from space to space.

The open office concept grew out of the need for:

1. better work and communication flow
2. better and more flexible use of space
3. improved ventilation and lighting
4. a cooperative environment

A well-planned design results in an attractive environment and improved employee morale. Also, open offices cost less to construct and reconfigure than enclosed offices.

For those whose work is of a confidential nature, or for personnel who need privacy in order to concentrate

and be creative, the traditional private office is still more practical. Employees with special needs must be provided with user-friendly access and workspace. Realistically, the open office is not the sanctuary of productivity it was assumed. The spontaneous nature of working closely with colleagues creates additional distractions; therefore, workflow is disrupted by the constant communication. Lack of privacy is cited as a concern for an open plan as well.

Closed Office Layout

The closed office, also known as an enclosed office, has distinct rooms for each department in the company as a separate space, and all employees working in the company have their own workspace. It provides privacy and speaks to the desire of the employees to have their individual working area. Additionally, the layout supports a reduction of distractions typically found in an open layout designs.

Arrangement of the Open Office

The **workspace** of employees whose work is related because of the kind of information being processed is often located in the same area. This is especially true when employees are primarily dealing with hard-copy material such as drawings, preprinted forms, or models.

Freestanding partitions are used to form individual workspace. The partitions usually do not go to the ceiling but are high enough to eliminate distractions and provide some privacy. Workers have the feeling of being with others. In some open offices, file cabinets and large plants are also used as space dividers.

Workspaces are arranged at angles in various configurations, in contrast to the monotonous effect of rows of separate enclosed offices. The arrangement of the workspace follows the natural flow of the work being processed. Workers who need to talk to each other about their tasks are placed in close proximity.

With an open office layout, it can be easy to create areas within the office used by team members who want to get into their workflow zone. As a best practice, designate one area or an office with a door as a collaboration workspace and allow team members to reserve the room for their private usage or for team collaboration. Optimally, an open office space allowing for individualization is helpful for improving morale and mood.

The **supervisor** may occupy a semiprivate office close to the workspace area under his or her supervision. It is usually private enough for conferences, yet open for those seeking advice or direction.

FIGURE 5-4 Open office layout.

Monkey Business Images/Shutterstock

Many offices have adopted a **mixed layout**. This allows for a combination of open spaces, with private meeting areas for discussions and closed offices for the higher-ranking employees where privacy is essential in order to meet the organization's objectives.

In a well-planned office, ample space is provided for easy movement from one workstation to another. Aisles follow the natural traffic pattern, which is usually not a straight line. Lighting, heating, air conditioning, and humidity are easier to control when the partitions do not go to the ceiling. Short partitions also facilitate the diffusion of ambient overhead lighting for the benefit and comfort of all workers. Task lighting may be used in addition to the ambient overhead lighting, to provide additional lighting where required. Better airflow and reduced energy costs should result from the open plan.

Decor

Colours that blend tastefully are used throughout each landscaped area. The colour scheme is harmonious, yet many contrasting colours are used to break up the monotony of look-alike workstations.

The partitions may be curved, adding grace to the design. Wall-to-wall carpeting and fabric surfaces of the partitions add elegance. Live plants are placed throughout the area to provide privacy, individuality, and beauty.

Living decorations, such as plants and aquariums stocked with tropical fish, add to personal enjoyment and interpersonal comfort during working hours.

Decorative appointments such as attractive light fixtures are also used. Because the decor of the landscaped area is artistically planned, it is **esthetically** pleasing—an important factor in maintaining employee morale and productivity.

High-Tech Office and Workstation Design

More and more companies are recognizing the impact that workplace design has on productivity and, by extension, the company's bottom line. Research indicates that millions are lost in productivity each year in Canadian businesses when the workspace design is not optimal. Many challenges accompany electronic equipment such as monitors, printers, and computers. For example, they often do not fit on traditional office desks. Fortunately, purpose-built office furniture can be purchased to provide a more efficient use of available space.

The workstation is a focal point for optimizing human factors in production areas. A **workstation** is an area where work of a particular nature is conducted. In an office, this is where a desktop computer or digital device is positioned for the individual employee to access.

The following tips help provide for a useful and comfortable workstation:

- Place the workstation in a position that works best for you from an access and comfort perspective. Height is an important consideration in utilizing a workstation effectively.
- Organize your desk according to the natural flow of the tasks you handle.
- Ensure that equipment you use most often is within easy reach.

Most organizations recognize the importance of an environmentally friendly office; many work actively to improve conditions to make the office a better place to work. Management will often seek advice in the design and optimal positioning of operational equipment such as computers, printers, and copiers. The proactive office professional will be prepared to make positive contributions to issues pertaining to office design and layout.

Research indicates that workers who spend long periods of time at a computer workstation may suffer from a number of health problems. For this reason, you must ensure that you will take periodic breaks to reduce the possibility of discomfort and fatigue. Complaints arise about eyestrain, backaches, muscle tension in the shoulders and neck, and headaches. The most common complaints of high-tech office workers are those symptoms associated with **carpal tunnel syndrome (CTS)**. CTS is caused by inflammation of the tendons in the tunnel at the base of the hand, which can normally be attributed to repetitive use of the hand and wrist.

CTS is, in fact, a **repetitive strain injury** (RSI) and can affect anyone whose work calls for long periods of steady hand movement. RSIs tend to come with work that involves prolonged and repetitive movement, such as keying. Typically, swelling occurs in the wrist sufficient to cause the median nerve to be pressed up against a ligament in the wrist, which may then result in numbness, tingling in the hand, clumsiness, or pain.

ERGONOMICS

The science of adapting the workplace to suit the worker is called **ergonomics**; it was previously known as *human factors engineering*. The office environment should be as safe, healthy, comfortable, and productive as possible. Everything that affects the worker must be taken into consideration—furniture, lighting, amount of space, quality of air, heating and cooling, acoustics, and placement of the equipment in relation to the worker.

Furniture

Office furniture manufacturers have designed **modular furniture** to carry out the landscaped office concept. Modular furniture consists of separate components that can be fitted together in various arrangements to meet the needs of users.

Modern desks are narrower than conventional ones and have fewer drawers. Some of them resemble tables with modesty panels. However, the modern workstation usually provides more working space than that available in a conventional office. Modular furniture can be arranged in many different configurations, giving the worker additional space on one side of the desk, behind the worker, or both. Some desks are adjustable.

If the work flow changes, creating a need for a change in working surface, the modular furniture can easily be rearranged.

The chair is one of the most important pieces of furniture in the office. A poorly designed or incorrectly adjusted chair can be a major contributor to physical discomfort. The height of the chair seat should be easily adjustable to accommodate the individual's height and size; the chair should provide adequate back support.

When the worker is seated, the angle at the knee should be 90 degrees, thighs should be parallel to the floor; the buttocks, not the thighs, should support most of the worker's weight.

Storage space may be integrated; easy-to-reach shelves can be added above the desk. Sometimes shelves are hung on a partition at the back of the desk. Credenzas can be included in the arrangement. However, storage space for files, or for manuals and books not currently in use, is not provided at a workstation. In open office environments, separate workspace is often provided for processing mail, assembling materials, and performing other highly repetitive jobs. See Figure 5-5 for a sample workspace arrangement.

Lighting

In addition to the diffused lighting over the entire area, referred to as **ambient lighting**, light fixtures are provided over individual workstations so that the intensity and direction of light for each worker's needs can be controlled. This is referred to as **task lighting**.

Natural light from windows is the greatest source of computer screen reflection and associated reading problems. A screen that faces directly into or away from a window can

FIGURE 5-5 A sample workstation arrangement.

cause eyestrain. For this reason, adjustable blinds should cover windows. Most modern monitors are built with antiglare screens; however, antiglare shields may be purchased to reduce or even eliminate glare from older technology screens.

Proper placement of lighting is also crucial; a light source directly behind the computer screen causes stress on the eyes of the worker, who must face the light source while at the workstation. The opposite case is also a problem: a light source directly behind the worker will result in direct glare on the screen. If you suffer from eyestrain or headaches while working, you can check for undue glare by switching off your monitor to determine what is reflected on your screen. The best way to deal with glare is to eliminate the source by closing the blinds or by tilting or moving your monitor. For optimum comfort, lower the ambient lighting and provide task lighting for deskwork.

Generally, the best orientation for a light source is for it to shine over the left shoulder of a right-handed worker (or over the right shoulder of a left-handed worker). The reason for this has to do with the shoulder action of the employee. A right-handed worker tends to lean forward in such a way that the right shoulder blocks light coming from the right side; this creates a shadow on the documents in front of the body.

Acoustics

The Canadian Centre for Occupational Health and Safety (CCOHS) suggests that noise is one of the most common occupational health hazards. Annoyance, stress, and interference with speech communication are the main concerns in noisy offices. To prevent adverse outcomes of noise exposure, noise levels should be reduced to acceptable levels.

CCOHS suggests that if you can answer yes to any of the following questions, your workplace may have a noise problem:

- Do people have to raise their voices?
- Do people who work in noisy environments have ringing in their ears at the end of their shift?
- Do they find when they return home from work that they have to increase the volume on their car radio higher than they did when they went to work?
- Does a person who has worked in a noisy workplace for years have problems understanding conversations at parties or restaurants, or in crowds where there are many voices and "competing" noises?

If there is a noise problem in a workplace, then a noise assessment or survey should be undertaken to determine the sources of noise, the amount of noise, and who is exposed and for how long. Temporary equipment such as earmuffs and earplugs may be used, but engineers and office designers must plan proper acoustical control so that unwanted sound does not disturb office work and conversations cannot be easily overheard.

Wall-to-wall carpeting, because of its sound-absorbing qualities, is used throughout the typical open office. The freestanding partitions are covered with carpeting or fabric. Ceilings are equipped with baffles. Sound-reflecting surfaces are limited or avoided.

Although manufacturers today are making electronic office equipment that runs more quietly than earlier models, much more has to be done to control noise in the office environment. For example, **white noise**, a continuous background noise evenly distributed, can be generated by electronic equipment. Installing floor-to-ceiling partitions can help to combat the problem of office noise.

There are provincial and territorial workplace noise level jurisdiction guidelines.

Position and Posture

In addition to the office environment, good work habits, correct keying techniques, and proper posture are important for prevention of musculoskeletal injuries. Musculoskeletal disorders (MSDs) include injuries that affect muscles, nerves, tendons, ligaments, joints, cartilage, blood vessels, and disks. They are the result of RSIs and are one type of injury attributed to ergonomic problems. For example, CTS, discussed previously in "High-Tech Office and Workstation Design," belongs to this category. Figure 5-6 illustrates proper posture at the computer, which can only be achieved with the correct positioning of equipment. Note that the chair and keyboard are set so that the thighs and forearms are parallel to the floor and that the wrists are straight and level. If the table is too high to permit this, you should find an adjustable chair; otherwise, you might need to put the keyboard in your lap.

While you are keying, your wrists should not rest on anything and should not be bent up, down, or to the side. You should use your arms to move your hands around instead of resting your wrists and stretching to hit keys with the fingers. When you stop keying for a while, rest your hands in your lap or on their sides instead of leaving them on the keyboard. Wrist rests are available and give you a place to rest your hands when pausing from keying. They are not designed to rest your wrists while you are keying.

In the illustration, you will note that the worker is sitting straight, not slouching, and does not have to stretch forward to reach the keys or read the screen. Good posture

FIGURE 5-6 Proper posture at the computer.

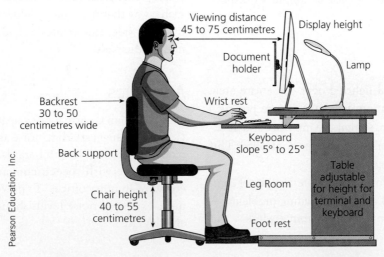

pro-Link
Work Away from Work

The popularity of virtual offices—offices located wherever employees happen to be—has increased the number of office professionals who work outside the confines of the traditional office building. Remote office workers should choose their workspaces carefully. It is quite possible that you will become a remote worker, perhaps working from home, so here are a few planning tips for *your* new home office:

- Locate the office as far away from temptation as possible: the cookie jar, the fridge, etc.
- Provide a business atmosphere: put a clock on the wall; provide a coffee station or a water cooler.
- Buy comfortable, purpose-built office furniture— you'll be spending a lot of time at the desk.
- Treat yourself to a decent sound system.
- Make full use of available technology: a fast and capable computer, company services, a wireless headset, for example.
- Use your phone service provider's voice mail and conference services—they appear more professional.
- Ensure that you have adequate and timely support for the technology on which you will depend.
- Keep your arms and hands warm. Cold muscles and tendons are at much greater risk for overuse injuries, and many offices are overly air conditioned.
- Pay attention to your body. Aches and pains are your body's signal that it is in discomfort. Learning what is comfortable or awkward for your body before you are in pain may prevent injury.

is not just about your hands and arms, but also about the use or misuse of your shoulders, back, and neck. These areas are equally as important as what is happening down at your wrists.

Anything that creates awkward reaches or angles in the body may create discomfort. However, even a perfect posture may result in problems if it is held rigidly for long periods of time.

Here are basic tips to avoid discomfort while keying:

- Relax.
- Use a light touch. Do not "pound" on the keys.
- Move and shift positions frequently.
- Wrists should not be bent to the side, but instead your fingers should be in a straight line with your forearm as viewed from above.
- Use an adjustable keyboard that permits optimal positioning, or tilt the back edge of your keyboard down and slightly away.
- Use two hands to perform double-key operations like Ctrl-C or Alt-F, instead of twisting one hand to do it.
- Move your whole hand to hit function keys with your fingers instead of stretching to reach them.
- Stretch and relax frequently. Momentary breaks every few minutes and longer breaks every hour or so work well.
- Hold the mouse lightly; do not grip it hard or squeeze it when **mousing**. Place it where you don't have to reach up or over. Place it close to the keyboard or learn and use keyboard equivalent commands.

QUESTIONS FOR STUDY AND REVIEW

1. Compare a functional organizational format to a matrix structure.
2. Compare line authority and staff authority management functions.
3. What is chain of command and span of control?
4. What is an organization chart?
5. Describe a horizontal linkage; how does it influence productivity?
6. Contrast the terms supply chain and value chain.
7. What is an informal organization?
8. What is the grapevine? How can managers use the grapevine effectively?
9. Why should an administrative professional be aware of informal organization?
10. What is the open office designed to accomplish?
11. Suggest three problems that accompany the open office layout.
12. What is the meaning of the term *ergonomics*?
13. Differentiate between task lighting and ambient lighting.
14. Describe the proper physical position for a person seated at a keyboard.
15. State three ways to reduce the risk of CTS.
16. Give four suggestions to avoid discomfort while keying.

Key Terms

administrative management 89

ambient lighting 93

authoritarian management 89

carpal tunnel syndrome (CTS) 92

centralization 87

chain of command 87

conscientiousness 89

division of labour 87

divisional 86

ergonomics 92

esthetically 92

grapevine 90

hierarchy 86

informal organization 90

line organization 87

line-and-staff organization 88

linkage 90

matrix 86

mixed layout 92

modular furniture 93

mousing 95

organization chart 90

participatory management 89

personal preference 89

repetitive strain injury 92

supervisor 91

supply chain 90

task lighting 93

value chain 90

white noise 94

workspace 91

workstation 92

EVERYDAY ETHICS

Sitting Pretty

Sally Chow, the office supervisor at Apogee Designs, has been with the organization for 12 years. Sally is respected for her knowledge of the processes and procedures in the office and, as a matter of fact, she authored the office's procedures manual. Unfortunately, it has not been updated for a few years because Sally is far too busy. She has a lot of control in the office, mainly because she has been working there for longer than most. Office personnel these days are mainly bright young graduates who fear upsetting the status quo, and Sally.

Over time, Sally has been given the authority to make direct purchases and orders from suppliers, including office supplies and furnishings. While it was no surprise to find Sally's workspace is a "cut above" that of other personnel, it was a huge disappointment to discover that one supplier and, indeed, one salesperson had serviced the office needs for quite a while. It was Bruce Bell, Sally's husband! Sally and Bruce have had a confidential and exclusive supply "arrangement" with Apogee Designs for the past eight years.

Bruce's supplies and furniture are okay, but you have noticed that service is mediocre and the quality of his furniture is not the best—except for what is in Sally's workspace.

Clearly, both Bruce and Sally are benefiting from this long-standing arrangement, but is that true for Apogee?

■ What, if anything, should you do about this situation?

Problem Solving

1. Your manager, Robert Wrigley, has 35 employees reporting to him. When he receives a memorandum from top management, he edits portions of it by condensing much of the material and asks you to rekey and make copies of what he has edited for distribution to the 35 employees. The employees often do not understand the summaries distributed to them and come to you for clarification. One co-worker, James Ellis, has demanded that he see the original memorandum. Should you show him the original memorandum or discuss the situation with Robert first? Why do you think your manager always rewrites the communications from top management before distributing them? Which management style do you believe Robert practices, and why?

2. You work in an open office area. The area works well for you most of the time. A concern you do have is that most of your colleagues are located several aisles away from you. The walk is not convenient when you are in a developmental thinking mode. You ask to meet your manager, Amber Rose, to discuss moving you closer to your colleagues. What reasons will you give for your request?

3. One of your temporary administrative office professionals, Martie Evans, is upset because she saw a memorandum written by a staff member in the Human Resource Department recommending that all temporary workers throughout the organization be laid off at the end of September. You suggested that she talk with your manager, Anthony Roberts, before reacting to the memorandum. You tried to reassure her by saying you could not produce all the work that was stacking up on your desk. Were you justified in suggesting to Martie that she talk with Anthony? Explain. Who will make the final decision about Martie's employment, and how does (or doesn't) this relate to organizational structure?

Special Reports

1. Research two prominent Canadian businesses who have been recognized in recent years as one of Canada's best-managed companies, locating their organization charts. Review each chart and then prepare a short report for your instructor addressing how many levels of management exist within each company identifying the organizational structure. In your report, discuss the similarities and differences of the two companies' organizational structures.

2. Consider the participatory management style and explain in a short essay why it may or may not suit your own work style.

3. Research what noise exposure limits are in Canadian jurisdictions. Identify in a response who has the highest standard and who has the lowest? Navigate to the Canadian Centre for Occupational Health and Safety, with respect to acoustics, on its website www.ccohs.ca. Prepare a paragraph identifying why noise measurement levels are assessed in industry.

PRODUCTION CHALLENGES

5-A A Personnel Problem

Supplies needed:

- *Plain paper*

Recently your office was redesigned and redecorated. The partitions that formed the private offices were removed, and a landscaped office design with smaller partitions and modular furniture was used. The office is beautiful. You work in a modular arrangement with Madison Stevens, administrative professional in purchasing, and Arista Compton, administrative professional in financial planning.

Madison and Arista spend much of their time talking. They remain at their workstations and shout over the "masking noise" in order to be heard. Their talking has decreased your productivity. The first week you tried to overlook the interruptions and worked overtime to keep up with your work. Later, Mr. Wilson asked you to plan your work so that you would not have to work overtime. You did not tell Mr. Wilson why you were working overtime. The next day you asked Madison and Arista to refrain from talking so much, but they have ignored your request.

You are getting so far behind with your work that you are taking it home with you.

Today you again asked Madison and Arista to stop talking so loudly and so much. Arista retorted, "Don't be such a nag." You became so upset that you felt ill. You took the afternoon off. All afternoon you worried about your work piling up and your inability to concentrate while Madison and Arista talk loudly.

What are the solutions to your problem? You decide that you need help with it. Capture in writing what you are going to do and what you will say.

5-B An Organization Chart Change

Supplies needed:

- *Organization chart template for the Marketing Department of PDI, Inc., Form 5-B, on the companion site*
- *Original organization chart for the Marketing Division PDI, Inc.,*

Figure In-3, *page* 10 PDI, Inc. is in the process of reorganizing itself to become leaner and more efficient. The vice president of Innovation and Design has resigned and there are no plans to replace him or the position. As a temporary step, the president of PDI has asked Noah Wilson, the vice president of Marketing, to oversee the activities of the both divisions of Marketing and Innovation and Design. The president has also asked Jim Schultz, director of Innovation and Design, to report directly to Noah Wilson. Jim Schultz directs the operations of the western and midwestern Innovation and Design through Raymond Jones and Eugene Liam. Noah Wilson has asked you to revise the marketing organization chart to reflect the temporary changes. Be sure to update the revision number on the organization chart.

Their names, titles, and addresses are as follows:

Jim Schultz
Director of Innovation and Design
Corporate Office
PDI, Inc.
320 Apogee Way
Winnipeg, MB R2R 4H6

Raymond Jones
Manager
Midwestern Innovation and Design
2202 Logan Avenue
Winnipeg, MB R2R 0J2

Eugene Liam
Manager
Western Innovation and Design
836 Carnarvon Street
New Westminster, BC V3M 1G1

Weblinks

Canadian Centre for Occupational Health and Safety
www.ccohs.ca
Canada's national occupational health and safety resource provides information on a wide variety of occupational health and safety issues, including ergonomics.

Canada Business Network
www.CanadaBusiness.ca
This website provides information related to organizational design, communication and structure.

Government of Canada
www.canada.ca
Provides an interesting insight into the organizational structure of the government of Canada.

Ergonomic Issues at the Workstation
www.healthycomputing.com/
This site has information specific to office administrators as well as a page on mobile device ergonomics.

Ergonomic Tips for Laptop Users
www.uhs.berkeley.edu/Facstaff/pdf/ergonomics/laptop.pdf
This site offers practical ergonomic suggestions to help reduce the health risks when using your laptop computer for short or long periods of time.

HR World
www.hrworld.com
This site contains ten easy tips regarding workstation ergonomics and numerous links to useful sites on the topic.

Mind Tools
www.mindtools.com
Provides an insight into Michael Porter's five forces to understand competitive forces to maximize profitability.

UCLA Ergonomics
www.ergonomics.ucla.edu
UCLA's website contains "How To . . ." tips on setting up your workstation, exercises, a computer workstation online self-evaluation, and much more ergonomic advice.

Exercises
www.mydailyyoga.com
Simple exercises you can do in your office or at your desk.

Chapter 6
Front-Line Reception

Rawpixel.com/Shutterstock

LEARNING OUTCOMES

After completion of this chapter, the student will be able to:

1 Understand the importance of the receptionist role.

2 Identify and explore workplace skills of an effective receptionist.

3 Describe how reception design influences organizational perception.

4 Explore current technological tools used to streamline the visitor experience.

5 Explain appointment, calendaring, and message management systems.

6 Discuss best practices for managing difficult and/or abusive customers.

A good first impression counts, and the front desk often serves as the initial point of contact the organization has to the outside world. The receptionist's role is vital to an organization's success, as an effective receptionist creates a welcoming yet professional environment. Receptionists are, by definition, the point person who welcomes all visitors as they enter an organization. Although a receptionist job designation is sometimes viewed as an entry-level position, companies need to be selective when hiring a receptionist, since it is the receptionist who makes the most important first impression for the organization. Commencing your career as an office receptionist provides an ideal training and development opportunity because the receptionist has a touch point with every person and every department within the organization. Keep in mind that since a receptionist communicates by phone, email, social media, and in person, the reception's role is highly visible. For clients who communicate only with the receptionist, in their view the receptionist *is* the organization. The first impression and the lasting impression that receptionists make with their voice, appearance, and expressions should be favourable. You create the atmosphere by the way you respond to people within and outside your organization. Successfully managing the front desk calls for an impressive line-up of technical and soft skills. These key traits include the following:

1. **Professionalism.** A receptionist is the brand, as in the face of the organization. This requires poise, as well as a friendly and presentable appearance. A receptionist should be well-groomed, clean, and professional—in appearance and in attitude.

2. **Communication.** Effective receptionists take the time to listen to clients while giving an appropriate, useful response. It is best for receptionists to speak in a soft tone to put clients at ease. They strive to be active listeners as they consistently navigate the variables of customer relationship management.

3. **Organization.** Being able to assist administrative staff with work overflow, work on special projects, and managing incoming clients are all attributes of a receptionist who is on point with his or her organization skills.

4. **Technology savvy.** Receptionists should be tech-savvy, meaning they can easily handle a multifunctional phone system, appointment software, and various computers apps. They update social media accounts, and they effectively use industry-specific software and programs.

RECEPTION DESIGN AND LAYOUT

The reception area represents an office or a business. Most visitors form an opinion about a business and how it is performing by viewing the reception area. Visitors should be able to walk in, look around, and understand what the company does. The reception area needs to be welcoming but also be interesting and surprising. Many think a company's reception area or waiting room should be separate from the rest of the work area. Visitors walking in should be able to get a glimpse of the rest of the office and of what happens in the company, but they should not be immediately be thrust into a workspace.

Organizations physically convey their unique brand and culture in many ways; designing an office layout space is an important aspect when communicating this to guests and clients. An open waiting area is foundational in terms of making clients feel connected with the people who are working for them, giving them a sense of immersion into the space and culture itself. A methodology to achieving this connection is to attractively post the company's values statement near the reception entrance to give guests a snapshot of what drives the organization. Here are some considerations to make when designing a reception area:

- **Comfort.** A welcoming reception area offers visitors a comfortable area where they can sit, relax, and possibly get work done. The arrangement should place the furniture far enough away from the door so that it will not be hit as people enter the area. Have chairs placed together so groups can sit and discuss business while they wait. Include various forms of media such as magazines or a TV monitor for solitary visitors to view while waiting. Lastly, consider a coffee maker; it is a nice touch for making clients, job candidates, and guests feel welcome and energized.

- **Reception Desk.** Curved desks are generally more expensive than straight desks, due to the amount of work that goes into their construction. They also take longer to produce. Straight desks generally cost less but may not offer the visual appeal you are trying to create. In addition, packages and deliveries are likely left at the reception desk on a daily basis, so it is important to have enough space to store these items until they can be picked up. Make the desk area large enough that packages can be placed on another desk surface or somewhere behind the main desk. Consider if the reception desk is purely functional in design or is it a statement piece aimed at dominating the whole area.

- **Branding.** The marketing aspect of creating a name, symbol, or design that identifies and differentiates a business or organization from another is known as branding. Trademark symbols are used to represent a company logo. The reception area should reflect your brand in setup and style. Consider decorating the area with your company's

Devika Bala

Devika Bala

Clerical Specialist
Royal Victoria Regional Health Centre
Barrie, Ontario
College Graduation:
Office Administration—Medical
Georgian College
Barrie, Ontario 2011

"The bottom line is positive attitude, aptitude, and being polite and professional."

Devika obtained a position after graduation at Royal Victoria Regional Health Centre in the role of office administration in the Project Management office, and then soon after that, in the Planning and Redevelopment office. This allowed her the time to acquire the knowledge of the business of running a hospital. She was very busy because the hospital was under a massive expansion at that time.

From there, she moved to a more clinical role as an administrative assistant to the director of Imaging Services. This very demanding position covered many different responsibilities, which included administrative duties such as transcribing meeting minutes, planning meetings, maintaining calendars and managing project databases, and organizing workshops and training sessions.

A new career opportunity presented itself a few years later as a nursing unit clerk working in Imaging's nursing area of 18 bays. This move gave Devika more valuable clinical and direct patient contact. In a fast-paced medical environment, she was a valued member of their team and provided service to 10 radiologists, 12 nurses, and 20 technologists caring

for patients who were pre- and post-interventional, as well as patients undergoing MRI and CT procedures.

Her most current role is now part of the Clinical Informatics Applications department as a clerical specialist. Now more familiar with the technology side of the hospital and its ever-changing and updating environment, she is in daily contact with employees and doctors alike, providing assistance and access to various programs.

Devika supports operations within the CIA to support MIS setup, all application user setup, and Provider Dictionary support and maintenance. She is responsible for documentation of key information for user setup for all applications. This role involves working closely with the CIA team and other internal programs and departments to confirm the appropriate user setup. As well, this role works with Finance, Decision Support, and Medical Affairs to confirm provider setup information. This position requires direct communication with CIA and IT service desk staff and other departments as required for clarification of user setup and requirements.

---

colors, placing the logo design on the wall or installing televisions playing your company's advertising near the sitting area.

Whether people are visiting your building for the first time or the tenth, they should always feel comfortable and welcomed. Large organizations have public relations departments that devote themselves full-time to creating and maintaining a favourable image of the organization. Public relations does not begin and end with a public relations department. Good public relations is every employee's responsibility. Every employee who encounters people from outside the organization is engaged in public relations and customer relationship management (CRM). Some of the important aspects of CRM discussed in this chapter revolve around effective telecommunications, appointment scheduling, receiving visitors, and managing difficult customers.

VIRTUAL RECEPTIONISTS

Some companies are outsourcing their reception needs by acquiring **virtual receptionists**. The person who handles the receptionist position for you is an actual receptionist but will not be sitting in your office at your front desk. Virtual receptionists (VRs) work from a remote location at home or elsewhere. An organization can hire and train a virtual receptionist any time. It can have all calls forwarded to this virtual receptionist, who will handle them as calls are processed based on specific instructions 24/7. Messages are gathered and calls are processed. Depending on an organization, a virtual receptionist can handle several tasks a traditional in-house receptionist manages. The VR could also handle tasks for more than one company at a time. What the VR opportunity provides for the administrative professional is a potential self-employment entrepreneurial business creation. Virtual receptionists can work independent of an employer and assume their own contracts, hire and train staff, and be an independent business owner.

VRs might perform any or all of these services:

- Answer the telephone with an upbeat greeting.
- Set up a conference call.
- Store and forward faxes.
- Forward calls.
- Respond to simple verbal commands.
- Schedule appointments.
- Record the caller's information, such as name and telephone number.
- Receive incoming calls while the user is checking messages.
- Store hundreds of names, telephone and fax numbers, and email addresses.

There is also a subcategory of VR that is digitally driven using artificial intelligence, or AI for short, discussed in the next section. Does the idea of a VR—or worse, a digital VR—make you worry about your future career? Stop worrying! Companies that hire receptionists recognize the value of personal customer service—a service that can best be offered by human beings. Companies that insist on having an individual receptionist are intent on establishing and maintaining good relationships with clients. They will hire you because you know the company better than any independent contractor or machine could.

Digital Assistants

A digital assistant is not exactly the same as a VR. A digital assistant is the technology evolution in voice activation. It removes the need to be typing into a keypad or pushing buttons on a phone to make calls, access apps, or play music. This technology is usually used at home and is tied to one person or group. Thanks to the latest voice-activated technology you can now do all this and more simply by talking into a device—whether that is a mobile phone, a computer, or one of the latest digital assistants. Using a third-party-developed platform, a business can enable this platform to perform tasks or services. Sometimes the term *chatbot* is used to refer to a digital assistant because it is generally accessed by online chat.

Most of these systems are entirely voice-driven, meaning the user does not have to touch the keypad. As well, the digital assistant has almost a human touch—it uses naturally spoken phrases like "Oh, hi," "How are you?" and "I'm back."

Who Uses a VR?

Small to midsize companies often use a virtual receptionist or digital virtual receptionist. These companies:

- look for cost efficiencies
- look for an effective way to handle receptionist responsibilities
- have service-oriented businesses
- have managers that spend considerable time out of the office
- want to be responsive to their customers
- want to portray an image of professionalism
- sometimes want to give the impression of being a larger company than they actually are
- do not want their customers to feel a machine is processing them

Using a VR with AI technology should be a receptionist's tool, not a receptionist's competition. Learn how to use this tool to your best advantage. Take pride in the customer relationship management role of your job and the personality you can inject into it.

Self-Check

1. List two attributes of receptionists.
2. What is a VR?

VISITOR MANAGEMENT SYSTEMS

Visitor management is the process of tracking everyone who enters your building or your office. A visitor may be a customer, a delivery person, a job applicant, a contractor, a consultant, or just about anyone. Essentially, anyone who is not a regular full-time employee is a visitor. The front desk in many organizations is always busy. Oftentimes signing in visitors can add up to a lengthy process: a minute for visitors to sign a logbook and then create a nametag. In addition, guests wait while a receptionist tracks down the person they are visiting. When a receptionist is focusing on the process, it may not leave the opportunity to connect with the visitor and provide a professional, warm welcome. Here are some examples of tools to enhance the visitor management experience:

- **Digital visitor sign-in.** Computer tablets are positioned at the front reception area where guests can digitally sign in upon arrival. From this, a badge could also be printed for the guest to wear.
- **Host notification.** Once a guest signs in, the meeting host in the organization is immediately notified of the guest's arrival and can prepare to greet them. The employee who is hosting the visitor can also send messages back to their visitors. For example, if an employee is running behind when the client signs in, the employee

FIGURE 6-1 Visitor management providers.

PROVIDER	SERVICE PROVIDED
Proxyclick®	Kiosk sign-in for visitors
SwipedOn®	Visitor in/out, photo capture, ID badge printing
iLobby®	Visitor management process and security
Alice Receptionist®	Real-time communication, securing employees, and processing visitors

can send a quick note back to tell the client it will be a few minutes.

- **Message forwarding.** Sometimes a visitor's primary contact is not available. A notification is sent to someone else within the organization, and if the secondary contact is not available, a third person can be notified. This provides an option for backup notifications and ensures you do not leave any visitors hanging without a next step.

- **Security.** To ensure the working environment is a safe place for visitors and employees, the option exists to capture a person's signature to be stored digitally in the system, which gives an organization an additional way to verify a visitor's identity. This adds another layer of security within the organization. See Figure 6-1 displaying visitor management tool providers.

ADDITIONAL RECEPTION TOOLS

Telecommunications

Effective phone techniques involve placing and receiving local and long-distance calls in the most efficient and cost-effective way. Talking with your friends over the telephone does not prepare you for handling business calls. When it is your responsibility to handle business calls, it is important to learn and remember effective techniques and to apply them consistently. Observe the techniques other professionals use when they call you or when they answer your call. Can those techniques be improved? If so, apply the improvements to your own calls.

Phone Communication Skills

Speaking clearly, using correct grammar, and listening actively are essential skills in communicating successfully and in projecting a professional image, and this is especially true in telephone communications.

Speak Clearly   Whether you are making or receiving telephone calls, it is important to remember that your voice projects an image of your company. Your tone of voice,

volume, and inflection are as important as the words you say when communicating via telephone. Because you cannot rely on nonverbal expressions such as body language and facial gestures to help convey a message, you must rely on your voice to convey a professional image of your company. Speaking clearly with a positive tone is essential to good communication. The image you project with your voice is determined by the following elements:

1. **Volume.** Speak as though you are talking to someone across the desk from you. Of course, if the person is having difficulty hearing you, you will have to adjust your speech volume to the appropriate level.

2. **Rate of speed.** Speak distinctly and at a rate that is not too slow and yet not too rushed. If you speak rapidly, your words may be jumbled, and the caller may ask you to repeat the information. Avoid speaking rapidly when answering the telephone. Because you use the company's greeting often, you may have a tendency to speak rapidly. Answer as if you were voicing the greeting for the first time; speaking at a controlled rate will enable you to appear confident and poised.

3. **Inflection.** Be aware of your voice tone. Vary it to show expression; avoid speaking in a monotone voice. Using inflection in your voice brings out the meaning of what you say and emphasizes important points in the conversation.

4. **Quality.** Smile when answering the telephone or when engaged in a telephone conversation. You don't need to paste on a giant clown smile! See Figure 6-2 showing an office administrator answering a phone with a poised smile. A slight uplifting of the corners of your mouth will ensure that you don't sound as if you are frowning or angry at the world. A voice that conveys a smile will project an image of a courteous and enthusiastic worker who is ready and willing to help—a professional image.

Use Correct Pronunciation and Grammar   Pronunciation means saying each word correctly, clearly, and distinctly by moving your lips, tongue, and jaw freely. Speaking clearly and distinctly is especially important

Tyler Olson/123RF

when communicating with people whose first language is not English and who may have difficulty interpreting run-together words. For example, avoid common grammatical errors such as:

"wouldja" for "would you"

"wanna" for "want to"

"gimme" for "give me"

"innerview" for "interview"

Using correct grammar is important both in projecting a professional image and in ensuring the message is conveyed correctly. Incorrect grammar includes both poor sentence structure and the use of jargon, technical terms, or local sayings that people not familiar with a particular culture, industry, or geographical region may fail to understand. Can you imagine the confusion that might result if you refer to an ordinary happening as a "run-of-the-mill" occurrence when talking to an international caller from a country where English is not spoken? If the caller is too "polite" to ask for clarification, the communication breakdown may have a negative impact on your organization.

Listen Actively Effective listening is active rather than passive. In passive listening, you absorb the information given. If the speaker provides a clear message and makes it interesting enough to keep your attention, you will probably get most of what the caller intended to communicate. In contrast, *active listening* requires you to understand the message from the caller's point of view. Hearing what the speaker says is easy, but active listening is hard work.

Improve your active listening skills when communicating via telephone by practicing the following:

- Give the caller your complete attention; concentrate on what is being said.

- Avoid letting your mind wander.

- Do not interrupt the speaker unless the conversation is wandering aimlessly. If this happens, ask direct, open-ended questions to bring the speaker back on track and to gather more information.

- Listen objectively; try to put yourself in the speaker's shoes.

- Wait until the speaker has finished before formulating a response. Thinking about what you will say in response to the speaker will result in a loss of concentration.

- Paraphrase your understanding of the message to ensure accurate communication.

- Jot down key points in the conversation.

- Avoid distractions such as using the keyboard while listening to the speaker.

Effective telephone practice also involves using telephone technology, such as voice mail, call forwarding, or conference calling to the best advantage of both the customer and the company.

Using Voice Mail

Voice mail is a computer-based system that processes both incoming and outgoing telephone calls. Special computer chips and software convert the caller's voice into a digital recording that is stored in the computer. Some organizations offer a single in-box feature that will allow you to process voice mail messages from an Outlook email in-box in order to review and respond to the message accordingly. The recording can then be retrieved at any time for playback.

Voice mail can help in the following ways:

1. Voice mail ensures that no telephone calls are missed.

2. Messages can be sent to voice mail systems regardless of time zones or work schedules.

3. Recorded messages can be left for people calling in with an access code. For example, if you are out of the office

and want to leave details about a scheduled meeting, give those people who are invited your access code and leave a descriptive voice mail message.

4. Voice mail allows messages to be recorded and saved in a mailbox.

5. A voice mail system can also forward messages to another location and/or to other office members.

6. Voice mail messages can be sent to a number of people at the same time.

7. Voice mail can serve as an automated telephone operator by answering your calls with a personal recording.

When it is used correctly, voice mail can eliminate the annoying practice of phone tag. **Phone tag** is an occurrence in which two parties attempt to contact each other by phone, but neither is able to reach the other for a conversation. Voicemail does, however, have its disadvantages:

1. Callers are often forced to listen to long, annoying messages.

2. Callers often prefer to initially talk to a person rather than leave a recorded message.

3. Recipients may not check their mailboxes regularly.

4. Recipients may not know that a message is waiting unless the system has a signalling feature.

5. Recipients may use voice mail to filter their incoming calls so they don't have to speak to people they wish to avoid.

Telephone companies provide voice mail systems with many sophisticated voice mail features. For example, your local telephone company may provide voice mail services in several different languages. With such features, voice mail can help employers handle language diversity in their workforce and help workers and customers access the company's voice mail without encountering a language barrier.

Although voice mail lacks the richness of direct communication, there are some fundamental practices you can follow that can help to improve voice mail interactions.

As a recipient of voice mail messages:

■ Change the message and date of your greeting on a daily basis. Doing so provides the caller with information that you are, in fact, accessing your voice mail system regularly.

■ Record an appropriate announcement on your greeting message when leaving for vacation or other extended periods to let the caller know you will not be checking your voice mail for incoming messages.

■ Provide clear instructions for your callers. If you wish to direct your callers to someone else in your organization, provide specific instructions in your recorded message.

As a caller, when you must leave a message for someone else:

■ Speak clearly, concisely, and politely.

■ Avoid leaving a lengthy message.

■ Be aware of your tone of voice and the impression that you will leave in your message.

■ State your message, your name, and your telephone number clearly and at a slow enough pace for transcription.

■ Specify the action you want to occur.

■ Indicate when you will be available to receive a return call.

■ Leave key pieces of information; if you think it would be helpful, restate your name and phone number at the end of your message.

The features and functions of voice mail systems are improving rapidly. Unless used correctly, however, voice mail systems can be annoying and frustrating for callers, which may have a negative impact on the organization. It is essential that organizations employ efficient procedures when using voice mail. The following three best practices will help minimize caller frustration:

1. Provide an opportunity for the caller to speak to a representative of the company at any time during the caller's

---

pro-Link
Voice Mail Jail

Voice mail is both a productivity enhancer and a potential problem! Many companies establish voice mail policies to address the fundamental question, "Do our customers really want to use voice mail in order to contact us?" Consider these concepts:

■ Customers may be uncomfortable speaking to a computer—many are!

■ Be sure your customers do not experience voice mail jail. This is where the customer is trapped in the voice mail with no option of getting out and speaking to a person.

■ Callers hear the same message each time they call you—keep your greeting messages short.

■ Allow customers to choose an option at any time rather than force them to listen to an entire list of choices first.

■ Research tells us that customers prefer to have contact with a person first—the person can then ask if the customer wants to be connected to the voice mail system.

What is your experience with voice mail?

voice mail interaction. This is often achieved by implementing what is known as a *zero out* option: the caller may press zero at any time during the call to speak to a live representative.

2. Maintain an organization policy for responding to voice mail promptly and efficiently. This will resolve the problem of messages not being collected or going unanswered.

3. Ensure that all staff are fully trained to use the voice mail message system. When a system fails to meet its objectives, it is often because of inadequate staff training.

Self-Check

1. Describe four elements of speaking clearly that can help project a professional image.
2. What is active listening?
3. What are two disadvantages of voice mail?

Using Automatic Answering Services The frontline reception of many companies is often an automated answering system rather than a live receptionist. These can be sophisticated telephone systems that handle incoming calls with efficiency and effectiveness. They are known as interactive voice response (IVR) systems.

IVR services can be programmed to do the following:

- Prompt the caller through a menu of options to acquire information or leave messages.
- Play a variety of announcements.
- Respond after a predefined number of rings.
- Respond between specific times of the day.
- Repeat messages based on the length of time the caller has been on hold.

IVR systems should not be confused with voice mail. Reaching a voice mail box is just an option that the IVR menu allows the caller to select.

Answering Promptly Answer the telephone by the first or second ring. Leaving the telephone to ring five or six times may convey an image of inefficiency. However, don't lift the receiver and let the caller wait while you finish a conversation with someone else—this is unprofessional and rude.

In order for the caller to understand you clearly, speak directly into the mouthpiece in a normal, conversational tone and volume, which will make your voice sound pleasant to the listener.

Identifying Yourself Let the caller know that he or she has reached the right office. If the incoming call is answered by a receptionist, he or she will say, "Good morning (or Good afternoon), Millennium Appliances." When the receptionist transfers the call to you, you can say, "Mr. Jamison's office, Linda McElroy speaking," or "Advertising Department, Linda McElroy speaking." Your manager may tell you specifically how to answer the telephone. If not, be sure to ask. Never answer a business telephone with "hello." "Hello" is considered far too casual for the business office.

It is courteous to let the caller know who you are. To identify yourself, use both your first and last names. A courtesy title—Miss, Mrs., Ms., Mr.—is not usually necessary; however, follow the procedure that is expected in your organization.

When phone calls come directly to your phone, first let the callers know they have reached the right organization; then add the identification for the particular telephone you are answering, and give your name. For example: "Millennium Appliances, Finance Office, Louisa speaking."

As an administrative office professional, you may not receive your manager's calls. Most managers have telephone numbers that ring directly through to their offices.

When you answer the phone for more than one manager, create a system to code each station or line on your phone so that you can give proper identification for each person whose calls you are taking. When you answer a phone call for a colleague, answer it in a similarly courteous manner, but use your name to let the caller know who is speaking. For example, "Brent Napier's desk, Linda Lewis speaking."

Being Courteous A greeting such as "good morning" or "good afternoon" is a courtesy when answering the telephone. Such greetings are also helpful because often callers do not hear the name of the organization if it is the first set of words spoken when a telephone is answered.

When you must leave the line to obtain information, explain why and how long it will take. Give the caller a choice. Ask whether:

1. The caller would prefer to wait.
2. The caller would prefer that you return the call shortly.

If the caller chooses to wait, avoid keeping him or her waiting for more than two minutes. When you return to the caller who is on hold, be sure to thank the caller for waiting.

During phone conversations, use "please," "thank you," and other courteous phrases. At appropriate times, use the caller's name.

If you discover that neither you nor your manager can help the caller, redirect the call to someone who can. Do not leave the caller stranded by saying that your department cannot handle the issue. Make a special effort to be helpful, and give the caller the name and number of the appropriate person. Let the caller know when you are looking up a number. It's your job to be helpful.

When the caller has dialled the wrong number, be especially courteous. Callers often reach a wrong number because they have looked at the wrong number on a list of frequently called numbers. The caller may be one of your current or future customers.

The person who initiates a telephone call should terminate it. However, you can bring the call to an end by thanking the person for calling or suggesting that you will give the message to your manager, or whatever is appropriate. When you initiate the call, let the other person know that you are going to leave the line. Do not end abruptly. You may close with "good-bye" or "bye." "Bye-bye" is too familiar, so avoid it.

Taking Messages

Despite the prevalence of automated phone systems, voice mail and phone trees, many companies still rely on humans to answer phone calls and take messages. Keep a small notebook, a pen, and a pad of telephone message blanks by the telephone. Some companies use a message-capturing platform for messages to be digitally entered and forwarded. Taking telephone messages may seem like a simple task. However, handling this task inefficiently wastes time and may cause loss of customer goodwill and business. A receptionist will want to capture these elements:

1. The date and time of call. The time of the call is important; for instance, if your manager talked with the caller at lunch, the manager needs to know if the call was made before or after lunch.

2. The complete name of the caller, spelled correctly. Remember that your manager does not know every Lawrence or Pierre who calls. If you do not know how to spell the caller's name, ask him or her to spell it for you.

3. The telephone number with area code. Some callers will say your manager or the person for whom this call is intended has the number. You can simply explain you would like to save your manager the time it would take to look up the number. Larger cities have more than one area code. For example, Toronto metropolitan area codes include 416, 647, and 905.

4. The name of the business that the caller represents.

5. All pertinent information to help the person for whom the call was intended to know what to expect when returning the call.

6. Always restate the message to assure both yourself and the caller that you have recorded it accurately and entirely.

Explaining Your Manager's Absence

Be careful how you explain your manager's absence from the office. Simply say, "Susan is away from her desk right now. May I ask her to call you?" or "Susan is not in her office at the moment. Would you care to speak to someone else?" or "She is not here at the moment. May I help you?" *Avoid* statements such as these:

- "She's playing golf this afternoon."
- "Susan is in Ottawa."
- "She is at a doctor's appointment."
- "She's still out for lunch."
- "She's tied up."

Transferring Calls

Nothing is more frustrating than to be transferred from one department to another two to three times during one phone call. Transferring calls properly not only involves knowing how to use the transfer feature on your telephone but also knowing who performs various functions within your company. The following suggestions can help you to increase your efficiency in transferring calls:

- Explain to the caller that you are going to transfer the call to someone else who will handle the call. For example, you might say, "Mr. Jenkins in our accounting department will be able to help you rather than Miss Truong in this department. May I transfer your call to him?"

- Be sure you transfer the call to the right person. Knowing "who does what" will ensure you know the appropriate person to handle a transfer call. Never transfer a call on the **speculation** that the person to whom you are transferring the call might be helpful.

- Never say, "I will transfer you; if I should lose you, Mr. Brighton's number is 531-6088." Say, "For your reference, Mr. Brighton's number is 531-6088. I will transfer you now." Give the caller the name and the telephone number of the person to whom he or she is being transferred, so the caller can place the call again if he or she is disconnected as you transfer the call.

- If your department cannot handle the request and you do not know who should handle it, tell the caller so. For example, you might say, "I don't know the answer to your question; I will be happy to make some inquiries. May I call you back in half an hour?" Another approach is to say, "I need to find out who has that information. May I call you back in half an hour?" Be sure to follow through on your promise.

- Limit transfers as much as possible. Callers often find themselves being transferred three or four times. Imagine how frustrating this must be for them each time they have to repeat their story. In addition, three or four people will have been interrupted by calls they cannot handle. When these callers reach you, stop the runaround. Offer to locate someone who *can* help.

Answering a Second Phone

If two lines ring at the same time, answer one and ask the caller if you may be excused to answer the other telephone. For example, "ABC Company. This is Shandra. I have another call coming in. May I put you on hold?" Do not leave the line until the caller agrees. Press the hold button and answer the second call. Then you might say: "ABC Company. This is Shandra. I am on another line. May I put you on hold?" When you return to the line of the first caller, say, "Thank you for holding, how may I direct your call?"

or

"Thank you for holding. How may I help you?"

What you need to do to answer multiple calls depends on whether the calls are local or long distance.

If the second call is a local one, you may ask the caller to hold or you may offer to return the call. Briefly explain why. If the second caller agrees to hold, press the hold button and return to the first caller. If the second caller agrees to be called back, hang up the second telephone and return to the first caller. As soon as this conversation ends, dial the second caller.

Knowing When to Answer

In most organizations, managers answer their own phone when they are in the office. Alternatively, you may be expected to take all phone calls and immediately put them through to your manager.

Know when to answer the telephone. For example, if you are not responsible for answering all of your manager's calls, be sure to answer your manager's telephone when a client or colleague is in his/her office. It would be inappropriate for your manager to have to interrupt a conversation with another person, regardless of who the person is, to answer the telephone.

Don't ask your manager to take a phone call when she or he has a visitor, unless you have been given specific instructions to interrupt if a particular call comes in. Let the caller know that your manager is not available at the moment and ask, "May I have Ms. Yee return your call?" Be sure to get the caller's name and number. Tell the caller your manager is not free to receive a telephone call *before* you ask who is calling. If you ask who is calling before you let the caller know that your manager is not available, you may give the caller the impression that your manager doesn't want to speak to him or her specifically.

Not all managers refrain from accepting calls when visitors are in the office. Again, it is best to clarify the desired procedures for different office personnel.

Distributing Messages

Distribute phone messages to office personnel as soon as the messages are received. If your manager is trying to work without interruption, he or she may wish you to send the message electronically. The plan your manager has for handling messages and returning calls will depend on individual schedules, preferences, and workload.

When members of your management team are not available to take calls, don't just take messages—take initiative! Many phone requests can be satisfied by you or by other employees.

Screening Calls

Many people on management teams have such heavy demands on their time that they want their calls to be screened.

If you must screen calls, probe courteously for information. Either respond to the caller yourself or determine what the caller's request is, and refer the call to someone else who can help. When **screening** calls, you are attempting to find out who is calling and what the caller wants.

Screening calls benefits in two ways:

1. It saves your manager time.

2. It ensures someone addresses the caller's request.

All incoming calls should be handled by someone in the office. The more knowledge you have about the organization, the easier your job of screening calls will be.

Conference Calling

A conference call takes place when three or more people are connected across a network that supports the conversation. Conference calls can be initiated by:

1. using the "conference" feature on most business telephone sets

2. using a temporary pass code created by a phone company

3. using specialized software like Skype, which permits up to 25 users to participate (24 plus yourself) in a conference call via the internet

With the first option, you use the convenient conference feature that most business phone sets have. You dial a number and ask the receiver of the call to hold while you conference another person into the call. You simply put the first caller on hold, press the conference button, and dial the second number. When the second caller is connected, you release the hold button to include the first person who has been waiting. A three-way conversation is now possible.

With the second option, the telecommunication provider sets up a pass code and temporary number information that participants call into.

With the third option, the host would set up a contact list for the conference group and then call the group when ready. A computer or mobile device is needed to use this option.

No special equipment is needed for conference calls. However, specially designed speaker/microphone conference sets, designed for boardroom use, may be used to enhance the clarity of the conference stations.

> ### Self-Check
>
> 1. Is it appropriate to end a business call with "bye"? Why or why not?
> 2. List the three essential elements of a completing a message.
> 3. What should you do to avoid unnecessary phone call transfers?
> 4. Why should you avoid saying that your manager *will* return the call?
> 5. What two purposes does screening calls serve?
> 6. Describe the main features of a conference call.

Using Phone Directories

The website www.Canada411.ca is an excellent resource for checking telephone numbers and addresses of individuals as well as businesses. At this site, you can perform a search that covers just your local area, or you can perform a much broader search to include international communities. Other sites are available that perform the same or similar services; however, Canada 411 produces quick and effective results.

International telephone directories can be accessed by using the website www.infobel.com. Directories are arranged by continents and then by country.

The **Yellow Pages** is a service that helps the general public and businesses locate specific business information and goods and services. Using the website www.YP.ca offers an efficient way to source resources and investigate products.

Paper-based directories have their place in the office. However, they are increasingly more awkward, slower to use, and take up more space than the more common electronic directories. Most offices use primarily computer-based systems.

Organizations generally provide their employees with an electronic record of their staff directory for calling other employees within the organization. An organization's directory will include, for example, the telephone numbers of its branch offices, plants, and distribution centres. These directories must be updated as staff and phone assignments change. It is most likely that the task of updating the office directory will be the responsibility of the administrative professional. If the responsibility is not assigned to anyone in particular, take this opportunity to demonstrate your initiative, and offer to update the directory.

Placing Local Calls

Before you place a call, assemble all the materials that you may need to reference during the conversation. Jot down the questions you want to ask and the comments you want to make. Be sure you have the correct number and name of the person with whom you wish to speak.

If the first person you reach is the receptionist, give the extension number of the person you are calling. If you don't know the extension number, give the receptionist the person's name and department.

When the person answers the call, identify yourself immediately. Use an appropriate identification, such as, "Good morning, this is Linda McElroy, executive assistant of Progressive Digital Innovations. May I speak to Ms. Delacroix, please?"

Managers often place their own calls, but at times you will be expected to get a caller on the line for your manager. When you are placing a call for your manager, make sure she or he is ready to talk before you get the other person on the line. It's inconsiderate to call someone and then ask him or her to wait while you search for the person who asked you to place the call. Your conversation might go something like this:

> Hello, Ms. La Roué. This is Linda McElroy calling. I'm executive assistant to Mr. Wilson of Progressive Digital Innovations. Mr. Wilson would like to speak with you about the order for Labrador office. Is it convenient for you to take Mr. Wilson's call at this time? Thank you, Ms. La Roué. I'll put Mr. Wilson through now. One moment please.

Placing Domestic Long-Distance Calls

Long-distance calls are all calls placed outside the local calling area. Domestic long-distance calls are those placed outside your local area but still inside Canada. Canada is divided into numerous areas identified by three-digit codes called **area codes**. Although area codes are necessary for dialling all domestic long-distance calls, they are also necessary for making local calls within certain major metropolitan areas. For example, within the greater city of Toronto, instead of dialling the familiar seven digits to make a local call, you must prefix the seven digits with either 416 or 647 to form what is known as a local 10-digit number. See Figure 6-3 for the Canadian numbering plan.

The number of Canadian area codes in use in Canada increases as the number of telephone numbers in use increases. If you have difficulty finding an area code, just dial the operator and ask for the correct area code.

FIGURE 6-3 Canadian telephone area code map.

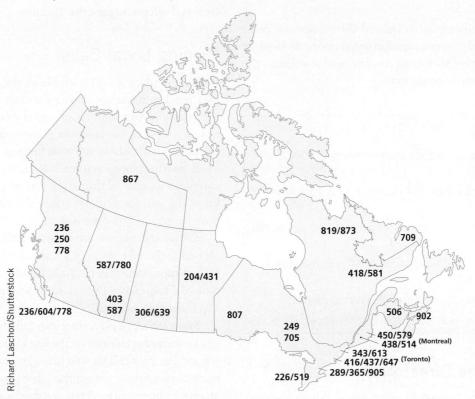

Richard Laschon/Shutterstock

Direct-Distance Dialling (DDD) Whenever possible, dial your number directly without the assistance of the operator. The cost of making a direct call is lower than that of an operator-assisted call.

To make a direct long-distance call, in Canada dial the access code 1, the area code of the geographic location you are calling, and the seven-digit local number.

Operator-Assisted Dialling Remember that of all the services offered by telephone companies, those requiring the intervention of a live telephone operator are the most costly. Therefore, you should always try to use automated services and avoid operator assistance whenever possible.

When would you need the operator to assist you with making long-distance calls? Here are some possible instances:

- You are having difficulty getting through to the destination.
- You wish to reverse the charges.
- You wish to bill a third party. Third-party billing means you don't want the charges to be applied to the telephone from which you are calling or to the destination telephone. Rather, you wish to have the charges billed to another telephone number, such as your home or business telephone number.

To place long-distance calls in Canada requiring operator assistance, use the **zero-plus dialling** method. Simply dial 0,

then the area code, and the seven-digit local number. After you have dialled the complete number, a short automated process will start, during which you will have the choice of entering your calling card number or speaking to a *live* operator for assistance in placing your call.

Many long-distance telephone companies have introduced a computerized operator. If you are placing a long-distance call and wish to use a special service such as reversing the charges, dial 0, the area code, and the local number. A computer-controlled voice will ask you which service you want, and then ask you to state your name clearly. When the call is placed, the computer-controlled voice system announces your name and the fact that you wish to reverse the charges or activate one of the other special services available. When you wish to reverse the charges, the person on the receiving end will accept or refuse the charges either by keying in a response on the telephone pad or by responding to questions with a simple yes or no.

Long-Distance Directory Assistance If you want to call long distance but you don't know the number of the party you want to reach, you need to access long-distance directory assistance. Similar to accessing directory assistance for local calls, dial 1, the area code of the geographic location you want, and 555-1212. You will reach the information operator or the automated directory system for the area you wish to call. First, provide the name of the city or town you want and then the name of the person or business. Write down the number that is given to you and hang up. Then dial 1, the area code, and the seven-digit number provided by the operator. This same procedure is used whether you are dialling inside or outside your own area code.

Time Zones in Canada

The Canadian provinces and territories are divided into six time zones:

1. Newfoundland
2. Atlantic
3. Eastern
4. Central
5. Mountain
6. Pacific

From east to west, the time in each zone is one hour earlier than the time in the adjacent zone. The only exception is the Newfoundland time zone, which is only half an hour ahead of the Atlantic time zone. The time and location where the call originates determine what long-distance rates apply.

During Daylight Saving Time (DST), clocks are turned forward one hour in each Canadian province except for Saskatchewan, which remains on Standard Time year round. For most time zones, DST begins at 2 a.m. on the second Sunday of March. DST ends and reverts back to Standard Time at 2 a.m. on the first Sunday of November. An easy way to remember how to set your clock is, "Spring forward and fall back." Check your local media for the actual dates to set your clock each year.

When you are placing a long-distance call, know the time zone of the city you are calling. For instance, when it is 3:30 p.m. in Victoria, British Columbia, you can expect that offices in Quebec City will be closed. When it is 5:00 p.m. in Quebec City, offices on the West Coast will still be open. Time zones around the world are explained in the following section and are illustrated in Figure 6-4.

Time Zones around the World

The world is divided into 24 time zones, which are based on degrees of longitude. The zones are one hour apart in time. Greenwich, England, is recognized as the prime meridian of longitude; in other words, standard time is calculated from Greenwich. Basically, each time zone covers 15 degrees of longitude; however, the time zone lines bend to accommodate local geographic regions.

The Greenwich zone is called the *zero zone* because the difference between standard time and Greenwich Mean Time is zero. A number representing the number of hours by which the standard time of the zone differs from Greenwich Mean Time, in turn, designates each of the zones.

Zones in west longitude are numbered in sequence from 1 to 12 and labelled *minus*; zones in east longitude are numbered 1 to 12 and labelled *plus*. In each zone the zone number is applied to the standard time (Greenwich Mean Time) in accordance with its plus or minus sign to obtain the time in that particular zone. For example, Toronto is in the –5 zone, as shown in Figure 6-4. When it is 0600 Greenwich Mean Time, subtract five hours to determine that it is 0100 in Toronto. Moscow is in the +3 zone. When it is 0600 Greenwich Mean Time, add three hours to determine that it is 0900 in Moscow.

The International Date Line is in the twelfth zone. It coincides with the 180th meridian, except that it zigzags so that all of Asia lies to the west of it and all of North America—including the Aleutian Islands—to the east of

FIGURE 6-4 Standard time zone chart of the world.

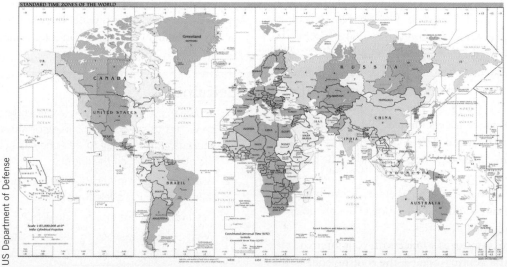

US Department of Defense

FIGURE 6-5 Understanding international time changes.

City	Calculating Time in the International Location	Time
Sydney	GMT + 10 *Standard Time*	Saturday 1010
Hong Kong	GMT + 8 *Standard Time*	Saturday 0810
Moscow	GMT + 4 *Daylight Saving Time*	Saturday 0410
Greenwich	0	Saturday 0010 *(10 minutes after midnight)*
Toronto	GMT − 4 *Daylight Saving Time*	Friday 2010
Vancouver	GMT − 7 *Daylight Saving Time*	Friday 1710
Honolulu	GMT − 10 *Standard Time*	Friday 1410

Pearson Education, Inc.

it. The 180th meridian divides the twelfth zone; therefore, the half in east longitude is *minus* 12 and the half in west longitude is *plus* 12. Each calendar day begins at the International Date Line. When crossing the International Date Line in a westerly direction, *advance* the date by one day; when crossing it in an easterly direction, set the date *back* one day.

The best way to determine times in cities around the globe is to check the world clock through the internet. This can be accessed at www.timeanddate.com/worldclock. Figure 6-5 compares the times of major cities around the world.

Placing International Calls

Making calls to the United States, Puerto Rico, the Virgin Islands, Bermuda, and other Caribbean Islands is like making long-distance calls within Canada. Each of these places has an assigned three-digit area code. Placing a long-distance call to Puerto Rico would require you to dial 1 + 809 (the area code for Puerto Rico) + the local number.

You can dial directly to most foreign countries. For example, to dial directly to a telephone number in Tokyo, Japan, you would dial 011 + 81 + 3 + the local number. The international long-distance access number 011 will direct your call out of Canada; the country code in this case is 81 for Japan. The routing code will direct your call to the region or city that you want to reach—in this case, 3 for Tokyo—and then the local number. Local numbers in Tokyo have four digits. International country and routing codes are given in many local telephone directories.

If you require operator assistance with your international call, dial 01 + the country code + the routing code + the

local number. For example, if you want to dial a number in Weymouth, in the county of Dorset, England, the procedure would be 01 + 44 + 1385 + the local number. At this point the operator will intercept, asking you what assistance you require. The routing code—1385, in this case—will direct your call to the region in Dorset.

Phone Equipment

The telephone is a valuable tool for conducting business. It is therefore imperative for the administrative professional to become familiar with the phone equipment used in his or her office. Refer to Chapter 7 for an overview of various types of telephone equipment features.

APPOINTMENT MANAGEMENT

Appointment scheduling is really the essence of a business. Managing schedules over time can have a major impact on

Self-Check

1. Your manager has asked you to call a client with whom he wishes to speak. Why is it important to make sure your manager is ready to take the call before you get the other person on the line?

2. Give examples of materials you should gather in preparation for making a telephone call.

3. Describe direct distance dialling (DDD).

4. What are two reasons to seek the assistance of an operator when making a long-distance call?

business. An organization needs to maximize a schedule in every way. Appointment preferences, administrative professionals knowledge, and scheduling tools are all components involved in the appointment coordination process. The flexibility in scheduling appointments will depend on a manager's preference and on the administrative professional's astuteness in scheduling. Self-scheduling of appointments by clients has become one of the most common online self-service tasks. It is a feature that is most prevalent in service-based industries like healthcare and personal services. It is gaining a stronger presence in the business community. Some recommendations for administrative professionals who are scheduling appointments on behalf of their manager include the following.

Scheduling Appointments

Use good judgment in scheduling appointments. Begin by learning:

1. Your manager's preference for scheduling appointments. For example, she may want to schedule out-of-office appointments for the mornings only, or no appointments after 3 p.m.

2. Which appointments your manager considers priority: perhaps those that are made by her president, her lawyer, or her partner.

3. What your manager considers is an optimum length of time for an appointment. Learning this will help you schedule a busy day for your manager. It will also enable you to further assist your manager in conducting efficient appointments by setting appropriate appointment finishing times.

Guidelines for Scheduling Appointments Here are some simple guidelines you can apply when scheduling your own appointments or those for management:

1. Avoid scheduling too many appointments on the manager's first day back after being out of the office for several days.

2. Avoid crowding a schedule with appointments the day before a trip. Preparation for the trip has priority.

3. Allow plenty of time before and after a top-priority meeting.

4. Avoid scheduling an appointment in another location too soon after a meeting that may run overtime.

5. Schedule free time between appointments. This gives opportunity to make phone calls, answer emails, sign documents, think about the next meeting, or just take a needed break.

6. Schedule appointments with others with whom your manager has a collaborative working relationship late in the afternoon. These appointments are easy to shift when your manager is unable to keep to the original schedule.

7. When someone requests an appointment, suggest specific times, giving the person a chance to select a time from at least two choices.

8. When you are arranging an appointment for a short period of time, let the person know the length of the appointment. For example, say tactfully, "Your appointment is from noon until 12:15."

9. When you arrange for an unexpected visitor to see your manager right away, let the visitor know if your manager has only a few minutes to spare. For example, you might say, "Ms. Campbell has another commitment in 10 minutes. However, she can see you for a few minutes before then if that's acceptable to you. Shall I show you to her office?"

10. Arrange appointments in another part of the city for first thing in the morning or late in the afternoon so that the manager can go directly from home to the early-morning appointment or not return to the office after a late-afternoon appointment.

Appointments Made by Phone or Email When someone telephones or emails your office requesting an appointment, determine the purpose of the appointment. Then decide who the best person is for the caller to see. Set the appointment, confirm the date, day, and time, and enter these details into the calendar. Where possible, send an appointment confirmation notice electronically allowing the parties involved in the proposed meeting the opportunity to accept the meeting request, sync the meeting with their electronic calendar, provide a response, and upload documents needed for the meeting, if applicable.

If your office is located in a difficult-to-find location, ask callers if they need directions. And, of course, always secure contact information in the event that you have to change the details of the meeting.

Appointments Made Online by Clients Many organizations integrate online web-based tools that allow clients to book their own appointments using preset parameters. Websites such as www.appointmentsonline. ca offer this capability. The software can be synchronized with other software such as Outlook to manage the schedule effectively. This ensures the appointment scheduling is ultimately managed by the organization. The variety of appointment scheduling apps has expanded significantly in recent years to meet the evolving expectations of industry.

Using Electronic Calendars

If your workplace has an integrated electronic network, you will use the computer to schedule appointments for management as well as your own appointments. The e-calendar system, such as the popular Microsoft® Outlook, is an excellent time-saver when used to check and organize calendars, find the common availability of a number of people and schedule all of them into a conference, cancel appointments, and create up-to-the-minute schedules. This system is a receptionist's super tool. (See Figure 6-6.)

Advantages of Electronic Calendars There are many benefits to using electronic calendar systems. Here is a list of

FIGURE 6-6 Electronic calendar displayed on computer screen showing daily and monthly views.

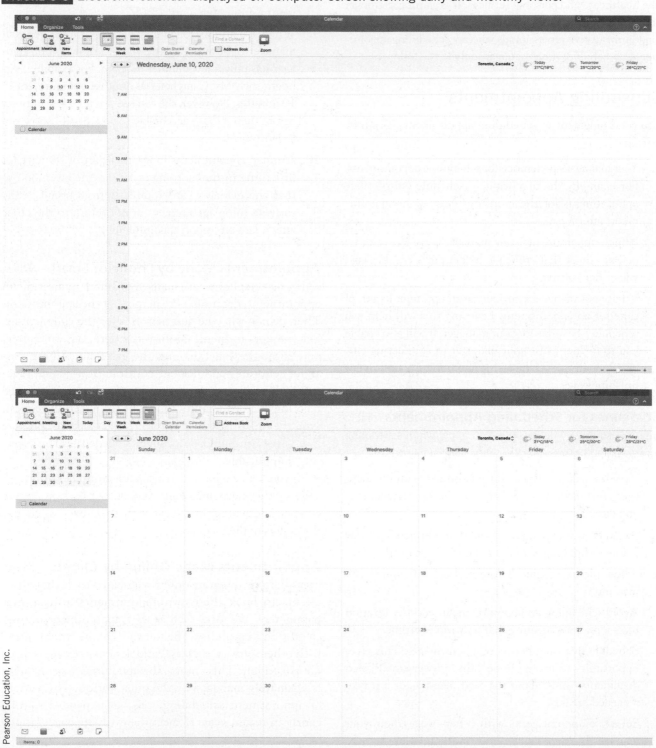

some of the advantages of using a networked electronic calendar system as opposed to using a traditional paper calendar system:

1. Electronic calendars can be set to remind you of your upcoming meetings.

2. They will produce a list of appointments as well as electronic to-do lists.

3. You can key a full set of details regarding each meeting because you are not working in the small blocks of space found in traditional paper calendars.

4. Using the electronic calendar makes cancelling or editing the details of an appointment very simple.

5. When you set up a meeting in your electronic calendar, the software gives you the flexibility of creating an invitation list and automatically sending an email asking each invitee to decline or accept the meeting. If they accept, the meeting is automatically entered into their electronic calendar. When they accept or decline, a message is automatically sent back to you, giving the status of their attendance.

For these reasons, the electronic calendar is always convenient to use as long as you have access to a computer system. For people who spend considerable time out of their office, at meetings, or travelling, a smartphone or a mobile device may be the answer (see Chapter 7).

Drawbacks of Electronic Calendars   The advantages of using e-calendars far outweigh the drawbacks. But here are two things to be aware of:

1. Unless you have reliable and exclusive access to a laptop computer or smartphone, you will need to back up your electronic calendar with a paper calendar. Being at a meeting without your electronic calendar will be unproductive when you can't refer to dates and times.

2. Many people are remiss at keeping their e-calendars up to date. This is frustrating for the receptionist trying to electronically schedule a meeting that includes these people.

Using Paper Calendars

Professionals who make commitments months in advance may prefer a full month displayed on one page, with small insert calendars for the preceding and following months. With a monthly calendar, they can review engagements without flipping through a lot of pages. People who make several appointments in one day may prefer a daily appointment calendar like the one shown in Figure 6-7. In this sample, each day is divided into 30-minute segments with the time printed in the left column.

Making Entries in Calendars

All appointments (even regularly scheduled meetings)—whether they are made by phone, electronically email, or in

FIGURE 6-7 Daily appointment calendar.

DATE — Monday, December 9, 20--

8	00	
	15	
	30	
	45	
9	00	
	15	Call for hotel reservation
	30	R. C. Thompson ABC Corp.
	45	
10	00	Manager's Staff Meeting
	15	
	30	
	45	
11	00	Explore procedure changes
	15	
	30	Ruth Raires, Ads
	45	
12	00	
	15	
	30	
	45	
1	00	
	15	
	30	Interview Applicant–
	45	Jane Allright
2	00	Assemble forms
	15	
	30	Lee Society Forms Design
	45	
3	00	
	15	
	30	Interview Applicant–
	45	Louise Petruzza
4	00	Complete Proposal
	15	
	30	
	45	Meet Jaxs Hunter – Airport
5	00	
	15	
	30	
	45	
6	00	AMA Meeting
	15	
	30	
	45	

person—should be entered into the calendar. When the days are very busy—and they will be—it is easy to forget even a regularly scheduled meeting. Be consistent and prompt in recording all appointments and commitments.

It's much easier to cancel or edit the details of an appointment when you are using an electronic calendar. Enter appointments in pencil when you are using a desk calendar. Even the firmest commitments can change suddenly. In the paper calendar, draw a diagonal line through each entry once the conference is held or the task is completed; this way, you will know whether items have been completed or not.

Because professional commitments are often made outside the office—at social or recreational events such as games of golf—it is imperative for people making these commitments to relay the information back to the administrative professional to make the appropriate entries into calendars.

Administrative professionals should plan a few minutes with their manager each morning to discuss the work scheduled for the day.

As you receive incoming mail, watch for announcements of meetings that managers will be expected to attend or might want to attend. Call attention to them, and make entries in the appropriate calendars.

At the end of the day, check the manager's calendar against yours to make sure you have all the correct and comprehensive appointment information. Transfer any items that still need attention to the page for the following business day. When you are clearing your calendar, if you are unsure whether managers have returned telephone calls or kept promises they have made, send emails as reminders.

Changing Appointments

When someone cancels an appointment, offer to schedule another one. Be sure to clear the manager's calendar and your own of the cancelled appointment.

When you cancel an appointment for the manager, let the person whose appointment is being cancelled know as soon as possible. Use the following guidelines for changing or cancelling an appointment:

1. Express regret on the manager's behalf.
2. Mention that the appointment must be changed.
3. State a reason in general terms.
4. Offer to schedule another appointment.

Think twice about what explanation you will give for the change. Be diplomatic and discreet when you change the appointment.

Self-Check

1. What three pieces of information about your manager will help you in scheduling his or her appointments?
2. List four guidelines that will help you to schedule appointments effectively.
3. When would it be more appropriate for a manager to use a monthly rather than a daily calendar?

GREETING VISITORS

As mentioned, visitors are influenced by their first impressions of the office and the receptionist. A favourable first impression, coupled with your courteous efforts to make visitors feel welcome, will create a receptive climate. The visitor's first impression should be that of an efficient receptionist working in a well-organized office.

As a person who welcomes the public, you should look like you belong in a professional office setting. Many offices have a casual environment, but they still want to convey a businesslike atmosphere to the public.

Immediate Attention

It's your role to make visitors, whether they have appointments or not, feel at ease. When visitors come to your office,

you should greet them the minute they arrive. As a visitor approaches your desk, look at the person directly, smile, and speak immediately. Nobody likes to be ignored, even for a few seconds. To continue keying or reading until you reach the end of the line or paragraph is extremely rude. To continue chatting with another employee is inexcusable.

Greet an office visitor formally by saying, "Good morning" or "Good afternoon." "Hello" or "hi" are too casual for most offices. Use the visitor's name whenever you know it. The greeting may go something like this: "Good morning, Mr. Oliver. I'm Chris Rogers, Mr. Sung's assistant. Mr. Sung is expecting you." If you don't know the visitor's name, don't guess it. Introduce yourself and ask how you may be of assistance.

Most business visitors will introduce themselves immediately and give you a business card. As soon as a new visitor arrives, repeat the visitor's name, introduce yourself, and add whatever statement is appropriate. For example, "Mr. Sung is expecting you," or "May I help you?"

The atmosphere in most organizations is informal enough that employees refer to managers by their first name. Regardless

---

pro-Link
Your Workstation Speaks

As a receptionist, you usually have the incredible responsibility of setting the first impression for your company. Consider yourself the office ambassador. The impression you make with clients is formed by such factors as your personality, your efficiency, and your appearance. It is also formed by the appearance of your workstation. What does your workstation say about you?

■ Does it project your personality? If you decorate your work area with personal items, it speaks to your personality. Is this what you want?

■ Does it say your company is organized? Are files neatly stacked, pens in holders, resource materials put away? If so, it may leave the impression that your company is organized but not busy.

■ Does it say business is slow? If your desk is so clean and organized that there is no activity to be seen, the impression will be that you need business because you have none.

■ Does it say your company is in chaos? It does if your workstation is a mess with adhesive notes stuck to everything, and files lying open in every direction.

The best impression to create is one that says your company is organized and busy. This can be created by ensuring everything is in place, activity is obvious at your desk, and decorations are restricted to ones that reflect the business.

---

of the informality of your relationship, it may be most appropriate to use your manager's last name in the presence of guests, especially international visitors. With experience you will determine how to address management in the presence of guests.

Preparing for Visitors

Will the meeting require materials from the files—correspondence and records? If so, locate them prior to the meeting.

You may have to compile data or collect information from other departments. Make sure you give the manager any information you have compiled well enough in advance of the meeting so that it can be reviewed adequately before the meeting. Anticipate any other items that will be needed during the meeting and have them ready. These materials might include:

- notes taken during previous meetings
- brochures to be distributed
- presentations to supplement a speech
- lists of names, addresses, and company affiliations of new members of a professional group, or anything else that is related to the purpose of the meeting

Introductions

Here are some easy guidelines for making introductions in the office:

- Gender and age have nothing to do with whose name you state first. In a business relationship, state the name of the person you want to honour first.
- Make the introduction sound natural. Just state their names. For example, "Mrs. Kensington, this is Mr. Adams." Or simply, "Mrs. Kensington . . . Mr. Adams." Reserve "May I introduce . . ." or "May I present . . ." for formal affairs and for very distinguished people.
- You can add the person's business after his or her name. For example, "Mrs. Kensington, this is Mr. Adams of Great Lakes EnviroTech." Or you can just use the visitor's name and hand the visitor's business card to your manager.

Visitor Who Have an Appointment Indicate to the visitor where to leave a coat, boots, or hat. Collect the visitor's business card. The business card will indicate the correct spelling of the name and the company the visitor is affiliated with. Ask the visitor to pronounce his or her name if it is difficult for you to pronounce. Escort the visitor to the correct office, and make the introduction. Pronounce the visitor's name and your manager's name distinctly when making the introduction. If the manager knows the visitor, you can be less formal. As soon as the manager is free, you can invite the visitor to go in. Invite visitors who must wait to have a seat. Keep current magazines, the morning paper, and other interesting reading material nearby so that visitors who must wait for any length of time can read. You are not expected to entertain the visitor by carrying on a conversation while the visitor is waiting. You should continue with your work.

A visitor who arrives early should expect to wait until the time of the appointment. As soon as the manager is free, tell the manager that the visitor has arrived, and ask if he or she is ready to see the visitor.

A visitor who has an appointment should not be kept waiting. Remember, the visitor's time is valuable. Asking the visitor to wait more than a few minutes is inconsiderate. Nevertheless, a busy executive may have difficulty keeping to an appointment schedule. This happens even when the manager and the administrative professional are making an effort to keep appointments on time. A previous visitor might take twice the expected time, or a high-level executive might drop by unexpectedly. When this occurs, the visitor with the next appointment often has to wait. In addition to making the visitor feel welcome and comfortable, you should assure the visitor that the wait shouldn't take too long.

The real test of how well you carry out your role as office host lies in how you act when the wait is long. Don't let your actions reveal that the day is hectic. When emergencies occur or the day is not going smoothly, slow down, put some of your work on tomorrow's list, and approach visitors in a very relaxed manner. Give each visitor the impression that your priority at that moment is to meet the visitor's needs.

Be cautious when you state the reasons for a delay. You can apologize and say that all appointments are running behind schedule, but do not explain why. Avoid statements referring to important business, problems, or inefficiency. The visitor is concerned about his or her own schedule and wants to know how long the wait will be. If you know that the manager is involved in a long meeting, tell the visitor approximately how long he or she will have to wait. The visitor may decide to postpone the appointment.

Don't forget about the visitor. If you can judge that a conference is ending, indicate to the visitor who is waiting that it is ending. If a visitor whose appointment is delayed cannot wait any longer, offer to make another appointment. Remember, this visitor has been inconvenienced and deserves special attention.

Staff Visitors A difficult part of every manager's job is maintaining good communication with the personnel. Whatever a manager's efforts to establish an easy, two-way flow of communication, breakdowns occur and misunderstandings arise. This is one reason why many executives maintain an "open door" policy for seeing personnel.

According to office protocol, a meeting between a subordinate and a superior is held in the superior's office.

Arrange for employees who report to your manager to meet in your manager's office or in a local conference room. When your manager's superior requests a conference, the implied message is that your manager will go to the superior's office unless a specific statement is made to the contrary concerning the place of the meeting.

Visitors without Appointments Be just as pleasant to the unexpected visitor as you are to one who has an appointment. Never judge a visitor by appearance. Appearance is not indicative of a person's contribution to the organization. Whether the visitor is a member of the family, a friend, or a business associate, always invite the visitor to be seated. If the manager is already engaged with another appointment, you could say, "Mrs. Kensington has someone in her office, but I'll let her know you are here." Find a method to make contact with your manager that works when interruptions such as this are necessary. If you interrupt your manager to tell him or her there is an unexpected visitor, the manager may step out of the office briefly to speak to this person. Visitors may come to your office and decide not to wait when they discover the manager is not immediately available. Always offer to help the person yourself. If you cannot be of assistance, give the visitor the option of leaving a message or making an appointment to see the manager.

When a sales representative calls unexpectedly, find out the purpose of the call to determine if any of these options is appropriate:

1. The sales representative should see someone else.
2. You should offer to make an appointment for the sales representative.
3. You should tell the representative the manager is not interested in the product or service.

However, due to increased security practices in most public and commercial places of business, visitors are no longer able to wander freely about the office. There will probably be a procedure for allowing an unknown visitor on the premises. Some offices simply require the visitor to wear an identification badge; others will require the visitor to be escorted to employees' locations. Make yourself familiar with the current security procedures in your office.

When you know your company won't want this representative's particular product or service, graciously tell the sales representative. The representative may still want to convince the manager of the need for the product or service. Invite the sales representative to leave a business card and literature about the product or service, and offer to contact the sales representative if the manager is interested in learning more about the product.

Remember that your job is to build relationships for the organization. Give a reason, at least in general terms, before

you say no. Visitors who are turned away should feel that they have been dealt with fairly.

Organizations should have definite policies, too, about dealing with **solicitors**. Know what the policies are. If you have been given the authority to handle solicitors, do so assertively but always with courtesy.

Terminating a Meeting

Arrange with the manager how you should assist in terminating a meeting.

On those days when the manager's appointment schedule is crowded, watch the time, and tactfully interrupt a conference following predetermined guidelines you have arranged with your manager. One appointment that runs overtime on a busy day can throw all the other appointments off schedule, inconveniencing many callers and giving the impression of inefficient planning. At the manager's request, you may have to interrupt a meeting in order to inform and dismiss visitors who overstay their allotted time.

When a second visitor arrives promptly for an appointment and someone is in the manager's office, if it is appropriate to interrupt, you might:

1. Send a text or instant message to the manager.
2. Enter the manager's office, apologize for the interruption, and give the manager the visitor's name on a slip of paper to indicate that the visitor has arrived. Say nothing more and exit the office.
3. Call the manager on the telephone, especially if you think he or she does not want to rush the first visitor.
4. Send the manager a priority message that will flash or signal on the computer screen.

Your interruption, either in person, by telephone, or by computer, may be all that is needed to prompt the visitor to leave. If not, it will be adequate to enable the manager to terminate the conversation.

Managers are typically busy people who need to navigate their responsibilities effectively. Most managers are skilled at terminating office visits. They thank the visitor for coming, stand, tactfully make statements that let the visitor know the conference is over, and lead the visitor to the door. At times, however, they rely on administrative professional to rescue them from persistent visitors.

Refusing Appointments

Many managers plan blocks of time in which they hope to work without interruption. At other times an executive will be forced by the pressure of a deadline to work full-time on a task that must be completed.

During periods when the manager is not seeing anyone, simply state that the manager cannot fit anything more into today's schedule, and then centre the discussion on future arrangements. Indicate when the manager will have time to see the visitor and invite the visitor to make an appointment.

Self-Check

1. Give an example of how you might show initiative in helping your manager prepare for a meeting.
2. How should you manage a visitor who
   a. arrives early for an appointment?
   b. does not have an appointment?
3. Consider how you might assist your manager to terminate a meeting when a visitor outstays the allotted time.

HANDLING DIFFICULT CUSTOMERS

Every administrative office professional will handle difficult customers or clients at some time in his or her career. Remember, difficult customers exist in every business, for every company, and even though you may want to suspend a relationship with them, ultimately and in most cases it is better to retain them if you can. Although this situation is undesirable, by handling it professionally you will benefit both your company and the customer.

The first decisions you must make will be based on whether the difficult person actually is a customer, whether the difficulty is based on dissatisfaction with your company's actions, and whether there is personal abuse involved. Clearly, if someone who is *not* a customer is personally abusive towards you, then civil action might be in order. However, here the discussion differentiates only between customers calling on the telephone and those visiting your office. The reaction and response to both is similar; the main difference is that you are dealing face-to-face with the visitor but are removed from the physical presence of a caller.

Difficult Callers

Difficult customers who call to voice their problems on the telephone are arguably easier to handle, the important difference being that there is no immediate and physical presence. These circumstances better allow you to maintain composure. You may even be able to read the procedural script that deals with difficult telephone callers in your office procedures manual—if it has been developed.

Fundamentally, difficult customers who call in should be handled in much the same way as those who appear in your office, with diplomacy, respect, and the help of the points outlined in the "Tips for Success" section on page 120.

Unwanted Visitors

How do you deal with a visitor who is obnoxious or one who makes you feel threatened? Many office buildings have security 24 hours per day. If this is the case in your organization, you would call security to have the individual removed. Dealing with unwanted visitors is something you need to discuss with your office team. Your colleagues may be able to provide names of people who have an abusive history with your office and are, therefore, not welcome. Your company may have an organizational policy for handling unwanted visitors. If so, follow it. If no policy exists, your office team should draft a policy and submit it to management for approval. Every organization wants to provide excellent customer service, but customer abuse towards employees should never be tolerated.

Complaining Customers

One unhappy customer may lead to two unhappy customers may lead to three unhappy customers . . . and so on. When you fail to convert a complaining customer into a contented one, you risk losing more than just one customer. You risk losing all the existing customers as well as potential customers as a result of the influence of one unhappy customer. The receptionist must be skilled at handling difficult people.

Ultimately, what you *don't* want is for your customers to go so far as to file an official complaint such as those submitted to the Better Business Bureau (BBB). There are 20 voluntary self-regulated Better Business Bureaus across Canada. Their objective is to promote and cultivate the highest ethical relationship between businesses and the public. The BBB can share with you reliability reports of businesses that are ethical and reliable; it can provide consumer tips, and it can provide information to consumers before they buy a good or service. It also investigates and exposes fraud against consumers and businesses, arbitrates disputes, and may report on cases of complaints made by both customers and its voluntary business members. While the BBB has no legal jurisdiction, its network and reporting processes may influence customers' and suppliers' behaviour across the country. Any negative exposure with the BBB may result in a loss of business for your company as customers leave and look for alternatives.

What you *do* want is to be able to offer advice and a solution in order to resolve the customer's problem. Remember, an unhappy customer who is allowing you to resolve his or her problem is actually giving you and your organization another chance to make things right. View this as an opportunity.

When dealing with unhappy customers, these simple principles will help you stay objective and better enable you to successfully resolve any problem:

- Don't get emotionally involved in the problem.
- Don't get defensive or aggressive—it never works.

- Provide solutions, not excuses.
- Customers are *not* always right, but don't tell them this.
- All customers have a right to be heard.
- Allowing a customer to abuse you is not acceptable.
- Promising action *without* action will lead to a customer service disaster.
- "Sorry" without corrective action is just an empty word.
- Preventing problems is easier than resolving them.

Abusive Customers

Abuse from customers can come in several forms. For example, a customer might attempt verbal abuse such as swearing, shouting, or even threatening employees. Physical abuse also takes place in offices where customers get angry enough to push people or throw items.

As an administrative professional, diplomatic and courteous treatment with colleagues and customers is essential. However, under no circumstances should you tolerate abuse. Model professional behaviour for people who are being abusive toward you. The best way to do this is to treat others with dignity and respect and in the way you would like to be treated in return. If a customer continues to be abusive, remain professional and courteous, but take control of the situation. If you have exhausted your diplomacy your next steps might be:

- Call your supervisor for assistance to deal with the abusive customer.
- Ask the customer to leave the premises and state that you will continue the conversation when the customer has calmed down.
- In extreme cases, tell the customer that his or her actions are not acceptable and you will call security.

Tips for Success

The following are tips for turning an undesirable situation into one that is satisfactory to both parties:

1. **Listen to the customer.** Listen to the spoken words, but also listen to the unspoken—that is, to the tone of voice and the body language. Often there is more information in what customers *don't* say than what they do say. Does the body language indicate anger or frustration? Has the customer omitted an important step in the process he or she is complaining about? If so, is there a reason for this omission? Listen quietly and carefully as the customer explains the source of distress. Take notes if necessary and ask questions to ensure clarity.

2. **Apologize if it is appropriate to do so.** Remember that customers are not always right, especially in situations where they have been dishonest or unethical. Where the company is not at fault, an apology might be phrased this way: "We apologize for any inconvenience our company may have caused. However, [company name] has done everything possible to provide you with a quality product [or service]."

   If your company has not performed to the highest of standards, a full apology is in order. Remember to use your tone of voice and your body language to reinforce the sincerity of your message.

3. **Show empathy and understanding.** Demonstrate that you have listened carefully and that you understand the customer's reason for distress. Paraphrasing the customer's story may be helpful. Example: "I understand how frustrated you must feel after receiving no response to your voice mail message."

4. **Promise follow-up.** Commit to assisting the person yourself or to having someone else take action. Tell the customer exactly what your action plan will be and when she or he can expect to hear from you. If you do not know what action is necessary, commit to finding out and to calling the customer within a specified time. Then check with the customer to see if your action plan has his or her approval.

5. **Follow through.** Carry out the action plan just as you promised you would. Be certain to keep the customer informed of your progress.

6. **Use common courtesies.** Learn the customer's name and use it along with the appropriate courtesy title (Mrs., Ms., Mr., Dr.). Be sure your tone of voice and body language always convey a positive and sincere message. Most important, do not reciprocate the aggression. It is easy to become defensive and annoyed at a customer who is complaining about your service or product. However, do not personalize the comments of a distressed customer. If you feel the situation is beyond your control and you have been unable to deal effectively with this individual, contact your supervisor for support.

If you follow these basic rules, a more satisfactory situation should result.

MANAGING DIVERSE SITUATIONS
Visitors and Language Barriers

Encounters with visitors can also be challenging if they do not speak your language and you do not speak theirs. Listen actively—you will have to listen more carefully to a visitor who is not fluent in the English language. Do not interpret and finish the sentence that the visitor is trying to say. Instead, paraphrase after your visitor has finished speaking to ensure understanding of what was said. Be patient. Just remember, the visitor's English may be a lot better than your Arabic, Japanese, German, or Spanish!

When they do not speak English at all, attempt to determine the native language of the visitors. The names of many languages are often recognizable in both English and the mother tongue. If you do not recognize the visitors' language, asking a one-word question ("Arabic?" for example), will likely get a response that you can understand. If the visitors do not speak Arabic, it is highly likely that they will recognize what you are asking and respond with the name of their language in a one-word answer.

If you do recognize the language and know someone in your area who speaks it, ask the visitors to take a seat (this may be done with hand motions). Then call the person who can speak with them, explain the situation, and ask if he or she would please assist you in helping the visitors by translating.

Don't assume the visitors do not *understand* your language. Ask. Many times a person can understand a language but not speak it. If your visitors understand English, you will be able to explain to them that you are going to ask a co-worker to translate.

Either way, display a positive attitude towards these visitors. Be careful what you say, verbally and nonverbally. Nonverbal communication can be as effective as voice in showing your interest and desire to help. Coming to your office can be a frustrating experience for those visitors, and your courtesy and understanding will contribute to their favourable impression of your company.

Visitors with Special Needs

Today's businesses deal with a diverse clientele, and you are likely to encounter a number of visitors with special needs, visible and invisible. Canada wide legislation exists which supports accessibility for those with special needs. For instance, in Ontario, the *Accessibility for Ontarians with Disabilities Act* (AODA) provides parameters to create an accessible Ontario for everybody. The AODA goal is to improve accessibility standards.

Be observant of visitors with special needs, and make them as comfortable as possible. If appropriate, offer to help; don't wait to be asked. Here are examples of ways in which you can demonstrate courtesy towards, and show consideration for, those visitors.

1. Hold open doors (if the door does not have buttons that automatically open) for someone who uses a wheelchair or for someone who has difficulty walking.

2. Make special arrangements to accommodate the needs of all participants of a meeting. Before booking meetings, ask whether special arrangements will be needed. If a visitor requires wheelchair access, ensure the meeting is booked in a room that has an adequate door opening to accommodate the wheelchair. If an interpreter is needed by a participant, arrange for one. Another type of special arrangement may be dietary such as vegetarians will be appreciative of your efforts in meeting their dietary requirements by providing a choice of nonmeat dishes at luncheon meetings.

3. Promote the acquisition of at least one telephone that is fitted with technology to aid the hearing impaired, and ensure that it is located in an area accessible to visitors but that will not compromise the confidentiality of your company. You can direct visitors who are hearing impaired to this telephone if they wish to make a call.

4. Encourage basic audio aids that will accommodate the needs of visitors who are sight impaired. If your office is accessed by elevator, point out to your employer the benefits of having the elevator equipped with audio signals, audible inside and outside the elevator, to signal each floor.

5. Show courtesy by facing the visitor with a hearing impairment when talking to him or her. This will help the visitor who lip-reads to compensate for the hearing difficulty. Speak up, and enunciate your words carefully.

6. Place a sign in both English and Braille next to a bell if visitors are expected to ring for service. If you do business with a large number of people who share a common language, include the message written in their language as well.

7. Post signs in the reception area to inform visitors of special accommodations that can be made. This will advise of services such as employees who speak languages other than English or who know sign language.

8. Familiarize yourself with the location of wheelchair-accessible restaurants, full-service gas stations, and other businesses in your area that accommodate special needs. Visitors will often ask you questions if they are unfamiliar with the area. Your knowledge and helpfulness will ensure that both you and your employer are perceived as a respectful and customer-oriented organization.

9. Arrange to have a supply of juice and liquids that can be made available to visitors with medical considerations such as diabetes. This small consideration will reap rewards in terms of goodwill if a visitor experiences sudden low blood sugar levels that require immediate attention while visiting your offices.

As you see, some accommodations for special needs that can be implemented by you, simply by your consideration and actions, can increase your visitors' comfort and satisfaction. In some instances, accommodation requests are outside your span of control and will require your employer to become involved, as they may even require financial expenditures. Be proactive in getting your employer involved. Impress them with your understanding of the benefits the company will accrue when it is recognized for its commitment to meeting the diverse needs of *all* its customers.

Your courteous manner and commitment to meeting customer needs will show visitors that your company is caring and wanting to help in any way it can. The benefits will far outweigh the costs of having a sign printed or of purchasing a telephone.

Self-Check

1. What is the main objective of the Better Business Bureau (BBB)?

2. How might you handle the situation if a visitor arrives who does not speak your language?

3. In addition to the examples provided, list two ways you might accommodate a visitor with special needs.

ETHICS AND VISITORS

Every so often you will have the opportunity to chat with visitors while they are waiting for your manager or another staff member. Remember to treat visitors in a fair, courteous, and respectful manner, while upholding the principles of the organization. Here are some guidelines to follow when dealing with waiting visitors:

■ Navigate confidential information, office gossip, and company successes or problems. Customers will sometimes ask questions of a confidential nature to gather information that may help them get ahead of any competition.

■ Treat each visitor equally. When two or more visitors appear, use the "first come, first served" rule. Acknowledge both visitors, but invite the second visitor to have a seat while you help the first.

■ Avoid asking questions of a personal nature. A visitor may be offended by questions that appear to be prying into his or her personal life. Don't discuss family, children, religion, or politics.

■ Do not assume that a visitor is from a particular foreign country, or from a foreign country at all, based on a stereotypical perception such as the colour of a person's skin. The visitor may very well be a Canadian who has lived in Canada for his or her entire life. You should never ask or make reference to a person's country of birth.

When handling visitors, keep in mind your organization's code of ethics as well as your own values.

QUESTIONS FOR STUDY AND REVIEW

1. Explain why the reception role is a critical element to the success of an organization.

2. Discuss two important attributes of a receptionist. In your opinion, are soft or technical skills more important in this role? Provide a reason to substantiate your response.

3. Name two ways that voice mail can enhance the efficiency of the administrative professional.

4. How can voice mail management eliminate telephone tag?

5. List three key considerations for an organization in terms of reception design and layout.

6. Describe a virtual receptionist. What are two disadvantages of acquiring a virtual receptionist?

7. What does visitor management involve? What systems exist to enhance the visitor experience?

8. Describe three best practices for telecommunications.

9. How would you introduce yourself if you were answering the phone for PDI?

10. Explain why it is important to record the time of the call when you are writing a telephone message.

11. State two comments you should avoid saying when you take calls for an absent manager.

12. State a guideline for transferring a call to another person.

13. Describe what to do when two phone lines ring at the same time and you are the only person in the office.

14. If a manager is trying to work without interruption, how should you get a telephone message to them.

15. Why do many managers want their calls screened?

16. Name a Canadian website that acts as a directory for Canadian telephone numbers.

17. How do time zones affect the administrative professional's work?

18. Where is the International Date Line? What happens when you cross it in an easterly direction? What happens when you cross it in a westerly direction?

19. Suggest how you can tactfully let people know that their appointments are for a short segment of time.

20. Suggest how the administrative professional can avoid scheduling conflicts in appointments.

21. State reasons why it is essential to record the telephone number of a person who has requested or confirmed an appointment.

22. Describe two proficiency advantages of using an electronic calendar.

23. Describe two pitfalls of using an electronic calendar.

24. What guidelines should you follow when you must cancel an appointment because the manager cannot keep it?

25. What should you say if a caller who has an appointment cannot wait and tells you he or she must leave?

26. What would you do if each of the following visitors did not have an appointment: the CEO of your company; the manager's spouse; the manager's former college friend from out of town; a sales representative your manager wants to keep in touch with but cannot see right now; a salesperson representing a product your company does not need; a person soliciting funds; and an aggressive and abusive person?

27. Explain why a customer complaint might be detrimental to your organization.

28. Explain what to do when a customer becomes abusive and you have exhausted your diplomacy.

Key Terms

area code 109

phone tag 105

screening 108

solicitors 118

speculation 107

virtual receptionist 101

visitor management 102

voice mail 104

Yellow Pages 109

zero-plus dialling 110

EVERYDAY ETHICS

Lying on the Job

You are a single parent, working as the receptionist for a fast-paced and aggressive law firm in Toronto. The firm maintains an impersonal work environment in which relationships are "strictly business" between the administrative office professionals and the lawyers. You are very efficient in keeping track of the lawyers, their whereabouts, and the cases they are working on. They rely on you to give out only information that assists them and not to jeopardize any personal or professional situations.

Kristin is an exceptionally busy lawyer with a heavy caseload. When she is unprepared to meet her clients, she asks you to give them false information, saying she is out of town or in court. Kristin is only one of many lawyers that expect your help in this way. If you refused to cooperate, you would be dismissed from your position.

When her husband calls, she expects you to continue with the same routine, saying she is in court or out of town for the day. You've been giving him false information for several years. Recently, you have begun suspecting that Kristin is having an intimate relationship with one of the other lawyers. When her husband calls, you give the standard excuse but are uncomfortable doing so because you suspect she is spending social time with her colleague.

- Why do you think you feel uncomfortable about this new situation?
- Could you have avoided this situation in the first place?
- What is the best course of action you can take?

Problem Solving

1. During your first job performance appraisal, you were criticized for the way you manage phone systems. You have been asking the caller to state the purpose of the call before you say whether or not your manager is in the office. After you find out who the caller is and the purpose of the call, you say, "Mrs. Burke is not in her office," or "Mrs. Burke is in a meeting." It is true that Mrs. Burke is not in her office when you say this, but apparently the callers are not convinced. What can you do to improve rapport with the callers?

2. You know that your manager, Mr. Perkins, is expecting an important long-distance call. He called Mike Brendl at 9:30 a.m., and he is expecting Mr. Brendl to return his call. At 4:30 p.m., Mr. Perkins was called to the president's

office. A few minutes later, Mr. Brendl calls. You feel that you should not interrupt Mr. Perkins in the president's office. You do not know whether Mr. Perkins will return to his desk before 5 p.m. What should you do? Do you have any alternatives?

3. Recently, Mrs. Garson has made three appointments with your employer, Mr. Stoney. Each time she has cancelled the appointment the day before—once because she was ill, another time because of bad weather, and the last time because she was too busy to keep the appointment. The last time she cancelled the appointment, Mr. Stoney said emphatically, "Please do not grant her another appointment!" This morning Mrs. Garson called requesting another appointment.

You told her that Mr. Stoney could not work in another appointment this week and that he would be out of town the following week. Mrs. Garson is furious and insists on talking with Mr. Stoney. What should you do? What will you say to Mrs. Garson?

4. Your manager, Mr. Harper, had a serious heart attack in his office late Tuesday afternoon. Today you are cancelling his appointments for the remainder of this week and next week. You are explaining that the appointments will be rescheduled with someone else. What can you ask in order to judge the urgency of each appointment? How much information can you give about Mr. Harper's illness? What can you say?

Special Reports

1. Accessing information is critical in the administrative professional role. Use the online Yellow Pages (www.yp.ca) of your directory to determine how the following are classified: educational services (public schools, private schools, colleges, and universities); food catering services; medical doctors (general practitioners and specialists); furniture for an office; office stationery; office computers; and airlines. Prepare a list and submit it to your instructor.

2. Have you ever worked or visited an office of any kind? If so, recall what you observed about how office visitors were received in the organization where you worked. Did the organization have a receptionist? Were the visitors escorted or directed to the offices of those with whom they had appointments? Were the salespeople's calls restricted? If so, how? What was the visitor's first contact with the

administrative professional? Provide a synopsis of what you recall, and share your ideas with the class. If you have never worked in an office, ask an administrative professional you know about how visitors are received in the organization in which he or she works.

3. In groups of two or three classmates, discuss positive and negative experiences you have encountered when calling an office for an appointment. Make a list of the positive points and the negative points and share it with the rest of the class. Come up with a list of three best practices to ensure positive experiences for clients visiting an office.

4. Research four online self-service booking apps. In a memo to your instructor, describe the features of each app and recommend which app in your opinion best meets client needs.

PRODUCTION CHALLENGES

6-A Receiving Phone Calls

Supplies needed:

- *Forms 6-A-1, 6-A-2, 6-A-3, and 6-A-4; Companion website*

When your managers are in their offices, they answer their own telephones. Today, August 11, Mr. Wilson, Alexander Rush, and Jacob Levine are not in their offices. You receive the following telephone calls:

9:15 a.m.—for Alexander Rush from Albert Sellars, 683-4750. He wants to know if his website has been enabled with security features. Please return his call.

10:30 a.m.—for Jacob Levine from Al Wilcox, 442-8761, about a printing order Jacob placed with him. Urgent. Please call.

11:00 a.m.—for Mr. Wilson from Bob Arnett, 366-8184, a speaker for the November Sales Seminar. He has a business

conflict and cannot attend the seminar on Wednesday. Please call.

11:15 a.m.—for Mr. Wilson from the Human Resource Department, Extension 5738, asking, "When can Mr. Wilson see an applicant?" Please call.

Complete the telephone message for each of the phone message you received today. Indicate the sense of urgency and therefore priority implied in each message.

6-B Placing Telephone Calls

Supplies needed:

- *Forms 6-B-1 and 6-B-2, Companion website*

Mr. Wilson asked you to respond by phone to the following. Here is Mr. Wilson's conversation with you:

"Mr. Arnett, who was scheduled to speak at the November Sales Seminar on Wednesday, November 12, at

10 a.m., cannot attend the Sales Seminar on Wednesday. He has an important business conflict. He is substituting for his manager, who had a heart attack and will not return to work for at least six months. Mr. Arnett must be in his Burlington office on November 12. He can attend the seminar on Monday and Tuesday."

"Find a speaker who can trade times with Mr. Arnett. Call James Epstein in Winnipeg, at 690-8699, who is scheduled to talk at 2 p.m. on Monday. If he can't do it, ask Abigail Agway in Vancouver, at 487-3232, who is scheduled to speak at 11 a.m. on Monday. Another possibility is Chris Morris from Margate, in England. Mr. Morris is a special guest on a panel on Tuesday afternoon. He may wish to stay over and speak in place of Mr. Arnett before flying back to England. Mr. Morris's number in England is 01843-386126."

"Be sure to call Mr. Arnett and tell him what arrangements you have made."

"Be sure to make the proper notations in the official copy of the program. It is necessary to write a confirmation letter to the person whose time is changed."

Note: When you called Mr. Epstein, he said he could not attend the seminar on Wednesday.

Before you place any calls, key or write a pre-plan for your calls. Record all essential information, such as names, phone numbers, dates, and times of day. Also record reminders about what you need to do after you have found someone who can trade times to speak with Mr. Arnett.

6-C Keying Messages

Supplies needed:

- *plain paper*

Mr. Wilson has a very busy week full of meetings with an international delegation that is visiting to discuss a new cybersecurity platform recently developed within the organization. The delegates are:

S. Abdalla from Egypt
C. Yoko from Japan
F. Schneider from Germany
J. O'Neill from Ireland

Throughout the week, you have a number of requests to interrupt the meetings. In each case, you key a message. Depending on the situation, you might take the message into the meeting and leave it with the appropriate person, or you might send a text message to his or her cell phone. Regardless, you key the text. If you want to give the guest a return phone number, be sure to provide the international access

code, country code, and city code when appropriate. Key messages for the following situations:

1. Tuesday, March 11 at 11:30 a.m.—You receive a call from Mrs. Yoko's son in Tokyo saying he needs to speak to his mother. When you tell him that she is engaged in a meeting, he says that his call is urgent and relates to his father's health. The phone number that shows on your electronic message system is 4314545.

2. Thursday, March 13 at 8:30 a.m.—You receive a call from the local Air Canada office regarding Ms. O'Neill's flight home to Dublin. Apparently, the flight has been cancelled and Air Canada is trying to reschedule people onto different flights. They are offering a flight out of Toronto tomorrow departing at 6:30 a.m. Because you know that she has an 8:00 a.m. meeting tomorrow, you suggested to the Air Canada agent that she needed a later flight. There is nothing available until Saturday evening at 8:30 p.m. The flight on Friday is direct, but the flight on Saturday goes to London where Ms. O'Neill will have to transfer to British Airways.

3. Thursday, March 13 at 12 noon—You receive a call from a Mr. Mohammed of North Africa in Cairo. This is the same company where Mr. Abdalla is the regional sales manager. He insists on telling Mr. Abdalla some very good news regarding a successful sale to one of the company's clients. He wants to talk to Mr. Abdalla immediately. The number showing on your electronic message is 1224557.

4. Friday, March 14 at 11:30 a.m.—A call is received, but you cannot understand the caller very well. He has a strong German accent. You believe he is requesting information regarding Mr. Schneider's flight arrangements. He has called twice leaving urgent messages. He tells you his number is 1445577.

6-D Scheduling Appointments

Supplies needed:

- *Mr. Wilson's appointment calendar, Form 6-D-1, Companion website*
- *administrative professional's appointment calendar, Form 6-D-2*
- *plain paper*

If you have access to an electronic calendar, perform the following challenge electronically. Otherwise, use the paper forms provided.

Mr. Wilson has been scheduling his own appointments. He uses a monthly paper calendar and crowds the appointments into the spaces. During a discussion with Mr. Wilson on Friday, he asked you to schedule his appointments for him.

You decided to use electronic appointment calendars—one for Mr. Wilson and one for yourself. Mr. Wilson has no appointments scheduled for Monday and only one for

Tuesday. He has the following appointments for Wednesday, August 6, entered in his monthly calendar:

- 10 a.m.—Pete Rollins, sales representative for PDI Inc. Toronto office, 416-741-2408
- 9 a.m.—Agnes Smith, sales representative from PDI Halifax office, 902-681-5432
- 11 a.m.—Joanna Hansen, manager of the Eastern Region of PDI Inc., and Jacob Rush, assistant vice president of marketing, Eastern Region
- 3 p.m.—Olivia Azam, assistant vice president of marketing, Western Region, to review marketing plans for fall
- 12 noon—Lunch with Ms. Hansen and Mr. Rush

You transfer these appointments to Mr. Wilson's daily calendar and yours.

On Tuesday, August 5, you receive the following telephone calls concerning appointments:

1. From Emma Yee, assistant vice president of marketing, Midwestern Region, saying that she must attend a funeral out of town on Wednesday. She has an appointment on Wednesday at 3 p.m. with O. C. Conners, president of Mapledale Homes, Inc., 905-872-1411. She asks if Mr. Wilson can see Mr. Conners for her at 3 p.m.

   Here is your response: "I'll try. Mr. Wilson has an appointment with Ms. Azam at 3 p.m. I'll see if I can move Ms. Azam's appointment to 2 p.m. I'll call you and let you know."

Later, you call Mrs. Yee and confirm that Mr. Wilson will see Mr. Conners at 3 p.m.

2. From Pete Rollins's assistant, saying that Mr. Rollins had an automobile accident, is hospitalized, and obviously cannot keep his appointment.

3. From Ray Rogers, co-chairman of the Eastern Region Sales Seminar, asking for an appointment on Wednesday to review plans for the November seminar. You suggest 10 a.m., and Mr. Rogers accepts.

4. From the Human Resources Department, asking Mr. Wilson to see a job applicant. You try to postpone this appointment, but the Human Resources Department insists that Mr. Wilson will want to meet this applicant while he is in the building on Wednesday. You schedule an appointment for Blake Horvath at 4 p.m.

Before leaving the office on Tuesday, you key Mr. Wilson's appointment schedule for Wednesday, August 6.

On Wednesday at 10:05 a.m., Jason Rhodes, a college friend from out of town, comes to the office for a brief visit with Mr. Wilson. You say you will schedule him for a few minutes between appointments at 10:45 a.m.

On his way to lunch, Mr. Wilson asks you to call the Lakeside Restaurant to tell the manager how many will be in his dinner party Wednesday evening. (Be sure to enter this in the reminder section of your calendar.)

Weblinks

Canadian Telephone Directories
www.Canada411.ca
Finding the names and addresses of people and businesses in Canada is made easy with this website. It offers more than 12 million listings, including postal codes, toll-free numbers, Yellow Pages, and City Guides in Canada.

Intelligent Office
www.intelligentoffice.com
This is the site of a company that offers virtual business assistance throughout North America. Informative videos explain how Intelligent Office works to provide remote reception and a complete line of administrative services to the businessperson on the go who does not need on-site office assistance.

Infobel
www.infobel.com
This is a site providing information on telephone directories worldwide.

Day-Timer
www.daytimer.com
This site includes Day-Timer's product information as well as articles with time management tips.

World Clock
www.timeanddate.com
The World Clock site allows you to determine the time in cities around the world.

Booking Calendar.com
www.bookingcalendar.com
On this site you will find one of many online calendar services that are offered for a fee as an alternative to application software such as Microsoft® Outlook.

Phone Etiquette
www.careerknowhow.com/ask_sue/officephon.htm
A weekly column about professionalism, etiquette, and problems in the workplace is featured on this site.

Chapter 7
Office Technology

Rawpixel.com/Shutterstock

LEARNING OUTCOMES

After completion of this chapter, the student will be able to:

1. Explain the importance of technology for industry, information flow, and the role of the administrative professional.

2. Identify types of digital computing devices, their capability, and usage.

3. Outline the input output format of computing.

4. Understand the importance of computer troubleshooting.

5. Examine various application software as it relates to industry and productivity.

6. Describe artificial intelligence (AI) and augmented reality (AR).

7. Develop a basic understanding of phone service capability and reprographics equipment.

Technology has an incredible impact on the way business performs. **Technology** refers to the application of information utilizing methods, devices, and systems to produce goods and complete task-based objectives. Emerging and evolving advancements continue to transform the role of the administrative professional. To ensure career and organizational success office professionals also need to keep up to date with new technological developments. Technology has revolutionized the way organizations conduct business by enabling business to level the playing field or move ahead based on the use and application of technology.

Changing technologies encompass new and innovative computer **hardware** and **peripherals** such as 3D printers as well as new and improved versions of application **software** that serve to improve productivity in the office and foster creativity. More importantly, office professionals are considered software experts, as they have the vested interest to know how this technology enhances productivity when used appropriately.

Office technology is acquired for many different purposes and may not be fully utilized in the contemporary office. Lack of utilization is often due to insufficient training, budget (to acquire the latest technology), or even time to learn the full extent of the technology's capability. It is the investment of time to learn the benefits of office technology that will eventually save you time with your tasks. This chapter explores a broad range of technologies, their application, and the potential productivity improvements they offer.

COMPUTER RESOURCES AND DIGITAL DEVICES

Computers are electronic devices capable of manipulating information, or data. They have the ability to store, retrieve, and process data at various rates of speed and capability.

Types of Computers

Consider the various types of computers from largest to smallest and their capability and usage.

Supercomputers   Supercomputers are those that perform at the highest operational rate currently possible for

---

Company Profile

Google

JHVEPhoto/Shutterstock

With over 60,000 employees worldwide and locations in over 50 countries, Google has always been a different kind of organization since its inception in a dorm room back in 1998. The first server used was formed out of Legos, affirming that this organizational approach was very different.

The founding goal for Google was to create an organization to improve the lives of as many people as possible through opportunity—opportunities to learn through their education division, opportunity to succeed, opportunity to be heard.

Google's products are countless and cover an extensive array of selections from their browsers, android apps, and analytic programs. Additionally, they boast an array of devices to support technological needs.

Google's mission involves making organization information available for everyone. Entrenched in their policies is a definite plan that supports their workforce, or googlers, as employees are referred. How they care for their employees is reflective of several core values. These include support for googlers and their family through a comprehensive benefit plans and extended parental leave. Google promotes healthy lifestyle approaches and choices for employees, offering on-site health and wellness facilities. It encourages a give-back approach within the team through community involvement and investment. Google encourages employees to take time for vacation, travel, and to unwind and relax when appropriate to be at their best to establish balance in their lives. Financial advisors are available to Google employers to ensure their financial fitness. Finally, lifelong learning opportunities are encouraged and offered for googlers.

Google boasts an inclusion-based employment policy whereby the company celebrates diversity as an equal opportunity employer. Google is determined to provide everyone the tools needed to develop and ensure digital well-being.

a computer. It is not simply a large and fast computer. The way a supercomputer processes information is unique, and it uses parallel processing instead of the serial processing that smaller computers use.

Mainframes   A mainframe is a computer working at a high rate of speed designed to support several smaller computers and peripherals.

Workstation/Personal   Computers (PCs) or **desktop computers** designed for use by one person at a time can be found at individual workstations in most offices. They are provided so that each member of that organization may share and distribute information and contribute to business goals.

Mobile Devices   Many office workers and business travellers will use a **laptop computer (notebook)** to retrieve and process information from the office, as it can offer 24/7 mobile computing; see Figure 7-1. Business professionals use the laptop computer at the office instead of a desktop PC. A businessperson can easily transport the laptop back and forth between offices, meetings, and home rather than having to manage a work file in the traditional capacity from the PC to a laptop or external storage for access at home.

Tablet Computers   A **tablet computer** is a portable personal computer equipped with a touch screen that has a virtual keyboard for data input in place of a traditional keyboard. Tablet computers are lightweight and smaller than typical laptops. A tablet, because of its wireless capability, offers significant flexibility in its usage.

Smartphones   A **smartphone** is a mobile phone that works on a mobile computing platform. These portable devices are much more than phones. They have built-in features such as cameras, music players, and global positioning systems (GPSs). Many smartphones have high-resolution touch screens and can access high-speed data using Wi-Fi (wireless fidelity) and mobile broadband technology. Application programming interfaces (APIs) allow smartphone users, depending on the operating system, to subscribe to third-party applications. For example, some of these applications allow users to track items they have shipped or to view and edit documents without a standard computer. Some additional features include the following:

- International data roam capabilities allow the traveller to stay connected with the office while out of the country without changing phones or phone numbers.
- Videoconferencing capability apps allow for face-to-face shared time utilizing the video feature of the phone to transmit and communicate at a distance with people over sharing digital screens.
- Instant messenger or text messaging allows users to send messages, images, attachments, and video clips to other phones.

Figure 7-2 shows a standard appearance of a smartphone. The laptop computer has many advantages over the desktop computer. Not only is it portable, but it offers the user the flexibility to **sign on** from locations remote to the workplace. Almost every laptop has wireless capability and requires only a location that provides wireless service. Many hotels provide wireless internet access in their guest rooms. Airports commonly offer wireless internet access, allowing business travellers to stay in touch with their offices. Access might be available throughout the airport or might be restricted to specified areas such as a designated room or waiting area.

FIGURE 7-2 Smartphones like this are handheld PCs designed to provide business people with remote access to their workplace computers.

FIGURE 7-1 Common digital devices (laptop, tablet, and smartphone).

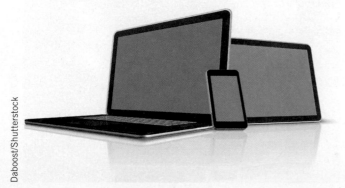

FIGURE 7-3 Input, processing, and output concept.

Gabor2100/Shutterstock · Indigolotos/123RF · Denis Tabler/Shutterstock

Computer Basic Functions

The amount of unique terminology surrounding computer technology is immense, but basic functions and vocabulary are useful to learn for simple communication purposes. Refer to Figure 7-3 for the visual concept of the following descriptions.

Central Processing Unit Commonly thought of as the brain of the computer, the **central processing unit (CPU)** is a **microprocessor chip**. The commercial computer was made possible in 1971 by the introduction of a silicon chip that was smaller than a dime and contained 2250 transistors. Chips today contain the equivalent of millions of transistors and can be found in many forms throughout the computer and its peripherals.

It is the CPU that seeks and interprets instructions from programs temporarily stored in **memory**. Based on its interpretation of the program instructions, the CPU directs all other functions of the computer, including the timing of **input** and **output** data. The CPU interprets millions of instructions and directions each second.

Input External information must be provided to the computer's central processing unit in a form that it can understand. Specially designed input devices change a keystroke or a **mouse** "click" into a computer-understandable form. Commonly used input devices are the **keyboard**, mouse, and **printer** used as a document scanner; see Figure 7-4. Other "input" may come from an externally connected PC, smartphone, or digital camera.

Output Various means of retrieving information from a computer are used, but you will be most familiar with the video **display** terminal (VDT) and printer. VDTs are more commonly known as **monitors** or screens and essentially display the information processed by the computer. Similarly, the printer displays a permanent, or printed, version of the information from the computer. There is no output until the computer is instructed to display, print, or send it to another peripheral. Smartphones may serve as another input and output device when the user is synchronizing with other devices.

Operating Systems The **operating system** gives fundamental operating instructions to the computer. It contains a number of internal **commands** needed to operate the computer. The operating system must be loaded into the computer's memory *before* **application programs** such as Word or Excel because the operating system is what enables the application program to make full use of the computer.

The application program must be **compatible** with the operating system of the computer. For example, Microsoft Windows is an operating system in which most common application programs that are **Windows** compatible can run; it is used widely in Canada. Mac OS is an operating system developed by Apple Inc. and installed on all Apple Mac computers sold.

Internal Memory This is the place where information and the instructions that tell the CPU what to do with the information are stored. There are two types of internal memory. One type is **random-access memory (RAM)**, also known as main memory. It is the primary memory in which information is held when being processed. Any data stored in RAM is lost when the computer is shut down.

Read-only memory (ROM) is the other form of internal memory that is used when **processing** information. It is used

FIGURE 7-4 Document scanner.

Sylvie Bouchard/Shutterstock

to store items that the computer needs in order to run when it is first turned on or booted up when a program such as Word is used. ROM is permanent and is not lost when the computer shut down.

External Memory In order to retain data created when using the computer and that must be kept permanently or for a period of time (e.g., a Word document), the data must be saved to an external memory device. Examples of external memory devices include the following:

- **Hard disk drive** (usually housed within the computer unit but sometimes outside). Some businesses choose to back up their critical files using external removable drives. The typical external drive usually connects via a USB port with plug-and-play capability. Data storage capacity of the hard drive varies substantially and evolves constantly to greater capacity.

- USB (universal serial bus) **flash drives** (sometimes called pen drives or memory keys). Flash drives plug into, or out of, any USB port on your computer. The miniaturized technology used in flash drives enables this wafer-sized device to provide permanent **removable storage** space. Once information has been copied from the computer and stored on the flash drive, it can be transported easily. Administrative professionals find the flash drive convenient for transporting selective information from workstation to workstation, or simply for backing up critical data.

A popular alternative for document data storage is cloud computing. Users access cloud-based applications through a web browser, allowing them to store and share documents. Individual users' data can be stored on servers at remote locations. Users can synchronize their mobile devices to gain access to and update their documents.

Web-enabled devices, when appropriately connected, allow users to communicate with each other and with a mainframe server **online**. Administrative professionals are among those who communicate with mainframe servers to obtain more information than is available on the local PC alone. Computers with secure access to online functionality through a coaxial cable connected to workstations is referred to as **broadband** connectivity. Signals are transmitted digitally to permit high-speed connection.

Several users may request information from the mainframe server at the same time. In theory, each user makes a request to the mainframe server quite independently, but due to the high speed of the mainframe server, it appears that all users obtain their requested information back simultaneously. This functionality is called **time-sharing**.

The online capability that provides instantaneous updating of data is known as real-time transaction processing. Updating takes place as the transaction happens. Commercial airlines' use of computer terminals for making airline reservations is one well-known example of time-sharing and real-time transactions.

With an online database or inventory control system, the inventory balance is immediately available. A sales representative in a remote branch office can enter an order directly into the home office computer. An executive or administrative professional can request desired data from remote computer files and receive an instantaneous response. The administrative professional will rely on it as an effective means of communication. For instance, if a customer calls about the status of his or her account, the administrative professional can consult the computer and obtain virtually instantaneous information for the customer. The process is so seamless that the user is not conscious that the information is retrieved from a remote source.

Networking Computers

Many organizations use **local area networks (LANs)** for connecting their internal computers. LANs by design not only provide a means of communication between users of computers but also facilitate the sharing of common documents, hardware, and software.

LANs typically connect computers that are in the same area. The computers are connected by fibre optic or coaxial cable (to permit higher transmission speeds) or by simple telephone cable. For enhanced capabilities, LANs commonly connected to a mainframe computer. LANs also can be connected to other **networks**, such as a metropolitan area network (MAN), which, as the name implies, provides networking facilities within a town or city. In much the same way, a **wide area network (WAN)** provides networking facilities over a yet wider area (perhaps an entire country, or even the entire world).

Campus area network (CAN) Larger than LANs, these types of networks are typically seen in colleges, universities, or businesses. This network is spread across several buildings close to each other so users can share resources.

Storage area network (SAN) A high-speed network connects shared groups of storage devices to several servers. This type of network does not depend on a LAN or WAN. Alternatively, organizations migrate storage resources away from the network and place them into their own network.

Wireless local area networks (WLAN) Originally developed by a consortium of companies including IBM, Intel, Nokia, Toshiba, and Microsoft, Bluetooth™ is considered short-range communication technology that replaces the cables connecting office computer hardware and peripherals while maintaining high levels of security. Offices can become virtually wireless by investing in Bluetooth-enabling products and turning on, or enabling, the Bluetooth technology that is integrated into the products. Bluetooth is not a wireless service that you purchase but, rather, is integrated into products by the manufacturer. In order for two devices to communicate wirelessly using Bluetooth, both must have the Bluetooth technology integrated and enabled. Laptops can communicate with printers, desktop PCs with laptops, and smartphones with office hardware over short distances without unsightly cables. This is especially advantageous in open offices, where wires can be an eyesore and a safety issue, and in small working areas such as work cubicles. There are also long-range Wi-Fi network capabilities available, as well as point-to-point communication.

Accessing the networks, an administrative professional can do the following:

1. Communicate with other employees through electronic mail.

2. Send draft copies of documents to individuals for validation or correction before committing them to final form.

3. Route a document for approval both sequentially and electronically.

4. Collaborate with several personnel on a single document or report.

5. Conduct **virtual** meetings.

6. Use the server as a common space where data can be saved and shared with authorized users.

Self-Check

1. List two input devices.
2. What does an operating system do?
3. Explain internal memory versus external memory.
4. What is Bluetooth technology?

COMPUTERS IN THE OFFICE

The Versatile Computer

When computers became an integral part of the office, they were used for word processing more than for any other application. As the speed and versatility of computers increased, so did the number of uses found for them.

Over time, varieties of new software versions and apps have emerged for word processing and many other document-creation tools. Each new release is an improvement on what was previously available. Also, computer hardware is continually being improved. This continual improvement model has leveraged computer devices as an essential tool in the office environment.

The computer's versatility is apparent in the range of software now available for business use: software to manage **spreadsheets**, graphics, electronic presentations, file and information management, telecommunications, accounting, and **desktop publishing (DTP)**. As well, your reliance on the speedy output of computers for decision making will increase as you begin to need it for tasks such as budgeting, scheduling, and general planning.

The computer is a powerful tool for productivity. Managers rely on computers for planning production, monitoring and controlling processes, and data. The administrative professional who has learned how to analyze and interpret data will also be an invaluable asset to any organization that employs advanced processes.

Artificial Intelligence (AI)

Artificial intelligence (AI) is revolutionizing the way humans interact with computers and technology. In a basic form, voice-activated devices provide information based on human command. This capability can find a local business supplier, prepare to-do lists and research various web-based information to facilitate information gathering and assessment. AI is possible because of mass distribution internet-connected devices, which generate huge amounts of data, cloud computing, and software algorithms that can recognize patterns within data and return information to the user. This allows the end user to appear smarter and work smarter. Imagine the support provided when completing a research report for an employer. Facial recognition capability is another stream and direction within AI. For more advanced features, consider how AI supports business initiatives in some of these ways:

- Source media specific to user preference.
- Prepare reports with relevant and current data.
- Help with marketing and product branding.
- Support decision making based on big data access.
- Protect confidential data.
- Act as your own virtual assistant.
- Improve productivity.

Artificial Intelligence Apps

Apps developed utilizing AI have exploded in industry and flooded the market in recent years. Some examples include:

1. **Cortana®.** Developed by Microsoft for Windows. With Cortana, a user can schedule a meeting and the application will do the rest. It will search the internet for information, send emails, and more.

2. **Hound.** A user can use Hound by speaking and get the results displayed almost immediately. With the app, a user can activate the app by saying, "OK Hound." Hound offers many features such as listening to music or video playback.

3. **Elsa.** This is an application to help with English pronunciation and translation. It will ask users their native

language and coach a user from that point forward to build skills. If someone is travelling to do business, it could greatly assist in communication processes.

4. **Google Assistant.** This is a personal assistant type app that helps with meeting objectives and tasks. It has a smart reply feature for message return.

Augmented Reality (AR)

Another developing technology is **augmented reality (AR)**. It is a direct or indirect live view of a physical, real environment, whose elements are available to view by computer-generated information. Businesses can set out virtual reality ability for someone with a specialized app to take a 3D tour of their office space. Retail AR apps can enable customers to try on an article of clothing without having to travel to a retail outlet—they can virtually try on clothes using their computer or smartphone. Augmented reality apps include programs such as the following:

1. **Google Translate.** Using this app, an individual can have a full conversation with someone who does not speak the same language. It can translate handwriting as well.

2. **My Augmented Reality.** This helps the users trace back to parts of a city or landmarks they have not yet visited. It is not the same as GPS. It allows you to geotag places you want to visit.

3. **Star Walk 2.** This app allows you to use your smartphone and position it to the sky. All the stars and constellations will be in full view on the phone screen.

Computer Troubleshooting

When working in a computer-based environment, it is inevitable that some challenges will arise. It is beneficial to understand some basic troubleshooting techniques to alleviate frustration and maintain productivity. Troubleshooting a computer problem involves knowing how to isolate the problem and then possibly fixing it. In an organization, it might not always be practical or cost-efficient to contact a technician when you have a computer problem. Knowing the basics of troubleshooting will save time and frustration. Consider these recommendations:

■ Always check your computer cables if you are having connectivity issues. Many issues originate when a cable or cord is unplugged or simply loose. A problem like the computer monitor not turning on might easily be due to a loose cable.

■ Use the process of elimination. Make of list of everything you have checked and ruled out as the potential problem.

■ When programs are running slowly, try closing and restarting the program. Check for any updates for the program.

---

pro-Link
Learning Lingo

Confused by computer terminology? Here are basic descriptions of commonly used terms to put computer information terminology in perspective:

■ A **directory** is a way to organize information. In your computer system, a directory contains a group of related files separated from other directories by a unique name. A familiar everyday example is the Yellow Pages telephone directory. Directories are also known as *catalogues* or *folders*.

■ A **file** is a related collection of *records*. For example, you might keep a record on each of your customers in a file.

■ A **record** consists of *fields* of individual data items, such as customer name, customer number, and customer address. A customer record contains all details of the customer.

■ A **field** is an area within a record that has a fixed size. By providing the same *information* in the same fields in each record (so that all records are consistent), the customer file may be easily used by a computer program.

■ **Information** is synonymous with *data*. Data are information translated into a form that is more convenient to manipulate by computers. It is often referred to in terms of *bits* and *bytes*.

■ A **bit** is the smallest unit of data in a computer. A bit has a single binary value, either 0 or 1. In most computer systems, there are eight bits in a byte.

■ A **byte** is a unit of information that is eight bits long. A byte is the unit most computers use to represent one character, such as a letter, number, or symbol.

■ A **kilobyte** means approximately 1000 (1 K) bytes or characters.

■ A **megabyte** refers to 1 000 000 (1 M) bytes.

■ A **gigabyte** refers to 1 000 000 000 (1 G) bytes.

■ A **terabyte** refers to 1 000 000 000 000 (1 T) bytes.

■ When a program is unresponsive, try using the task manager to end it. (In Windows systems, you can open the task manager by pressing the ctrl, alt, and delete keys and then selecting the task manager.)

■ Check computer or software manuals, as they may offer a solution to a problem.

■ Finally, if you can't resolve the problem, make a note of any error messages and follow up with a technician. Know who to call in this situation.

Accuracy of Input Information

People are familiar with the expression, "Garbage in, garbage out" (or **GIGO**). This expression is particularly significant when applied to the use of computers.

The usefulness of output information from the computer is only as good as the accuracy of the input information. Accuracy and completeness of the input information, or data, are key to obtaining accurate results. If the user provides inaccurate or incomplete input data to the computer, inaccurate or incomplete output data will result.

Consider for a moment the speed at which a computer processes information (typically millions of instructions each second). Inaccurate input data are processed and distributed so rapidly that the results may create long-term and difficult-to-correct problems. If an address is entered incorrectly, it will impact reports generated and documents created. In company terms, such problems have the potential to negatively affect the customer or financial records on which the company's survival depends.

Data input is sourced from documents. Source documents include orders, invoices, incoming cheques, time cards, and sales tickets. Source documents are assembled in originating departments and then submitted for processing. Regardless of where the data entry specialist is located, the originating department is responsible for ensuring the accuracy and completeness of the source documents before turning them over to the data entry specialist. Similarly, the data entry specialist is responsible for accurately entering source documents into the computer.

Do everything you can to decrease errors in source document information. If errors are detected, keep a record of the following:

- frequency of errors
- types of errors that occur

- originator(s) of the errors

Analyze the problem to determine how to do the following:

- Decrease the frequency of errors.
- Eliminate errors altogether.
- Improve the process.

Your responsibility as an employee and your role as an administrative professional include both preventing problems and attempting to resolve those that do occur. If the internal or external customer who has been a victim of a "computer error" calls you, be attentive to that customer's position. Demonstrate your commitment to customer support and your willingness to help correct the problem. Customer follow-up is exercised any time there is an inconvenienced or dissatisfied customer. For the sake of retaining the customer's investment, a written response or telephone call should be made by an appropriate company representative.

Using Computer Storage

The promise of going paperless in specific businesses is still a dream. Many are hopeful that paper files will gradually be replaced by computer-based and computer-assisted filing systems. These systems use media that require much less space than traditional paper files and storage systems. For the near future in industry, paper is here to stay; but a variety of information technology-based storage media options are now available to hold the use of paper in check and support environmental sustainability. Typically, the choice of medium will depend on availability and your specific requirements. Figure 7-5 provides a practical guide to computer-based storage media; it illustrates

FIGURE 7-5 Relative capacities of computer-based storage.

COMPUTER BASED	CAPACITY*	APPROXIMATE EQUIVALENT IN FULL PAGES OF TEXT	IMAGE
Optical disks OD	25 Gigabytes	10 800 000	Langdu/Shutterstock
Pen drive flash memory	2 Gigabytes	540 000 000	Dslaven/Shutterstock
Hard (disk) drive	1 Terabyte	270 000 000 000	Faraways/Shutterstock

*In operation, 10% to 15% of the capacity of each medium would be used for directory and page-formatting information.

FIGURE 7-6 Online data storage options.

SERVICE	STORAGE CAPACITY
Microsoft OneDrive	5GB, 50GB, 1TB
Dropbox	2GB to With 1 TB (1000 GB)
Apple iCloud Drive	50GB, 200GB, 2TB
Google Drive	100GB, 1TB, 10TB, 20TB, 30TB

capacities of external computer-based storage and the approximate equivalence in full pages of text.

Both information access and retrieval speed are dramatically improved by computer-based and computer-assisted filing systems. However, the fact that those systems are susceptible to loss or damage is a definite disadvantage; the loss of information on one flash drive or OD could result in lost hours or even weeks of work. Consequently, making a **backup** copy of your information and storing information in two places are essential. Figure 7-6 provides examples of online cloud-based data storage options, which often prove more reliable than traditional storage methods.

Self-Check

1. List two steps to take when troubleshooting a computer problem.
2. What is cloud-based storage, and why would it be beneficial?

APPLICATION PROGRAMS

Application programs, often referred to collectively as application *software*, are written to perform specific tasks such as word processing, spreadsheet production, graph and/or desktop publishing, and information management. Electronic mail usually requires its own special application program such as Outlook, a comprehensive time manager, calendar, and email application from Microsoft.

Word Processing

In most organizations, document creation and editing is one of the main administrative responsibilities. Expert navigation skills utilizing word processing software are essential for productivity. In a more detailed overview, word processing may include creating, editing, storing, printing, and even transmitting documents to others within or outside the organization. Remember that the goals of organizations that install text-editing equipment are to increase productivity and to improve communication.

Input for Word Processing　Information in its original form is called **raw data**. Raw data for word processing can be obtained from any of the following sources:

- keyed data
- form letters or documents—the author of text material dictates the variables (addresses, dates, amounts of money, etc.)
- flash drives
- optical disks
- document scanners (using an optical character reader)
- voice input

The flash drive or OD containing stored material must be compatible not only with the equipment being used but with the data itself. The data must be in—or converted to—the correct format for the word processing application in use.

A document scanner reads printed material previously keyed with a font style the scanner can recognize. As the keyed material is scanned, it is transferred to the memory of the computer.

Computer **voice-recognition software** converts recognizable voice input into computer data and presents it to the word processor as text.

Impact of Word Processing　The use of word processing has resulted in improved document accuracy and a decrease in the time needed to produce documents. Document originators are no longer reluctant to make revisions when they know that the entire document does not need rekeying.

Administrative professionals enjoy working with word processing applications because most mundane tasks are eliminated. Word processing software can, for example, establish margins and tabs, paginate, assemble a table of contents, and tabulate endnotes and footnotes. Recent versions of Microsoft Word convert typed lists of items seamlessly into attractive graphic representations of the data using the SmartArt feature. One result might be a professional-looking organization chart showing the hierarchy of employees in an organization. Merging variable information such as names and addresses with form letters is known as **mail merge** and is one of the most valuable word processing features that support the tasks of the administrative professional. The administrative professional can key and store the variables to be merged; the system can then produce hundreds of letters while the administrative professional is focused on another task.

Advanced word processing features allow administrative professionals to compare documents side by side, create tables of contents, translate documents, and produce brochures, sales bulletins, and other documents with a variety of headings, columns, graphics, and designs to standards that come close to matching those of professional printing companies.

You will need to plan your work carefully in order to increase your productivity. Be sure to save what you have keyed. When you work with revisions, make sure that what is to be moved, deleted, added, or changed is clearly marked on the hard-copy draft. Make sure that if you saved the original data in two versions, you avoid accidentally retrieving and using unrevised data at a later date. You need to understand and use proofreaders' marks. The appendix illustrates the most commonly used proofreaders' marks. Data and file management are essential in this capacity.

Spreadsheets

Spreadsheet applications—simply called spreadsheets—are computer programs that enable you to create and manipulate the numbers in a spreadsheet electronically. In a spreadsheet application, each number occupies a *cell*. You can define what type of number is in each cell and how different cells depend on one another. This defined relationship between cells is called a "formula," and the names of cells are called *labels*.

Once you have defined the cells and the formulas for linking them together, you can enter your numbers. You can then modify your numbers to see how all the other related numbers change accordingly. This enables you to study various "what-if" scenarios. See Figure 7-7 for a typical spreadsheet window.

A simple example of a useful spreadsheet application is one that calculates loan payments for a car. You would define five cells:

1. total cost of the car
2. deposit
3. interest rate
4. term of the loan
5. monthly payment

Once you define how these five cells depend on one another, you could enter numbers and play with various possibilities. There are several spreadsheet applications available, Excel and Quattro Pro being the most popular. The more powerful spreadsheet applications provide graphic features that enable you to produce sophisticated charts and graphs from the data.

Desktop Publishing

Desktop publishing (DTP) is the process of using your computer to develop and print professional-looking literature, a task that was once the exclusive domain of professional printers. Some desktop publishing can be achieved by using word-processing applications, but the special visual and printing features of DTP software allow you to develop a more professional look for your design.

Desktop publishing is best done with a computing device, special desktop publishing software (Microsoft Publisher or Adobe Illustrator, for example), and a high-quality printer. With this combination, you can combine text and graphics to produce documents such as newsletters, brochures, books, and graphic advertisements.

Desktop publishing software is an excellent tool for the administrative professional to create visual communications for the office. However, training on this software environment is invariably required for optimal use.

Importance of Learning Desktop Publishing
Mastering the skill of desktop publishing benefits the administrative professional in a number of significant ways.

FIGURE 7-7 An active spreadsheet.

Courtesy of Microsoft Corporation

	Date	Receipt No.	Details	Amount
1	Cash receipts and payments for Commerce Department - ESA			
2			Cash Receipts	
3	Date	Receipt No.	Details	Amount
4	06-Feb-20	1	Industry of Technology	$5,000
5	12-Feb-20	2	Cash from Al Thomas General Trading & Real Estate Ltd.	$2,000
6	27-Feb-20	3	Cheque from National Bank	$1,000
7	16-Mar-20	4	Cheque from NOC	$6,000
8	21-Mar-20	5	Cheque from Arthue Smith	$3,000
9	22-Mar-20	6	Cheque from General Petroleum Corporation	$5,000
10	05-Apr-20	7	Cheque from National Bank	$1,500
11	10-Apr-20	8	Cheque from Habtoor Co (LLC)	$2,400
12			TOTAL	$25,900

Here are seven benefits:

1. DTP allows the user to exercise creative skills. A great deal of personal satisfaction is derived in this way. DTP brings enjoyment to what might have been a mundane task.

2. DTP increases the effectiveness of the document. The professional appearance will attract attention and increase credibility.

3. Illustrations and charts can be added to documents without difficulty. These deliver the message more clearly than words alone.

4. The turnaround time is shorter when documents are produced in-house. Before desktop publishing, professional-looking documents could only be produced by sending the project out to a typesetter.

5. Professional documents can be prepared at a lower cost when the administrative professional can produce them in-house.

6. Individuals who master the art of desktop publishing will have a competitive edge when applying for administrative assistant positions. Desktop publishing is an advanced skill, and one that will impress prospective employers.

7. Administrative professionals who are adept at desktop publishing have greater career opportunities. Employers seek administrative assistants who have diverse software training.

Presentation Software

Oral or written presentations accompanied by visual representation of information in the form of charts and graphs are more quickly and easily absorbed and understood than when presented in written or verbal form only. Augmenting a speech or an oral presentation with graphics and charts created using **electronic presentation software** is considered routine practice in the workplace. The administrative professional will be required to convert an outline of a speech into a digital format using presentation software such as Microsoft PowerPoint or the online platform Prezi. The application software is used to prepare a digital slideshow of the main points of a speech and incorporate graphics, illustrations, and graphs to enhance the audience's understanding of the material. Animation, music, and sound effects, as well as video clips, can be added to the presentation for additional emphasis. See the example provide in Figure 7-8.

Integrating Application Software

As an administrative professional, you will be expected to create spreadsheets using spreadsheet software, create business documents using word processing software, and create electronic presentations using electronic presentation software. But, more than that, you will also be expected to have expertise in **integrating application software**, that

FIGURE 7-8 Electronic presentation software enhances the oral presentation.

Kzenon/Shutterstock

is, connecting data created in one software program (e.g., Excel) with another (e.g., PowerPoint) in its original form. For example, you might be asked to create a spreadsheet in Microsoft Excel that shows estimated quarterly sales profits for the year. You might then be required to create a digital presentation that would include a slide containing that spreadsheet in its Excel form. This can be done by either embedding or linking (hyperlinking) the original spreadsheet to the presentation. When there is a hyperlink created between the spreadsheet and the electronic presentation, if the values in the original spreadsheet cells are changed, they will be updated automatically in the electronic presentation when it is next activated. This automated feature can save valuable time, and being skilled in using those advanced software features will increase your value to the organization.

Increasing Your Productivity

After completing an administrative program, you will possess skills in accurate keying and word processing, and you will be familiar with application programs for spreadsheets, digital presentations, and desktop publishing. You may also have skills in information management, project management, and accounting applications. The job-ready technical skills are foundational, and additional ongoing opportunities to learn more on the job is present. Be receptive to the opportunities and challenges that come your way. Accept change readily.

Learn new computer applications. Develop a plan for improving and maintaining your technical skills. Take advantage of in-house training sessions. Study manuals, read technical magazines, and attend night classes. Continually search for ways that the computer helps to support task management.

The speed with which the computer handles information will enable you to be more productive. Master the flow of information in and out of your office. Plan your work carefully; set priorities. Use spare time to think, to listen to customers' needs, to communicate, to apply critical thinking to solve problems, and to be creative.

PHONE TECHNOLOGY

Office phone systems have remained about the same for the last several years. A physical Private Branch Exchange (PBX) hardware system is installed somewhere in the office and lines are connected from the local phone service provider. The PBX hardware creates the different extensions as well as traditional office phone features such as voicemail and call transfers between extensions.

Voice over internet protocol (VoIP) technology and high-speed internet connections are becoming the norm in new offices set up across Canada.

Telecommunications is a term used to describe sending information over a distance. This can include not only telephone communications but also fax transmissions, radio, and television.

Today, almost all phone systems are digital. The advantage of digital service is that it doesn't require wires dedicated for use on your phone system. It usually utilizes the internet to send voice signals. VoIP enables people to make voice and video calls over an internet connection. VoIP is sometimes referred to as IP Telephony, or internet protocol telephone system. This type of service can greatly reduce the cost of calls, especially international calls, since VoIP not only provides inexpensive call rates but also allows users on the same network to make free calls. To set up and use VoIP communications, one must have an internet connection and VoIP-provider software.

Interconnect Equipment

Interconnect equipment is the term used to refer to phone equipment that organizations purchase or lease from suppliers other than the phone companies. The manufacturers of phone interconnect equipment have placed new switchboards and other equipment with hundreds of features on the market.

Most of the new features of modern phone systems are controlled at the central office (previously known as the *telephone exchange*), usually owned by the local telephone company. These modern (electronic) digital exchanges replaced old mechanical equipment at the central office and are program-controlled, offering users a variety of services. These are collectively known as **call management services** and include features such as:

- displaying the caller's number on your telephone

- forwarding your call to another number when you are busy or away from your desk

- having the telephone system monitor a busy number and inform you when that number becomes free

Other call management features can enhance your telephone effectiveness:

- A special button feature will allow the administrative professional to speed dial a predefined number.

- A previously dialled number may be redialled by pressing a single designated key.

- A list of names and/or numbers may be stored in the electronic memory of most contemporary telephones for convenient recall and dialling.

Many more phone features are gaining popularity as enhancements to productivity: bilingual displays, built-in cameras or visual displays to communicate with callers, and supplemental features such as lightweight headsets that enable the user to work hands-free; see Figure 7-9.

Wireless Phones

Wireless telephone service (commonly called mobile phone service) provides mobile communication. This phone network uses radio waves rather than telephone wires to transmit messages. However, mobile telephone users may communicate

FIGURE 7-9 A lightweight headset containing a miniaturized mouthpiece allows the administrative assistant to communicate with hands free.

Racorn/123RF

with conventional phone users, since wireless systems interconnect with local and long-distance telephone networks.

Mobile phone users can take advantage of most of the features offered to regular phone users, including voice mail. Technology has enabled owners to use cell phones as remote internet terminals, digital cameras, and global positioning system (GPS) receivers.

Phone Messages

Organizations often make arrangements for the phone to be answered after regular business hours or when it is inconvenient for employees to answer the telephone. Commonly used systems are automatic recording machines, answering services, and voice mail.

Digital Recording   With a phone recording system, a user can turn on a recorded message at the end of the business day. The message may tell callers when the office will be open and invite the callers to leave their number or a message. Sometimes, customers are encouraged to place orders at night through a system that enables automated recording. Recently, advances have allowed these messages to be transferred to the intended party by way of appearing in the emailing listing as a playable audio recording for playback and response.

Voice Mail   Voice mail (VM) is by far the most popular form of phone messaging system in use today. In fact, it is essential. From a technological point of view, VM is a computer-based system that processes incoming and outgoing telephone calls by converting speech patterns into digital data, which are then stored and manipulated in the computer.

Hardware for VM systems may be independently purchased and programmed for the organization that intends to use it. Alternatively, the local phone service provider may provide adequate VM.

THE WEB

The most popular means of communicating and researching information is the internet, or the information superhighway. The internet is a public global communications network that enables people to exchange information through a computer.

Internet Networking

In its simplest form, the web is a global network of computer-based information available to anyone with a computer, a modem, and a subscription to an Internet Service Provider (ISP). More accurately, the internet is a network of networks with international telecommunications facilities connecting them.

The telecommunications data network that links the internet together employs **routers**, devices that route information from one network to another. Routers allow independent networks to function as a large **virtual network** so that users of any network can reach users of any other.

While there are many private commercial computer networks, the internet is the largest collection of networks in the world.

Unlike traditional voice or data networks, there is no charge for the long-distance component of the internet. There is also no charge for exchanging information on the internet. However, internet providers will charge users a fee for the local connection to the internet.

Uses for the Internet

What can you do with the internet? Some of the main basic activities that people participate in on the internet are as follows:

1. **Sending and receiving text.** Email or digital text can be addressed to another internet user anywhere on the global network.

2. **Transferring data files.** Data file transfers allow internet users to access remote computers and retrieve programs or text.

3. **Joining newsgroups.** A newsgroup is a collection of users who exchange news and debate issues of interest.

4. **Using social media.** Users of social networks such as Facebook interact through various media, including email and instant messaging. Sharing of photographs and videos, as well as posting messages on other users' pages, are popular activities. Social networks can be used as a marketing tool for business. Personal use of social networks is often frowned on in the workplace due to the distraction factor and, by extension, the loss of productivity.

5. **Performing remote computing.** Those programmers and scientists who need the power of remote computers, or those who need to tap into large information databases, do remote computing.

6. **Researching topics of interest.** Students and business professionals alike research topics of interest. Clearly, the internet supplements more familiar resources, such as books and periodicals.

7. **Conducting ecommerce.** These activities focus on buying and selling products on the internet.

Collectively, these seven basic activities provide a vast and rich resource for the administrative assistant. Office productivity is directly influenced by such activities as email, research, information feeds, the delivery of large document files, and office commerce. The resulting influence of the internet has enabled greater office productivity.

In addition to the seven basic internet activities already discussed, the following activities are also popular in the business world.

Webcasting (or Netcasting)   Webcasting (or netcasting) is broadcasting live or recorded audio and/or video transmissions via computer. For example, a business might record a videotape of a news release to be aired as a webcast at a designated time simultaneously on several media websites. Similarly, your local TV channel will likely record, and make accessible via the internet, webcasts of its news broadcasts. This will enable the public to "watch the news" at their convenience.

Web Conferencing   Using web conferencing software, employees can take part in real-time conferencing via the internet from their own computers, much as they would take part in teleconferencing via their own office telephones. In some instances, access to the conference gained using downloaded application software, either free or purchased through a vendor. See Chapter 8 for more information.

USING REPROGRAPHICS

The term **reprographics** refers to reproduction processes from the highest-quality **offset printing** to the simplest photocopying. The reprographics industry produces a vast array of high-tech products; however, the reprographics equipment most often used by administrative assistants is a copier. For this reason, the following discussion will focus on copiers only.

Copiers

In its simplest form, a copier is used to reproduce exact copies of original documents. At the other end of the spectrum, a copier will also do the following:

- Act as a fully active unit in the office network so it can receive documents and instructions directly from all office computers.
- Act as a multifunctional device permitting scanning and faxing of documents through the office network.
- Format a document from a computer file so the end product is in book format with adjusted headers, footers, margins, and page numbers.
- Print in colour so well that the copy looks just like the original.
- Print and bind the document so it has the professional appearance of a brochure or booklet.
- **Duplex** the document—that is, print on both sides of the paper.
- Staple and hole-punch the papers.
- Enlarge or decrease the size of the document.
- Use a variety of sizes, weights, and qualities of paper.

The list goes on. Copiers are classified as low-, mid-, and high-volume machines. The differences between categories are evident in the following discussion.

Personal Low-Volume Copiers   Low-volume copying machines, called **convenience copiers** or personal copiers, are mostly used in home offices, small businesses, or in decentralized areas to save the user travel time. These compact copiers have numerous features. Low-volume copiers can do the following:

- Be networked into the office system for two to four users.
- Receive documents and instructions directly from computers.
- Print in good-quality colour.
- Reduce and enlarge documents.
- Accommodate a variety of paper sizes.
- Automatically feed documents.
- Print 15–25 pages per minute.

Low-volume copiers used in small businesses are often multifunctional units that include any of the following features: fax, copier, printer, and/or scanner; see Figure 7-10.

Mid-Volume Copiers   Mid-volume copiers have all the features of the low-volume copiers, along with some additional features. Most mid-volume copiers are appropriate for 5 to 20 users and can do the following:

- Operate through touch control screens.
- Accommodate more paper sizes and weights.
- Store multiple instructions.
- Print in high-quality colour.
- Sort and stack multiple copies.
- Staple and hole-punch documents.

FIGURE 7-10 A combination fax, copier, and scanner.

Supertrooper/Shutterstock

- Bind documents into book-style covers.
- Centre an image on the paper.
- Print 36–55 pages per minute.

High-Volume Copiers With all that low- and mid-volume copiers can do, is there more that high-volume copiers can handle? High-volume copiers (see Figure 7-10) are appropriate for 20 or more users and can:

- Produce documents in book format with adjusted headers, footers, margins, and page numbers.
- Hold large supplies of paper.
- Sort at faster speeds.
- Insert tabs and coversheets where programmed to do so.
- Print in colour with even better quality.
- Produce 95–105 pages per minute.

How to Select a Copier

Given all the available features, how do you select the right office copier for your office needs? To begin, determine your current and future needs. Collecting input from the people who use the office copier would be a good way to find out the needs of the office. See Figure 7-11 depicting a high volume copier.

To find the office copier needs.

1. Form a group of people who use the office copier.
2. Together, create a survey that will solicit information about current and future copier needs.
3. Give the survey to everyone who uses the copier.
4. Collect the surveys and collate the data.

Find the Right Vendor Once you know your requirements, it is time to talk to the right vendor in order to find the right product.

1. Ask other people who have recently purchased or leased copiers what vendor they recommend.
2. Research products and vendors through the internet, newspapers, etc., to determine what products and vendors appeal to you.
3. Contact vendors and set up appointments to view their products.
4. During appointments, share the results of your survey with the sales representatives.
5. Keep in mind that it is the sales representative's job to help you solve your problem—the problem of finding the right copier for your office.
6. Get more than just a sales demonstration. Try the equipment yourself.

FIGURE 7-11 High-volume copier.

Maksym Bondarchuk/Shutterstock

Find the Right Service When you think you have found the right equipment, you're not finished. The company must be prepared to provide the best service, too. What should you look for in service?

- The machine should have a warranty that covers all parts and labour for at least one full year.
- There must be a service agreement that includes routine maintenance calls as well as on-call emergency service with a quick turnaround time. It's acceptable to wait four hours for the repairperson to arrive, but it's not acceptable to wait four days. All parts should be available within 24 hours.

Find the Right Price Prices will vary depending on the company, the product, and whether you are planning to purchase or lease the equipment. Shop around for the best product, service agreement, and price.

> ### Self-Check
> 1. What is a multifunctional device?
> 2. Differentiate between low-volume, medium-volume, and high-volume copiers.

QUESTIONS FOR STUDY AND REVIEW

1. What are the basic functions of a computer?

2. Which input devices are widely used in offices? Provide an example of an output device.

3. Name two types of removable portable data storage.

4. Which type of computer-based storage has the greatest capacity?

5. Discuss both artificial intelligence and augmented reality. Suggest how each affects the industry and how task are performed utilizing it.

6. Give three examples of application software.

7. Why has the computer placed such a premium on accuracy?

8. What are source documents? Why should they be checked for accuracy and completeness?

9. What advantage does word processing provide document originators?

10. Discuss cloud-based computing and how is it a beneficial tool for data storage.

11. What is desktop publishing?

12. State two things you would check if you were trouble-shooting a computer that would not turn on.

13. What is meant by the term *reprographics*?

14. What are two important steps in selecting a vendor when purchasing or leasing a copier?

15. Discuss why the service agreement is so important when selecting the right equipment vendor.

16. State two factors you should look for in a service agreement.

Key Terms

application programs 130

artificial intelligence (AI) 132

augmented reality (AR) 133

backup 135

bit 133

broadband 131

byte 133

call management services 138

central processing unit (CPU) 130

command 130

compatible 130

convenience copier 140

desktop computer 129

desktop publishing (DTP) 132

directory 133

display 130

duplex 140

electronic presentation software 137

field 133

file 133

flash drive 131

gigabyte 133

GIGO 134

hardware 128

information 133

input 130

integrating application software 137

interconnect equipment 138

keyboard 130

kilobyte 133

laptop computer (notebook) 129

local area networks (LAN) 131

mail merge 135

megabyte 133

memory 130

microprocessor chip 130

monitor 130

mouse 130

network 131

offset printing 140

online 131

operating system 130

output 130

peripheral 128

printer 130

processing 130

random-access memory (RAM) 130

raw data 135

read-only memory (ROM) 130

record 133

removable storage 131

reprographics 140

routers 139

sign on 129

smartphone 129

software 128

spreadsheets 132

tablet computer 129

technology 128

terabyte 133

time-sharing 131

virtual 132

virtual network 139

voice-recognition software 135

web-enabled device 131

webcasting (or netcasting) 140

wide area network (WAN) 131

Windows™ 130

EVERYDAY ETHICS

Long-Distance Code

Tessa has been employed as an administrative professional for the last three years with a small but growing manufacturing company. About six months ago, business was expanded beyond Canada. As overseas business has increased, so has the need to make a significant amount of long-distance phone calls to coordinate orders and deliveries. Tessa was given a special authorization code to key into the phone system whenever she makes a long-distance call. When employees use the long-distance codes, the company receives a reduction in the actual cost for the call. In the last few weeks, Tessa has started using her code for some personal long-distance calls before or after her shift. Tessa has mentioned that she is using the company code to make some personal calls, and she doesn't believe she is doing anything wrong because she is not making the calls on company time.

- Do you see anything fundamentally wrong with her reasoning?
- What might be unprofessional about Tessa's attitude?

Problem Solving

1. You are an administrative professional supporting the general sales manager in an organization that has four sales regions. You are responsible for overseeing that specialized equipment requested by the regions are shipped promptly from manufacturing plants. You operate a PC that is connected to the web and to the offices of the sales regions and the manufacturing plants. Recently, the regions have been receiving the correct number of the equipment ordered, but the colours have not been the ones that were requested. You analyze the input data that you have used for the past month. What should you look for in your analysis? What recommendations could you make to improve your accuracy?

2. You are teaching an assistant to input data. This week, the assistant has entered the input for all the orders. Every Friday the main computer prints a summary of all the orders for the week. This Friday, the computer did not print the summary of your orders for the week. What do you do now to obtain a summary? What else should you do?

3. The day started well. All the people in the office were able to start their computers, find their work, and continue from yesterday. Then it happened. At about 11 a.m., all PCs in the accounting department stopped communicating with the other departments. Interestingly, the order entry group and the administrative professionals could still communicate both with the web and with each other. Luckily, each group was able to continue using their application software. Mr. Wilson heard about the situation and asked you to phone the appropriate technical support to resolve the issue. Would you call the local communications provider or the computer support people? Why?

Special Reports

1. Research, using the web, to find three artificial intelligent (AI) apps not identified in the chapter. Create a table showing the apps, their features, and how they would support business purposes. Submit your findings.

2. Compare the features of two smartphones and identify which one you would recommend using in business. Provide your rationale for your recommendation. Prepare a table for your instructor showing your comparisons.

3. Your local office expansion recently expanded from 15 to 28 permanent employees, and you are tasked with the research and evaluation of an appropriate telephone exchange system to support the expanded staff. Develop a brief report comparing features and benefits of the various systems described in this chapter. Conclude your report with a recommendation.

4. Interview an administrative professional and ask the following questions about the office technology:

   a. What three software do you use most frequently?

   b. What features do you need to have an advanced skill set to manipulate data using these software apps?

   c. How do you stay current and learn new apps as they become available?

   Report your findings to your instructor.

PRODUCTION CHALLENGES

7-A Preparing a Final Draft of Material on Copier/ Printer Project

Supplies needed:

- *Draft on Online Copier/Printer project, Form 7-A on Companion Website*
- *Common Proofreaders' Marks, on Companion Website*

George Andrews is a procurement officer for PDI Inc. and is frustrated by the indecision over a new online copier/printer purchase plan that seems to have stalled. George has drafted a memorandum to the CEO in an attempt to get the stalled project moving again. Form 7-A is a draft of what he has written, including notations that he made in the margins of the draft copy. Proofread the draft memorandum and rekey the corrected copy. Perform this job in three steps:

1. Using (the draft copy) Form 7-A on the companion website, the Common Proofreaders' Marks on the companion website, and your pen, carefully mark all the edits that George has indicated in the margins of Form 7-A before you begin to key.

2. Using your edited copy, key the complete document in its edited form.

3. Print one copy of your final document. Give your instructor the printed copy of your final document as well as Form 7-A with the penned edits.

Weblinks

Microsoft Office Tools
www.office.microsoft.com
This site provides the latest downloads, how-to articles, and more.

PC Webopedia
www.webopedia.com/
This online dictionary and search engine for computer and internet technology includes, among other things, a text messaging abbreviations listing.

PC Magazine
www.pcmag.com
This site allows users to access technological product guides, tips, news, product reviews, and test drives.

Computer Hope
http://www.computerhope.com
This site provides information on how to troubleshoot common computer issues.

The Phone Lady
www.thephonelady.ca
This site provides articles and tips on phone management as well as techniques for marketing and effective best practices related to effective phone management.

Voices of VR Podcast
www://voicesofvr.com/
An information site with podcasts focused on virtual, augmented, and artificial technologies.

Chapter 8
Web Tools and Security

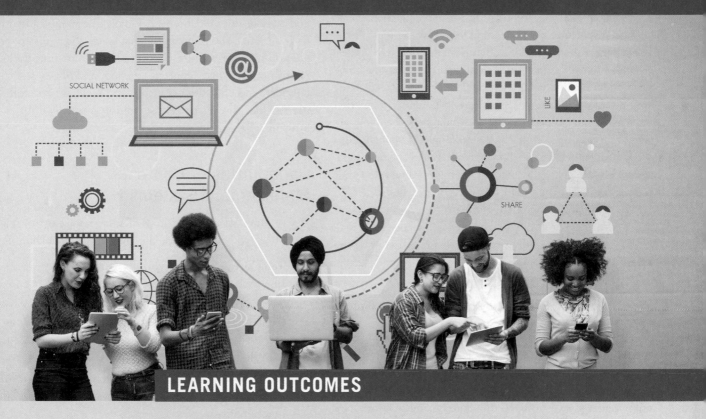

Rawpixel.com/Shutterstock

LEARNING OUTCOMES

After completion of this chapter, the student will be able to:

1 Identify and explain the relevance of web presence in relation to organizational success.

2 Explore web content management systems, recognizing capabilities and advantages.

3 Understand network types.

4 Discuss the difference between Web 1.0, 2.0, and 3.0.

5 Explore web application tools.

6 Understand and identify potential cybersecurity threats.

7 Recognize strategies to combat internet security issues and to keep data secure.

From website design to social media and everything in between, managing a web presence is integral for most businesses. Business websites need to be both appealing and functional. They serve to reinforce an organizations brand, supports marketing strategies, and facilitates a connection with clients. A **website** is the virtual equivalent of a physical company in the real world. While some organizations have their own branded content, many are looking for administrative professionals with expertise to manage their web presence.

A web presence or website consists of a collection of web files on a specific topic that includes a starting file called a home page. An organization will provide its home page address or single domain in its promotional material. From the home page, additional individual webpages are accessed based on the specific informational needs of the website user. These other sections of the business website and their associated links are referred to as deep web links. By building and maintaining a website, organizations can display their services and build credibility. Most people will search for a service online before they purchase to verify the organization's credibility first.

To navigate through this consistently evolving landscape, the office professional develops knowledge and a skill set to support opportunities serving to strengthen web presence initiatives within the organization.

BENEFITS OF WEB PRESENCE

Whether it is a website, an ecommerce platform, a social media page, or a combination of all three, having a web presence will reap major benefits. Even if an organization does not conduct business online, customers and potential customers are expecting to do some business online. Not being online, a business runs the risk of missing opportunities to increase a customer base and increase general awareness about business services. Consider the following list of additional benefits:

- **Availability 24/7.** The internet never rests or closes, and an online presence gives a business a virtual 24-hour showroom. Potential customers can research a product or service after business hours.

- **Cost-effective.** From a marketing perspective, businesses traditionally depended on print ads, direct mail, and television advertisements. For the most parts, these methods still work, but they come with a substantial price tag. If a business has a website, marketing online can be a simple, cost-effective way to reach your target audience. With online marketing tools, the business brings its message directly to customers who are already interested in and looking for specific products and services.

- **Branding.** Building and sustaining a corporate brand does not transpire overnight. It takes time to develop and

cultivate. In this social media age, social media serves a variety of purposes, including social selling and customer support. Social media gives you the perfect opportunity to reach your target audience and build your brand.

CONTENT MANAGEMENT SYSTEMS

A **website content management system (WCMS)** is a software application or set of related programs used to create and manage digital content. It usually allows multiple users with minimal web programming language the ability to create and manage website content. Typical features include publishing webpages, content creation, and library services, check-in and check-out controls, and security. The following sections discuss the considerations and capabilities of utilizing a WCMS.

Capabilities of Content Management Systems

A vast array of content management systems exist to select from; however, most provide the following beneficial tools:

1. **Templates.** Systems typically permit the creation of standard templates. These templates can be the foundational basis to add or modify content.

2. **Content modification.** Various pieces and components of pre-existing content have the ability to be modified with simplicity by nontechnical users.

3. **Expandable or scalable components.** WCMS platforms provide plug-ins or add-ins to enhance an existing site's functionality.

4. **Upgrade for web.** Current WCMS software receives continual updates with new enhancements to keep the system up to current web standards.

5. **Workflow management and collaboration.** Controls deployed on an as-needed basis to ensure content creation follow a process cycle of creation. This could involve content being reviewed by those assigned to company website hosting prior to publishing the content live. WCMS software may provide an opportunity for collaboration. Many users retrieve and work on assigned content. Individual changes can be tracked as well as authorized for publication prior to going live on the web. See Figure 8-1 for examples of WCMS.

Getting Connected

The internet has become a constant fixture in almost all organizations. Businesses consider the internet as an indispensable tool for their daily operations for uses ranging

Herjavec Group

The Herjavec Group was founded in 2003 by Robert Herjavec, promoting cybersecurity. It quickly became one of North America's fastest growing technology companies. They are viewed as a global leader in information security by offering protection-based solutions for industry. They pride themselves on the ability to support current and emerging technology worldwide. This is accomplished by developing and supporting state-of-the-art security operations centres (SOS). Herjavec Group has offices in Canada, the United States, and the United Kingdom. The foundational operational now extends into consulting, professional services, and incident response.

Herjavec Group commenced operations as a vendor for Checkpoint firewalls, supporting complex networks in Canada, moving through managed security services, and, in 2010, adding Security Operations Centres. In 2014, the group expanded its operations to the United States and later, in 2015, expanded operations to Europe. Revenue generated in 2007 topped C$16 million and C$120 million in 2012.

In 2016 Herjavec Group was awarded the Hot Managed Services Provided from *Cyber Defense Magazine*. In 2018, *Cyber Defense Magazine* also recognized the company for expertise in Identity and Access Management, Managed Security Services Provider, and Security Company of the Year. The Herjavec Group was named number 10 on the top 500 cybersecurity listing.

When seeking talent, Herjavec Group seeks individuals who are excited to work in a fast-paced environment, interested in learning and developing, and prone to be self-starters. Opportunities exist for those who seek it in terms of promotion and advancement. Mentorship is another core value represented.

At Herjavec Group, a focus on local community involvement to make a difference is pervasive. Every employee is provided a day off each year to volunteer in his or her local community. Community involvement covers education, healthcare, and the environment.

FIGURE 8-1 Web content management systems.

CMS	KEY CAPABILITIES
1. WordPress	▪ CMS for blogging
	▪ Documentation deployment
	▪ Auto update core
2. Text Pattern	▪ Ease of use
	▪ Structured elements using HTML
	▪ Single file download
3. Radiant CMS	▪ Flexible template layout
	▪ Plug-in extension system
	▪ Management of users/permissions
4. Silver Stripe	▪ Configurable options
	▪ Uses modules and themes for content
	▪ Content version controls
5. Drupal	▪ Multiple levels of content types
	▪ Plug-ins
	▪ Forums and user blogs

from video conferencing, employee training to data file downloads. As internet technology evolves, so does the need for efficient and fast internet connections. Businesses understand selecting sufficient broadband and an internet service provider (ISP) provider means careful consideration is needed based on the business needs. **Bandwidth** refers to the volume of information per unit of time that an internet connection can handle. Consider bandwidth to be like a water pipe—the wider the pipe, the more water can flow through. This is one of the key requirements managers should thoroughly evaluate to ensure selection of the bandwidth size is appropriate for the organization. An administrative professional's responsibility may include sourcing potential ISPs on behalf of the organization. Bandwidth needs will depend on the nature and size of an organization. To begin an assessment of broadband needs consider the following questions:

- How fast does the internet connectivity need to be?
- How many devices may be transferring data on a regular basis?
- What rate of data transfer does the business require considering download and upload speed?

Methods of Connectivity

Copper Digital Subscriber Line (DSL)   The connection provided is always on. This service uses a two-wire copper telephone line that transmits a digital signal. Symmetric digital subscriber lines (SDSLs) permit equal upload and download speeds. It is often referred to as a high-speed connection because it has high bandwidth. In addition to offering a high-speed connection, one of the advantages of DSL is that several users can access the internet at the same time without influencing the bandwidth. Since DSL only requires telephone lines, it is easy to install compared to other types of business internet connectivity.

Cable   By using a cable modem, a user can access broadband internet service over TV lines. A coaxial cable is connected to the computer's modem, which enables data transmission. This is another type of connection that is always on. The service provider for uploading and downloading data reserves separate TV channels.

A disadvantage to this type of access is that bandwidth may be limited, depending on the number of users accessing the service at the same time. That is, the more people accessing the service at the same time, the slower will be the data transmission speed.

Fibre Optic Cable   Fibre optic cable is a technology that uses glass (or plastic) threads (fibres) to transmit data. A fibre optic cable consists of a bundle of glass threads, each of which is capable of transmitting messages modulated onto light waves. Fibre optic cables have a much greater bandwidth than metal cables or DSL; this means that they can carry more data than a standard metal cable. In addition, telephone companies are steadily replacing traditional telephone lines with fibre optic cables, clearly because of the advantages fibre offers over metal cables.

Satellite   A satellite is an object that orbits the Earth transmitting a two-way digital signal to satellite dishes located on Earth. A satellite connection is another form of broadband (high-speed) connection. It is usually 10 times faster than a typical modem but not as fast as DSL or cable. Satellite offers an option for high-speed internet access in locations where DSL and cable may not be available.

Wireless   Wireless is another form of broadband connectivity. Instead of using a cable or a telephone line to connect to the internet, a wireless connection uses radio frequency. Users remain consistently connected, providing they stay within the prescribed network coverage range. Of course, the greatest benefit of wireless is the mobility it provides. Users can move about from location to location within the organization and access many resources connected to the network without needing to plug in.

Types of Networks

A **network** is a set of connected devices. Devices or computers on a network are called nodes. Connected networks can share resources, like access to the internet, printers, file servers, and others. A network is a multipurpose connection, which allows a single device to do more than what is installed to the device.

Wireless Fidelity (Wi-Fi)   Wi-Fi is a wireless network set up for public access. In places like a library, airport, or even a coffee shop, you may find a connection for your mobile device. A **hotspot** is a site that provides a wireless local area network with a router connected to a link to an ISP. Recently, some concerns have been raised about possible health risks associated with this type of technology, prompting some to evaluate its use. Wired networks use cables to connect devices, such as laptop or desktop computers, to the internet or another network.

Intranets   Organizations sometimes set up a private computer network to share proprietary websites, information, and resources. Such a network is known as an intranet. By using an intranet, a company can ensure that internal communication and collaboration access are restricted to only those within the organization. In many cases, intranets are protected from unauthorized external access by means of a network firewall (see "Internet Security" section). An intranet's websites look and act just like other websites, but the firewall surrounding an intranet fends off unauthorized access.

Extranets   An extranet provides various levels of accessibility to outsiders. Commonly, a user can access an extranet only if he or she has a valid username and password. Sometimes an organization will determine which components of the extranet a user can view, based on his or her identity. An organization may also set up an extranet to communicate with suppliers and customers alike.

Search Engines

A search engine is a program that enables the user to search online for information. By entering key words or phrases, users can generate real-time results, including online databases, documents, and webpages. There are many search engines available, and it is important to note that results generated by one search engine may not be the same as those from another one. Here is a list of some available search engines:

- Google
- Bing
- Yahoo!

- Ask.com
- DuckDuckGo

Self-Check

1. List two capabilities of web content systems.

2. State one benefit of an intranet.

WEB APPLICATIONS

A **web application** is any application that uses a web browser as a client. The application can be as simple as a message board or a guest sign-in book on a website or as complex as a word processor or a spreadsheet program.

The new landscape for web applications is crossing the line into applications that do not normally need a server to store information. A word-processing application, for example, stores documents on the device and does not need a server. Web applications can provide the same functionality and gain the benefit of working across multiple platforms. For example, a web application can act as a word processor, storing information and allowing you to save the document onto the device hard drive. Google docs is an example of a web application where you create, edit, share, and access your documents wherever you are. You can collaborate with several people on the same document at the same time using this web app.

Web 1.0, 2.0, and 3.0

When the web was first introduced, it was linear. That is, a webmaster would create a webpage, and the viewer would visit the site and read the information, and very little interaction was possible. Those early days of the internet are often referred to as Web 1.0.

Web 2.0 presents the web to the user with interactive data. Unlike Web 1.0, Web 2.0 facilitates interaction between webusers and sites, so it allows users to interact more freely with each other. Web 2.0 encourages participation, collaboration, and information sharing. Examples of Web 2.0 applications are YouTube, Wiki, Flickr, and so on.

Web 3.0 is presentation of the web with dynamic applications, interactive services, and machine-to-machine interaction. Web 3.0 devices can interpret information like humans and intelligently generate and distribute useful content tailored to the needs of users. One example of Web 3.0 is TiVo, a digital video recorder. Its recording program can search the web and read what it finds to you based on your preferences. This is a form of artificial intelligence technologies. We do not just use the web; we connect with it: it is engaging, interactive, and social. Web tools (see Figure 8-2)

FIGURE 8-2 Web 2.0 tools.

that have enabled this dynamic assimilation are described in the following sections.

Examples of Web Tools

Blogs   A blog is short for weblog. A blog can best be described as a journal available on the web. The person or organization responsible for it updates it on a regular basis. A business blog is the perfect resource to give the company an official and authoritative voice on the web. Moreover, it can give customers or clients a way to discover more about what a business offers.

Wiki   A wiki is a collaborative website that allows its users to add, modify, or delete its content via a web browser. Designed as a simple-to-use cooperative tool, wikis have risen through the ranks of content management systems. Businesses have found that wikis are a perfect tool for groups to share information (e.g., human resource policies) with larger groups within the organization. Companies may also use a wiki to share or answer frequently asked questions (FAQs) raised by their internal and external customers.

Social Media   Social media is a general term used to describe web-based tools that encourage exchange of information by users. Some examples of social media sites include YouTube, Twitter, Flickr, and Facebook. What distinguishes social media sites from ordinary websites is that they are based on user-generated content (UGC). Businesses have discovered social media can provide significant opportunities to highlight services, events, and community initiatives. It is also worth noting that in recent years there has been a tremendous shift in how employers view employee use of social media. Although previously it was discouraged, it is now strongly encouraged in collaboration with company values.

Live Meeting   Depending on the system the office has in place, this tool can be used to conduct meetings with a facilitator who has the ability either to share his own desktop image or to have attendees share theirs. This tool is great for hosting a meeting across multiple sites and locations, and it is often used as a virtual training tool.

SharePoint   Developed by Microsoft, SharePoint is an online database where documents can be stored and then shared throughout an organization. For instance, administrative professionals from multiple locations may need to work together on an annual budget for the management teams they support. Instead of each individual administrative professional having his or her own copy, and tasking someone with rounding them all up and combining them each month, SharePoint allows for one report to be updated by many individuals while maintaining the report in one location. This also simplifies the process and allows each user to see progress as it is made.

SlideShare   SlideShare is an online presentation management system. Users can upload a slideshow presentation to be viewed publicly or privately, depending on preference. Users can search topics of interest and download or remix slide presentations. SlideShare and similar tools promote collaboration and idea sharing with a wider audience.

Quick Response (QR) Code   QR Code is software that allows camera-equipped mobile devices to read and scan special barcodes. A user can quickly scan the barcode, and the information on the barcode is then automatically entered into his/her device (see Figure 8-3). Some companies have placed a QR code on promotional t-shirts using the technology as a marketing tool to promote their corporate image.

Web and Video Conferencing

Web conferencing is, as its name suggests, a way of conducting a conference online. Participants gain access to the conference from their own computers, from the comfort of their own offices. Web conferencing is ideal for small collaborative groups or meetings where the participants must not only hear or view a presentation but also be able to communicate with each other. Enabling collaboration online is one of the strengths of web conferencing. Organizations appreciate the ability to create a workspace online that in the past required members to travel in order to collaborate. The emergence of

FIGURE 8-3   Quick response code.

powerful and reliable smartphones has shifted the attention of this technology towards mobile devices. Most conferencing platforms facilitate fast content sharing. Participants are instantly invited to a meeting, record minutes of a meeting, create follow-up emails, present discussion slides, and support multiple computer monitors. Audio is captured and transmitted through voice over internet protocol (VoIP). In some cases, a web conference platform also requires users to download proprietary software before accessing the presentation or sharing content. Video conferencing (VC) usually requires specialized equipment on both ends for a successful connection or live streaming. Skype for business is one of the world's most popular calling and video conferencing apps.

Webcasting

A webcast is a media file distributed over the internet using streaming media technology to distribute a single content source simultaneously to many listeners/viewers. Often a webcast has accompanying PowerPoint slides. A webcast may be distributed either live or on demand.

Essentially, webcasting is "broadcasting" over the internet. Ideal for engaging larger online audiences, webcasting is a "one-to-many" form of communication, in which one speaker or panel of speakers presents to many attendees. Since it is broadcast over the internet, it can accommodate thousands of viewers simultaneously.

Webcasts are browser-based and require no additional software download. Because audio is integrated into the platform, no phone line is needed. A user can listen to the presentation through speakers or headphones.

Typically, a webcast is a professionally produced program in itself, or it might involve coverage of a live event, streamed with almost any combination of interactive features, from question-and-answer tools to surveys, polls, and social media sharing.

Podcasting

A podcast involves transmission of media files via the internet; the files are then synced or downloaded to an MP3 player, handheld computer, laptop, or desktop computer for listening at the user's convenience. The files are usually received by subscribing to what is called a podcast feed. The key benefit of podcasts is that the files are portable.

Webinars

A webinar is a seminar delivered over the web, and it is a strategic application often used for marketing and training. To transmit the webinar, either a webcast or a web conference platform is used. Webinars typically include interactive features to allow viewers to submit questions to speakers and participate in polls. Other tools relied on in conducting webinars include registration pages to capture audience information, reminder emails to encourage good attendance, source-tracking URLs to monitor how users are finding the program, and departure surveys to collect immediate feedback from attendees. If your organization is planning a webinar, all of these features should be integrated into any webcast or web conference platform you use. In addition, consider the following tips for hosting a successful webinar:

- Send out reminders to your participants reminding them of the time and date of the presentation; this gives participants an opportunity to ask questions, such as how many other individuals will be taking part in the webinar.
- Set up and check in early. You may want to have your presenters online 10 to 15 minutes before the session begins to avoid any last-minute technical issues.
- Do a roll call to make sure all participants are able to connect.
- Once ready to begin, review the agenda.
- During the webinar, ensure the conversation is kept on track; discussion can easily be hijacked if not controlled.
- Collect feedback.
- After the session, follow up. You may want to send thank-you emails or notes to speakers.
- Use feedback for planning future seminars.

Web Usage in a Professional Setting

As wonderful as the various web tools are, consideration must be given to appropriate use of this technology within the context of a business environment. Employers are encouraged to develop policies and procedures addressing concerns related to user security, privacy, and reflection of corporate image. An effective corporate web-usage policy will help employees understand what is expected of them, as it affects their work as necessary. Organizations will define what employees can say or do on work-provided devices or employee-owned devices that are used for or involve employees, workplace, or the organization. Guidelines within a policy provide clear direction for employees. A policy example may state that employees are not to publish images of themselves with their co-workers at work events. Additionally, an organization may determine in its policy that any device or computer including, but not limited to, desk phones, smartphones, tablets, laptops, and desktop computers that the business provides for use should only be used for business. A helpful model and directive in this regard is the policy standard published in 2016 by the Government of Canada, *Policy on Acceptable Network and Device Use* (link available in Weblinks section of this chapter). Companies need to have employee-friendly policies governing the use of this technology, but they also need to maintain their security. Some questions companies have to consider include the following:

- How do we protect confidentiality and intellectual property?
- How do we protect our brand while promoting it?
- How do we avoid public relations disasters while still engaging our staff and customers?

---

pro-Link
Web Lingo

With the explosion of the web and especially social media, understanding some basic terminology will help you to get the most of this powerful tool. Here are some key terms:

- **Algorithm**—a set of formulas that allow programs like Facebook to develop content-sharing platforms
- **B2B**—Business to business
- **B2C**—Business to consumer
- **DM**—Direct messaging
- **Hashtag**—a word or string of characters that starts with a number sign; usually used with Twitter to create a searchable category
- **HootSuite**—a social media management system that helps businesses streamline campaigns across several social media sites
- **Mashup**—the use of two or more sources to create a new graphic, presentation, or audio or other media file
- **RSS (Real Simple Syndication) feed**—also called web feed; a personal delivery system for news content from several places
- **RT**—Retweet
- **Traffic**—the number of visitors to a website
- **Trend**—an indication of how many users are viewing the same article or link
- **UGC**—user-generated content in written and visual context
- **Viral**—a term to describe a video made popular through internet sharing

---

DATA SECURITY

Most businesses use computers, devices, servers, and networks to send and store vital information, often managing financial or private information belonging to customers and clients. Every day, new threats appear that can compromise the security. An intruder who breaches security can recover data an organization hosts, see website personnel, and access emails sent. If a company's computer security is compromised, unauthorized individuals might learn confidential information about the organization. The consequences of a security breach include the cost of correcting the breach, client notification, network repairs, and lost revenue. It is essential, therefore, for an organization to be aware of the various types of data security risks, as well as countermeasures for protection.

General Data Security Risks

A risk all businesses take when managing data is having the data breached or compromised. Organizations must consider the possibility that unauthorized parties might access private or sensitive information. Following is a list of descriptions of the most common security data risks facing businesses but often overlooked.

Uninformed Personnel   At times, personnel within an organization may not have the necessary training to be aware of best practices as those relate to data security. They may select weak passwords, visit unauthorized websites, or click on links provided in an email. All of these examples present an enormous risk for an organization. The solution is to invest in training for all personnel on cybersecurity risks.

Mobile Devices   Data theft is a high vulnerability when employees are using mobile devices, especially their own, to share data or access company information. A solution is to have a carefully spelled out bring-your-own-mobile-device (BYOD) policy in place. This will ensure employees are better educated on device expectations and companies can better monitor email and documents downloaded to company or employee-owned devices.

Cloud and File Sharing Applications   Various applications permit the storage of data in this newer technology platform. An employee can be using a cloud application to store easily accessible organizational data. What might be unknown are the security restrictions in place for this application and how easily others can access the data. Many companies have been slower to adopt cloud-based computing for this reason. A solution is to use data encryption security. **Encryption** is the process of converting information or data into a code, especially to prevent unauthorized access.

Third-Party Providers

Organizations are relying more on outsourcing through various software vendors. These third-party vendors often grant remote access to the platform they host for the organization. Additionally, for simplicity they provide a standard password for all company personnel. If a hacker guesses a password, the hacker then has access to sensitive company data. A solution is for a company to research the vendors to determine if the vendors will accept or provide a multifactor authentication when users access their platform remotely.

Methods of Cybersecurity Threats

Cybersecurity is the body of technologies, processes, and practices designed to protect networks, computers, programs, and data from attack, damage, or unauthorized access (see Figure 8-4 and Figure 8-5). Here is a list of additional security risks facing all users of technology.

Computer Viruses

Viruses are destructive programs written and designed to load and run undetected by users. Viruses can delete or corrupt files and programs, duplicate themselves, travel across networks and via email, and even destroy operating systems and shut down computers.

FIGURE 8-4 Web security.

Sky Motion/Shutterstock

Worms and Trojan Horses

Worms and Trojan horses are often inaccurately described as computer viruses, but they are in fact different in some important ways. A worm, unlike a virus, needs no human action; it can travel unassisted. For instance, a worm can send out messages to all the contacts in your computer email system. Likewise, a Trojan horse will first present itself on the computer as useful and helpful software. Once activated, however, it will do significant damage to your computer.

Hacking

A hacker is a slang term referring to someone with an advanced understanding of computers and computer networks. Hacking allows the hacker to benefit by exposing weaknesses in a computer or computer network. Whether motivated by protest or profit, hacking can unleash significant havoc for a computer network, often corrupting or permanently destroying data.

Denial of Service (DoS)

This occurs when users receive a message stating that they can no longer access the platform or application they may need on a regular basis. Further, a user might have to log on and change or supply their password to have access granted. A hacker is counting on retrieving the user's password and related access codes when this happens.

Credential Reuse

This occurs when a hacker has breached a website and accessed passwords. The expectation in that the passwords will be reused. This means that if an employee used one password to access the company website, he or she might use the same password to access bank accounts or other personal information.

Malware

Short for malicious software, malware is software used or created by hackers to disrupt computer operation, gather sensitive information, or gain access to private computer systems. Malware includes computer viruses, worms, Trojans, spyware, adware, and other malicious programs.

Phishing

Phishing is the practice of fraudulently attempting to obtain secure information, such as a password, by masquerading as a trusted source. This is considered a method of potential identity theft. The fraud often works by sending out an email that looks like an authentic request for information from a bank or credit card company, asking you to use a link or pop-up window and enter confidential information.

Spam

Spam is the use of electronic messaging systems to send unwelcome bulk messages. The most widely recognized form of spam is email spam. Many organizations are aware of the extensive influx of spam and have responded by investing in **spam-filtering software**. This software is designed to detect or block unwanted messages from reaching a user's in-box.

FIGURE 8-5 Common security issues and possible solutions.

THREAT	ISSUE	SOLUTION
Intrusion/hacking	Unauthorized access to network	Firewall
Virus	Destruction of files and programs	Antivirus software
Malware	Disruption of computer activity, information theft	Antimalware software
Denial of service attack	Attempts to make a network resource unavailable	Intrusion prevention systems
Spam	Possibly tricking users into buying nonexistent service	Antispam software
Stolen laptop/mobile device	Access to confidential files stored on device	Encrypt files
Clickjacking (social media)	Tricking users into clicking on a fake webpage	Avoid visiting nonwork-related sites

Bluejacking   The Bluejacker program was originally designed to share information, such as cell phone contacts, from device to device through Bluetooth technology. However, it has become a method of sending anonymous, unwanted messages to other users with Bluetooth-enabled mobile phones or devices. Bluejacking is relatively harmless and can be more bothersome than malicious. For instance, a bluejacker might send out offensive or obscene material.

Cookies   Cookies are files stored on your computer that allow websites to remember your information. They can compromise your confidentiality, as others may be able to review your computer search history, but cannot steal your data.

Mousetrapping   This security threat prevents the user from leaving a website. The user will sometimes be directed to a fake website. After the user repeatedly attempts to quit, another browser will open, showing the same site from which the user is trying to escape. The best way to avoid this is by using a favourite bookmark for your frequently visited sites.

Pagejacking   Pagejacking involves webpage links that direct the user to navigate to another webpage for more information. The new page is often a duplication of a real page. Many times scammers use this to advertise a service and generate more revenue, as some sites are paid per visitor.

Pharming   Pharming redirects the user from a legitimate website to a fraudulent copy, allowing scammers to steal any information you enter at the bogus website.

Maintaining Internet Security

Internet security is a central concern for businesses in every industry. The following tools can help users to protect the security of company as well as personal data.

Antivirus Programs   This software can prevent, detect, and immobilize potential threats such as viruses or spyware. Internet service providers frequently recommend or offer software at significantly discounted pricing. To maximize the benefits of antivirus software, take the following steps:

- Activate real-time continuous scanning.
- Schedule regular system scans.
- Check frequently for updates.
- Ensure renewal when necessary.

Passwords   The purpose of a password is to ensure privacy and security on computer networks (see Figure 8-6). Many hackers, however, can be successful in their attempts to steal your information because they can figure out your password. Here are some tips to consider for password security:

- Avoid simple and short passwords; choose a password at least seven characters in length.
- Choose a password that is easy to remember but hard for others to figure out.
- Use a combination of uppercase, lowercase, and numerical characters.
- Change your password frequently, since this reduces the opportunity for detection.
- Do not write your passwords down, as they can be found and used by unauthorized individuals.
- Never give your password out in an email.
- Consider using a password manager program to store multiple passwords; this way you only have to remember the password for the program.
- Use a password strength analyzer. This free software will classify your password as weak, fair, or strong.

FIGURE 8-6 Login security.

Ron Dale/Shutterstock

Data Encryption Software When information is transmitted, **encryption software** can scramble the data to make it unreadable if intercepted. A password supplied by the sender will convert the data to plain text to be viewed by the intended recipient.

Firewall A **firewall** is hardware or software used to control network traffic. A firewall will have preset determinants directing what can pass in or out of the network it is protecting. Intranets utilize firewalls to prevent external networks from breaking through.

Clearing the Cache This is a tool that requires no special program. Your browser's memory is called the cache; every time you visit a website, a copy of it is saved in your computer's cache. After each internet session, close your browser to ensure the cache is cleared.

Website Site Advisor This is a browser plug-in that will check the safety of a website before you actually select it to use. A rating icon is displayed indicating the website's level of risk.

QUESTIONS FOR STUDY AND REVIEW

1. State what opportunities exist for an organization to ensure that it has a web presence.

2. Describe two organizational benefits for having an online presence.

3. State two reasons why content management systems are helpful for website development.

4. Why might a company set up an extranet?

5. In what form are results generated from a search engine?

6. How does Web 2.0 differ from Web 3.0?

7. Provide two reasons a business would host a webinar.

8. Explain why a company would adopt a professional web-usage policy.

9. Describe two ways an organization may experience a data breach.

10. Suggest three best practices to employ when working with passwords.

11. How does a firewall protect computers and computer networks?

12. Describe three ways to maximize your antivirus program.

13. What purpose does data encryption software serve?

14. What does clearing the cache mean?

Key Terms

bandwidth 147

blog 150

cybersecurity 153

encryption 153

encryption software 155

fibre optic cable 148

firewall 155

hotspot 148

network 148

satellite 148

social media 150

spam 153

spam-filtering software 153

virus 153

website 146

web application 149

website content management system (WCMS) 146

Wiki 150

EVERYDAY ETHICS

Sick Day

You work as an administrative professional for McMillan & Partners, a medium-size law firm located in Calgary. You get along well with most of your co-workers, and for the most part you enjoy your work. You work closely with another administrative professional, Suzanne. Often you cover each other's phone lines when you take lunch or have a break. Last Thursday, Suzanne called in sick. She took the day off, and you did your best to pitch in and help out where you could.

You and Suzanne have embraced using social media, and you have access to each other's Facebook page. On Saturday, you were updating your Facebook page and noticed an update from Suzanne that caught your attention. It was a picture of Suzanne sitting on the beach sipping her favourite drink. The caption read, "Having a great 'sick day.'" Naturally, you were shocked and surprised.

- Will you ask Suzanne about what you saw on Facebook?
- Should you say anything to your supervisor? Why or why not?
- Do you think it is a good idea to "friend" a co-worker? Why or why not?

Problem Solving

1. It is your first month on the job. Your supervisor, Samuel Barnes, vice president of marketing, met with you today to discuss your performance this past month. Overall, he is very pleased with your administrative skills and your take-charge attitude. He especially likes how computer and internet savvy you are. Based on this, Mr. Barnes would like you to find and recommend two web application programs for creating slideshow presentations. Because Mr. Barnes spends so much of time away from the office meeting customers and making presentations, he wants a dynamic tool that he can access anytime on any of his mobile devices. He also wants to be able to import presentations he has already created into the new program. What steps would take to find a program that would work for Mr. Barnes?

2. You are training a new receptionist for the group medical practice you manage. So far, the training has gone well, and you believe the new person will fit well with the team. Today, you happen to notice a slip of paper sitting by the new receptionist's workstation when she is out for lunch. You pick up the piece of paper and quickly realize the patient database login is written on the piece of paper, along with the password. It has been a very busy day, with three of the five physicians and 60 to 70 visitors in the office. Since you have no idea if anyone else has seen this information, what should you do?

3. It is almost the end of a busy workweek. You feel you have been confronted by every challenge imaginable. You just received a panicked call from your immediate supervisor, Julianne Kwong, who is leaving on a business trip to Germany in a few hours. She is taking her tablet computer and plans to remotely access all the documents she will need by using the company's intranet. Ms. Kwong has just realized, however, that she does not know how to do this, or even if it is possible to do this, and she has asked you to find out if and how she can access her documents remotely. You are now going to contact the IT department. What information do you believe the IT specialists will want to know before giving you an answer? What questions will you ask?

Special Reports

1. Research two webinar creation or hosting programs. List the advantages and disadvantages of both and present your findings to the class.

2. Interview an administrative office professional and ask the following questions:

   a. Does your organization have a social media presence? If yes, what programs are used?

   b. Are you directly involved in the web content preparation and updating?

   c. How often are you required to change your password for the various platforms you access? Do you use third-party vendor platforms to access remotely?

   d. Do you know what measures are in place to protect internet security when you go online?

3. Conduct online research using three of the search engines listed in this chapter. Use the following key phrases:

   a. Latest in cloud computing

   b. Computer viruses

   c. Internet security

   Write a summary of your findings, identifying the similarities and the differences.

4. Inquire about the media services available at your school. Determine if your school is equipped to conduct a webinar. Find out what technical support is available if you have any trouble. Report your findings to the class.

PRODUCTION CHALLENGES

8-A Identifying Appropriate/Inappropriate Use of Technology

Supplies needed:

- *Identifying Appropriate/Inappropriate Use of Technology, Form 8-A on the Companion Website*

Review Form 8-A. Decide whether the examples provided are appropriate or inappropriate uses of technology in the workplace. Hand in your completed form to your instructor.

8-B Web 2.0 in Action

Supplies needed:

- *Plain bond paper*
- *Access to the internet*

Visit two of the following three blogs written by administrative office professionals (or ones of your choosing):

1. secretaryhelpline.blogspot.ca/

2. www.theeffectiveadmin.com

3. www.theprofessionalassistant.org

   Your supervisor, Mr. Barnes, has decided a blog would be a great tool for announcing events and generating interest in the company. He would like you to review the listed blogs and write a one-page report outlining your findings.

Weblinks

Audio, Video, and Networking Products

www.polycom.com

Polycom, now a division of Plantronics, is a leading producer of networking systems that enhance office voice and video communication. Specification and application information may be found at this site.

Government of Canada—Policy on Acceptable Network and Device Use

www.tbs-sct.gc.ca

This site for the Treasury Board of Canada Secretariat provides recommendations covering best practices for acceptable network and devices usages for business.

Norton Antivirus Software

www.symantec.com

Information on Norton software products, including antivirus and anti-spyware software, can be found at this site.

McAfee Antivirus Protection

www.mcafee.com

Visit this site to find information on McAfee software products, including antivirus and anti-spyware software.

SlideShare

www.slideshare.net/

This website offers slideshow presentations on a number of topics.

Center for Internet Security

www.cisecurity.org/

The Center for Internet Security (CIS) is a site providing useful information regarding issues related to internet security.

Bitdefender Resource Centre

www.bitdefender.com

This site displays a searchable encyclopedia of computer viruses. It indicates the level of threat as low, medium, or high. The site also lists the date the virus was discovered.

Chapter 9
Incoming and Outgoing Mail

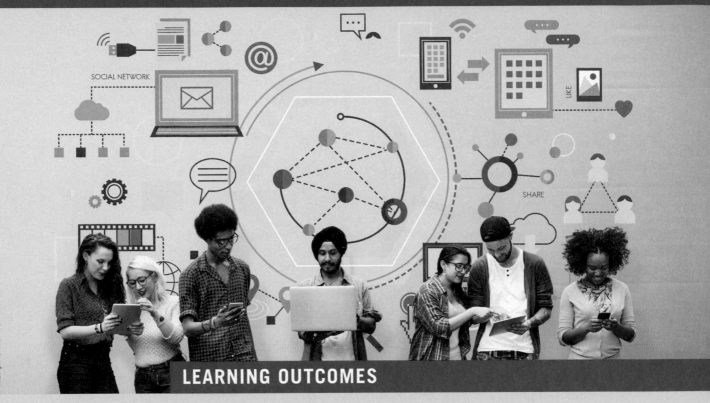

LEARNING OUTCOMES

After completion of this chapter, the student will be able to:

1 Identify the benefits of electronic mail (email).

2 Explore alternative methods of technology-based mail.

3 Explain the procedures for processing incoming mail.

4 Understand the privacy expectations that accompany the role of the administrative professional in mail management.

5 Describe the purpose and variety of mailing services available from Canada Post (CP).

6 Identify what items are prohibited from within the inclusion of mail.

7 Develop an awareness of alternative delivery methods available in Canada.

8 Demonstrate proper addressing according to Canada Post guidelines.

Whether you are an administrative professional in a large organization or a small one, mail will arrive daily—probably more than once during each business day. Electronic mail, courier services, and other distribution alternatives have seen a significant increase in recent years. At the same time, traditional mail services still provide an effective means of moving information from one location to another.

Each mail transaction represents a contact with someone outside or within your organization, and the promptness of responses provided is an important factor in building good-will and increasing the effectiveness of your organization.

As an administrative professional, you may or may not have direct contact with the post office—this may depend on whether or not the organization for which you work has a central mailing department. Nevertheless, you should become knowledgeable about all distribution and shipping services because as you prepare outgoing mail you will have to indicate how it is to be sent. Become familiar with the Canada Post (CP) website (www.canadapost.ca). As postal rates and services are subject to frequent change, you will find this site an invaluable tool and a source of current information.

While far from comprehensive, this chapter introduces alternatives and advice for dealing with selective technology-based mail services, as well as the traditional incoming and outgoing mail. See Figure 9-1 for an overview of general distribution services typically available in Canada.

OVERVIEW OF BUSINESS SERVICES AVAILABLE FROM CANADA POST

Canada Post offers a variety of business-related services and solutions. Knowing what these services are helps to position the resources available in the most successful way to meet the needs of the business:

- **Postal service.** Businesses normally mail in higher volumes than residential clients. Discounts are available through CP for sending letter mail or other mailable items in bulk.

- **Shipping.** CP is the number one parcel delivery in Canada. CP has positioned this to its advantage by providing reliable parcel shipping services to businesses at a competitive price point.

- **Marketing.** A variety of tools are available to support direct marketing campaigns.

- **Ecommerce.** An assortment of tools is available to support ecommerce shipping needs and online businesses.

FIGURE 9-1 Overview of general distribution services.

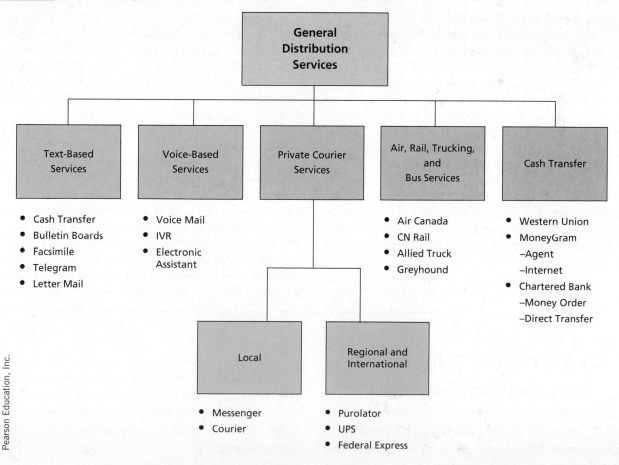

Pearson Education, Inc.

Vanessa McInnis

Vanessa McInnis

Holland College, Prince Edward Island
Office Administration Medical
Graduate 2010

"Believing in yourself and then loving what you do, you will succeed in your career path."

In May 2010, Vanessa graduated from Holland College, Medical Support Services with a Medical Secretary Profile. Her on-the-job training was at a long-term care facility, Beach Grove Home. Her first casual position was at Prince Edward Home. Just after graduating from Holland College, she already had her foot in the door with two positions as a Clerk 4. Vanessa's experience shows that how hard you work during your work placement can provide a positive outcome for your career. Believing in yourself and then loving what you do will help you succeed in your career path. Put in your best efforts and do your best. As you grow and learn new skills as a student, you will learn what it takes to become a professional in the workplace.

With these positions her responsibilities were providing general office duties such as answering telephones; organizing charts for the house physician; preparing new resident charts; accessing decentralized files; interacting with residents; producing meeting minutes; stocking supplies; and updating lists. She also covered as the receptionist providing professionalism, as the first contact greeting the public; transferring calls to appropriate areas; filing; providing receipts for cheques; and posting job positions.

September 2009–2012, Vanessa volunteered at Holland College orientation to give feedback on this program/career to new students starting out. She had a very positive experience at Holland College and grew to have a successful career. She enjoys talking about her experiences and providing advice.

In November 2010, Vanessa enrolled in the Health Unit Coordinating Certificate Program at Holland College to compliment her diploma and increase job opportunities. In September 2012, Vanessa accepted a permanent part-time position with the Admitting Department at the Queen Elizabeth Hospital.

With this position, her responsibilities were management of beds by maintaining admissions/discharges/transfers; maintaining patient/information confidentiality; registration through CIS; cashier services 24/7, retrieving patient files from medical records; maintaining census stats and providing inpatient lists to hospital departments; preparing inpatient charts; and performing general office duties.

From 2010–2014, Vanessa worked in 13 different areas of healthcare during her career thus far. If the shifts slowed down, she continued to find work looking for more opportunities. Vanessa loved her career choice and was determined to get full-time employment. At the Queen Elizabeth Hospital, she now has experience working in the Emergency Department, Orthopedic Clinic, Special Testing Services, Unit 2/7/8, and Dialysis. Additionally, Vanessa has also worked with Public Health Nursing, Health PEI Programs, and Primary Queen East.

In April 2014, Vanessa accepted a permanent full-time position as a Clerk 3 at Hillsborough Hospital on Units 7 & 8 and continues to work there today. Her responsibilities are providing clerical support and assistance to the nursing units; communicating with patients and co-workers; shopping for required patient/unit supplies; preparing/maintaining/organizing patient records; sending referrals for patients discharge; preparing and relaying information for payroll processing; filing; maintaining forms; and ordering supplies.

HANDLING OFFICE TECHNOLOGY

Automated Mail Services—Email

Because of its speed and accessibility, **electronic mail (email)** is one of the most popular and cost-effective mail system found in business. Many companies use private communication systems known as an **intranet**, which connects employees' together in a messaging system. Companies usually also subscribe to the larger, external internet, but in either case, employees are provided with a unique email address to which both internal and external users may send email.

Email systems vary widely, both in configuration and screen appearance, but all have certain controls in common. Most commercial email systems run within a Windows™ operating system, or Android™ tablets, phones, iPad or iPhone® in which controls and options are presented to the user in an **icon** format. Many businesses have adopted an Office 365 subscription to access Outlook for email and additional MS Office messaging-based applications, such as Skype instant messaging.

If the user is *sending* an email, the system will present the send screen, or template (see Figure 9-2A). Certain fields on the send template will already have information added, such as the date, time, and the sender's network address. These are already recorded by the device's operating system.

However, to prepare the message for sending, you must provide certain information. Specifically, you must enter:

1. the name or unique email address of the intended recipient

2. the names and unique email addresses of any users who are to receive a copy of your email, or group distribution

3. the subject title of your message (strongly recommended but not required)

4. the message text

Options such as *mark as urgent, acknowledge,* or *cancel* may also be selected from this screen.

When options (if any) are selected and the message is complete, the user may instruct the computer to "send" the message across the network to the addressee.

Similarly, when you read incoming email, your message will be displayed in a message display template (see Figure 9-2B). The message will be received complete with:

1. the identification of the sender

2. the subject title

3. the date and time that the message was sent

4. names of those who were copied on the message

5. the message's priority status

6. the incoming message itself

FIGURE 9-2A An email message being composed for sending.

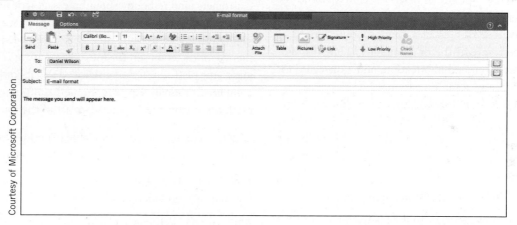

Courtesy of Microsoft Corporation

FIGURE 9-2B An incoming email message.

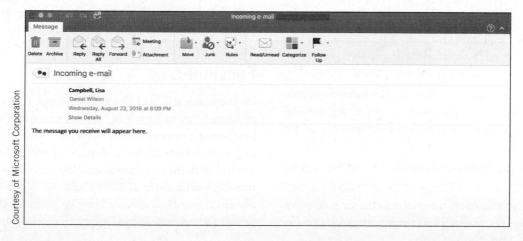

Courtesy of Microsoft Corporation

The recipient is not given the option to edit incoming mail directly, but typical options provided with incoming messages may be:

1. Reply—Reply to the originator using the same subject title.
2. Forward—Forward this message to another user.
3. Delete—Erase the message.
4. Print—Print the message on a printer.
5. File—Copy the message to a separate file (storage location).

The administrative professional should quickly become familiar with the email system used in order to communicate effectively. However, the explosive growth of digital messaging through communication tools such as email presents its own challenging issues. More organizations are recognizing that emailing and other platforms for communications require guidelines in order to be effective.

Researchers have discovered that while the exchange of email is a way of life, unacceptable and inconsistent email practices can develop into potential problems, ranging from system overload to public relations and legal issues. Unless the organization has a policy in place, users may not know they are using email incorrectly. Unintentional email problems include overuse of messages, inappropriate length of messages, failure to credit the original author, impulsive or inappropriate use, poor communication, and a disregard for the impact of one-way communication.

The office professional should remember that while the printed word has long been governed by widely accepted rules, the guidelines for using email are still evolving. To retain the meaning of the message and to ensure it will be read, remember to do the following:

- Learn to use all the email features appropriately.

- Clearly identify the subject so the reader can determine if the message is important. Be similarly clear and precise in your message. Be aware of privacy concerns in terms of others seeing the email on your computer screen. Be clear but think confidentiality as well.

- Avoid using bold, italics, or fancy lettering, as they may be misinterpreted by the reader as expressive or denoting urgency, even when this is not your intent.

- Avoid using special formatting. Special formatting commands in email word processing programs are not universal and may be garbled during transmission to readers who do not have identical programs.

- Ensure that you do not send emails with spelling or grammatical errors.

- Temper the speed and efficiency of email by carefully proofreading every document for accuracy, tone, and content.

- Never forward confidential mail to others without obtaining permission.

- Avoid sending highly emotional, sensitive, or controversial information.

- Make sure you do not burden the receivers with unnecessary information.

Implementing suggestions like these will be easier if you remind yourself that a person, not just a computer, is on the receiving end of your electronic message.

Email Alternatives—Integrated Business Messaging Platforms

The evolving nature of technology is creating a focus on alternatives to traditional email messaging services. Studies are showing that the use of email has declined steadily over the last several years. Customers are looking for ways to interact with businesses, how they want, when they want. A significant driver of this shift reflects the desire for faster, more efficient communication channels. Speed often equals success. Convenience is also a driver as clients are looking for greater results-based tools as life continues to get busier. Customers tend to believe email messages are ignored or are never responded to and phone calls disrupt workflow. Messaging provides the right mix of instant speed and convenience for the end user. Business teams are also migrating to messaging platforms for an enhanced collaborative approach compared to email services. Some examples of messaging platforms enabled in business consist of the following.

Slack   This is a chat tool available to businesses. Documents can be shared by drag-and-drop methods and editing capability.

HipChat   This platform has an instant messaging feature, file sharing, and video-conferencing capability.

Microsoft Teams   Creates a chat-based workspace focused on collaboration. It integrates with Skype video service to speak with guests and/or clients in real time.

Google Hangout Chats   A consumer friendly chat service. Offering one-on-one and threaded messages.

Facsimiles

Do businesses still fax? Resoundingly, yes, they still do! Surprisingly, a recent survey of business confirms the use of fax has gone up in recent years, not down. Faxing is evolving into a cloud-based service. Most business users have integrated fax services with other technologies like email, customer relationship management (CMR) tools, and specialized systems like electronic medical record (EMR) systems. Some business believe fax services are more secure than email and log a paper trail in legal matters. With e-fax, a traditional fax machine no longer is required—just a faxing platform accessible through the web using a digital device. This is the primary way of faxing now, compared to a standard traditional fax machine.

The traditional **facsimile**, commonly known as the *fax machine*, remains a component of office equipment (see Figure 9-3). Fax machines can electronically send copies of original documents from one location to another. The fax machine will send almost any kind of hard-copy document—keyed text, charts, photographs, drawings, longhand messages, and so on. The document will be reproduced on paper at the destination fax or computer.

Fax transmission uses telephone lines or internet services to send documents—in fact, sending a fax is as easy as making a telephone call. Fax machines operate automatically, allowing you to send documents without first notifying the recipient. The general procedure is very simple:

1. Place the document prepared for transmission in the sending fax unit.
2. Dial the fax number of the receiver.
3. Press the send button.

Whether enabling a traditional or cloud methodology for faxing, each fax transmitted should be accompanied by a cover page, called a **transmittal sheet** (see Figure 9-4). The transmittal sheet gives full details of who the sender is and who the receiver should be.

If you work for a small company that does not own a fax machine, you can lease one or use an online platform. Many CP outlets are equipped with fax machines for public use. Hotels will allow their guests to use their fax machines and often locate a fax machine in the lobby for public use. Most courier services are equipped with fax equipment that can be used for a fee.

Another precaution to take may be the inclusion of a *confidentiality request statement* at the foot of the cover sheet. The statement could reflect the following: *The information contained in this message is confidential and intended for the addressee only. Please treat this message as confidential and deliver to the addressee. Please inform us immediately if you do not recognize the addressee.* The administrative professional may wish to modify the confidentiality request statement or have a separate set of fax cover sheets for critical or confidential faxes.

Sending Money Electronically

If you wish to send or receive money over a distance, it can be achieved through most chartered financial institutions using their web-based banking options. You can also use a service such as Western Union or MoneyGram. These services require the sender to provide funds through a major credit or debit card. The initial transfer of funds may be limited to a maximum amount $2500. In more populated centres, transfers are almost immediate; in the worst case of a remote location, the complete transfer and notification process might take as long as a few days.

Electronic Services

Canada Post (CP) has invested heavily in technology to meet the evolving needs of contemporary business and consumers. CP has combined its long experience of moving mail with advanced technology to develop a unique Mail Production and Delivery™ service that simply requires you to provide CP with mailing information, and CP can look after the rest.

These comprehensive electronic services may assist with your mailing lists, mail processing, custom programming and artwork, formatting and printing of your mail, and delivery, either electronically or in hard-copy format.

Original information in electronic data format may be sent to CP via:

- PosteCS™
- file transfer protocol (FTP)
- optical disk
- tapes

Once CP has received your information, it offers consultation and production options that include:

- mail printing
- custom programming
- design and layout
- information management

FIGURE 9-3 Fax system.

Iakov Filimonov/Shutterstock

FIGURE 9-4 Fax transmittal sheet.

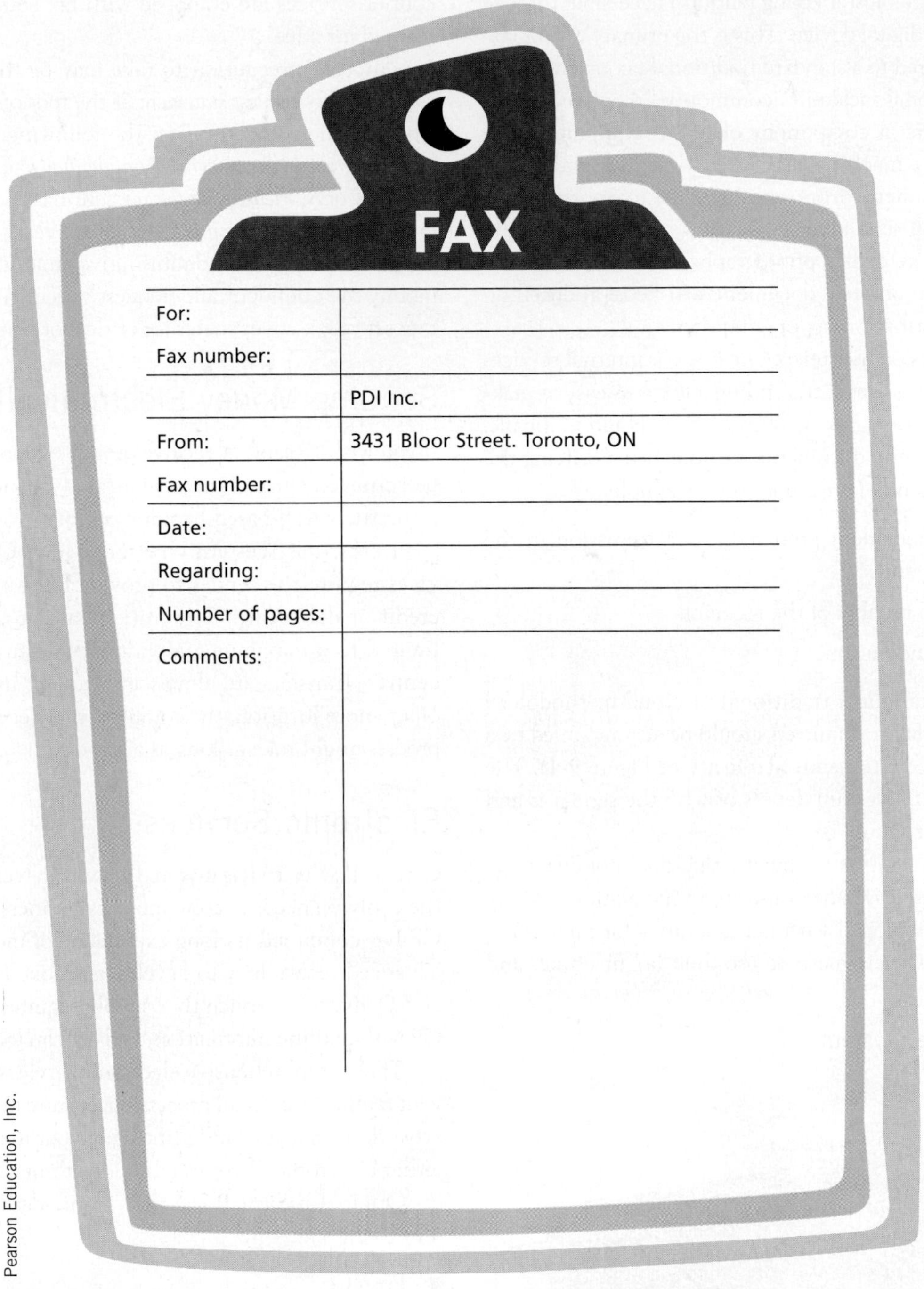

FAX

For:	
Fax number:	
	PDI Inc.
From:	3431 Bloor Street. Toronto, ON
Fax number:	
Date:	
Regarding:	
Number of pages:	
Comments:	

Pearson Education, Inc.

- address management
- return mail management

Finally, more options provide your organization with a choice of delivering its information electronically or in hard copy.

The two electronic services provided by CP are known as:

- epost™—for bill payment and receipt
- SmartFlow™—a document management service

These services automate high-volume document production for secure internet delivery. Examples of their use include secure invoices, monthly bank statements, and bill presentation and payment, all of which can be managed with confidence as a result of CP's focus on providing internet security for its clients.

The three hard-copy delivery services are known as:

1. Lettermail™
2. Addressed Admail™
3. Incentive Lettermail™

These options provide a hassle-free alternative to the volume "printing, production, and delivery" projects that are common tasks of the administrative assistant.

Electronic Post Office

CP provides the ability to send and receive mail electronically. Mail, in this case, refers to invoices, forms, and other correspondence that would normally be delivered as physical mail. The Electronic Post Office uses the internet to deliver your mail to a secure virtual electronic post office box known as an epost™ box. Individuals and participating companies send mail to your epost™ box just as they would send physical mail to a letter mailbox. You can store documents up to seven years in your mailbox.

You will choose the invoices you want to receive electronically from the list of participating companies. You may pay the bills in a number of ways: directly from your organization's bank account, a credit card, or by forwarding your invoices to your financial institution's banking facility.

All personal and confidential information remains secure because of encrypted codes and passwords. Only the sender and the recipient are able to see the contents of your mail. The email is stored on CP's own secured servers and not on public internet servers.

From the participating company's point of view, the Electronic Post Office eliminates the cost of paper and postage. The company may also maintain accurate records of mail and invoices as they are already presented in electronic format.

Email sent via the Electronic Post Office increases the flow of information in and out of the office. Since speed of communication is the main advantage of using email, the administrative assistant must be alert to email that arrives on his or her system but is intended for someone else in the office. Deliver or transfer the email without delay; however, if this type of email is received frequently, delivery schedules should be worked out.

Electronic Lettermail may arrive in the regular mail and should be processed along with the other items. However, the fact that it is electronic mail indicates that there is some urgency for its receipt.

Voice Mail

Because of its name, **voice mail** must be mentioned in this chapter.

In its simplest form, voice mail allows callers to access or record voice information from a list of prerecorded options.

Self-Check

1. Define the term *intranet*.

2. What information must you provide when sending an email?

3. How might you ensure the confidentiality of a fax you are sending when it arrives at the recipient's company?

To better understand this technology, refer to Chapter 6, "Front-Line Reception."

HANDLING INCOMING MAIL

Although most organizations now use email, every office continues to receive paper mail, and handling the mail is a high priority for an administrative professional. When the mail is handled accurately and expeditiously, other office employees are able to respond more efficiently to the needs addressed in the items of mail.

The information provided here on incoming mail is extensive. For an administrative professional to perform all these steps would be too time-consuming. While it is not expected that every office will handle mail with this degree of care, the administrative assistant is certain to perform at least some of these steps:

1. sorting mail

2. opening mail

3. inspecting the contents

4. date-time stamping mail

5. reading and annotating mail

6. presenting mail

7. distributing and routing mail

Some large organizations have central mailing departments, although with the decreased volume of paper mail, one encounters fewer of these. Such departments are responsible for receiving *all* of the organization's mail and for routing it to the correct departments or individuals. Usually, the mailing department provides at least one pickup and delivery to each department every day. At one time, central mailing departments opened, date-time stamped, and distributed the mail. They rarely do so now; instead, recipients open their own mail, or the administrative professional performs this task for the executives or for the whole department.

When the mail is delivered to one location, someone must sort the mail and deliver it to the appropriate workstations. If this task should be assigned to you, sort and make the deliveries at once so that other administrative assistants may start processing their own mail.

Sorting Mail

Mail may come to your desk unopened. When it does, read the information on the envelopes and sort it into the following groups:

1. mail sent with urgency (electronic or courier)
2. Lettermail, including bills and statements
3. interoffice mail
4. personal mail
5. newspapers and periodicals
6. booklets, catalogues, and other advertising materials
7. parcels

The administrative professional may have to sign for couriered mail and other insured, registered, or expedited pieces of mail before they can be received. Keep the priority mail separate from the rest of the mail, open it as soon as it arrives, and then put it on the addressee's desk in a way that calls attention to it. Priority mail refers to electronic mail, couriered mail, and all CP mail that is delivered via an expedited service.

In the stack of mail to be opened immediately, assemble Lettermail and interoffice memoranda. All interoffice mail is important. Each item either requires a reply or provides your manager with information she or he needs.

Do not open anyone's personal mail. Definitely do not open letters marked *Confidential*, *Personal*, or *Private*. Unless you receive explicit instructions to open them, place the personal letters on your manager's desk unopened.

Do not open, but quickly distribute, any mail specifically addressed to another employee in your work area. Any mail that has been delivered to you by mistake should be promptly forwarded to its intended recipient or returned to the post office.

You will have to decide whether mail addressed to an employee who is no longer with the organization is personal or business correspondence. If the letter appears to be personal, write the forwarding address clearly on the item and put it in the outgoing mail. If the letter is addressed by title to someone no longer with the organization, you can assume that it is a business letter. When you distribute the mail, deliver it unopened to the new employee who has this title or is responsible for the work implied by the title.

As you sort, put all circulars, booklets, advertisements, newspapers, and periodicals aside until you have opened and processed the more urgent mail.

Opening Mail

Before you begin opening the mail, assemble the supplies you will need: opener, date-time stamp, pencils, stapler, transparent tape, paper clips, your Mail-Expected Record, and your to-do list.

Slit the envelopes of all the important mail before you remove the contents from any of them. To reduce the possibility of cutting the contents, tap the lower edges of the letters on the desk so that the contents fall to the bottom.

Should you open a letter by mistake, seal the envelope with transparent tape, write "Opened by mistake" and your initials on the envelope, and distribute or forward the letter to the addressee.

Inspecting the Contents

Be certain to remove *all* the contents from envelopes. A thorough inspection is necessary to avoid throwing enclosures out with the envelopes. Keep the envelopes until you are certain that all the enclosures and addresses are accounted for.

Inspect each letter for the address and signature of the sender, the date, and enclosures. If the sender's address *or* signature is missing from a letter, look for the address on the envelope. If it is there, staple the envelope to the back of the letter. When a letter is not signed, the envelope may help identify who wrote the letter.

When a letter is not dated, write the postmark date on the letter and staple the envelope to the back of the letter. Also, if you notice a major discrepancy between the date on the letter and the date of arrival, staple the envelope to the letter.

Check the enclosures received against the enclosure notations. If an enclosure is missing, inspect the envelope again; if you do not find the enclosure, make a note on the face of the letter beside the enclosure notation that the enclosure is missing. Underline the reference to it and add a note in the margin. You will have to fax or telephone the sender to request the missing enclosure; enter a reminder on your to-do list at once.

When appropriate, if enclosures are letter-size or larger, staple them to the back of the letter. Fasten small enclosures to the front of a letter. Use paper clips to fasten an item temporarily that a staple would mutilate—for example, a cheque or a photograph. Fold a small piece of paper over a photograph to protect it from the paper clip.

Date-Time Stamping Mail

The time of arrival of certain correspondence has legal significance. For example, the date a payment is received is a factor in allowing a cash discount, and a specific time of day is set for opening bids. When correspondence is received too late for the recipient to comply with a request, the date received is protection for the addressee.

Organizations do not prejudge which correspondence should be date-time stamped. With the exception of a few documents that should not be marred in any way, organizations stamp all incoming mail either with the date or with both the date and the hour of arrival. The entry is made in one of three ways:

1. Write the date in abbreviated form, such as 21/9/2020, in pencil.

2. Stamp the word *Received* and the date with a mechanical date stamp, on which the date must be changed daily.

3. Stamp the minute, hour, and date of arrival with a date-time recorder. Mailing departments use a date-time recorder, which has a clock built in with the printing device.

Stamp or write the date received on each piece of correspondence in an area of white space at the edge. If you date-stamp all the mail as you read it, you will know as soon as you see the stamp that you have already seen and read a particular piece of correspondence. Consistently stamp booklets, catalogues, and periodicals on either the front or the back.

Reading and Annotating Mail

You can save a lot of time for your manager and yourself by marking and grouping correspondence according to the next step to be taken for each piece. You do this by reading the correspondence in search of the important facts, underlining key words and dates, and writing notes in the margins. In some cases, you will not know what the next step should be; in other cases, your manager will not agree with your notations. Even so, by using good judgment you can organize the correspondence so that your manager can spend time on the letters and memoranda that truly need attention.

Some managers prefer that nothing be underlined or written in the margins of incoming letters. For this reason, Post-It Notes or Info Notes have become a popular alternative to writing notes in the margin of a letter.

Read the correspondence rapidly, concentrating on the content and using a systematic method of making notes on which you can rely for following through. Develop a questioning attitude—one that will ensure that you pick out significant facts and help you decide what the next step should be. For instance, keep your eyes open for letters that:

1. Contain the date of an appointment that must be entered in the appointment calendars.

2. Mention that a report is being mailed separately.

3. Confirm a telephone conversation.

4. Request a decision that cannot be made until additional information is obtained.

Use a pencil to underline and make notes. Underline sparingly; otherwise, your attempt to emphasize will lose its effectiveness. Underline key words and figures that reveal who, what, when, and where.

Provide your manager with additional information in the form of notes. This is called **annotating**. Use small handwriting and make your notations brief. See Figure 9-5 for an example of an annotated letter.

Jot down what you would remind your manager of if you were talking to him or her about it. For example, if the letter is a reminder to send a booklet that was requested earlier and it has been mailed, write "Mailed" and the date of mailing. If an item referred to in a letter arrived separately, write "Received."

Annotating is preferable to verbally reminding your manager. The use of marginal notes eliminates interruption; also, your manager is able to refer to those notes as she or he answers the correspondence. On the other hand, she or he might prefer that no marks be made on a letter—for example, in cases when that letter might be presented to a manager for consultation and action, or if the letter might be circulated. Marginal notes can confuse readers, and underlining can irritate the readers to whom a letter is circulated. Although your usual practice may be to underline and annotate, refrain from marking certain letters. When in doubt, do not mark them.

As you read correspondence, pay close attention to the items that require following up. Make the entries in the proper places in your reminder system. Your follow-up plan needs to be foolproof; do not rely on your memory. Use a to-do list.

If you discover that your manager will need previous correspondence, make a note in your to-do list to obtain it. As soon as you have finished reading the mail, obtain the earlier correspondence and attach it to the back of the respective incoming letters. However, do not delay getting the mail to your manager. You can obtain earlier correspondence, locate facts, and verify figures while your manager is reading the mail.

Be sure to enter reminders on your to-do list to request missing enclosures. Occasionally, the sender will discover that an enclosure was omitted and will send it separately. Unless an enclosure is urgently needed, wait a day to request it. At other times, the enclosure will be needed immediately, and you will need to fax a message or make a telephone call to check on it.

If an enclosure is money, make sure the amount received matches the amount mentioned in the letter. When it does not, indicate the amount received and the difference in the margin of the letter.

FIGURE 9-5 Sample annotated letter.

PDI Inc.

3431 Bloor Street, Toronto, ON M8X 1G4
www.PDI.com

August 1, 20XX

Mr. Kyle Rhodes
Manager, Sales Office
PDI Inc.
3152-45th Avenue
Vancouver, BC V6N 3M1

Dear Mr. Rhodes,

November Sales Seminar

One of the speakers for the November Sales Seminar is in the hospital. Therefore, he will not be able to present a program for the sales seminar.

The members of the Executive Committee have suggested that you would make and excellent additional speaker. If you accept our offer to speak, you will receive VIP hospitality and an honorarium to cover all out of pocket expenses that you may incur.

The dates for the Seminar are Tuesday, November 11 and Wednesday, November 12. We would ask that you present your topic twice, once on each day.

Your presentation should last approximately one hour and delivered to an audience of 50 sales professionals. May we suggest that your topic relate to your successful methods of team building? I am enclosing a list of topic that will be used by other speakers at the Seminar.

Your acceptance of this invitation would be greatly appreciated.

Sincerely,

N. Wilson

N. WIlson
Chairperson, Sales Seminar

lr
Enclosure

YOU HAVE A CONFERENCE PLANNED FOR NOV 11, WITH H. THOMAS AND B. ROSS

NO ENCLOSURE WAS SENT

Pearson Education, Inc.

Presenting Mail

When placing mail on your manager's or colleague's desk, follow these simple rules:

1. Remember that the mail is a priority; act on it as quickly as possible.

2. Place the most urgent items on top and the least urgent items on the bottom. When items are couriered or faxed they may be urgent; however, you will need to determine this by reading the content. The longer you have worked for a particular organization or manager, the better your judgment will be in separating urgent mail from routine mail.

3. Mail should be placed in such a way that it is not visible to people visiting your manager's office in his or her absence. Often, you can protect the confidentiality of the mail by placing it in a large envelope or a folder.

HANDLING PACKAGES, PUBLICATIONS MAIL, AND ADVERTISING BY MAIL

Packages should receive priority over periodicals and advertising materials. Expedited parcels should receive the same priority as Lettermail. In some cases, you will be watching for the arrival of packages. Packages that have letters attached or that are marked "Letter Enclosed" should be processed with the important mail. However, do not open a package or separate a letter from it until you have time to check the contents carefully against the packing slip or invoice. Always avoid opening a package with the intention of checking the contents later.

Do not throw advertising materials away until your manager has had a chance to glance at them. Managers want to know about new products in their fields; perusing advertising materials is one way to become aware of what is new. If your manager asks you to screen advertising materials, be sure you clearly understand which items she or he has no interest in.

After your manager has seen the advertising materials, booklets, catalogues, and so on, you will have to decide what to do with them. Which ones should you keep? Which ones should you route to someone who has an interest in a particular subject? Which ones should you throw away? Ask your manager to initial anything that might be looked at again.

Figure 9-6 shows a sample Mail-Expected Record. Many offices use these to track packages and expected mail to ensure proper follow-up procedures are used to locate mail, especially those that are time sensitive in nature.

Distributing Mail

A manager distributes mail to others to do the following:

1. Obtain information so that she or he can reply.

2. Ask someone else to reply directly.

3. Keep others informed.

Important mail can be delayed and can even get "lost" on someone else's desk. Nevertheless, top management expects mail to be answered. Your manager is still responsible for the reply to a letter, even when the actual writing of it has been delegated to someone else.

As a general rule, your manager will make notations on letters or send memoranda asking others to comment, provide information, or reply directly. Some managers attach "Action Requested" or routing slips as they read the mail so that they do not have to handle the same pieces of correspondence again. However, much of this responsibility can be handled by an administrative professional. When given the responsibility for making requests, realize that a considerate tone will play a significant part in getting someone to comply. In contrast, a demanding tone will detract from your efforts and sometimes result in the letter getting "lost."

For informal requests for action, use an Action Requested slip similar to the one shown in Figure 9-7. For example, attach an Action Requested slip to a letter that has been misdirected to your manager and obviously should be handled in another department. Write the recipient's name, and check "Please handle."

Sometimes a letter requires two types of action, one of which your manager can handle and another that someone in another department must handle. When this situation arises, let the other person know precisely which part of the letter she or he is to answer. In the margin of the letter, indicate the part on which your manager will follow through.

Decide whether the person who is to reply will require earlier correspondence. If you think she or he will need it, attach it to the letter being distributed.

To obtain information, you will be dealing with co-workers in numerous departments throughout the organization. Make an effort to get acquainted with them, at least by telephone. When you must obtain information from a service

FIGURE 9-6 Mail-Expected Record.

MAIL-EXPECTED RECORD			
EXPECTED FROM	DESCRIPTION OF DOCUMENT	DATE RECEIVED	FOLLOW-UP SENT
L. Crawford	map	Nov. 1	—
D. Duggin	photos	Nov. 16	yes — thank you
I.B.M.	brochures		
Unitel	annual report		

Pearson Education, Inc.

FIGURE 9-7 Action Requested slip.

	ACTION REQUESTED!
TO:	Janice Miller
FROM:	Edward Kaye
DATE:	May 2
√	**PLEASE RUSH** – immediate action necessary!
	For your information; no need to return.
	Let's discuss.
	Note and return to me.
	Note and file.
	Please handle as you see appropriate.
	Please respond to this document.
	Your comments, please.
	Other –

COMMENTS:

The Kentworth Project can't go ahead without the third communiqué. We need to push this through.

Please complete action by _May 2_

Pearson Education, Inc.

department, you should be aware of the work schedule followed by that department. Find out how much time must elapse between the time you place a request and the time the material will be ready. Often you will be pressed by a deadline, and you must communicate this. You may have to request special service in order to meet your deadline.

When you ask someone who is not following a predetermined schedule to assemble facts for you, request that the information be ready by a designated time. Suggest a realistic deadline. Often, work that can be done when it is convenient to do gets relegated to the bottom of the stack.

Attach a routing, or circulation, slip to mail that is to be distributed to more than one person. A routing slip is a small sheet of paper on which are listed the names of the people to whom an item is to be distributed. Each recipient should initial and date the slip after she or he has seen the material and then forward it to the next person on the list.

When mail is often circulated to the same people, the names can be preprinted. On a preprinted slip, you can change the order in which material is to be circulated by

writing numbers in front of the names on the list. For an illustration, see Figure 9-8. Be sure to include "Return to" near the bottom of a routing slip.

When you distribute a letter, memorandum, or report to inform others, you will have to decide whether to attach to the original a routing slip listing the names of the recipients, make a copy and attach a routing slip, or make a copy for each person on the list. When deciding, consider the important factors, such as the number of pages, whether each person on

FIGURE 9-8 Routing or circulation slip.

ROUTING SLIP			
Sequence	Team Member	Date	Initial
4	J. Adamson		
	B. Best		
3	L. Singh		
	M. Paoli		

the list must be informed at the same time, your immediate need for the original, and the risk that the original will be lost while it is being circulated. Also consider paper wastage when you ask yourself how many copies are actually necessary.

Your records should show what information has been disseminated. When a circulated item is returned to you, staple the routing slip to the document. This makes a permanent record of who saw the item and the date she or he saw it. When you do not use a circulation or routing slip, and must make separate copies for each individual, write on your file copy the names of the people to whom you sent the item.

Answering Mail in the Manager's Absence

What happens to the mail when your manager is away from the office depends on his or her preferences and length of absence, and on the time and attention she or he can give—or chooses to give—to what is going on at the office while she or he is away.

Email may be dealt with in a number of ways: auto response, remote access, or with the direct support of the administrative assistant. Contemporary email systems provide an auto notice function that will automatically inform every email correspondent that the intended recipient, your manager in this case, is away from the office and that a full response will not be forthcoming until his or her return date. Alternatively, your manager may want to deal with his or her email while away from the office by accessing the office email system remotely. With the use of appropriate connections and passwords, your manager may access and deal with email as if he or she were in the office.

Active businesses of all types maintain their pace based on the free flow and exchange of critical information through email. If you are charged with the responsibility of monitoring and responding to email in the manager's absence, it will first be prudent to understand the nature and deemed priority of your manager's email. Determine which, if any, email should be forwarded to the manager or a higher authority during the manager's absence from the office. What remains in your manager's email is that which requires a response or that which can be saved until your manager returns.

You should process the postal mail as promptly when your manager is out of the office as when she or he is there. The first steps are always the same: classifying and sorting; opening, removing, and inspecting contents; date-time stamping; reading and annotating; and rerouting mail that does not belong in your department.

You will have the additional responsibilities of making a summary of all incoming mail, answering and acknowledging letters yourself, and seeing that correspondence requiring immediate action receives it.

If your manager is away from the office for only a day or two, his or her preference probably will be for you to put aside all the mail you cannot answer. However, never put aside correspondence that must be handled immediately. If there is no one at the office who is authorized to reply to an urgent message, call your manager.

Send letters that require immediate action to the person designated to answer them; make copies of these letters and write the name of the person receiving each one on the letter itself. Put the copies in a folder for your manager marked *Correspondence to Be Read*.

Answer the letters that you can answer. Acknowledge nearly all the Lettermail not being answered immediately, indicating that your manager will be back in the office on a specific date and that the sender can expect a reply soon after she or he returns. Note and reply to the email address (if any) on the incoming mail. This form of response is expedient and can provide a concise record of your actions. If no email address is evident, write a brief letter to explain the situation. The recipient of your acknowledgment will either wait for your manager's reply or contact someone else within your organization. You may say that your manager is on vacation, but do not say where. When your manager is on a business trip, remember that you would be giving out confidential information if you told where she or he is. (See Chapter 14 for examples of acknowledgment letters.)

Organize in folders all the business mail that accumulates during your manager's absence. Place the folders, along with your summary of the mail, on your manager's desk in the order listed below. Keep personal mail in a separate folder and put it on your manager's desk in a separate place. The folders might be labelled:

- *Correspondence for Signature*—for letters you prepared for his or her signature.

- *Correspondence Requiring Attention*—for all correspondence your manager must answer.

- *Correspondence to Be Read*—for copies of letters you and others have answered, and copies of your replies. Often, as a courtesy, the people answering will send your manager a copy of their replies. When they do, staple these replies to the letters they answered.

- *Reports and Informational Memos*—for all informational items.

- *Advertisements*—for advertising brochures and other literature for your manager's perusal.

When dealing with your manager's email and postal mail, always remain cognizant of the expectations and individual rights surrounding privacy. Chapter 1, "Human Relations," under "Keep Confidential Information Confidential," discusses confidentiality and the responsibilities that accompany your critical role as an administrative professional. If you wish to find out more about this topic, the Office of the Privacy Commission of Canada has prepared a guide for individuals to learn about their rights and the rights of others under the *Personal Information Protection and Electronic Documents Act (PIPEDA)*, Canada's private sector privacy law. For more discussion on *PIPEDA and privacy laws*, see Chapter 11, "Information Management."

Self-Check

1. List three reasons why your manager would distribute mail to others.

2. When would you use a routing slip? An Action Requested slip?

3. How should you process mail when your manager is away from the office?

HANDLING OUTGOING MAIL[1]

Outgoing mail handled by Canada Post (CP) may have a domestic destination, a U.S. destination, or an international destination. **Domestic mail** is mailable matter that is transmitted within Canada; this includes the 10 provinces, Yukon Territory, Northwest Territories, and Nunavut. Mail addressed to a point in any state of the United States, or to any U.S. territory or possession, is considered **USA mail**. Mail addressed to any destination outside Canadian or U.S. territory is considered **international mail**. These three destination groupings determine the cost of the mailing service. Of course, the size, weight, and delivery service required will also all have a bearing on the cost of the delivery. See Figure 9-9 for an overview of business services provided by CP.

CP publishes brochures that provide product and price information for these three destinations. However, because rates change rapidly, as do definitions of services, CP now provides a toll-free number and a comprehensive website for Canadians to visit. If you require the most current information on services provided by CP to any destination, call 1-888-550-6333. If your office requires a printed document with detailed information and rates for all services available from CP, the *Canadian Postal Guide* is available for reference at all Canadian postal outlets. Or, you may review and print it by connecting with CP's online information website at www.canadapost.ca.

---

[1] Information for the "Handling Outgoing Mail" section has been extracted from the *Canadian Postal Guide and Reference Tools* and the *Addressing Guidelines online tools*, both available through and by Canada Post.

Types of Domestic Mail

The basic types of domestic mail are Lettermail, Publications Mail, Admail, and Parcels. Your knowledge of available services should enable you to choose expeditious and economical means of sending mail.

Lettermail   Among the items classified as Lettermail are:

- letters, postcards, or similar communications completely or partly keyed or handwritten

- receipts, invoices, or similar financial statements relating to a specified sum of money

- any other mail that the sender chooses to post at Lettermail rates of postage

Lettermail items mailed without sufficient postage are returned to the sender. If the item has no return address, it is forwarded to the addressee for collection of the deficient postage and an administrative charge.

Publications Mail   To be eligible for mailing at the publications rate, a newspaper, magazine, or newsletter must be produced at least twice a year and mailed in Canada for delivery in Canada. Further qualifications require the publication to be either individually addressed or in bundles of unaddressed copies.

When you want to mail a single copy of a newspaper, magazine, or newsletter, you should use Lettermail.

Again, due to the dynamic nature of this service, it would be prudent for the administrative assistant to review current criteria for a mailing to qualify for Publications Mail. For more information, see available documents guides from www.canadapost.ca.

Snap Admail™   Admail is advertising mail that is posted in Canada for delivery in Canada and that meets the conditions and requirements for such mail referred to as direct mail as well. Alternatively, also through the CP Admail services include marketing campaigns appearing on digital devices as opposed to traditional door-to-door delivery. Addressed Admail offers your company the ability to target promotional messages to specific people or groups of people.

Parcels   Parcel service is used to send goods, merchandise, and so on. CP will accept parcels within a broad range of sizes and weights. To be accepted, parcels must conform to the packaging requirements of CP and must not contain dangerous or prohibited articles.

Parcel service includes:

1. **Commercial parcels.** Commercial parcels are those the mailer has weighed and applied sufficient postage to, before bringing them to CP for mailing.

FIGURE 9-9 Business services from Canada Post.

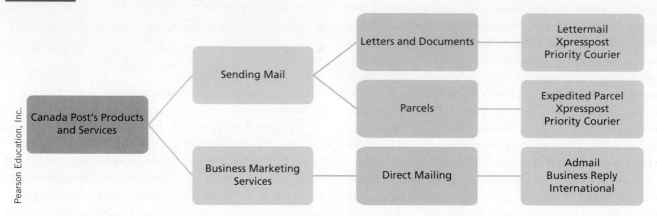

2. **Counter parcels.** Counter parcels are those parcels that the CP counter staff must weigh and calculate postage.

The minimum acceptable size for a parcel is a small packet; the maximum size depends on the length, width, and depth of the package. Within certain limits, oversize items may be acceptable, but these may be charged higher rates. The maximum weight allowable is 30 kg. Refer to Figure 9-10 for guidance when you need to determine which service to use. Remember, for exact specifications you must check CP's website. If you find it necessary to send a package exceeding the size or weight limits, you should consider alternatives to CP. Among these alternatives are services offered by private courier companies and by airline, train, truck, or bus companies.

Sometimes special services are required. When this is the case, items usually sent as parcels may be sent Priority Courier. Refer to the next section of this chapter for more information on the Priority Courier service.

CP publishes information on the *ABCs of Mailing* for business, which recommends proper packaging methods

for ensuring the safe arrival of goods. Unless properly packaged, a parcel's contents could suffer damage; parcels could even cause harm to postal workers and damage other mail. Remember that a parcel containing damaged goods is a poor reflection on your company and also on the product it promotes.

To determine precise weights, sizes, and standards for the service you are using, refer to the *Canada Postal Guide* or Canada Post's website.

You are not permitted to enclose a letter in a parcel; however, certain enclosures are acceptable. These include:

- an invoice or statement of account relating exclusively to the contents
- a return card, envelope, or wrapper
- a card or slip of paper giving a brief identification or directions for the contents

When a letter is enclosed or attached, it must be paid for at the Lettermail rate, and the item must bear the following endorsement: *Amount includes Lettermail postage for letter attached/enclosed.*

FIGURE 9-10 Maximum and approximate sizes for Canada Post mail services.

	EXAMPLE OF CONTENT	MAXIMUM WEIGHT	MAXIMUM SIZE
Standard Letter	Letter	50 grams	245 mm × 156 mm × 5 mm
Oversized Letter	Book	500 grams	380 mm × 270 mm × 20 mm
Parcel	Notebook Computer	30 kilograms	No one dimension may exceed 2 m (78.7 in.) Maximum length plus girth = 3 m (118 in.)

Note: To determine precise weights, sizes, and standards for the service you are using, refer to the *Canada Postal Guide* or Canada Post's website.

Priority Courier   Priority Courier is CP's top-priority service. It is a guaranteed delivery service for urgent, time-sensitive items. Priority Courier items, deposited at a post office in any major Canadian location and addressed to another major Canadian location, will be delivered on the next business day. However, this one-day Priority Courier guarantee applies only to shipments within Canada. For international courier delivery service, Canada Post offers service through Purolator™ International. This service guarantees on-time delivery of time-sensitive documents and packages to the United States and to over 220 countries worldwide.

The fee for Priority Courier covers $100 worth of insurance; additional insurance can be purchased up to a maximum of $5000. If you require further details, contact your local service and sales representative at CP.

Xpresspost   Xpresspost™ service combines speed with verification of delivery. CP guarantees that Xpresspost™ will be delivered in one business day for local destinations and in two business days between major Canadian urban centres. Xpresspost™ can also be used for time-sensitive delivery to the United States and other parts of the world. Service delivery is guaranteed within three to five days for the United States and four to six days internationally. It is intended to be faster than regular delivery and less expensive than Priority Courier.

It is available for both documents and packages up to 30 kg. Because an identification number and access code are printed on the sender's receipt, the customer may access information on the delivery status by using CP's tracking system.

Self-Check

1. Define domestic mail, USA mail, and international mail.
2. List the types of domestic mail.
3. Define commercial parcels and counter parcels.
4. What is the name of Canada Post's top-priority service?

Supplemental Services

As an administrative professional who prepares outgoing mail, you should know what special services are available from CP and when to use them. The following is a discussion of some of the services that enable office workers to handle correspondence effectively and efficiently. CP has an increasing number of services. If you require a service that is not discussed below, contact your local CP sales and service representative or review CP's website.

Registered Mail   Registered mail is an option with most of CP's services. For an additional fee, registered mail provides mailing and delivery confirmation for valuable mail items such as:

- important letters: for example, confirmation of appointment or a message from a dignitary
- critical documents: for example, contracts or land titles
- jewellery and other negotiable items: for example, stocks, bonds, precious stones, and metals

It also includes built-in insurance for loss or damage to the mail piece.

Registered mail is coded with a red identification sticker and is available for Lettermail services both domestically and internationally. You can also print registered mail barcodes directly on your mail items, using your own computer and printer. Check with your IT department to ensure your systems are capable of printing the required barcodes.

The sender's receipt bears an identification number that enables the sender to track the delivery status of domestic items through either:

- the CP automated inquiry system at 1-888-550-6333, or
- www.canadapost.ca

Partial tracking of U.S. and international items is also available.

Registered items must be turned in at an authorized postal outlet or given to a rural mail courier; they may not be dropped into a mailbox. On the delivery end, CP must obtain a signature from the addressee or the addressee's representative before delivery is considered complete. The receiver may inquire as to the name and address of the sender but may not inspect the contents before accepting receipt of the item.

For registered items going to the United States or international destinations, an optional Advice of Receipt is available at the time of mailing. This card accompanies the registered item and will be returned to the sender with the date and signature of the addressee.

Advice of Receipt   An Advice of Receipt provides proof of delivery (including the date and signature of the addressee) in hard copy. For selective services, Advice of Receipt can be purchased at the time of mailing. The actual advice receipt card is attached to the mailed item and returned to the sender by the destination postal administration.

The Advice of Receipt service is only available for registered mail to the United States and other international destinations.

Insurance   CP offers insurance coverage on its distribution services. Coverage for loss or damage up to $100 is built into the fee charged for many distribution services, including:

- Priority Courier
- Xpresspost™
- Purolator International

Additional coverage is available up to a maximum of $5000 for domestic services and $1000 for U.S. and international services, depending on the destination country. Again, it is important to reference CP's website for current and complete insurance details.

Articles to be insured must be handed in at the post office or given to a rural mail courier. They may not be dropped into a street letter box.

For insured items, a receipt for proof of mailing is always given to the sender. As with registered mail, the codes given on the sender's receipt permit the sender to access the tracking system in order to check the status of delivery. Refer to the section on "Registered Mail" for the correct telephone number and internet address.

In all cases, the signature copy of the receipt is available to the sender for an additional fee and will be forwarded by Lettermail or faxed within three days.

COD   By means of *collect on delivery* service (COD), the seller who wishes to mail an article for which she or he has not been paid may have the price of the article and the postage fee collected from the addressee when the article is delivered. COD articles must be sent by parcel only or at parcel rates. However, customers wishing to use the COD service for letter-size packages may pay Xpresspost service plus the COD fee.

CP will collect payment up to $1000 for a cash payment on a COD item. A cheque or money order is also accepted up to a maximum of $5000. When the addressee makes payment by cash or by cheque, CP will forward a Postal Money Order payable to the sender. This service cannot be used to collect on items that were not ordered or requested by the addressee or to collect money owing on previous accounts. The CP official acts only as a type of liaison in the transaction—delivering the goods, collecting the payment, and forwarding the money to the sender.

This service is available only for domestic mail. The item may be mailed at any postal outlet in Canada and may be delivered to any postal outlet or mail delivery route in Canada.

Return to Sender   Domestic business Lettermail is returned to sender:

- if it does not bear a sufficient address
- if the addressee has moved without providing a forwarding address
- if it is refused by the addressee, or
- if the addressee does not pay the postage on demand (no return address shown on cover)

Depending on the type of mail, the cost to the sender can vary from no charge, a fixed or negotiated amount, or an amount equal to the original postage.

Dangerous Goods

Articles or substances that could be dangerous to postal workers and postal equipment, or that could damage other mail, are prohibited from being mailed both domestically and to points outside Canada. It is an offence to use the domestic service to deliver:

- explosives
- flammable solids and flammable liquids
- radioactive material
- gases, oxidizers, and organic peroxides
- corrosives
- toxic and infectious substances
- miscellaneous dangerous goods, such as asbestos, airbags, and dry ice

A list of restricted items is available for international mail as well. If you are in doubt about any item you wish to mail, contact CP for a complete list of prohibited mail.

U.S. and International Mail

CP offers a number of services for Lettermail, Admail, parcels, and other items subject to customs clearance and duty.

Purolator International courier service provides guaranteed delivery to 19 000 U.S. cities and over 220 countries worldwide. It also includes:

- online tracking
- convenience packaging
- Saturday delivery to selected U.S. zip codes

  Xpresspost–USA offers:

- guaranteed service of three to five days between major centres in Canada and the United States
- availability for both documents and packages

Specific item barcodes and documentation for customs clearance in the United States are required. Like their domestic counterparts, delivery confirmation is available by using CP's tracking system.

As CP's U.S. and international mail services are designed in conjunction with other international postal services and are therefore subject to frequent change, it is advisable to obtain current and complete details of specific services from:

- Distribution Service Customer Guide
- www.canadapost.ca

Other Delivery Options

Courier Services   Courier service is available for sending documents or packages across town or across the world. It guarantees expeditious delivery; however, the cost of this service is high relative to that of CP's Priority Courier. Courier services are privately owned and represent strong competition for CP.

Many courier services offer one-hour pickup and delivery in the same city, overnight delivery to all major cities in Canada and the United States, and door-to-door delivery of sensitive packages and business documents. When an administrative assistant is responsible for having an item delivered within a very short time, a courier service is often the best option.

Airline Services   Canada's airlines offer competitive delivery service to all destinations they serve. If urgency of delivery is not the major factor, you may ship documents and goods via air cargo services. This service will transport almost any size of cargo, and pickup and delivery are available. Shipments are guaranteed to move on the first available flight. This service is much more economical than express services.

However, if you wish to ensure that your shipments arrive the next business day, you should use the airline express or priority services. Of course, these services cost more.

Bus Express   The most rapid means of delivering a package to a small town in your geographic area (or to more distant points not served by an airport) may be *bus express*. Most bus companies offer a shipping service on a round-the-clock basis, including Sundays and holidays. Packages often get same-day or next-day delivery. Call the local offices of bus companies for information on rates, restrictions, and schedules. Also inquire about pickup and delivery services.

Freight Shipments   Freight service is used for sending heavy, bulky goods in large quantities. Carriers include railway companies, trucking companies, and shipping lines. Airline transport is not as economical but is more expeditious. If the decision to ship goods by freight is based on economics alone, the sender will likely choose the railway, trucking, or shipping lines.

Self-Check

1. When would you send correspondence via registered mail?

2. What is Canada Post's COD service? How does it work?

3. Give three examples of dangerous goods that are prohibited from being mailed both domestically and to points outside Canada.

4. What are three mail delivery options besides Canada Post for sending nonelectronic mail?

Proper Addressing

CP uses computerized systems that can scan a wide range of addressing styles; this includes both handwritten and keyed addresses. To increase the speed and efficiency of mail handling, CP has designed a consistent format for users. For efficiency, CP utilizes a standard machineable mail service. Several pieces of addressed mail are placed in to an automated system, which is known as a Multiline Optical Character Reader (MLOCR). When the mail is addressed correctly following CP's requirements, it is processed quicker through this system. When it is not, it slows down the process, as each piece of mail needs manual scanning. CP requests that we use this *optimum* format whenever possible but recognizes some other formats as acceptable for computerized scanning. This is especially important for mail addressed in some languages other than English. Especially important in Canada is the fact that the *acceptable* formats encompass the accents, upper- and lowercase characters, full spellings, and punctuation used in the French language. For the sake of brevity, this textbook will deal only with the optimum format as defined by CP.

Canada Post's *Addressing Guidelines* can be found and downloaded from CP's website at www.canadapost.ca. Here is a simple example of addressing an envelope to a Canadian address courtesy of Canada Post. See Figure 9-11.

This comprehensive guide provides illustrated examples of different types of addresses, including:

- civic
- post office box
- rural route
- general delivery
- bilingual
- military
- U.S.
- international

The *Addressing Guidelines* also provide acceptable bilingual names and abbreviations for:

- street types
- street directions
- unit designators (flat, apartment, etc.)
- province and territory symbols
- U.S. and possessions symbols
- English and French country names

Properly addressed mail saves time and avoids errors in delivery. While the following information is designed to help the administrative professional properly prepare addressed mail, the *Addressing Guidelines* will remain an essential professional reference.

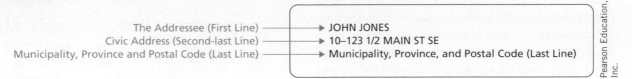

FIGURE 9-11 Guidelines for addressing envelopes from Canada Post.

The Addressee (First Line) ——————→ JOHN JONES
Civic Address (Second-last Line) ——————→ 10–123 1/2 MAIN ST SE
Municipality, Province and Postal Code (Last Line) ——————→ Municipality, Province, and Postal Code (Last Line)

Address Format The sequence of components for mail originating in and addressed to a destination within Canada is as follows (see Figure 9-12):

Addressee Information

Delivery Address Information

Municipality Province Postal Code

1. The bottom lines of the address are the most critical, since the automated equipment scans from the bottom lines upwards.

2. Attention or information data must always appear at the top of the address block.

3. Addressee information, delivery address information, municipality, province, and postal code must always be the bottom three or four lines of the address block.

4. Address components and elements on the same line will be separated from each other by one blank space.

The postal code, however, must be separated from the province by two blank spaces and must contain one space between the first three and last three characters.

5. Where symbols exist for address elements, these should be used rather than full names.

6. Province and state names should always be written in the two-letter abbreviation format. A table format is shown later in this chapter.

7. All lines of the address should be formatted with a flush-left margin.

8. Uppercase letters are preferred on all lines of the address block.

9. Punctuation such as the number sign (#) should not be used as a delimiter between address elements. Use punctuation marks only where they are a part of the place name (e.g., ST. ALBERT).

FIGURE 9-12 Guidelines for addressing envelopes.

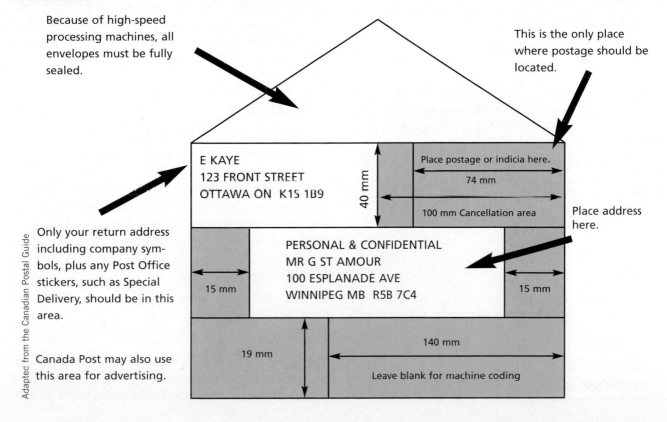

Because of high-speed processing machines, all envelopes must be fully sealed.

This is the only place where postage should be located.

Only your return address including company symbols, plus any Post Office stickers, such as Special Delivery, should be in this area.

Canada Post may also use this area for advertising.

E KAYE
123 FRONT STREET
OTTAWA ON K15 1B9

40 mm

Place postage or indicia here.

74 mm

100 mm Cancellation area

Place address here.

PERSONAL & CONFIDENTIAL
MR G ST AMOUR
100 ESPLANADE AVE
WINNIPEG MB R5B 7C4

15 mm

15 mm

19 mm

140 mm

Leave blank for machine coding

10. The name of the addressee is the last line scanned; this means that the automated equipment has already determined the destination before it reads the addressee's name. Therefore, punctuation is acceptable on this line. However, for consistency this text will adhere to the rule of all capital letters and no punctuation except where these are part of the place name. Both of these are quite acceptable:

```
MR. W. ROSS
     or
MR W ROSS
```

11. The return address should follow the same format as the main address. This is of little value in the original scanning for sorting and delivery of the item; remember, however, that if the address cannot be deciphered, the item may need to be returned to the sender. Use the same format, since the CP staff are accustomed to it. For items leaving the country, be sure to include the country of origin as part of the return address.

Non-Address Data   Non-address data refers to any additional information that you put on the envelope. The data should be located above all other lines in the address. Refer to the following sample.

```
ATTN: MR B CLARKE
MARKETING DEPARTMENT
IMPERIAL OIL LTD
PO BOX 9070 STN B
ST. JOHN'S NL A1A 2X6
```

Civic Addresses   In an English address, the street type always follows the street name. In a French address, the street type appears before the street name unless the street type is numeric, in which case the street type follows the street name. The street type should always be identified by the official CP symbols. Two samples follow; in the first, the French address has a street name, and in the second the street type is numeric. See the complete list of symbols in Figure 9-13.

```
B GUTHRIE
225 RUE FLEURY O
MONTREAL QC H3L 1T8
```

```
R MANN
2061 36E RUE
SHAWINIGAN QC G9N 5J9
```

Street Direction   Street direction, where required, is identified by a one- or two-character symbol, as shown below.

```
W WEEKS
548 GEORGIA ST E
VANCOUVER BC V6A 1Z9
```

For a complete list of CP's street direction symbols, refer to Figure 9-14.

Unit Designator   This designator indicates the type of unit, such as an apartment or suite, and should be identified by the official CP symbol.

```
MRS A DALE
415 HERITAGE CRES SUITE 102
SASKATOON SK S7H 5M5
```

Where the number of characters is too long on a line, the unit information may be placed on a line by itself above the street information. Refer to the following example.

```
MME R HUGHES
UNITE 509
169 RUE NOTRE-DAME-DES-VICTOIRES
STE. FOY QC G2G 1J3
```

Unit Identifier   The unit identifier is the specific number of an apartment, suite, house, or building. It must appear in numeric format; therefore, you would never see an identifier written as SUITE TWO.

```
MRS A DALE
415 HERITAGE CRES SUITE 102A
SASKATOON SK S7H 5M5
```

Where the unit designator is not stated in the address, the unit identifier may be placed before the street information. The proper separation between the identifier and the street information is a single hyphen. Refer to the example below.

```
MR W RIDDELL
104-2701 23RD AVE
REGINA SK S4S 1E5
```

Mode of Delivery   The mode of delivery refers to postal boxes, rural routes, general deliveries, and so on. The numeric identifier is separated from the mode of delivery

FIGURE 9-13 List of street types and corresponding symbols.

STREET TYPE	SYMBOL	STREET TYPE	SYMBOL
Abbey	ABBEY	Dell	DELL
Acres	ACRES	Diversion	DIVERS
Allee	ALLEE	Downs	DOWNS
Alley	ALLEY	Drive	DR
Autoroute	AUT	Echanger	ECH
Avenue	AVE (E)	End	END
Avenue	AV (F)	Esplanade	ESPL
Bay	BAY	Estates	ESTATE
Beach	BEACH	Expressway	EXPY
Bend	BEND	Extension	EXTEN
Boulevard	BLVD (E)	Farm	FARM
Boulevard	BOUL (F)	Field	FIELD
By-pass	BYPASS	Forest	FOREST
Byway	BYWAY	Freeway	FWY
Campus	CAMPUS	Front	FRONT
Cape	CAPE	Gardens	GDNS
Carre	CAR	Gate	GATE
Carrefour	CARREF	Glade	GLADE
Centre	CTR (E)	Glen	GLEN
Centre	C (F)	Green	GREEN
Cercle	CERCLE	Grounds	GRNDS
Chase	CHASE	Grove	GROVE
Chemin	CH	Harbour	HARBR
Circle	CIR	Heath	HEATH
Circuit Close	CIRCT CLOSE	Heights	HTS
Common	COMMON	Highlands	HGHLDS
Concession	CONC	Highway	HWY
Corners	CRNRS	Hill	HILL
Cote	COTE	Hollow	HOLLOW
Cour	COUR	Ile	ILE
Court	CRT	Impasse	IMP
Cove	COVE	Inlet	INLET
Crescent	CRES	Island	ISLAND
Croissant	CROIS	Key	KEY
Crossing	CROSS	Knoll	KNOLL
Cul-de-sac	CDS	Landing	LANDING
Dale	DALE	Lane	LANE

FIGURE 9-13 (*Continued*)

STREET TYPE	SYMBOL
Limits	LMTS
Line	LINE
Link	LINK
Lookout	LKOUT
Loop	LOOP
Mall	MALL
Manor	MANOR
Maze	MAZE
Meadow	MEADOW
Mews	MEWS
Montee	MONTEE
Moor	MOOR
Mount	MT
Mountain	MTN
Orchard	ORCH
Parade	PARADE
Parc	PARC
Park	PARK
Parkway	PKY
Passage	PASS
Path	PATH
Pathway	PTWAY
Pines	PINES
Place	PL (E)
Place	PLACE (F)
Plateau	PLAT
Plaza	PLAZA
Point	PT
Pointe	POINTE
Port	PORT
Private	PVT
Promenade	PR
Quay	QUAY
Quai	QUAI
Ramp	RAMP

STREET TYPE	SYMBOL
Rang	RANG
Range	RG
Ridge	RIDGE
Rise	RISE
Road	RD
Rond-point	RDPT
Route	RTE
Row	ROW
Rue	RUE
Ruelle	RLE
Run	RUN
Sentier	SENT
Square	SQ
Street	ST
Subdivision	SUBDIV
Terrace	TERR
Terrasse	TSSE
Thicket	THICK
Towers	TOWERS
Townline	TLINE
Trail	TRAIL
Turnabout	TRNABT
Vale	VALE
Via	VIA
View	VIEW
Village	VILLGE
Villas	VILLAS
Vista	VISTA
Voie	VOIE
Walk	WALK
Way	WAY
Wharf	WHARF
Wood	WOOD
Wynd	WYND

FIGURE 9-14 List of street directions and corresponding symbols.

STREET DIRECTIONS AND SYMBOLS			
ENGLISH STREET TYPE	SYMBOL	FRENCH STREET TYPE	SYMBOL
East	E	Est	E
North	N	Nord	N
North East	NE	Nord-est	NE
North West	NW	Nord-ouest	NO
South	S	Sud	S
South East	SE	Sud-est	SE
South West	SW	Sud-ouest	SO
West	W	Ouest	O

designator by one space. Do not use a number sign (#) before the mode of delivery identifier. Refer to the following examples showing the official CP symbols used see Figure 9-15.

Sometimes the identifier is alphanumeric, as in the next example.

```
MS B COLLINS
SS 4
SPRUCE GROVE AB T7X 2V1
```

```
MR BRIAN HUNTER
PO BOX 6001 LCD 1
VICTORIA BC V8P 5L1
```

Postal Code A unique alphanumeric code is used to identify the delivery address for a mail item. It is the first set of alphanumeric characters that CP's high-speed sorting equipment reads. The purpose of the **postal code** is to enable the automatic sorting equipment to read and sort millions of items each day. As the sorting process is an integral part of delivery, a speedier delivery of the mail item can take place. Addresses are considered incomplete if the postal code is missing. The sequence for the characters in Canadian postal codes is letter, number, letter, space, number, letter, number.

Since the postal code is read by a scanner, it is important that the characters not overlap each other or other parts of the address.

Canada has approximately 20 distinct postal code zones. The letter for each zone begins all six-character postal codes within that zone. The next two characters represent a region within that zone. The last three characters

of the postal code identify a smaller section of the area. A correct postal code will lead the mail carrier to the correct side of a specific street, or even to an exact building. Canada's postal code zones are shown in Figure 9-16.

Postal codes are now available from a number of sources:

- Some phone books publish the postal codes for all areas under the jurisdiction of the telephone book.
- A very effective postal code lookup search engine can be found on CP's website at www.canadapost.ca.

The postal code should be placed on the same line as the municipality and the province unless the line is too long; in this case, the code may be placed on the line below. Refer to the following examples.

```
MS DULAC
GD
COLD LAKE AB T0A 0V0
```

```
MARIELLE HOBBS
913 RUE DES MARRONNIERS
ST-JEAN-CHRYSOSTOME-DE-LÉVIS QC
G6Z 3B1
```

The lists in Figure 9-17 on page 183 show the preferred two-letter abbreviations for the provinces, territories, states, and districts.

Country The country name is used only on mail items to be delivered outside Canada. Use the official English- or French-language spelling for the country name. It should appear alone on the last line of the address block.

FIGURE 9-15 List of delivery address symbols.

DELIVERY ADDRESS SYMBOLS			
ENGLISH DELIVERY INSTALLATION TYPE	SYMBOL	FRENCH DELIVERY INSTALLATION TYPE	SYMBOL
Letter carrier depot	LCD	Poste des facteurs	PDF
Post office	PO	Bureau de poste	BDP
Retail Postal Outlet	RPO	Bureau auxiliaire	BA
Station	STN	Comptoir postal Succursale	COP SUCC
ENGLISH DELIVERY MODE TYPE	**SYMBOL**	**FRENCH DELIVERY MODE TYPE**	**SYMBOL**
General Delivery	GD	Poste Restante	PR
Mobile Route	MR	Itinéraire motorisé	IM
Post Office Box	PO BOX	Case postale	CP
(for lock box/bag service)		(pour service de cases postales/ sacs)	
Rural Route	RR	Route rurale	RR
Suburban Service	SS	Service suburbain	SS

An administrative professional may be called upon to prepare envelopes for delivery to foreign countries. For this reason, it is important to know the regulations that pertain to international addresses. CP defines *international mail* as mail items addressed to countries other than Canada and the United States. During processing of international mail, CP equipment reads only the country name.

Canada is involved in significant trade arrangements with the United States; an administrative professional in Canada may often have to prepare envelopes for delivery in that country. The CP processing equipment reads the country name, municipality, state, and zip code. Therefore, the lines that include these pieces of information should follow the CP regulations for envelopes being delivered in Canada. Other information in the address block is used by the U.S. Postal Service and should be prepared according to U.S. standards. The American standards are very similar to those used in Canada:

1. The full municipality name should be separated from the two-letter state abbreviation by two blank spaces.

2. The zip code will appear on the same line as the municipality name and state abbreviation. Separate the state abbreviation from the zip code with two blank spaces.

3. The zip code will be either five or nine digits in length. When the zip code is nine digits, a single hyphen is used to separate the fifth and sixth digits.

4. The guidelines for names and street addresses in the United States are the same as those in Canada.

MR B ROSS
4417 BROOKS ST NE
WASHINGTON DC 20019-4649
UNITED STATES OF AMERICA

MR THOMAS CLARK
17 RUSSELL DR
LONDON W1P 6HQ
GREAT BRITAIN

KARL HAUSER
LANDSTRASSE 15
4100 DRUSBURG 25
GERMANY

FIGURE 9-16 Map of Canada showing postal code areas.

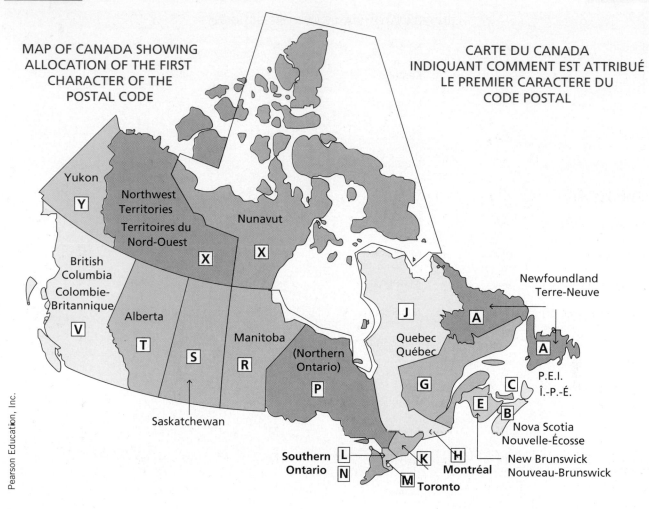

MAP OF CANADA SHOWING
ALLOCATION OF THE FIRST
CHARACTER OF THE
POSTAL CODE

CARTE DU CANADA
INDIQUANT COMMENT EST ATTRIBUÉ
LE PREMIER CARACTERE DU
CODE POSTAL

Pearson Education, Inc.

FIGURE 9-17 Two-letter abbreviations for destinations in Canada and the United States.

CANADA (PROVINCES AND TERRITORIES)			
Alberta	AB	Nunavut	NU
British Columbia	BC	Ontario	ON
Manitoba	MB	Prince Edward Island	PE
New Brunswick	NB	Quebec	QC*
Newfoundland and Labrador	NL	Saskatchewan	SK
Northwest Territories	NT	Yukon Territory	YT
Nova Scotia	NS		

FIGURE 9-17 (*Continued*)

UNITED STATES (STATES AND POSSESSIONS)					
Alabama	AL	Kansas	KS	Northern Mariana Islands	MP
Alaska	AK	Kentucky	KY	Ohio	OH
American Samoa	AS	Louisiana	LA	Oklahoma	OK
Arizona	AZ	Maine	ME	Oregon	OR
Arkansas	AR	Marshall Islands	MH	Palau	PW
Armed Forces Africa	AE	Maryland	MD	Pennsylvania	PA
Armed Forces Americas	AA	Massachusetts	MA	Puerto Rico	PR
Armed Forces Canada	AE	Michigan	MI	Rhode Island	RI
Armed Forces Europe	AE	Micronesia	FM	South Carolina	SC
Armed Forces Pacific	AP	Minnesota	MN	South Dakota	SD
California	CA	Minor Outlying Islands	UM	Tennessee	TN
Colorado	CO	Mississippi	MS	Texas	TX
Connecticut	CT	Missouri	MO	Utah	UT
Delaware	DE	Montana	MT	Vermont	VT
District of Columbia	DC	Nebraska	NE	Virgin Islands	VI
Florida	FL	Nevada	NV	Virginia	VA
Georgia	GA	New Hampshire	NH	Washington	WA
Guam	GU	New Jersey	NJ	West Virginia	WV
Hawaii	HI	New Mexico	NM	Wisconsin	WI
Idaho	ID	New York	NY	Wyoming	WY
Illinois	IL	North Carolina	NC		
Indiana	IN	North Dakota	ND		
Iowa	IA				

*Note that the province of Quebec uses QC as its official abbreviation. In the past, both PQ and QC were acceptable; however, PQ is no longer considered correct.

Bilingual Addressing Bilingual addressing is the use of address information in both English and French. The standard bilingual format is two side-by-side address blocks: the left block in French, the right block in English. The address blocks should be separated by a solid black line at least 0.7 mm thick. The following sample illustrates bilingual addressing.

MASTER CARD	MASTER CARD
BANQUE DE MONTREAL	BANK OF MONTREAL
CP 6044 SUCC A	PO BOX 6044 STN A
MONTREAL QC H3C 3X2	MONTREAL QC H3C 3X2

Return Address A mail item should display a return address that includes a postal code. The return address should appear in the upper left-hand corner of the face of the mail item. The same rules regarding components and format of the mailing address apply to the return address. Sender's name, address information, municipality, province, and postal code lines are mandatory.

Metered Mail

Many organizations use in-house postage meters. Metered mail need not be cancelled when it reaches the post office; however, it must be turned in at a postal outlet counter and not simply dropped into a mailbox.

Metered mail is sent directly for sorting, since it does not need cancelling by CP. **Cancelling mail** refers to the process of printing bars over the stamps, as well as printing the date, time, and municipality where mail processing has occurred. This process prevents a person from reusing the postage; more importantly, it also allows the receiver to track the actual time, date, and place where processing occurred.

Since properly prepared metered mail can go directly to the sorting machine in the postal centre, it may be dispatched slightly sooner than mail that must be cancelled. However, the real advantage to the user is the convenience of not using stamps but being able to apply whatever amount of postage is needed. Additionally, not waiting in line at the postal outlet is a great time-saver. Postage meter machines vary in size from lightweight desk models to fully automatic models that feed, seal, and stack envelopes in addition to printing the postage, the postmark, and the date of mailing.

Manufacturers of postage meter machines must have the approval of CP before distributing the machines. The meter impression die is the property of CP. Only an authorized representative of CP may set, lock, and seal a postage meter.

The user of a basic postage meter must take the meter to the post office and pay for a specified amount of postage. The meter dials are then set for this amount by a CP agent. Each time an envelope is imprinted with an amount of postage, the unused balance on the meter is decreased by that amount. When the unused balance runs low, the meter must be taken to the post office to be reset.

Most offices use a computerized postage machine that provides efficiency. These machines have a number of features, including electronic weighing, metering, and sealing. Computerized postage machines are leased from an authorized dealer. They are designed so that you can buy postage electronically without having to go to CP. Because the service is computerized, you can purchase postage at any time, even when the leasing agents are closed. The Electronic Postage Setting System (EPSS) allows the user of designated postage meters to reset meters at his or her place of business. The customer can remotely reset these meters over the telephone. The meter supplier provides the customer with a code via telephone, which allows the customer to reset the meter.

The following examples apply to mail prepared in Canada to be delivered to countries other than Canada.

If you use a postage meter, check the manual dials or electronic readout to make sure the correct postage will be printed on the mail. Also check the date to be certain it is the correct date of mailing, not the previous day's date.

In order to work efficiently, group your mail, and stamp all mail requiring the same denomination in one batch. Put pieces of mail requiring irregular amounts of postage aside until the rest of the mail is stamped.

After you have processed all the mail, reset the machine so that the next user will not waste postage because the meter was set for the wrong amount.

Try to avoid making mistakes when stamping mail, but if you do make a mistake, you can request credit from the leasing agent. When complete and legible meter stamps cannot be used because of misprints, spoiled envelopes or cards, and the like, the agent will credit the postage. You should note that in order to receive a credit, you must supply the complete envelope as proof, not just the meter impression.

Self-Check

1. When addressing envelopes for domestic mail, what information should appear in the last line of the address block?
2. What does the first letter in a Canadian postal code represent?
3. What does cancelling mail mean?

EXCEPTIONS

The mail does not always go through without problems. What happens to undelivered mail? Is it possible to recall a piece of mail or to refuse mail? As an administrative professional, you will encounter these situations, and you will have to make decisions regarding what to do when there is an exception or a change in procedure.

Changing an Address

When the organization for which you work changes its address, someone within the organization must notify the local postal outlet of the change. This can be enabled by purchasing through CP a business mail forwarding option. The mail forwarding option once set up with CP will automatically reroute the mail to the new address. There are some restrictions as to what CP will not forward such as prepaid envelopes or parcels delivered through Xpresspost.

In the event that you are sharing your address with more than two other businesses, CP will not be able to accept your change of address, and different arrangements will have to be made. Such arrangements are usually made in cooperation with company mailroom personnel or the person that accepts the mail on your company's behalf.

Returning Undelivered Mail

Keep mailing lists up to date, and address envelopes and labels with absolute accuracy to avoid the cost and delay involved when mail is returned. A returned letter must be placed in a fresh envelope, correctly addressed with new postage.

If the addressee has moved or simply refuses to accept mail, if there is insufficient postage or an incorrect or incomplete address, or if for other reasons the mail cannot be delivered, CP will return the item to the sender. Where the item is sent as Lettermail and contains a return address, the item is returned to sender at no charge.

However, charges may apply to other types of mail that must be returned to the sender. For example, if for any reason unaddressed Admail items cannot be delivered, they may be returned to the sender by specific request. The cost for this additional service is the applicable regular parcel counter price. Conversely, all Admail pieces that do not have the proper endorsement are disposed of locally.

Lettermail and Parcel items that are without a return address are sent to CP's National Undeliverable Mail Office. If necessary, CP will open the items to look for an address and, if one is found, will return the item to the sender. There is a fee for returning these items. If no return address is found, mail with no obvious value is destroyed. If the item contains cash, the money is deposited to the credit of CP. Saleable merchandise found in the undeliverable items is sold, and again, the monies are deposited to the credit of CP; merchandise that is not saleable is destroyed. Customers wishing to inquire about undeliverable mail should contact CP's customer service department.

Refusing Mail

The recipient of unsolicited mail, such as books and other items of some value, is not obligated to pay for the item or to return it. However, if unsolicited mail arrives at your desk and you wish to return it, you may do so without paying postage if you have not opened it. Simply write "Return to Sender" in clear words on the exterior of the item and drop it in the local mailbox. However, often mail becomes solicited without intention. Be certain to read the fine print carefully before agreeing to receive information through the mail. Often when people agree to receive information, they are also agreeing to receive merchandise that has a cost.

> ### Self-Check
> 1. What happens to mail that has insufficient postage?
> 2. What happens to mail that cannot be delivered and has no return address?

ETHICAL ISSUES REGARDING EMAIL

Every office employee should be aware of just how public the office email system is and take responsibility for learning the company's expectations regarding monitoring of email and other computer activity such as web browsing. While Canadian laws recognize an employer's right to monitor employees' email and internet use at work or while using company resources, controversy continues over what can be considered "reasonable" levels of surveillance. One factor to be considered in determining reasonable monitoring might be the reason for the surveillance.

Employers will cite a number of valid reasons to justify surveillance of their employees' computer use. Their concerns include the following:

1. maintaining the company's professional reputation and image
2. increasing security
3. preventing employee disclosure of confidential information
4. improving employee productivity

Companies vary in their degree of surveillance. Some companies rarely, if ever, monitor email use. Other companies may restrict any internet browsing or personal email use by employees while at work or while using company resources. Still others may restrict personal use of the employer's computer resources while at work to break times.

What is an acceptable balance between security and employee privacy? Companies are struggling to establish a balance between the two. If your company has no formal guidelines or policies regarding personal email/internet use, check with management regarding appropriate behaviour in these areas. Volunteer to work on a team to develop reasonable policies that would be acceptable to both employer and employee. Without a doubt, employees will be more likely to buy into the practice of surveillance if they understand the logical reasoning behind the measure.

Company policy or not, play it wise. Use company email for company use only. Set up your own email account through a provider and use it exclusively for personal correspondence. Furthermore, access that account only outside the office. That way, regardless of company policy, you will be confident that your privacy is not being invaded, that you are not using company resources and time for your personal use, and that you are not jeopardizing the security of the company's electronic data.

Further information on Government of Canada legislation regarding privacy laws and access to information is presented in Chapter 11.

International Holidays and Mail Service

People who conduct international business know how important holiday information can be when mailing or faxing important documents. Did you know that the dates of many holidays celebrated each year change from year to year? Some countries have such diverse ethnic populations that they observe religious holidays for ten or more major religions. How does this knowledge affect the way you and your manager conduct your business communications?

A surprisingly common reason for getting no response to a fax you have sent to an international number is that you are faxing the document on that country's national or local holiday. Conducting business may be difficult if people take extra days off from work in order to take advantage of the long holiday. Before you try to mail or fax an important document or package to a country outside Canada, check out that country's schedule of holidays. For a current list, access a search tool such as Google, and search under the key words *international holidays*.

QUESTIONS FOR STUDY AND REVIEW

1. List five guidelines that you might employ to make your email more targeted.

2. What alternatives exist to traditional email? Identify a reason as to what is driving the shift to these messaging choices.

3. List three postal services offered by Canada Post.

4. Explain why nobody but the sender and recipient is able to see the contents of a subscriber's epost™ box.

5. What should you do with a personal letter addressed to a former employee of your department?

6. What are the correct steps to take if you open a letter by mistake?

7. Why is date-time stamping important?

8. What is annotating? Why is it helpful?

9. The recommended methods for placing mail on a reader's desk are to put it in a folder or in an envelope. Why?

10. Give reasons for opening booklets and advertising mail daily.

11. What information should be recorded in a Mail-Expected Record? Why is the follow-up significant?

12. Suggest ways to group mail that has arrived in your manager's absence before presenting it for review.

13. State what happens to Lettermail items that are mailed without sufficient postage.

14. If you wish to include a letter in a parcel, mailed at parcel rates, what must you do?

15. What advantages do private courier services offer over Canada Post?

16. Can registered mail be put in a street letterbox, or must it be handed in at the post office?

17. Provide two reasons why you would send an item registered mail.

18. State five items that would be considered dangerous goods.

19. Where does the postal code go on a properly addressed envelope?

20. What punctuation is acceptable in the address on an envelope?

21. What is the rule for bilingual addressing on an envelope?

22. Why do many organizations use electronic postage meters?

23. What would be the most economical and fastest method of sending a bulky parcel to Whitehorse, Yukon?

Key Terms

annotating 167

cancelling mail 185

domestic mail 172

electronic mail (email) 160

facsimile 163

icon 161

international mail 172

intranet 160

postal code 181

transmittal sheet 163

USA mail 172

voice mail 165

EVERYDAY ETHICS

Trick or Treat?

Could it be that dogs recognize the shape of their biscuits? Canada Post believes they do!

Recently, Canada Post successfully lobbied Pet Valu Canada, a chain of pet stores in Manitoba and Ontario, to stop selling their most popular dog biscuits. The Bark Bar, a biscuit made in the United States, comes in several flavours and shapes. Most popular are those manufactured in the shapes of cats and letter carriers—traditional adversaries of the domestic canine.

The president of Pet Valu agreed to discontinue the Bark Bar after he received a persuasive letter from Canada Post's legal department. Pet Valu and its executive were accused of being insensitive to the dangers posed to letter carriers by dogs that ate the Bark Bar. Interestingly, there were no formal complaints from cat lovers.

For Canada Post, the whole affair was very serious and in very bad taste considering the hazards that letter carriers face each day. Pet Valu, on the other hand, reported that the product had not been withdrawn from any other market. In fact, some letter carriers in the United States are reportedly carrying Bark Bars to pacify their would-be archenemy.

- Is this a David and Goliath story?
- Did Canada Post take advantage of its overwhelming profile for other reasons?
- Did Pet Valu have any moral reason to stop selling Bark Bars?
- Was Canada Post morally responsible to protect its letter carriers in this case?
- What do you think? Support your answer with good reasoning.

Problem Solving

1. Desmond Clive is an administrative professional at a very busy office. He handles correspondence for five managers. When he processed the mail today, he opened a letter for one of his managers. He soon realized it was of a very personal nature, even though it was not marked *personal*. How should he handle any letters he receives in the future from the same return address?

2. Your manager, who is head of the accounting department, forwarded a letter to the sales manager requesting a reply. The situation is difficult to handle. The customer is dissatisfied with a product and has threatened to send it back rather than pay for it. Your manager is convinced that the sales manager must handle the problem. Here is the chain of events that follow: The sales manager's administrative professional immediately sends the letter back to you. You attach an Action Requested slip to it and send it right back to the sales manager. The sales manager's administrative professional calls you on the telephone and says, "We just sent this back to you, and here it is on my desk again." She demands that your manager answer the letter. What should you say to her? What should you do next?

3. As you open the mail, you find the following items:

   a. a letter that mentions two enclosures, but that only contains one enclosure

   b. a confirmation of an appointment your manager requested by letter

   c. a reference to a catalogue being sent separately

   d. a memorandum requesting forms that you supply to others

   e. a memorandum from your manager's superior, reminding your manager that she wants to approve the final draft of a sales bulletin before she leaves town on Thursday afternoon

f. a second letter from a customer whose first letter was sent to another department a week ago requesting a reply

g. a letter being sent to another department requesting a reply to one part of it

h. a letter including a price quotation that you requested by telephone

What notations would you make, and on which document or form?

Special Reports

1. Research online and find the following international rates and fees from CP:

a. the rates for sending a letter to China, Portugal, Russia, and Taiwan

b. the cost of sending a parcel weighing 1 kg to Australia, Israel, Spain, Great Britain, and Peru

2. Using information from CP, find the cost of the following:

a. an Advice of Receipt obtained at the time of mailing

b. an Advice of Receipt requested after the item has been mailed

c. a letter-size Xpresspost travelling to a destination 500 km away

d. insurance for a package valued at $60

e. registration for an item with a declared value of $2700

f. a 4.50-kg parcel mailed within your local postal zone

3. By searching the CP website, determine the service standards for:

- Lettermail
- Admail
- Periodicals

PRODUCTION CHALLENGES

9-A Processing Incoming Mail

Supplies needed:

- *Notes on Incoming Mail for Monday, July 14, Form 9-A-1, on Companion Website*
- *Mail-Expected Record, Form 9-A-2, on Companion Website*
- *To-do list, Form 9-A-3, on Companion Website*
- *Routing Slips, Forms 9-A-4, 9-A-5, 9-A-6, and 9-A-7, Companion Website*
- *Plain paper*

Mr. Wilson is out of the office during the week of July 14. You are processing the mail on Monday morning, July 14. Mr. Wilson always wants mail from a region routed to the respective assistant vice president for the region. However, Mr. Wilson expects you to open the letters and to keep a record of the mail forwarded to the assistant vice presidents. You route magazines and advertising letters from other organizations to the assistant vice presidents. On your to-do list, put reminders to yourself and notes about items that you should follow up on. Put the other letters, memoranda, and important items in a folder for Mr. Wilson. For your instructor, make a list of the items you will put in a folder for Mr. Wilson.

9-B Correcting Addresses and Postal Codes

Supplies needed:

- *Access to CP's website and the Postal Code Look Up web page*

- *List of names and addresses from Noah Wilson, Form 9-B, Companion Website*
- *Plain paper*

A. Privately, Noah Wilson is organizing a high school reunion. He has asked you to help in your spare time. The challenge is that while Mr. Wilson knows the names of his old classmates really well, he has vague recollection of their last known addresses. That's where you can help. Using CP's Postal Code Look Up webpage, determine the full, correct address. Key the address in the way that it will appear on an envelope, including the correct format and postal code. You will find the address information from Mr. Wilson on Form 9-B.

B. Martin Beard will be the treasurer of the high school reunion. Noah Wilson has asked you to determine the closest postal outlet to Martin's location to enable cash transfers. Provide the complete address of the postal outlet to Noah Wilson in the form of a memo.

9-C Checking Postal Services

Supplies needed:

- *Information from CP*
- *Postal Services question sheet, Form 9-C, Companion Website*

Collect information from CP. Read and interpret the information in order to answer the questions on the question sheet, Form 8-C.

9-D Determining Which Service Is Best

Supplies needed:

- *Mail Service Options, Form 9-D-1, Companion Website*
- *Mail Service Selections, Form 9-D-2 Companion Website*

Weblinks

Canada Post
www.canadapost.ca
Here users may locate rates, access product information, track mail items, obtain postal code information, and link to Canadian retailers online.

FedEx
www.fedex.com
FedEx's Canadian site provides details of online services, free software, shipment tracking, delivery options and rates, international shipping documentation, and much more.

PIPEDA
www.priv.gc.ca
This site from the Office of the Privacy Commission of Canada contains a guide on individual rights under the *Personal Information Protection and Electronic Documents Act* (*PIPEDA*).

Western Union
www.westernunion.ca
This site lists the company's business solutions services plus its messaging services such as Money Transfer.

Determine which class of mail or special service you would use to send the items listed on Form 9-D-1. Arrange each item on Form 9-D-2 indicating the service you would use and why.

https://www.canadapost.ca/tools/pg/videos/default-e.asp

Purolator
www.purolator.com
This site lists Purolator's online shipping products and services, including shipping estimates, shipment tracking, and an online shipping demo. Purolator™ International is a courier delivery service offered by Canada Post, as an agent for Purolator. This service provides on-time delivery of time-sensitive documents and packages to the United States and to over 220 countries worldwide. Details may be found on the Canada Post website.

UPS
www.ups.com
This site lists the UPS products and services and allows you to find out whether and when your package was delivered and who signed for it.

Greyhound Courier Express
www.shipgreyhound.ca
This site provides information on Greyhound's shipping services. The company offers domestic and international shipping services.

Chapter 10
Project Management

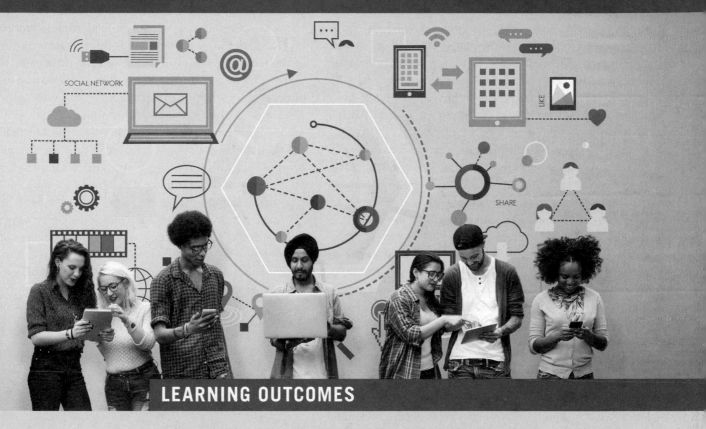

Rawpixel.com/Shutterstock

SOCIAL NETWORK

LIKE

SHARE

LEARNING OUTCOMES

After completion of this chapter, the student will be able to:

1 Recognize and understand the defining components of a project.

2 Understand concepts related to the theory of project management.

3 Define the role and core competencies of the project manager and project assistant.

4 Describe the five phases of a project's life cycle.

5 Explore project management certifications.

6 Discuss project management tools.

7 Identify project software options.

8 Understand common project management terminology.

Today, in addition to their ongoing daily responsibilities, administrative professionals are often called upon to work with their managers on special projects. These projects typically involve individuals from different departments and areas of an organization who work together for a limited time; usually a project manager, or PM, directs these activities. Administrative professionals handle and track a project from beginning to end in conjunction with a PM. These projects can range from conferences and physical relocations to major events and change management ventures. To be successful in these assignments, apply the skills of project management. The skills of project management are designed to provide the exactitude and discipline required to deliver a project on time, on budget, and within expectations.

Expectations extend to supporting a manager's participation on such projects. When a manager is supervising a special project, the administrative professional role will involve working as a project assistant. This will demand a large investment of time, and it will require an advanced skill set—to coordinate the work involving several people, gather resources, and assist management in setting goals and identifying project requirements.

This chapter will explore key theoretical concepts related to project management, the roles and responsibilities of project managers and assistants, essential tools for project management, and some of the challenges associated with managing special projects.

WHAT IS PROJECT MANAGEMENT?

To understand **project management**, we first need to understand what a project is. A project typically has a defined goal and a set outcome. The Project Management Institute (PMI) describes a project as temporary, having a clearly defined beginning and end, with a defined scope and resources. Additionally, a project is unique, going beyond a routine act or task, designed to accomplish a singular goal (Project Management Institute, 2017). For example, planning the Olympics would be considered a project to be managed that has a defined beginning and ending. Projects differ from ongoing work or tasks in that they often bring together, for a limited time, people who normally would not work together. Projects may also draw on a variety of organizational resources. A project is considered successful when its promised outcome is delivered, within budget, and on schedule. The primary challenge of project management is to achieve all of the project goals within the given constraints. For example, a constraint could be the scope, time, and costs involved in order to successfully complete the project.

According to the PMI, project management is the application of knowledge, skills, tools, and techniques to an extensive range of actions in order to meet the requirements of a particular project (PMI, 2017).

A project manager has the responsibility of planning, implementing, and concluding the project. The chief challenge facing the project manager is to achieve the project goal while dealing with constraints of time and resources.

In general, many of the skills an administrative professional enables on a daily basis are the same tools for successful project management deployment. The ability to use effective business writing skills to capture and conceptualize the project is essential. Prioritizing is also one of the most targeted project management strategies, as it allows a focus on tasks based on their deadline and level of importance. A large project may be perceived as overwhelming until it is dismantled into smaller, manageable pieces. Effective information-gathering skills will reduce the need to repeat or duplicate steps or processes. If called upon to work on a project team, plan to do a step each day on a long-term project to avoid rushing to complete many tasks at the last minute.

As noted, the administrative professional serves a vital role in meeting various challenges arising during the management of projects. As a project assistant (PA), you will work closely with the project manager from conception to completion of the project. Seamless collaboration between the project manager and the PA is essential for a successful outcome of the project. To equip this functionality, a foundational understanding of project management phases is helpful.

PHASES OF PROJECT MANAGEMENT

Each project has a life cycle, and within this life cycle there exist five distinct phases. Here are working descriptions of the project management phases (see Figure 10-1).

FIGURE 10-1 Phases of project management.

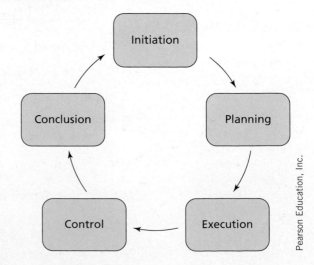

Pearson Education, Inc.

Fusion Projects
Vancouver British Columbia

Victor Zastolskiy/Alamy Stock Photo

Located in Vancouver, British Columbia, Fusion Projects is a project management company specializing in design builds focusing on tenant improvements. They believe the keys to their success is their integrity and operational excellence. These goals are achieved by providing value to their partners and clients through solutions to support increased productivity and employee retention. They pride themselves on the ability to bring an extraordinary quality personal approach to each project they manage.

Working towards a common goal of creating business interior solutions, Fusion Projects strives to deliver projects on budget and on time. Its talent pool of employees consist of project managers, coordinators, superintendents, executive assistants, and administrators. Employees are profiled,

detailing their title, credentials, and experience as it relates to project management. Fusion Projects boasts that its team is experienced with superior project management skills. The team skills, highlighted as they relate to project management, include time management, customer service, prioritization, field report compilation, quality assurance, and quality control. Part of Fusion Project's vision is to be recognized as an industry leader while delivering a positive project-based experience.

Another goal for Fusion Projects is to attract, develop, and retain outstanding employees. Fusion has a strong reputation for being a progressive employer, promoting the professional development of its employees. Fusion Projects encourages employees to take an active role in managing career development while providing an environment supportive of continuous learning. The commitment involves reimbursing employees who venture to enroll into approved business-related degrees, seeking diplomas and professional designations. Fusion Projects continually seeks to increase its talent pool with project management professionals who share a similar vision for the industry. Employees work a flexible schedule and are entrusted to manage their own time and work schedule. They are permitted to take needed personal time to meet family obligations. The workplace culture values respect, accountability, and open and honest discourse.

As a final point, Fusion Projects has an employee code of conduct policy to promote ethical guiding principles to follow while conducting company business.

1. **Initiation.** When an idea for a project is considered, it needs to be carefully evaluated to determine how it will benefit the organization. This evaluation usually takes the form of a business case that defines the project's objectives, scope, and purpose, as well as the deliverables required. Some questions addressed in this phase include the following:

   - Why do we need to do this project?
   - Who will partner with us?
   - What is the feasibility of this project?
   - What is seen as the high-level objective?
   - How is this project funded?
   - What are the constraints?
   - Who are the stakeholders

   - What internal and external dependencies should we be aware of?

   As part of this process, an organization will usually undertake a feasibility study to determine solutions for the business problem or need identified. Within the range of the study, a number of possible pathways will be reviewed and considered. Potential risks for each pathway will also be highlighted. Once the study is completed, a report is compiled and presented in order to gain the support necessary to move forward.

2. **Planning.** Once approval is given to move forward with the project and the team is assembled, the planning phase of project management begins. This phase involves putting the plans in place to guide the team

through the project process. In addition to creating an overall schedule for the project, several individual plans are created during this phase, including the following:

- quality plan
- financial plan
- resource plan
- risk plan
- acceptance plan
- communication plan
- procurement plan
- phase review plan

Together, these plans are known as the project plan. Not only does the project plan enable the team to focus on the project's goals, but it also helps in the management of staff and external factors to ensure that the project is delivered on time and within budget.

3. **Execution.** This is the part of the project and product life cycle where the tasks that build the deliverables are executed or launched. Project execution should be in accordance with the approved project plan. In this phase, you know what needs to be done and when it needs to be done. The start of one activity is dependent on the completion of another activity. This is why it is essential, during the planning phase, to create an effective schedule. Tracking the progress of completed activities is also a focus of project execution. Once work is completed by a contractor or supplier, it must be approved, or validated, to confirm that the work meets the plan specifications.

4. **Control.** The project control phase involves monitoring the actual performance and comparing it with planned performance and then and taking appropriate corrective action or directing others to take action that will facilitate the desired outcome in the project when significant differences exist. Controlling also involves anticipating and monitoring for possible challenges that could affect project cost, completion target, and outcome. Projects usually fail because challenges are not anticipated and effectively controlled. **Quality control** consists of the observation techniques and activities used to fulfill requirements for quality. **Quality assurance** is about ensuring that the project is produced in the right way. It is proactive and concerned with the processes and activities during the project's development. To differentiate between both, remember that quality control is about evaluating whether the product of your project meets quality standards. It is also important to remember that phases

2, 3, and 4 will be continuous, interactive activities throughout the project.

5. **Conclusion.** This phase involves the finalization and acceptance of the project. The project manager will ensure the deliverables are handed over to the customer. All contracts related to the project are settled. Sometimes a post-project review is conducted to assess the lessons learned through the process itself and to prepare for future project initiatives.

Self-Check

1. What is a project?
2. What role does the administrative professional fulfill in project management teams?
3. List the five phases of project management.

THE PROJECT TEAM
The Project Manager

Successful project management is a collaborative team effort, and a results-oriented team leader is vital in order for the mission to attain its goals. The leader is often referred to as the project manager. Since the administrative professional will work closely with the manager, an understanding of this role is essential. The primary duties and responsibilities of a project manager are described here.

Staffing and Development   To effectively lead a team, a project manager must:

- Build the project team by recruiting, selecting, orienting, and assigning duties to members.
- Establish all procedures.
- Provide training and coaching where needed.
- Lead and motivate the team and provide support for the client.
- Resolve conflicts between team members and relieve client concerns.

Plan Management   To ensure that the project stays on track, the manager must:

- Arrange resources by securing equipment, tools, and appropriate contracts.
- Establish project timelines.
- Meet financial objectives.
- Provide updates on project progress while identifying problems and solutions.
- Work directly with project stakeholders.

Interpersonal Management In addition to the practical skills listed previously, the project manager should have soft skills, or people skills, that will allow team members to interact productively. A project manager should:

- Communicate clearly and concisely.
- Maintain a positive attitude, even when things do not go according to plan.
- Provide leadership in order to manage by example (MBE).
- Be influential. With this skill the manager can often remove roadblocks presented by others in the department or organization.
- Delegate responsibilities to other members of the team. Managers will often fail when they fail to delegate.

Although simplified, this list provides a general overview of the duties and responsibilities of a project manager. See Figure 10-2 as it relates to the desired traits of a project manager.

Administrative Professionals Duties and Core Skills

From the project assistant's perspective, organization is key at the outset of the project assignment. Project assistants support project managers in balancing the time, money, and scope of a particular project. As support staff, the PA must be able to assume a wide range of responsibilities. The PA may be expected to clarify the objectives of a particular project and to assist in its overall operation. Duties can include handling the logistics of gathering information for progress reports, collecting and tracking time sheets, preparing job cost reports, making agendas, and maintaining and updating websites related to the project.

Although the PA's primary responsibility will be to the project manager, he or she will provide a variety of administrative support functions to the project team. A typical job description for a PA might consist of the following:

- Assist in the development of the project work plan.
- Compose, revise, and edit a variety of routine correspondence, reports, technical charts, tables, and other specialized materials, ranging from routine to complex.
- Produce materials to promote the project, including brochures, newsletters, and flyers.
- Prepare minutes of team meetings.
- Arrange appointments for the project manager, receive visitors, and screen calls.
- Maintain office systems, such as a filing system for project-related documents.
- Collect financial, statistical, and specialized data from multiple sources for the project team.
- Assist in solving complex problems by consulting with team members, including senior management.
- Provide logistical support.

Again, this is only a partial list. The PA may need to assume additional support functions, since each project is as unique as the project team.

It is important to remember that you may be assigned to serve as a PA on a project in addition to your other ongoing duties. Learning how to juggle the two roles can present some unique challenges. The ability to manage your time, work, and resources, as discussed in Chapter 3, is essential in order to find a balance when working in this type of environment. The following list outlines five key fundamental skill sets for a PA:

1. **Time management and organization.** Possessing these skills allows project assistants to keep project managers on track and to ensure deadlines are being met. A PA should be organized and should manage time effectively, being aware of the status of the project at all times. This is crucial in helping to keep the project on time and within budget.

2. **Adaptability and stress management.** A PA handles many of the unknowns, which accompany most projects. Objectives will constantly shift throughout the project phases, and setbacks are likely to occur. Managing through errors is essential to keeping the project on track.

FIGURE 10-2 Traits of a project manager.

TOP 10 PROJECT MANAGER QUALITIES	
✓	Communication
✓	Organization
✓	Competence
✓	Integrity
✓	Delegation
✓	Enthusiasm
✓	Being Visionary
✓	Team Building
✓	Problem Solving
✓	Flexibility

3. **Computer and math.** A PA should be skilled in the use of project management software as well as other digital communication tools related to the project. Budgets are key pieces of the project requirements, and the PA often assists the project manager in costing and estimating projects, hence the math skill requirement.

4. **Communication.** The ability to communicate project information is key for the success of the initiative. According to statistics, 75% of successful project completions have effective communication strategies as the common element. The PA role is foundational for ensuring that information is conveyed in a timely and proficient manner to all stakeholders.

5. **Leadership and problem solving.** The significance of leadership and problem-solving skills cannot be overstated. At times when the project manager is unavailable, the project assistant may assume some of the project responsibilities. The ability to take a leadership charge and evaluate situations to determine a best course of action is one of the most important qualities for a project assistant to possess.

Building the Project Team

The project team is critical to the success of the project. In selecting the team, the project manager must determine if the skills of each potential team member will match the project. It is important to have the right people working on the right projects. The project manager may prepare checklists to ensure that each member of the project team has the skills and abilities to reach the targets of the project. Getting the right balance of skills, knowledge, and ability is difficult but essential for the smooth implementation of a project plan.

When the team is assembled, the background and benefits of the project will be explained. This will establish the foundation for execution of the project plan. It is important that all members of the team fully support the overall project as well as the methods for its implementation. All team members need to be flexible, and the team leader needs to set reasonable and realistic expectations.

The importance of good communication among team members cannot be underestimated. The project manager is ultimately responsible for the way in which information and updates are communicated and for creating an environment in which members feel free to share their ideas. Everyone has a preferred approach to communicating, so it is important, where possible, to accommodate and adapt to these preferences. This will make team members more comfortable and more confident in their abilities. Whatever method of communication is chosen, it should be easily accessible to ensure that team members always have the most up-to-date information.

In addition, the project leader must provide encouragement and **motivation**. Being overly critical will have a negative effect and discourage team members from fulfilling the requirements of the project. The project leader should also schedule meetings, either face-to-face or online, so that team members can ask questions and set action lists. Problems can also be addressed and resolved during these routine meetings.

Finally, the team needs to trust the project manager. They need to have confidence that the project manager will lead the team effectively, and they need to know they can come to the project manager with questions and concerns. Team members will also look to the leader to set the tone for how the team will function. It is very difficult to solve problems in a distrustful environment. Similarly, when team members trust each other, they are much more likely to work well together and accomplish their goals.

Self-Check

1. Name three recommended skills for a project manager.
2. Name two tasks a project assistant will perform.

Certifications and Credentials

Certification requirements for project management professionals as set forth by the PMI are globally recognized as providing the standard for knowledge and skills in this continually growing and evolving field. Project assistants may consider securing certifications and/or credentials offered by PMI to boost career opportunities in this area.

PMI refers to over 650 000 professionals worldwide holding a project related certification and the numbers continue to grow (PMI, 2018). PMI was the first organization to offer certification for project managers. As of 2018, PMI offers eight certifications. Here is a sample of the certifications offered.

Certified Associate in Project Management (CAPM)®

This is an entry-level certification for someone who is new to project management but who wants to embark on a career in this field. Certification eligibility for each credential is based on several factors such as project management experience and education. To formalize the process, an exam is usually required to obtain this certification. Generally speaking, to be eligible to write the exam, you are required to demonstrate that you have either approximately 1500 hours of experience related to project management or 20 to 25 hours of in-class project management education.

Project Management Professional (PMP)® This certification attests to the ability to lead projects and teams. To obtain this certification, a candidate normally requires several years of practical experience in project management.

Program Management Professional (PgMP)® This is an advanced certification for project managers who have handled multiple projects to satisfy organizational goals.

PfMP® Portfolio Management Professional (PfMP)® Portfolio management certification recognizes the advanced experience and skill of portfolio managers. The PfMP demonstrates proven ability in the coordinated management of one or more portfolios to achieve organizational objectives.

PMI Agile Certified Practitioner (PMI-ACP)™ This certification is awarded to professionals who possess the demonstrated technique of developing and delivering incremental components of business functionality, product development, or process design.

---

pro-Link
Project Management Terms

Professionals often use terminology that is unique to their area of expertise. The field of project management has its own specialized terminology. Familiarizing yourself with these terms will help you to communicate more effectively when you are assigned to a special project:

1. **Acceptance.** The formal process of accepting delivery of a product or intermediate project deliverable after having assured that it meets the stated requirements.
2. **Acquisition.** Obtaining under contract the supplies and services to meet the needs of a project.
3. **Assumptions.** Factors that, for planning purposes, are considered to be true, real, or certain. Assumptions affect all aspects of project planning and are part of the progressive elaboration of the project. Project teams frequently identify, document, and validate assumptions as part of their planning process. Assumptions generally involve a degree of risk.
4. **Baseline.** A formally approved version of the project schedule and/or budget that is used as the benchmark for comparing future progress as the project is completed. A baseline cannot be changed without going through a change approval process. It is usually used with a modifier (e.g., cost baseline, schedule baseline, performance measurement baseline).

5. **Chain.** A series of elements joined together in sequence, such as a logical series of activities or occurrences.
6. **Deficiency.** All or part of an item that does not comply with its governing requirements or specifications.
7. **Deliverable.** Any measurable, tangible, verifiable item that must be produced to complete the project. The term is often used more narrowly in reference to an external deliverable, which is a deliverable that is subject to approval by the project sponsor or customer.
8. **Forecast at completion (FAC).** Scheduled cost for a task.
9. **Gantt chart.** Henry Gantt designed a graphic display to show a schedule of related information. In the typical Gantt chart, activities are listed down the left side of the chart, dates are shown across the top, and planned activity durations are shown as date-placed horizontal bars. This is also called a bar chart.
10. **Handover.** A process of transfer of responsibility for all or part of a project or its deliverables. Typically, this takes place at the end of a project or a major part thereof.
11. **Key.** In project management, if something is key it typically means an item is a deciding factor, that is, is critical, instrumental, or central to arriving at some determination.
12. **Medium term.** Anything occurring over or involving an intermediate time period, that is, between long term and short term.

PMI Professional in Business Analysis (PMI-PBA)® The PMI-PBA highlights expertise in business analysis. The certification shows the ability to work effectively with stakeholders to define business requirements, shape the output of projects, and drive successful business outcomes. It requires approximately 7500 hours of business analysis experience or a combination of education and experience.

PMI Risk Management Professional (PMI-RMP)® This certification recognizes the professional manager's unique expertise and competency in assessing and identifying project risks, mitigating threats, and capitalizing on opportunities, while still possessing a baseline knowledge and practical application in all areas of project management.

PMI Scheduling Professional (PMI-SP)® This certification recognizes the professional manager's unique expertise and competence to develop and maintain project schedules, while still possessing baseline knowledge skills in all areas of project management.

These are an example of some of the certifications available to project managers. There are a number of other institutions, each with its own curriculum and requirements, that offer project management credentials.

PROJECT MANAGEMENT TOOLS

As with any task or responsibility, in project management a variety of tools can be used to maximize success. One of the duties of the project manager is to determine, in collaboration with the project team, which tools will be most effective.

Tool Categories

According to Project Management Tips, a collaborative blog located at www.pmtips.net offering advice on a number of project management topics, there are three categories of tools that can be used during a project: individual, collaborative, and integrated:

1. **Individual.** These are tools individual members on the program team will use. An individual tool could be something as basic as a task manager program or a spreadsheet stored on an individual's computer or device.

2. **Collaborative.** These are tools that more than one person on the team can access and contribute to, such as a document made available on an intranet site. Another example might be a wiki that team members can use to resolve a challenge they are facing.

3. **Integrated.** This tool can take data from different sources and make it available in one place. Calendars and instant messaging systems are examples of integrated tools.

Project Management Software and Apps

Because special projects often depend on many different people, departments, and outcomes, they can be complex. Project software can help in managing some of these factors. For example, project management software can determine which events depend on one another, how exactly they depend on each other, and what happens if things change or go wrong.

There are many different types of project management software—even the definition of it varies widely—and what software your organization will use is likely to depend substantially on the size and scope of the project. Some types of project management software are designed to help organize

a project from start to finish. Software is also available that provides task and resource management, tracking, and outcome report standards.

If your organization decides to invest in project management software, it can be obtained in a few formats.

Desktop Applications A desktop package typically gives the most responsive and graphically intense **interface**. Desktop project management applications typically store their data in a file. Although some versions offer the ability to collaborate with other users, the desktop format does limit collaboration significantly. Some desktop programs permit users to store their data in a central database. Multiple users can then share file-based project plans or data. Microsoft Project (see Figure 10-3) is an example of this type of software.

When using desktop project management software, it is important to keep the version current. All users should regularly obtain software updates.

Client Servers Server-based collaborative project management applications are also available. These are designed to support multiple users who are working on different parts of a project. Server-based project management systems hold data centrally and can also incorporate collaboration tools so that users can share knowledge and

FIGURE 10-3 Screen capture of Microsoft Project.

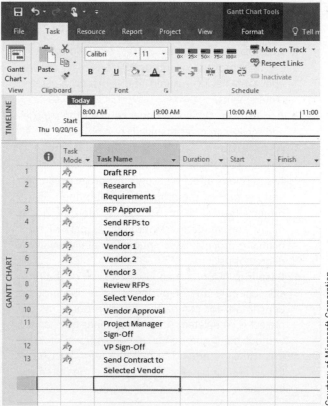

expertise. Microsoft Project is also available as a server-based application.

With client server software you are in control of updates, and you can cut ties with the provider if you do not need upgrades or technical support. A drawback to server-based products is that they usually cost more than desktop software; licensing fees are often charged on an annual basis.

Web-Based Software Project management software can be obtained as a web application. Web-based software is accessed through an intranet or extranet, or the internet itself, using a web browser. Users can access the application from a computer or mobile device without needing to install the program on their computers. They will always have the most recent version, as the provider will automatically update it. One of the greatest advantages of web-based programs is that they support multiple users. A drawback to this type of software is that, unlike a desktop application, the software is not available when the user is not online.

Mobile Apps For teams on the go, a project management app is helpful to keep everyone productive. Some examples of these mobile apps include WorkflowMax, Wrike, and Trello.

Problem Solving and Decision-Making Techniques

In a perfect world, problems are solved with little to no effort. The project team (see Figure 10-4) must work together to solve problems quickly and efficiently. When a problem occurs, people on the team need to take ownership of it by involving those individuals most familiar with it. This will promote prompt resolution. When the problem is defined and all options are weighed, a solution can often be found. Here are some basic guidelines to follow when problem solving collaboratively within the project team:

- Define the problem. What prevents this aspect of the project plan from working?
- Identify alternatives. Consider a variety of solutions.
- Avoid blaming. Focus on solutions, not blame.
- Be creative. Encourage a different approach.

FIGURE 10-4 A project management team.

Konstantin Chagin/123RF

QUESTIONS FOR STUDY AND REVIEW

1. What is the difference between a project and ongoing work?

2. What title are administrative professionals often given for their support role in project management?

3. What does PMI stand for?

4. Describe the initiation phase of project management.

5. List two types of plans developed in the planning phase.

6. Contrast quality assurance and quality control.

7. Identify staffing and development responsibilities of the project manager.

8. Discuss three abilities a project manager should possess. State why these qualities are essential for effective project management.

9. List two certifications available through PMI.

10. Describe tools that can be used during a project.

11. Identify one of the benefits of using desktop-, server-, web-based, or mobile apps for project management.

12. Identify a disadvantage of using desktop-, server-, or web-based software for project management.

13. Suggest three important considerations a project manager should take into account when building a project team.

14. Explain what happens during the execution phase of a project.

15. Define the following project management terms:

    acquisition

    chain

    deliverable

Key Terms

interface 198

motivation 196

project management 192

quality assurance 194

quality control 194

EVERYDAY ETHICS

The Presentation

You have been working at a construction firm for three years as an administrative professional. Two months ago you were asked to assume the role of project assistant on a new project proposal. This new responsibility has required you to work closely with a new sales manager, Maureen Frances. Ms. Frances is responsible for putting the initial proposal together for the large project, which, if successful, will generate a significant industry-related recognition for the company. You are nearing the end stage of the proposal preparation; a meeting has been set to present the proposal to the senior management team for final endorsement next week. Ms. Frances has asked you to take the information she has gathered so far and create a slide show to "wow" the senior team.

Following Ms. Frances's instructions, you placed significant key points from the feasibility study, including the financial analysis and the risk management analysis, into the slide show. The day before the presentation, Ms. Frances asked to review your slide show. After viewing it, she thanked you and appeared pleased with the work you did.

Today, Ms. Frances presented the slide show to the senior team and received full endorsement to move forward with the proposed project. You should be happy, as this means you will continue as the project assistant and receive bonus, but you are not. Your concerns are based on the presentation Ms. Frances gave. Many of your slides involving the potential risks of the project were either removed from the presentation or changed to make the project more attractive to the senior team. You believe the senior team did not receive the full information necessary to make an informed decision.

■ Should you ask Ms. Frances about the altered slides? If yes, how will you approach her? If no, what are the possible consequences of your silence?

■ Should you speak to the senior team members about what happened? Why? Alternatively, why not?

■ Do you have any other choices in this situation?

Problem Solving

1. You have been working on a new project team for the last couple of weeks, and you find you are often the liaison between the project manager and the client. When you communicate with the client, you feel you get vague instructions, and several times the client has changed his requirements. Today, the project manager has asked you to contact the client to set up a Skype meeting in one week's time with the project team to discuss the status of the project. The status update meeting is a periodic meeting that offers team members an opportunity to address issues and concerns. How will you address your concerns about the client's vague instructions and unexpected requests for changes?

2. The project manager, Ray William, has asked you to call two subcontractors to set up a meeting for tomorrow morning to discuss some urgent work to be completed, as the project has come to a standstill. You make the necessary calls, and both of the contractors tell you that they will consider a meeting only after they have received some key pieces of information. You agree to forward these documents to them electronically very shortly. Unfortunately, you have been very busy today, as a computer emergency took up a lot of your time and your son came home from school sick. It is now 4 p.m. and you have not sent the information to the contractors. Is there anything you can do now to fix the situation?

3. You are approaching the midway point of a project, and the date of the next status meeting is fast approaching. You have almost everything you need to put the status report together for the stakeholders. You are working with five members of the team. Four of them have been wonderful about sending you updates, but one team member, Christopher Rays, is consistently behind schedule. The team uses web-based software so that everyone can see when a task has been completed. You have repeatedly reminded Christopher that he needs to send you timely updates. Each time he promises he will be more punctual in sending you the updates. Still, you feel you are spending a lot of your energy in following up with Christopher, and his updates still come in late despite your best efforts. Is there anything you can do?

Special Reports

1. Working in groups of two or three think of a time you have been part of a project team. In your groups, discuss the following:
   a. the main objective of the project
   b. the project outcome
   c. what was positive about the experience
   d. what was negative about the experience
   Report your findings to the class.

2. Interview a project manager asking the following questions:
   a. Describe the core skills you need in your project assistant.
   b. How would you recommend that someone gain experience in project management?
   Prepare a memo to your instructor sharing your findings.

3. Review the University of Chicago's Project Management webpage here: http://itspmo.uchicago.edu/ and then select *success stories*. Select and review two projects completed as outlined on the webpage, and prepare a brief report outlining the scope of each project, the methodology used and address why it was successful.

PRODUCTION CHALLENGES

10-A Assigning Duties and Tasks

Supplies needed:

- *Project Responsibilities, Form 10-A, Companion Website*

Read over the checklist presented on Form 10-A. Several duties and responsibilities are listed on this form. You are to decide who is responsible for each task listed, the project manager or the project assistant. If you believe both are responsible, place a check in the "both" column and provide a rationale for your choice in the comments section on the form. If you think someone other than you or the project manager is responsible, place a check mark in the "other" column and again provide a reason for your decision.

10-B Determining Resources

Supplies needed:

- *Determining Software Resources for Project Management, Form 10-B, Companion Website*
- *Access to the internet*

Your supervisor, Patricia Johnson, has just given you a "wish list" (provided on Form 10-B) detailing her requirements for project management software. Ideally, she would like to have you provide three top choices that are web based and two mobile app based. Then she will consult with her team and make a decision based on your findings. This is a significant task, as you know the success of a project can be compromised if the wrong tools are used.

After conducting some research online and comparing the wish list, you are ready to pick three potential prospects. Complete Form 10-B using the instructions and requirements outlined. Hand in your completed form to your instructor for evaluation.

Weblinks

Project Management Institute
www.pmi.org
This site provides information about globally recognized standards for the profession of project management.

Project Management Tips
www.pmtips.net
This site provides tips and tricks for project management practitioners.

Project Management Podcast
www.project-management-podcast.com
This site provides downloadable podcasts on a variety of topics related to project management.

10-C Project Problems
Supplies needed:

- *Project Management Challenges, Form 10-C, page, Companion Website*

Working in small groups, discuss the three problem scenarios presented on Form 10-C. As a group, brainstorm and determine how your team would approach solving the problems, and identify any resources required.

Hand in one form on behalf of the team with all the members' names clearly identified.

Project Connections
www.projectconnections.com
This site offers a variety of articles related to project management.

Major Projects Management Office
www.mpmo-bggp.gc.ca/
This is a Canadian government website detailing major project proposals submitted to the federal government.

Business Balls
www.businessballs.com
This site provides free information on tools, processes, plans, and planning tips for project management.

References

Project Management Institute. (2018, March 26). Retrieved from https://www.pmi.org/

Project Management Institute and Agile Alliance. (2017). *A guide to the project management body of knowledge PMBOK guide*, 6th edition. Pennsylvania: Project Management Institute, Inc.

Chapter 11
Information Management

Rawpixel.com/Shutterstock

LEARNING OUTCOMES

After completion of this chapter, the student will be able to:

1 Describe encompassing components in maintaining effective and efficient records management in the digital age.

2 Explain legislation and privacy laws surrounding records management.

3 Describe the rules and processes of organizing information for both visible and electronic filing systems.

4 Identify the factors governing retention and transfer of records.

5 Understand the life cycle of a record and the four classifications of records for retention.

6 Index and alphabetize names for the alphabetic filing system.

7 Compare alphabetic, subject, geographic, and numeric filing systems.

Keeping good records is vital to every business. Collecting, storing, and effectively analyzing your data is critical. There are also legal obligations to maintain reasonable records. **Filing** is one segment of a broad office function called **information management**. Filing involves classifying, arranging, and storing materials according to a systematic plan for quick reference, for preservation, and—most important of all—for retrieving an item readily when it is required. It is not how fast you file a document but, rather, how fast you access documents that is important. This chapter will provide effective filing and records management procedures that will assist in knowledge and skill development, positioning the administrative professional as an efficient manager of information.

Managing information can involve both paper and electronic files. In fact, technology has made it possible for offices to maintain records without needing a printed-paper copy. An effective administrative professional, however, will be skilled in handling paper and electronic information in the digital age.

PROTECTING INFORMATION

Information is one of the most valuable resources of any business. It is important to protect this information from abuse and misuse. This can range from sharing personal information about employees to exposing corporate plans and budgets. As an administrative professional, you are responsible for protecting information according to company policy as well as various government legislation.

The Canadian government has legislated the *Access to Information Act*, and some Canadian provinces and

---

Graduate Profile

Tracy Staunton

Tracy Staunton

Clarke Transport Inc.
Customer Service | National Accounts
Brampton, Ontario
College Graduation:
Executive Office Administration Diploma
Georgian College—2010

"Never the same day twice."

The year 2018 marked Tracy's seventh year with Clarke Transport. Her journey there began the year following her graduation from the Office Administration Executive program at Georgian College's Barrie Campus. She has utilized the skills and upgrading she learned at Georgian as well as her 20+ years in working in customer service. She started as a clerk in the billing department for five months before being offered a position as a call taker in the customer service department. Her skills and dedication in processing customer pickup orders and her attention to detail when following through earned her the position in 2014 for delay clerk, where her duties included coding train units and advising customers of any transit delays.

Within her sixth year, Tracy was offered the position she holds currently, customer service agent of national accounts. Her days now consist of time-sensitive tasks, including updating and sending off customer reports, answering all inquiries concerning the accounts she oversees, as well as providing backup for the customer service department phone queue and emails.

Organization and follow-through are still must-haves—using standard Microsoft Office programs, as well as the AS400 system for tracking and dispatching, Tracy must make sure all the information is in the right place so that there are no errors along the line. Proper identifying numbers must in place, proper billing must go to correct accounts, etc. When something is amiss and she cannot correct things on her own, she works closely with Billing and Rates to have things corrected.

When dispatch needs critical information on freight pickups of any of her accounts, Tracy must contact the shipper or her customer to obtain this information. Most of her communication, around 70%, is via email, and the rest is through the phone with customers and colleagues alike.

The best part of her job is her work environment: "I love the atmosphere of teamwork here at Clarke; everyone is supportive and is always willing to help me with this ever-changing industry."

Tracy would still like to upgrade her language skills. She has taken a basic French class with the Toronto Board of Education and intends to continue with various programs offered in the Greater Toronto Area. Although the road to post-graduation employment was a little rocky, Tracy urges future graduates not to get discouraged. It is important to start your job search early, even before your course is completed. Then, consider registering with a temporary agency—it may lead to a great job, as it did for Tracy, but even if it does not, it will add valuable work experience to your résumé.

It has been an incredible journey, but Tracy has immensely enjoyed the skills and learning curve she gets at Clarke, as there is never the same day twice there.

territories have legislated a *Freedom of Information and Protection of Privacy Act*. This legislation has motivated public and private organizations and business to do the following:

- Establish formal information management systems.
- Set up policies and procedures based on the legislation.
- Design training programs to ensure staff knowledge and understanding of the policies.

This legislation establishes records management as a priority function in the office.

Privacy Legislation

Several factors determine the application of the privacy laws and who oversees it. The Government of Canada has legislated protection of information through two privacy laws: the *Privacy Act* and the *Personal Information Protection and Electronic Documents Act* (PIPEDA).

The Privacy Act primarily deals with personal information the government has collected about its citizens. It ensures that all Canadians have access to their personal information and provides for privacy, ethical handling, and correction by the individual if necessary. PIPEDA has been fully in effect since 2004. It legislates the use of personal information for all commercial activities in Canada. It sets strict laws regarding what information a business can collect about its customers, how long it can keep that information, how it can use that information, and how it can share that information with others.

The key purpose of PIPEDA is to help businesses manage personal information and, at the same time, allow individuals to protect their personal information.

Not only is information protected under federal government legislation, but also some provinces and territories of Canada have legislation that affects privacy and access to information. Where the federal government deems that a province or territory does not have fully adequate privacy legislation, PIPEDA applies.

Access to Information Guidelines

The *Access to Information Act* gives Canadians the right to obtain copies of federal government records. These records could be in any format, including letters, emails, photographs, audio and video recordings, and the like. The premise of the act is that government information should be made available to the public.

For some Canadian businesses, these laws have meant a heavier workload and new procedures for handling information, both paper and electronic. These laws have enforced the cautious handling and protection of customer/client information.

Personal Information

Personal information is data about a person. Pieces of information applied together make an individual identifiable. Protection of all aspects of this information is essential in business data collection. Components of personal information consists of:

- age
- marital status
- religion
- ethnicity, race or origin
- financial information
- connected numbers—like Social Insurance Number (SIN)
- gender
- employment, medical history
- income level

Canada's Anti-Spam Legislation (CASL)

Spam is unsolicited bulk email (UBE). For business that send out commercial electronic messages (CEMs) via email or text for promotion, there is a requirement in Canada to follow Canada's Anti-Spam Legislation (CASL). In order for a business to send this bulk information out, it must gain consent, and the requirement must include an unsubscribe feature in every message sent out. There are two types of consent, implied and express. Express covers the aspect in which the person has clearly agreed to receive the bulk email; while implied is not consent freely provided by a person, but rather indicated by a person's actions, especially in the case of inaction or silence. If a recipient of CEM unsubscribes, an organization is required to stop sending messages. Additionally, the legislation covers the definition of an existing business relationship (EBR).

A business has the obligation to prove that it has consent. This is part of the legislation that ensures compliance; in order to demonstrate this and as a company best practice, organizations should maintain hard copy and electronic records of consent, CEMs, and unsubscribe requests and demonstrate business procedures implemented and followed.

> **Self-Check**
>
> 1. Define the word *filing*.
> 2. What two Government of Canada privacy laws legislate protection of information?
> 3. When does PIPEDA take precedence over province or territory legislation?

ORGANIZING INFORMATION

Information management involves much more than placing a sheet of paper in a folder. The administrative professional's role in filing involves the following:

- Setting up both electronic and paper systems so they are synchronized and systematized. This means that they will work together and that they will follow a solid set of rules and procedures.

- Preparing paper and electronic documents for filing.

- Managing and maintaining the systems. This is a responsible aspect of the role that can be difficult due to the nature of the work-related variables involved. See the word cloud in Figure 11-1 for a reminder of key words surrounding privacy.

Among many other tasks, administrative professionals ensure that staff members follow strict procedures for filing, retrieval, and replacement of files. Especially with electronic systems, people tend to make multiple copies and file the documents in numerous places, except the one place you are expecting to find the document.

Managing information is a comprehensive responsibility and involves a critical set of procedures for the efficient and effective office.

Preparation for Visible Filing

What is visible filing? Visible filing is simply the most current word used to describe paper filing. This section will provide an overview of visible filing, but most activities we do in paper filing are possible and even more efficient in electronic filing. With the progressive movement towards electronic filing methodologies, many offices still maintain paper records or a combination of electronic and paper, and this manual process of paper filing will remain an activity and task in an office in the foreseeable future.

When not maintained effectively, paper records are untidy and disorganized. We have all seen stuffed and worn file folders crammed into overcrowded cabinets. These same files often have handwritten labels, no **charge-out** system, and redundant information. No wonder filing is the task least enjoyed by many administrative professionals. However, by following the procedures suggested here, filing can become efficient, effective, and satisfying. The procedures to follow, before placing a paper inside a file folder, are:

1. reviewing
2. indexing
3. coding
4. cross-referencing
5. sorting

Reviewing Review each document before you determine how to file it. Follow these guidelines:

- Check papers that are stapled together, and decide if they should be filed together.

- Staple together related papers where one document refers to the other.

FIGURE 11-1 Word cloud of key words related to privacy.

Mindscanner/Shutterstock

- Remove paper clips and extra staples.
- Keep the routing slip with the appropriate documents. You may need to determine later to whom the document was circulated.
- Determine if documents are duplicates and should be deleted/destroyed or filed.

Indexing   Indexing is thinking about how you will file each paper. It is the mental process of determining the key word or number under which a paper will be filed. Careful indexing is the most important part of the process of filing papers. The key word can be a name, a number, a subject, or a geographic location. For example, if you wanted to file a document where the name is *Mr. Benjamin Ross,* you would determine that the most important word for filing is *Ross.*

When you are filing correspondence by name, scan the correspondence to decide which name to use. Note that

1. Incoming letters are often called for by the name of the organization appearing in the letterhead, so index them by that name.
2. Outgoing letters are often called for by the name of the organization appearing in the inside address, so index them by that name.

To learn how to index for the variety of names you will encounter, follow the standardized indexing rules presented later in this chapter under "Alphabetic Filing Rules."

Coding   After you decide how a paper should be filed, mark the indexing caption on the paper. This process is called coding. To code by name, underline the name with a coloured pencil.

In the following three examples, the key words have been bolded and the number of indexing units has been identified. The order in which to consider the units for filing is shown with a number above the unit. The first unit or the most important word in the sequence has been underlined.

(3rd) (2nd) (1st)
- Mr. **Benjamin Ross** = three indexing units

(1st) (2nd) (3rd)
- **National Geographic Photography** = three indexing units

(1st) (2nd) (3rd)
- **Ontario Publishers** Ltd. = three indexing units

The code on the paper should be complete enough that you can return the paper to the same folder each time it has been removed. As you study the indexing rules, you will learn how to determine the order of units within a name.

Cross-Referencing   When a document is apt to be called for by two different names at different times, you should be able to locate it by looking under either name. To make this possible, file the document according to the name by which it is most likely to be requested. Also prepare a reference to it by a second name. This is referred to as **cross-referencing**.

The purpose of cross-referencing is to send you to the correct file and eliminate filing similar documents in more than one place. An electronic or paper card filing system is an effective way to manage cross-referencing.

To make a cross-reference card, use a card of the same size as the primary card in the file but use a different colour. Notice in Figure 11-2 the two cards prepared for Maclean Hunter Limited. The information printed below "SEE" on the cross-reference card is the same caption as that on the primary card.

Avoid preparing unnecessary cross-references, but if you are in doubt, make one: it may help you locate a paper when you need it. There are various situations in which cross-referencing is necessary. Consider the following:

1. Correspondence pertaining to individuals may be filed by subject (e.g., Temporary Employees) instead of by the name of the employee.
2. It may be difficult to determine the individual's surname. Consider names like Abdalla Mohammed, Chen Yu, or Kent Ross. What are the surnames? How can you determine which is the last name? In this case, you may have to gather further information confirming which the surname is, you may have to ask directly and not assume.

For the example of Kent Ross, if the surname is Ross, the correct file will read *Ross, Kent,* and the cross-reference card will read:

Kent Ross

SEE Ross Kent

3. The names of married women can be confusing to file and may need support from cross-referencing. For example:

Written or Indexed	Name before Marriage (if she uses her maiden name as her surname)	Name after Marriage (if she marries Robert Whyte and adopts his surname)
As Written	Ms. Heather Ross	Mrs. Heather Whyte
As Indexed	Ross Heather Ms.	Whyte Heather Mrs.

A cross-reference will be necessary for two of the three cases. Most commonly, correspondence would be filed under either Ross Heather Ms. or Whyte Heather Mrs. Only one file should be set up to hold the documents. One primary card will be needed, but two cross-reference cards will be needed for the card file.

FIGURE 11-2 Primary card; cross-reference card.

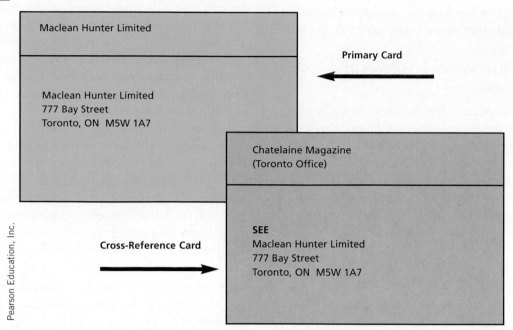

Maclean Hunter Limited

Primary Card

Maclean Hunter Limited
777 Bay Street
Toronto, ON M5W 1A7

Chatelaine Magazine
(Toronto Office)

Cross-Reference Card

SEE
Maclean Hunter Limited
777 Bay Street
Toronto, ON M5W 1A7

Pearson Education, Inc.

4. Subdivisions of a parent company are filed under the name used on the subdivision's letterhead; documents are not filed under the parent company name. To avoid confusion, file correctly under the name of the subdivision, but prepare a cross-reference for the name of the parent company. For example, a subdivision business called Pizza Town with a parent company called Pizza Enterprises would have the correspondence filed as Pizza Town, but a cross-reference card for Pizza Enterprises would send the records manager to the Pizza Town file.

5. Some organizations are referred to by their acronym because they are better known that way—for example, IAAP (International Association of Administrative Professionals) and CNIB (Canadian National Institute for the Blind). Check the organization's letterhead or business card to see how the organization refers to itself. Whether you file by the full name or by the popular abbreviation, *consistency must prevail.* A cross-reference will be necessary to keep all the correspondence in the same file.

6. A business name may include several surnames. For the law firm Baines, Jones, and Samuelson, file the original by Baines and cross-reference Jones and Samuelson.

7. A company may change its name. File by the new name, and record the date of the change. Retain the old name in the cross-reference card system.

8. Names of foreign companies and government agencies are often written in both English and the respective foreign language. File by the English name, and make a cross-reference card with the foreign spelling.

9. A foreign company is handled differently than a foreign government. For a foreign company, file the documents by the name as it is written on the letterhead or business card and make a cross-reference card under the English translation.

10. When confusion exists concerning a filing rule, alleviate the confusion by making a cross-reference. A cross-reference will send the reader to the correct file.

11. When a department is renamed because of restructuring within the organization, internal correspondence filed by department name will be affected. File the correspondence by the new name and create a cross-reference card under the old name.

Sorting   This is prearranging papers in the same order that they will be filed before the actual filing begins. By sorting paper documents, you eliminate unnecessary shifting back and forth from drawer to drawer or from shelf to shelf as you file the documents. As a result, you work more efficiently.

Portable vertical sorting trays with dividers and guides are available in a variety of sizes. Use a sorting tray to hold the papers until you file them. If you accumulate a stack of papers in the to-be-filed basket each day and do not have sorting equipment, request it. In the meantime, use the following efficient method of sorting manually.

Sitting at your desk or a table, first divide the papers into manageable groups. For example, if you are sorting by name, first stack the papers in groups A–E, F–J, K–P, Q–T, and U–Z. Next, arrange the papers in the first group in A, B, C, D,

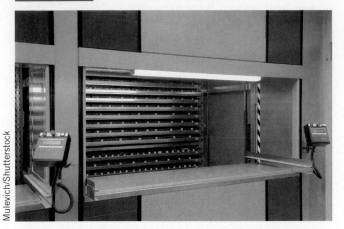

FIGURE 11-3 Automated sorting system.

and E stacks, and then assemble the papers in each stack in alphabetical order. Sort the remaining groups in the same way. Remember, where two pieces of correspondence share the same name, the most recent document is placed on top.

Where there is a very large amount of paper filing to handle, automated sorting systems are available.

See Figure 11-3 for an example of an automated sorting system.

Techniques for Assembling Papers

One of the steps of filing is the placing of papers in folders. Allow at least 30 minutes a day in your schedule for this activity.

Many administrative professionals rate filing as their most disliked task. When unfiled papers stack up, a simple task becomes a burden. You will spend more time locating a paper in an unarranged stack than in one that is properly organized. Note also that you run the risk of losing papers when they are disorganized. It is crucial that you keep up with filing on a daily basis.

In any new office job, you will be placing and locating materials in files that were maintained by your predecessor. Do not try to reorganize the files in your office until you are familiar with what they contain. Allow yourself several months to learn the system. In the meantime, become thoroughly familiar with the contents of the files. Write down your suggestions for improving the filing system.

The following are very important practices for placing papers away. If your office is not currently doing them, implement them as quickly as possible.

■ Always file the most recent correspondence at the front of the file (on top).

■ When a file folder is held horizontally, all documents should face forward. For 8½" × 11" documents, the stapled edge of those documents should be on the upper left side of the document and sit into the crease of the folder while documents that are 8½" × 14", the stapled edge should be in the upper right-hand corner of the document and the spoiled edge will be positioned well above the creased area facing forward.

Charge-Out Methods

Charge-out methods do not apply to electronic filing. In fact, one of the advantages of electronic systems is that when you retrieve a document from the filing system, you just take an electronic copy. This means, of course, that there is never any reason to return the document to the folder, since the original never left the folder.

However, paper filing is a very different story. Since materials are kept in active files for use, effective charge-out methods must be followed if you are to keep track of materials that have been borrowed from the files and are to be returned.

Charge-out procedures can be electronically controlled. This reduces the time spent searching for files. Software can provide the location of a file and determine whether it is in the filing system or has been charged out.

Manual charge-out systems are very popular. A manual system uses special cards, folders, and pressboard guides with the word "OUT" printed on the tabs to substitute for papers and folders that have been taken from the files. When only a few sheets of paper are removed from the files, an **out guide** is placed inside the folder; when the entire folder is removed, an **out folder** is substituted. If new documents must be filed after the original folder has been removed, the out folder will hold the documents until the original is returned.

Charge-out guides have printed lines for writing a description of the materials removed, the name of the person who has taken the file or the materials, and the date the materials were taken.

The method you use for keeping track of materials removed from the files you maintain will depend on what works best in your organization. Here are some suggestions:

■ When important documents are removed from the files, and there is no electronic copy, make a paper copy. Everyone occasionally loses or misplaces documents; this happens to even the most organized people.

■ If time permits, you or other administrative professionals who are trained in the charge-out procedures should handle all the removals and returns of materials. When other employees attempt to remove and return the files on their own, charge-out and refiling procedures are not completed, and files go missing.

■ When it's not possible for the administrative professional to control all the charge-outs and returns of files, train all the staff on the charge-out system. Be sure to let them know how important this is to the smooth operation of the business.

> **Self-Check**
>
> 1. List two features of the administrative professional's responsibility in filing.
> 2. List basic steps in preparing records for filing.
> 3. Why is it important to sort paper documents before placing them away?

ORGANIZATION OF ELECTRONIC FILES

Because most organizations depend heavily on electronic filing methods as well as paper filing methods, it is essential that the administrative assistant has an effective and efficient means of filing and locating documents on the office network and on removable storage.

In some ways, the electronic system works much like the paper system. Put simply, in the paper system we have cabinets that contain folders that contain files that contain documents. Refer to Figure 11-4 for a screen capture of electronic folders and files.

In an electronic system, we have **directories** that contain folders that contain files that contain documents. A directory is a section of the network allotted to certain people for their files. Having your own directory is like having your own filing cabinet.

When using the office network, certain directories are allotted for your use. In these directories, you can create folders, as you need to open them. Other directories will be available for you to access and read but not to alter, while still other directories will be completely off limits for your use. This is comparable to confidential paper files.

You will need to set up and maintain an organized system for both your removable media as well as the office network. Removable storage comes in many forms. Popular forms for storing information include **pen drives**, cloud-based platforms, optical disks, and portable hard drives. Removable storage is enabled as a primary means of electronic storage or as a backup for documents stored on the office network.

When labelling your directories on the network or on removable media, be sure to use descriptive naming conventions to easily return to the directory, folder, or file at a later date and know exactly what to find there. As well, it is essential to be consistent with your labelling. If you identify your letters as "Correspondence—February" on one folder, don't label the next directory as "Corr—March." Consistency in labelling is an important key to locating information efficiently.

FIGURE 11-4 Electronic folders and files.

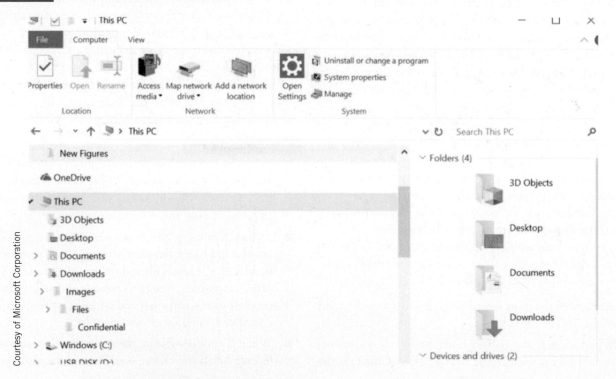

Courtesy of Microsoft Corporation

Benefits and Drawbacks of Electronic Filing

Electronic filing viewed as an efficient and effective way of managing information. However, it has both benefits and drawbacks.

Benefits The fact that documents take up much less space is a major advantage. No large and awkward metal filing cabinets are required to house electronic documents compared to the systems used to house bulky paper files. In addition, offices can conserve paper and avoid unnecessary printing, thereby practicing environmental sustainability. Speed of accessing information is increased by using electronic systems.

The fact that files can be accessed by any authorized person using an internet connection, from just about any location, at any time of the day or night, has given office professionals the flexibility they need to be competitive in business.

Drawbacks Because documents are easily accessible to many people through the office network, a number of different authorized people can access the same **e-file**, take a copy, and then file it into another system. The problem increases when people edit the original document to suit their own purposes, resulting in confusion as to which is the original document and how many edited versions are filed outside the main system.

Just as consistent labelling of directories is important, consistent naming of electronic records is essential for timely retrieval. Management would be wise to ensure that employees receive training in electronic file management to avoid "lost" records.

Other drawbacks like easy manipulation of documents and unethical distribution also exist. Better controls for electronic filing continue to develop.

Records management, defined as the systematic control of all business-related documents throughout their life cycle, is a vital component of successful business practice. From an employability perspective, record managers are employed to organize, maintain, and protect a company's information database, in both paper and electronic forms.

Electronic filing can be expensive. If your office doesn't already have a scanner, one will need to be purchased. You may also have to upgrade your computer system to handle the increased storage demands.

Self-Check

1. Define *directory* as it relates to electronic files.
2. Why is it important that employees be trained in electronic file management?

ORDERING SUPPLIES ONLINE

Products for both visible and electronic filing should make your systems more organized, efficient, effective, and interesting. There are numerous products, styles, sizes, and shapes available to make a filing system work well for the organization. Many products will be available at the local stationery store; however, to get the greatest variety in products, use ecommerce—as a search term to shop online through the web.

The following is a brief discussion of some basic items that are essential to manage your records. Once you have the basics, you will need to enhance and improve on what you have.

Supplies for Visible Filing

Guides Dividers in conventional filing drawers are called guides. They serve as signposts, separating the filing space into labelled sections. Guides also help to support the folders in an upright position.

Guides will have a tab projecting from the edge. Tabs are available in a variety of sizes and colours. While you can purchase blank tabs in order to customize your system, you can also purchase tabs that list the days of the week, the names of the months, or alphabetic letters.

Guides for open-shelf filing differ from guides for vertical file drawers. Figure 11-5 shows open-shelf filing. Note that the tabs on the guides are along the side and not on the top, as they would be on vertical files.

Folders Folders are the containers for holding the correspondence and other paper. Since folders tend to take a lot of abuse, they are constructed of a heavy paper. They can be purchased in a variety of colours, sizes, and weights.

FIGURE 11-5 An office worker locates a file in an open-shelf filing system.

Michaeljung/Shutterstock

FIGURE 11-6 Variety of tab cuts.

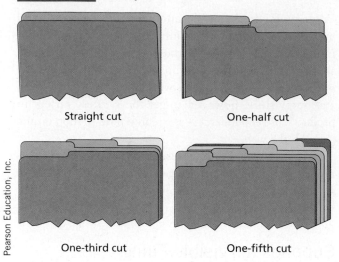

Straight cut   One-half cut

One-third cut   One-fifth cut

FIGURE 11-7 Hanging file folder.

The tabs on the folders also come in a variety of places and sizes. Figure 11-6 shows some of the possible tab cuts.

All folders should have creases at the bottom. The creases are called *scores*. When the folder begins to fill with correspondence, the score allows you to fit more documents in the folder without damaging the papers.

Expandable folders are available for oversized files. The folders have a gusset instead of a score; gussets allow a folder to expand more than a conventional folder.

Suspension, or hanging, folders are popular for active files. Hanging folders are suspended by extensions at their top edges across a metal frame within the file drawer, which means they don't rest on the bottom of the cabinet. Materials filed in suspension folders are easily accessible because the folders open wide and slide smoothly on the hanger rail. Attachable tabs are inserted into slots at the top of the folders and are used in place of conventional guides and tabs. Figure 11-7 shows a suspension folder with labels.

Labels Labels help us find our way through the file cabinet. Each folder and each guide needs a label. Labels come in a variety of sizes, shapes, and colours so you can customize your filing system to meet the needs of your organization. Colours should not be used at random. Use colours to represent a topic or the status of a file.

Labels can be purchased either on a continuous strip or on flat sheets, which work well with a printer. They are self-adhesive and pressure sensitive.

If the labels can be read from both sides, such as with open files, be sure that both sides of your label bear accurate and attractive information.

Key the names on your labels in the indexed order. Use an easy-to-read font and do not use all capital letters. Words keyed in all capital letters are sometimes more difficult to read. Above all, remember to be consistent with labelling through your system.

The captions on the labels of your files should resemble an aligned list of names, as shown in Figure 11-8.

Label drawers or sections of files with either open or closed notations. A closed notation indicates the entire

FIGURE 11-8 Aligned labels on folder tabs.

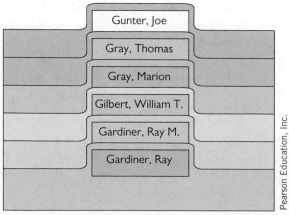

Gunter, Joe

Gray, Thomas

Gray, Marion

Gilbert, William T.

Gardiner, Ray M.

Gardiner, Ray

span of the contents. A typical example of a closed notation would be:

Correspondence

A–H

A typical example of an open notation would be:

Correspondence

Supplies for Electronic Filing

One of the advantages of electronic filing is that very few supplies are needed. Depending on the requirements of your office, you will need a supply of pen drives, optical disks, or an external hard drive. Each medium has a different storage capacity.

Self-Check

1. List three types of supplies required for visible filing systems.
2. How should you key names on file folder and guide labels?

STORING INFORMATION

Paper correspondence is usually filed in drawers. Information printed on cards is filed in a variety of ways—in drawers, in trays, on wheels, in panels—to make it easily accessible to the operator. Some filing units are automated, so that the operator can bring the files or cards within easy reach by pressing a button.

Storing Visible Documents

Paper correspondence is usually filed vertically, standing upright and supported by guides and folders in file drawers. The two types of popular filing cabinets for paper are the vertical filing cabinet shown in Figure 11-9. Another file cabinet style is shown in Figure 11-10. The type you choose will depend on your office space available and your personal preference.

Lateral files save space because 25% to 50% less aisle space is needed to pull out a lateral file drawer than is needed to pull out a vertical file drawer.

Cabinets may be used as single units or may be grouped together to serve as area dividers. They can be adapted to store almost any kind of record such as disks, letters, legal documents, or cards.

One type of lateral file is open-shelf. This type is used to save floor space, filing and retrieval time, and initial

FIGURE 11-9 Vertical filing cabinet.

Dan Barbalata/123RF

installation costs. For open-shelf filing, the tabs project from the side of the folder.

Lateral files are equipped to handle either regular or suspension folders. The folders may be arranged either

FIGURE 11-10 Filing cabinets.

Chad McDermott/Shutterstock

FIGURE 11-11 Wire organizer.

Pearson Education, Inc.

side-by-side or from front to back. The tabs are at the top of the guides, and the folders are arranged in closed drawers.

A popular device designed to hold files upright inside the filing drawer is the wire organizer. With the wire organizer, folders may be placed directly into the file drawer without any suspension folders being used. Folders remain upright, and space is saved. Time is also saved, since duplicate labels for the hanging folders are not needed. See Figure 11-11.

Automated filing equipment is available for both visible card files and folder files. This equipment is constructed so that an operator can bring a shelf of folders, or cards assembled in trays, within easy reach by pushing a button.

Storing Electronic Media

Flash drives and optical disks are not very susceptible to changes such as temperature fluctuations within the surrounding environment.

All critical information needs to be backed up for safety. The backup copy may be kept on another removable medium or on the computer system. Whatever you decide, store the original and the copy away from each other so that the same accident will not destroy both copies.

Storing Business Contact Information

Most business professionals keep their own list of contacts. They develop an electronic database from all the business cards they collect from clients, customers, agents, competitors, etc. Executives will either maintain their own database or ask for help from the administrative professional. Often professionals store a contact list within their email account to ensure easy access for ongoing contact. Microsoft Outlook is one of many software programs used today to store and organize basic contact information.

The database should consist of the client's name, title, company, geographical address, email address, and telephone and fax numbers.

Administrative professionals often collect all client information into one database and make it accessible to all employees. The database will only be effective if it is frequently updated. Refer to Figure 11-12 showing an MS Outlook contact listing.

Electronic Databases

Computer records lend themselves perfectly to storing and sorting lists of just about anything, including records on employees, projects, products inventory, and paper files and descriptions of their contents. A variety of computer software is available for creating databases. Refer to Figure 11-13 and imagine it placed into an electronic file.

- A name or number, such as a family name, postal code, email address, or telephone number, is called a *field*.

- The complete information about one person or one item is called a *record*. An example of a record would be all the information about Henry Ross.

- A collection of records is called a *file*. An example of a file would be all the records of employees in the finance department.

- A *database* is a set of logically related files. An example would be all the department files for a company.

FIGURE 11-12 Sample MS Outlook contact list.

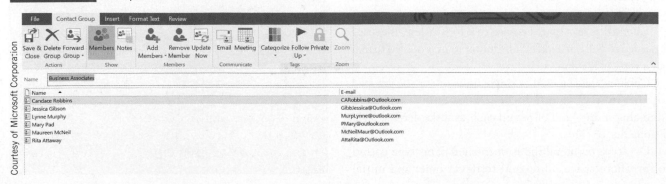

Courtesy of Microsoft Corporation

FIGURE 11-13 Sample information for the Quality Flooring Company illustrates a character, a field, a record, a file, and a database.

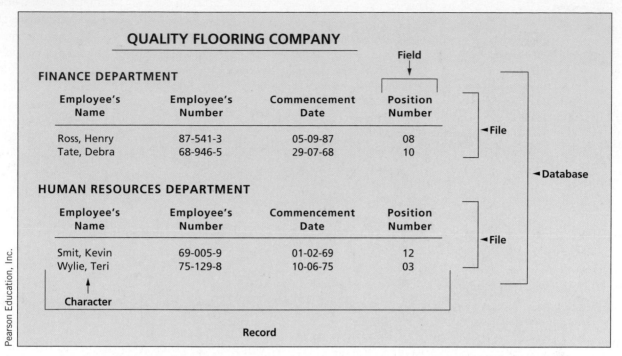

Please refer to Figure 11-14 for an illustration of an electronic database.

Electronic databases are essential to the efficiency of a professional office. Accessing information through a database saves a lot of time. Remember that having the ability to locate information gives you a professional advantage over people who do not possess these skills. Take every opportunity to learn how to use the electronic databases in the office.

RETAINING AND TRANSFERRING RECORDS

When the file cabinets or your removable electronic storage systems become full of files, what do you do? Should you destroy them? Should you transfer them to another location? These decisions cannot be made at random. Records retention and transfer is strictly governed by the policies of both your organization and your government.

Life Cycle of a Record

Most records have a standard life span from the creation to its preservation or disposal. While various models of the records life cycle exist, they all feature the same parts from the creation or receipt, use, and disposal. Here are the four stages of a record life cycle:

- **Creation.** A record begins its life cycle when created or received.
- **Active.** Records used or accessed frequently are active.
- **Inactive.** Records no longer in use or archived are inactive. They are required to be maintained for legal regulatory rules or administrative or historical purposes.
- **Disposition.** Records are destroyed when they no longer serve a purpose nor are required to be maintained.

Paper Records Retention

The following factors determine how long records must be preserved:

1. the nature of an organization's business operations
2. provincial or territorial statutes of limitations
3. regulations or statutes of the federal government

Each province has its own statutes of limitations, specifying the time after which a record cannot be used as evidence in the courts. An organization is subject to the statutes of limitations of the province or territory in which it operates. Among the records affected by provincial statutes of limitations are written contracts, injury claims, and accident reports.

FIGURE 11-14 Electronic database.

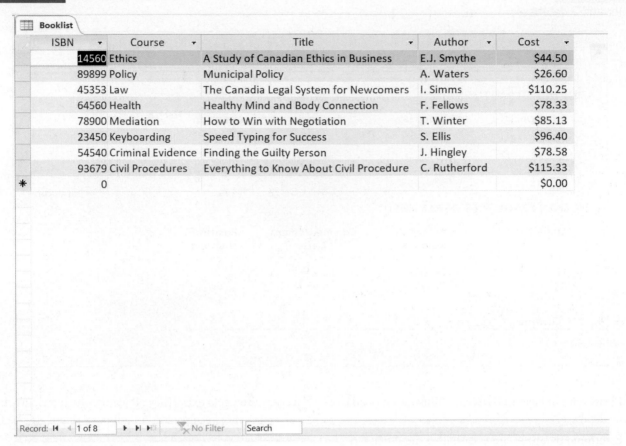

ISBN	Course	Title	Author	Cost
14560	Ethics	A Study of Canadian Ethics in Business	E.J. Smythe	$44.50
89899	Policy	Municipal Policy	A. Waters	$26.60
45353	Law	The Canadia Legal System for Newcomers	I. Simms	$110.25
64560	Health	Healthy Mind and Body Connection	F. Fellows	$78.33
78900	Mediation	How to Win with Negotiation	T. Winter	$85.13
23450	Keyboarding	Speed Typing for Success	S. Ellis	$96.40
54540	Criminal Evidence	Finding the Guilty Person	J. Hingley	$78.58
93679	Civil Procedures	Everything to Know About Civil Procedure	C. Rutherford	$115.33
*	0			$0.00

Record: 1 of 8 — No Filter — Search

Banking records, records of employees' taxes, and aircraft operation and maintenance records are examples of records covered by the federal government's regulations and statutes.

Determining which records to keep and for how long is a critical function. An administrative professional should not dispose of any records or papers from the files without a clear knowledge of retention legislation.

Record Classification for Retention

Records are classified based on their importance and retention practices. Consider the following:

- **Vital records.** These are records that must be maintained forever by an organization. They can include articles of incorporation, mortgage records, minutes of meetings, and insurance policies. These records should always be considered active as they are irreplaceable. Vital records usually account for 3% of records maintained by an organization.

- **Important records.** These records are very important to the business; they should be retained for five to seven years. These can include financial statements, cancelled cheques, and inventory records. These documents can be replicated, but doing so would require a very costly and involved process.

- **Useful records.** Items that are useful are usually retained for one to two years within the organization. These can include correspondence, employment applications, and petty cash vouchers.

- **Nonessential records.** Items that have only an immediate need to the organization, such as telephone messages and some emails, do not need to be retained.

These are some general considerations. It is essential to familiarize yourself with your organization's rules for maintaining records. Check before disposing of any record if you are unsure.

Paper Records Transfer

The most accessible file spaces are used for active files; this means that the less active papers or stale dated papers will be moved from time to time in order to free up the most accessible space for the current papers. Organizations use two methods of transfer: perpetual and periodic. Paper storage can consume a great deal of space. When the inactive records are transferred, they are either moved to a back room or a storage site away from the office.

Perpetual Method *Perpetual* transfer is a method of continually transferring files to inactive storage as a project or case is completed. It is highly applicable for records kept by organizations that handle projects or cases, such as legal firms or construction companies. All the records for one project or case are transferred at the time they are completed.

Periodic Method The *periodic* method provides for transferring files to inactive storage at predetermined intervals, such as every 6 months, year, or 18 months. The inactive files are transferred to the storage centre, leaving more space to house the active documents.

Electronic Records Retention

Like paper records, inactive electronic records are transferred into storage. This process is called **archiving** and usually involves moving records from the computer system onto portable media storage. Both the perpetual and periodic transfer methods apply to electronic files.

Records managers are expected to retain and protect electronic records in the same way they do paper records. According to Canadian federal law, all business records should be kept for a minimum of six years. However, company policy could dictate a longer period.

Government policy affecting electronic records also stipulates that records must be easily converted into a readable format. This means that if you change your software application, you must ensure that related documents less than six years old can still be quickly accessed and clearly read. With the rapid upgrades in technology, it is a challenge to ensure that yesterday's technology and software are kept available and in operating condition in the event you are expected to produce readable documents compatible to the old system.

When government officials request documents, they must be available immediately. This is another good reason why maintaining and managing a highly organized electronic filing system is essential.

Maintaining Records in Medical and Legal Offices

Rules for regulating standards for medical records are similar across Canada. The College of Physicians and Surgeons governing a jurisdiction ultimately sets the standard. Generally, medical records are to be maintained for a period of 10 years after the last entry. Electronic Medical Record systems, or EMRs, are the standard for data entry and records management in healthcare settings. Significant training in software usage is required to effectively maintain an EMR.

The Law Society of Upper Canada publishes guidelines for lawyers and paralegals providing guidelines and recommendations for retention of files based on the nature of the documents and the case. The guidelines also provide information on the contents of a client file, organization of the file, and closing a file.

Disposing of Records

Records maintained for the required life span need eventual discard or disposal. Factors influencing disposing of these records consider these aspects:

- Maintaining privacy is still crucial.
- If you utilize a commercial shredding service, research how secure the services are.
- Equipment should be available on-site in the organization for document disposal purposes.

---

pro-Link
Paper Preference

For years we've been told that offices would become paperless. It's as if the paperless office has become the professional destiny. However, in many office tasks we are seeing less use of paper, but in others we are seeing a greater use of paper.

We use less paper when we.

- Use electronic calendars.
- Send attachments on email.
- Leave voice mail messages.
- Take notes on a keyboard.
- Store files electronically for teams to access and source.

Some offices are becoming more paper dependent. You see this when people:

- Insist on working from tangible records.
- Worry about the security from the electronic system and want records backed up on paper.
- Print their email messages and place them into paper files.

With the proliferation of communication, offices that like to print their documents have more to print than ever before. It is unlikely that paper suppliers and photocopier vendors have much to fear in the near future.

Self-Check

1. List three factors that determine how long records are preserved.
2. Briefly describe the life cycle of a record.

ALPHABETIC FILING PROCEDURES

All filing systems are based on the alphabet. The main filing systems are alphabetic, geographic, subject, and numeric.

The *geographic* system is arranged alphabetically, but geographic locations, such as provinces and cities, provide the primary subdivisions.

The primary subdivisions in a *subject* filing system are the functions of the organization; the topics in the subject system are filed alphabetically.

The *numeric* system is an indirect system. Each person (or topic) is assigned a number, such as a Social Insurance Number. The information is filed in sequence by number, but an alphabetic index of the individuals (or topics) to whom numbers have been assigned is also maintained. Several combinations of subject and numeric filing systems have been devised.

The *alphabetic* system is the arrangement of names or other captions in order from A to Z. Organizations do not follow identical filing rules; however, with few exceptions the names are usually indexed according to the rules presented and explained in the next section of this chapter. (Variations in the rules are explained at the end of this chapter.)

To set up the simplest alphabetic system in strict sequential order for filing correspondence in regular folders, you need:

- primary guides
- individual name folders
- miscellaneous folders
- special guides
- colour coding (optional)

Primary Guides

Primary guides divide a file into alphabetic sections. A guide is placed at the beginning of each section. Guides direct the eye to the section of the file in which the folder being sought is located.

Guides are not needed with hanging folders, as the folders are supported on a metal frame and the guide tabs are attached directly to the folders. When guides are used, the correspondence is filed in either individual or miscellaneous folders placed behind the guides. Normally, miscellaneous items are placed at the end.

Individual Name Folders

When you accumulate at least five items for one correspondent, or when you determine from the current letter that much communication will take place between the correspondent and your manager, prepare an individual folder with the full name of the correspondent keyed in indexed order in the caption.

Arrange individual folders in alphabetical order immediately following the appropriate primary guide, as shown in Figure 11-15. File correspondence within individual folders in chronological order, so that the correspondence bearing the most recent date is placed at the front of the folder.

Miscellaneous Folders

For every primary guide in your file, there should be a miscellaneous folder with a caption corresponding to the caption on the primary guide. Miscellaneous folders belong *behind* individual folders. File in the miscellaneous folders the papers to and from all correspondents for whom you do not have individual name folders.

Within a miscellaneous folder, arrange the papers in alphabetical order by name. When you have two or more papers for one correspondent, arrange them in chronological order, so that the one with the most recent date will be in front of the others. Staple related papers together to increase the ease of locating them.

Special Guides

Special guides direct the eye to individual folders that are used frequently. Special guides are also used for subdivisions of the alphabet or to mark the section of a file containing individual folders for several correspondents with the same surname, such as Smith.

Colour Coding

Colour coding can be applied to any filing system—alphabetic, numeric, geographic, subject, or chronological. Colour coding is popular because:

1. It provides easy identification for sorting, filing, and finding.
2. It confirms that the folders have been filed in the right places.

All types of filing supplies are available in a variety of colours. If you develop your own filing system, you should use colour. First determine how you are going to use colour, and then be consistent in following your plan.

> ### Self-Check
> 1. What are the four main filing systems?
> 2. Where would you place a miscellaneous folder in a particular alphabetic section of a visible file system?
> 3. List two advantages of colour coding your filing system.

FIGURE 11-15 Arrangement of guides and folders in alphabetic filing system.

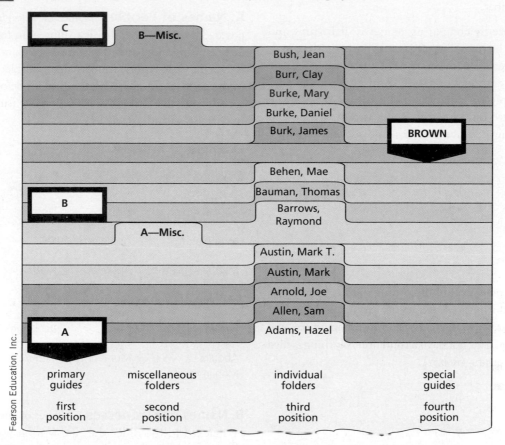

ALPHABETIC FILING RULES

Standardization of alphabetic filing rules is very important because it allows office procedures to be consistent and efficient. In 1960, the Association of Records Managers and Administrators (ARMA) recognized the need for standardization and so published the first standardized rules for alphabetic filing. Although the association still refers to itself as ARMA, it has expanded its role to include training, publications, and development of ethics and standardization of the most sophisticated records management systems. The full name for ARMA is now the Association for Information Management Professionals. However, because the name ARMA is so highly respected and recognized, it's likely that the ARMA acronym will continue to be used for years to come. The best way to contact ARMA is through its website at www.arma.org.

The alphabetic filing rules presented in this chapter are based on standardized and simplified rules suggested by ARMA and adapted to meet Canadian needs.

Order of Filing Units

Before you begin any filing process, it is important that you understand the following three terms.

Unit   Each part of a name that is used to determine the filing order is called a *unit*. For example, the name *Steven Andrew Watson* has three units: *Steven, Andrew, Watson*. The business name *The Wacky Wig Boutique* has four units: *The, Wacky, Wig, Boutique*.

Indexing   Names are not always filed in the same way they are written. In preparation for alphabetic filing, the format and order of a name is often altered. This process of arranging units of a name for filing purposes is referred to as *indexing*. An example of indexing is where *Steven Andrew Watson* has his name indexed as *Watson Steven Andrew*. Indexing always precedes alphabetizing.

Alphabetizing   Placing names in an A-to-Z sequence is considered alphabetizing. This process is necessary to maintain an alphabetic filing system. For example, placing the name *Adamson* before the name *Boulton* is alphabetizing.

This process appears relatively simple; however, because the English language is made up of words from other languages, word derivatives, prefixes, suffixes, compound words, and other combinations, the filing process may become complicated and inconsistent unless rules are applied.

Before working with the rules, there are some basic principles to remember:

1. Alphabetize by comparing names unit by unit and letter by letter. When first units are identical, move on to compare the second units; when second units are identical, compare third units; and so on. For example, in comparing the following indexed names you would need to make the distinction in the third unit, since the first and second units are identical.

Unit 1	Unit 2	Unit 3
Black	Jeff	Peter
Black	Jeff	Robert

2. Nothing comes before something. Thus, in comparing the following indexed names, you would file *Ross William* first, since the first two units are identical, and *Ross William* does not have a third unit. Nothing is filed before something (*Robert*).

Unit 1	Unit 2	Unit 3
Ross	William	
Ross	William	Robert

Another example of this principle would be

Unit 1	Unit 2	Unit 3
Chatham	Bus	Depot
Chatham	Business	College

In this case, *Bus* would come before *Business* under the principle that nothing comes before something.

3. All punctuation marks should be ignored when indexing. Examples of punctuation marks found in names include periods, quotation marks, apostrophes, hyphens, dashes, and accent marks. Where words have been separated by a hyphen or dash, consider them together as one indexing unit.

4. When the name of a person or business is known in more than one format, file it in the way that it is written on letterhead and business cards. Then prepare a cross-reference. Refer to the discussion on cross-referencing in this chapter for further details on this process.

Rule 1—Basic Names

A. Names of People   Names of individuals are transposed. The surname is the first filing unit, followed by the first name or initial, and then the middle name or initial. If it is difficult to determine the surname, consider the last name as the surname. Because nothing comes before something, initials (such as M) are filed before a name (such as Martha) that begins with the same letter.

Example of Rule 1A

AS WRITTEN	AS FILED		
	Unit 1	Unit 2	Unit 3
M Appleton	Appleton	M	
Martha Appleton	Appleton	Martha	
Martin A Appleton	Appleton	Martin	A
Benjamin Frank	Frank	Benjamin	
Abdulla Mohammed	Mohammed	Abdulla	

B. Names of Businesses   Names of businesses should be indexed in the order they are written by the business. Therefore, a surname in a business is not necessarily the first unit. Always use the business's letterhead or business card as your guide, or telephone the business receptionist to confirm the correct name of the business.

Example of Rule 1B

AS WRITTEN	AS FILED		
Ben Frank Submersibles	Ben	Frank	Submersibles
Donald Chow Services	Donald	Chow	Services
Ice Delights	Ice	Delights	
Stony Plain Restaurant	Stony	Plain	Restaurant
Tim Tucker Trucking	Tim	Tucker	Trucking

Rule 2—Symbols and Minor Words

Symbols should be indexed in the way they are pronounced. Examples of such symbols include:

AS WRITTEN	AS INDEXED
$	dollar/s
#	pound or number
&	and
%	percent or percentage
+	plus

Minor words include conjunctions, articles, and prepositions. Examples of these minor words are:

CONJUNCTIONS	ARTICLES	PREPOSITIONS
and	the	on/off in/out
or/nor	a/an	at by
but		with of

Each is considered as a separate indexing unit and is not moved in the indexing process. "The" is the only exception. When the word "The" appears as the first word in a business name, it is considered as the last indexing unit.

Example of Rule 2

	AS FILED		
AS WRITTEN	Unit 1	Unit 2	Unit 3
A Catered Affair	A	Catered	Affair
Bailey & Shaw	Bailey	And	Shaw
$ Store	Dollar	Store	
Dots and Spots	Dots	And	Spots
Lacy of Linwood	Lacy	Of	Linwood
Million $ Baby	Million	Dollar	Baby
Play the Game	Play	The	Game
Service +	Service	Plus	
The Sock Shop	Sock	Shop	The

Rule 3—Punctuation

A. Names of People   Both given and surnames are sometimes hyphenated. In these cases, ignore the hyphen and write the two words together as one indexing unit.

Example of Rule 3A

		AS FILED	
AS WRITTEN	Unit 1	Unit 2	Unit 3
Irene Dale-Scott	DaleScott	Irene	Dale
Irene Dale Scott	Scott	Irene	
Laura Lee Wilkes	Wilkes	Laura	Lee
Laura-Lee Wilkes	Wilkes	LauraLee	

B. Names of Businesses   Ignore all punctuation marks. Where a hyphen separates two words, disregard the hyphen and index the two words as one unit.

Examples of Rule 3B

		AS FILED		
AS WRITTEN	Unit 1	Unit 2	Unit 3	Unit 4
Fab-Abs Gym	FabAbs	Gym		
Lotta Dots!	Lotta	Dots		
Marty Allen's Beauty Salon	Marty	Allens	Beauty	Salon
Mr. Lube	Mr	Lube		
When (Pink) Pigs Fly!	When	Pink	Pigs	Fly
Who's Coming?	Whos	Coming		

Rule 4—Abbreviations and Single Letters

A. Names of People   Abbreviated and shortened personal names are indexed as they are written. Do not spell out the short form of the name.

Example of Rule 4A

		AS FILED	
AS WRITTEN	Unit 1	Unit 2	Unit 3
Ed Kaye	Kaye	Ed	
Edward G. Kaye	Kaye	Edward	G
Geo. Little	Little	Geo	
Bob N. Ross	Ross	Bob	N
Robt. Ross	Ross	Robt	

B. Names of Businesses

When abbreviations and single letters are used in business names, they should be filed as they are written. They are spelled out only when the business writes them that way on letterhead or business cards. Check to see if initials are separated by spaces. If they are separated, then each initial is a separate indexing unit. It does not matter if initials are separated by periods because punctuation is ignored. If the letters are separated by periods but without spaces, the letters will be considered as one indexing unit. Television and radio station letters are indexed together as one unit.

Example of Rule 4B

AS WRITTEN	AS FILED			
	Unit 1	Unit 2	Unit 3	Unit 4
A B C Moving	A	B	C	Moving
AT&T Wireless	ATandT	Wireless		
C.P. Bell Travel Co.	CP	Bell	Travel	Co
CROC Radio	CROC	Radio		
MSS Inc.	MSS	Inc		

Rule 5—Titles and Suffixes

A. Names of People

Titles (Dr., Ms., Sir, Sheikh, Mayor, Senator) are written before a person's name. Make the title the last indexing unit. The exception to this rule is religious or royal titles that are followed by only one name. In this case, index them exactly as written.

Suffixes (MBA, Ph.D., Sr., II) are written after a person's name. Keep them in place and use them as indexing units. Disregard punctuation.

Example of Rule 5A

AS WRITTEN	AS FILED			
	Unit 1	Unit 2	Unit 3	Unit 4
Sister Mary Adamson	Adamson	Mary	Sister	
Sheikh Mohammed Ahmed	Ahmed	Mohammed	Sheikh	
Daniel Hart II	Hart	Daniel	II	

AS WRITTEN	AS FILED			
	Unit 1	Unit 2	Unit 3	Unit 4
Daniel Hart III	Hart	Daniel	III	
Daniel Hart CPS	Hart	Daniel	CPS	
Dr. Phil Hart, MD	Hart	Phil	MD	Dr
Reverend Edward Kaye	Kaye	Edward	Reverend	
Mother Theresa	Mother	Theresa		
Queen Elizabeth	Queen	Elizabeth		
Mayor Joseph Reimer	Reimer	Joseph	Mayor	
Joseph Reimer, Sr.	Reimer	Joseph	Sr	
General Newton Ross, MBA	Ross	Newton	MBA	General
Sister Mary	Sister	Mary		
Ms. Eleanor Vaugh, B.Ed.	Vaugh	Eleanor	Bed	Ms
Ms. Eleanor Vaugh	Vaugh	Eleanor	Ms	

B. Names of Businesses

This rule is simple to apply. Write the titles and degrees in the order they appear.

Example of Rule 5B

AS WRITTEN	AS FILED			
	Unit 1	Unit 2	Unit 3	Unit 4
Sister Sara Sue Sweets	Sister	Sara	Sue	Sweets
Dr. Phil Dentistry	Dr	Phil	Dentistry	
King Edward Hotel	King	Edward	Hotel	

Rule 6—Prefixes

Prefixes such as De, Des, Du, El, La, Les, Mac, Mc, O', Van, Vonder, St., and the like are indexed with the name that follows the prefix. It does not matter if there is a space between the prefix and the following name. They still become one unit. Note that the prefix rule applies to both personal and business names alike. Also, note the prefix examples provided here are only a small sampling of prefixes.

When a large number of names begin with a particular prefix, the trend is to treat that prefix as a separate group and to file the prefix group preceding the basic listing; for example, *Mac* and *Mc* may be filed before the other M names.

Example of Rule 6

	AS FILED		
AS WRITTEN	**Unit 1**	**Unit 2**	**Unit 3**
Jose El Toro	ElToro	Jose	
Louis O'Connor	OConnor	Louis	
A. R. MacNaughton	MacNaughton	A	R
A. R. McNitt	McNitt	A	R
Louis St. Denis	StDenis	Louis	
Michelle Ste. Denis	SteDenis	Michelle	
Adam Vandermallie	Vandermallie	Adam	
John Vander Mallie	VanderMallie	John	
Ray L. Van der Mallie	VanderMallie	Ray	L

Rule 7—Numbers

For names containing numerals, observe the following guidelines:

- Names using either Arabic numerals (e.g., 7, 54) or Roman numerals (e.g., IV, X) are filed in ascending (lowest to highest) order before the alphabetic characters. Arabic numerals are filed before Roman numerals. So the ordering is Arabic numerals, then Roman numerals, and finally alphabetic characters.

- When a number is spelled out, such as "twelve," it is treated as an alphabetic unit, so disregard its value. Numbers as words go into the mix with all the other words—again, ignore its value; treat the alphabetic number "twelve" merely as a word. Therefore, 100 would precede twelve.

- When a digit is used in an ordinal number, such as 1st, 2nd, or 3rd, ignore the suffix (st, nd, rd, or th) and index only the number itself. Therefore, 1st is indexed as 1, 2nd is indexed as 2, 3rd as 3, 4th as 4, and so on.

- When a numeral is separated from a word by a hyphen, as in 2-Much Fun Shoppe, the hyphen is ignored and the numeral joins the word to become one unit—2Much Fun Shop.

- When a number is spelled out and hyphenated—for example, Seventy-Seven Sunset Shop—the hyphen is ignored, and the two numbers become one unit—SeventySeven.

Example of Rule 7

	AS FILED			
AS WRITTEN	**Unit 1**	**Unit 2**	**Unit 3**	**Unit 4**
1–2 Corner Dollar Store	12	Corner	Dollar	Store
1st Street Bistro	1	Street	Bistro	
4-By-4 Sales	4By4	Sales		
8-1 Convenience Store	81	Convenience	Store	
XVIII Century Costumes	XVIII	Century	Costumes	
XXI Century Designs	XXI	Century	Designs	
AA Advertising	AA	Advertising		
Fat Fred's 50s Club	Fat	Fred's	50s	Club
Forty-Two Club	FortyTwo	Club		
One Hour Cleaners (Hyphen removed)	One	Hour	Cleaners	
Salon on 5th	Salon	On	5	
Salon on 7th	Salon	On	7	

Rule 8—Organizations and Institutions

Examples of names that fit this category are unions and associations, financial institutions, hospitals and care homes, clubs, schools, hotels, magazines and newspapers, and religious and charitable organizations.

Index the names of institutions and organizations just as you would any business name (see Rule 1B and Rule 2). Remember to confirm the names of institutions or organizations by checking their letterhead or business cards.

Example of Rule 8

	AS FILED			
AS WRITTEN	**Unit 1**	**Unit 2**	**Unit 3**	**Unit 4**
4-H Club	4H	Club		
Alvin Buckwold Sanatorium	Alvin	Buckwold	Sanatorium	
Chinese Baptist Church	Chinese	Baptist	Church	
Edmonton Journal	Edmonton	Journal		
Habitat for Humanity	Habitat	For	Humanity	
Jewish Historical Society	Jewish	Historical	Society	
Ramada Hotel	Ramada	Hotel		
Rashid Mohammed Mosque	Rashid	Mohammed	Mosque	
Royal Bank of Canada	Royal	Bank	Of	Canada
Saskatoon Convalescent Home	Saskatoon	Convalescent	Home	
Toronto Sick Children's Hospital	Toronto	Sick	Children's	Hospital
United Grain Growers	United	Grain	Growers	
United Way	United	Way		

	AS FILED			
AS WRITTEN	**Unit 1**	**Unit 2**	**Unit 3**	**Unit 4**
University of New Brunswick	University	Of	New	Brunswick
The Vancouver Philharmonic Orchestra	Vancouver	Philharmonic	Orchestra	The

Rule 9—Identical Names for People or Businesses

At times, two or more names will be identical. In such cases, use the geographical address to determine the filing order. Consider the following elements in this order:

- **City/municipality name.** When the names are the same, compare the names of the cities/municipalities.
- **Province/territory/state name.** When the cities/municipalities have the same name, compare the names of the provinces/territories/states.
- **Street name.** When the names of the provinces/territories/states are the same, compare the street names. File street names as they are written following the same principles learned in the rules for filing business names. Remember that numerals written as digits come before the alphabetic numbers (22 Street, Second Avenue). Remember that numerals are considered in ascending order (22 Street, 43 Avenue). Compass directions (North, SE, Southwest) are indexed as they are written.
- **Building number and name.** When the street names are the same, compare the building names or numbers. This refers to buildings of all sizes (houses, apartment blocks, business towers, and the like). Always try to compare building numbers, but when a building's number is unknown, you will have to use the building's name for the comparison. As always, numerals come before words. Remember that numbers are placed in ascending order before words (11 Saskatoon Drive, 22 Saskatchewan Crescent, Sampson Medical Building). Postal codes and zip codes are always ignored.

Example of Rule 9

NAMES AND ADDRESSES	UNIT COMPARED
General Assurance Agency **Milton,** Ontario	**City/municipality**
General Assurance Agency **Toronto,** Ontario	

NAMES AND ADDRESSES	UNIT COMPARED
Top Travel Vancouver, **British Columbia**	**Province/territory/ state**
Top Travel Vancouver, **Washington**	
Kids' Korner 222 – **5th Avenue** Halifax, Nova Scotia	**Street**
Kids' Korner 4 **Baxter Avenue** Halifax, Nova Scotia	
Classique Coffee Café 11 Deer Foot Trail Calgary, Alberta	**Building number or name**
Classique Coffee Café 55 Deer Foot Trail Calgary, Alberta	
Classique Coffee Café **Calgary Investment Building** Deer Foot Trail Calgary, Alberta	

Rule 10—Government Names

A. Provincial/Territorial/Municipal The first indexing unit should be the province/territory or municipality that has control over the government department. The next indexing unit is that of the most distinctive name in the department, agency, or ministry.

When the name includes "Department of," "City of," or similar, consider each word as a separate indexing unit.

Indexing government names can be a confusing task if you aren't sure which level of government has jurisdiction over the department. When in doubt, check the local telephone directory's government listings. (Example of Rule 10A is at the bottom of the page.)

B. Federal When the jurisdiction is the federal government, the first two indexing units will be *Canada Government of*. (Example of Rule 10B is on the next page.)

C. International When filing the names of foreign governments, always use the English spelling of the country name as the first unit. The next units will include the most distinctive name of the department, then bureau, commission, or board.

Variations in Alphabetic Filing Rules

Because conflicts in alphabetic indexing have existed for many years and continue to exist, you need to be aware of the conflicts as well as the standardized rules. When you report for a new work assignment, you will have to retrieve papers that have been filed by someone else. Furthermore, the organization for which you work may have its own rules for indexing and alphabetizing. If so, learn them and apply them, so that the files you maintain will be consistent with the other files in the organization.

Watch for the following variations in indexing and alphabetizing names of individuals:

1. The hyphenated surnames of individuals might be treated as separate units rather than as one filing unit.

2. Names beginning with *Mac* and *Mc* might be filed before names beginning with M.

3. A nickname used in the signature might be filed under the true given name, such as *Lawrence* instead of the nickname *Larry*.

Example of Rule 10A

AS WRITTEN	UNDER JURISDICTION OF	AS FILED						
		Unit 1	Unit 2	Unit 3	Unit 4	Unit 5	Unit 6	Unit 7
Department of Bylaw Services Winnipeg, Manitoba	**Municipality/City**	Winnipeg	City	of	Bylaw	Of	Department	of
Department of Social Services Whitehorse, Yukon Territory	**Province/Territory**	Yukon	Territory	Social	Services	Department	of	

Example of Rule 10B

| AS WRITTEN | UNDER JURISDICTION OF | AS FILED | | | | |
		Unit 1	Unit 2	Unit 3	Unit 4	Unit 5
Health Canada	**Federal**	Canada	Government	of	Health	Canada
National Defence	**Federal**	Canada	Government	of	National	Defence

Example of Rule 10C

| AS WRITTEN | UNDER JURISDICTION OF | AS FILED | | | |
		Unit 1	Unit 2	Unit 3	Unit 4
Ministry of Tourism Bahamas	International/ Foreign	Bahamas	Tourism	Ministry	Of
Industrial Development Commission Netherlands	International/ Foreign	Netherlands	Industrial	Development	Commission

4. Numeric seniority designations, such as II and III, might be filed as spelled out rather than in numeric sequence; also *Sr.* might be filed before *Jr.*

5. The name of a married woman might be filed under her husband's name instead of her own name.

There are many variations in the alphabetic filing rules for business establishments, institutions, and other group names. Watch for the following variations:

1. Each part of a hyphenated business name made up of surnames might be indexed as a separate filing unit, instead of the hyphenated name being treated as one filing unit.

2. Geographic names beginning with prefixes might be filed as two separate units rather than one.

3. Words involving more than one compass point (northeast, northwest, southeast, and southwest, and their variations) might be treated as two words instead of being indexed as written in the company name.

4. Geographic names that are spelled as either one or two English words—such as *Mountain View* and *Mountainview*—might be filed inconsistently, with the result that papers pertaining to one business establishment are filed in two different places.

5. Names beginning with numbers expressed in figures, as opposed to being written out, might be filed in regular alphabetical sequence with all the numbers spelled out

in full rather than filed in strict numeric sequence preceding the entire alphabetic file.

6. The *s* following an apostrophe might be disregarded, so that the word is indexed without the *s*.

Self-Check

1. What services does ARMA's expanded role encompass?
2. Define *unit, indexing,* and *alphabetizing.*
3. What is the first filing unit in a personal name?

OTHER FILING SYSTEMS

Alphabetic filing is a *direct* system for finding filed documents. A document's indexed name, if known, can be located easily by going *directly* to the files, looking through the alphabetized folders for the folder with the appropriate caption, and retrieving the document from this folder. Most offices dealing with individuals and companies use some form of alphabetic name system for filing papers. There are, however, other filing systems that may be more useful for particular types of businesses.

Subject Filing

With *subject filing,* records are arranged by topics rather than by personal, business, or organization name.

A furniture manufacturer might want to keep documents dealing with tables, chairs, sofas, and beds in separate file folders. In this case, these topics or *subject* headings would be written (coded) on the appropriate documents, and the papers would be put away in folders bearing the same captions.

Care should be taken to choose subject headings that are specific enough that documents are likely to be requested by these headings. A major subject heading should be subdivided into more specific headings if this will make for faster and easier location of papers. If a document deals with more than one subject, cross-reference sheets or photocopies should be placed in the other subject folders.

There are two methods of subject filing:

1. the encyclopedic system
2. the dictionary system

The *encyclopedic system* is used for both small- and large-volume filing. In this system, the major topic is broken down into related subheadings, and folders appear behind each subheading. An example might be:

BEVERAGES	(MAJOR TOPIC)
Coffees	(Subtopic)
■ Decaffeinated	(Folder)
■ Gourmet	(Folder)
FOOD	(MAJOR TOPIC)
Breads	(Subtopic)
■ Brown	(Folder)
■ Rye	(Folder)
■ White	(Folder)
Vegetables	(Subtopic)
■ Potatoes	(Folder)
■ Tomatoes	(Folder)

The dictionary system is not effective where a large volume of files exists. Topics are filed alphabetically, with no grouping by related topics—hence the term *dictionary system*. An example might be:

FOOD	(MAJOR TOPIC)
Brown Bread	(Folder)
Potatoes	(Folder)
Rye Bread	(Folder)
Tea	(Folder)
Tomatoes	(Folder)

Subject filing requires the records manager to refer to an index or list of topics before searching for a folder; for this reason, it is considered an indirect access system. The list is called a **relative index**.

The relative index is an alphabetic listing of all topics that appear in the system. Before returning a folder to the system or searching for a folder, the records manager consults the index to establish which topic the folder is kept under. Refer to Figure 11-16 for an example of a relative index.

Geographic Filing

A real estate company may wish to keep its records of houses for sale arranged by street names and numbers. A large organization with many branch offices across the country may wish to file its records by branch office location. A company that does work internationally may choose to file its records by country name. The arrangement of files by location is called *geographic filing*.

In geographic filing, the largest locations—street, city, province/territory, or country—are used as main divisions, arranged alphabetically by guides. Individual document folders pertaining to these main divisions are arranged behind the division guides, also alphabetically. The system can be as simple or as complex as desired. To meet the needs of customers, office supply companies maintain a wide variety of prearranged geographic, subject, and alphabetic filing systems with guides.

Geographic filing is usually a direct filing system. If the name under which the document is filed is known, the document can easily be retrieved by going directly to the files and looking for it in alphabetical order behind the appropriate guide. However, a geographic system in which an index must be consulted before a file can be located is an indirect filing system.

Geographic filing may use either the encyclopedic or the dictionary system (as explained in the section "Subject Filing"). Which one is used will be determined by the volume of topics.

How a geographic system is divided will depend on the company. One company might find it convenient to use guides with the names of provinces/territories and then further subdivide the filing system by city names. Another company, if it operates in only one city, might use guides that divide the city by districts. They would then further subdivide the filing system by street names. A company that works internationally might divide the filing system by country and then possibly subdivide by city.

Numeric Filing

Numeric filing is an *indirect* method of storing records. In numeric filing, even if you know the name, subject, or geographic heading of a document, you cannot simply go to the files and find it in alphabetical order. In numeric filing, each document is given a number and put in a folder with that number on the label. The numbered folders are arranged in the files in sequential order. Refer to Figure 11-17.

FIGURE 11-16 Relative index.

RELATIVE INDEX FOR RECREATION TOPICS

TOPIC OF FOLDER	REFER TO THE GUIDE ENTITLED
Bait	Fishing
Boating Registration	Fishing
Competitive Swimming Rules	Swimming
Court Fees	Tennis
Cycle Helmets	Cycling
Golf Clubs	Golfing
Knot Types	Sailing
Mountain Bikes	Cycling
Racquets	Tennis
Reflective Clothing	Running
Shin Splint	Injury
Sun Stroke	Injury
Tacking	Sailing
Tred-Fast	Athletic Shoes

Pearson Education, Inc.

To find a document filed under a numeric system, you must first consult an alphabetic index to determine the number assigned to that particular document. The index will be kept on a computer database that may be in card format. The index will relate alphabetized file names to their file numbers.

FIGURE 11-17 Numeric filing arrangement.

Splain2me/E+/Getty Images

Retrieving and updating information in a numeric system is extremely quick. The computerized database shows the number that has been assigned to the file. It may also show other helpful information such as postal and email addresses, telephone and fax numbers, and the date the file was created.

Once the file has been recorded on the database, the new folder is placed numerically in the filing system. The number of the file is coded on all documents that go in this folder. Inside the folder, the documents are filed chronologically, with the most current document on top.

While numeric filing may seem cumbersome, it has many advantages over straight alphabetic filing. Here are three:

1. **Time.** Once filed, document folders are faster and easier to find if they are arranged in numeric rather than alphabetic sequence.

2. **Filing Expandability.** In an A–Z alphabetic system, if the B section becomes overcrowded, all sections behind it must be moved to accommodate the overflow. In a numeric system, because each new name gets the next available number, the file folder is simply added to the end of the files; this does not disarrange the previous file folders.

3. **Privacy of Files.** Numeric filing protects the privacy of files because numbers rather than names are printed on the file folder labels.

Self-Check

1. Why is alphabetic filing considered a *direct* system?
2. In what order are records arranged in subject filing?
3. Is geographic filing a *direct* or *indirect* method of filing? Explain.
4. List three advantages of using a *numeric* filing system.

ETHICAL ISSUES IN RECORDS MANAGEMENT

In recent years, it has been quite common to hear news reports of unethical behaviour in the workplace and in records management in particular. Loss of important documents, improper disclosure and alteration, discovery of confidential or personal information stored in unsecured areas, and disposal of sensitive information in regular garbage without being shredded or otherwise withholding records made inaccessible are issues that have made headline news.

Employers are expected to be aware of various laws and principles that promote the rights of their employees and customers. The person responsible for managing the company's records must be knowledgeable about laws pertaining to the confidentiality and security of employee and customer records. Some of the issues related to ethical principles of records management are:

- confidentiality of personal information
- security of physical equipment such as desktop and laptop computers, as well as paper file cabinets and portable storage media such as USB flash drives
- validity of information
- disposal of records

- improper use of personal identification numbers (PINs) that intentionally or unintentionally allows unauthorized persons (other employees, internet users, or internet hackers) access to confidential or personal information

As an office professional, you should be aware that customer and employee records and emails, as well as other correspondence, are often used as legal documents, and that legal actions may be taken if records are not handled in a safe and secure manner.

INTERNATIONAL STANDARDS IN RECORDS MANAGEMENT

Standards create a professional environment of "best practice" procedures. The International Organization for Standardization (ISO) is a global network that identifies what international standards are required by businesses and government, develops them in partnership with the sectors that will put them to use, adopts them through procedures based on national input, and delivers them to be implemented worldwide.

The ISO is recognized worldwide for establishing the baseline for excellence in records management programs. The ISO states that records management includes:

- setting policies and standards
- assigning responsibilities and authorities
- establishing and sharing procedures and guidelines
- providing a range of services relating to the management and use of records
- designing, implementing, and administering specialized systems for managing records
- integrating records management into business systems and processes

More information on the ISO can be found at its website, www.iso.org.

QUESTIONS FOR STUDY AND REVIEW

1. List information management responsibilities of the administrative professional.
2. Explain the purpose of the federal Access to Information Act.
3. Explain the purpose of the federal Personal Information Protection and Electronic Documents Act (PIPEDA) and Canada's Anti-Spam Legislation (CASL).
4. What is the meaning of the term *visible filing*?

5. What is indexing? What is coding?
6. Explain how a cross-reference can be helpful in locating a paper in the files.
7. Describe the proper way to place paper documents in a folder.
8. Why do charge-out procedures not apply to electronic documents?

9. How is the filing system organized with electronic files?

10. State a benefit and a drawback to having an electronic filing system.

11. Explain the difference between a guide and a folder.

12. What are the most common supplies needed for electronic filing?

13. What is the difference between vertical and lateral filing cabinets?

14. What is the purpose of a wire organizer in a filing cabinet?

15. What is the most efficient way to store business contact information?

16. What is a field? a record? a file? a database?

17. State factors that determine how long records must be retained.

18. Define the following terms: *perpetual transfer method* and *periodic transfer method*.

19. How are electronic files archived?

20. What does government legislation say about retaining electronic records?

21. In filing rules, what is the meaning of the rule "nothing comes before something"?

22. How are two identical names for different people filed in an alphabetic system?

23. Compare the encyclopedic system and the dictionary system of subject filing.

24. What is the purpose of a relative index for subject filing?

25. In geographic filing, what is the first indexing unit?

26. Why is the numeric filing system an indirect system?

27. A paper that is urgently needed is missing from the correct file folder. Describe the steps you will take to locate it.

Key Terms

archiving 217

charge-out 206

coding 207

cross-referencing 207

directory 210

e-file 211

filing 204

indexing 207

information management 204

life cycle 215

out folder 209

out guide 209

pen drive 210

relative index 227

spam 205

visible filing 206

EVERYDAY ETHICS

Financial Records

Lyndsay has recently started working for a small office supply company as an administrative professional. One of her key responsibilities is updating and maintaining a number of records for the organization. It is nearing year-end, which means financial records need to be prepared for the accountant to submit a summary of business activity to Canada Revenue Agency (CRA). Today, Lyndsay called you on her lunch break; she sounded very upset and did not know what to do. Her immediate supervisor, Mr. Brown, had asked her to omit some expense reports for the accountant.

Lyndsay realizes this omission could have some serious consequences for the company and possibly for herself. Lyndsay feels her new position is in jeopardy if she does not do what is asked. She has just started this job and has told you how much she needs it. She thinks she should ignore Mr. Brown's request and submit all of the expense reports to the accountant—without telling Mr. Brown

■ Is this the best course of action for Lyndsay? Why or why not?

■ How would you recommend Lyndsay handle this situation?

Problem Solving

1. You work with three administrative professionals in a publishing company. You share a centralized paper filing system for the business files. To stay organized, you spend at least 20 minutes each day filing, as does your co-worker Dylan. Unfortunately, your other co-worker, Ashley, hates to file and rarely does any filing; instead, she puts the files

in a pile on her desk. Often when you are searching for a file, you cannot find it in the file system, but eventually you locate it on Ashley's desk. You are getting increasingly frustrated with having to search for missing files, since this wastes a considerable amount of time. How should you address this issue?

2. You are convinced that your predecessor made up his or her own filing rules. You have been working for three weeks, and you are having difficulty finding anything your predecessor filed. Your office supervisor has asked you to redo the files and to set up your own system. You are eager to set up a better filing system, but this is the peak season for your department. It will be at least two more months before you have time to redo the files. What can you do in the meantime?

3. You have set up an electronic filing system for your office, complete with directories and folders. At numerous staff meetings you have asked the managers in your organization to please file their completed proposals into the correct folders that you have set up. However, whenever you have to search for a proposal, you rarely find it in the correct folder or even in the correct directory. What ideas do you have for solving this problem?

Special Reports

1. Visit three websites that sell filing supplies and equipment online. Select five items that you would need in order to set up a filing system. Prepare a brief report for your instructor comparing the products and the prices listed on the three websites. Be sure to state the website addresses and names. Use an electronic spreadsheet to display your information.

PRODUCTION CHALLENGES

11-A Indexing and Filing Names

Supplies needed:

- *35 7.6 cm × 12.7 cm cards*
- *Set of alphabetic guides, A to Z*
- *Answer Sheet for 10-A, Form 10-A, Companion Website*

You have many names, addresses, and telephone numbers stored on cards. Since the cards are worn and inconsistent, you have decided to make new cards. The names, addresses, and telephone numbers are computer stored. You have requested a new computer printout of address labels for all your cards. Key the names in indexing order at the top of each card. In the upper right corner of each card, key the corresponding number for each name. (You will need the number to record and check your answers.) The first day you work on this project you key 35 cards.

After you have keyed Cards 1 to 35, separate the cards into five groups, arrange the cards in alphabetical order, and file them in correct sequence. Complete Answer Sheet for 10-A and check your answers.

Do NOT remove the 35 cards from your file. In Production Challenges 10-B and 10-C you will add more cards to your file.

Here are the names for Cards 1 to 35:

1. James R. Larsen
2. Bob O'Donald
3. Helen Vandermallie
4. Martha Odell-Ryan
5. Sister Catherine
6. George Harris, Ph.D.
7. Mrs. Georgia Harris
8. Father Jenkins
9. Ty Chen
10. Martha Odellman
11. Allens Swap Shop
12. J. T. Larson
13. Herbert Vander Mallie
14. George Harris, M.D.
15. Mary Allen's Beauty Shop
16. Marshall Field & Company
17. Georgia Harris
18. Allens' Print Shop
19. Trans-Continent Truckers
20. George Harris
21. James Larson
22. Hubert Vander Mallie
23. George E. Harris
24. Cayuga Industries
25. North East Fuel Supply
26. AAA Batteries
27. CHAM Radio
28. Higgins Cleaners
29. Electronics Laboratory, General Electric Company
30. Niagara Office Supply
31. Over-30 Club
32. Prince Arthur's Hair Styling

33. C & H Television Repair
34. First Baptist Church
35. Hotel Isabella

11-B Indexing and Filing Names

Supplies needed:

- *35 7.6 cm × 12.7 cm cards*
- *The card file prepared in 10-A*
- *Answer Sheet for 10-B, Form10-B, Companion Website*

The next time you work on your filing project, you key 35 more names in indexing order on cards. (Be sure to key the corresponding number on each card so that you can record and check your answers.)

Here are the 35 names:

36. James Danforth, Jr.
37. Burns Travel Agency
38. Strathcona County Water Department
39. Norton R. Henson
40. Sister Marie O'Doul
41. The Lone Ranger Riding Supplies
42. The Jefferson Party House
43. El Rancho Inn
44. Cecil Young-Jones
45. RCT Manufacturers
46. Administrative Management Society
47. Hotel Baker
48. Triple-Star Enterprises
49. Miss Robert's Charm School
50. Acadia University, Wolfville, Nova Scotia
51. Bob Guerin
52. William T. Au
53. Thomas Kaplan, M.D.
54. Irene McGregor
55. Arthur P. Van der Linden
56. Ontario Municipal Board
57. John Wilkins Supply Corp.
58. Southwestern Distributors
59. Department of Employment and Immigration
60. Four Corners Answering Service
61. Reliable Answering Service
62. Montgomery Ward & Co.
63. South East Pipeline
64. Webbers' Home for the Aged
65. People's Republic of China
66. Prince Albert Printing Co.
67. The Mercantile Bank of Canada
68. Aero Bolt and Screw Co., Montreal
69. Strong Memorial Hospital
70. Surv-Ur-Self Pastries, Inc.

After you key the names on the cards, separate the cards into five groups, arrange the cards in alphabetical order, and file them with the 35 cards you filed in 10-A. Complete Answer Sheet for 10-B and check your answers.

Next, prepare for Finding Test No. 1, which will be distributed by the instructor. If you had a card filed incorrectly, find out why. Before you take Finding Test No. 1, be sure that all 70 cards are arranged in correct alphabetical order.

When you have completed Finding Test No. 1, you are ready for 10-C. Leave the 70 cards in your file in order.

11-C Indexing and Filing Names

Supplies needed:

- *43 7.6 cm × 12.7 cm cards*
- *The card file prepared in 10-A and 10-B*
- *Answer Sheet for 10-C, Form 10-C, Companion Website*

You key 40 names in indexing order to complete your list of names. Here are the names:

71. Jason Wayne Suppliers
72. Prudential Assurance Co. Ltd., Winnipeg, Manitoba
73. Prince Charles Tea Shoppe
74. Federal Department of Consumer and Corporate Affairs
75. Hank Christian
76. East Avenue Baptist Church
77. CKY Television
78. Maudeen Livingston
79. Jim Waldrop
80. Department of Highways Alberta
81. The Royal Inn
82. Human Rights Commission, British Columbia
83. Ellen Jan Elgin
84. Robert E. Kramer, D.V.M.
85. Robert E. Kramer
86. United Hauling, Ltd.
87. Prince James Portraiture
88. Harold Roberson
89. London-Canada Insurance Co., Toronto, Ontario
90. The Royal Bank of Canada, 2411 Bellrose Drive, St. Albert, Alberta
91. Harold O. Roberson
92. Maverick
93. Mrs. Maudeen Livingston
94. George Zimmer Corporation
95. Simon Fraser University
96. Rain or Shine Boot Shoppe
97. M. T. Torres
98. Marion Burnett

99. Harold Robertson
100. John R. de Work
101. Del Monte Properties
102. Mason-Dixon Consultants
103. Robert E. Kramer, M.D.
104. La Belle Arti Furniture Manufacturing
105. Camp Edwards
106. Northern Alberta Pipeline
107. Frank T. Forthright
108. Bill Carter Petroleum Corporation
109. London & Midland General Insurance Co., London, Ontario
110. George Johnston Museum, Teslin, Yukon Territory

You anticipate that you may have difficulty finding cards 71, 75, and 79, because they could be called for by different names. Therefore, make cross-reference cards for them. In the upper right corner of each cross-reference card, key 71X, 75X, and 79X, respectively.

After you have keyed all the names on the cards, including the cross-reference cards, separate the cards into five groups, arrange the cards in alphabetical order, and file them with the 70 cards you filed in 11-A and 11-B. Complete Answer Sheet for 11-C and check your answers.

Next, prepare for Finding Test No. 2, which will be distributed by the instructor. If you had a card filed incorrectly, find out why. Before you take Finding Test No. 2, be sure that all the cards are arranged in correct alphabetical order.

11-D Setting Up E-Folders and E-Files

Supplies needed:

- *List of Electronic Folders and Files, Form 11-D, Companion Website*

You have neglected your electronic filing for the past week. Thirteen electronic documents you've created for Mr. Wilson are not yet in folders. The following list gives the document names that you have given to each document. Determine into which electronic folder you should place each document.

1. Minutes November 10
2. Sales Training
3. Annual Leave Request Wilson
4. Guest Speakers October Conference
5. Northwest Budget 20XX
6. Agenda December 7
7. Minutes December 7
8. Halifax Appliance Manufacturers
9. Annual Leave Request Levine
10. Invitations November Sales Seminar
11. Vancouver Better Homes Builders
12. Agenda November 10
13. Records Management Training

11-E Taking the Privacy Test

Supplies needed:

- *Plain paper*

Mr. Wilson has concerns about how the Canadian privacy laws relate to the electronic documents at PDI Inc. He wants all the administrative staff to receive training. He asks you to visit the Office of Privacy Commissioner of Canada at www.priv.gc.ca and watch the video *PIPEDA and Your Business: What you need to know about protecting your customers' privacy* and report back to him. He asks you to do the following:

- Provide a summary of the content presented in bulleted points.
- Comment on the effectiveness of the video and helpful media for PDI Inc.'s administrative staff.
- Explore the website and recommend three additional content resources for training purposes and for Mr. Wilson to incorporate into the training.
- Note the provinces in Canada possessing their own privacy laws separate from PIPEDA.

Prepare your responses in a keyed document or in an email message to Mr. Wilson.

Weblinks

ARMA International
www.arma.org
This site of the Association for Information Management Professionals includes a list of local chapters, upcoming conferences, and other useful information, including a download of disaster recovery plans and forms.

Filing Systems Online
www.filingsystems.com
This site contains information on records management products.

Vital Records Protection
www.vitalrecordsprotection.org
This site provides information on records protection. A variety of articles are available for reference, and relevant links are provided to assist with understanding how to manage business information.

Privacy Legislation

www.priv.gc.ca

This Office of the Privacy Commission of Canada site contains a description of privacy legislation and how it affects Canadian businesses.

Canada's Anti-Spam Legislation

www.fightspam.gc.ca

This site provided a detailed description of the anti-spam legislation and addresses frequently asked questions.

The Law Society of Upper Canada

http://www.lsuc.on.ca

This site provides guidelines for lawyers on records management.

The Canadian Medical Protective Association

www.cmpa-acpm.ca

This site publishes information on how to set up and maintain electronic medical records.

International Organization for Standardization (ISO)

www.iso.org

ISO's website provides information about the organization, membership, their strategies and policies, and the scope of their authority in implementing ISO standards.

Chapter 12
Travel Arrangements

Rawpixel.com/Shutterstock

SOCIAL NETWORK

LIKE

SHARE

LEARNING OUTCOMES

After completion of this chapter, the student will be able to:

1 Explain business travel concepts.

2 Describe key components of travel planning navigation.

3 Understand the services provided by a travel consultant.

4 Describe the procedures for making flight, car, and hotel reservations.

5 Discuss the requirements for acquiring passports, visas, and immunizations.

6 Prepare travel itineraries and other travel related documentation.

7 Make an airline reservation.

8 Research destination countries and compile information that the traveller should know before departing.

Forming business travel arrangements for a colleague, manager, yourself, or others while keeping it as stress-free as possible for the traveller requires planning. There are significant details to oversee, reservations to make, and schedules to coordinate. Even if all details are planned out and reviewed, there is still no guarantee that a travel obstacle will not occur. Planning business travel is no simple matter, and an experienced administrative professional knows this. Each traveller has personal preferences and unique inclinations that make travel planning a detailed process. Working with a manager who travels frequently requires the administrative professional to become thoroughly familiar with the organization's travel policies. Sourcing travel arrangements and how to schedule them is also essential.

PLANNING THE TRIP

Preparation is everything. Making travel arrangements is a perfect example of a task that requires thorough organizational skills. Breaking this planning aspect into phases is helpful. Consider the following as distinct phases:

1. **Information gathering.** Before proceeding to make travel arrangements, asking specific questions will assist in gathering timely and accurate information to support phase 2. In this phase ask questions such as:

   - Who is responsible for making travel arrangements?
   - Do designated administrative professionals handle travel arrangements within the organization?
   - Business class or economy class?
   - What is the policy concerning the use of private cars and car rental services?
   - Does the organization prefer a particular airline?
   - If so, what are the policies for using it?
   - How are payments for reservations handled?

2. **Laying the groundwork.** Make the reservations and construct a complete travel plan that coincides as closely as possible with scheduling needs and travelling preferences.

3. **Confirming.** Prepare or secure a travel itinerary for all travellers. Review the itinerary with the travellers and ensure they know how to source assistance if travel plans are interrupted or changed at the last minute.

Company Profile

Travel Masters

Webphotographeer/iStock/Getty Images

Organizations are seeking alternatives to facilitate company travel and are turning to businesses such as Travel Masters to help support the travel navigation pieces. Travel Masters completes the arrangement components many businesses find challenging or may not have the resources to undertake this task effectively.

A business initiates the contact and Travel Masters develops a customized travel plan to fit within the company policy. Travel Masters supports the business needs by ensuring they seek out exclusive lower fares, review the company strategic travel plan, systemic travel reporting, 24-hour on-call support, and up-to-date travel profiles.

Travel Masters satisfies business requirements by offering one-on-one personal attention, mindful of the needs of the business traveller. Travel Masters also boasts of its access to the world's best reservations systems, along with 20-years-plus supplier relationships to provide upgrading options to its clients. It also utilizes a travel app with clients called TripCase, which removes the need for paper confirmations—itinerary changes are seen in real time, as are flight delays.

Based on their business model and service to industry, Travel Masters received recognition for their attributes through various associations and organizations. These acknowledgements range from recognition such as a Top 10 Travel Agency, Circle of Excellence, Top Producer, and Outstanding Sales Accomplishment.

Since its startup as an economy travel provider in 1994, the key to Travel Masters' success is its team of travel specialists with the latest information and access to the most current and exclusive travel options possible. Vancouver is the location of the head office; there are also offices in Alberta as well as Saskatchewan. Even for business travellers who do not reside near a current location, Travel Masters will find a travel specialist located closest to the business traveller to provide assistance.

As soon as you have answers to a few of these questions, you will know whether to turn the arrangements over to someone else or make them yourself. Regardless of who makes the arrangements, try to request all reservations far enough in advance to ensure that you can obtain the travel arrangements and accommodations desired.

Digital Travel Services

Using digital technologies to make airline bookings is efficient and accurate. Going online offers an abundance of information that will help the administrative professional plan business trips. By searching the website of a travel service company, the administrative assistant may access information regarding:

- passports
- visas
- tourism
- flight schedules
- latest pricing
- phone numbers
- travel tips
- email, fax, and postal mailing addresses

When reservations are made using digital technologies, usually, the subscriber pays for the tickets with a credit card number. In addition to providing an instant confirmation number that can be printed or viewed on a device, travel providers follow up with an email including a ticket voucher containing trip details to the subscriber. This documentation replaces the traditional paper ticket when the traveller checks in at the airport.

More travel providers are integrating their technologies to address concerns before there is a problem. Using a travel app on mobile device, the traveller could be made aware that a connecting flight may be delayed and offer solutions before the traveller boards the first plane and well in advance before they arrive for the connecting flight.

Travel Consultants and Agencies

In the digital age, travellers have more choices and are better informed compared to in the past. The business models in the travel industry have evolved and the value propositions offered by traditional retail travel agencies are still relevant. This is because they offer incentives for corporate and group travel. Travel consultants often can find much lower prices. Agencies form relationships with travel suppliers, and therefore, the client often receives the best prices possible as compared to booking online. The expertise provided by a travel consultant along with the special business relationships permit consultants to source information it may otherwise have difficulty in obtaining, as well as their time-saving, stress

relieving, and problem-solving navigation skills. The services of a travel consultant when arranging for international travel are a definite asset. Many agencies guarantee 24-hour telephone access to travellers who run into problems, such as flight delays or cancellations during the trip.

Travel consultants receive their commissions from the airlines, hotels, and other organizations whose services they sell. Some agencies also may bill an organization a small fee for service.

If you are concerned about finding a reputable travel consultant or agency, call the Better Business Bureau or the Alliance of Canadian Travel Associations (ACTA) or check online for a listing of ACTA members. ACTA's membership includes travel consultants in all major Canadian cities. ACTA has high standards and a rigorous code of ethics; the group's members are reliable and efficient.

The International Air Transportation Association (IATA) approves most travel consultants. IATA is a conglomerate of international airlines. It allows travel agencies that meet its stringent requirements to use its insignia. An agency seeking IATA's approval must have a solid reputation, as well as the financial backing to ensure its own stability.

Travel consultants use digital technologies to maintain up-to-the-minute information on all airline schedules and hotel accommodations. Because of their experience and business connections, travel consultants obtain information quickly.

Travel consultants typically represents *all* the transportation lines, hotels, and motels, not just certain ones. The administrative professional of course, must provide the consultant with all the details needed. When planning a trip, attempt to work with only one person at the agency, and rely on that person to prepare the complete package.

The travel consultant will prepare the itinerary, secure tickets, make hotel reservations, arrange for car rental, and perform other services related to the trip.

For international travel, the consultant will provide information on the need for visas and how they can be obtained, how much luggage is allowed, luggage size restrictions, the countries being visited, the local currency, and the regulations for bringing foreign purchases through Canadian Customs.

They do not give advice on immunizations. That advice should be obtained through a local health authority such as a travel clinic.

Trip Information Needed

As soon as the manager mentions a trip, start compiling information. Before you contact a travel consultant or a carrier, compile the details concerning:

1. the destination
2. intermediate stops, outward and inward bound

3. date of departure and date of return

4. date and time of the first business appointment and the time needed between arrival and the appointment

5. preferred time of day for travel

6. method of travel—air, rail, automobile

7. type of service—business class, economy class

8. preferred service provider (i.e., airline)

9. preferred seat selection (aisle? window? front of the airplane?)

10. special accommodations (extra legroom, wheelchair access, dietary restrictions)

11. hotel preference or the desired location of the hotel within the city

12. hotel amenities required (conference facilities, wireless internet, multimedia equipment)

13. need for transportation at the destination or at intermediate stops

14. make or size of the car preferred if car rental is involved

15. events and meetings occurring during the travel stay

For use in planning future trips, maintain an electronic data folder containing general trip preferences. When the traveller returns from a trip, make comments about the transportation and hotel accommodations as a reminder for the next trip. In this folder, keep comments and all other information that will help you recall preferences when you are planning another trip to the same city or part of the country. If you plan trips for more than one person, maintain several subfolders with travel preferences specific to each person.

Self-Check

1. What are the key benefits of acquiring the services of a travel consultant?

2. List five pieces of information an administrative professional should have before contacting a travel consultant to make a reservation.

ARRANGING TRAVEL

Making transportation arrangements for international travel is similar to making transportation arrangements for domestic travel. However, an additional factor to take into account when planning international travel is the effect of a long trip through different time zones. International travellers commonly suffer from **jet lag**, the disruption of the body's natural rhythm that comes from high-speed jet travel. Effects (such as fatigue and irritability) and severity vary with individuals, directions travelled, and the number of time zones crossed.

Many, but not all, people report that easterly travel makes adjustment more difficult. The important thing to remember is international travel is both physically and mentally wearing on the traveller. When planning an overseas trip, allow an adequate rest period following arrival in the country you are visiting and following the return home.

To make travel arrangements with ease, you should know about air travel services and other types of transportation, including car rental services; how to make hotel reservations; how to obtain **passports** and **visas**; and what is involved in meeting immunization requirements.

---

pro-Link
Trusting Travel

Dreaming of faraway places? Cruising online to make your arrangements to visit them? It's interesting to know that only a small percentage of businesses rely on booking travel arrangements online. Why?

- Many offices don't trust online access for something as important as booking flights and hotels.

- It's easier to make a single phone call to a travel consultant and let the agent do the rest of the work.

The reluctance by businesses to use online services for travel arrangements is not likely to change dramatically until airlines and hotels offer greater incentives, such as reduced prices, for online bookings.

Air Travel

Because many managers are required to fly to meetings in different cities, the need to be informed about air travel services is essential.

Sources of Air Travel Information You can obtain air travel information about a specific trip by direct contact with a local travel consultant or airline. However, all this information is easily accessible digitally as well.

As well, the Canadian Transportation Agency has made available a number of free brochures of information about air travel.

Types of Flights Flights that encounter the fewest delays and inconveniences are considered the most desirable. When making travel arrangements, consider the flights available in this order:

1. a **nonstop flight**, which is uninterrupted from point of departure to destination

2. a **direct flight**, is a flight that goes between two points with one or more stops but no change in flight number

3. a **connecting flight** with another flight of the same airline

4. a connecting flight with another flight of another airline

When a passenger changes aircraft without changing airlines, the gate for the connecting flight should be near the deplaning gate. The distance between the boarding gates of two different airlines at a major airport can be great and walking or being shuttled from one gate to another is time-consuming. If the first flight is delayed, the passenger may not have enough time to get to the connecting flight.

Because delays cannot always be predicted, use wise judgment when making reservations; if the traveller must make a connection, allow adequate time between the flights. Remember that many airports have more than one terminal and that some cities have two airports. A connection between two different terminals or airports in the same city can take two hours, or even longer. Think of the activities involved: deplaning, getting transportation to the second airport, and locating and boarding the next flight.

Commuter flights are short, direct flights between two neighbouring cities. These neighbouring cities need not be in the same province, but they must be close enough that significant numbers of travellers use the service as a convenience. There are commuter services between Vancouver and Victoria, Edmonton and Calgary, Toronto and Ottawa, and various other Canadian cities. Many business travellers rely on commuter flights to meet with clients or colleagues in neighbouring cities and even to go to work each day. These flights leave frequently—often every hour. Although reservations are recommended, they are often not required because of the frequent schedules.

Classes of Service
The services passengers receive aboard the plane—especially where they sit and the food and beverages served—are purchased by class of service. The basic classes of service are business class and economy class. The priority services for business-class travelling include expeditious check-in and boarding as well as additional comfort and service during the flight.

Airlines sometimes refer to business-class service as first-class service. When an airline offers both first-class and business-class service on the same flight, the first-class service offers even greater seating comfort, at a proportionately greater cost. Some airlines, particularly on international flights, include extra-wide seats that recline fully into beds for their first-class passengers.

Some organizations require their personnel to fly *business class* because it is considered more prestigious and because it provides greater comfort, such as wider seats with more legroom and working room—an important consideration on long flights. Other organizations, for obvious financial reasons, require personnel to fly *economy class*, the most popular

FIGURE 12-1 First-class airline cabin seating.

Agnieszka Olek/Caiaimage/Getty Images

class of airline tickets. Disadvantages of economy-class air travel include longer check-in lines at airports, crowded cabins, and limited food service. The obvious advantage of economy-class travel is the cheaper ticket cost. Figure 12-1 depicts the typical seating of first class.

Flight Reservations You can make a flight reservation yourself online or by simply phoning the airline reservations office.

Most airlines provide digital tickets (e-tickets). The system works like this:

- Book the reservation over the phone or online.
- Use a credit card or charge account to pay for the tickets.
- Receive an emailed itinerary and confirmation from the airline carrier.
- An electronic boarding pass can be accessed online anytime within the 24-hour period prior to departure. Timelines will vary depending on whether the flight booked is domestic or international. Be sure to confirm electronic boarding pass requirements at the time of booking. You print your pass and proceed to the gate.
- Many airlines are offering a mobile device boarding pass option. When the electronic boarding pass is issued, it can be saved as a PDF file to the traveller's smartphone or tablet, which can then be scanned at the gate. Ensure the airline has a mobile scanner with which to scan your device appropriately. Alternatively, you can search for the mobile app of the airline to store your digital boarding pass.

Before you contact the airline reservations office, collect all the trip information you need for making a flight reservation. The reservations agent will be using a computer system that stores all the reservations. The agent will establish whether the space you want is available. If it is, make the reservation during the initial contact. When the traveller does not know the return date, purchase an **open ticket**. As soon as the traveller knows the return date, call the agent and make the return reservation.

If space is not available on the flight you want, proceed with alternative plans. Inquire about earlier and later flights with the same airline and with other airlines. If you cannot select an alternative flight, ask that the manager's name be placed on a waiting list in case there is a cancellation on the flight desired.

Reconfirmation of airline reservations is required on international flights. The traveller should reconfirm reservations for each leg of the trip.

Making Online Reservations
Booking the airline reservations online can be very efficient for the office professional. The administrative professional can access the availability of flights in minutes. Alternative schedules can be printed and then compared and selected by the travellers. Keep in mind that travel and flight plans change frequently and rapidly. While the administrative professional can save time and make changes promptly online, travel agents are more up to the minute on price and schedule changes that may have occurred since the reservation was made.

Many professionals within an organization like to make their own reservations. In this case, they may require some training on how to access flight information and book flights online. This way the traveller can quickly change plans without involving others.

Cost of Tickets and Payment
While fares for all scheduled intra-Canadian airline flights are deregulated, the Canadian Transportation Agency still evaluates tariffs and monitors competitive economy fares between Canadian destinations. International fares are regulated by IATA based on bilateral agreements between international carriers. Fares may vary minimally between Canadian airline companies. However, one company may offer a seat sale or an excursion fare.

In order to compete, some smaller airline companies offer **no-frills flights** for reduced prices. No-frills flights usually do not offer the in-flight cabin services of flight attendants, and passengers are required to provide their own food and drink. Even larger Canadian airlines such as Air Canada no longer provide meals to economy travellers on many of their domestic routes. Economy passengers on other routes may have the option to *purchase* prepackaged food from the airline during the flight. All travellers should check on the availability of food services before embarking on lengthy flights. All airlines include food and beverage service on their international flights.

Most airlines today offer travel incentives to their customers. Travellers who become members of an airline's travel plan earn points each time they fly. Points are earned in relation to the distance flown and class of service purchased. They can be redeemed for free travel with the airline or one of its partner airlines at a later date. Points are earned in the name of the traveller rather than the organization and are often influential in the traveller's choice of airline carrier. Air Canada's travel plan is Aeroplan, and members can use accumulated points for future travel with Air Canada or one of its partners, including international airlines such as Lufthansa and Air New Zealand.

Another way to save money is to make reservations well in advance of travel, since costs of remaining seats tend to rise as seats are sold for particular flights. While booking in advance can save the organization money, spontaneous travel plans are more common for business travellers. When a passenger must change travel plans or cancel a reservation, the passenger should call the nearest reservations office of the airline at once. Unused airline tickets and unused portions are sometimes redeemable where full fares have been paid. When discounted tickets are involved, there is a penalty for making changes or cancelling reservations. Penalties vary between airlines and with the type of ticket purchased. Refund regulations should be investigated at the time of booking.

Reading the 24-Hour Clock
For air travel, the times shown are often based on the 24-hour clock. This is to eliminate confusion between a.m. and p.m. Under this system, time begins at one minute past midnight (0001) and continues through the next 24 hours to midnight (2400). Likewise, a flight at 5:30 p.m. would show up on the boarding pass as 1730. See Figure 12-2.

FIGURE 12-2 Time conversion for the 24-hour clock.

1:00 a.m.	=	0100	1:00 p.m.	=	1300
2:00 a.m.	=	0200	2:00 p.m.	=	1400
3:00 a.m.	=	0300	3:00 p.m.	=	1500
4:00 a.m.	=	0400	4:00 p.m.	=	1600
5:00 a.m.	=	0500	5:00 p.m.	=	1700
6:00 a.m.	=	0600	6:00 p.m.	=	1800
7:00 a.m.	=	0700	7:00 p.m.	=	1900
8:00 a.m.	=	0800	8:00 p.m.	=	2000
9:00 a.m.	=	0900	9:00 p.m.	=	2100
10:00 a.m.	=	1000	10:00 p.m.	=	2200
11:00 a.m.	=	1100	11:00 p.m.	=	2300
Noon	=	1200	Midnight	=	2400

Ground Transportation   Airports are usually located 5 to 30 (or more) kilometres from cities; for that reason, one or more types of ground transportation—airport limousine, taxi, shuttle bus, and car rental—are available at all airports.

The distance and direction of the airport, the travel time needed, the types of ground transportation available, and approximate costs are all listed in the Official Airlines Guide (OAG) for most destination cities.

To determine what arrangements to make for ground transportation, ask the airline reservations agent or your travel consultant.

Limousines and shuttle buses operate on a regular basis between the airport and downtown hotels. They leave the designated hotels in time to get the passengers to the airport for departing flights, and they meet incoming flights.

Air taxi is a helicopter or small airplane service available at some airports. Helicopters operate between two airports of a destination city, between an airport and downtown heliports, or between the destination airport and an airport not served by jet aircraft. Compared to other types of transportation, air taxi service is expensive, but it saves time.

A traveller who must make a connecting flight at a different airport may need air taxi service in order to make the connection. On domestic flights, avoid scheduling a connecting flight that involves a second airport. When people travel abroad, they may have to make a connection involving two airports because the traveller's incoming flight may arrive at one airport and the international flight may depart at another. Before making a reservation for air taxi service, find out about airport limousine or bus shuttle service between the terminals serving the airports involved.

Car Rental Services

The largest car rental agencies offer both domestic and international car rental services, publish worldwide directories of their services, provide a toll-free number for making reservations, and have a website with reservation facilities.

When you are making arrangements for car rental, specify the following:

- city, date, and time
- size of the car desired
- location where the car is to be picked up
- name of the person who will pick up the car
- location where the car is to be left
- length of time the car will be used
- the method of payment for the charges
- availability for GPS mapping driving directions

A car can be picked up at the rental agency right at the airport. All the traveller has to do on arrival is go to the airport car rental office, state that there has been a reservation, present a driver's licence, and complete arrangements for payment of the charges. Allow time in your schedule for the agent to inspect the car for damage and discuss insurance options with you. Know in advance whether your company's insurance will cover damages to the vehicle in the event of an accident or act of God (hail, flood, falling tree).

Charges incurred are payable at the completion of the rental, but the arrangements for payment must be made in advance. Major credit cards are accepted. An organization may have arrangements with car rental agencies entitling you to a discount.

Self-Check

1. What is jet lag?
2. What is the difference between a nonstop flight and a direct flight?
3. Distinguish between business-class and economy-class airline tickets.
4. What is an e-ticket?

Hotel Reservations

Many hotels provide a toll-free number for making reservations. You can obtain the toll-free number from the hotel's website or by calling 1-800-555-1212. Be aware that if you call directory assistance, there might be a charge.

If you are not familiar with the hotels in the destination city, contact a local travel consultant. Most international accommodation information changes so rapidly that agents consult online, which is updated frequently. Many of the larger hotels and resorts have their own websites, so it is very possible to access this information and make your own reservations. Most hotel and resort websites provide online booking services and toll-free phone numbers. There are also many discount travel sites that offer significant reductions in accommodation costs.

Always secure confirmation of a hotel reservation. A confirmation number or an electronic confirmation note is the typical format; be sure to attach it to the itinerary so that the traveller will have it if there is any question about the reservation.

Hotels usually require a credit card to hold the reservation and sometimes require a deposit, especially when you request that a room be held for late arrival. A room that is being held for a possible late arrival is called a *guaranteed* reservation. Make the request and provide a credit card number as a deposit if there is the slightest chance that your manager might arrive late. Late arrival time usually starts between 4 p.m. and 6 p.m. Major credit cards are accepted by hotels, and providing the credit card information simplifies the process of making a deposit for a guaranteed room reservation. The benefit of a guaranteed reservation is that your manager should assured of a room regardless of the arrival time. However, if travel plans change and the guaranteed reservation is not cancelled before a specified time on the arrival date (e.g., 6 p.m.), the cost of the room will be billed to the credit card number, and the authorized owner of the card will be required to pay the cost. In addition, if there is a chance that the traveller will arrive very late (such as after 11 p.m.), the hotel should be notified so the room will continue to be held. If there is huge demand for rooms, even guaranteed rooms have been given to other guests after a certain time.

Passports and Passport Substitutes

A passport is a travel document, given to citizens by their own government, granting permission to leave the country and to travel in certain specified foreign countries. A passport serves as proof of citizenship and identity in a foreign country. It asks other countries to allow the bearer of the passport free passage within their borders. It entitles the bearer to the protection of her or his own country and that of the countries visited. Any Canadian citizen who goes abroad must carry a Canadian passport.

As an alternative, Canadians citizens travelling by *air* to the United States are required to present a valid passport; a NEXUS card is also acceptable when used at a NEXUS kiosk. This card is issued to applicants who pass rigorous security checks and is approved by both countries. It is intended to expedite border crossings. Crossings by land or sea require a passport to cross the Canada–U.S. border. The FAST pass can also be sourced and used as a program, as it preapproves commercial truck drivers for travel between the United States and Canada.

To apply for a passport, a person must complete an application form. The passport application is available free of charge at any post office or passport office and at most travel agencies. The passport office is an agency of the Government of Canada. Along with the completed application, the applicant must submit (1) two identical passport photos taken within the previous 12 months and certified on the back by an eligible guarantor and (2) an *original* document as proof of Canadian citizenship. A photocopy of a birth certificate is not acceptable. Payment must be submitted with the application form and must be made in the form of cash, money order, or a certified cheque made payable to the Receiver General of Canada.

Passport applications may be made in person at a regional office or can be submitted through the mail; processing time is longer in the latter case. If a passport is urgently required, processing can be expedited at an extra cost when presented in person.

Under current regulations, a Canadian passport is valid for 5 years or 10 years and may not be renewed or extended. An **ePassport** is also known as a biometric passport. It looks like a traditional passport book, but it has an electronic chip that is encoded with the same information found on page 2 of the passport (surname, given name, date of birth, and sex). It also has a digital picture of the bearer's face and issuing authority.

The ePassport is designed to reduce tampering. Border crossings are equipped with an ePassport reader in order to scan the chip on the ePassport.

Visas

Many countries require foreign travellers to hold a visa. A visa is a stamped permit to travel within a given country for a specified length of time. It is granted by the foreign country's government and is usually stamped or attached inside the passport. However, some countries provide loose visa documents so that the visa can be removed when travelling to uncooperative countries.

Global Affairs Canada maintains a website that contains information for Canadians who travel abroad. It promotes different cultures and values worldwide; it can be located at www.international.gc.ca/international/index.aspx?lang=eng. It includes a link to Canadian government offices abroad where you can get up-to-date visa information. Additional information is found using this link www.travel.gc.ca/travelling. The site provides current travel updates on conditions of foreign destinations, political unrest, threatened security and health conditions, entry requirements, and consular contact numbers. Information that pertains to foreign countries, including visa requirements, is subject to change. Well in advance of the departure date, a traveller should check passport and visa requirements with the consulates of the countries to be visited. Most countries require the Canadian passport to be valid for a specified period of time past the scheduled departure date from that country.

The traveller should obtain the necessary visas before going abroad. Visas are obtained through consulates and embassies located in Canada. Most foreign consular representatives are located in principal Canadian cities, particularly Ottawa, Toronto, and Vancouver. The addresses of foreign consulates in Canada may be obtained by consulting Global Affairs Canada through the Office of Protocol's website, http://www.international.gc.ca/protocol-protocole/reps.aspx?lang=eng. This comprehensive website includes an inquiry service. If you wish to contact Canadian embassies and consulates abroad, these can be searched by location or city at http://travel.gc.ca/assistance/embassies.

The traveller must send his or her passport to each consulate involved to obtain visas. The time (and level of patience) it takes to process a visa after it reaches a consulate office varies between one day and three weeks. Allow plenty of time and use prepaid courier services whenever possible. Some travel consultants are experienced in obtaining visas, but because the process is usually straightforward, you should not need to rely on travel consultants.

Immunization Requirements

The International Health Regulations adopted by the World Health Organization (WHO) stipulate that certain vaccinations may be required as a condition of entry to any country. The WHO recommends that all travellers whether domestic or international should be up to date with routine immunizations. The WHO sends communiqués to local health departments advising them of required and recommended **immunization** for travellers. Additional information on major health risks to travellers to various countries can also be found on their website at www.who.int.

For travel to many countries, an International Certificate of Vaccination is not required. If you need one, you can obtain it from the local health clinic. The form must be stamped by the clinic where the vaccinations are administered.

Refer to your local health authority well in advance of trips to developing countries. Canadian websites that contain information related to immunization requirements are the Public Health Agency of Canada, under "Travel Health," at www.travelhealth.gc.ca and Health Canada.

Carry-On Luggage

Airlines differ with regard to their regulations for carry-on luggage. Policies may vary concerning some airlines have developed a sizing device to help with the acceptance and refusal of carry-on baggage. Carry-on baggage must fit within the dimensions of this sizing device. These devices are generally located near the check-in and gate areas. Other considerations related to carry-on luggage include:

- the number of pieces allowed
- the weight of the carry-on

Travellers are generally allowed only one or two pieces of carry-on luggage. All pieces must be small enough to fit under the seat or in the overhead cabinets of the aircraft.

Carry-on luggage is scanned as it passes through security. The Canadian Air Transport Security Authority (CATSA) provides detailed information on carry-on baggage limitations as well as specific information on what items are considered unacceptable to pack. If any suspicious items show up on the scan, the luggage is checked by hand. It is forbidden to carry any items deemed to be potentially dangerous. More information can be obtained by visiting and searching items for travel at www.catsa.gc.ca.

Security

All travellers, both national and international, should be aware of security issues. Global travel faces a number of security threats. Corporate travel buyers are dealing with a growing number of traveller concerns. Many airports now use full-body scans to look for concealed weapons or objects. For the administrative professional who makes travel arrangements and who helps the business traveller prepare for the trip, here are some factors to consider:

- Travel to and through some countries can put Canadians at risk. When booking flights, choose flights that are reputable and ones that avoid countries that are unfriendly to Westerners.
- Location is a critical consideration when booking hotels. Be certain that you book reputable hotels in safe locations.
- Security at airports is heavy. Business travellers who travel should expect to have their mobile devices and briefcases thoroughly examined before they board a flight.
- Prescriptions and over-the-counter drugs that are legal in Canada (e.g., codeine) may be restricted in other countries. Keep the original prescription and the original container while the medication is being taken and even after the treatment is finished since traces of certain medications can still be detectable in the system for a period of time.
- Batteries in the travellers' mobile devices should be charged. With increased airport security, people carrying electronic devices may be asked to start these machines to prove they are truly business tools and not explosive devices.
- Many airports insist on jackets and shoes being removed as travellers pass through security.
- Some countries deny entry to travellers whose passports indicate travel in countries on their "uncooperative list" within a certain period of time. Travellers should check to see if restrictions apply between countries they intend to visit.
- Travellers should expect to answer questions about why they are travelling to certain countries. Is it for business? If so, what business?
- Travellers should carry their passports and their immunization cards (in some countries) since government officials can request these at any time.
- Gifts for clients should not be wrapped prior to boarding the flight. Airport security can insist that you unwrap all parcels for inspection.

- Travellers should expect to be patted down by security officers if any level of metal registers as the traveller passes through the metal detection gate.
- Increased security at airports throughout the world often results in longer delays in boarding airplanes than in the past. Take this into consideration when determining how early to arrive at the airport.
- Travellers should never carry any device or substance that security will deem as dangerous. If found in your carry-on luggage, these items may be confiscated and charges could be levied.

To avoid any unnecessary risks, check the Global Affairs Canada website prior to the trip. Give this website address and the Canadian embassy coordinates for the foreign country to the business traveller before the trip.

Self-Check

1. (a) How would you make a guaranteed hotel reservation?
   (b) What is the benefit of having one?
2. How does immunization relate to international travel?

FOLLOWING THROUGH

While administrative professionals can rely on a travel consultant when planning a trip, they are directly responsible for checking the completeness and accuracy of the final arrangements.

Prior to the Trip

Just before the business traveller leaves on a business trip, the main responsibilities may include checking the tickets, securing funding for the trip, preparing the itinerary, assembling materials for the trip, and identifying instructions surrounding special areas of responsibilities during the absence.

Checking the Tickets   Obtain the tickets in enough time to check them carefully. First compare the information on the tickets with what was requested; then thoroughly check each item on the tickets with the itinerary. The information on the tickets and the travel portion of the itinerary should be identical.

Funding the Trip   Credit cards such as American Express, Visa, and MasterCard make it possible to travel without carrying large sums of money. Most people rely on credit cards while travelling. Companies pay for necessity items using a variety of methods, the most common being to reimburse the employee after they have submitted their receipts. Other companies may use a nonaccountable per diem system. In this system (discussed more fully in the next section), a business provides a flat payment to its employees to cover business expenses incurred each day but the employee does not have to substantiate the expenses or return advance payments in excess of the amount actually used.

To cover the expenses of the trip, however, some travellers prefer cash. In this case, many organizations will provide a cash advance to employees who travel. If this is the policy in your organization, complete the required form, and obtain the cash. Figure 12-3 shows a **travel fund advance** form. Although forms vary, it is important on all forms to fill all appropriate blanks with accurate information. This will help avoid delays in receiving the travel advance.

Whether you are obtaining cash from a bank or through a direct deposit from an organization, get some small bills to be used for tips.

Most business travellers take limited cash and carry their Visa, MasterCard, or American Express credit cards. Cash in the foreign country's local currency is readily available through automatic teller machines found in most international hotels.

FIGURE 12-3 Travel fund advance.

Progressive Digital Innovations Inc.

Travel Advance Form

Employee Last Name: ☐ Smith.

Employee First Name: ☐ Sylvia.

Employee ID: ☐ 245.

Email Address of Employee: ☐ S. Smith@PDI.ca.

Reason for Travel:

Destination:

Departure Date: ☐ Click or tap to enter a date.

Return Date: ☐ Click or tap to enter a date.

Amount Requested: ☐ Choose an amount.

Preferred Method of Payment: Direct Deposit: _____

Approval Manager:

Pearson Education, Inc.

Understanding Per Diems

One of the first things you will need to understand is the **per diem rate**. *Per diem* is a Latin term meaning per day. It means an amount of money, determined by the company, that it will pay per day for expenses to an employee who must travel for business. There is usually a meal per diem and sometimes an accommodation per diem.

The Canada Revenue Agency publishes the rates that Canadian government employees are reimbursed for their expenses when travelling abroad. They must publish this because they are accountable to the Canadian taxpayer. Appendix C: Meals and Allowances provides useful information for travel in Canada and the United States (search "meal allowance" at www.canada.ca). Many nongovernmental Canadian organizations use these published rates as their own policy within their organizations. Travel expense policies vary greatly among nongovernmental organizations. Some companies allow travellers to claim more than the per diem if receipts can be provided, while other companies expect their travellers to cover their own expenses beyond the per diems allowed.

As an administrative professional, be sure to confirm your company's per diem rates and policies before you make travel arrangements.

Travel Expense Voucher

If you are not sure about your company's policy with regard to expense claims, consult a policy manual so that your work on the voucher is accurate. Completeness and accuracy are the two necessary ingredients for ensuring a quick return of funds owing to the traveller.

Note that all expenses must have the approval of a senior organization representative. Although these forms vary from company to company, most require at least the following information:

- the date the expense was incurred
- the location where the expense was incurred
- the cost of transportation
- the cost of the hotel where the traveller stayed
- the cost and explanation of other business expenses that relate to the trip (including telephone calls, laundry services, or a necessary business item that was purchased)
- the cost of company-related entertaining
- the cost of meals
- the amount of any travel fund advance that may have been received prior to the trip

This amount is deducted from the amount the employee will now receive from the company. Remember that most claimed expenses must be verified by receipts and must not exceed costs specified by company policy.

These forms are completed by anyone who has a legitimate company expense. This may include any level of employee. If the travel expense voucher form is stored on your computer, you can key the information. If not, it is acceptable to submit these documents in handwritten form.

Preparing the Itinerary

Usually, an **itinerary** is a combined travel/appointment schedule. However, the travel itinerary and the schedule of confirmed appointments can also be prepared as two separate lists. An itinerary shows when, where, and how the traveller will go. It should include:

- the day
- the date
- the local time of departure and arrival
- the name of the airport
- the flight numbers
- the place of departure and arrival
- the name of the hotel for each overnight stay on the trip

The itinerary should also include details about confirmed appointments. Examples of such details might be:

- The names and titles of the people the traveller will see. Include brief information that will be helpful in the introduction if this is a first-time contact.
- Personal notes about people the traveller may see. These comments are intended to aid conversation and familiarity. They may include reminders about family members, recent achievements or personal interests.
- Dates and times of the appointments. All times should be shown as local times.
- The purpose of the appointments. This should be a simple summary.
- Software and/or documents required for the appointments. If specific power cords or cables are required, note that.

These details are illustrated in the itinerary in Figure 12-4.

As soon as the travel and hotel accommodations and the appointments have been confirmed, you can prepare the final itinerary. Make a step-by-step plan that is so complete that the business traveller will know where to go, when, and what materials will be needed by referring to the itinerary.

Preparing an itinerary is time-consuming because you need information from several different sources. Arrange the papers relating to hotels and appointments in chronological order. Give the itinerary an appropriate heading. Use the days and dates as the major divisions, and list the entries under each division in order according to time. Check the final itinerary more than once to make sure it is 100% correct.

FIGURE 12-4 Itinerary.

```
                ITINERARY FOR IAIN BROWN

                Toronto—Vancouver—Toronto
                April 5—April 7, 20XX

Monday, April 5

0905            Depart Toronto Pearson International Airport for
                Vancouver on AC167.

1030            Arrive Vancouver International Airport.

                Reservations are at the Westin Bayshore. Hotel confir-
                mation attached.

1230            Lunch with Benjamin Edwards and Bob Ross at Olives
                Restaurant in the Westin Bayshore.

1430            Conference with Sales Team, Vancouver Branch. The
                meeting is scheduled to be in the Pacific Room, 2nd
                floor.

Tuesday, April 6

1000            Meet with William Mack, Manager Victoria Sales
                Branch.

                Mr. Mack will meet you in the lobby of your hotel.

1300            Lunch with Christine Bollen, Editor of Sales Unlimited
                magazine.

1930            Dinner with Sandy Wolfe, President of Avanti
                Products, at the Pines Restaurant in the Westin
                Bayshore.

Wednesday, April 7

0730            Depart Vancouver International Airport for Toronto
                on AC443.

1710            Arrive Toronto Pearson International Airport.


                HAVE A PRODUCTIVE TRIP!


Note: All times are shown as local times.
```

Pearson Education, Inc.

FIGURE 12-5 Working en route with a wireless laptop computer.

Phovoir/Shutterstock

Prepare the itinerary in the style a manager prefers. However, if the travel consultant has already prepared a detailed itinerary, instead of rekeying it to add the appointments, prepare a separate schedule of appointments.

Just prior to departure, when all the details have been finalized, send an electronic copy of the itinerary to the traveller. Keep a copy in the office information system as a record. Many people travel with a laptop computer, as shown in Figure 12-5.

Special Instructions　Record key instructions if the manager is the business traveller; the manager may provide directives about how to navigate situations during her or his absence. Find out how and when correspondences should be forwarded and any special responsibilities to be handled in the manager's absence. Be sure to understand how to follow through on important correspondence and phone calls.

Printing Business Cards　A business traveller who is conducting organization business in a foreign country may request to have new business cards printed for the trip—one side containing the usual information in English, the reverse side printed in the foreign language. Foreign business contacts will view this as a courteous gesture.

During the Manager's Absence

When a manager is away, as a best practice administrative professionals should continue to work at the same pace as they normally work. This is an excellent opportunity to work on assignments they may have put off.

Managers will typically access their email remotely while they are away from the office in order to keep up with information and work. They will check in with touch points with the office regularly to keep informed. Be ready to report on significant events, important mail, and phone calls. Record a summary of what you should discuss. If the manager keeps in touch with the office through email, you can provide this information on a daily basis and get the manager's feedback immediately.

Many organizations use an email provider such as Microsoft Outlook that includes an "out-of-office" feature. This feature can be set to alert senders of incoming emails that the recipient is out of the office for a specified time.

Plan your schedule so you can spend the first day the manager is back in the office following through on work generated by the trip.

When the manager is away, you will have added responsibilities and may need to allow extra time to handle them. For example, you will want to read the manager's email and other correspondences to determine if any of the information is urgent and needs to be handled by you or someone else within the organization. Offer your assistance if you can perform any of these responsibilities. Try to keep the manager's calendar free of appointments for the first day following the trip.

After the Manager Returns

Activities on the manager's first day back after a trip will centre on briefing the manager on what happened during the trip, following up with correspondence, assembling receipts for the expense report, and filing materials your manager brings back.

Report the most significant happenings first. Put the following items on your manager's desk: correspondence that arrived in your manager's absence, arranged in folders as explained in Chapter 8; the summary of appointments; a summary of important phone calls that were not left on voice mail; and a list of who came to the office to see the manager.

Early in the day, call attention to anything that requires immediate action.

Review your list of the materials the traveller took on the trip that must be returned to the files. Locate these materials and file them. Also, file materials your manager acquired during the trip. This includes business cards that have been collected. Copies of materials from the files that your manager took on the trip can be disposed of. First, however, check carefully for notes that may have been made on them.

Discuss the trip with your manager. Record any problems encountered with hotels, car rentals, or other arrangements so that you may avoid such problems in the future. Likewise, note particularly good service your manager received. This will be valuable information to consider in the future when opportunities to use those same services arise.

Write messages of gratitude to people who hosted your manager. Offer your support to complete reports related to the trip. Of course, one of the most important responsibilities is to collect receipts and prepare the expense account for the trip (including phone calls, laundry services, or a necessary business item that was purchased).

Self-Check

1. What is a travel advance? How would you go about requesting one?
2. Define *per diem*.
3. List the items to be included in an itinerary.

ETHICAL ISSUES IN REPORTING TRAVEL EXPENSES

Employers expect employees to operate in accordance with the highest attainable standards of ethical business conduct. They also expect employees to take action against improper conduct by reporting it if they are aware of it.

When an employee demonstrates unethical behaviour, it may begin with peer pressure or a supervisor's direct request to violate the company's code of ethics. Consider the situation of Nada, who routinely assisted in the preparation of travel expense reports. What began as a one-time request from her supervisor to "pad" expenses became a mountain of bogus entries. Once found out, Nada's employment was terminated.

Although companies have their own policies, there may be grey areas in expense regulations that often lead employees to "fudge" the numbers in their favour. What if you are asked to falsify an expense report for your manager? You have several options: (1) inform your manager you feel it is wrong to inflate the numbers and ask for his or her support in your decision; (2) report the request to your ethics officer or a human resources representative before you do anything; (3) honour the request, but inform your superior you will not do it again; or (4) comply with your manager's request.

Employees are expected to follow the travel expense policies to ensure honest and efficient use of company funds. If you prepare travel expense records or certify the accuracy of information in such records, you must be diligent in ensuring the accuracy and integrity of this information.

Culture and International Travel

Customs vary widely from one country to another, and understanding and observing these cultural variables is critical to a traveller's success. Helping a business traveller learn something about the culture of a country before doing business there will enhance the chances of a successful outcome and help him or her develop prosperous, long-term relationships.

1. Research national holidays and important events in the country the traveller will be visiting. Then she or he can show respect for those occasions by honouring customs and restrictions associated with special events and holidays.

2. Help the traveller learn a few foreign words and phrases such as *Hello, How are you? Please, Thank you, Goodbye, It was a pleasure to meet you.* Books on language translations of common terms are readily available for purchase in many bookstores.

3. Learn to correctly spell and pronounce the names of your hosts and business associates, and ensure the traveller does too. Both your efforts will be appreciated and accepted as a gesture of respect for and acceptance of their culture.

4. Research the local habits and restrictions of countries the traveller will be visiting. For example, did you know it is unacceptable in some countries for women to appear in public without arms and knees covered, even for casual events? Are you aware that while a gift wrapped in red might be well received in Denmark where red is seen as a positive colour, the same wrapping might offend the recipient in an African country where red represents witchcraft and death? The traveller will appreciate it if you inform her or him of any pertinent information you learn in this area.

Self-Check

1. Why is it important to help the traveller learn a little about the culture of a country before she or he leaves to conduct business there?

2. Describe two customs of foreign countries that are not normally practised in Canada.

QUESTIONS FOR STUDY AND REVIEW

1. Organizations have definite policies concerning business travel. Name some areas in which you would expect policies to be clearly stated.

2. How can access to digital technologies help the administrative professional make travel arrangements?

3. What services will a travel consultant perform for domestic travel? For international travel?

4. What general information relating to a trip should an administrative professional compile before contacting a travel agency or carrier?

5. Distinguish among the following:
   a. nonstop flight
   b. direct flight
   c. connecting flight
   d. commuter flight

6. Explain how jet lag can affect travellers and how this relates to business trips.

7. If the flight reservation a traveller desires is not available, explain how to proceed to make alternative plans.

8. What is meant by reconfirmation of an airline reservation? When is it necessary?

9. Using the 24-hour clock, write 6 a.m., 2 p.m., 9:20 p.m., noon, and midnight.

10. What ground transportation is available at airports?

11. What is an air taxi? What is a heliport?

12. What information should an administrative professional compile before securing arrangements for a car rental?

13. Suggest two ways to make hotel reservations.

14. Why should an administrative professional always ask for a written confirmation of a hotel reservation?

15. What is an ePassport?

16. List the items that must be submitted along with a passport application.

17. What is a travel visa? Who can issue a visa?

18. What information might the administrative professional obtain from the World Health Organization pertinent for travel?

19. State two factors to consider when packing carry-on luggage.

20. List three security precautions that travellers should be aware of before air flights.

21. What is a travel per diem?

22. What information should be included in an itinerary?

23. Explain how an administrative professional's time can be used efficiently during the manager's absence.

24. State four ways to help a business traveller learn about the culture of a foreign country prior to a business trip to this country.

Key Terms

commuter flight 239

connecting flight 239

direct flight 238

ePassport 242

immunization 243

itinerary 245

jet lag 238

no-frills flights 240

nonstop flight 238

open ticket 239

passport 238

per diem rate 245

travel fund advance 244

visa 238

EVERYDAY ETHICS

Exaggerated Expenses

You work for Craig, the executive director of Power Product Corporation. Craig has just returned from a two-week business trip to Asia and has handed you a stack of receipts to organize. It's your responsibility to prepare Craig's travel expense report.

You sort through the receipts and find some that you doubt can be considered as business expenses. These include bar expenses, tickets for sightseeing trips, and an expensive amethyst necklace purchased in Canada prior to the trip. You separate these receipts from the others and broach the issue with Craig. Craig insists that these entertainment and gift expenses are a necessary part of doing business in Asia. The necklace, he explains, was given as a corporate gift to the Asian client. He tells you to put these expenses under the entertainment column on the expense form. According to Craig, the trip cost him a lot of personal money, and he is in a hurry to get reimbursed.

He doesn't want the hassle of having to explain his expenses to the vice president who must approve his expenses. So he instructs you to hide the words "amethyst necklace" and write "company gift" in its place. His tone edges on being aggressive. You are uncomfortable with this but feel convinced that these expenses are just a part of corporate life. You treat the expenses as Craig has requested. Craig signs the expenses and you send them to the office of the vice president for approval.

Then it happens! The day after you submit the expenses, Craig's wife appears at the office wearing a dazzling amethyst necklace.

- Whose actions have been unethical?
- What do you say to Craig?
- Should you contact the administrative professional in the vice president's office and request that the expenses be returned to you?
- What will you do when Craig submits the next bogus expense claim?
- Will your work on the expense claim reflect poorly on you or on Craig?
- Is there a chance you will lose your job?

Problem Solving

1. The manager is planning a business trip to one of the organization's branches located across the country. At the time that the manager asked you to make a reservation for her, all the tickets had been sold for the date she requested; her name was placed on a waiting list for both directions of the trip. Today you checked with the airline and found that space is available to the destination city at the time your manager requested but that she still would have to be on a waiting list for the return trip. Should you accept the reservation to the destination city? Explain.

2. When the office manager, Mrs. Orlando, arrived in Saskatoon, she could not find her luggage. Her notes for the talk that she is to give at the conference are in her suitcase. Another copy of the notes is in Mrs. Orlando's desk at the office. She calls you at home on Saturday morning and asks you to go to the office, find the notes, and get them to her. How will you get the notes to her? What suggestions would you make about packing notes for future talks?

3. You work for three executives. Two of them are planning to attend a national management conference in Toronto, and you have made travel reservations for them. Now the third executive has decided to attend the conference. He has asked you to make travel reservations for him for the same time the other two executives are travelling. You call the airline. A reservation is not available at that time. What should you do while you are talking with the reservations agent?

4. This was the first time you made travel arrangements for your manager. He manages his multiple sclerosis well, but fatigue aggravates the symptoms. Your manager had the following problems on his trip. How would you prevent these problems from reoccurring on the next trip?

   a. The hotel room was guaranteed for arrival, but an accessible room was not requested. Because of a large convention being held at the hotel, your manager could not get an accessible room when he arrived.

   b. Although you told your manager that a car had been rented, the rental agency did not have a reservation. Your manager could not rent the type of car that he prefers.

   c. A schedule of appointments was not included in the travel file given to your manager.

Special Reports

1. Find a local airline schedule online. Select the departure city and a destination city. List the schedules of service available between these two cities.

2. Research the following foreign locations: Berlin, Germany; Beijing, China; and Bangkok, Thailand. For each location, obtain the latest information and prepare a report on one of the following topics:

   a. visa regulations and where they can be obtained

   b. immunization requirements

   c. ground transportation to and from the local airport

   d. recommendations for city transportation

3. Search online for information on current airline fares. Compare the fares of two airlines travelling between Calgary and Vancouver. Then compare the fares for the same airlines travelling between Halifax and Montreal.

4. Go online to research the status of working women in China, Saudi Arabia, Russia, Cuba, and England. Explain how their work status compares to that of Canadian women. Prepare a keyed report for your instructor and present your findings to your class through presentation software.

PRODUCTION CHALLENGES

12-A Preparing an Itinerary

Supplies needed:

- *Notes on Mr. Wilson's Trip to Midwestern Region, Form 12-A, Companion Website*
- *Plain paper*

Noah Wilson, vice president of marketing at PDI, Inc., will make a business trip to the Midwestern Region during the week of September 11 to 14. He will visit the Midwestern Regional Sales Office of PDI in Regina and the regional office in Winnipeg. He will speak to the Sales Management Club at Red River College.

Prepare Mr. Wilson's itinerary.

12-B Making an Airline Reservation

Supplies needed:

- *Plain paper*

Mr. Wilson asked you to make an airline reservation for him from Toronto to Vancouver on Tuesday, October 10. Since Mr. Wilson does not know how much time he will spend in Vancouver, you are to request an open return ticket. You know that Mr. Wilson prefers to travel in the morning and that he prefers an aisle seat on nonstop and direct flights.

You call the airlines. A nonstop flight is not available. You make a reservation for him with Air Canada. Flight AC895 leaves Toronto at 1005, arrives in Winnipeg at 1210, leaves Winnipeg at 1230, and will arrive in Vancouver at 1345. He will be on the same airplane for the entire trip. His tickets will be ready at the counter.

Key Mr. Wilson a note giving him complete information about the airline reservations.

12-C Preparing a Travel Fund Advance

Supplies needed:

- *PDI Travel Fund Advance, Form 12-C, Companion Website*

Mr. Wilson has requested an advance for his trip to Vancouver. The purpose of this trip is to visit Ms. Singe, sales manager. Together they will attend the annual Sales Strategies Seminar. Mr. Wilson will require the advance the day before his departure. He prefers to receive it in the form of a direct deposit. The per diem rate is $180.00 for his accommodation and $50.00 for his meals. He estimates that he will remain in Vancouver for three days. The airline tickets will be prepaid by the company; therefore, Mr. Wilson will not be required to claim this as a personal expense. His employee number is 847254. Complete the form electronically

12-D Preparing an Open Itinerary

Supplies needed:

- *Plain paper*

Although you do not have complete information for Mr. Wilson's trip to Vancouver, you still need to prepare an itinerary. Use the information provided in 12-B, Making an Airline Reservation, and 12-C, Preparing a Travel Fund Advance, to complete the best open itinerary possible. Do not use the information from 12-E, Preparing a Travel Expense Voucher, since this information is unknown prior to the trip. You will be booking the Westin Bayshore for Mr. Wilson for Tuesday, Wednesday, and Thursday evenings.

12-E Preparing a Travel Expense Voucher

Supplies needed:

- *PDI Travel Expense Voucher, Form 12-E, Companion Website*

Mr. Wilson returned from Vancouver on Friday, October 13. He has requested that you complete a travel expense voucher on his behalf. He has provided receipts for all his expenses. The receipts give you the following information:

- He stayed at the Westin Bayshore using the full per diem rate each evening.
- Meals for each day were:

Tuesday	–	Dinner	=	$25.62
Wednesday	–	Breakfast	=	$10.50
		Lunch	=	$15.10
		Dinner	=	$21.10
Thursday	–	Breakfast	=	$10.50
		Lunch	=	$14.18
		Dinner	=	$25.80
Friday	–	Breakfast	=	$12.10

- Please note—charge the per diem amount for the two full days but only the actual expenses incurred for Tuesday and Friday.
- PDI has prepaid Mr. Wilson's airfare through its associated travel consultant; therefore, this expense will not show up on the travel expense voucher.
- On the day Mr. Wilson arrived in Vancouver, he hired a taxi. The fare was $52.00. The day he left Vancouver he again hired a taxi, for $56.50.
- On Wednesday he rented a car for three days. His receipt shows a total charge of $187.83.
- He had one miscellaneous receipt showing a charge of $50.35 for a portfolio purchased on Wednesday.
- One receipt showed an entertainment expense of $135.50. This was incurred on Thursday, when he bought theatre tickets for Mr. and Mrs. Singe.

First, refer to the information in 12-C, Preparing a Travel Fund Advance. Complete the Travel Expense Voucher, Form 12-E, from the Companion Website.

12-F Planning an International Business Trip

Supplies needed:

- *Plain paper*
- *Online access*
- *Directions*

Mr. Wilson has asked you to plan his international business trip. He is making a presentation in Mexico City and Guadalajara one month from today. His first presentation will be in Mexico City.

1. Mr. Wilson needs reservations at the Hilton Hotel in each of the two cities he is visiting. Reservations will be for one week at each hotel. He has asked you to determine specific information about these two cities. Your findings must include the following:

   a. travel times
   b. time zone changes
   c. travel documents needed
   d. medical requirements
   e. airlines to use
   f. approximate cost for transportation and lodging
   g. nearest Canadian embassy location
   h. international country and city telephone codes
   i. average weather temperatures
   j. holidays during his stay

2. To assist him in understanding the hosts' cultural and business practices, Mr. Wilson asked you to research the following:

   a. greetings, handling of introductions, using appropriate titles, exchange of business cards, and any other important points of business etiquette
   b. gift giving for the hosts
   c. the hosts' work-hour practices
   d. the hosts' attitudes towards time in general
   e. nonverbal communication patterns as they relate to the hosts
   f. the country's currency and exchange rates
   g. letter-writing styles

3. Because you are already working on completing a large project, you have asked one of the assistants in your work group to help gather this information.

4. Summarize your team's findings in a memo to your instructor.

5. Be prepared to present your findings to the class.

12–G Keying Vacation Requests

Supplies needed:

- *Vacation Requests, Form 12-G, Companion Website*
- *Plain paper*

It's Monday, May 12. Mr. Wilson has asked you to key a list of the department's employees and their vacation requests in chronological order. He explains that he has not yet scheduled two weeks of his vacation, and that he has a policy of not taking a vacation when any of the assistant vice presidents of marketing are on vacation. He said a chronological list will quickly point out the weeks when he should be in the office.

You set up and key the vacation information from Form 12-G. You send it to him electronically as an attachment to an email message.

Weblinks

Expedia.ca
www.expedia.ca
This Canadian travel site lists airlines, hotels, and car rentals, as well as travel news and advice.

Travelocity.ca
www.travelocity.ca
This Canadian travel site lists airlines, hotels, car rentals, European and Canadian rail information, as well as travel news and advice.

World Time Zones
www.worldtimeserver.com
World Time Server provides current local times anywhere in the world.

Treasury Board of Canada Secretariat
https://www.canada.ca/en/treasury-board-secretariat.html
This site provides information about the financial management of Canada's affairs and the departments that manage the wealth. This is the location for finding the Treasury Board's Travel Directive for allowable hospitality rates for government employees travelling within and outside Canada.

Converting Currencies
www.xe.com
There are many sites that convert worldwide currencies. This particular site is easy to use and works with the most current conversion rates.

Passports in Canada
https://www.canada.ca/en/immigration-refugees-citizenship/services/canadian-passports.html
This site provides up-to-date information on the requirements for obtaining a passport in Canada

International Business Etiquette, Manners & Culture
www.cyborlink.com
Learn about doing business in many other countries and cultures by accessing the links on this informative site.

WorldWeb Travel Guide
www.worldweb.com
This comprehensive online travel and tourism guide provides resources for travel to destinations worldwide.

World Health Organization
www.who.int
This site is a valuable resource for people seeking information on health risks to travellers to various countries. Comprehensive information on health statistics in countries throughout the world is also provided.

Canada Travel and Tourism
www.travel.gc.ca
This site provides information and assistance for Canadians travelling abroad, including a traveller's checklist, reports on safety and health issues in various countries, and a list of Canadian government offices abroad.

It provides easy-to-access travel reports and warnings on various countries, contact information for Canadian embassies and consulates abroad, passport information, and numerous other links to valuable information for international travellers.

Global Affairs Canada
www.international.gc.ca
This direct link to Global Affairs Canada, which has safe-travel publications for the Canadian public who are travelling abroad is a wealth of information. Of particular interest are publications in the general category, such as those for women travelling alone, Canadians who hold dual citizenship, and traveller's checklists. Publications related to specific countries and situations are also available for downloading.

Chapter 13
Meetings, Events, and Conferences

SOCIAL NETWORK · LIKE · SHARE

LEARNING OUTCOMES

After completion of this chapter, the student will be able to:

1 Recognize the similarities and differences between meetings, events, and conferences.

2 Describe the administrative professional's role in meetings and conferences.

3 Explore the basic steps involved in meeting and conference planning.

4 Understand the purpose and preparation of documents involving meetings and conferences.

5 Review strategies and best practices for successful meetings.

6 Identify the benefits of virtual meetings, conference calls, and web conferencing.

Among the myriad skills administrative professionals need in today's corporate environment, meeting, event, and conference planning is increasingly a significant component of the role. Responsibilities will range from coordinating small on-site meetings to planning larger off-site conferences. An administrative professional often is tasked with securing vendor proposals and booking travel and accommodations for group trips and events. This can sometimes be a complex process requiring clearly defined objectives and goals coupled with a systematic approach.

The difference between meetings and conferences is a **meeting** is a gathering of two or more people for the purpose of achieving a common goal through interaction, such as sharing information or reaching an agreement. A meeting is called at any time, in a space available. It may involve handling all the preliminary activities—arranging the meeting **venue** and time, inviting the participants, preparing the **agenda**, assembling materials needed during the meeting, and arranging for food and accommodation—as well as follow-up activities such as transcribing the minutes and reminding personnel to carry out the commitments made during the meeting.

In addition to handling the preliminary activities and the follow-up, the administrative professional is often expected to participate during the meeting, making valuable contributions to the decision-making process.

An office that is skilled in teamwork has learned that conducting meetings effectively involves having input from all team members associated with the meeting agenda. It is vital to remember that each team member has something important to contribute. The extent of the contribution is based on the participant's experience and expertise.

A **conference** is most often formal and will have a program of activities planned. Some conferences will span over a number of days, and the delegates will participate in team building and other activities. All meetings are events but not all events are meetings. As a distinction, an **event** is typically designed to commemorate, celebrate, or raise awareness. A recognition award ceremony would be an example of an event. This chapter will examine meetings and conferences from fundamental planning components to successful deployment.

CONFERENCES

Nothing compares to a good conference: the atmosphere of immersion in a crowd of people who share a similar passion, the valuable lessons learned with like professionals, frequently involving new industry contacts. A successful conference re-energizes attendees. Many attendees, also known as delegates, leave full of zest for their jobs and bursting with new ideas. These are the eight basic steps for organizing a conference:

1. Define and brand the conference.
2. Set the budget.
3. Gather requests for proposals.
4. Review room setup and seating plans.
5. Organize food and beverages.
6. Engage speakers and entertainment.
7. Manage technology.
8. Arrange accommodations and travel.

Defining and Branding the Conference

Clarify and define the purpose while also determining goals and objectives of the conference. These definitions cultivate easier when a clear outcome from the conference is imagined. Once the purpose is established, branding is an essential component. A brand is a name, term, design, symbol, or other feature that distinguishes an organizational event. **Branding** remains one of the best ways to differentiate your events from others.

Setting the Budget

The conference budget is an estimate of costs and potential income if it is profit driven. Developing a budget provides financial control. With the purpose of the conference defined, the budget can help assess the needs for conference cost estimating. Start by listing all fixed and variables costs. If data from a past conference are available, review those records for costing benchmarks. General fixed and variable cost examples include the following:

- **Venue.** Event and meeting space, the setup and breakdown, equipment rental and setup
- **Food and beverage.** Food costs per person, beverages, and taxes and gratuities
- **Communications.** Invitations, website and social networks, handouts, signage, and banners
- **Accommodations.** Rooms, hospitality suite, and other fees
- **Transportation.** Airfare, taxis, chartered buses, and or shuttles
- **Other costs.** Accounting, staffing, security, insurance, and advertising

Gathering Request for Proposals

For larger conferences, approach a selection of venues and encourage them to bid on the project. This is known as a **request for proposals.** Ensure the request for proposal documentation is clean, clear, and precise. Be sure to include the venue requirements, preferred location, type of event, event start and end time, company information, and contact information. Set aside time to perform site inspections to ensure that choices meet expectations.

Reviewing Room Setup and Seating Plans

Dynamic conferences foster effective interaction and, by extension, learning as well. Attention to room setup based on needs leads to enhanced success. Review the room comfort level, doors, walls, overall room(s) appearance, lighting, sound, and table shapes. In advance of the conference, decide on seating plans. This is dependent on the type of activities planned, such as an open forum based around significant discussion during the conference. Figure 13-1 visually represents some common seating styles. Seating plans to consider:

- **Classroom.** Rows for seating. Optimally used when demonstrating a product or concept to all delegates at the conference.

- **Conference.** Usually limited to 40 or fewer people where all delegates are seated at the same boardroom table. Used often when a group leader or a panel is leading a discussion.

- **Banquet.** Involves several tables arranged in a room with 8–12 groups of people seated together at each table. Optimally used for collaboration and round-table discussions in smaller thinking clusters.

- **Auditorium or theatre.** Appropriate for a short lecture or larger groups that do not require extensive note taking, similar to classroom seating.

Organizing Food and Beverage

F&B, or food and beverage, is a critical part of the conference plan and success. Delegates should have an opportunity when registering for the event to indicate food preferences, special needs, or allergies. Be sure to negotiate guidelines for F&B with your vendor or caterer. Choose a food service format, arrange tasting, know the pricing per head count, sign a contract, understand what happens when additional attendees are added, and finalize the menus, including special need requests. For buffets, makes sure they are double-sided and provide healthy, fresh-food choices for snacks. Personalize meals by having the organizational logo on display or choose linens and napkins that reflect your branding theme and organization.

Engaging Speakers and Entertainment

From a guest speaker's point of view, determine the guest's purpose. Is it to educate, entertain, or persuade? Hiring a guest speaker often necessitates meeting in person and discussing specifics about the presentation to avoid surprises and to focus on the target. Ensure that the venue can accommodate the type of presentations missioned. If staff members are speaking, they may need additional supports or public speaking training. If you are considering a virtual speaker, look for someone with broadcast experience.

Managing Technology

Manage this aspect of the meeting well in advance. Know how delegates get connected, use a videoconferencing facility, have webcam-equipped laptops, leverage social media such as Twitter or Eventbrite, and organize press releases. Arrange for digital projectors and use closed-circuit video in large rooms with satellite screens throughout the audience. Make sure you have all the necessary connection cords so that presenters can connect to the venue's interactive whiteboards or other technology.

Arranging Accommodations and Travel

Research accommodations well in advance to ascertain how flights will be booked for the event while selecting an official airline. Best airfare pricing generally is found 90 days in advance of travel. Encourage delegates to use the official airline with incentives such as frequent-flyer points. For ground transportation, check with the hotels and facilities to determine if they offer shuttles, research taxicab fares, or provide pre-paid vouchers to delegates. Charter buses are sometimes available through public transportation or private companies in host cities.

> **Self-Check**
> 1. Define the term *request for proposals*.
> 2. What are the eight steps for organizing a conference?

FIGURE 13-1 Common meeting and event seating styles.

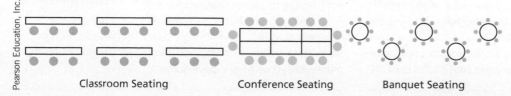

Classroom Seating   Conference Seating   Banquet Seating

BUSINESS MEETINGS

Meetings will range from informal meetings in a manager's office to formal meetings for boards of directors in large conference rooms. Depending on the formality, you may be responsible for any or all of the following:

- arranging the date and time
- reserving the meeting room
- sending notices
- preparing the agenda
- planning for supplies, equipment, and software
- planning for food and refreshments
- assembling materials
- attending the meeting
- handling interruptions
- recording the meeting
- following up
- preparing and editing minutes

Minutes are records of meeting discussion, informally called notes. They are the instant written record of a meeting or hearing.

Creating an Action Checklist

How will you ensure that you remember all the necessary steps and that you are organized? It is best to work from an action checklist. You may require more than one checklist if you have substantial responsibilities for the meeting or conference. The following checklist is just a guide—you will have to customize your own list for your own purposes:

- Find a common date and time when key members can attend.
- Book a meeting room.
- Invite members to the meeting.

Company Profile

Canadian Society of Professional Event Planners (CanSPEP)

Robert Kneschke/Alamy Stock Photo

CanSPEP is a Canadian society focused on the professional practice of event planning. One of their fundamental goals is to be a Canadian leader in entrepreneurial event management. CanSPEP formally known as the Independent Meetings Association of Canada before they rebranded in 2007 under the current name, the association was originally incorporated in 1996. Their main goal is to promote professionalism and generate mindfulness of the skills that independent event planners provide. They support their independent members through access to exclusive event planning resources, liability insurance, education, training, and development, as well as key opportunities to expand event and business opportunities.

CanSPEP partner members are experts in event management, and organizations are encouraged to acquire the services of their expert event planners to ease the burden of planning events. This is a planners-only group. It boasts the ability to provide quality services and decrease the time and money organizations spend in the logistical functions surrounding corporate events. Partner members are governed in their practice as they subscribe to a set of professional principles.

Located on the association website is a membership directory where industry can search for the services of a corporate event planner. Additionally, CanSPEP also has a request for proposal option open to accept proposal requests in the context of having a partner member manage a professional project. These initiatives provide partner members with the opportunity to market their services as they develop a profile, which highlights the strengths of the member partner.

Each partner member is proficient in strategic planning, supplier relationships, and the ability to network with other partner members to ensure that meetings and events for companies, associations, nonprofits, and government agencies are planned with successful deployment.

As a professional planning group, CanSPEP hosts a variety of events and conferences for its membership. The group also encourages and practices a social responsibility approach by participating in activities supporting contributions related to cancer research funding.

Finally, CanSPEP has a Partnership Advisory Council, also known as PAC. The advisory council shares best practices with members to strengthen and enhance membership professional growth and development.

- Confirm attendance of members.
- Prepare an agenda.
- Send the agenda to participants at least two days ahead of the meeting.
- Ensure the facilities are adequate and in good working order for the meeting (chairs, presentation equipment, computer, tape recorder, etc.).
- Prepare materials.
- Order food and/or refreshments.
- Forward telephone calls to voice mail.

Arranging the Date and Time

Arranging meetings of several people is easy if:

- The meeting participants use electronic calendars and keep them up to date.
- The calendars are not classified as private and, therefore, are available to other people on the office network.

When you have electronic access to calendars of the attendees, let the software find a time when all the participants are free, schedule the meeting, and then send the information about the meeting to the participants by email. Using phone calls to find a convenient time for all the participants to meet is too time-consuming.

Another option once you have isolated a few possible meeting times is to use scheduling polling software such as Doodle®. Such programs allow you to survey the group with suggested times for a meeting. Each group member selects a preferred meeting time, and the most commonly selected time is chosen for the meeting. This provides everyone with an opportunity to have input.

Executives Scheduling Their Own Appointments
Many executives schedule all their own appointments, while others prefer that the administrative professional schedule all the appointments. Still others prefer a combination. Because many executives travel and do much of their work outside the office, the tendency is for executives to make some of their own appointments, while, back in the office, the administrative office professional is also making appointments for the executive. It is imperative that the schedule is kept accurate and current. Otherwise, there will be duplication of bookings.

When arranging a meeting for 8–10 executives, you probably will not find a time when all of them are free, unless you book well in advance. Schedule the meeting for a time when most of them—especially the principal members—can attend. At an executive level, corporate politics often determine attendance. Notify all participants of the time and place of the meeting. Any executive who has a time conflict must decide how to resolve it.

Reserving the Meeting Room

Reserve a room as soon as you know the date and time for the meeting. It's best to know the location when you send out the meeting invitations. The type of conference room needed will depend on the equipment required for the presentations, the size of the group, and the activities that will take place during the meeting. For example, specially equipped rooms are needed for a videoconference, a computer presentation, or an interactive whiteboard presentation. The right equipment is very important since it will greatly enhance a presentation at a meeting. (See Figure 13-2.)

The size of the room will depend on how many people are planning to attend. You can estimate this by checking the list of expected participants. As well, the space required will depend on the activities planned during the meeting. Will the participants remain seated, or will they move around during the meeting?

Whenever possible, make a special effort to inspect the room in advance. Before you determine which room is right, ask the following questions:

- Will the participants remain in the same room for refreshment or lunch breaks?
- Will the team be required to perform some physical routines, or will the members remain seated throughout the meeting?
- Will the team need to break out into smaller rooms?
- Will special equipment requiring significant space be used?
- Will the meeting be an audioconference or **videoconference**?
- Will there be a guest speaker? Does the speaker have special requirements for the room?

FIGURE 13-2 An interactive whiteboard acts as an effective presentation tool during a meeting.

In order to get the best room, reservations are made far in advance of a meeting date. Be alert to any changes in meeting dates, times, and rooms. If changes occur, follow-up immediately. Several days before the meeting, confirm the room reservation. Remember that change happens all the time. Keep on top of it. Otherwise, you will be left without a good room after all your preparation and attention to detail.

If the meeting or conference has been arranged in an external facility such as a hotel or conference centre, become familiar with the terms and conditions of your booking agreement—particularly the cancellation and refund policy.

Sending Notices

A **notice of meeting** is a designed document to notify shareholders or directors of the time, date, and place of a corporate meeting. Business professionals are busy people, so it is important to announce meetings as soon as possible. Most participants have heavy schedules and prefer plenty of advance notice.

As soon as you have established a date, times, and venue, send out the notices by email. Refer to Figure 13-3 for an example of a meeting notice that shows essential information.

When composing notices, always specify:

- the purpose of the meeting
- date and time
- venue
- deadline for accepting agenda items
- action to take if member will attend
- action to take if member cannot attend

Participants for a meeting are sometimes asked to submit topics for the agenda. Requests for items should be made early enough that the administrative assistant has time to prepare a final agenda based on the replies received. Clearly state the deadline for the latest time you will accept agenda items.

Self-Check

1. What is the purpose of an action checklist?
2. What would you do if you were trying to arrange a team meeting and you could not find a time when all members were available?
3. What factors should you consider when booking a meeting room?

Preparing the Agenda

Chairpersons or team leaders follow prepared agendas as they conduct meetings. Preparing the agenda is the responsibility of the administrative professional.

FIGURE 13-3 Notice of meeting.

Notice of Meeting

The Progressive Digital Innovations Inc., also known as, PDI, Inc. shareholders are advised of a Shareholders' meeting to be held on May 31, 20XX at 14:30 hours at the corporate head office 3431 Bloor Street Toronto, ON in order to consider the following proposed agenda items:

1. Approval of PDI's financial statements for the fiscal year ending in 20XX
2. Related party agreements and commitments
3. Ratification of selection vote of Board of Director, David Romphfman
4. Powers to accomplish formalities
5. Renewal of Board of Directors mandate for four terms

Courtesy of Microsoft Corporation

An agenda is a list of topics to be addressed and acted upon during a meeting. It is arranged in the order in which the topics will be discussed. Refer to Figure 13-4 for a sample agenda.

Use the following list of topics as a guideline in preparing an agenda for a *formal meeting*:

1. call to order by presiding officer
2. roll call—either oral or checked by the administrative professional
3. approval, amendment, or correction of minutes of previous meeting
4. reading of correspondence
5. reports (in this order):
   - officers
   - standing committees
   - special committees
6. unfinished business from previous meetings
7. new business
8. appointment of committee
9. nomination and election of officers—once a year
10. announcements, including the date of the next meeting
11. adjournment

Use the following list of topics as a guideline in preparing an agenda for an *informal meeting*:

1. check-ins or warm-ups (optional)
2. review goals of agenda or purpose of meeting
3. review roles of members (optional)
4. review ground rules (optional)
5. discuss issues listed on agenda

FIGURE 13-4 Sample agenda.

AGENDA
MEETING NO. 4
QUALITY CONFERENCE COMMITTEE

Date:	Wednesday, June 10, 20—
Time:	1500–1630
Place:	Conference Room 3
Chairperson:	Jeffrey Keaton
Recorder:	Gina Darroch
Committee Members:	Jodi Alford, Satvinder Bhardwaj, Allan Kohut, Kenneth Skoye, Benjamin Ross, Brian Van Bij, Marian Weston, Edward Woods

TIME	TOPIC	MEMBER RESPONSIBLE
1500	Adoption of Minutes from Meeting No. 3	J. Keaton
1510	Facilities Report	B. Van Bij
1525	Registration Report	A. Kohut
1540	Budget Report	S. Bhardwaj
1555	Public Relations Report	B. Ross
1610	Other Business	J. Keaton
1625	Adjournment	J. Keaton

Pearson Education, Inc.

6. review follow-up actions that members have committed to

7. closure

8. determining date and time for next meeting, if necessary

If you are responsible for preparing the agenda, key it and send it out as an email attachment. Or place it on a cloud-based platform for the team to access digitally. Even for a very informal office meeting, an agenda should be accessible to all the members. Prepare the agenda early enough that the members receive it several days before the meeting. They will need time to prepare for the meeting. The more prepared people are, the more productive the meeting will be.

Planning for Supplies, Equipment, and Software

The list of meeting supplies and equipment will be different for every meeting. How many supplies and the type of equipment necessary will depend on the type of meeting, the style of presentations to be given, and the guests who have been invited. The following is a general checklist for any meeting:

- digital device for presentation hook-up or for note taking
- computer for presentations with media storage
- online mapping tool to capture visually ideas as creativity flows within the meeting
- professional presentation software, such as MS PowerPoint
- data projector
- laser pointer for presentations
- projection screen
- digital media player
- remote control for DVD or computer
- flip chart tripod or support for paper block
- flip chart paper
- adhesive tape or putty to suspend flip chart paper around the meeting room
- coloured markers for flip-chart paper
- name tents or tags, and a marker to write the names
- scissors
- whiteboard markers and eraser
- writing block for each participant
- writing pen or pencil for each participant
- promotional items such as lapel pins, key tags, or pens with company logo
- enough chairs for all participants

Planning Refreshments and Food

At many meetings there will be international guests and members of various religions and cultures. There may also be vegetarians and people with special-needs diets. So it's important to include a variety of foods and beverages if you wish to ensure the comfort of all participants.

If you schedule a luncheon or dinner meeting at a hotel or restaurant, call the venue manager to help you with the refreshment and lunch requirements. Inquire about food options and costs. You may have to guarantee a minimum number of attendees.

Participants perform at their best when their energy is high. For that reason, it is important to provide beverages and often food at meetings. The types of beverages will depend on the participants and on the time of day. Some beverage guidelines follow:

Beverages

- North Americans are, in general, health conscious. Keep this in mind when arranging the menu.
- Most participants enjoy coffee and tea regardless of the hour. Supply some decaffeinated coffee and herbal teas for those who cannot tolerate caffeine.
- Juices are popular at morning meetings. Supply both sweetened and unsweetened juices. Many people avoid excess sugar intake.
- Participants at afternoon breaks often enjoy juice or soft drinks. Remember to provide both regular and unsweetened varieties.
- Bottled mineral water is appreciated at both morning and afternoon meetings. In this case, smaller is better. Larger bottles are awkward to handle and inappropriate.
- During a lunch meeting, all of the previous choices are acceptable, as is milk. Low-fat white milk (*not* skim) is the safest choice.
- The key is to provide some variety. At the very minimum, provide coffee and juices for any of the meeting breaks.
- At each break, you can expect that participants will consume one or two beverages.
- Ensure that fresh water and glasses are available throughout the meeting.

The break should bring renewed energy and relieve stress caused by the meeting. Therefore, supply light foods that provide energy. Some food guidelines follow:

Food

- Some participants will have special-needs diets (such as no meat, low-calorie, low-sugar, or low-cholesterol).

Don't wait for a participant to identify this ahead of time. Plan enough variety to accommodate differences.

- Never make pork the only meat option. For religious reasons, many people do not eat any form of pork.
- Participants enjoy fruit and muffins for morning breaks.
- Order food in small, manageable pieces. People generally converse during breaks, and most find that small sandwiches or fruit sections are easiest to handle.
- If you want the participants to maintain a high level of energy, stay away from heavy desserts or starchy foods.

Assembling Materials

Before a meeting, assemble the materials needed during the meeting. For a formal meeting, you will need:

- extra copies of the agenda
- minutes of previous meetings
- a list of standing committees
- a list of special committees
- a list of action items that have not yet been completed by members
- documents related to the agenda items
- copies of materials that have been prepared for distribution

If possible, prior to the meeting, send out all these documents to the participants through email attachments or make them available through a secure online file-sharing program. This gives the participants an opportunity to review them and print their own copies before the meeting.

Even if you distribute all the documents available prior to the meeting, you will still need to bring extra copies of them to the meeting. It's highly unlikely that all members will remember to bring their copies.

Certain supporting materials may be called for during the meeting that you did not expect. If your electronic and paper filing systems are in good order, you should be able to retrieve these materials without too much difficulty.

Self-Check

1. What is an agenda?
2. What are three factors that you should consider when determining the supplies and equipment needed for a meeting?
3. Why is it important to send copies of all meeting documents to participants prior to a meeting?

Recording the Meeting

When the meeting is more formal, it is usually recorded and later keyed into minutes. As an administrative professional, you may be assigned the task of recording and transcribing the minutes of a business meeting. Although your office may provide an informal setting, your manager may be the chairperson of a committee where the meetings follow very formal rules. Senior administrators are often members of charitable organizations, hospital boards, and community service organizations.

Your manager may need your assistance in preparing a record of the meeting, especially if the manager's role on the board is that of corporate secretary.

Using a Digital Voice Recorder   A voice recorder is used to obtain a verbatim record of a meeting for the purpose of:

- preparing a word-for-word transcript
- assisting the administrative professional in keying accurate minutes
- securing a record of discussions on controversial topics

Audio recordings may be made on digital recorders or on software designed for recording meetings, such as Soniclear. Keep each recording until the minutes have been approved, or for a longer time when the topics are controversial or may become controversial. Some groups save the minutes in a digital file permanently. Check the company and government policy before erasing the file.

Although audio recordings are very useful, you still need to be aware of what information is not being recorded and, when necessary, take notes. For instance, when a chairperson acknowledges a speaker, the chairperson does not always call the speaker's name. Likewise, a chairperson does not always restate a motion. An audio recording may not indicate who made and who seconded a motion. When one of the participants is reading from distributed materials, the section to which the speaker is referring is not always clear from the recording. Use your notes to supplement the recording.

The best way to take notes at a meeting is with a computer or digital device.

Using a Laptop Computer   Most meetings do not require a verbatim transcript. In this case, the best practice is to key notes onto a laptop computer during the meeting. Your job of transcribing your notes into minutes will be mostly complete when you leave the meeting. All that will be required is some reformatting and editing. Refer to Figure 13-5, which shows a laptop computer being used during a meeting.

During a meeting, a computer can be used for more than recording notes. A laptop computer may operate

FIGURE 13-5 Laptop computer used during a meeting.

Deklofenak/123RF

independently but may also be connected online to the office network. The online connection gives the ability to access information that may be needed to make informed decisions during the meeting.

Tips for Successful Note Taking Taking notes effectively at business meetings is a skill that takes time to master, and in the business world, you will no doubt have to master this skill because you will need to attend business meetings where note taking is critical. Taking notes at a meeting can be a challenging assignment. Here are some tips for successful note taking:

- Before the meeting, study the minutes of similar meetings. Become familiar with the format used.

- Prior to the meeting, create a template with as much information as possible. During the meeting, have the template on the screen of your laptop computer so you can add information as the meeting progresses.

- Position yourself near the chairperson so you can assist each other.

- Ask the chairperson to secure a copy of all materials read or discussed. These materials are a part of the record and should be attached to the minutes. Do not wait until the end of the meeting to collect them.

- Arrange a signal, such as slightly raising your hand, with the chairperson to let him or her know that you need assistance in getting details.

- Before the meeting begins, record the name of the group, date, time, and place of the meeting. Also record the names of those people in attendance and those who are absent.

- Indicate in your notes the names of people making motions.

- Record the exact words of people who ask that their views be made a part of the record.

- Listen to the informal discussion that sometimes follows the adoption of a main motion. This discussion centres on implementation of the action—the details about who will do what, when, and how. Record each detail as it is suggested. After a detail is agreed upon, write "agreed" beside it. Each of these items must be followed up. Be sure to take notes on any obligations your manager assumes during the meeting.

- While a committee is being appointed, record the name of the committee, the full names of the members, and who accepted the position of chairperson.

- When officers are elected, record their names and their respective offices.

- Record the place, date, and time of the next meeting.

- Write the time of **adjournment**.

- As soon as the meeting adjourns, verify any points about which you are doubtful. You may need to ask about a person's title, the full name of a product or a place, the correctness of a technical term, or any small details you need in order to prepare complete minutes.

Following Up

Immediately after a meeting, prepare a to-do list of all the actions you need to take. Some items might include:

- Make entries in the calendars for deadlines on work to be completed.

- Send materials digitally to members who were absent.

- Prepare a list to remind your manager of his or her commitments.

- Enter the time of the next meeting in the calendars.

- Make edits to the minutes of the previous meeting.

- Complete the minutes.

- Arrange for equipment return.

- Book a room and equipment for the next meeting.

All distributed materials that were introduced and discussed are a part of the minutes and should be referred to in the minutes and attached to them. To simplify your own work and to extend a courtesy to those who were absent, provide copies of any materials distributed but not discussed.

Keep in mind that the record of a meeting must be meaningful in the future to those who were not present. The record must show that the decisions made were actually carried out.

Preparing Minutes

Given adequate information, you can prepare minutes without having attended the meeting yourself. If your manager is a recording secretary for a civic or professional organization, the manager will probably do one of the following:

- Give you a recording of the meeting and anticipate you will transcribe it into minutes.

- Give you detailed written notes and expect you to turn them into minutes.

- Give you an electronic copy of the minutes that have already been roughly keyed and ask you to edit and improve on the format.

If you wonder why preparing minutes for a civic or professional organization is a part of your job, remember that being an active participant in these organizations may be part of your manager's job. Corporations, institutions such as universities and hospitals, and various types of businesses encourage managers to participate in civic and professional organizations. As the administrative professional, you provide essential support to the manager's role.

Key the minutes immediately following the meeting. Ask questions while the meeting is fresh in your manager's mind. If you recorded the minutes of the meeting yourself, you will be able to organize the motions and amendments and summarize the discussion much faster if you do these things soon after the meeting.

Before you prepare a final version, key a rough draft of the minutes, double-spaced, and submit it to your manager for approval. Then submit the final copy to the organization's secretary or presiding officer for signature.

There are two purposes for preparing the minutes:

1. Include all the essential information as a record that will be meaningful to others in the future.

2. Make it easy for the reader to locate information.

Refer to Figure 13-6 for a sample of meeting minutes.

Informal Meetings
When a meeting has been conducted informally, there will be no motions and no voting. Instead, agreement may be made by consent. In this case, include the essential facts in the minutes. For an informal meeting, include:

- the purpose of the meeting
- date and time
- location
- who attended and who was absent
- summary of discussion and decisions
- summary of the follow-up

Formal Meetings
For formal meetings, use the following as a guide:

1. Either single- or double-space minutes.

2. In all capital letters, key a heading that fully identifies the meeting: MINUTES OF THE PROGRAM PLANNING COMMITTEE, PDI INC. Key the date as a subheading and double-space below the heading. Repeat the date on each page. If the group holds special meetings, the subheading could read: "Special Meeting, October 22, 20–."

3. Use the past tense, and write complete sentences. In the opening paragraph, state the name of the group, where the meeting was held, both the time and the date, who presided, and whether the meeting was regular or special. When the meeting was "called" (i.e., when it was "special"), add the purpose of the meeting, since it was called for an express purpose.

4. State whether the minutes of the previous meeting (mention its date) were "approved as read," "approved as corrected," or dispensed with.

5. Use side headings or marginal captions to help the reader locate items. The agenda will be helpful in organizing the minutes.

6. Mention all reports presented by officers, standing committees, and special committees in the order they were presented, and tell what actions were taken. Usually a member of a group moves that the report be accepted, another member seconds the motion, and the group votes to accept the minutes. These actions should be reported in the minutes.

7. To make each distributed report a part of the official record, refer to each one in the appropriate section of the minutes. You could say, "The attached report on Revised Plans for Issuing Supplies was distributed by Tamara Yee, Chairperson of the Committee on Reducing Office Costs." In the same paragraph, state who made the motion and the action taken.

8. Key verbatim all reports read orally and treat them as quoted material; that is, indent five spaces from the left and the right. This way, the format will reflect the origin of the material. If a report that was read is lengthy and in a form that can be copied, you can say, for example, that "the report on Downtime for Reproduction Equipment, presented by Norman Hanover, was copied and is attached."

9. Treat each main motion (and the amendments related to it, if any) as a separate item. Be sure to include in the minutes all motions made and how they were disposed of. State each motion verbatim, along with who made it, that it was seconded, whether it was adopted or defeated, and the votes cast for and against it. For some groups, also include the name of the person who seconded the motion.

10. When a motion has been made from the floor, you can begin the paragraph by saying, "Lillie Williamson

FIGURE 13-6 Meeting minutes.

MINUTES OF THE EXECUTIVE TEAM OF CONTINENTAL TECHNOLOGY INC.
Meeting No. 9 - July 8, 20--

The Executive Team of Continental Technology Inc. met in a regular session at 1030, Wednesday, July 8, 20--, in Conference Room 3. The following members were

PRESENT:		
	Verna Chiasson	(Quality Advisor)
	Penny Handfield	(Guidance Team)
	Maurice Ingram	(Team Member)
	Daniel Lawrence	(Team Member)
	Laura Milton	(Team Leader)
	Betty Noble	(Guidance Team)
	Paul Noel	(Team Member)
	Gregory Patrick	(Recorder)
	Dana Rahn	(Facilitator)
	Michelle Savard	(Team Member)
	Gayle Schmitt	(Team Member)
	Mike Sherman	(Team Member)
	Wendy Scarth	(Team Member)

ABSENT:

Maurice Ingram moved to approve as read the minutes of meeting no. 8. This motion was seconded by Mike Sherman. The following topics were then discussed:

REDUCTION IN ADMINISTRATIVE COSTS:

The ideas presented at the June 10 meeting for cutting administrative costs were revised and the following decisions were made:

Travel. Effective August 1, 20--, all executives of Continental Technology will no longer travel Executive Class; economy fare only will be paid by the company, with the exception of Executive Class fares approved by the Vice-President. Where Continental executives are taking major clients on business trips, the Executive Class will automatically be approved by the Vice-President.

Sales Incentive Trips. The consensus was that the yearly sales incentive trips, given to sales executives reaching their quotas, should be shortened in length. The trips will be shortened from one week to four days. As well, these trips will no longer be to extremely distant points; they will now be to warm weather North American resorts. It was felt that this would reduce both the air fare and accommodation charges considerably. This will be effective May of next year.

EMPLOYEE EVALUATIONS:

Laura Milton circulated copies of a new Employee Performance Evaluation which has been designed to follow ISO 9001:2005 principles. The Executive Team voted unanimously in favour of using the new form beginning September 1.

ANNOUNCEMENTS:

Catalogue. A new product catalogue will be available July 25. Copies can be obtained by calling Betty Noble.
New Team Member. Wendy Scarth joined the team as of July 1. However, she is currently on a training course and was absent from meeting No. 9. Wendy works in the Marketing Department and was previously employed by CanTech in Montreal.
Next Meeting. The 10th regular meeting will be held in Conference Room 3 at 1030 on Thursday, August 15, 20–.

ADJOURNMENT:

The meeting was adjourned at 1145.

July 10, 20xx

Date

G. Patrick

Gregory Patrick, Secretary

moved [not made a motion] that . . .," or "It was moved by Lillie Williamson and seconded by Raj Falfer that . . . ."

11. When a motion is amended, give the history of the motion in the minutes. First, state the motion, who made it, and that it was seconded. Next, take up the amendments in the same order as they were made. State each amendment verbatim, who made it, that it was seconded, and the votes cast for and against it.

12. The debate concerning a motion does not have to be included; nevertheless, reasons for a decision are often helpful to the current officers and to others in the future. Therefore, discussion can be included in the minutes. Summarize the debate in broad, concise terms. Try to include all the main ideas—both pros and cons—but do not overload the minutes with who said what.

13. Motions should appear in the minutes in the same order that they were taken up during the meeting. Minutes shift abruptly from one topic to another. Just separate them with side headings, or triple-space between them when you use marginal captions.

14. An agenda item that has been addressed but not completed becomes unfinished business on the agenda of the next meeting; therefore, indicate with some detail any information that will be helpful when this item is addressed again.

15. Group announcements near the end under the heading "Announcements." Some of the announcements may have been made at the beginning of the meeting or during it, but they can be grouped together.

16. Include the time, place, and date of the next meeting, and the time of adjournment.

17. Minutes that are to be read aloud are signed by the secretary; minutes that are to be distributed are signed by both the chairperson and the secretary.

18. Provide a place for the signature and the date of approval, such as

_____	_____
Date	Secretary

OR

_____	_____
Date	Chairperson
_____	_____
Date	Secretary

19. Arrange the file copy of the minutes in chronological order. Arrange all attachments in the order they were introduced in the minutes.

Correcting Minutes Once minutes are signed and distributed to members, some members may request amendments. These requests usually take place electronically immediately after the minutes have been distributed. If they are not urgent, they wait and take place at the next meeting.

Never rekey minutes to correct them. Make the changes so anyone reading the minutes can tell what corrections and additions were made and when they were made.

Minutes that are distributed are usually approved at the start of the next meeting. However, sometimes the approval of minutes is dispensed with, and then several sets are approved at a later meeting. The place provided for the date of approval appears at the end of the minutes. To be able to tell at a glance which minutes have been approved, write "Approved" and the date of approval at the top of the first page of the file copy immediately after the meeting where the minutes were approved.

> **Self-Check**
>
> 1. List three instances where you will likely need notes to supplement audio recordings of meetings.
> 2. Think of two reasons why you should key the minutes immediately following a meeting.
> 3. List two purposes for preparing minutes of meetings.

TEAM MEETINGS

The team concept of meetings focuses on equal participation. Each participant's input is considered significant as that of all other participants, from the junior clerk to the chief executive officer of the company. The team concept is effective because each member is empowered to participate, regardless of his or her organizational status.

Teams make decisions at their level of authority. If a decision resolves at a higher level of authority, the team forwards a recommendation to management.

Because team meetings encourage all participants to express their views, conflict and team dynamic challenges may occur. Please refer to Chapter 1 under the section "Nonproductive Behaviours" to learn how to work through challenges at meetings.

Preparation for the Meeting

A meeting that follows team techniques requires the same preparation as any other meeting—a convenient time is established, people are invited, and an agenda is prepared and delivered to participants prior to the meeting.

When team techniques are followed, careful attention is given to issues that arise even at the preliminary stages.

- Choosing an appropriate time is important. You want the attendance and full attention of every team member.

- The people who form the team may be from all levels of the organization. All people who are involved in the issue that will be discussed at the meeting must be invited.

- All team members carry equal status. No one person dominates the meeting. Refer to the section "Roles of the Participants" for an understanding of each team member's responsibilities.

The agenda is much like that of a more traditional meeting. However, agenda items are sometimes determined in the meeting, so agenda topics may be very general. Refer to Figure 13-7 and an earlier section in this chapter, "Preparing the Agenda."

Roles of the Participants

Part of the team philosophy is to get input from people who are actually working within the process. In other words, the people who know the most about a topic should be at the meeting to discuss it and to make wise recommendations and decisions about it.

Each role in the team is equally important. The following briefly discusses the roles of team participants.

FIGURE 13-7 Agenda for a team meeting.

AGENDA
MEETING NO. 1
ADMINISTRATIVE TEAM

Date:	Wednesday, June 10, 20– –
Time:	0830–1130
Place:	Conference Room 3
Leader/Facilitator:	Jeffrey Keaton
Recorder:	Gina Darroch
Guidance Team:	Kenneth Skoye, Donna Welch
Team Members:	Jodi Alford, Satvinder Bhardwaj, Chris Dennison, Allan Kohut, Benjamin Ross, Brian Van Bij, Marian Weston

TIME	ACTIVITY	LEAD PERSON
0830	Check in	Jeffrey
0845	Brainstorm issues affecting Admin Team	Jeffrey
0930	Use NGT to vote on issues	Benjamin
0945	Refreshment break	
1000	Discuss priority issues and make recommendations	Jeffrey
1100	Discuss any other business (AOB)	Jeffrey
1115	Review "Next steps"	Gina
1130	Bring closure • *Determine time and date for next meeting*	Jeffrey

Pearson Education, Inc.

1. **Team leader.** The team leader acts as a chairperson, directing the meeting, moving from one topic to the next, and keeping on schedule.

2. **Guidance team.** The guidance team should consist of two or more people who are very familiar with the organization. Because of work constraints and time pressures, the guidance team may send only one member to a meeting. Often a management position; this enables the guidance team to provide information that other members may be unaware of and that will be helpful when team decisions are made. The guidance members should be people who have the authority to make changes and the influence to put decisions into practice.

3. **Project team members.** All members who take part in the discussions and vote on issues are considered project team members. This includes the team leader, but it does not include the guidance team. The votes of the project team members are critical to the decision-making process.

4. **Facilitator.** The team leader often carries both the roles of team leader and facilitator. When there are enough staff members available or when any type of disagreement or friction is expected at a meeting, it is important to have a separate person act as facilitator. The facilitator's responsibility is to make the meeting process flow with ease. The facilitator will ask the participants questions to help clarify their ideas.

   The facilitator structures the comments into a simple list, a flowchart, or a cause-and-effect diagram. (Refer to the section "Brainstorming" for more information on cause-and-effect diagrams.) These visual aids make the participants aware of comments presented.

   The facilitator's task is a demanding one; therefore, he or she will often ask a team member to assist by recording the comments on a flip chart or erasable board.

   The facilitator must be completely nonbiased about the topics discussed. For that reason, the facilitator is often a person from a different department who has no stake in the direction the team takes. The facilitator does not vote.

5. **Recorder.** The recorder's task is to prepare minutes. Recording topics discussed, decisions, and follow-up actions part of the minutes. The recorder is also responsible for forming the priority list of issues after the participants have voted.

The task of recording is often rotated among team members so that no one team member always has the additional responsibility of taking notes at each meeting. When a team member has the responsibility of taking notes, the attention needed for the task often eliminates her or him from part of the meeting discussion.

This task is made infinitely easier by the use of a notebook computer at the meeting. A further explanation of this process is found in the section "Nominal Group Technique."

Off to a Good Start

With the team process, considerable effort in making meetings productive is desired. Therefore, it is very important to get the meeting off to a good start.

1. **The team leader starts early.** He or she should arrive before any of the other participants in order to write the agenda in a place that is visible to all members. A flip chart or an erasable board works well.

   If house rules are established at a prior meeting, the leader will want to place these rules in a visible location. The leader should make sure the room configuration is conducive to team participation. Do the chairs and tables need arrangement in a circle? Is there an area for the coffee and juice containers?

   As each member arrives, the team leader should give him or her a warm welcome in order to establish a friendly environment for sharing information and ideas.

2. **The meeting begins and ends as scheduled.** Do not wait for late arrivals. People appreciate a team leader who starts and ends a meeting on time. Once late arrivals learn that the meetings begin exactly on schedule, they will try harder to be on time.

3. **Warm-up.** If the members do not know each other, the team leader should start the meeting by having all people introduce themselves. Introductions considered part of the meeting warm-up. Many activities initiated for team warm-ups. If the members of the team already know each other, the warm-up is not required.

4. **Check-in.** "Checking in" is an opportunity for each team member to express his or her present state of mind to the whole team. It is not necessary for everyone to check in; however, most people cannot simply switch off their feelings and become active participants. When possible, it is best to check in with the team. Checking in may sound something like this.

   - "I've been looking forward to getting some of these issues resolved, so I'm very happy to have been invited to this meeting."
   - "My desk is loaded with work, and I have a paper due for my night school class. If I seem a little stressed, that's why."
   - "I've just had a super weekend; my energy has returned, and I'm ready to participate."

5. **Agree on the goals.** Once the check-in is complete—that is, once all those who wish to check in have done so—the team leader should review the agenda.

6. **Review the roles of the team.** At the first meeting, the roles of the team leader, guidance team, quality advisor, facilitator, and project team members are reviewed by the team leader. Of course, this will be necessary only for the first or second meeting. Once the team members have exercised their roles, they will know what is expected.

7. **Establish the house rules.** The next step towards a successful project is establishing the house rules, also referred to as the "ground rules." The team should suggest and agree on some general house or ground rules before the meeting progresses. When rules are not adhered to, any team member may point this out and bring the meeting back on track. Suggestions for house rules might be as follows:

- Everyone will be given an equal opportunity to speak.
- Any person wishing to speak must raise his or her hand.
- Criticize only the issue, not the person with the issue.
- Side conversations are not allowed.
- Each person must focus on the speaker.
- Expect unfinished business.
- The meeting will begin and finish on schedule.
- Everyone will focus on the topic and will not interrupt the team's work for outside reasons.
- No negative body language is allowed.

Brainstorming

If the agenda is general and the team expects to provide the issues for discussion, the next step is team brainstorming. Even if the topics for discussion have been predetermined, brainstorming is a useful tool to apply now. Brainstorming will help the team develop many ideas in as short a time as possible.

Brainstorming is performed in one of two ways: structured or unstructured.

1. **Structured.** The structured method works well if the point is to avoid having one or two people dominate the meeting. It also works to encourage introverted members to share their ideas.

   When structured brainstorming is used, every person is given a turn to express opinions, concerns, or ideas.

The opportunity to speak rotates among the participants; people wishing to express their ideas must wait their turn. The rotation of ideas is repeated until all ideas have been expressed. As each member states a problem he or she would like to deal with at the meeting, that person should also state why it is an issue.

During the rotation, any member may forfeit the opportunity to share an idea.

Each of the ideas is recorded by the facilitator (or the facilitator's assistant) and by the person responsible for preparing the minutes or the meeting log.

2. **Unstructured.** The unstructured method of brainstorming has an unrestrictive atmosphere; participants express their ideas as they think of them. No rotation or waiting for turns is involved. Although this creates a very relaxed atmosphere in which to brainstorm, the problem of domination by one or two members may arise.

Whether the atmosphere is structured or unstructured, the facilitator will work hard to make the ideas clear and relevant and to balance the participation. All ideas must be recorded where the participants can view them. As well, all team members must agree on the wording.

The recorder remains busy during the brainstorming session, documenting all the issues that the team has identified. The issues are prioritized by the group according to their importance.

Nominal Group Technique

Once the problems have all been listed, and assuming there are no duplicate problems, the team should establish by vote which issues are most important and need immediate attention.

To ensure that the most vocal or persuasive participants do not dominate the proceedings, the nominal group technique (NGT) is applied. Without NGT, concerns raised by less forceful participants might not be resolved.

The recorder should prepare a form similar to the one in Figure 13-8. With this form, each participant can vote on each problem separately. Weighting is based on the following:

3 = This problem is of high priority and should be dealt with now.

2 = This problem is of medium priority and should be dealt with as soon as possible.

1 = This problem is of low priority and should be dealt with when possible.

0 = This problem does not affect me or my work.

Once the voting on issues is complete, the importance of the issues is calculated. The weighting on each listed

FIGURE 13-8 Voting sheet.

VOTING SHEET FOR NOMINAL GROUP TECHNIQUE					
ITEM NO.	ISSUES FOR DISCUSSION	TOTAL VOTES			
		3	2	1	0
1.	Ticketing of cars parked in the south lot				
2.	New payment schedule for per diem expenses				
3.	Criteria for Employee of the Month award				
4.	Lack of nutritious food in the staff cafeteria				
5.	Purchase of more voice mailboxes				
6.	Upgrading of fax machine				
7.	Purchase of a colour photocopier for the Reprographics Department				
8.	Extension of office network				
9.	Further leadership training for administrative assistants				
10.	Dissatisfaction of customers due to delayed billing				

REMEMBER: 3=This problem is of high priority and should be dealt with now.
2=This problem is of medium priority and should be dealt with as soon as possible.
1=This problem is of low priority and should be dealt with when possible.
0=This problem does not affect me or my work.

Pearson Education, Inc.

problem illustrates which issues the team wishes to discuss and resolve first. The recorder should sort these weightings on the computer and provide all team members with the revised list. Refer to Figure 13-8 where NGT has helped the team to reach a **consensus**.

Discussion and Solution

The problems that receive the highest priority under NGT are discussed and resolved first. To encourage brainstorming, the facilitator might now draw a cause-and-effect diagram.

The cause-and-effect diagram is referred to as a fishbone diagram, shown in Figure 13-9. The lines on the diagram (which appear as fishbones) represent the causes of the problem. The facilitator usually starts with four to six major categories such as the ones shown in Figure 13-9 (Equipment and Software, Procedures, People, External Sources). These major categories help to get the team thinking. The participants add to the diagram by suggesting more specific causes that fit under these major categories. It is important to use as few words as possible but to make the causes very clear.

The rectangle on the right of the diagram (the fish's "head") represents the effect, or the major problem, and the causes are the bones.

A structured or unstructured brainstorming technique is used to fill the diagram with all the possible causes of the problem. Once all the causes are identified, the team leader leads a discussion in which solutions are sought. The team leader will probably ask the team members why each of the causes happens. No doubt this will encourage discussion. During the discussion and solution phase, the team must remain respectful of the house rules. Any infraction of the rules should be brought to the attention of the team.

Team members may use their meeting logs to write personal notes, while the designated recorder makes a more detailed record of important discussion points, solutions, recommendations, and planned follow-up. The meeting log will form the official record of the meeting.

Closure

Although discussion of the topics has now concluded, it is important to spend a few minutes debriefing. The debriefing session allows participants to express their feelings.

FIGURE 13-9 Cause-and-effect diagram.

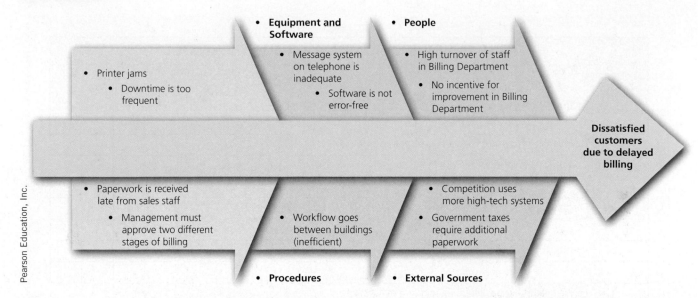

Pearson Education, Inc.

Each participant is invited to **debrief**, or "check out"; however, it is not required.

During the debriefing phase, you might hear comments such as the following:

- "I feel this was a successful meeting today. The candour of the participants was very helpful in reaching decisions."

- "I feel some scepticism at the decisions made today; however, I am willing to work with these new ideas."

- "Because I'm tired, I was ready to check out some time ago. Although it seemed a long meeting, plenty was accomplished."

Self-Check

1. What is the "team philosophy" underlying team meetings regarding participants?

2. In team meetings, which role in the team is most important?

3. List several suggestions for ground rules (or house rules) for team meetings.

4. What are two ways in which brainstorming is deployed?

5. Who determines the priority of items when using the nominal group technique?

6. What is debriefing? Is participation in debriefing by all team members mandatory?

MEETING DYNAMICS

One of the many roles of the office professional is to attend and contribute to meetings. However, many administrative professionals are taking an active role by leading and facilitating meetings. This means they develop a comfortable approach with meeting dynamics or the interplay that happens between meeting participants. Please refer to Chapter 1, under the sections "Be a Team Player" and "Avoid Nonproductive Team Behaviours," for discussions of interpersonal relations in the office. Many of the behaviours described in Chapter 1 become obvious at meetings. In addition, some unique behaviours occur at meetings.

Poor Body Language

Nowhere is it easier to see body language in action than at a meeting. In a meeting environment, participants may sit for long periods of time in close proximity. It is easy to get your message across to others without even opening your mouth. Common negative body language messages found at meetings will include:

- I am bored.
- You are wrong.
- I'm too busy to be here.
- I need to get out of here.
- I don't want to be here.
- Your comments are not important.
- Your comments are foolish.
- I'm frustrated.
- I don't agree with you.

Tardiness

When a meeting is scheduled for 0800, it means being in the correct meeting room, having your coat off, being seated, and being prepared to start at 0800. It does not mean flying through the meeting room door at 0810 and making loud apologies for your busy schedule and late arrival.

Although people know this, many continually show up late and interrupt the meeting with their arrival. The message that they are giving to the other participants is that their work is more important—more important than the meeting and more important than the work of the other participants.

Being Unprepared

What is more frustrating than participants who attend meetings without being prepared? This may include:

- not completing the activities you have agreed to at the previous meeting
- not reading the agenda before the meeting
- not preparing handouts for your presentation
- not reading background documents sent prior to the meeting

This lack of preparation is completely unfair to the other participants.

Not Participating

Preparing for a meeting is work. Attending a meeting is work. Following up from a meeting is work. The person who comes to a meeting expecting to get a break or socialize is doing a disservice to the other members.

Some people are masters at avoiding meeting follow-up. When they leave the meeting, everyone else has an action list to follow, but they leave without a follow-up list of activities.

During the meeting, they may offer verbal suggestions or advice, but they do not offer to prepare background reports, statistics, or any concrete evidence of work. Some nonparticipants remain completely quiet at meetings and simply occupy the chair.

Being Rude

Rudeness comes in many forms at a meeting. Rudeness might include:

- speaking over the top of other participants
- not listening to others
- ignoring the ideas of other people
- discounting the ideas of others
- speaking directly to one person and shutting out a third party (This is often done through body language, not responding to the third person's attempts to get into the conversation, and not making eye contact with them.)
- coming late to a meeting
- holding side conversations
- reading or working on unrelated materials during the meeting
- using vulgar language or stories to make a point
- rushing to finish the meeting regardless of where you are on the agenda and regardless of what you have not yet accomplished

Creating Solutions

The study of meeting dynamics is fascinating, and the list of nonproductive behaviours found at meetings could be very long. Meeting dynamics make leading a meeting a difficult challenge. However, strategies a meeting facilitator or leader takes help solve some of the difficulties. Here are some suggestions:

- Rely on the ground rules. The ground rules are created during the first meeting of the team. The team members create them, so they are likely to buy into them. When a member's behaviour does not follow the ground rules, stop the meeting shortly, point to the rule, and ask the member to get back on track.
- Start the meeting on time every time. It does not matter if only half the members are there. Move ahead. Once members see that the leader is serious about getting started on time, they will make a greater effort to be ready on time.
- Do not stop the meeting when people arrive late with loud interruptions. You can acknowledge them with a facial gesture but do not let the flow of the meeting be interrupted.
- The leader should speak privately to errant members at the break or after the meeting. A one-on-one private conversation about poor behaviour will be more effective than challenging the person head-on during the meeting in front of the other members.
- Sticking to an agenda and using printed time charts and action plans that are on display at every meeting will help to remind and encourage people about their needed activities and their deadlines.
- The team leader or facilitator can discourage poor behaviour and encourage productive behaviour by managing the input during the meeting. A diplomatic and assertive request for participation or for productive team behaviour can be very effective.
- Be sure that the team leader has the respect of the team members. If the team members have selected the leader, there will be a greater chance for respect and better behaviour at the meetings.

- Pay attention to what is discussed after the meeting. Do not get involved in side meetings held outside the main meeting or criticism of the leader or decisions made inside the meeting, but be aware of what is taking place outside the walls of the meeting.
- Strive for consensus by the team members. If all the team members agree or at least can support recommendations made by the team, the behaviour will be productive.
- Meetings should be enjoyable as well as productive.

Self-Check

1. Identify one way to increase the likelihood of the team leader demonstrating respect for all team members.
2. What should the facilitator do when people arrive late for the meeting?

VIRTUAL MEETINGS

Many companies use communication tools in the office to conduct virtual meetings, including conference calls, web conferences, and videoconferences. These forms of meetings reduce travel costs and losses in productivity that result from time spent away from the office.

Service providers and technology vendors support their customers with the latest virtual conference tools to ensure the greatest possibility of success. They may provide complimentary training on the virtual meeting service, live help during the conference call, or a **hotline** into their technical support facility.

Before selecting a virtual meeting, spend some time to consider your real needs. If simple communication is all that you require, then a conference call is the least complicated and most cost-effective approach. If your virtual meeting necessitates the sharing or presenting of data and other material, then **web conferencing** will meet your needs. In Chapter 8 web conferencing is covered from a technical requirement standpoint.

Teleconferences

Teleconferences, also known as **conference calls**, are telecommunication-based meetings that use ordinary telephone lines to bring together three or more people at various locations. Teleconference services offered by your local telephone company can connect dozens of people to the same call. They can involve local, national, or international calls. Office professionals will often find themselves arranging or participating in teleconferences.

Many business telephones have a simple conference function that allows the conference coordinator to dial up participants and put them into the conference call. This does not require operator assistance. The conference coordinator may control the teleconference from a touch-tone telephone using commands on the keypad. There are no additional fees except for the "collective" cost per minute of conference.

However, for more complex conference calls, the traditional process of contacting your local service provider to reserve a common **bridge** or dial-in number for participants is probably the safest method. There are a number of somewhat inflexible conditions that surround these reserved teleconferences such as a predetermined number of lines for participants and a fixed length of conference time, and there is invariably a charge for services.

To ensure a successful teleconference, always remember that you are part of a meeting involving many people. Here are some specific teleconferencing suggestions:

- Identify yourself when speaking, and direct your questions or comments to people by name.
- Remember that comments not specifically directed to an individual are perceived as intended for the entire group.
- Speak naturally as you would during any phone call, but pause for others to comment.

Web Conferences

Web conferences allow participants to be online in real time via the internet. Using your computer and web-conferencing application software, often found in your web browser, you can establish an inexpensive and reliable way to share information through screen sharing, computer software applications, presentations, or anything enabled on your computer with others in online meetings.

As the coordinator, you can guide participants through the conference, supporting them to see what you display on your PC screen.

Coordinating a conference call to coincide with a web conference may enhance web conferencing and encourage those without the benefit of a reliable device to participate.

Videoconferences

Videoconferences can be an important vehicle for collaborative office communication. They allow participants in scattered geographic locations to see and hear one another on computer or television monitors by way of images transmitted over special telephone lines or satellite.

Videoconferences typically cost 20% to 50% less than face-to-face meetings, but they remain the most expensive form of virtual meetings.

It is very popular for people to hold meetings through their computers, just using their screens and keyboards. By simply downloading software from the internet, participants can engage in real-time key conversations. Audio and video options are available as long as the participants have the right multimedia software, a computer microphone and speaker, and a simple web camera placed near the screen. The cost is minimal, the procedure is simple, and the result is highly effective.

ETHICAL BEHAVIOUR IN MEETINGS

As you know, ethics is a system of deciding what is morally right in a given situation. You may find yourself in situations where you might not want to tell the truth to avoid hurting someone's feelings. For instance, imagine you are a new participant in a team meeting. After the meeting, the facilitator asks you if you enjoyed the meeting and learned a lot of helpful information. In fact, you were really bored and already knew everything discussed. Is it wrong to say, "Oh, yes,

pro-Link
Warm-Up with an Icebreaker

When people come to meetings, their minds are busy with other priorities, deadlines, and pressures that they bring with them to the meeting. That's why a meeting facilitator will often use a simple exercise at the start of the meeting to help get people focused. These exercises are called icebreakers or warm-ups. These same activities, when used at the end of meetings, are cool-downs. Here's an example:

Select comic strips from the newspaper. Cut out each frame in the strip. Place all of the frames into a large container. When the meeting begins, ask each participant to take one frame out of the container. Start the clock! The participants must find the other frames that belong to the same comic strip. Once all the frames have been located, they are ordered chronologically so that the comic strip can be read correctly. If the facilitator wants the participants to work in groups, it is an easy way for group formation. Participants have actively moved about, they may have met new people, laughed at the comic strip, and now are ready to start the meeting.

Figure 13-10 depicts types of virtual meetings and their usages.

FIGURE 13-10 Virtual meetings type and use.

Type of Virtual Meeting	Use of Meeting
Teleconference	A conference using ordinary telephone lines and sets, with three or more participants. Teleconferences are used for local, national, or international voice conferencing wherever there is a telephone service. They are "verbal only" and may be both impromptu and informal meetings.
Web Conference	A conference of two or more people at different workstations connected to the internet. Participants may share documents, applications such as PowerPoint, and video images. Used in conjunction with a teleconference to enhance participation. Web conferences are inexpensive and reliable.
Videoconference	Videoconference facilities using special telecommunication lines or satellite services are often set up and administered by third-party specialists. This type of virtual meeting involves a corporate-wide audience or a smaller, more focused audience in a single office. Videoconferences provide the best quality of all virtual conferences but remain the most expensive and require the participant to have skills in coordination to participate.

I really enjoyed the meeting," to avoid hurting the facilitator's feelings? It would be an outright lie. You may want to learn to sidestep a question or issue without being brutally honest when it is simply a matter of avoiding hurting someone's feelings. Your response to the facilitator could be, "I really did find several points you made interesting and helpful."

What if the situation has damaging consequences? For instance, while attending your manager's presentation, you notice certain figures in the sales report changed to report higher sales. After the meeting, you question him about it, and he tells you he increased the figures because the department is under pressure to increase sales. If you do not report this behaviour and he does it again, he can say you helped him change the figures because you did not report it the first time you noticed it.

You have the responsibility to do the right thing based on your own values, and you should report any unethical behaviour from the beginning. By doing so, you will be following your company's code of ethics. Adhering to ethical behaviour in meetings, as well as in any personal interaction, involves making choices that will build positive qualities—trust and credibility.

INTERNATIONAL CONFERENCING

As global communications become more commonplace, you may find yourself helping your manager prepare for an international meeting or conference. In addition to your usual responsibilities in making routine meeting arrangements, you might also find yourself responsible for other aspects of planning. Examples might include:

- arranging hotels and transportation
- tracking and handling finances and payments, including exchange rates
- arranging interpreters

- arranging business cards, printed in both English and the language of the host country
- providing protocol advice to your manager
- making security arrangements
- researching the names of major political leaders, sports figures, and other celebrities
- compiling a dossier on the host country, including information on business philosophy, social customs, and seasonal climate

The following guidelines will help you to deal effectively with cultural and language differences during your consultations with people from the country to which your manager will be travelling:

- Learn courtesy greetings in the language of that country. A simple "Good morning," "Thank you," and "Goodbye" in that language at the beginning and end of a telephone call will make a favourable impression.
- Educate yourself as to the geography and transportation systems of the country so that you will be somewhat familiar with distances, terrain, and mode of transportation when discussing meeting locations and time schedules with your counterpart in the country being visited.
- Gather information on major landmarks and their histories in the host country. This will enable you to make informed decisions when collaborating with your counterpart in preparing a schedule of meetings and activities for your manager during his visit.
- Determine the preferred times for calling to discuss your manager's pending visit, and make an effort to adhere to those preferences.
- Become familiar with the religious beliefs, social customs, business philosophy, and family structure of the country where the meeting is to be held. This will ensure that you do not unintentionally give offence during consultations.

As you research communication and cultural barriers that may arise between cultures, keep an ongoing file of pertinent information. Realize, though, that the information will have to be updated from time to time. You will give yourself an edge as you plan or progress through your career and gain the reputation of an "expert" in international conferencing protocol.

QUESTIONS FOR STUDY AND REVIEW

1. Explain the statement: "All meetings are events, but not all events are meetings."
2. Discuss four steps to consider when planning a conference.
3. How can automation be helpful in arranging the date and time for meetings?
4. What information should be included in a meeting notice?

5. What items might appear on an agenda for a formal meeting?

6. What items might appear on an agenda for an informal meeting?

7. State five guidelines to follow when ordering beverages for a meeting.

8. What supporting materials will be required for a formal meeting?

9. How are digital devices useful at meetings?

10. List three tips for successful note taking during a meeting.

11. What are two actions that might appear on your to-do list following a meeting?

12. What would you include on the minutes of an informal meeting?

13. What would you include on the minutes of a formal meeting?

14. How is a team meeting different from a formal meeting?

15. What is the role of the team leader at a meeting?

16. What is the role of the facilitator at a meeting?

17. State five house rules you believe would help make team meetings more productive.

18. Differentiate between structured and unstructured brainstorming.

19. Explain how the nominal group technique is used.

20. What is the purpose of a cause-and-effect diagram?

21. How does debriefing take place at a team meeting?

22. What is the meaning of meeting dynamics?

23. Describe five poor behaviours that are often witnessed at meetings.

24. What is the meaning of a *virtual* meeting?

25. Suggest two advantages in holding virtual meetings instead of face-to-face meetings.

Key Terms

adjournment 262

agenda 254

branding 254

bridge 272

conference 254

conference call 272

consensus 269

debrief 270

event 254

hotline 272

meeting 254

minutes 256

notice of meeting 258

request for proposals 254

teleconference 272

venue 254

verbatim 261

videoconference 257

web conferencing 272

EVERYDAY ETHICS

Cove or Conference?

You work in the Public Relations department of the Southern Saskatchewan Petroleum Institute (SSPI). SSPI has paid your expenses to attend a business conference in Halifax where you are representing the company. Your participation includes leading a one-hour seminar in public relations issues for Canadian petroleum companies. You spent one full weekend preparing your materials and making sure that you would represent your company in the very best way possible.

Then you travelled to Halifax after working hours on a Tuesday evening. Your presentation was held on the first day of the two-day conference. You performed in an excellent fashion, and you know that positive reports will get back to your management team in Regina.

You are expected to attend other people's seminars on the second day—but in your judgment, there appears to be nothing of interest for SSPI. However, there is a full-day tour available from the hotel lobby that takes tourists to Peggy's Cove and to other tourist points in Halifax. You have never been to Halifax and have always wanted to see Peggy's Cove. You feel you "deserve" the time off in lieu of all the personal time you put into preparation for the conference. Instead of attending the second-day seminars, you board the tourist bus. Edward Graham, a business associate, sees you leaving on the bus.

■ What are your next steps?

Problem Solving

1. You arranged an all-day meeting for a group of 25 executives within your office and national branch offices. You have planned and arranged the location, agenda, and meals for this meeting. Everything is going well until lunchtime. Five executives had requested a vegetarian lunch, but when lunch arrives from the caterers, none of the meals are vegetarian. Everyone is ready to eat, but there are no meals for the five executives. What should you do?

2. You have planned a conference for your organization. The company has a key product launch in the works and is planning a product demonstration to be held outside at the venue. Of course, the day of your conference arrives, and it is pouring rain. What can you do?

3. Your manager, Lee Chung, is the chairperson of a regional group of office managers. The group meets once a month. Mr. Chung plans to hand out keyed minutes from the last meeting during the meeting, as he has found that when he sends them electronically in advance of the meeting, nobody reviews them. Today you keyed and duplicated the minutes of the January meeting. Mr. Chung is leaving the office to attend the February meeting, and he plans to take the minutes of the January meeting with him for distribution. As you are looking over the notes of the January meeting, you discover that you omitted a motion that had been voted upon. Mr. Chung does not have time for you to rekey the minutes and duplicate them. Should Mr. Chung take the minutes you have prepared? How can the correction be made?

Special Reports

1. Ask to shadow an administrative assistant who is responsible for preparing minutes of meetings. Find out how the minutes are prepared (from written notes, a recording, etc.). Ask your interviewee to share five tips for minute preparation. Prepare a report for your instructor detailing your findings.

2. The Olympics is held every four years. This international sporting celebration is a mammoth event to organize. It requires a lot of time and money but mostly a team of highly skilled people to manage the event.

   a. Locate the website for the next Olympic Games.

   b. Consider that you are working with the Olympic organizing team. You have been assigned as the team leader for managing one particular sporting event. Select one of the activities from those listed on the site. Then become familiar with this activity through internet research.

   c. Make a comprehensive list of all the sub-teams that you, as the team leader, will form to take care of all aspects of this sporting event. For example, if you have chosen downhill skiing as your sporting event, you might form a sub-team for housing the athletes, another sub-team for transporting the athletes, and so on. Be as thorough as possible.

   d. Now select one of your sub-teams and brainstorm all the potential barriers/problems that you will have to avoid. For example, if your sub-team is transportation for the downhill skiers, one of your potential barriers might be lack of suitable racks to carry the skis on the bus. Again, make your list exhaustive.

   You do not have to write paragraphs. This is a "thinking" exercise. Use enumerations and bullets for your two lists. There are no right and wrong answers. Instead, this is a brainstorming exercise and a chance for you to think through the complexities of organizing a major event.

3. You have been asked to arrange a workshop for your classmates on career planning to be held at your campus in one month. This will be a three-hour workshop. Research event planning online and prepare an event-planning checklist that includes all of the items to consider when arranging this type of event. Hand in the checklist to your instructor for feedback.

PRODUCTION CHALLENGES

13-A Composing a Notice of Meeting

Supplies needed:

- *Plain paper*

The current date is September 3. Mr. Wilson has called a meeting of the executive committee of the November Sales Seminar, and he has asked you to send the notices. The meeting will be held at 1700 on Wednesday, September 10, in Mr. Wilson's office at PDI Inc. The purpose of the meeting is to finalize plans for the November Sales Seminar. The names and contact numbers for the executive committee members follow.

Mr. Wilson needs to determine if each committee member can attend the September 10 meeting, if he or she has a report to make, and if he or she thinks that an October meeting of the executive committee will be necessary. Invite all members by email and request all members to email their responses to Mr. Wilson's address, which is NWilson@PDI.ca.

Mr. Michael Wong
Electronic Systems
Tel: 905-322-5839
Wong.M@ES.ca

Mr. Jasim Mohammed
CanTech Industries
Tel: 705-429-7192
JMohammed@CanTech.ca

Ms. Louise Witherspoon
City Centre
Fax: 298-781-7498
Tel: 298-781-6735
Email: louisew@cca.com.ca

Ms. Dimitra Theodorakopoulos
Seneca College of Applied Arts and Technology
Tel: 416-366-9981
Email: dimitrat@senecac.on.ca

13-B Composing and Keying Minutes

Supplies needed:

- *Notes on September 10 Meeting of the Executive Committee for the November Sales Seminar, Form 13-B on Companion Website*
- *Plain paper*

Mr. Wilson put his notes for the September 10 meeting of the executive committee of the November Sales Seminar in your in-basket. The following note was attached: "Please compose and key these minutes."

13-C Event Management

Supplies needed:

- *Plain paper*

You are all currently working on a team with the goal of improving customer relationship management within PDI. Mr. Wilson has asked your team to organize a seminar for the company.

For the seminar, the team has decided to bring in an expert guest speaker. You search the internet and find sites that give profiles of speakers who will travel to your city to work with your team. One such site that you have located is www.leadingauthorities.com.

Prepare a three-paragraph biography about the speaker you have chosen that you could use to convince Mr. Wilson to give you approval to book this expert for your upcoming seminar.

Then create a document that will capture a list of all your potential expenses for hiring the guest speaker. In your document, list all the potential expenses, a justification for each expense, and your educated estimate of each expense. Don't forget to consider the following in your list of potential expenses:

- services
- travel
- accommodation
- meals
- products
- shipping
- transportation
- equipment and supplies
- rentals and leases
- communication
- miscellaneous
- gifts

Weblinks

Canadian Association of Professional Speakers (CAPS)
www.canadianspeakers.org
This site is the number one internet resource for the Canadian speaking industry. It includes a bulletin board for CAPS members.

Canada Business Network
www.canada.ca
Go to the website for the government of Canada and put Canada Business Network in the search bar. The Canada Business Network provides links to event and conference-planning resources.

Cvent
www.cvent.com
Provides guidance in planning, executing, and measuring meetings and events of various sizes, and complexity.

CanSPEP Canadian Society of Professional Event Planners.
www.CanSPEP.ca
An association of partner members who offer professional services in event management and planning.

Meetings Mean Business
www.meetingsmeanbusiness.ca
An advocacy group that supports and encourages the benefits of hosting face-to-face business meetings.

Chapter 14
Business Communication

Rawpixel.com/Shutterstock

SOCIAL NETWORK

LIKE

SHARE

LEARNING OUTCOMES

After completion of this chapter, the student will be able to:

1 Describe the impact of standard communication channels.

2 Understand communication in relation to personal space, eye contact, posture, and facial expressions.

3 Demonstrate ways to improve your listening skills and factors surrounding constructive feedback.

4 Review the components of presentations and public speaking.

5 Describe the standard qualities of an effective business letter.

6 Compare the techniques for writing letters of differing business purposes.

7 Inspect letter format styles.

8 Discuss common reports styles, sections, and components.

9 Review in-text citations, references, and bibliographies.

Effective communication is the responsibility of every person in an organization. As organizations increase their dependence on technological advances, the volume of work that everyone is expected to manage increases. This greater amount of responsibility is accompanied by increased communications in many formats. One of the most important foundational skills for an administrative professional is communication. The organization needs to know that it can count on your skill set to represent the company in face-to-face interactions as well as in handling correspondence from others within the company, its customers, and suppliers.

INTERPERSONAL COMMUNICATION

The term **interpersonal communication** refers to personal interactions between individuals or members of a group. Whether you are discussing with a colleague the implementation of a new process or conversing with your friend about anxiety over an upcoming job interview, you are engaging in interpersonal communication. This communication includes the use of verbal (words and voice), nonverbal (body language, image), and listening skills; and its effectiveness depends on the level to which those skills have been developed.

Various studies tell us that in a conversation or verbal exchange:

- Words are 7–10% effective.
- Tone of voice is 38–40% effective.
- Nonverbal clues are 45–50% effective.

How effective your communication is depends as much on *how* you say something as on what you say. Whether your message is clear depends on the method of communication you choose to use to deliver it.

VERBAL COMMUNICATION

Verbal communication can mean a phone conversation, a voice mail message, a formal meeting, or even an informal chat with a colleague at lunch. Much of the communication in the office is verbal, and the degree to which communication occurs depends on the skills of the individuals involved in the interchange. The most effective verbal communication takes place in a comfortable atmosphere and on a one-to-one basis. Effective verbal skills can be developed. Strive to continually improve those skills by following these guidelines:

Company Profile

Alectra Utilities

Alectra Utilities

From left to right: Nathan Scheewe, Manager Government Relations, Alectra Utilities; Max Pacheco, Government Relations Coordinator, Alectra Utilities; Tamar Heisler, Director Government Relations, Alectra Utilities; Brian Wilkie, President and CEO, Niagara Peninsula Energy and incoming EDA Chair, Board of Directors; Brian Bentz, President and CEO, Alectra Inc

Alectra is a newly formed electricity distribution and integrated energy solutions company providing services to nearly one million customers in Ontario's Greater Golden Horseshoe area. Alectra delivers approximately 22% of Ontario's electricity and services over 15 communities. Alectra has been acknowledged for several recognition awards, most notably, an industry award from the Electricity Distributors Association (EDA) for communication excellence. The communication strategy that the Government Relations team developed with the organization's six key municipal stakeholders is what earned them this award. Some key elements of this strategy consist of face-to-face meetings with stakeholders and the creation of a quarterly newsletter, alectraNews, aimed at keeping constant and open lines of information and communication.

- **Listen and watch for verbal and nonverbal feedback.** Many factors affect how someone reacts to what you are saying. Among them is past experience—what happened to that person in a similar situation.

- **Choose your words carefully when the topic you are discussing is sensitive or controversial.** You may wish to withhold your opinion entirely if you know your view will offend the listener, put the listener on the defensive, or force the listener to disagree with you.

- **Encourage the other person to talk: communication should be two-way.** Communication will be open and honest if the person trusts you; it will be restricted if the person does not. A growing trend in business is one-way communication. A message is sent, and the receiver does not acknowledge it. This lack of acknowledgment on the part of the receiver can change the tone of communication, creating a barrier, and the sender may demonstrate a reluctance to engage the receiver in future communication unless mutually necessary.

- **Give the other person your undivided attention.** Performing another task while you are talking is distracting and rude. This is equally important whether you are talking face-to-face or over the phone.

- **Avoid talking incessantly.** Pause often to give your listener an opportunity to respond.

- **Summarize the important points in logical order and give the listener a chance to ask questions at the end of a conversation.** Communication does not take place until the listener truly understands what you are saying.

You can improve your own speech patterns by being aware of any negative habits you may have developed. For example, do you say "uh" or "you know" when you are talking? Words such as "like" or "well" are examples of *filler words* and will cause the listener to lose interest and stop listening. Those or similar repetitive phrases can be quite distracting to the listener. A person once said, "I counted 104 'uhs' in another person's message." It is doubtful whether the listener heard any of the intended message through the "noise" of the repetitive phrase. "You know what I mean?" is an example of another habit that detracts from the intended message being sent. Be careful not to pick up those and other similar habits that you find distracting in others.

In order to convey the clearest message possible, be aware of the tone and volume of your voice when speaking. Consider the following:

- **Slow your speech.** When you talk fast, you may appear to be nervous and unsure of yourself.

- **Avoid talking in a monotone.** Inflection helps convey meaning. When you want to make a point or emphasize something, put a dip in your voice by lowering it briefly.

Raising your voice slightly at the end of a statement makes it a question.

- **Avoid talking loudly.** If you are standing close to someone, keep your volume down. Increase your volume depending on the distance between you and the person. Avoid speaking so softly that your listener has to ask you to repeat what you are saying.

- **Speak clearly.** Avoid mumbling. When you hear "huh?" or "pardon?" that is a warning you are not speaking clearly.

- **Use the correct pronunciation.** Misuse occurs from hearing words mispronounced by others so often that we begin to mispronounce them ourselves. Have you heard "candidate" mispronounced "cannidate"? or "especially" mispronounced "expecially"? Pay particular attention to correct pronunciation; common misuse or mispronunciation neither makes the habit acceptable in business nor conveys a professional image.

- **Use the right word.** If you are not clear of a word's meaning, do not use it.

Self-Check

1. What skills are included in interpersonal communication?

2. Discuss a guideline for improving verbal communication.

3. How can you use your voice to improve the clarity of the message being sent?

NONVERBAL COMMUNICATION

Most people are skilled at communicating a message without speaking even one word. Our facial expressions, our body gestures, and the way we present ourselves often express our feelings and opinions better than our spoken words. Make certain, however, that the person with whom you are communicating does not misinterpret what are often seen as subtle nonverbal cues. It is imperative that your actions convey a clear meaning—that is, the meaning you intend. Verbal communication can be completely discredited by the nonverbal kind. The following are some of the ways through which people interpret nonverbal messages.

Image

It is no surprise that the way we dress sends a message to customers and colleagues. Accurate or not, people do form immediate perceptions of your professionalism, your competence, your credibility, and your ability based on your personal appearance. Promotions may be affected based on your professional presence or appearance.

Conservative dress conveys the message that you are a professional and to be viewed as a serious contender in business. While formal dress is still adhered to in some organizations, especially for top management, the trend, overall, is towards more relaxed business attire. Many professional companies consider business-casual clothing to be quite appropriate. Take your cue from the other workers you see in the office, or determine if there is an official dress code. When in doubt, dress up rather than down.

The location of the office, the style of management, organizational culture, and the type of industry you work in will all dictate the level of professional dress that is required. If you work in an organization whose clientele consists of trendsetters, you will likely find the dress code to be cutting-edge stylish but professional. On the other hand, a high-profile corporate law firm will likely require employees to dress in a more formal manner in keeping with their corporate clientele. Consider your customers. In our multicultural society, customers come from varied demographics, and the image you convey through your appearance should be one that will avoid offending.

Regardless of the casualness of the office environment, do not confuse social dress with business dress. Consider attire and accessories, too; these help to create your image, and wearing accessories conservatively will portray a professional image to both your customers and your supervisors.

It is common practice among many Canadian offices to designate Friday as **casual day**. This policy allows employees to dress in a casual style that is still attractive and presentable. However, customers and clients may be unaware of this convention and receive the incorrect message that the office is less than professional. You might consider taking the initiative to create an attractive, tasteful sign explaining "casual day," and getting permission to post it in a public area to attract clients' attention.

Be conservative in using perfumes, colognes, and scented products! Many Canadian offices and buildings have banned the use of scents altogether because of increased allergic reactions to ingredients used in the manufacture of many of the products. Ask about the policy in the office or building where you work and adhere to any restrictions that are in place.

Personal Space

Canadians, like all other nationalities, have expectations about their **personal space**. Personal space refers to the distance apart from another at which one person feels comfortable talking. People who stand too close are viewed as aggressive or perhaps overly friendly; people who stand too far away may be seen as aloof. Always be considerate, and do not violate another person's personal space.

Perception of personal space varies among cultures. We live in a multicultural society, and it is important to understand the difference between our perception of personal space and that of a co-worker from another culture. We should not assume someone is being rude because their communicating distance is shorter or longer than we are used to.

Eye Contact

It takes confidence to look directly into someone's eyes when you are speaking to them. Eyes are one of our most important nonverbal language tools—we use them to read the other person's body language, and in turn, they give off our own nonverbal messages. In Canadian culture, direct eye contact tells the receiver that you are interested and listening. In other cultures, direct eye contact can make a person feel uncomfortable or even threatened. Avoid prolonged eye contact in such instances, but bear in mind that a total lack of eye contact can send a message of disinterest or even arrogance.

If you find it impossible to look someone directly in the eye, try looking at a facial feature near the eyes; for example, the nose. This will give the appearance of making eye contact and may prevent that person's interpreting your discomfort as a sign of shiftiness or dishonesty.

Posture

Your posture, the way you stand, sit, and walk, tells others a story and can convey your level of confidence. By leaning towards someone, you show attentiveness; likewise, leaning away can show lack of interest and some level of reserve. When you hunch your shoulders and keep your head down, it appears you have low **self-confidence**. When you cross your legs and arms, you may be perceived as being closed to the ideas of the person with whom you are communicating; uncrossed legs and arms may lead individuals to believe you are more open to the conversation.

Remember that your posture may not be telling the story you intend to tell, so be cautious about how your posture is perceived. A relaxed body posture will help you appear and feel more relaxed and confident.

Facial Expressions

The face is the most expressive part of the body. It is capable of many expressions that reflect our attitudes and emotions. In fact, the face speaks a universal language. Many cultures share the same expressions of happiness, fear, anger, or sadness. Others interpret your meanings from your facial expressions. You can reverse a misrepresentation of appearing aloof, disapproving, or disinterested by simply smiling. Your smile is the strongest tool you have. It can help you appear warm, open, friendly, and confident. Be aware of the impact this powerful nonverbal tool can have.

Because nonverbal language is far more powerful than verbal communication, it is imperative that you pay attention to the messages your body language sends. Smiling, making eye contact, using open gestures, and using good posture can project self-confidence. Being aware of your body language can help you send a consistent message.

Self-Check

1. Why is it important to dress conservatively in the workplace?
2. What does one's posture say about a person? Give examples.

LISTENING AND PROVIDING FEEDBACK

Few people listen as attentively as they are capable of doing, and those who do have trained themselves to listen. Real listening, including providing constructive feedback, is an active process.

Active Listening

Being an active listener does the following:

- It shows the other person you care and want to understand.
- It shows the other person you are receptive to him or her talking to you.
- Active listening fosters more meaningful, more helpful, closer relationships.
- Really listening may reduce prejudice or negative assumptions about others because you get to know them better.
- Others might view you as an enjoyable conversationalist and might open up more.

Recognize that good listening skills can be learned, and adopt a plan for improving your listening skills. Tips to help you improve in this area include the following:

- Give your full attention to the person who is speaking. Concentrate on what is said and on grasping the meaning of what is said. Avoid saying you understand when you do not.
- Become aware of your listening barriers, such as allowing your mind to wander, planning on what you are going to say next, or being close-minded about what is being said.

- Let the speaker finish before you begin to speak.
- Actively listen to what the speaker is saying.
- Repeat information (paraphrase) to ensure complete understanding. Ask questions if you are not sure you understand what the speaker has said.
- Take notes and confirm that what you understand is what was meant. Listen for key ideas.
- Avoid judgment until you fully comprehend what the other person is saying.
- Give feedback. Sit up straight and have good eye contact with the speaker. Nod your head now and then to show you understand. When appropriate, smile, frown, laugh, or be silent. These clues help the speaker know you are listening.

Constructive Feedback

One of the best skills an administrative professional can possess is the ability to give and receive constructive feedback without sounding or appearing to be critical. Giving and receiving constructive feedback requires diplomacy, as well as sensitivity to the needs of other people. It also requires a level of high function, self-reflection, maturity, and experience.

Giving Constructive Feedback   If you are inexperienced in giving constructive feedback, the following tips will help you to be more effective:

1. If you make a practice of giving positive feedback when appropriate and on a regular basis, the negative feedback will be easier for the listener to accept. Your comments will be more credible if the listener is accustomed to receiving your positive feedback.

2. Phrase your comments as constructive feedback and not as criticism. Be certain to include what the listener has done well and what you see as areas of improvement. Ask the recipient for an opinion on how to improve matters. Perhaps the person will have a better solution than your own.

3. Be certain to describe the context of the problem. Always review the actions that led up to the problem. Just commenting on the problem without providing the details that surround it will lead to confusion and possibly no resolution.

4. Provide constructive feedback only when *you* are capable of doing so. If you are carrying around *personal baggage*, or if your emotions are running high, your chances of being effective are minimal.

5. Provide constructive feedback only when the listener is capable of receiving it. If it is obvious that the

recipient is suffering from low self-esteem, perhaps offering friendly assistance is more appropriate than offering constructive feedback at this particular time.

6. Provide the correct environment. Never offer constructive feedback to an individual when there is an audience present. Show respect for the receiver by creating a confidential atmosphere.

7. Describe the facts; do not generalize or exaggerate. If the person has been late five times for your 10 team meetings, say, "You have been late five times," not "You are late all the time." Ask yourself if your data is accurate. What you don't know for certain should not be promoted as fact.

8. Don't be judgmental. Comments such as "That's the worst report I've ever read" tend to belittle others. If your intent is to elicit a mature response, use discretion in how you choose your words. A better comment would be this: "I have detected five typographical errors and two missing sections in your report."

9. Don't state your impression of the person; instead, describe the problematic actions of that person. For example, if you say, "You are lazy," you are likely to receive an angry response. But if you say, "You have not completed your last three reports on time," you may get a more cooperative response.

10. Do not be a conduit for other people. Speak only for yourself. Comments such as "Everyone is concerned about . . ." are unjust. Rather, say, "I feel concerned when you. . . ."

11. Do not ask the listener a question about her or his behaviour. Instead, state a fact. If you ask, "Have you been late for the last five meetings?" you are inviting defensive behaviour and encouraging the listener to lie for the sake of self-preservation. Simply state: "I have observed that you were late for the last five meetings."

12. Use a strategy that expresses how the person's actions make you feel, and ask for the person's feedback. Examples:

   ■ "I have observed that you have been late for the last five meetings."

   ■ "When you are late, I feel disappointed because your input at the meetings is valuable."

13. Allow the receiver to comment, and leave the door open for a discussion.

   ■ "I would appreciate it if you would attend every meeting on time because, as your team leader, I am depending on your commitment."

   ■ "How do you feel about this?"

Then discuss alternatives and a possible compromise.

Receiving Feedback   When your supervisor is giving the feedback, there is no guarantee that it will be positive or constructive. The following tips are designed to help you work through an uncomfortable situation:

1. Attempt to relax. An employee who is being criticized for perceived lack of performance often finds this advice very difficult to follow. Remember to breathe deeply. When we become tense, we often breathe shallowly; when we do that, we aren't providing our body with the oxygen it needs to perform at its best.

2. As your supervisor is explaining the problem, listen very carefully. Take notes if possible and appropriate.

3. To clarify the situation, ask your supervisor questions that will help you to understand her or his point of view.

4. If you agree that you have mishandled a piece of work, apologize. Also, acknowledge valid points that are made by your supervisor.

5. Remember, if you feel uncomfortable with your supervisor's comments, you can ask for time before responding. You might say, for example, "Thank you for explaining this; however, I feel uncomfortable with this situation. I'd appreciate some time to think about your comments. May we continue discussing this tomorrow?" Use this time to speak to a mentor and, if necessary, to collect facts. Be certain that you have regained your composure before meeting with your supervisor. This is preferable to responding in a way you will later regret.

Self-Check

1. List two professional benefits of being an active listener.
2. What is an example of a listening barrier you should avoid?
3. What are some benefits of constructive feedback?

PUBLIC SPEAKING

Be at Ease in the Spotlight

Speaking to an audience is the number one phobia for many people. Some speakers can learn to overcome this fear simply with practice, while others have a great deal of difficulty conquering the phobia. What works for one speaker does not work for another. Here are some useful suggestions that may help:

■ Do not rush to a presentation. Give yourself plenty of time to travel to the location, find the room, and set up. You will need time to lay out your handouts, set up the computer, projector, flip charts, pens, and other materials.

- Know your topic in detail and develop a passion about it. Your passion should override your nervousness.

- Stand behind a podium if possible. This barrier will help to hide shaky legs and hands.

- Prepare excellent visual aids. These will highlight your key points and act as a guide for your presentation.

- Prior to the presentation, prepare yourself in a way that typically assists with coping strategies. Use music and relaxation exercises, and think of the best highlights of your presentation.

Given time and practice, most people can improve their verbal presentation skills so they can offer informative and entertaining presentations.

Avoid Anxiety

A great presentation requires a lot of planning and organizing of details. Whether you are giving the presentation or it is your responsibility to introduce or host the speaker, you want everything to go without a single hitch. With some serious attention to detail and thoughtful preparation, you can improve the odds. Here are some points to prevent presentation anxiety:

- If you are introducing the speaker, be sure you have adequate and accurate information to introduce that person.

- Be certain that the speaker arrives in plenty of time. This may include changing air flights or picking up the speaker at the airport. If there is plenty of time, there is reduced panic and pressure for both the speaker and the organizer.

- Most presentations require technical equipment, and technical equipment leaves plenty of opportunity for mishap. That is why it is imperative to have a backup plan whenever technical equipment is involved. For example, if a speaker is using a computer presentation, you should prepare overhead transparencies and arrange for an overhead projector and extra bulb—just in case! Does the microphone work? How does it work? Does the speaker need a mobile microphone? Does the speaker need a remote control for the computer projector? If you are uncertain about the technical setup, learn all you can about the equipment ahead of time, or you might arrange to have a technician in the room prior to the presentation.

- When you book the presentation room, if you are not familiar with it, visit the room to be certain it will accommodate the presenter, the audience, and the equipment.

- Rooms are full of surprises! You can never depend on the condition that the last group left it in. Chairs and tables may need to be rearranged. Flip chart paper and pens may need to be replenished. Where is the switch that dims the lights? Where is the switch that lowers the projection screen?

- Know the audience. Anticipate their needs, concerns, interests, and questions. If you do not do this research ahead of the presentation, you may be opening up yourself or the speaker to a potentially embarrassing situation. Not all audiences are patient and polite.

- If you are the presenter, know where your presentation can be shortened. Presentations often have a delayed start. If you need to stretch your presentation, some well-prepared questions for the audience will extend the presentation without too much extra work.

---

pro-Link
Presentation Jitters

What will happen if you forget your words in the middle of an oral presentation? Will you stammer and stutter? Will you look foolish in front of the audience? These are common concerns that presenters often face. Here are some tips to prevent you from becoming speechless:

- Use your computer presentation or overhead transparencies as your guide. These visual aids are not intended just for the audience; they are also for you.

- Keep a set of notes, just in case you need them. If you do, the worst thing that can happen is that you have to read your notes. You will find comfort in knowing you have notes to rely on.

- Know your topic so well that you are the expert—better, get passionate about the topic so you are the passionate expert.

- Ask yourself what is making you so nervous that you are drawing a blank. If it's a particular person in the audience, stop looking at him or her. Your eyes can glance around the entire room and still avoid a particular person or location.

- If your presentations are usually peppered by pause words such as "um" and "ah," it may be a habit you need to break. Try attending public speaking classes.

Self-Check
1. Compare constructive feedback with criticism.
2. How can you prepare yourself for a successful presentation?

ETHICS IN PUBLIC SPEAKING

When you speak to an audience, your audience must believe you to be credible, truthful, and qualified. Every statement you make, each figure you show, and each conclusion you draw must be supported by fact or based on credible information. Your audience will be attentive to your presentation, so ensure that your research has been thorough and that you are presenting accurate information. Use only information that you can confirm should someone question it.

What happens if inaccurate or incomplete information is presented? Consider the case of Olivia. As a guest speaker at a workshop, she presented information that she had researched. After she spoke, several participants came to her and said they were familiar with the research behind the topic she had presented and were offended that she had not given appropriate credit for the material. Olivia apologized for not identifying the source. Even though this error was not intentional, it may affect her future presentations with this group; her apology may not have been enough to rebuild her credibility.

Always give credit where credit is due, whether presented in oral or written form.

WRITTEN COMMUNICATION

Excellent writing skills are among the most important skills you can possess. The business letter is one of the main vehicles for transmitting messages between the organization and its customers. Additional written communication includes reports and requests for proposals, for example.

You need to develop techniques that enable you to write well, just as you would use effective techniques in developing interpersonal communication skills. The remainder of this chapter will address various forms of written communication.

BUSINESS LETTERS

The business letter is still the main vehicle for transmitting official messages to and from customers. An administrative professional skilled in composing letters may write replies and originate correspondence. Some of these will be composed for the signature of another person; others will be signed by the administrative professional as a correspondent for the organization.

Whether letter writing becomes one of your major responsibilities will depend on the letter-writing talent you exhibit and on your team's willingness to delegate the responsibility. Let the manager know that you are interested in composing letters, and give the manager a chance to see your ability. Occasionally, answer a letter that has just arrived in the incoming mail. Key a draft of your letter, attaching it to the letter you are answering, and put it on the manager's desk in the stack of incoming mail. Be certain not to delay the usual letter-answering process by hanging on to the incoming letter too long.

Communicate Effectively

Writing business letters is a significant endeavour. Think of the business letter as your organization's representative, going out alone to be the point of contact. Keep in mind that communication does not take place until the reader comprehends and responds to the message. Realize that the effectiveness of each letter you write depends on how well you have equipped it to accomplish its task. As you compose a letter, ask yourself this question: Will the letter get the results I am seeking? Although you may learn many guidelines for writing letters, recognize the significance of giving more thought to reactions and to anticipated results than to rigid procedures for writing letters. Figure 14-1 demonstrates two colleagues reviewing correspondence.

The person who writes outstanding business letters has learned to concentrate, weigh each word, anticipate the reader's reaction, and carefully organize every piece of correspondence to accomplish its purpose.

An effective business letter contains the essential facts. The words have been chosen precisely, and the sentences are grammatically correct and carefully structured. The letter indicates that the writer knows business procedures and policies and thinks logically. It delivers the message the sender intended.

Letters that convey a favourable message are organized differently from letters that convey an unfavourable message, and persuasive letters are organized in still another way. The basic principles for organizing different classes of letters are discussed as separate topics in this chapter. Certain qualities,

FIGURE 14-1 Excellent communication is necessary in both electronic and personal formats.

however, are common to all effective letters. Incorporate these qualities in all the letters you write.

An effective business letter:

1. centres on a key purpose
2. focuses on the reader
3. conveys a meaningful message completely, correctly, coherently, concisely, clearly, and courteously
4. reflects a positive, sincere, and appropriate tone
5. uses a natural style with readable, vivid, and varied language

Know Your Purpose

The purpose of a letter may be to inform, to create understanding and acceptance of an idea, to stimulate thought, or to get action.

Isolate the main purpose of the letter you are writing and develop your message around it. Make other points secondary to the main purpose; give the secondary points a subordinate position. Use one letter to do the job when you possibly can, but do not overwork your letter. Sometimes you will need a series of letters to accomplish one purpose. Unrelated topics that require answers should be presented in separate letters.

Focus on the Reader

Keep in mind that you are writing for the reader. Know who your audience is, and show consideration for that person. You can do this by putting the reader's needs first, emphasizing words and ideas that will be meaningful and of interest to the reader.

Try to put yourself in the reader's place. Get to know the reader through the letters in your correspondence files, and try to visualize the reader in the reader's type of business. When you are persuading readers to accept ideas or to carry out suggested actions, remember that self-interest is a potent force. In your letter, show the same interest in the reader's needs that you would if you were talking in your office or over the phone.

Convey a Meaningful Message

To ensure that your message will be meaningful to the reader, check it for completeness, correctness, coherence, conciseness, clarity, and courtesy (sometimes called the six Cs of business writing).

Completeness   If you are responding to a letter, in order for your reply to be complete your goal is to answer all the questions the reader asked or discuss all the subtopics mentioned in the reader's letter. When you are making a request, ask all the questions for which you need answers. When you are originating correspondence, always anticipate the background information the reader will need in order to grasp the full meaning of the message. Also, anticipate the questions the reader will have when reading your letter; include the response to these anticipated questions.

Correctness   Accuracy in every detail is **correctness**: accurate data in the content, perfect spelling of every word, flawless grammar and punctuation in every sentence, an absence of errors, and an esthetically pleasing arrangement of the letter on the page. Inaccurate facts will confuse and possibly irritate the reader. Furthermore, they will likely delay the response. Always try to eliminate the confusion and extra correspondence generated by inaccurate, incomplete, or vague information.

You could contend that a letter containing misspellings and incorrect grammar and punctuation can still be meaningful, and you would be correct. However, inaccuracy of any kind reveals carelessness. A customer would be justified in wondering whether an organization that carelessly misspells the customer's name and omits essential punctuation would be equally careless in manufacturing its products or rendering its service. Just as the sales representative must make a good first impression, so must your letter. The only contact the reader has with your organization may be by letter. Give all the letters you send out a chance to make that all-important first impression. Do this by displaying them in an attractive professional **format** and by ensuring that they are correct in every detail.

Coherence   The arrangement of words and ideas in logical order in representative of **coherence**. Words and ideas arranged in a manner that flows naturally within each sentence, within each main paragraph, and in the transitional paragraphs that hold an entire communication together. A coherent communication is woven together so carefully that the reader is always sure of the relationship of the words and ideas. Numerous writing guidelines exist. See the following list of some of the more important guidelines for achieving coherence in writing:

1. **Put modifiers next to the words they modify.**

   WRONG: The rough draft was mailed on May 9 that contains the original specifications in plenty of time for you to revise it.

   RIGHT: The rough draft that contains the original specifications was mailed on May 9, in plenty of time for you to revise it.

2. **Express parallel ideas in parallel form.**

   WRONG: Jessica's additional responsibilities this year have been writing letters and to handle travel arrangements.

RIGHT: Jessica's additional responsibilities this year have been writing letters and handling travel arrangements.

3. **Complete comparisons (or eliminate the comparison).**

   WRONG: The prices of the new homes in the Lakeside Addition are much higher than the Southside Addition.

   RIGHT: The prices of the new homes in the Lakeside Addition are much higher than the prices of those in the Southside Addition.

4. **Connect an agent to the right word.**

   WRONG: Before seeking applications for the position, a detailed job description should be written.

   RIGHT: Before seeking applications for the position, you should write a detailed job description.

5. **Place a pronoun close to a definite antecedent.**

   WRONG: Jason and Steve went squirrel hunting, but they were unable to find any.

   RIGHT: Jason and Steve went hunting for squirrels, but they were unable to find any.

6. **Use conjunctions in pairs to connect coordinate ideas.**

   WRONG: Mr. Arnett hoped to be transferred to Victoria or that he would remain in Halifax.

   RIGHT: Mr. Arnett hoped either to be transferred to Victoria or to remain in Halifax.

7. **Hold the same point of view.**

   WRONG: You either may deliver the claim papers to our branch office in Prince Albert, or they may be mailed to our home office in Regina.

   RIGHT: You may either deliver the claim papers to our branch office in Prince Albert or mail them to our home office in Regina.

Conciseness   To write concise messages, use all the necessary words, but no more. Send the reader a complete message, but avoid obscuring the thought with needless words. To distinguish between completeness and a profusion of words, watch for irrelevant details, obvious information, and unnecessary repetition of words and ideas, and then eliminate them.

Concise is not the same as *brief*. When you concentrate on brevity, you run the risk of writing a message that is incomplete or curt, or both. A good approach is to write the full message and then stop. Notice the contrast in the following paragraphs:

■ **Wordy:** Should any premium that becomes due not be paid before the expiration of the grace period, which in reference to the above-noted premium will be June 15,

20—, said premium automatically will be charged as a loan against the policy in accordance with the automatic premium loan provision contained in your policy.

■ **Concise:** If this premium is not paid before the end of the grace period, which is June 15, 20—, it will be automatically charged as a loan against your policy.

Sentences can become loaded with words and phrases that add nothing to the message. Wordiness detracts from the message by slowing down the reader. To write concise sentences, study your phrases and omit the needless words. Compare the phrases in the "wordy" list to the words and phrases in the "concise" list:

WORDY	CONCISE
A cheque in the amount of	A cheque for
At the present time	Now
During the year 1812	In 1812
For the purpose of providing	To provide
In accordance with your request	As requested
Make an inquiry regarding	Inquire about

Wordiness also results from the inclusion of expressions—often called *trite expressions*—that convey no meaning. They are obstacles to concise writing because they are used in place of meaningful words.

For example:

■ **Trite:** It is as plain as the nose on your face.

   Better: It is obvious.

■ **Trite:** Our staff meets once in a blue moon.

   Better: Our staff meets infrequently.

Clarity   Clarity in writing cannot be isolated entirely from completeness, correctness, coherence, and conciseness, but it does involve an added dimension: choice of words. Words have different meanings to different people. Therefore, you must choose words that will have the intended meaning for the reader.

To write a message that is understood is not enough; your goal is to write a message *that cannot be misunderstood*. Assume that if the message can be misunderstood, it will be; then make an effort to eliminate any chance of misunderstanding. This will force you to learn the precise meanings of words, to use familiar words, to explain technical words, and to avoid colloquialisms, slang, and coined phrases.

Words are symbols; they are tools of thought. Your goal is to choose words that will penetrate the reader's mind and create the image you want. To do this, you need a vocabulary large enough that you can select the word that will convey your precise meaning. You must understand both the denotation and the connotation of the words you use. *Denotation* is the explicit dictionary meaning of a word. The suggested idea or overtone that a word acquires through association, in addition to its explicit meaning, is referred to as its *connotation*. Avoid any word with a connotation that would be distasteful to the reader.

Write to express an idea, not to impress the reader with your vocabulary. This involves choosing words that are familiar to the reader. Avoid **colloquialisms**, slang, and coined phrases because they may not be familiar. The reader may not know the meaning you give a word or phrase and may have no way of checking on the meaning you intend.

Use a technical term when it conveys the meaning better than, any other word, but write so skillfully that the reader grasps the meaning of the technical term. First, use the term; then, explain it either in a phrase or in a subsequent sentence or paragraph. Here are illustrations of this approach from news stories; the same techniques for using technical terms can be applied in writing business letters:

1. **Descriptive phrase:** The president of the corporation envisioned a hypersonic plane *capable of flying 8000 km an hour.*

2. **Phrase set off by commas:** On Friday, the country's largest banks boosted to 11% their prime, or *minimum,* lending rates to large corporations, making the higher charge almost industry-wide.

3. **Phrase set off by dashes:** The minister underwent a tracheotomy—*a windpipe incision*—yesterday to aid his breathing.

4. **Subsequent sentence:** A total of five companies competed for the contract to install a local area network (LAN). A LAN is a system for communicating electronically among a number of PCs located within close proximity.

Courtesy   Your attitude towards the reader will have a noticeable effect on the tone of the letter. Even though your attitude is not described in the letter, it has a way of creeping in. Therefore, regardless of your feelings towards the reader, show consideration and courtesy by using words like *please* and *thank you.* Consider how different the following sentences might appear to the receiver. In the first, you are giving an order; in the second, you are asking.

1. You must tear along the above perforation and keep this portion for your records.

2. Please tear along the above perforation and keep this portion for your records.

Establish an Appropriate Tone

Your attitude towards the reader will have a noticeable effect on the tone of the letter. Even though your attitude is not described in the letter, it has a way of creeping in. Therefore, to set the appropriate tone, examine your feelings towards the reader. Show consideration for the reader. Reflect a sincere attitude.

The tone of each letter conveys appropriateness for the given situation. Whenever it is appropriate, write informally and radiate a warm, friendly tone. Be courteous and tactful. Do not write sentences or inject words that you will later regret.

One way to achieve tact in business letters is to replace negative words and phrases with words and phrases that are positive in tone. Watch for negative words; try not let them creep into your writing. Compare the tone in the following phrases. The italicized words in the left column are negative in tone. They have been omitted from the phrases in the right column.

NEGATIVE	POSITIVE
We are disappointed at your *failure* to include	We had hoped to receive your report
If you would *take the trouble to*	Please
You are probably *ignorant* of the fact	Perhaps you did not know
It is *not* possible for us to	We are unable to
We *must* ask that you send us	Please send us

Develop a Natural Style

Writing style is a distinctive way of expressing ideas. Develop your own style. Give your letters personality. Be natural. Sound like yourself in your letters. Write as naturally as you talk—not exactly as you talk, but with the same naturalness. Trade in stilted and time-worn phrases for natural ones. Compare the phrases in the following list:

STILTED AND TIME-WORN	NATURAL
As per our phone conversation	By phone
At an early date	(Refer to a definite date.)
Enclosed please find	Enclosed is
This will acknowledge receipt of your letter	(Refer to the letter by date.)
Under separate cover	Separately

To make your letters vivid, choose words that give life to what you say:

- Use active verbs, except when you want the statement to be impersonal.

- Make the subject of the sentence a person or a thing.

- Use specific, meaningful words. Use general or abstract words only when a concept has not yet been reduced to specific terms.

- Use familiar words and phrases in place of the unfamiliar.

- Use short words instead of long words. Here are some examples of short words that can be substituted for multisyllabic words:

MULTISYLLABIC	ONE SYLLABLE
endeavour	try
interrogate	ask
demonstrate	show
encounter	meet
purchase	buy
obtain	get

For variety, mix simple sentences with compound and complex ones. Choose the type of sentence that will most effectively convey the idea.

Careful writing will contribute to the readability of your message. To increase readability, control the length of the sentences and the arrangement of the letter on the page. The following are some suggestions for increasing readability.

Sentence Length   To change the pace and to increase reader interest, vary the length of your sentences. Write some short sentences and a few long ones. Short sentences are emphatic, but too many short sentences make the letter seem choppy and elementary. A few long sentences are effective, but too many of them will cause the reader to lose interest and will make the letter harder to understand.

Authorities who have studied sentence patterns have found that copy with sentences averaging 17 words in length is highly readable. For business letters, write sentences that average between 17 and 20 words in length. Do not attempt to limit the length of your sentences to 17 or 20 words; be concerned only about the *average* length of all the sentences in one message. Most software programs have a **grammar check** feature that will send a message when the sentence is too long or incomplete.

Arrangement   Arrange the letter on the page so that it is easy to read. Keep the paragraphs short. Try to condense the opening paragraph into four keyed lines or less. A one-sentence opening paragraph in a business letter is permissible.

Divide the rest of the letter at the logical points—that is, at the places where there is a change in thought. However, if a paragraph develops into more than seven or eight keyed lines, divide it into two paragraphs. Tie the letter together by arranging the ideas in logical order so that one idea naturally follows another.

If possible, vary the arrangement so that all the paragraphs are not the same length. End with a short paragraph. The end of the letter, like the opening, is a place for emphasis.

Self-Check

1. What are the qualities of effective letters?

2. What are the six Cs of business writing?

3. How can you increase readability in your business letter?

TYPES OF BUSINESS LETTERS

Most business letters fall into one of three distinct classifications:

1. a favourable message

2. a disappointing message

3. a persuasive message

Beyond these classifications, letters can be described as pertaining to appointments, requests, orders, routine replies, acknowledgments, follow-ups, notes of appreciation, and many more. Some require your manager's signature and others require your own. An effective letter must be planned. The classification of a letter provides clues for organizing it.

In order to supply a yes or no response, give an explanation, or speak convincingly, you must know what the organization's policies are concerning the topic being discussed. You must be absolutely sure that your reply reflects the current policy, not one followed at an earlier time or one that is being considered but has not yet been approved. If in doubt about a policy, always check to make certain your reply falls within the current policy guidelines of the organization. Correspondents who make statements that are not supported by, or are in disagreement with, the organization's policies can find themselves in embarrassing predicaments.

Incorporate the basic writing principles discussed here in your business letters. Use them as general outlines for organizing favourable, disappointing, and persuasive messages. You should not follow these principles rigidly; you should use them only as guides. You must alter them to fit each individual case and vary them to emphasize the specific purpose. You will find the favourable letter the easiest to write, for you know at the time you are composing the letter that the reader will be receptive to what you say.

Favourable Letters

Replies that carry a yes message, requests that you anticipate will be granted without persuasion, and goodwill letters are classified as favourable. You can use the following guidelines for writing all favourable letters:

1. Begin favourable letters directly with a favourable statement. Do not waste words getting the letter started.

2. Make sure the content is complete, correct, and clear.

3. Use a tone that reflects consideration for the reader.

4. When you finish the message, either stop or write an appropriate closing paragraph. Not all favourable letters need a specially prepared closing paragraph. Include one only when it improves the tone of the letter enough to warrant the time you spend composing it.

Replies   When you are writing a reply, establish in the opening that you are doing what the reader has asked you to do. State this in the first sentence, preferably in the first main clause. For example:

> Your antique eight-day clock, which arrived this week, can be repaired and adjusted to keep accurate time. It has been carefully inspected by our service department.

When you are sending something, say so in the opening lines. Thus:

> All 16 rugs that you ordered are on their way. Riverton Truck Lines should deliver them to you on or before March 27.

When you are partially complying with a request, establish in the opening sentence what you are doing; then use the rest of the letter to explain why you are complying with only part of the request.

Do not restate the obvious. "We have received your letter . . .," "This is an answer to . . .," "I am writing this letter to tell you . . .," and "This will acknowledge receipt of your report . . ." are not effective openings.

Check carefully that your reply is complete, correct, and clear. If the reader asked questions, answer every question, whether it was direct or implied. Whenever possible, make one letter do the job.

Some replies should end when the explanation is finished. When you write a closing paragraph, always end confidently. Avoid statements such as, "I hope that I have answered your questions," or, "I trust that this is the information you are asking for." An expression of willingness to comply, when it is used, is much more appropriate in the closing than in the opening. At times, an expression of willingness to comply can be used to avoid the possibility of sounding curt.

All replies should be prompt; delay is disappointing and detracts from a favourable situation.

Direct Requests   When you write a request that you anticipate will be granted without persuasion, make your major request in the first line of the letter. Do not hint; write directly. For example:

> Please send me a copy of your booklet, "Tips for Successful Management of a Word Processing Centre," which you offered to those of us who participated in the word-processing seminar you conducted in Quebec City on May 15.

If you use a subject line in your letter, do not depend on it to introduce the topic in the body of the letter. Instead, write the letter as though you had not used the subject line.

When you must ask questions, include all the questions to which you want answers, and arrange them in logical order. Word your questions to get the information you want. Do not imply that a yes-or-no answer will be adequate when you need a more complete answer. If you have a series of questions, number them so that they can be read quickly. Numbering them will also increase your chances of getting answers to all of them.

Provide the reader with an adequate explanation. If the explanation applies to the request as a whole rather than to a specific question, put it in a separate paragraph either before or after the questions. If, however, the explanation applies to a specific question, put the explanation close to the question it relates to.

When you are asking for confidential information, state that the information will be handled confidentially. Here are two examples:

> We shall appreciate you answering these questions and supplying any other confidential information concerning Mr. Green's managerial qualifications.

> All the information you supply us will be kept confidential.

Your title, plus a statement within the letter, should show that you have a right to be making a confidential inquiry.

In the closing paragraph, express gratitude cordially in first person, future tense: "I would appreciate . . ." or, "I would be grateful. . . ." Avoid thanking the reader in advance. It is appropriate to express thanks only after someone has complied with a request. Set a deadline if it is appropriate or if it will expedite the reply. Note the following closing paragraph:

The 20— directory of the Bridge City Chapter of IAAP is ready to go to press, and we want to include your name on the Education Committee. Please let me know by July 16 that we can count on you to serve on the Education Committee.

Special Goodwill Letters   Thank-you notes expressing appreciation for a favour or for special cooperation, congratulatory notes to a business associate on a promotion or to an employee on an important anniversary with the organization, and a welcoming note to a newcomer are examples of goodwill letters. These letters should be concise, appropriate in tone, and timely.

The letter must convey that the sender delighted in writing it. The most important single element common to all goodwill letters is timeliness: they must arrive promptly. (Timeliness and appropriate tone are also the two important elements of sympathy letters.) The following letter was used to congratulate a business associate on an important promotion:

How exciting to read about your promotion in this morning's edition of the Edmonton Journal. *Congratulations! Those of us who have worked closely with you know how much you deserve this promotion to executive vice-president. Best wishes for your continued success!*

Repetitive Favourable Replies   Save yourself writing time by speeding up the way you handle favourable messages. When giving the same response over and over, stop composing individual letters. The method you choose for replying will depend on the number of replies and the equipment and personnel available. Consider the following ideas:

1. When you are mailing a catalogue or literature about your products or services, either send it without a letter or enclose a preprinted letter. Make a note on the request that the literature was mailed.

2. Use a form letter, but print it individually for each recipient. Prepare the form letter (primary document). Then merge the date, inside address, salutation, and any other variable information with the primary document. Each form letter will have the appearance of a unique document.

3. Prepare and store form paragraphs. At the time you are answering the letter, compose only the opening and closing paragraphs. Then merge these new paragraphs with the stored paragraphs.

4. Macro functions may be used with software so that merging and printing a letter is a very quick and efficient process. The macro function allows you to program a series of instructions and store them under a single command. The instructions can then be carried out with a few simple keystrokes.

Letters of Disappointment

The letter of disappointment requires a lot of planning. Typically more words are needed to say no than to say yes.

Use the opening paragraph to reflect a pleasant, cooperative attitude. Perhaps you can agree with the reader on something. Begin closely enough to the subject of the letter for the reader to know that you are answering her or his letter. It often helps to think of a general statement you can use to begin the letter. Avoid stating the refusal in the opening, but at the same time, avoid giving the impression that the answer is favourable. Also, refrain from recalling dissatisfaction or stating dissatisfaction any more than is absolutely necessary.

If you are complying with a part of what was requested, either start with a discussion about what you are doing to comply or include this discussion in the first paragraph.

The opening paragraph, or *buffer paragraph*, should lead naturally into the second paragraph. Your opening paragraph will not be effective if it is not a natural transition to the main content of the letter.

Your explanation should be courteous and convincing. Give at least one reason for the disappointing news before you actually state it. Whenever you can, flush out reasons that are for the benefit of someone other than yourself or your organization. Make the disappointing news a logical outcome of the reasons you have presented.

Phrase explanations in impersonal terms. For example, say, "Your order was incomplete," instead of, "You failed to state the size of the sweaters you ordered."

To avoid delaying the disappointing news too long, do not give *all* of the reasons first; provide some of these afterwards. To improve the tone, subordinate the disappointing news; put it in the middle of a paragraph and in a dependent clause. For example: ". . . which we have not stocked for two years," or ". . . that are commercially unsuccessful."

When you are refusing a request, avoid leaving any room for doubt about the refusal. Do not apologize for the refusal. Eliminate negative words and phrases such as *impossible, must refuse,* and *very sorry to tell you that we cannot.* State what you *can* do instead of what you *cannot* do.

If you can suggest an alternative plan, do so at the end of your letter; then provide the reader with information on how to take up the suggestion. Otherwise, use an ending (often unrelated to the problem discussed in the letter) that will provide a pleasant tone.

The following three paragraphs are excerpts from a reply received by a teacher who had requested copies of teaching materials used in office administration courses. The first excerpt contains:

- a general opening statement
- an agreement with the reader
- a partial compliance

You can provide your office administration students additional employment opportunities by offering a specialized program for students interested in becoming executive administrative professional. I am sending you the associate degree requirements for the executive admin program at our college and a list of the topics covered and the textbooks used in each of four specialized executive admin courses.

The second excerpt contains:

- a courteous explanation
- a reason for being refused
- subordinated refusal
- additional reasons

The students purchase kits of practice materials that I have prepared for use in the executive administrative courses. Since I am planning to publish these materials, I cannot release them at this time. As the students use the materials in each kit, I make the essential revisions and hope to publish these materials, along with teaching suggestions, in the form in which I actually used them in my classes.

The third excerpt provides a pleasant ending:

Submit your proposal for an executive admin program for approval. If you have specific questions that I might be able to answer about the development of your program, please write to me again.

Persuasive Letters

Persuasive letters are enabled for selling products, services, and ideas. The informative office memorandum should also be persuasive; that is, it should persuade the recipients to accept the ideas or changes mentioned in the memorandum. When you write a job application letter, be persuasive; after all, you are selling your qualifications for a job.

Letters selling ideas can follow the same plan as a sales presentation:

1. Gain the reader's attention and interest.
2. Create a desire.
3. Convince.
4. Stimulate action.

Instead of beginning a persuasive letter directly, use the opening statements to get the reader interested in what you are saying. Wait until the second paragraph to start explaining your proposal. In the opening paragraph, avoid:

1. using a question that can be answered obviously yes or no
2. depending on an explanation to arouse interest
3. using obvious flattery to win the reader's attention

Use facts to convince. Give the necessary details to show that your request warrants consideration and action. Do not phrase the explicit request until most of the reasons leading up to it are stated. When you do make the request, state it directly; do not hint.

Maintain a tone of positive confidence. Do not apologize for your request, and do not supply excuses that the reader can use to refuse the request. When a negative element is involved, discuss it as a part of the explanation. Omitting necessary parts of an explanation usually results in additional correspondence and delay.

Close the letter by expressing appreciation and by restating the action you want the reader to take. Establish your appreciation cordially in first person, future tense. The recipient, having finished reading the letter, should know what is expected, how to do it, and the reasons for prompt action. If you have discussed these points at various places throughout the letter, you may need to summarize them in the closing. Discard generalities such as "early reply" and "at your convenience"; cleverly suggest a deadline.

The following four excerpts are from a persuasive letter about new parking procedures. Before the Miller Company purchased the parking lots, the employees parked on these same lots and paid high daily or weekly rates. Employees could park on any lot where they could find a space. In the letter, the Miller Company is asking each employee to cooperate by using the parking lot designated for him or her. The approach here is to point out the advantages that will accrue to each employee.

The first excerpt is designed to do the following:

- **Gain attention and interest.**

  Beginning Monday, June 1, you may park your car near the main office of Miller Company. The company has purchased seven parking areas near the main office to provide ample parking space for Miller employees.

The second excerpt is written to:

- **Create a desire to cooperate.**

  To assure each of you a parking space near the building entrance close to your work area, we have assigned employee parking by departments. The parking areas have been designated by numbers, and parking area stickers have been distributed to the department heads.

The third excerpt will:

- **Provide ample facts and make desired action clear.**

  To obtain entry and to park your car in a company area, obtain a sticker from your supervisor and display it on the lower-left side of the windshield of your car.

The fourth and final excerpt will:

- **Explain the benefit of action.**

  Using designated parking areas should result in a smooth flow of traffic around the main office of Miller Company and enable you to enter and leave your area with ease.

Correspondence for the Manager's Signature

Writing letters for another person's signature requires a special skill. It is not an easy assignment because the letter must sound as though the person signing the letter actually wrote it.

The letter that is the easiest to write for another person's signature is the letter report setting forth a series of facts. This is because the personality of the writer is not so apparent in factual reports. If the message is lengthy, another way to carry out the assignment is to write an informal report, accompanied by a covering letter actually written by the person over whose signature the information is transmitted.

When you have the assignment of writing letters for someone else's signature, study previous letters to become thoroughly familiar with vocabulary and style. Where possible use the same phrases; use the same salutation and complimentary close; and organize the letters in the same way. "Lift" paragraphs, making appropriate changes, from similar letters the originator has written. When feasible, prepare a draft of the letter and ask the originator to review it and make changes before you key the letter in final form. Be tactful; do not advertise that you are writing letters for someone else's signature.

Correspondence for the Administrative Professional's Signature

From the first day on your job, you may be writing correspondence for your manager and team members. As the need arises, you will write correspondence for your own signature.

In carrying out your daily work, you may find yourself writing letters that you sign yourself concerning such things as appointments, requests, orders, routine replies, acknowledgments, transmittals, delays, and follow-ups. For your **courtesy title**, use Ms., Miss, Mrs., or Mr. Use appropriate courtesy titles when you are addressing others. Ms. is a female courtesy title that does not denote marital status. Use Ms. for women who prefer it and for women who do not indicate a

preference. When a woman specifies her courtesy title, add it to your address list and use it. Do *not* use Ms. when a woman has given you another courtesy title.

Appointments   Appointments requested, granted, confirmed, changed, cancelled, and sometimes refused are a part of regular business procedure. Typically, appointments are handled entirely by phone, email, or voice mail. However, there are occasions where letters are required.

Letters concerning appointments should follow the same guidelines used when appointments are arranged by phone:

1. Refer to the purpose of the appointment.
2. Clearly set forth the date, day, time, and place.
3. Request a confirmation of the appointment when it is applicable.

When postponing or cancelling an appointment for an indefinite period of time, always express regret and suggest some provision for a future appointment. When you are postponing the appointment, suggest another specific date, and ask for a confirmation. The following examples illustrate different situations that arise when appointments are handled in writing:

- **Appointment requested; time suggested**

  Mr. Robert Arnet will be on the West Coast during the week of July 17. Scheduled to be in Nanaimo on Thursday, July 21, and Friday, July 22.

  Mr. Arnet requested and arranged an appointment with you concerning the production problems you described in your letter of July 7. Will it be convenient for you to meet with Mr. Arnet on Thursday afternoon, July 21, at 2 p.m.?

  Sincerely yours,

  Ms. Karen O'Brien

  Administrative Assistant to Mr. Arnet

- **Appointment granted; time suggested**

  Mr. Harrison will be glad to talk with you while you are in Charlottetown during the week of January 24. Will Wednesday, January 26, at 3 p.m. be convenient for you?

  Mr. Harrison is looking forward to seeing you again and to hearing the plans you have outlined for the Ritter project.

- **Appointment confirmed**

  Mr. Hanson will be expecting you on Thursday, May 15, between 10:30 a.m. and 11:15 a.m. in his office, Room 783, to discuss the need for improved shipping containers.

- **Appointment confirmed in manager's absence**

  Before Ms. Wilcox left on an out-of-town trip, she asked me to tell you that she will return on Thursday, June 12, in time to meet with you to discuss the need for temporary help in your area.

- **Change of appointment**

  Ms. Thompson has been called out of town on business and regrets that she must postpone your appointment with her for 9 a.m., Thursday, July 16. Ms. Thompson will be back in the office on Monday. She suggested Tuesday, July 21, from 9 a.m. until 10 a.m. as a time when she could see you.

  Please let me know if July 21 will be satisfactory. When you arrive, come directly to the fourteenth floor and ask the reception for Ms. Thompson.

- **Cancellation of appointment**

  Mr. Darnell suddenly was called to our Edmonton office because of the tornado damage to our plant there. He regrets that he cannot keep his appointment with you for Thursday, July 29, at 3 p.m.

  When Mr. Darnell returns, I will contact you in order to arrange another appointment that will be mutually convenient.

Routine Requests, Inquiries, and Orders

Use the suggestions presented earlier for writing favourable letters as a guide for writing routine requests and inquiries. Expect that the reply to your letter will be favourable. State the request or inquiry directly, include only essential information, and create a pleasant tone. These letters will be short. If the letter seems curt because it is too brief, add a sentence or two to improve the tone. Observe how these points are achieved in the following excerpts from letters:

- **Request for a publication**

  Please send me a copy of your booklet, "21 Ideas: Tested Methods to Improve Packing, Shipping, and Mail Room Operations." We are continually searching for methods to improve our mailing operations. We look forward to receiving your booklet.

- **Request for information**

  Mr. R. T. Wilson is interested in obtaining information about the notebook computer you have made available to your employees. Please send me the brand name of the computer and the name and address of the company that manufactures it.

- **Inquiry**

  Ms. Jessica Williams would like to purchase 125 copies of a booklet recently published by your organization, "Tips on Using Word-Processing Apps for Desktop Publishing." Is this booklet available in quantity? If so, what is the charge for 125 copies?

Orders are usually submitted on an order form. If you do not have an order form, include the essential information in a letter. Be sure to give the order number, quantity, an adequate description, the unit price, and the total price. When you are ordering several items, tabulate the information for easy reading. If you do not enclose a cheque, state how payment will be made.

Routine Replies

When a response is favourable, state it in the opening sentence. If you are declining a request, give at least one reason before you state the refusal. The message of a favourable reply carries a favourable tone; for this reason, even a brief message is effective. In a reply that may be disappointing to the recipient, add a sentence or a paragraph to cushion or soften the message.

When the reply concerns a meeting, repeat the date, day, time, and place. Following are some examples of routine replies:

- **Favourable reply about meeting**

  You can count on Mr. Stephens to attend the Area 5 Board of Directors meeting scheduled on Friday, March 24, at the Four Points Hotel, Kitchener, Ontario. Mr. Stephens plans to arrive Thursday night and anticipates his presence at the 7:30 a.m. breakfast meeting on Friday.

- **Favourable reply; material sent**

  We welcome the opportunity to furnish you with the Right-Way teaching aids you requested. The material is scheduled for shipment to you from our Winnipeg warehouse. If we may be of further help in your in-service office course, please let us know.

- **Request temporarily declined**

  Because of the heavy demand for the booklet "Guidelines for Today's Consumer," our supply is exhausted. This booklet is currently undergoing an update and in turn reprinted in quantity. I have recorded your request for eight copies of "Guidelines for Today's Consumer" and will forward them to you as soon as they are available. We appreciate your interest in this publication. If we can be of service to you in any other way, please let us know.

Acknowledgments

Most acknowledgments either state or imply that another communication will follow. The administrative professional often has the responsibility of writing acknowledgments when the manager is away from the office for an extended period.

Acknowledge correspondence promptly—preferably on the same day received. Be cautious about giving away business secrets; make statements about your manager's absence in general terms. Avoid making promises or commitments your manager cannot keep or would prefer not to keep. Make copies of the letters you refer to others and the letters you forward to your manager.

What you say in an acknowledgment depends on what you are doing about the correspondence. You can acknowledge the letter without answering it, supply the answer yourself, say that you are referring the letter to someone else for reply, or let the reader know that you are forwarding the letter to your manager for reply.

Other uses of acknowledgments are to let the sender know that important business papers have arrived and to confirm an order when the recipient is not expecting immediate shipment.

Following are examples of the many ways acknowledgment letters can be used:

- **Acknowledgment; letter not answered**

  Mr. Martin will be out of town on business for the next two weeks. Your letter, which arrived this morning, will be provided to Mr. Martin for his attention on June 3, the date he is scheduled to return to his office.

- **Acknowledgment; letter answered**

  Mr. Argyle has set aside every Wednesday afternoon to talk with sales representatives. Mr. Argyle is out of town on business, but he plans to return to the office on Friday of this week. He is glad to see you any Wednesday afternoon that is convenient for you. Please respond to set up a definite appointment.

- **Acknowledgment; letter referred**

  Your letter, outlining the difficulties with the equipment you recently purchased from us, arrived today. Mr. Chung will be out of the office for an indefinite time. In his absence, Mr. Walter Barbato, equipment specialist, is handling all of Mr. Chung's correspondence concerning equipment. I have referred your letter to Mr. Barbato, and you should hear from him soon. If you wish to call Mr. Barbato, his contact information is supplied below.

- **Acknowledgment; letter forwarded**

  Ms. Anderson is away on vacation. Since I do not know the title of her talk scheduled at the Third Annual Conference of Fashion Designers, and because your letter seems urgent, I forwarded it to Ms. Anderson. You should hear from her before your April 10 deadline.

- **Acknowledgment of business papers**

  Today we received the Substitution of Trustee and the Notice of Default in the case of Hamilton Life Insurance Company v. John R. Hilton, along with your confirmation of recording them. Thank you for recording these documents and returning them to us.

Cover Letters   A cover letter may be brief. It should, however, state what is being transmitted and from whom it has been sent. The cover letter often mentions a focal point or a major highlight of the attached report. Here is an example of a short covering letter.

- **Cover letter**

  Here is your copy of the report "Ten Years Ahead." Mr. Daigle asked me to send each member of the Camp Warwa Committee a copy of this completed report.

He requested that all members take special note of the section on fiscal restraint.

Notices of Delay   Because success in business depends on quality of service as well as quality of products, you may be asked to notify a customer whose delivery of merchandise will be delayed. In the letter, include an explanation for the delay, and tell the customer what he or she wants to know most—when the merchandise can be expected. Do not promise delivery by a date that your organization cannot meet. The following is an excerpt from a letter sent when the delay was only 24 hours:

- **Notice of delay**

  Your printing order for 20 000 customer order forms was arranged for shipment today. Unfortunately, because of a breakdown in equipment and the additional delay of obtaining a part for the machine from Dartmouth, we are 24 hours behind in our printing schedule. Our machine is operating this morning. We will ship your order forms tomorrow.

Follow-Up Letters   Write a follow-up letter when you have not received something promised or due, or when you have not received a reply to a letter after a length of time. Keep a careful record of missing enclosures and other items promised, and write follow-up letters to obtain them. Write follow-up letters also as reminders.

Be specific about what is requested. If you are referring to an unanswered letter, send a duplicate of it. Avoid making the reader feel at fault. Notice the core content of the follow-up letters:

- **Follow-up letter; missing enclosure**

  In your letter of May 16 to Mr. Balint, you indicated you were enclosing a biographical sketch inserted in the brochure for the 47th Annual Conference of RNA. However, your biographical sketch was not enclosed with your letter. Since the conference brochure is scheduled for printing by May 22, will you please send your biographical sketch in the next mail?

- **Follow-up letter; order not received**

  On March 12, we ordered 25 copies of your book, Management Under Stress. We have not received the books or an acknowledgment of the order. Since we need these books for a seminar that begins two weeks from today, please ship us 25 copies of Management Under Stress immediately. Mail the invoice to Mr. Arthur Shepherd, Director of Education, who will forward it to the accounting department for payment.

- **Reminder**

  Ms. Yates plans to use your report on basic changes in inventory control when she meets with the Executive

Committee on March 16. *This note is a reminder that Ms. Yates should have the report on March 14 in order to become thoroughly familiar with it before her presentation on March 16.*

- **Reminder; lapse of time**

  We have not received your expense report covering the period from October 1 to October 31. As you know, we cannot reimburse any of the sales representatives until all the expense reports for October receive approval by the comptroller. Unfortunately, our October report has gone astray. Please mail us another copy.

- **Reminder to confirm**

  This note is to confirm our meeting, Friday, May 31, at noon in the chamber of commerce dining room with the purpose of discussing membership activities in the Lethbridge Chapter of CMA for the coming year.

Appreciation Letters Many opportunities arise in business for expressing appreciation. Do not neglect to write thank-you letters. Be prompt in sending them, for they lose their effectiveness if delayed.

To let the reader know the letter was prepared especially for the recipient, be specific, as illustrated:

- **Thank-you letter**

  Thank you for sending your proposal for needed changes in the contract with dealers. Ms. Wilroy asked me to express her appreciation to you. Your proposal arrived in time for Ms. Wilroy to present your ideas to the Executive Committee, which meets this Thursday.

Self-Check

1. What are the three basic classifications of business letters?

2. What considerations are important when writing a letter for the manager to sign?

FORMATS OF BUSINESS LETTERS

With the efficiency of email messages and messaging apps, fewer formal letters are being prepared. Further, unless the letter is very formal, contemporary letters usually adopt a basic style. The most popular and recognized formats are the full-block and modified-block letter styles. However, it is important to note there are many acceptable formats for letters. The letters shown in this chapter are to provide context and a basic guideline to follow. When you are new to an office position, begin by following the letter style already used in the office. Once you have established some credibility, you may want to introduce one of the styles described in this section.

Organizational Document Style Guide

A style guide is a detailed document provided by an organization that outlines guidelines for the way the business brand is presented from both a graphic and language perspective. The purpose of a style guide is to ensure that everyone in an organization create a clear and cohesive manner reflective of the corporate style and ensures brand consistency with everything related to writing. Most organizations have part of the guide focused on the visual display in graphic form. Items such as letterhead, logo, and general branding trademark pieces relate to all documentation created inside the business. Another guide component will focus on the editorial part of documentation created within the organization. This part of the guide often lists key words of preference and templates or samples of various documents. Be sure to read the guide thoroughly and adopt the style presented by the organization.

Components of a Letter

To ensure a letter is complete, review the following common components of a letter accepted in business today:

1. **Dateline.** A dateline appearing below the letterhead. A date should appear on all letters for historical reference and when action is needed in a time-sensitive matter.

2. **Inside address.** According to mailable standards, a complete address of the receiver is usually keyed about four single lines below the date line.

3. **Salutation.** Often referred to as the greeting. The greeting tends to start with Dear Sandy or Dear Ms. Smythe.

4. **Body.** Typically commences two single lines below the greeting and contains the words making up the content of the letter.

5. **Complimentary closing.** Usually keyed two single lines below the body ending. Suitable closing phrases include "Sincerely," and "Regards," among others.

6. **Signature block.** The name of the letter signer. Usually keyed four single lines after the complimentary closure.

7. **Enclosure, attachment, and/or copy notation.** These notations may or may not appear on a letter, depending on circumstance. When enclosing or attaching something along with a letter, a notation is noted on the letter indicating this circumstance, such as the word "enclosure," usually two single lines after the signature block. Copy notation is included if the letter is copied to another person or organization.

FIGURE 14-2 Letter completeness checklist.

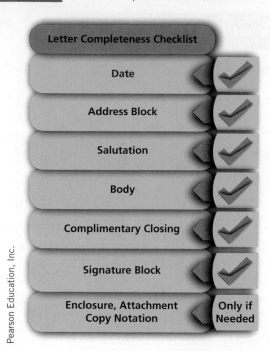

Letter Completeness Checklist

Date	✓
Address Block	✓
Salutation	✓
Body	✓
Complimentary Closing	✓
Signature Block	✓
Enclosure, Attachment Copy Notation	Only if Needed

Pearson Education, Inc.

Use this handy checklist when you prepare a letter to ensure all required components are included in your letters. See Figure 14-2.

Full-Block Letter Style

Figure 14-3 illustrates a full-block letter style. Note that:

- Every single line from the date to the initials begins at the left margin.
- Paragraphs are single-spaced.
- A double-space separates paragraphs.

Figure 14-3 demonstrates a two-point punctuation (also commonly known as mixed or closed punctuation). This popular punctuation style uses only a colon after the salutation, a comma after the complimentary close, and no other punctuation at the ends of lines outside the body. These are general guidelines; the spacing format will vary depending on software and templates used.

FIGURE 14-3 Full-block letter style with two-point punctuation.

Progressive Digital Innovations

3431 Bloor Street, Toronto, ON M8X 1G4

www.PDI.com

September 1, 20XX

Sage Jenkins
Director of Architecture Design
Abbotsford Contemporary Housing
100 Mountain View Street
Abbotsford, BC V2T 1W1

Dear Sage:

We are pleased to read about your recent promotion to Director of Architecture and Design at Abbotsford Contemporary Housing. No doubt, you will add to your already dynamic and progressive team.

Please call on me once you are settled. We should have lunch together and discuss a potential business opportunity. I am enclosing a brochure detailing our digital solutions.

Again, congratulations on your new role and good luck with your new challenges. I look forward to hearing from you.

Sincerely,

Olivia Ozam
Assistant Vice President of Marketing

lr

Enclosure

Pearson Education, Inc.

FIGURE 14-4 Modified-block letter style.

Progressive Digital Innovations

3431 Bloor Street, Toronto, ON M8X 1G4

www.PDI.com

September 1, 20XX

Sage Jenkins
Director of Architecture Design
Abbotsford Contemporary Housing
100 Mountain View Street
Abbotsford, BC V2T 1W1

Dear Sage:

We are pleased to read about your recent promotion to Director of Architecture and Design at Abbotsford Contemporary Housing. No doubt, you will add to your already dynamic and progressive team.

Please call on me once you are settled. We should have lunch together and discuss a potential business opportunity. I am enclosing a brochure detailing our digital solutions.

Again, congratulations on your new role and good luck with your new challenges. I look forward to hearing from you.

Sincerely,

Olivia Ozam
Assistant Vice President of Marketing

Pearson Education, Inc.

Modified-Block Letter Style

Another style is the modified-block letter. Note that the format is the same as the full-block style with the exception that:

- The date, complimentary closing, and signature lines begin at the centre and are keyed to the right of centre.
- Although not shown in Figure 14-4, the paragraphs are sometimes indented. However, the preference is to block them at the left.

> ### Self-Check
> 1. What is the difference between full-block letter format and modified-block format?
> 2. What are the seven components of a letter?

CLASSIFICATION OF REPORTS

Reports in an academic setting are generated:

1. to demonstrate research/data
2. to explain technical components or findings
3. to define experiments/lab work

Reports used in business are primarily:

1. to inform
2. to provide decisions and recommendations
3. to enable proposals, such as a request for proposal (RFP)

Mastery of report writing at the academic level will support business report composition. Some reports are prepared merely to keep a record. Much reporting consists of presenting data in statistical form. For the data to be meaningful to the reader, however, someone who understands them must interpret them to determine what they mean and to express their meaning in clear language. Consequently, reports are prepared for the reader's benefit.

Reports can be classified in many ways. Some reports are classified on the basis of function, others on the basis of form.

Reports that inform without giving conclusions and recommendations are called *informational reports*. Examples of informational reports are personnel booklets on employee benefits and progress reports on the construction of a new building.

Reports that present an analysis or interpretation of data, and that perhaps recommend action as well, are called *analytical reports.* Market surveys and analyses of business conditions are examples of analytical reports.

Some reports are specialized. The annual reports of corporations are financial reports to the shareholders, but in addition, these annual reports perform a significant public relations function. *Requests for proposals* are another example. Administrative professionals often have the responsibility of seeking out suppliers and providers of various products. This often requires the preparation of a request for proposal (RFP). The key purpose of an RFP is to transmit the list of the requirements for a project to suppliers who have the ability to provide solutions. The RFP is a written document that both you and the supplier use to establish your mutual understanding of the requirements.

Reports vary in size from a short, one-page memorandum to enough pages to make a thick book. Reports also vary in writing style and format. Some are formal; others are informal. Whether a report is formal or informal depends on the relationship between the reader and the originator, the purpose of the report, and its length. Informal reports, in contrast to formal reports, do not always follow a prescribed format.

As an administrative professional, you should first learn about the format and organization of reports. Eventually you will compose reports. The following sections discuss informal and formal reports.

INFORMAL REPORTS

An informal report may take the form of:

1. a letter
2. a short internal report
3. an email memorandum report

Letter Reports

Letter reports generated as both internal and external means of communicating information, analyses of data, and recommendations. Commonly printed on letterhead stationery, and their layout is the same as that of a letter. Letter reports may contain all the parts of a business letter, but sometimes the inside address and the complimentary close is omitted. Letter reports are signed. The name of the originator is keyed at the end of the report, with adequate space allowed for the signature. Reference initials appear on the letter report in the same position as on a letter.

Letter reports differ from business letters in two main ways:

1. Headings are often inserted in the letter report to guide the reader to the different points covered in the report.
2. Tables are often used to summarize data.

Much of the content of a report is factual. Facts are presented objectively, written without being filtered or influenced by the writer. An objective presentation removes all statements indicating personal opinions or impressions. To achieve objectivity, the writer presents the facts in the third person. However, a letter report can contain some statements written in the first and second person—for example, "*I* interviewed the managers of the Southern, Western, and Midwestern regions," or "Having studied the facts gleaned from these three managers and presented here, will *you* approve the recommendations contained in this report?"

A subject line may be used; if it is, it should appear immediately preceding the body of the report to serve as a title for the text of the report. Double-space before and after the subject line. The subject line may begin flush with the left margin.

The headings within a letter report may be either centred or left-aligned. For emphasis, they should be underscored, keyed in bold, *or* placed in all capitals. At times you may have to leave additional white space at the bottom of a page to avoid separating a heading from its text.

Formal tables have titles, called *captions* or *headings*. If more than one formal table appears in the same letter report, the tables should be numbered. The table number, such as TABLE III, should be in either capital or lowercase letters, but the title of the table should be in all capitals. Sometimes a subtitle is also used. Key a subtitle in lowercase letters with the first letter of each main word capitalized. The table number, main title, and subtitle should be centred. See Figure 14-5.

Arrange the data in the table in columns under appropriate headings. It will often be necessary to show the source of a table. Key the source a double-space below the last line of the table.

FIGURE 14-5 Numbered table with subtitle.

DISTRICT	DOLLARS THIS YEAR	DOLLARS LAST YEAR	DOLLARS INCREASE/ DECREASE
TABLE III COMPARISON OF DISTRICT SALES Information Technology			
Northern	300 000	350 000	(50 000)
Western	560 000	500 000	60 000
Eastern	725 000	700 000	25 000
Southern	300 000	345 000	(45 000)

When a letter report contains tables, spend some time planning the layout of the letter. Observe the following two rules for inserting tables:

1. When possible, an entire table should appear on the same page.

2. A table should be mentioned in the text before it appears.

Use 2.5 cm margins for letter reports. Key the second and subsequent pages on plain paper of the same quality and colour as the letterhead. Key a heading on each additional page, using a form acceptable for the heading of the second page of a letter. Indicate the subject of the report, the page number, and the date.

Short Internal Reports

Short reports used within an organization are formatted in an informal style. The tone as well as the organization of the report is informal; thus, first-, second- and third-person writing may be used in combination, and the report may be organized in a variety of ways. Informal reports differ from formal reports in length and purpose; however, the text of an informal report can contain the same divisions as the text of a formal report. Usually, the preliminary pages used in formal reports—letter of transmittal, cover, title page, letter of authorization, table of contents, list of illustrations, and other items—are not included.

An informal report should have a title and contain at least the following three divisions:

1. **Introduction.** The authorization for the report, its purpose, and the procedures and limitations for compiling the data are stated.

2. **A presentation of facts.** If the purpose of the report is informational, a presentation of facts is sufficient. If the report is analytical, a presentation of facts will include an analysis of them.

3. **Summary.** This may or may not include conclusions and recommendations.

A detailed explanation of these divisions is given in the section concerning the divisions of a formal report (see "Organizing the Report").

Informal reports are keyed single- or double-spaced, depending on how the reports will be used. The margins are even—2.5 cm on the right and left—because the reports are not bound.

Headings and tables are used to speed up the reader's comprehension of the report. The suggestions given for incorporating tables in letter reports may also be followed when tables are inserted in the text of informal reports. You have more leeway in incorporating tables in informal reports than you do in letter reports. If the tables are long, you can key each table on a separate page and then insert these pages, properly numbered, at the appropriate places in the report. Doing this will save time you otherwise would spend planning the text so that each inserted table comes at the logical point in the text and also fits on the page.

Informal reports often follow a deductive arrangement of ideas. In the basic format of the deductive arrangement, the conclusions and recommendations are presented first and the supporting facts are presented last. In many ways, the deductive arrangement is the reverse of the logical arrangement, which is the standard format for a formal report. The ideas in an informal report, however, can be organized according to either the deductive or the inductive (logical) arrangement.

Email Reports

The email report has largely replaced the traditional informal memorandum report as a means of internal communication. Email is always less formal than letter reports and can be written using a combination of first, second, and third person. Inherently, email has TO, FROM, DATE (automatically stamped), and SUBJECT headings, which in the past distinguished the memorandum from other forms of informal reports.

Because email is a computer-based document-distribution service, memoranda and documents are quickly copied from one computer to another. The growth, speed, and convenience of this medium require the user to exercise caution and forethought before communicating. Many unintentional problems occur as a result of overuse and inappropriate length of messages, failure to credit the original author of text, impulsive or inappropriate use, and simple poor communication.

The administrative professional should compose email with the same diligence as traditional memoranda in an effort to avoid many of the common problems associated with office email. Pay special attention to the following guidelines for using email:

- **Become familiar with the application.** Learn to use all features, including those that provide security and confidentiality.

- **Check punctuation and spelling.** Do not distribute an email document without proofreading for spelling and grammatical errors.

- **Ensure confidentiality.** Obtain permission of others before forwarding confidential content.

- **Do not assume privacy.** Emails are not secure. A good rule of thumb is that you should not send anything by email that you would not want posted—with your signature.

- **Special formatting.** Avoid the use of special fonts, italics, or bold type. Special characters are often read as emphasis and could be misinterpreted as adding an aggressive tone to your communication. In addition, if the receiver does not have that font, the text could show up with strange symbols or boxes.

- **Include a salutation.** If you would normally address a person as Ms. or Mr., use "Dear Mr. Jones" or "Mr. Jones" as your salutation. If you would normally address the recipient of the email by his or first name, you may use "Dear Ann" or "Ann." Avoid "hey," "hi there," or a greeting too informal in a business setting.

- **Use a meaningful subject line.** Recipients scan subject lines to determine the level of priority to the email. "Change in Policy" will not deliver as much impact as "Change in Vacation Policy."

- **Keep each email to one subject.** If you have two concerns to discuss, send two emails to ensure the email is not overlooked or ignored.

- **Flag an email as important only if it is.** If you use the email feature to flag all mail you send as priority, you run the chance of having all of your mail handled as unimportant since recipients will not take the top-priority notice seriously.

- **Copy only people who really need the information.** Don't reply to all. Reply to only the individual(s) who should receive the information, especially if the information should be kept private.

- **Avoid inappropriate language.** Use courtesy and tact just as you would in regular postal mail. Do not use swearing or offensive language. In some companies, email administrators are assigned the responsibility to check emails. You could be risking your job if you write something inappropriate.

- **Do not open suspicious email.** If the subject says, "YOU HAVE WON THE LOTTERY," do not believe it! Either delete the message without opening it, or if you are doubtful, inform your email administrator so it can be dealt with properly. The message will likely contain a virus that, if opened, could harm your computer. Also be cautious of emails that have legitimate-sounding subject lines, such as "Change in invoice" but have a link without the kind of text you would expect. Before replying or clicking on any links, click on the email address to see if it is coming from a trusted source or is masking another address.

FORMAL REPORTS

The format and writing style of a report are determined largely by its purpose and length. Reports moving upward to top management are more likely to be formal than reports moving horizontally between departments. Long reports are easier for the reader to follow when they are arranged according to a prescribed format. For this reason, formal reports, which tend to be long, usually follow a prescribed format. Note here that any report presented formally or informally depends on the preferences of the originator. The following discussion includes guidelines for preparing a formal report and for the proper arrangement of its parts, as well as suggestions for composing formal reports. Keep in mind as you review the guidelines provided in this chapter that many companies will have their own format that they will want you to follow. Some organizations prepare a style guide for all employees to follow when composing a report. Be sure to download the standard guidelines followed by any templates provided to develop the documents covered by the style guidebook.

Guidelines for Formatting

Your first encounter with a formal report will be when you key it. Someone else may compose the report, but it will be your responsibility to prepare in final form nearly all—if not all—parts of the text. You may also perform some of the necessary research for the report.

The material may not resemble a report when the originator first hands it to you. Take time before you begin the report to plan the layout and to itemize what is to be included in the final report.

Preliminary Steps Read enough of the report to understand its overall plan. Check all of the following items carefully:

- headings
- tables
- graphics
- accuracy of data
- possible inconsistencies

Ask questions such as these:

- Does the draft contain all the headings that are to be used in the final copy?
- Are the headings correctly flowing from one to another?
- Are headings at each level constructed in a parallel fashion?

An oversight concerning a heading usually results in the need to reformat more than one page. To avoid an oversight, list the headings in outline form and consider how they relate to one another. Headings of the same level should be of equal importance.

To achieve parallel structure, notice the parts of speech used in the headings. If one secondary heading begins with a present participle (an "–ing" word), *every* secondary heading must begin with a present participle. If one subheading under a topic is a noun phrase, *every* subheading under this topic must be a noun phrase. However, subheadings under a given topic need to be parallel *only to each other*—not to subheadings used elsewhere in the report.

Before you begin, decide which tables should be inserted on the same page as the text that refers to them, and which should appear on "stand-alone" pages.

Determine whether any graphics (charts, illustrations, drawings, or photos) are being prepared for inclusion in the report. If there are, how many, and where will they be inserted? All visual materials are treated as belonging to the numbered pages and should be numbered. Allow for them as you number the pages of the text. Make a list of them so that you will not overlook a page that is to be inserted as the report is being assembled.

If you have any doubt about the accuracy of the data in either the tables or the text, get verification. Statistical analyses in the text are often based on data provided in tables and charts; this means that one wrong figure in the basic data can affect several pages of analysis.

Word choice and format should be consistent throughout a formal report. Inconsistencies often occur when more than one person is responsible for the writing of the report and because a number of formats are acceptable. Be alert to shifts from one acceptable format to another. Select a standard style and be consistent throughout the report. Be alert, too, for poor grammar.

Margins   The margins of a report should be uniform after the report is bound. Allow 2.5 cm margins, exclusive of the part of the page used for binding. Leave extra white space at the top of the first text page. Twelve or so blank lines is the suggested amount.

Always begin a new major section on a new page unless the report is too lengthy. In this case, be certain to number all the sections.

Before you begin, you need to know how the report will be bound. For most reports, a binding allowance of 1.3 cm is adequate. If the report is to be bound at the left, use a 3.8 cm left margin, unless you have determined that it should be more. If the report is to be bound at the top, allow at least a 3.8 cm top margin. Also keep in mind that when the report is bound at the left, the margin allowance for binding affects all centred headings. Of course, when word processing is used, the software automatically adjusts for this.

Spacing   Formal reports may be either double- or single-spaced, depending on how the report is to be used and the preference of the author. Reports that are reproduced in quantity are often single-spaced and printed on both sides of the page to save paper and filing space. Reports to be mailed are often single-spaced and printed on both sides of the paper

to save mailing costs. A periodic report should be prepared with the same format—including the same spacing—that was used in previous reports.

Double-spacing should be used between the paragraphs of single-spaced material. Single-spacing is used in double-spaced reports to display a list of items.

Even when the report text is double-spaced, single-space the following:

1. quoted material of more than three lines
2. an enumeration that occupies two or more lines (double-space between the items)
3. a bibliographical entry that occupies two or more lines (double-space between the entries)
4. a two-line notation below a table indicating the source of the data, even when the table is double-spaced
5. tables that have headings, unless the table is very short or appears on a page by itself and needs to be expanded to fill the page
6. a title in the table of contents, in a list of tables, or elsewhere (exceptions to this guideline are the main title of the report, a chapter, or major section, where the heading is too long to occupy one line)

Paragraph Indention   Indent the paragraphs of a double-spaced report either 5 or 10 spaces to indicate where they begin. Five-space or 1.27 cm indention is most common. When using word-processing software, set the paragraph format to indent the first space of the paragraph automatically so that the indent is consistent throughout.

Since paragraphs in single-spaced reports are separated by double-spacing, paragraph indention in single-spaced reports is optional.

Subject Headings   Headings and subheadings are used to show the reader the organization of the report. They point the reader to where the reader has been and is going. A good heading should indicate clearly the content below it. Headings enable the reader to locate specific sections of the report and to read or reread only those portions of the report that supply the information the reader is seeking.

The form and location of a heading should make its relative importance clear at a glance. Headings for all divisions of equal rank must be in the same format and occupy the same location on the page. Each heading must either be in a different form or occupy a different location than its superior (of which it is a part) and its inferiors (which are its subdivisions).

Centred headings are superior to side headings in the same format. "All-caps" headings are superior to those with lowercase letters. Headings appearing above the text are superior to those starting on the same line as the text.

Headings should not be depended on as the sole transitional elements in a text. If all the headings were removed, the report should still flow easily from one section to the next.

Here are examples and explanations of headings most frequently used:

FIRST-LEVEL HEADINGS

The title of the report is the first-level heading. Since there is only one title, this heading should be written at the highest level, and no other heading should be written in the same form.

Second-Level Headings

Second-level headings are used to indicate the major divisions of a report. They are centred horizontally. The first and last words are always capitalized. So is the first letter of every other word, unless it is an article or a preposition of four letters or less. The heading is usually underscored and/or printed in bold type. There should always be at least two second-level headings.

Third-Level Headings

Third-level headings are used as subdivisions under second-level headings. They are usually formatted exactly like second-level headings, except that they are placed tight against the left margin.

Fourth-Level Headings. For further breakdown, fourth-degree headings are used. These are placed at the beginning of the paragraph on the same line as the text. They may be written in the same form as the second- and third-level headings. They should be separated from the paragraph by a period, and they should be underscored or printed in bold. They are often called run-in headings.

Fifth-level headings Can be handled as a part of the first sentence of the first paragraph about each separate topic, as illustrated by this sentence. The key words at the beginning of the sentence are underscored or printed in bold, but the sentence is written as a regular sentence. Only the first letter of the first word is capitalized.

When any level of heading is used (i.e., beyond the first-level or title heading), there must be at least two headings, If a section of a report contains only one heading and does not logically divide into two parts, write the entire section without subdivisions. Each section of a report is subdivided independently of the other sections; that is, third-level headings can be used in one section without being used in the others; fourth- and fifth-level headings can be used only where they are needed.

Two headings should not appear in a report without intervening text. Often, the discussion between headings of different degrees is a transitional paragraph that tells the reader what to expect next. Transitional paragraphs may be written last; for that reason, they are sometimes forgotten. When you are studying the layout of the report and find a heading that is immediately followed by another without intervening text, ask the originator to add the essential paragraphs. Or, better, compose them yourself and submit them for approval.

Page Numbers Number the pages in the preliminary section with small Roman numerals.

All pages of separate tables and graphic illustrations are counted and should be numbered when it is possible and attractive to do so. More than likely, the report will be collated and bound by someone who is not familiar with the report. Numbering all the pages is a guard against omitting and misplacing pages.

In the preliminary section, count the title page as *i* but do not print the number. Number the remaining preliminary pages *ii, iii, iv,* and so on; centre these numbers horizontally 2.5 cm from the bottom of the page.

When a report is reproduced on both sides of the paper (*duplexed*) and bound on the left, it is best to centre page numbers at the bottom of each page. If page numbers appear at the top right on odd-numbered pages, they should appear at the top left on even-numbered pages. When you choose to alternate the page numbers from left to right, remember that this will also alternate the running heads. A running head is a heading printed at the top of each page.

Tables Tables should be inserted in the text immediately following the paragraph in which reference is made to the table. A paragraph should not be divided by a table. A table less than one page in length should not be spread over two pages.

If there is no room on the page for the table to follow the paragraph referring to it, continue the text to the *next* page and insert the table immediately following the *next* paragraph.

A table that requires a full page should follow the page on which the reference to it is made. You can save time and avoid a last-minute rush by printing each table that almost fills a page on a separate sheet of paper. Following are the reasons why:

1. Tables are usually prepared before the report is written. You can prepare many of the tables in final form while you are working on drafts of the report. If you are not sure of the order of the tables at the time you are preparing them, you can number them before you print the final draft.

2. Preparing the text is faster when tables are not inserted on the page with the text.

3. Tables, because they consist of numbers and headings, can be keyed by someone else on different software and still harmonize with the prepared text.

All the tables in the report do not have to conform to the same spacing. That being said, tables usually are single-spaced. Treat each table independently, displaying the data in the most readable and attractive manner possible. A table may be landscaped (placed broadside on the page). When it is, the page should be numbered in the usual way, and the table should be inserted with the top at the left edge of the report.

Tables should be numbered or lettered consecutively throughout a report. When there are many tables, key the table number, such as Table III or TABLE 3, in either lowercase or uppercase letters. Centre it horizontally above the title of the table. Key the title in all-caps above the column headings. If the title contains a subtitle, key the subtitle below the title. The guidelines for arranging titles, subtitles, column headings, and sources in a letter report apply to all formal tables. By using shading and double-lines, and by changing the width of lines, you can create attractive tables.

Quotations

Short direct quotations of three lines or fewer should be enclosed in double quotation marks and incorporated into the text. The lines should extend from margin to margin. See the following example:

> The study concluded that "most customers preferred to deal directly with a company representative" (Lyons, 2009, p. 74). This conclusion supports our recommendation to hire additional support staff.

Direct quotations longer than three lines should be set off from the text, indented five spaces from both the left and right margins, and single-spaced. A quotation that is set off from the text is not enclosed in quotation marks. Refer to the following example:

> Lyons (2009) surveyed corporate clients from several different industries to determine their preferences regarding customer service. He arrived at the following conclusion:
>
> Regardless of their industry, most customers preferred to deal directly with a company representative. Survey respondents indicated that they were able to resolve their problems effectively and efficiently when customer service representatives replied to phone and email requests within three hours. (p. 74)

To indicate a quotation within a quotation, use single quotation marks if the quoted material is enclosed in double quotation marks. However, where quoted material has been set off from the text (and thus is not enclosed in quotation marks), use double quotation marks to indicate a quotation within a quotation.

Occasionally words are omitted from quoted material. This is permitted if the original meaning is not changed. An omission less than one paragraph in length is indicated by an ellipsis, which is three periods in a row. An ellipsis may be "open" (spaces between the periods), or "tight" (no spaces). However, there is always a space *before* and *after* an ellipsis.

Documentation

The proper documentation has the following purposes:

- Give credit to the source of ideas quoted directly or indirectly or paraphrased.
- Enable the reader to locate the quoted material.
- Lend authority to a statement not generally accepted.

In business and scientific reports, citations are often placed within the text. This is known as in-text citation. Do one of the following:

1. State the facts as naturally as you would if you were presenting them orally.
2. Use the author's name or some other reference to the source at the logical point in the sentence, followed by the documentation in parentheses.
3. Give the citation at the end of the sentence—either state the author, date, and page number in parentheses or refer to a reference list, arranged alphabetically, at the end of the report.

At times you will need to refer to a source named in your reference list. There are many acceptable ways to credit sources. One effective approach, using MLA style, is to state the author's surname and the page in the source from which the reference is taken. The following is an example of a quotation where the source is given credit.

> "People from other nations may be more attentive listeners" (Smithson 337).

This tells the reader that the quotation was extracted from page 337 of Smithson's book, which is listed in the works cited list.

Business reports often use APA style to cite sources. When using APA style for in-text citations, you should list, in parentheses, the author's surname, the date of publication, and the page number for the quotation you have used. The following is an example of an in-text citation using APA style:

> "This technique can be difficult for people to learn, because proper resources may not be available" (Smith, 2010, p. 207).

If you wish to refer to an author directly by name before quoting him or her, the date of publication should follow the author's name:

> According to Smith (2010), "Some people had trouble following the instructions, which prevented them from succeeding" (p. 207).

These parenthetical citations let the reader know that the quotations are from a work by Smith, published in 2010, which is listed in the references list at the end of the report. Refer to Chapter 4 for more information on both MLA and APA styles.

Preliminary Sections

Key and assemble the preliminaries of the report after you have completed the text of the report. Among the items placed in the preliminary section of a report are the following:

- letter of transmittal
- cover
- title page
- executive summary or **synopsis**
- acknowledgments
- table of contents
- list of tables
- list of illustrations

Examples of some preliminary pages are shown in Figures 14-6, 14-7, and 14-8.

Supplementary Sections

Materials that add to the report but do not belong in its text are placed in supplementary sections. The pages of the supplements are numbered as a continuation of the page numbers used in the report text. There are any number of sources that explain how to format supplement pages. If you need more detail than provided here, consult a current office reference manual or internet reference source such as *The Research Guide for Students.*

References   All sources used in preparing the business report are listed in the **references**, also called the works cited list or **bibliography** in academic reports. References you have cited in the text (see the section "Documentation") will necessarily appear in the references list, but in addition to those references, all work that you read but did not use directly in your report should also be listed. The reference list should include all references for information and ideas consulted in the preparation of your report. In-text citations are included in the reference list. A bibliography list all works consulted whether in-text citations are used or not. A report based entirely on the organization's own data (as numerous business reports are) would not have a reference list.

Material obtained from the web is noted in the list of references. However, some material found on the web is more "temporary" than that found in traditional publications, such as books, and should be cited with the date that you last accessed the information. Refer to the web entry on the example of an APA-style reference examples, Figure 14-9.

FIGURE 14-6 Sample title page.

MSS BUSINESS SYSTEMS INC.

PROPOSAL FOR

ADVANCED COMMUNICATION TRAINING

Prepared by

Amelia Jane Ross
Director of Training and Recruitment
MSS Business Systems Inc.

February 22, 20--

FIGURE 14-7 Table of contents.

TABLE OF CONTENTS

Topic	Page
List of Tables	iii
List of Illustrations	iv
Introduction	2
Establishing Guidelines	5
Identifying Training Needs	9
Identifying Positions Involved	15
Identifying Hardware Training	20
Identifying Software Training	26
Establishing Follow-Up Procedures	29
Evaluating the Project	35
Conclusions	37
Recommendations	40
References	50

APPENDICES

A - Graph - Cost of Program	51
B - Line Graph - Expected Learning Curve	53
C - Statistical Summary of Completed Questionnaires	55

ii

FIGURE 14-8 List of tables.

LIST OF TABLES

Table		Page
I.	Number of Memoranda Written to Employees	6
II.	Number of Questionnaires Sent to Departments	10
III.	Communication Difficulties Classified by Type of Hardware	23
IV.	Communication Difficulties Classified by Type of Software	26
V.	Areas Where Follow-Up Is Required	29

iii

Pearson Education, Inc.

A reference page appears at the end of the manuscript on a separate page or pages. Entries are listed alphabetically by the author's last name. Page numbers for reference entries are included only if the material cited is part of a larger publication, such as a book or journal.

As more graduate administrative professionals apply their skills to productive office work, traditional titles and headings for the supplementary sections are blending with those from the academic world. Though the titles and headings of supplemental pages may differ, the purpose remains to give credit to the authors of material from which you derived your information or ideas.

Appendix Supporting data that the reader will refer to while reading the report should be incorporated as part of the text; any additional supporting data should be placed in a supplementary section, called an *appendix*, at the end of the report. Examples of items placed in the appendix are:

- a copy of a questionnaire used in an investigation
- sample forms and letters
- detailed summaries of data
- graphs and charts

Not all reports contain appendices. When only one item is appended, its title is APPENDIX. If more than one

FIGURE 14-9 References for websites.

REFERENCE LIST CITATION

A specific page within a website	**Single author:** Freitas, N. (2015, January 6). *People around the world are voluntarily submitting to China's Great Firewall. Why?* Retrieved from http://www.slate.com/blogs/future_tense/2015/01/06/tencent_s_wechat_worldwide_internet_users_are_voluntarily_submitting_to.html **Multiple authors:** Nafees, Q., Yilong, Y., Andras, N., Zhiming, L., & Janos, S. (2014, November 19). *Anonymously analyzing clinical data sets.* Retrieved from http://arxiv.org/abs/1501.05916 **Corporate author:** Sea Turtle Restoration Project. (2006). *Threats to sea turtles.* Retrieved from http://www.seaturtleinc.org/rehabilitation/threats-to-sea-turtles/ **In-text citations:** (Freitas, 2015) (Nafees, Yilong, Andras, Zhiming, & Janos, 2014) (Sea Turtle Restoration Project, 2006)
Entire website	If you refer to an entire website, you do not need to include an entry for it in your reference list but must identify the source clearly in the text of your paper. For example: The Sea Turtle Restoration Project homepage presents a wealth of compelling, well-researched information on the struggle to save the world's sea turtles from extinction (http://www.seaturtles.org).

Source: University of Maryland. APA Citation Examples. Retrieved from http://sites.umuc.edu/library/libhow/apa_examples.cfm#websites

item is appended, each item should be numbered or lettered under its own heading: APPENDIX A, APPENDIX B, APPENDIX C, and so on.

The appendix begins with a cover sheet stating the appendix number and the contents of the appendix. (See Figure 14-10.)

The appendices are the final items of the report. They follow the references. Each appendix, along with the page number on which it begins, is listed in the table of contents. Refer back to Figure 14-7.

Guidelines for Composing the Report

Your first step in preparing a formal report should be to study the purpose of the report to determine precisely what the expected outcome is. You should be able to state the purpose of a report in one clear sentence.

Next, list the problems that must be solved in order to achieve the purpose of the report. The answers to the problems to be solved will become the main text, or body, of the report.

Do your research thoroughly and accurately. The content presented in the body of the report will be the result of one of the following:

■ an analysis of data on the organization's operations

- secondary research, which is information gleaned from published sources
- primary research

The methods of primary research are:

1. observation
2. questionnaire
3. interview
4. experimentation

In other words, to obtain your facts you may need to carry out an investigation, conduct interviews, confer with a few authorities, send out questionnaires, analyze existing data, and/or do bibliographical research.

Before you begin writing, review the purpose of the report to make sure you have arrived at solutions to all parts of the problem. Those solutions will form your conclusion. Also, check the accuracy of your facts and figures.

Organizing the Report Give your report a title that is broad enough to encompass all the topics presented in the report. Divide the report into at least three main divisions:

1. introduction (see Figure 14-11)
2. body
3. summary

FIGURE 14-10 Appendix cover sheet.

APPENDIX A

Graph showing cost of program

Page 51

Pearson Education, Inc.

FIGURE 14-11 Introduction to a formal report.

A COST ANALYSIS FOR MAINTAINING TERMINALS DURING A THREE-YEAR PERIOD

As authorized by Mrs. Monica Pascini, Manager of Financial Services, MSS Business systems, we have analyzed the cost of repairing terminals at ABC Insurance during a three-year period. The methodology used in this analysis compared the cost of maintaining terminals on a per-call basis with the cost of maintaining the same terminals under a service contract. The results indicate the most cost-effective method of terminal maintenance for ABC Insurance.

Procedures Used for the Analysis

The data on the maintenance cards for the 2063 terminals and the 2263 terminals used in the offices of ABC Insurance were analyzed.

Maintenance Study for the 2063 Terminals

The installation of the 2063 terminals took place in January of 20--; therefore, the study was limited to maintenance during the last three years. Twenty-four 2063 terminals were a part of this study. Terminals that were kept for standby situations were not included. The cost of preventative maintenance was analyzed as a separate item.

The provisions and costs of three service contracts were obtained from three local companies. Copies of these contracts may be found in Appendix A of this report.

In some respects, the study of these workstations was in less detail than the study of the 2263 terminals

Maintenance Study for the 2263 Terminals

Because the 2263 terminals were installed in March of 20--, we were able to collect more extensive data on these particular workstations.

At this time, there are no 2263 terminals that are considered as standby equipment; therefore, all 2263 terminals were included in the analysis. Fifty-one such terminals are currently in use with this company.

Five service contracts among three different companies were obtained and used for the study. Copies of these reports are included in Appendix B of this report.

Pearson Education, Inc.

Next, prepare an outline for the body of the report. Each problem you solve should become a separate division or subdivision of the body. Assign an appropriate heading to each one.

Use a logical arrangement of ideas. State the problem and how the study deployment occurred. Take the reader systematically, in logical order, through all the procedures you followed to arrive at the conclusion. Use facts to convince the reader. Present all the facts, and use tables and graphics to make it easy for the reader to grasp the facts. Lead the reader logically from the facts to the conclusion or conclusions. Any recommendations you make should be a logical outcome of the conclusions.

Writing the Report   Reports must be factual and impersonal; therefore, they should be written in the third person. Strive for objectivity. Do not let "we," "I," and "you" detract from the objectivity of the report. Another way to achieve objectivity in writing is to report statistical findings, for example:

Sales in the first quarter of 20— were $77.9 million, a gain of 15% over the $67.8 million in the previous year's first quarter.

Avoid using words or phrases that reflect your reaction to the findings. Instead of saying, "It is interesting to note that the increase in net profit closely parallels the increase in sales," make a direct statement about the relationship between sales and net profit for the period. A more objective way of expressing this would be, "There is a direct relationship between the increase in sales and the increase in net profit."

Write as much of the report as possible in the present tense. A combination of past and present tenses may be used. The discussion about how the study, investigation, or analysis conducted is expressed in past tense to show the reader that the work is completed, not still in progress. Some business reports express past tense because the facts reported were true only on a given day or for a definite period. Examples of such reports are accounting reports, such as the balance sheet and the profit-and-loss statement.

When describing conditions that definitely have changed since the day the facts collected, use the past tense. Use the present tense to describe conditions that will still exist after the report is finished.

Write first the part of the report that is easiest for you to compose. Consider each main division and each subdivision as a separate topic. Most of the time, you can develop these topics in any order.

Before you begin developing a topic, carefully check data related to the topic. Next, list your subtopics in the order that you will present them. Prepare the tables and graphics you will use to illustrate the topic you are writing about. Carefully label all the columns of your tables and graphics. You can work from a draft or a sketch while these graphic illustrations are prepared in final form, but keep copies of the illustrations in front of you as you write.

The graphic illustrations belong in the text of the report. Introduce the reader to each illustration before it appears by referring to it in the report. You may want to assign numbers to tables and letters to graphics in order to avoid confusion.

After you introduce a table or graphic, take the reader completely through it, to help the reader understand the concept illustrated. Avoid constructions such as "Table 3 shows . . ." or "Chart 4 illustrates. . . ." Instead, begin sentences with the subject of the table or chart. Example: "A sharp increase in computer sales is illustrated in Chart 4."

Avoid beginning sentences with "There. . . ." You can strengthen the report by placing the key word of the topic being discussed in a prominent position at the beginning of the sentence. For example: "Telecommunications has made global business a reality."

Write your report so that the reader can grasp the important facts from the written copy without having to study the graphic illustrations. The reader should not have to read the headings to understand the topic.

A well-written report will be clear and meaningful even when all the headings and illustrations are removed.

Interpret data at appropriate points so that they will be meaningful to the reader. Tell the reader what the facts mean in a natural, logical way. For the most significant data, give both the figures and percentages, or other computations. By interpreting the data, you will be presenting a picture, not just a string of data. Present the data to the reader systematically in the same logical order you followed when analyzing them.

Summarize your facts in the final section of the report. If you provided a summary sentence or paragraph as you developed each main topic, restate the content of the interim summaries in the last section of the report. Do not include new facts or new interpretations in the summary section. The conclusions and recommendations, if you write them, belong in the summary section and should be the logical outcome of the facts presented in the report. Make sure the recommendations relate to the conclusions. At the time you provided the assignment, establish whether you are expected to include recommendations. Sometimes when an executive assigns a report to a writer, the executive prefers to write the recommendations.

Usually more than one solution exists for a business problem. In the summary section, present all the alternatives.

Present the most feasible alternative first; then present the others in any order, or in decreasing order of feasibility.

If you require a synopsis at the beginning of the report, write a synopsis and place it in the preliminary section of the report immediately preceding the first page of the text. When you include a synopsis, do not change the summary section; both belong in the report.

The introduction to the report is composed either first or last. The introduction should be brief. Subheadings are optional. Write the purpose of the report and the authorization in the opening paragraph without a heading other than the title of the report. In the paragraphs that follow, describe the methods of collecting the data and the scope and limitations of the study. Using the outline of the text of the report, list the topics in a paragraph in the same order in which they will be discussed in the report.

Read the entire report through from beginning to end at one sitting to examine how all the parts relate to one another. Do you need to add transitional paragraphs or sentences? Transitional paragraphs are guideposts that introduce what is coming next. They give direction to the reader. They are often written after the draft of the report proper is finished; in fact, it often saves time to write them last, because you can compose them more easily when you know precisely what you are introducing.

Writing the Letter of Transmittal
The letter of transmittal should do the following:

1. Transmit the report.
2. Refer to the authorization (or request).

The letter of transmittal should indicate why the report was prepared; for that reason, the subject of the report, the authorization or request, and the date of the authorization or request should be included. These facts can be stated in the opening of the letter. Refer to the following three examples:

1. Here is the report on the web, television, and radio advertising possibilities that you requested on June 24.
2. In accordance with the authorization given in your letter of May 11, 20—, I have completed the branch plant location survey of Windsor, Ontario, and I am submitting a detailed report of my findings.
3. Following the instructions contained in your letters of July 2, 20—, and August 22, 20—, I am submitting the data you will need for selecting a brand of car to replace the two-year-old models now in the sales fleet.

The letter of transmittal should be factual. It should be written in a direct style because the main message is a positive one. Do not use the letter of transmittal to persuade the reader to accept your conclusions, and do not use it to defend your findings.

You may write in an informal style, using first person, even if the letter accompanies a report written entirely in the third person. You may use the past tense in the letter to show that the report is completed, thus:

I presented the analysis of the compact cars first because of the cost savings. In the second section of the report, I have made a detailed comparison between compact and medium-sized cars.

Letters of transmittal are usually short. Even so, they can also serve the following purposes:

1. Show the purpose of the investigation and of the report.
2. Indicate how the facts were collected.
3. Give significant findings.
4. Orient the reader to the report.
5. State the scope and the limitations of the report.
6. Point out special problems or special considerations.
7. Mention whether the report marks the completion of the investigation or is a progress report.
8. State conclusions if it is feasible to do so.
9. Call attention to another study or investigation that is needed.

Arranging the Report
Reports may be arranged according to any of the following styles: inductive, deductive, or chronological.

The **inductive** arrangement is used when a report is lengthy, when it is difficult to understand, or when the reader must be convinced of something. The arrangement of ideas is in a logical order. The reader is systematically brought through all phases necessary to arrive at the conclusion.

The **deductive** arrangement used when the writer knows that the reader will be receptive to the findings in the report. Executives prefer reports organized by the deductive arrangement because they are easy to read. Because the significant findings appear at the beginning, the executive can read the first part only or the first part plus selections from the supporting data.

The content of a report is the same whether it is arranged inductively or deductively; only the arrangement of ideas differs. The elements in a deductive arrangement are usually presented as follows:

1. an introduction, which includes the purpose of the report, the authorization, and how the study was conducted
2. a summary of the findings and conclusions
3. the recommendations, if any are given
4. the supporting data

Variations of this outline may be used.

Some reports consist mainly of historical background to a problem. When you must refer to situations that occurred at different times over an extended period, the best way to organize the report may be according to the time sequence, using the dates as the subheadings.

Chronological reports are easy to write but difficult for the reader to comprehend. The chronological arrangement does not help the reader see how the parts of the report relate to the problem. For this reason, do not use the chronological arrangement when you can organize the data inductively or deductively.

Self-Check

1. When is an informal report the best option?

2. Why is it important to study the purpose of a formal report before beginning the report?

3. What should be included in the preliminary sections of a formal report?

ETHICS IN WRITING

Many businesses today have a written code of ethics that encompasses everything from ethics in business practices to ethics in receiving and writing email. Whether or not your employer operates under a *written* code of ethics, use the following guidelines to ethical standards in your writing:

- Make certain the information included in your writing is correct. Verify that your source is a credible one.

- Keep confidential information away from prying eyes. Place sensitive information in a folder when you are not working on it rather than just in your in-basket or on your desk where others might read it.

- Ensure the information you write is your own. Always give credit where credit is due when you use others' work.

- Never violate copyright laws. A copyright identifies the legal right of authors or artists to protect their work against unauthorized reproduction. Make certain you have the permission to use copyrighted material before you copy it.

Maintain integrity in your communications. Everyone in the organization is accountable for their actions, including you as an administrative professional. Never agree to cover for someone else's mistake that might compromise your position. Ensure that you know where the information you work with comes from, and keep supporting documents should you be asked to justify or verify information.

INTERNATIONAL CORRESPONDENCE

You cannot assume that all the rules you have learned about business writing in Canada apply to other countries. Just as you must recognize the differences in cultures, you must recognize and adjust to the differences in rules for writing in those cultures. With the globalization of our economy, your learning must include international information to build your skills in this area.

Addressing Envelopes

When addressing envelopes to countries outside Canada, type the entire address in all capital letters. The postal delivery zone should be included with the city, when required. The country name must be typed in English, in all capital letters, and as the only information on the last line. Do not abbreviate the name of the country. For example:

> MR THOMAS CLARK
> 117 RUSSELL DRIVE
> LONDON W1P6HQ
> ENGLAND

Correspondence being sent to the United States will have *UNITED STATES OF AMERICA* as the last line of the address.

Writing Letters

Many Canadian companies have offices or plants outside Canada or do business with international companies, and it is highly likely you will encounter letters from outside the country. Letters from abroad are translated to English before being sent to your company. The wording may differ greatly from what you have learned in this chapter or in a Business Communications class. For instance, the usual format for a letter written in Canada that gives bad news to the reader would begin with a neutral first paragraph that softens the blow by reviewing the facts leading to the bad news; then there would be an expression of the bad news; finally, a polite closing would be included to maintain rapport with the reader. In Germany, however, the buffer might be omitted, going right to the bad news. In Latin America, the letter might avoid the bad news altogether. In Japan, the letter may present the bad news so politely that someone from Canada wouldn't even recognize it.

Be aware that misunderstandings are possible, not only in the different writing styles but also in the translation from one language to another. It is sometimes difficult for translators to find the words to exactly describe a sentiment being expressed by the writer, and the message delivered may not be exactly as intended. The more opportunities you have to read and analyze business letters from abroad, the more you will become familiar with the differences in style and wording. Here is a beginning sentence from the translation of a Spanish letter into English.

I am grateful for the opportunity to write to you to offer you my catalogue. . . .

If you received this business letter from someone in Canada, you might consider the language flowery and wordy.

We would say, "Thank you for requesting our catalogue. . . ." Yet again, if the letter came from Germany, the writer would likely be more straightforward and say, for example, "We are enclosing our catalogue. . . ."

Your acceptance of cultural diversity should extend to business letters from abroad. Be patient, tolerant, and understanding, and remember that the sender's culture is different from your own. This difference is reflected in both the writing and formatting of the correspondence.

QUESTIONS FOR STUDY AND REVIEW

1. Detail examples of documentation prepared in business.

2. Explain two guidelines for coping with the fear of giving oral presentations.

3. Discuss two methods for preventing the anxiety caused by presentation hazards.

4. What nonverbal messages are conveyed through the amount of personal space you provide others?

5. Describe how eye contact can make the receiver feel comfortable or uncomfortable.

6. Discuss how posture can send a message of interest or disinterest.

7. Why are facial expressions considered a universal language?

8. Suggest two ways to improve listening skills.

9. Suggest how an administrative professional can take initiative in replying to correspondence.

10. List qualities common to all effective letters.

11. When the writer is originating correspondence, what guidelines should be used to check the completeness of the message?

12. What is achieved through coherence in a communication?

13. Compare conciseness with brevity.

14. Compare connotation and denotation.

15. Summarize the techniques for using technical words effectively in business letters.

16. State the requirement for an effective opening sentence in a favourable reply.

17. What can the writer say to let the reader know that confidential information will be protected?

18. What is the most important single element common to all goodwill letters?

19. When should the actual request be stated in a persuasive letter? How should the request be phrased?

20. Contrast the following letter styles: full-block and modified-block.

21. What are the primary uses of business reports?

22. What guidelines concerning parallel structure should you follow when composing headings?

23. Explain the main differences between fourth- and fifth-level headings.

24. What guidelines are followed for keying direct quotations of fewer than three printed lines? What are the guidelines for more than three printed lines?

25. Describe the ordering of the supplementary sections in the report.

26. What are the differences between an in-text citation and a reference page?

27. What is the difference between works cited/references and bibliography pages for academic reports?

28. State the guidelines a report writer should follow to help the reader understand the tables, charts, and graphs used in a report.

29. Compare the inductive and deductive arrangements of reports.

Key Terms

bibliography 305

casual day 281

chronological 310

cite 304

clarity 287

coherence 286

colloquialism 288

concise 287

correctness 286

courtesy title 293

deductive 309

format 286

grammar check 289

inductive 309

interpersonal communication 279

personal space 281

reference 305

self-confidence 281

synopsis 305

EVERYDAY ETHICS

The Computer

Your supervisor, Mr. Sims, Vice-President of Sales, has been away for three weeks on vacation and still has another week to go. You have been able to keep up with replying to a variety of inquiries, when needed, on behalf of Mr. Sims. Today, you receive a letter of complaint from a customer named Ms. Jans about a computer she recently purchased at one of your company's stores. The customer tried to return the computer to the location where she purchased it, but the store manager would not accept the return and told the customer that there was nothing wrong with the computer. In frustration, the customer has written to your office looking for resolution. Ms. Jans's complaint is that the computer is taking too long to start up.

You believe this can be quickly resolved by offering to replace the computer Ms. Jans bought with another model your company sells. In fact, your company sells three different models, each with its own unique specifications. It is a very busy day, but you want to prove to Mr. Sims that you can resolve any issue. Without confirming the specifications of the alternative computer, you draft a letter to Ms. Jans offering her the exchange. You mail the letter today.

■ What are the potential problems with your action?

Problem Solving

1. You are eager to write letters, and the manager needs help to keep up with the correspondence. This morning as you processed the mail, you selected six letters that you believed you could answer satisfactorily and put them in your desk drawer. At about 11 a.m. a customer called the manager and asked if he had received the letter that the customer had written to him. Your manager asked you about the customer's letter. You had to admit that you were attempting to answer it. What did you do wrong? What would be a better plan for getting an opportunity to write letters?

2. The manager, Kathy Shapiro, left you an email with an attachment. Her email asks you to have 12 copies of the attached report ready by 8:30 a.m. tomorrow. The report needs to be edited, and tables need to be inserted. The tables are computer printouts that have been left on your desk. Kathy is out of the office for the day. With your normal daily workload—opening the mail, answering the phone and email, and handling clients—you cannot complete the report before tomorrow morning. What should you do?

Special Reports

1. Obtain information about two similar office products that you have seen advertised in an office technology magazine or on the web. Develop and write an informal report comparing the two products. Present both the final report and your rough development work to your instructor.

2. Imagine that you are employed in a professional office where the office manager is out of town for two weeks. Before she left she provided you a proxy to her email, which you can access. However, you are not to answer the emails; simply acknowledge them. Draft an email message you can use as a guide for acknowledging the office manager's emails in her absence. Your manager does not wish to have an automated response in her outlook set out; she wants you to personally respond in real time.

3. Consider the excerpts from (i) a letter of disappointment and (ii) a persuasive letter addressed in the chapter. Rekey these excerpts and identify the component parts according to headings in the text. For example, which sentence or phrase is the "general opening statement"? Which is the "subordinated refusal"?

PRODUCTION CHALLENGES

14-A Writing a Letter of Request

Supplies needed:

- *The web*
- *Plain paper*

You want to know more about desktop publishing. Search the current website for information about desktop publishing equipment and/or software. Write a letter to a vendor of desktop publishing software requesting information. Submit the letter to your instructor.

14-B Preparing the Final Draft of a Manuscript

Supplies needed:

- *Draft for Work Improvement Methods, 14-B on Companion Website*
- *Plain paper*

Linda Yee is preparing an article on work improvement methods for publication in the company magazine. Key the manuscript in Form 14-B in final format using edits indicated to make changes. Watch for all formatting, grammatical, and spelling errors. Use double-spacing; print one copy for Mrs. Yee's files. Note: More error and formatting corrections are required than those indicated by Mrs. Yee, and you are responsible for making the article error-free.

14-C Correcting a Letter

Supplies needed:

- *Letter for Correction, Form 14-C, on Companion Website*
- *Common Proofreaders' Marks, on Companion Website*

You were experimenting with your new software and quickly keyed a letter. You were not pleased with what you printed and decided to mark the corrections with your pen. The letter you keyed is Form 14-C. Mark the corrections needed using your pen and the Common Proofreaders' Marks.

Weblinks

Grammar Slammer
http://englishplus.com
This site contains a number of links to English grammar and composition reference materials.

A Research Guide for Students
www.aresearchguide.com
This site provides all the necessary tools to do research and to present your findings.

Intelligent Editing
http://www.intelligentediting.com/writingastyleguide.aspx
This site provides practical information on how to design a style guide for your organization.

The Balance Careers
www.thebalancecareers.com
Visit this site for a practical guide to business-related items from career issues and report writing.

Chapter 15
Office Commerce and Record Keeping

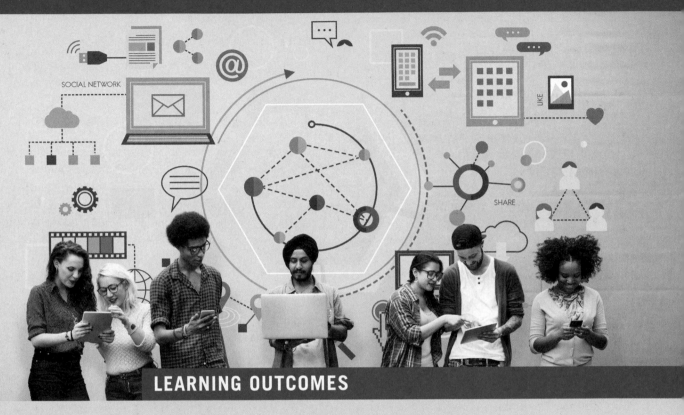

Rawpixel.com/Shutterstock

LEARNING OUTCOMES

After completion of this chapter, the student will be able to:

1. Describe ecommerce and understand functions related to financial transactions.

2. Recognize privacy matters related to financial transactions.

3. Define technical terms related to financial transactions.

4. Prepare cheques and compare endorsement formats.

5. Explain bank statement reconciliation processes.

6. List the standard protocol for maintaining a petty cash fund.

7. Describe payroll processing, including mandatory deductions and calculations.

8. Explore the administrative professional's role in budget preparation.

Handling office commerce is one of the more typical duties of the administrative professional who works for a private company or for a small office such as a physician's office. This part of the administrative role includes handling banking transactions, payments received, bank deposits, cheque management, bank reconciliations, and, in some instances, payroll. When a business engages in commercial activity, records are generated, and the business transactions must be accurately recorded. These types of records include paper or electronic receipts, payroll information, expenses and revenue, and taxes collected. A general guideline for retention of these records is a period of six years from the end of the last tax year to which they relate.

In large organizations, there is usually a department designed for the purpose of handling these commercial activities. Depending on the nature of the business, this could be called the Finance, Accounts Payable or Receivable department, or simply the Administration department. All incoming cash and cheques are forwarded to that department. After invoices and statements are approved for payment, they are forwarded to the same department for payment.

Funds transferred electronically in small private companies and larger organizations alike typically establish **electronic funds transfer (EFT)** as an efficient and cost-effective method of moving money between accounts. Electronic funds transfer is one facet of ecommerce (synonymous with ebusiness) that is referenced by the Canada Revenue Agency (CRA) as the delivery of information, products, services, or payments by phone, computer, or other automated media.

The Canada Revenue Agency's (CRA's) definition includes a broad range of businesses transactions that use electronic equipment to conduct trade. In fact, it covers any business transaction that may use the phone, fax,

automatic teller machine (ATM), credit card, or debit card, or involve a government service, business over the internet, or banking.

This chapter will introduce ecommerce from a banking perspective, as well as provide traditional banking and record-keeping functions essential to the professional administrative professional.

ECOMMERCE

A major step in the evolution of business is the concept of exchanging goods or money (commerce) because of advanced (electronic) technology. Electronic commerce, or **ecommerce**, is simply an applied term for electronic file transfer, although ecommerce is also a broader concept. Ecommerce may be considered as electronic file transfer between businesses or between businesses and their customers, but in each case, it is a different application.

Business-to-business (B2B) transactions typically use private communication networks. These networks were originally built to automate and speed up the exchange of data and information between companies that regularly conduct business together. Financial institutions are a typical example of this type of exchange. Banks have been using **electronic data interchange (EDI)** for many years, exchanging account information and adjusting balances based on any number of activities. Despite being relatively unknown, EDI still forms the basis of most ecommerce transactions on the web. It provides a standard exchange of business data from one computer to another computer. Documents exchanged in the EDI process contain the same information that you would expect to find in bank transaction, catalogue, payment system, or shipping information.

The web is the network of choice for business-to-customer (B2C) transactions. Consider Canadian Tire at www.canadiantire.com, one of the millions of businesses that provide e-shopping opportunities around the globe. The company offers a wide selection of hardware and household items in addition to building and garden materials. Customers can use the web to virtually shop their local store by browsing Canadian Tire's online catalogue, loading a virtual shopping cart, and choosing to pay by several methods. Delivery is scheduled, and you may sit back and wait for your goods. Personal banking, stock trading, and tracking a package with Canada Post are other examples of the way both businesses and consumers engage in ecommerce.

Ecommerce is popular for several reasons:

- It increases productivity.
- It improves internal business processes.
- It improves the relationship between business partners and the company.
- It increases sales.
- It reduces the cost of doing business.

Concerns with ECommerce

Sending orders and account information across a network is cheaper, faster, and more convenient than a traditional method of conducting business transactions. However, it comes with a few issues regarding privacy and security.

Privacy Establishing ecommerce business facilities, it is practical to study correspondents' privacy policy to be sure it agrees that customers' sensitive information will not be shared or sent over the web without encryption. Encryption means converted into code. Many organizations subscribe to a certificate process for improved privacy and security. One form of certification confirms the identity of the web user. The Financial Transactions and Reports Analysis Centre of Canada provides methodologies to confirm the existence of an individual or other entity concerning financial transactions. Forms of personal certification are used when you send personal information over the web to another user who needs to verify your identity. Other website certificates ensure that the website is safe and trustworthy. It is wise to check the certificates not only of websites that will receive your sensitive information but also those that deliver information—you need to know that such information comes from a known and reliable source. Many organizations supporting trustworthy websites subscribe to a third-party certification process that requires them to provide a safe, legal, and ethical internet environment.

Security Through legislation, the government is supporting the reduction and control of ecommerce abuse in Canada. All regulations and laws that affect traditional business apply equally to those that practise ebusiness. However, certain business practices in the areas of consumer protection and privacy are of special interest. A working group committed to consumers, businesses, and government protection has developed a set of guiding principles for ebusiness. The principles call for eight assurances:

1. clear disclosure of a business's identity, the goods and services it offers, and the terms and conditions of sale
2. a transparent transaction confirmation process
3. payment security
4. protection of personal data
5. restriction of unsolicited commercial email (spam and antispam legislation)
6. a fair balance of liability in the event of transaction problems

7. timely and affordable means of complaint handling and redress

8. effective consumer education

Similarly, the government of Canada acts to protect personal information with the *Personal Information Protection and Electronic Documents Act (PIPEDA)*, which covers matters such as the collection and disclosure of personal information and the protection of information and privacy. The act generally considers email addresses as protected personal information. For reference and research, review the information provided by the Office of the Privacy Commissioner of Canada. Detailed information available includes: broad coverage of PIPEDA, outlines and definitions of personal information, federal and provincial laws, as well as highlights of industry sector privacy laws such as those involved in the provision of healthcare.

Web-Banking

Most chartered banks offer business banking, investing, and insurance facilities to their customers online. **Web-banking** provides easy management of banking transactions online wherever you have access to the internet. Primary functions of such services are to enable business customers to make electronic transfers between accounts and get real-time information on balances and transactions. Accounts may be viewed and manipulated "on screen" just as you might with more traditional methods of banking.

Establishment of a web-banking account is achieved by first visiting the company's bank to provide a company profile and, perhaps, to acquire software that is loaded to your PC or computer network. This software will allow you to make the connection with the company's bank and its accounts. In some cases, downloading the software may provide the connection. In either case, web-banking should be established with the assistance of a commercial banking expert at your company's bank.

Access to your web-banking services will depend on the financial institution with which your company is partnered, and your company's unique identification and password. A unique password can be established for each authorized user of the business account. Commercial banking services are comprehensive but varied in their design.

Mobile Banking

As a variation to web-banking, most banks offer **mobile banking**—that is, banking using a smartphone or tablet. Most chartered banks offer customers with digital devices access to banking services similar to web-based banking.

Automated Teller Machines

A gain in efficiency is often accompanied by a loss of personal contact. This is true of the teller service provided by the **automated teller machine (ATM)**. The customer's contact is entirely with the ATM and not with a bank representative. ATMs, located inside or outside of banks, enable customers to obtain cash, make deposits, check the status of their accounts, transfer money between accounts, and pay bills. To access the ATM or cash machine, the customer simply activates the machine with a plastic magnetically coded card referred to as a debit, payment, or cash card. Standard cards have an embedded smart card chip, and the user enters a personal identification number (PIN) for access to the account. The chip encrypts information to help increase data security when making transactions at terminals or ATMs that are chip-enabled. Some cards are co-branded with the financial institution and another provider like a retailer. The magnetic stripe located on the back of the card can be black, brown, or silver in colour and contains three distinct pieces of data or tracks. Each track is about one-tenth of an inch wide. The first and second tracks are encoded with information about the cardholder's account, such as the credit card number, full name, the expiration date of the card, and the country code. Added information can be stored on the third track at the discretion of the issuer. Many cards have a tap and pay feature. These cards allow the user to pay for some purchases by tapping the card on a secure payment terminal instead of inserting or swiping the card and adding the PIN. ATMs may be used in conjunction with web-banking accounts for access to information and cash.

Direct Payroll Deposit

Direct payroll deposit enables an organization to pay its employees without writing cheques. Instead, the organization furnishes the financial institution with a description of all payroll disbursements to employees. The bank credits the account of each employee with his or her net pay and withdraws the amount from the account of the employer. The employer then sends a statement to the employee. The statement, often produced by a third party, shows gross payment, types and amounts of deductions, and the net payment. Usually, an organization arranges for direct payroll deposit with several banks.

Preauthorized Payment

Another type of automated transfer of funds is the preauthorized payment. A preauthorized payment transfers funds from one account to another within the same financial institution. For example, a customer can arrange payment from a company chequing account to a loan account on a regular basis. In the office, preauthorized payments may be useful for repaying business loans or petty cash accounts. It can remove the potential for human error in terms of forgetting to pay a loan on time.

Self-Check

1. Define the term *ecommerce*.
2. What type of issues does the *Personal Information Protection and Electronic Documents Act (PIPEDA)* address?
3. How does direct payroll deposit work?
4. Why would a business use preauthorized payments in its banking?

NONELECTRONIC TRANSFERS

Traditional banking services continue to play a major role in office commerce. Customers buy goods with cash and cheques, employees need petty cash, and some suppliers may not have access to an e-banking service—but they need to deal through a company bank account.

A company establishes a corporate account at a financial institution as a convenient means of transferring funds. In addition to the electronic transfer, a more traditional non-electronic instrument used for transferring funds is the ordinary cheque, which is defined as *a written order of a depositor upon a commercial bank to pay to the order of a designated party or to a bearer a specified sum of money on demand*.

The cheque is, in fact, a written contract between two parties in a financial transaction. The major benefits of using a traditional cheque are that the cheque is portable and that neither party needs an active computer network in order to initiate the transaction—the written cheque is simply handed over.

The parties to a cheque are the *drawer*, the person who draws the cheque on her or his account; the *drawee*, the bank upon which the cheque is drawn; and the *payee*, the person to whom payment is made. See Figure 15-1 and the itemized components found on a standard cheque.

At the time that the depositor opens a chequing account, the depositor places on file with the bank a signature card showing her or his authorized signature. A depositor should always use that authorized signature when signing cheques. If you are to sign cheques for the organization where you work, your manager will ask the bank to honour your signature. You will be asked to fill out a signature card, thereby placing your authorized signature on file with the bank.

In addition to the ordinary cheque, the following are other nonelectronic methods used to transfer funds:

- certified cheque
- bank draft
- money order

Certified Cheque

A *certified cheque*, also known as an official cheque, guarantees payment to the payee by the drawee bank. To obtain certification, the depositor completes the cheque in the usual

---

FIGURE 15-1 Cheque with notations.

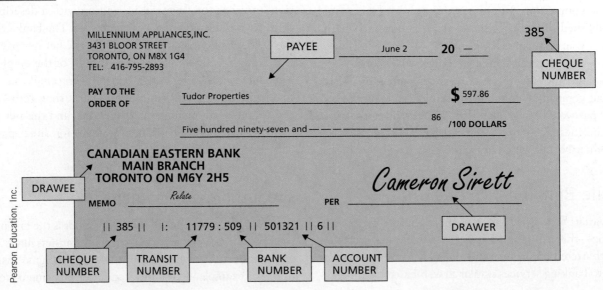

way and then takes it to the bank where the depositor has an account. After ascertaining that sufficient funds are in the depositor's account to cover the amount of the cheque, a representative of the bank certified, accepted, or guaranteed across the face of the cheque, signs her or his official name, dates the cheque, and immediately charges it to the depositor's account. The "acceptance" written across the face of the cheque is the bank's acknowledgment of its obligation to pay when the cheque is presented for payment. The drawer of a certified cheque cannot stop payment on it.

A depositor whose financial status is unknown to the payee can use a certified cheque as a means of payment. Certified cheques are commonly used when large amounts of money are involved. A certified cheque is required in certain business transactions, such as the purchase of real estate.

If a certified cheque is not sent to the payee, it should be deposited back to the depositor's bank account. This is because a certified cheque has effectively been withdrawn from the depositor's account upon acceptance and a reversal must be made to keep the account in order. A certified cheque should never be destroyed.

Bank Draft

A *bank draft* is a cheque drawn by a bank on its own funds (or credit) in another bank. The draft is made payable to a third party, who upon endorsing it may cash it at the bank on which it is drawn.

A bank draft can be used to transfer money to another person or organization in another geographic location. A bank draft payable in foreign currency may be purchased.

The process of obtaining a bank draft is quite easy. Simply provide the desired amount of money in the form of cash, a personal cheque, or a business cheque made payable to the bank. The bank will additionally charge a nominal administration fee. In exchange, you will receive a bank draft made payable to the person or organization specified as payee.

Money Order

A *money order* may be obtained from a bank. The service is used mainly by people without chequing accounts to send relatively small amounts of money through the mail.

A bank money order is negotiable and requires the endorsement of the payee to transfer it. It may be cashed at any bank. The fee for obtaining a money order is nominal. The amount for which a single money order may be written is limited; for instance, Canada Post limits a single Canadian money order to $999.00 but the number of money orders that may be issued to the same person to be sent to one payee is not restricted.

Self-Check

1. What are two advantages of the traditional cheque?
2. Who are the three parties to a cheque?
3. Besides the traditional cheque, list two other nonelectronic methods used to transfer funds.
4. How does a certified cheque differ from a traditional cheque?

WRITING CHEQUES

Blank cheques are assembled in various forms, but the information to be entered in the cheque does not vary. Follow standard rules for writing cheques.

Many organizations use computer software such as Quick-Books to prepare cheques. Some businesses use cheque-writing machines as a safety measure against possible alteration of cheques.

Chequebooks and Cheque Forms

A bank will supply books of single cheques, as well as large books with three cheques to a page. One type has the cheque stub attached to each cheque; another type comes with a separate book for recording information about each cheque written.

Although banks will supply depositors with cheques, an organization may wish to use its own printed forms, called *voucher cheques*. The form of voucher cheques varies. When cheques are written by the computer, attached to the voucher cheque is a perforated form, called a *stub*, for recording the details of the cheque, such as gross payment, type and amount of deductions, and net payment. Some cheques are unbound in multiple copy packs. All cheques must bear a unique sequence number for identification and processing.

Rules for Writing Cheques

Follow these rules when you are writing cheques with a printer or a pen:

1. Make sure that sufficient funds are in the account to cover the cheque and bring the chequebook balance up to date.
2. If you are preparing cheques by computer printer, use a dark-colour ink cartridge whenever possible. If you are preparing cheques by hand, use a pen. (Faintly printed figures and letters are easy to alter; so are handwritten ones.)
3. If the cheque is in a chequebook that contains a stub record, number the stub to agree with the number on the cheque being written.

4. Complete each stub or voucher statement as you write a cheque. Fill in the stub before you write the cheque. When you are paying two invoices with one cheque, show each separately on the stub or voucher statement.

5. Date the cheque as of the day it is being written. Postdating a cheque in anticipation of having additional funds in the bank by the date entered on the cheque could result in an overdraft because the payee might present the cheque before the date shown and may even be paid. Postdating a cheque is permissible, but doing so should be avoided to protect the financial reputation of the organization. (If you receive a cheque that is not dated, write in the date on which you received it.)

6. Write the name of the payee in full without a title—such as Ms., Mrs., Miss, Mr., or Dr.—preceding the name. If the payee is serving as treasurer or chairperson, or in some other capacity, include the official title following her or his name to indicate that the payee is not receiving the money personally. Begin the name at the extreme left.

7. Before entering the amount, verify that the amount of the payment is correct.

8. Take precautions to protect the cheque against alteration. Enter the figures first, placing them as close to the dollar sign and to each other as possible. For even amounts, be sure to fill in the cents space with xx ("xx/100"). Notice how the figures are written in the cheque in Figure 15-2.

9. Enter the same amount in words. Capitalize only the first word. Begin the words close to the left margin and fill in the space following the words with dashes or a wavy line. Express cents as a fraction of 100. Write large amounts with the fewest number of words. For example, $4365.73 may be written in the following two ways, but the second example occupies the least space:

*Four thousand three hundred sixty-five and 73/100 ....
.................Dollars*

*Forty-three hundred sixty-five and 73/100 ....
...........Dollars*

10. Verify that the amount expressed in words agrees with the amount expressed in figures. When the figures and words do not agree, the bank may choose to not honour the cheque.

11. If you make a mistake, do not erase or cross out the error. Although some people cross out, correct, and initial their errors, it is better to write "VOID" across the face of the cheque and the stub and start over with a new cheque. File the voided cheque in numerical order with the cancelled cheques from the bank, if the bank returns your cancelled checks. Alternatively, scan a voided business cheque and maintain it for the duration of your associated financial records.

12. If your manager is an authorized signatory, present the completed cheques to your manager for signing. Your manager should sign them in ink. Be prepared to disclose the original invoices and your calculations including applicable discounts.

Stop-Payment Notification

At the request of the drawer, a bank will stop payment on a cheque at any time until it has cleared the bank upon which it is drawn. Stopping payment is a safety measure that should be taken when a cheque has been lost or stolen; it may also be taken when a cheque is written for an incorrect amount,

FIGURE 15-2 Keyed entries on cheques.

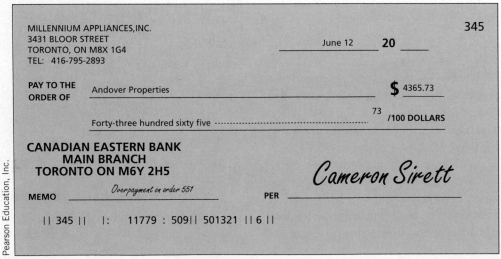

when certain conditions of an agreement have not been met, or for other reasons.

As an administrative professional, you may stop payment of a cheque signed by your manager. To do so, first call the bank or access web-banking and request that payment be stopped. Give the names of the drawer and the payee, the date, number, and amount of the cheque, and the reason why payment must be stopped.

The bank will request confirmation of the verbal order to stop payment. The bank will ask you either to complete a stop-payment electronic form or to write a letter of confirmation.

When you are certain that payment has been stopped, write "stopped payment" across the stub of the cheque and add the amount to the current chequebook balance. Later, if the cheque is returned to you, mark it void and treat it as a voided cheque. Depending on the circumstances, you may need to write a replacement for the cheque on which you stopped payment. There is often a charge for this bank service.

Cash Withdrawals

A depositor can withdraw funds from her or his personal chequing account by writing the word "Cash" on the line provided for the name of the payee, filling in the amount, and signing the cheque. However, since a cheque written in this way is highly negotiable, a depositor should fill in the cheque only when ready to receive the money.

One of your responsibilities may be to obtain cash from your manager's personal chequing account. If your manager hands you a cheque made payable to "Cash," be especially careful with it. Anyone who comes in possession of it can cash it.

Handle cash as inconspicuously as possible. Put the cash you obtain for your manager in a sealed envelope. Always keep cash that you obtain for others separate from your own funds.

Endorsing Cheques

A cheque presented for cash or deposit must be signed (endorsed) by the payee on the reverse side of the cheque—preferably at the left end. A bank will accept for deposit cheques that have been endorsed by a representative of the payee. The endorsement may be made with a rubber stamp, or it may be handwritten in ink.

The payee should sign her or his name exactly as the payee's name is carried on the bank account. If the payee's name is written differently on the face of the cheque, it should be endorsed twice—first as it is written and then exactly as the payee's account is carried.

Restrictive Endorsement

A restrictive endorsement limits the use of a cheque to the purpose stated in the endorsement. Words such as "For deposit only" or "Pay to" are written before the organization's name or the depositor's signature. As a result, further endorsement of the cheque is restricted. A restrictive endorsement should be used when deposits are sent to the bank by mail.

Since most organizations deposit all the cheques they receive, the restrictive endorsement is the most widely used on business cheques. On cheques to be deposited, the endorsement can be made by a rubber stamp. As the endorsement merely transfers the cheque to the depositor's account, a handwritten signature is not usually needed.

Blank Endorsement

A blank endorsement consists only of the signature of the payee. Because a cheque endorsed in blank is payable to the bearer, the holder should use a blank endorsement only when he or she is at the bank depositing or cashing the cheque.

Full Endorsement

A full endorsement transfers a cheque to a specified person or organization. "Pay to the order of" followed by the name of the person or organization to whom the cheque is being transferred is written on the cheque preceding the signature of the endorser.

When a cheque that has been received is forwarded to another person or organization, a full endorsement should be used to ensure that only the specified payee can transfer or cash it. To further negotiate the cheque, the endorsee must sign it.

Self-Check

1. How might you protect a cheque you are issuing against alteration?

2. Give three reasons why you would stop payment on a cheque.

3. How should the payee endorse a cheque for deposit when the name on the cheque is written differently than the name on the bank account?

DEPOSITS

While web-banking is taking care of day-to-day transfers between accounts and information on balances and transactions, businesses still need to deposit money into their accounts. Many organizations use ecommerce applications, which accept electronic deposits from customers, but cash deposits remain an administrative function of many retail-oriented and small businesses.

If making cash deposits is one of your administrative functions, make them regularly. In between times, keep cash and cheques in a secure place.

Present coins, paper currency (bills), cheques, money orders, and bank drafts to the bank teller for deposit, along with a deposit slip in duplicate listing what is being deposited.

Preparing Deposits

Use coin wrappers supplied by the bank to package a large number of coins in rolls. Write the account name on the outside of each roll. The numbers of coins that can be packaged in different rolls are shown in Figure 15-3.

Put coins insufficient for a roll in a sealed envelope on which you have written the account name and the total value of the coins enclosed.

Stack bills face up according to denomination, and then enclose them in bill wrappers supplied by the bank. Write the account name on each wrapper.

Stack bills of varying denominations face up with the largest denomination on top and the lowest on the bottom. Place a rubber band around them.

Examine each cheque to determine that the amount of the cheque is correct, that the amount written in figures agrees with the amount written in words, and that the cheque is properly signed and not postdated.

Ascertain that the cheques are correctly endorsed either by a rubber-stamp endorsement or by a handwritten signature. Group together all cheques drawn on a given bank. Endorse money orders and bank drafts as though they were cheques.

Preparing the Deposit Slip

Keep on hand a supply of deposit slips, which are obtainable from the bank. These are often available as multiple-copy sets encoded with the depositor's account number.

FIGURE 15-3 Coin roll format.

COIN	NUMBER IN ROLL	VALUE OF ROLL
Nickels	40	$2.00
Dimes	50	$5.00
Quarters	40	$10.00
One Dollar	25	$25.00
Two Dollars	25	$50.00

FIGURE 15-4 Deposit slip.

Key the current date, the name exactly as it appears in the account, and the address. Add the account number if it is not already on the deposit slip. Some banks require a separate listing of coins and paper currency. See the sample deposit slip in Figure 15-4.

List each cheque by the drawer's name or the drawee's name. Use whatever system works best for your record-keeping purposes. Whichever you use, be consistent. When you cannot list all the cheques on one deposit slip, either staple two deposit slips together or show on the deposit slip the total of the cheques being deposited and attach a separate list of the cheques. Present the cheques to the customer service representative in the order in which you list them.

List a money order as "money order." List a traveller's cheque as "traveller's cheque."

Make sure that the total shown on the deposit slip is correct.

Depositing after Hours

Some organizations that collect cash and cheques after the close of banking hours use the night depository. For this purpose, the bank provides the depositor with a bag with a lock. The depositor places the deposit and deposit slip in the bag, locks it, and takes it to the bank at any time during the night.

From the outside of the bank, the depositor drops the bag through a slot that leads into the vault. The next day the deposit is completed in one of two ways:

1. The bank teller unlocks the bag and makes the deposit.
2. The bank leaves the bag locked until the depositor arrives to make the deposit in person.

Self-Check

1. Describe preparing a deposit.
2. What is one acceptable procedure for making a deposit after hours?

RECONCILING THE BANK STATEMENT WITH THE CHEQUEBOOK BALANCE

Bank reconciliation is the practice of comparing your records against the bank records. A monthly reconciliation helps to identify any unusual transactions caused by fraud or accounting errors. Each month, the financial institution issues a current bank statement to the depositor.

If requested, the bank will also return all cancelled cheques that coincide with the current bank statement (see Figure 15-5). The cancelled cheques are the ones that have been paid by the bank. The statement shows the previous month's balance, deposits made, cheques paid, bank charges, and the ending balance.

Reconcile the bank statement with the chequebook balance as soon as you receive the bank statement and the cancelled cheques. Compare the final balance on the statement with the balance in the chequebook, and then account for the difference. Usually, the two balances do not agree because some cheques that have been written have not been presented for payment, deposits made since the date on the statement are not listed, and automatic subtractions and/or additions may have been made by the bank. For example, if there is a service charge for the account, the bank will deduct the charge. If monthly rental payments or other types of income are deposited directly to the account, the amounts will be added to the statement.

To make the reconciliation statement, assemble:

1. the current bank statement and cancelled cheques
2. the bank reconciliation statement for the previous month
3. duplicate deposit slips representing the deposits made since the last one listed on the previous month's reconciliation statement
4. the chequebook or cheque register

FIGURE 15-5 Bank statement.

Carter Enterprises
P.O. Box 782
Station A
Toronto ON M6Y 2J6

CANADIAN EASTERN BANK
MAIN BRANCH, TORONTO

Account Number: 820116742

CODE	DESCRIPTION	DEBIT	CREDIT	DATE	BALANCE
	Balance Brought Forward				4 061.74
CH	Cheque #66	26.17		04/11	4 035.57
LN	Loan Payment	500.20		04/11	3 535.37
MB	From Bank 2749-11		2 500.00	06/11	6 035.37
NS	Cheque Return NSF	200.36			5 835.01
SC	Service Charge	10.00		06/11	5 825.01
DC	Other Charges—Cheque Print	23.00		07/11	5 802.01
IB	Inter-Bank Transfer		8 274.92	09/11	14 076.93
DD	Direct Deposit		624.25	12/11	14 701.18
CH	Cheque #67	490.00		15/11	14 211.18
CH	Cheque #68	762.60		15/11	13 448.58
INC	Interest		56.07	17/11	13 504.65
DS	Chargeable Service—Insurance	79.64		18/11	13 425.01
SC	Service Charge	3.50		18/11	13 421.51
CH	Cheque #71	4 270.50		20/11	9 151.01
CH	Cheque #72	100.00		21/11	9 051.01
DD	Direct Deposit		272.82	23/11	9 323.83
DC	Other Charges—Cheque Back Fee	5.00		29/11	9 318.83
IND	Interest	21.00		30/11	9 297.83
	TOTAL BALANCE FORWARD	**6 491.97**	**11 728.06**		**9 297.83**

Pearson Education, Inc.

Adopt a Consistent Method

The process can be as formal or informal as you need. Some businesses create a bank reconciliation template using a spreadsheet based application program, but the most important thing is to review each transaction from each source reflective of your records and the bank's records match those transactions and compare your account balance at the end of each period. Again, the period could be monthly, daily, or any other period you choose.

Where can you find the information you need? The accounting system utilized should have everything you need. Financial institutions normally provide online access to the account, allowing you to view and download transactions regularly.

Use the same method each month to prepare the reconciliation statement. By working systematically and checking carefully, your objective should get the bank balance and the chequebook balance to agree.

Prepare the Reconciliation Statement

To prepare a bank reconciliation statement similar to the one shown in Figure 15-6, proceed in this way:

1. Key an appropriate heading, including the company name, the name of the form (bank reconciliation), and the date.

2. Enter the chequebook balance and the bank statement balance across the top of the page. In the example, Figure 15-6, the chequebook balance is given as $9401.42.

3. List any credits to the account that may have been deposited automatically or without your knowledge.

An example of an automatic credit is interest earned on your account. Add the credit to your chequebook balance.

4. List and add to the bank statement balance all deposits to the account that are not shown on the previous month's statement. In Figure 15-6, a deposit of $149.00 was made on November 30. This deposit does not appear on the previous bank statement.

5. List, add, and finally deduct the total of all bank charges from your adjusted chequebook balance. These charges would appear on the previous month's statement. Service charges and nonsufficient cheque charges, also known as NSF, are examples of these deductions.

6. Deduct the sum of all outstanding cheques from the adjusted bank statement balance.

7. Show both the adjusted chequebook balance and the adjusted bank statement balance. They should be equal.

Search for Errors

If the adjusted bank statement balance and the adjusted chequebook balance do not agree, first find out how much the balance is off and look for that figure. Then, check the reconciliation statement. Are the figures accurate? Have you added when you should have subtracted?

Next, look for omissions of cheques and/or deposits. Have all the cheques written been subtracted from the chequebook balance? Have all the cheques that have not cleared through the bank been listed as outstanding cheques on the reconciliation statement? Have all the deposits been included on the reconciliation statement?

FIGURE 15-6 Bank reconciliation statement.

BANK RECONCILIATION Carter Enterprises December 1, 20xx					
CHEQUEBOOK BALANCE		$9401.42	BANK STATEMENT BALANCE		$9297.83
ADD: Interest Earned	$56.07	$56.07 $9457.49	ADD: Deposit of *11/30*		$149.00 $9446.83
DEDUCT: NSF Cheque Plus Service Charge Cheque Printing Charge Interest Charge Cheque Back Fee Service Charge	$210.36 23.00 21.00 5.00 3.50	$262.86 $9194.63	DEDUCT: Outstanding Cheques No. 69 No. 70	$180.00 72.20	$252.20 $9194.63

If you still have not located the error, check for an arithmetical mistake in the cheque stubs. When you find one, mark the correction in two places. On the stub where the error occurs, write "Should be" followed by the correct amount. Make the compensating adjustment at the bottom of the last stub used or in the first blank line of the cheque register.

File Cancelled Cheques

Organizations that are committed to web-banking often do not request the return of their cancelled cheques. Instead, they rely on the virtual bank statement for reconciliation. For those that prefer the security of possession of the cancelled cheques, they do offer legal and tangible evidence of payment.

The system you use for filing cheques will be governed by the frequency with which you must refer to them. Physically or electronically, file the current bank reconciliation statement to ensure accessibility next month. File statements in chronological order when using a physical filing system, placing the most recent in front. You can either keep the cancelled cheques inside the folded bank statements or file the cheques separately in numerical order.

The retention period for the cheques and the method of disposing of them will be determined by the organization's policy. The person in your organization who is responsible for records retention will provide you with information about destroying cheques. Records retention was discussed in Chapter 11.

> **Self-Check**
>
> 1. What items are required in order to prepare a reconciliation statement?
> 2. Why do some companies prefer to have all the cancelled cheques in their possession?

KEEPING RECORDS

Most organizations keep their accounting records digitally in a secure platform. Accounting is a separate business function, performed by accountants; record keeping occurs wherever a record originates. Consequently, office professionals maintain and assist with various financial records. Some administrative professionals, especially those who work for owners of small businesses, help their managers with personal business records.

Anticipate overseeing a petty cash fund, assisting with payroll records, and keeping records involving office supplies.

Petty Cash Fund

Petty cash refers to small amounts of cash kept on hand in a business. When the amount of an office expenditure is small and payment is made immediately, it may be more convenient to make the payment by cash than by cheque. To provide cash to pay for incidental items, such as ad hoc courier service, postage due on packages, or emergency purchases of office supplies, organizations establish a petty cash fund. Petty cash works on the imprest system, in which an initial amount of money is put into an account, utilized for specific purposes. When the account goes below a certain specified amount of cash on hand, the system is continually replenished as required. Since debit cards are used in many places, the need for petty cash kept in a cash drawer has diminished. A transaction occurs each time cash serves for purchase. Importantly in this system, documenting the transaction for accurate accounting and record keeping is essential. These funds usually range from $50 to $100 or more, depending on the cash needs for a period of time—perhaps a month. Even though the petty cash is used to make miscellaneous payments, it must still be accounted for.

Generally, an administrative professional is responsible for handling the petty cash fund. When you are the one who keeps track of petty cash, observe the following standard procedures:

1. Keep the cash and completed voucher for each purchase in a box or an envelope, and put them in a safe place. They should be in a locked desk drawer or file or in an office safe. Balance the petty cash record at least once a week. If the cash and vouchers are left unlocked, balance the record at the end of each day. See Figure 15-7.

2. Prepare a petty cash voucher for each expenditure you make. The voucher, which is a receipt, should show the amount paid, the date to whom the payment was made, the purpose of the payment, the expense category to which the payment will be charged, and the signature or initials of the person authorizing payment. Some organizations also require the signature or initials of the person receiving payment. Unless the accounting department stipulates that the vouchers be machine printed, write them, using a pen; this way, you complete the voucher quickly at the time you are making the payment and without interrupting work you may have in the printer.

3. Keep an accurate petty cash record, using either a petty cash book or a distribution sheet or log. For each payment from the petty cash fund, enter the date, the amount. See Figure 15-8.

Some petty cash books provide columns for expense categories; others do not. The columns and the appropriate headings for the petty cash record can be printed on a sheet of paper or an envelope. Accounting departments

FIGURE 15-7 Petty cash voucher.

PETTY CASH

NUMBER	DATE

DESCRIPTION OF ITEM/SERVICE PURCHASED	AMOUNT
CHARGE TO ACCOUNT TOTAL	

A-9072/T-3008

RECEIVED BY ____________ APPROVED BY ____________

> ## pro-Link
> ### Fraud Filter
>
> Fraud in the office can be an expensive proposition for any organization. Small business is the most vulnerable to three main types of fraud and abuse: misappropriation, fraudulent statements, and bribery and corruption.
>
> Here are some preventative tips for *your* office:
>
> - Designate a front-line point person to open the mail and systematically list all cheques before passing them on to the accounting department.
> - Develop cheque-signing limits. For example, the administrative professional may sign for $100, the manager $1000, the executive $10 000, etc.
> - Pay attention to your bookkeeping practices. Have your work periodically reviewed by a colleague as a "sanity" check.
> - Establish a dual signature practice for cheques, but do not sign cheques in advance of your absence.
> - If you are about to ask someone new to handle the accounts, make sure the person is in good standing with the company—not just qualified to do the work.
> - Create an office atmosphere that encourages everyone to be honest and on the lookout for fraud. Each employee has a vested interest in the well-being of the company.
>
> Can you think of more?

often supply envelopes imprinted with columns and headings for the petty cash record, including columns for the distribution of payments.

4. Replenish the petty cash fund soon enough to keep an adequate supply of cash on hand. In some organizations, petty cash is replenished at a predetermined time—for instance, when only one-fourth of the cash is on hand. In other organizations, replenishing the petty cash fund is left to the judgment of the office professional responsible for maintaining the fund.

5. To replenish the petty cash fund, balance the petty cash record, formally request a cheque for the amount needed, and prepare the petty cash report.

Begin by balancing the petty cash record: count the cash on hand, total the columns of the petty cash record, determine the amount needed to replenish the petty cash fund to the original amount, and enter the balance in the petty cash record. Verify that the cash on hand plus the total amount of the vouchers equals the original amount of the fund. Also, add the totals of the distribution of payment columns as a check that the total amount distributed equals the total amount spent.

Request the amount needed to replenish the petty cash fund to its original amount, unless you have been authorized to decrease or increase the fund. In some organizations, the person in charge of the fund is expected to write the cheque. If you write the cheque, make it payable to "Petty Cash," and present it to the person who is authorized to sign it.

FIGURE 15-8 Petty cash log.

PETTY CASH LOG

REPORTING PERIOD

FROM

TO

DATE	NUM	PAID TO/ RECEIVED FROM	PURPOSE	APPROVED BY	CASH OUT	CASH IN	BALANCE
			BEGINNING BALANCE				
TOTAL							

PETTY CASH RECONCILIATION

FINAL BALANCE	
CASH ON HAND	
DIFFERENCE	
PETTY CASH REIMBURSEMENT	
BALANCE FORWARD	

Vertex 42

With the request for cash, submit the records called for by the accounting department. When the accounting department supplies a petty cash distribution envelope, the usual procedure is to submit the envelope with the supporting vouchers enclosed. Before you release an envelope, make a copy for your files. Attach the petty cash vouchers.

6. Cash the cheque. Enter the amount and the date in the Received column of the petty cash record. If you are using a new petty cash distribution envelope, transfer the balance of the old envelope to the Received column of the new petty cash envelope, together with the amount of new cash received.

Payroll Processing

In a small business, you may be responsible for processing payroll for team members and for yourself. In larger organizations, a payroll or accounting department would oversee this function. Even with a payroll department you may still be required to track hours worked and submit reports based on any changes in hours or employment terms.

To complete payroll you need to be aware of legal requirements and regulations set forth by the federal and provincial governments, as accurate payroll records must be maintained by all businesses. Employer and business entities are required to have a program account with CRA and receive an account number, which will identify the business. The make-up of the account with CRA consists of the nine-digit business number (BN), a two-letter code, which represents the type of payroll program, and finally, a four-digit reference number to identify each account in a program account a business has. A business is required to open a payroll program account before the first remittance is due. The remittance is due on the 15th of each month unless the organization has another arrangement with the CRA. The remittance involves the calculations of deductions.

Here are four key points to keep in mind:

1. Calculation of earnings and deductions must be made for each payment processed.

2. For each employee, three mandatory deductions must be recorded: Canada Pension Plan or Quebec Pension Plan, Employment Insurance (EI), and income tax.

3. Each employee must receive a statement detailing earnings and deductions. This statement will show gross pay, which is the total amount earned before any deductions are made, and the net pay, which is earnings after deductions are made.

4. On a monthly basis, prepare and remit payment to Canada Revenue Agency (CRA), specifically the Receiver General, for the three mandatory deductions. There are variations in the remittance schedule depending on the organization; some organizations remit on a quarterly basis.

The CRA provides several online tools showing calculation tables for the mandatory deductions. As a starting point, obtain CRA's publication T4001, available in PDF or HTML format: *Employers' Guide—Payroll Deductions and Remittances. Failure to Comply With Canadian Payroll Requirements*. The penalties for noncompliance with Canadian payroll requirements range from fines of $1000 to $25 000, imprisonment for up to 12 months, or a combination of both.

Several payroll software packages are also available to assist with accurate payroll preparation.

Canada Pension Plan (CPP) The Canada Pension Plan (CPP) provides contributors and their families with partial replacement of earnings in the case of retirement, disability, or death. Almost all individuals who work in Canada outside Quebec contribute to the CPP. In Quebec it is referred to as the Quebec Pension Plan. If an employee is 18 years and older and in a pensionable employment arrangement and the individual does not receive a CPP retirement or disability pension, the employer is required to deduct CPP contributions from the pay. For an individual 65 years old and under 70 and working and receiving CPP or QPP pension, the employer continues to deduct contributions. There are calculations table tools guiding the deduction rates and annual maximum contribution for employers to follow. After calculations are made on the payroll, the employer is responsible for ensuring the remittance on behalf of the employees.

Employment Insurance (EI) Unlike CPP, there is no age limit for deducting EI premiums, as they are called. The benefit of EI assistance provides for income support during times of pregnancy, illness, unemployment, and caring for a newborn, adopted child, or seriously ill family member. Employee and employer pay deduction-based premiums. Calculation tools like CPP exist through the CRA. Here as well there are annual maximum premium deductions.

Income Tax The employer also considered the payer will calculate the amount of tax to deduct from an individual's gross income. A new employee is provided with a TD1 Form prepared from CRA. Based on the requirements and completed form, a tax rate is calculated, again using CRA taxation table tools. See Figure 15-9 for the representation of a TD1 form.

Office Supplies on Hand

Administrative professionals should replenish their office supplies during the time of day or week that they are the least busy. Yet they need to plan well enough that they are not searching for supplies when pressed for time to complete a rush job. Sometimes an administrative professional is responsible for stocking office supplies for an entire floor or a department. Inventory control is essential to maintain a constant supply of needed materials. To manage this, you need a record, preferably kept in longhand, of supplies on hand.

An easy way to determine supplies needed is to keep an electronic file indicating inventory of each item required in the supply listing. These cards, when completed, are known as perpetual inventory files. When you check supplies out of the main supply department or order them directly, enter the amount of each item received in the file, and then add the amount to the figure in the balance column. When you take supplies from the supply cabinet or shelf, enter the amount in the checked-out column, and then subtract the amount to show the new balance. Encourage others who check out supplies to follow the same procedure.

By looking at the perpetual inventory file, you can decide:

1. whether the item you need is on hand in sufficient quantity
2. when it is time to order additional supplies

Self-Check

1. When would a company's petty cash fund be used?
2. How is a petty cash voucher used? Explain.
3. What are the three mandatory deductions required by law when preparing payroll?

BUDGET PREPARATION

A **budget** is a yearly plan a business uses to determine revenue and expenses. This document is critical for planning for future growth and development. Businesses take the compilation of an annual budget seriously. In large organizations, each department may have a portion of the budget it is required to complete. An administrative professional will assist with the budget process by gathering and recording financial data from sources such as monthly financial statements, expense reports, and income summaries. Here are some helpful guidelines to consider if you are preparing the budget documents:

1. Use a reliable template to confirm all areas of the budget are identified and addressed.
2. Ensure data are entered correctly. An error will affect the entire budgetary outcome.

FIGURE 15-9 TD1 Form for income tax deduction calculation.

Canada Revenue Agency   **Agence du revenu du Canada**

2018 Personal Tax Credits Return

Protected B when completed

TD1

Read page 2 before filling out this form. **Your employer or payer will use this form to determine the amount of your tax deductions.**
Fill out this form based on the best estimate of your circumstances.

Last name	First name and initial(s)	Date of birth (YYYY/MM/DD)	Employee number
Address	Postal code	For non-residents only – Country of permanent residence	Social insurance number

1. Basic personal amount – Every resident of Canada can claim this amount. If you will have more than one employer or payer at the same time in 2018, see "More than one employer or payer at the same time" on page 2. If you are a non-resident, see "Non-residents" on page 2.

11,809

2. Canada caregiver amount for infirm children under age 18 – Either parent (but not both), may claim $2,182 for each infirm child born in 2001 or later, that resides with both parents throughout the year. If the child does not reside with both parents throughout the year, the parent who is entitled to claim the "Amount for an eligible dependant" on line 8 may also claim the Canada caregiver amount for that same child who is under age 18.

3. Age amount – If you will be 65 or older on December 31, 2018, and your net income for the year from all sources will be $36,976 or less, enter $7,333. If your net income for the year will be between $36,976 and $85,863 and you want to calculate a partial claim, get Form TD1-WS, *Worksheet for the 2018 Personal Tax Credits Return*, and fill in the appropriate section.

4. Pension income amount – If you will receive regular pension payments from a pension plan or fund (excluding Canada Pension Plan, Quebec Pension Plan, Old Age Security, or Guaranteed Income Supplement payments), enter $2,000 or your estimated annual pension income, whichever is less.

5. Tuition (full time and part time)– If you are a student enrolled at a university or college, or an educational institution certified by Employment and Social Development Canada, and you will pay more than $100 per institution in tuition fees, fill in this section. If you are enrolled full time or part time, enter the total of the tuition fees you will pay.

6. Disability amount – If you will claim the disability amount on your income tax return by using Form T2201, *Disability Tax Credit Certificate*, enter $8,235.

7. Spouse or common-law partner amount – If you are supporting your spouse or common-law partner who lives with you and whose net income for the year will be less than $11,809 ($13,991 if he or she is **infirm**), enter the difference between this amount and his or her estimated net income for the year. If his or her net income for the year will be $11,809 or more ($13,991 or more if he or she is **infirm**), you cannot claim this amount. In all cases, if his or her net income for the year will be $23,391 or less **and** he or she is **infirm**, go to line 9.

8. Amount for an eligible dependant– If you do not have a spouse or common-law partner and you support a dependent relative who lives with you and whose net income for the year will be less than $11,809 ($13,991 if he or she is **infirm** and you **cannot claim the Canada caregiver amount for children under age 18 for this dependant**), enter the difference between this amount and his or her estimated net income. If his or her net income for the year will be $11,809 or more ($13,991 or more if he or she is **infirm**), you cannot claim this amount. In all cases, if his or her net income for the year will be $23,391 or less **and** he or she is **infirm and is age 18 or older**, go to line 9.

9. Canada caregiver amount for eligible dependant or spouse or common-law partner – If, at any time in the year, you support an **infirm** eligible dependant (aged 18 or older) **or** an **infirm** spouse or common-law partner whose net income for the year will be $23,391 or less, get Form TD1-WS and fill in the appropriate section.

10. Canada caregiver amount for dependant(s) age 18 or older – If, at any time in the year, you support an **infirm** dependant age 18 or older (**other than the spouse or common-law partner or eligible dependant you claimed an amount for on line 9, or could have claimed an amount for if his or her net income were under $13,991**) whose net income for the year will be $16,405 or less, enter $6,986. If his or her net income for the year will be between $16,405 and $23,391 and you want to calculate a partial claim, get Form TD1-WS and fill in the appropriate section. You can claim this amount for more than one infirm dependant age 18 or older. If you are sharing this amount with another caregiver who supports the same dependant, get the Form TD1-WS and fill in the appropriate section.

11. Amounts transferred from your spouse or common-law partner – If your spouse or common-law partner will not use all of his or her age amount, pension income amount, tuition amount, or disability amount on his or her income tax return, enter the unused amount.

12. Amounts transferred from a dependant – If your dependant will not use all of his or her **disability amount** on his or her income tax return, enter the unused amount. If your or your spouse's or common-law partner's dependent child or grandchild will not use all of his or her **tuition amount** on his or her income tax return, enter the unused amount.

13. TOTAL CLAIM AMOUNT – Add lines 1 to 12.
Your employer or payer will use this amount to determine the amount of your tax deductions.

Source: Retrieved from CRA 42. https://www.canada.ca/en/revenue-agency/services/forms-publications/td1-personal-tax-credits-returns/td1-forms-pay-received-on-january-1-later/td1.html

3. Take time to readjust your figures when necessary.
4. Obtain input from all departments involved in the budget process—information gathering is essential in this process.

ETHICS IN ACCOUNTING PROCEDURES

You may remember hearing news items about the financial collapses of well-known companies without warning, often companies with spotless reputations and histories of positive financial reports. What went wrong? The inevitable question is, "Where were the auditors and the accountants as these financial statements of well-being were released?" The problem often appears to be one of a lack of ethics. Could the financial troubles have been hidden deliberately to ensure strong investor support or to maintain a strong presence in the industry? Were they the result of fraud or embezzlement? The unfortunate result is that investors lost millions of dollars, and our trust in those involved in accounting practices was shaken.

Ethics can be taught and learned. An internet search will reveal multiple options for classes on ethics for administrative professionals.

Because of the high cost of dishonesty, you must be a person others see as having high values and integrity-based processes. You must be a person who would not compromise those values, especially when working in the accounting area and even at the request of your manager or supervisor. High ethical standards are required in every phase of the administrative professional's job.

INTERNATIONAL CURRENCY EXCHANGE

With international business travel so commonplace, it is very possible that you will be required to provide current currency exchange rates when personnel from the organization travel abroad. You might have to arrange to exchange Canadian money into a foreign currency before the employee leaves—and back into Canadian money when your employee returns from the trip abroad.

You can check the current exchange rate for any country's currency in a number of ways. You could search the web and contact your financial institutions. If the travelling airport handles international flights, you will likely find a company there that exchanges currency. Likewise, destination airports handling international flights will usually have currency exchange companies on site.

A word of caution. Canadian currency can be easily exchanged in Western countries. However, smaller countries or those in the Far East and Middle East will not necessarily deal in Canadian currency exchange. It is important to research the destination country to confirm that Canadian currency is accepted at exchange centres. If in doubt, exchange currency before personnel leave Canada. Always arrange for the employee to have small amounts of local currency upon arrival in another country to cover such things as transportation and food.

Credit cards are widely accepted throughout the world. Charges are made in the currency of the country where the purchase is made and converted to Canadian currency when it appears on your credit card statement.

QUESTIONS FOR STUDY AND REVIEW

1. What do the letters EFT represent?
2. What are the two main broad categories of ecommerce?
3. Explain how an administrative professional can obtain a certified cheque for a business financial transaction.
4. How does a bank draft differ from an ordinary cheque?
5. Provide two guidelines for preparing cheques.
6. Describe the steps an administrative professional would take to stop payment on a cheque.
7. When should each of the following endorsements be used: blank, full, restrictive?
8. A representative of an organization can endorse cheques being deposited. Explain a time-saving way to make endorsements.
9. How should money orders and bank drafts be endorsed?
10. What information is needed for preparing a bank reconciliation statement?
11. Why do the bank statement balance and the chequebook balance seldom agree?
12. Summarize the steps involved in making a bank reconciliation statement.
13. When your bank reconciliation statement does not balance, how should you proceed to locate errors?
14. How should a cancelled cheque be managed?
15. What is the purpose of the petty cash fund?
16. How can you be sure you have kept an accurate petty cash record?
17. When you replenish the petty cash fund, how do you determine the amount of money to request?
18. Where can you locate information to calculate mandatory payroll deductions?
19. To show the distribution of expenditures, why should you use categories predetermined by the accounting department rather than your own?

Key Terms

automated teller machine (ATM) 317

budget 328

ecommerce 316

electronic data interchange (EDI) 316

electronic funds transfer (EFT) 315

mobile banking 317

petty cash 325

web-banking 317

EVERYDAY ETHICS

Sales at Any Cost?

Call centres have often been compared to pressure cookers; calls are monitored for proper conduct, speed, and accuracy, as well as quota. At the Barkley Trust Bank's Call Centre (BTBC), the operators, or associates as they are called, are not only expected to handle the incoming and outgoing calls but also to "upsell" the client caller with other products such as investment accounts, mutual funds, or insurance coverage. The bonus is good, but high pressure is always on!

One of BTBC's associates, Rita, is determined to exceed her quota but seems to be experiencing only "high-maintenance" calls today—complaints! By chance, she picked up her headset this morning to hear Bryan telling a customer that he was not able to talk to the customer's business associate about bank products because he was too busy dealing with other business.

Rita did not say a word. She quietly noted the associate's details and decided then and there that if Bryan couldn't be bothered to take this opportunity to sell something, then she would! After all, any sale generated from any customer is revenue for BTBC. She rationalized that it does not matter which associate or by which method the associate gets the sale—a sale is a sale! Right?

- What's the main issue in this case?
- What principle, if any, was violated?
- Do you agree with Rita's assessment of the situation?

Problem Solving

1. You work for an investor. Your responsibilities include keeping a record of money received and preparing cheques for expenses. When you reconciled the bank statement for March, you had a difference of $550 between the chequebook balance and the bank statement balance. The bank statement was $550 more. You rechecked every entry. You finally remembered that your manager had recently purchased a house to rent and had instructed the renter to mail the rent cheque to the bank. You went through the cheques and other items returned from the bank. There was a deposit slip for $550. What entry should you make in the chequebook?

2. When you reconciled the balance of the bank statement for September with the chequebook balance, the bank statement balance exceeded the chequebook balance by $1100, a difference for which you had difficulty accounting. You finally discovered that this was the amount of a cheque issued for supplies that were never delivered. The cheque was returned to you by the vendor. What adjustments, if any, would you make to the chequebook balance side of the bank reconciliation statement?

Special Reports

1. Search the web and locate three providers of computerized, bookkeeping/accounting software. Create a table comparing the features of each product and write a brief recommendation for the software you would choose providing a rationale for your answer. Submit the table and your written recommendation to your instructor.

2. Interview two administrative professionals to find out how involved they are with banking procedures. Do they perform all banking-related tasks? How do they perform the banking tasks, in person or online? How do they maintain their banking records? Identify any challenges they experience with banking procedures. Prepare a brief report and present it to your instructor or your class.

3. Visit a local chartered bank branch and find out about business banking services offered at this branch. Prepare a brief report outlining the key business services offered at this bank and present it to your class or instructor.

PRODUCTION CHALLENGES

15-A Making Deposits

Supplies needed:

- *Deposit slip, Form 15-A-1, Companion Website*
- *Cheque Register, Form 15-A-2*

Jacob Levine is in charge of registration for the November Sales Seminar, and you are assisting him.

On Tuesday, November 4, you received cheques from four registrants as follows:

Leroy McGovern, $75.00
Janet Temple, $75.00
Kevin Smythe, $75.00
Laura Cole, $75.00

Make out a deposit slip for the November Sales Seminar account (by Noah Wilson) for November 4. The account number is 09-04156. Also, record the amount of the deposit in the cheque register, and show the balance. The account has a balance of $360.27.

During the week, you received cheques from the registrants for the following amounts:

Nov. 5	$1500.00	20 registrants
Nov. 6	$3000.00	40 registrants
Nov. 7	$2250.00	30 registrants

On Monday, November 10, the first day of the seminar, eight more people registered; the total amount of cheques was $600.00.

Assume that you made out daily deposit slips, took the deposit slips and the cheques to the bank, and entered the daily amounts in the cheque register. (In an actual situation, you would also make out a receipt and a name tag for each registrant.)

15-B Writing Cheques

Supplies needed:

- *Blank cheques, Forms 15-B-1 through 15-B-12, Companion Website*
- *Cheque Register used in 15-A*

On Thursday, November 13, the November Sales Seminar is over, and you are writing the cheques for the expenses incurred because of the seminar. Mr. Wilson signed the signature card at the bank for the November Sales Seminar account, so he must sign the cheques.

Prepare cheques for the following expenses:

- *Parker's Restaurant for banquet, $1224.00*

- *A & R Breakfast House for Tuesday's breakfast, $510.00*
- *Jane's Pancake House for Wednesday's breakfast, $450.00*
- *BJ Florist, $96.00*
- *Ramco Signs, $78.25*
- *Al's Print Shop, $1700.00*
- *City Equipment Rental, $25.00*
- *William Wilson, reimbursement for postage, $60.00*
- *Parker's Hostess Service, for coffee and rolls at morning and afternoon breaks, $300.45*
- *Louise Barclay, keynote speaker, $500.00*
- *Raymond Clevenger, banquet speaker, $500.00*

15-C Reconciling the Bank Statement

Supplies needed:

- *Cheque Register used in 15-A and 15-B*
- *Bank Statement, Form 15-C, Companion Website*
- *Plain paper*

On November 26, you received the bank statement for the November Sales Seminar account. On November 23, you received a cheque from Al's Print Shop for $170.00 as a 10% discount for paying promptly. You mailed this cheque to the bank, but it is not shown on the bank statement.

Reconcile the bank statement with the cheque register for the November Sales Seminar. Key the bank reconciliation statement.

15-D Handling Petty Cash

Supplies needed:

- *Petty Cash Envelope, Form 15-D-1, Companion Website*
- *Petty Cash Vouchers, Forms 15-D-2 through 15-D-13, Companion Website*
- *Plain paper*

Martin Kline, who had been handling petty cash transactions for the Marketing Department, was transferred to another division, and you were asked to handle petty cash.

You started with a clean petty cash envelope. The balance in the fund was $100.00. Write $100.00 in the Received column.

You paid out cash for the following items:

- *December 1, paid Stationery Store $5.12 for a special drawing pen.*
- *December 3, paid $5.55 to the post office for stamps.*
- *December 3, paid $7.16 to post office for postage and insurance for a package.*

- December 4, paid City Taxi $10.25 to deliver a package to Airlift Freight office.
- December 5, paid Williams Drugstore $12.58 for two magazines for the reception area.
- December 8, paid BJ Florist $18.50 for plant for Mr. Wilson's office.
- December 8, paid Williams Drugstore $4.56 for fertilizer tablets for plants at the office.
- December 9, paid Rapid Courier $19.50 to deliver a telegram.
- December 9, paid Meyers Stationery Store $5.63 for a set of markers.

Your cash fund is getting low. Record the totals for the Paid Out column and the Distribution of Payment columns. Carry the balance forward to the Received column, but label it as "Balance." On plain paper, key a petty cash report and ask for enough money to bring the petty cash fund balance back to $100.00. Attach the petty cash vouchers to the report. You are authorized to sign the vouchers.

15-E Checking on Privacy

Supplies needed:

- Plain paper
- Access to the internet

There have been customer complaints of rudeness towards them by Jacob Levine, the AVP of Marketing for the Northwestern region. Noah Wilson has asked you to confidentially record all customer-related calls from Jacob Levine so that he may judge how improper the calls really are. You are not comfortable with this request and feel that it may violate Jacob's privacy rights.

Noah empathized with your concerns and suggested that you research the issue and provide a brief report of your findings before you record Jacob's calls.

Go to the Federal Privacy Commissioner's website at www.priv.gc.ca to determine whether it is illegal for you to record Jacob Levine's calls without his consent.

Write a brief one-page report of your findings for Noah Wilson.

Weblinks

Bank of Montreal
www.bmo.ca
Bank of Montreal's main site provides links to all of its services, initiatives, and economic reports.

RBC Financial Group
www.royalbank.ca
RBC's main site offers access to personal, business, and corporate products and services, plus a wide variety of topics from international trade to starting a business.

TD Canada Trust
www.tdcanadatrust.com
TD Canada Trust's main site offers access to a wide range of banking, investment, insurance, and small business products, services, and information. It also offers brokerage services through its partner, TD Waterhouse.

Canada Revenue Agency
https://www.canada.ca/en/revenue-agency.html
Provides detailed information for personal and business taxation. Additionally, provides payroll preparation for business with calculation tools, etc.

Office of the Privacy Commissioner of Canada
http://www.priv.gc.ca
See the guide for businesses and organizations concerning the *Personal Information Protection and Electronic Documents Act* (PIPEDA). Valuable resources are available for individuals and businesses.

Innocation, Science and Economic Development Canada, Office of Consumer Affairs (OCA)
http://oti.ic.gc.ca/eic/site/oca-bc.nsf/eng/h_ca02214.html
Read about the *Canadian Code of Practice for Consumer Protection in Electronic Commerce*.

Scotiabank
www.scotiabank.ca
Scotiabank's main site provides interest rates, personal and business banking services, and economic reports.

ECommerce Guide
www.ecommerce-guide.com
Ecommerce business owners are offered ecommerce news, hardware and software reviews and tutorials, online business solutions, and much more.

Make Use Of
www.makeuseof.com
Trustworthy website certification information for various transactions.

Canadian Marketing Association
www.the-cma.org
The Canadian Marketing Association is the industry's leading advocate on legislative affairs; electronic commerce is one of the many areas for which it develops self-regulatory policies.

Universal Currency Converter
www.xe.com/ucc
Convert world currencies quickly and easily using up-to-the-minute currency rates.

Chapter 16
Employment Strategies

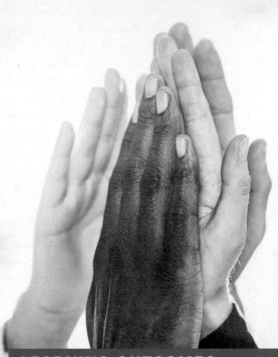

Flam ngo Images/Shutterstock

LEARNING OUTCOMES

After completion of this chapter, the student will be able to:

1 Describe components of The Conference Board of Canada Employability Skills.

2 Recognize methods for locating employment opportunities.

3 Understand the steps involved in an effective job search campaign.

4 Develop an understanding of preparing a résumé, cover letter, and assorted employment seeking and follow-up documentation.

5 Explore portfolio development illustrating accomplishments and skills.

6 Prepare for an employment interview and explore various interview question styles.

7 Analyze interview experiences.

8 Review the components of preparing employment documents for electronic scanning.

Seeking an opportunity in a new career is intimidating for most people. Knowing how to navigate these important components will facilitate a satisfying transition from the academic to professional world. An environmental scan of employment prospects is helpful to cast a net for potential opportunities. It is important to be sure you are employable and that you know how to drive an effective job campaign.

Preparing the skills to ensure marketability, as well as aligning it with your academic credentials, often positions individuals for success. The administrative career choice offers rewards not only monetarily but also in terms of job satisfaction and opportunities for promotion. Securing employment will involve seeking out professional openings, preparing job-hunting materials including a résumé, cover letter, and portfolio. Unless you have specialized in the legal or medical field, do not limit yourself to seeking a job in a specific department, such as human resources, accounting, or sales. Remain open to opportunities; often, getting your foot in the door is the first step to gaining experience and eventually getting the position and advancement desired.

Office administrative skills are transferable and portable from location to location. Often the same basic skills are required in different departments; therefore, as a best practice, do not limit your opportunities by expressing interest in working only for one department—instead, express interest in working for the organization. Demonstrate flexibility and willingness to adjust to the needs of the organization. Experienced interviewers will strive to match you to a position that will maximize your talents.

Start your job campaign several months before graduation or several months prior to transitioning to a new position. Identify by making a job prospect list using the sources listed in this chapter. In addition, most academic institutions have career centres to support employment search strategies.

EMPLOYABILITY SKILLS

A main end goal as a student is to gain employment skills that will secure you job satisfaction as well as a good income. Once you secure that opportunity, you will enable a host of skills to position you in a manner to keep your job and then

Company Profile

Office Team

Smith Collection/Gado Images/Alamy Stock Photo

This organization dates back to 1948. Founded by Robert Half, Office Team has an extensive history as a staffing agency serving the evolving needs of industry. Companies seek out Office Team to secure talent for their business.

Office Team sources temporary or full-time professionals to fit client organizational needs. It also provides support to those seeking employment opportunities. Recruiters boast the ability to help locate jobs that bring about satisfaction and happiness on the part of the job seeker.

A core value is promoting a positive work environment for clients and the professionals seeking an opportunity.

They consider themselves workplace happiness experts as they conduct significant industry scans and research that lends itself to assist organizations with a view to increase employee engagement and satisfaction.

Annually, Office Team publishes a Salary Guide. Of course, the publication includes salary standards from industry and also captures employment trends to help organizations with their recruitment processes, ensuring they remain competitive when offering a salary benchmark in their own organization. Additionally, Office Team conducts research in several employment sectors such as administrative, accounting, and marketing areas.

Office Team prides itself on being an international organization generating $5 billion in professional services. In 2018, Office Team was again named first in the industry on *Fortune* magazine's list of "World's Most Admired Companies." In 2017, the chairperson and CEO was name to Staffing Industry Review's—Staffing 100 Hall of Fame.

Finally, its core values are described as leadership by example, ethics first, openness to new ideas, and a dedication to excellence. Office Team has a full department based on training and development that is available to all employees whether in person or online. With hard work and talent, there are no limits to opportunity for those who are motivated for success.

to progress in your career. Exactly what skills will make you desirable in the workplace?

Ready for Work

Although each opportunity posting in the workplace requires unique targeted skills, most jobs require a common set of skills. Essential employability skills can be leveraged with most opportunities. These include, for example, critical thinking and problem solving, ability to work with others, demonstrating positive attitudes, communicating effectively, and acting responsibly. Become a graduate with a package of skills that will give you the leading edge in the job market. Continuously look for ways to improve your own employability skills.

The Conference Board of Canada

As discussed in the introductory chapter, The Conference Board of Canada is a not-for-profit Canadian organization. It is a specialized organization adept in research. Every year The Conference Board hosts conferences and holds leadership development programs. It has among its members representatives from Canadian private industry and business, the military, government, and education.

One of The Conference Board's mandates is to act as an advisory board to guide the education sector in preparing students to be productive members of the Canadian workforce. Both educators and employers consider The Conference Board of Canada informative and content published surrounding employability skills are highly regarded.

It is key to be familiar with the most current *Understanding Employability Skills* publication that lists skills needed to enter and progress in the workforce. The Conference Board breaks these skills into the following three categories:

- **Fundamental skills.** These are the foundational skills needed to secure and progress at work and achieve positive results.
- **Personal management skills.** A combination of skills, attitudes and behaviours necessary to secure, keep, and progress in a position.
- **Teamwork skills.** This category relates to the importance of being able to work with others on the job to achieve the best results. See Figure 16-1 showing a poster of The Conference Board of Canada essential skills mapping.

Self-Check

1. When should you start your job campaign?
2. What three categories of skills are listed in the *Employability Skills Poster* publication?

SOURCES FOR JOB PROSPECTS

Sources for job prospects are the web, college career centres, social media, job fairs, private and public employment agencies, government service announcements, chambers of commerce, and your network of friends and associates.

Use all of these sources, not just one, to find job leads. Once you begin your job campaign, keep it going. Be persistent in following through on what is available for someone with your qualifications and interests. It has been said that looking for a job is a full-time job. Whether your job hunt is simple and quickly successful or difficult and protracted, you will need all the contacts you can get.

Networking

Put in simple terms, **networking** means exchanging information. Information is the most powerful asset a business professional can have. If you have information and are willing to share it, you will be viewed as a valuable person to have on staff.

During the job hunt, networking is an essential step towards gaining successful employment. Sharing employment information with a network of people is probably one of the most effective methods of obtaining employment. As a student, you can begin to build your network by attending functions such as career fairs, where prospective employers will be available to meet students. Attend and participate in seminars and other functions where office administrators will be present. By expressing your desire for employment and by leaving a positive impression, you will be increasing your opportunity to learn about possible employment prospects.

The early stages of forming a network should include discussing your employment goal with your course faculty and with business friends of the family. Tell your neighbours, relatives, and business contacts that you are actively seeking employment and that you would appreciate their help in finding out about job openings.

When your contacts give you job leads, follow through on them, or they will not share additional leads with you. Then let the person who told you about the lead know the results. This is a simple courtesy and a way of thanking this person for his or her assistance. Remember that networking is an *exchange* of information, not a one-way effort. The more information you give, the more information you usually get back. To be a good networker you must be a good listener. By applying your best listening skills you will collect accurate information. This, in the long run, may save you time and effort in your job search.

By listening to the needs of other networkers, you will be able to offer them greater assistance. In this way, you will be viewed as a valuable network partner. As previously stated, the more information you provide others, the more

Employability skills are the skills you need to enter, stay in, and progress in the world of work—whether you work on your own or as part of a team.

Fundamental Skills

These are the skills needed as a basis for further development. You will be better prepared to progress in the world of work when you can:

- communicate
- manage information
- use numbers
- think and solve problems

Personal Management Skills

These are the personal skills, attitudes, and behaviours that drive one's potential for growth. You will be able to offer yourself greater possibilities for achievement when you can:

- demonstrate positive attitudes and behaviours
- be responsible
- be adaptable
- learn continuously
- work safely

Teamwork Skills

These are skills and attributes needed to contribute productively.

You will be better prepared to add value to the outcomes of a task, project, or team when you can:

- work with others
- participate in projects and tasks

 The Employability Skills profile was developed by members of The Conference Board of Canada's Employability Skills Forum and the Business and Education Forum on Science, Technology, and Mathematics. For more resources on education and skills go to: www.conferenceboard.ca/topics/education/learning-tools.aspx.

conferenceboard.ca

Source: Employability Skills, https://www.conferenceboard.ca/docs/default-source/public-pdfs/spse_skillsposter_en.pdf

people will reciprocate. Networking is a developed skill that will help you enhance your life and your career. It will increase your ability to be employed and to advance.

The following are suggestions for improving your networking skills:

1. If you have recently been employed, choose a corporate mentor. A corporate mentor usually holds a position at a higher level than yours. This person can offer you information and advice about the organization and give you career direction.

2. Never limit your contacts by missing an opportunity to meet new people. Your network may include business associates, friends, neighbours, past graduates from your college, relatives, and many other groups of people. A network should become a vast chain of information. The more effort you put into networking, the more the network will expand, and the greater your chances of career success will be.

3. Make yourself visible. Becoming a leader of a professional organization or volunteering to serve on a committee will open networking doors.

4. If you have not already, secure your voice mail setup. Missed messages may mean lost contacts.

5. Increase your reading of business materials. Remember that information is power, and reading will build your information base.

6. Develop an organized database of your contacts. A computer database will be invaluable as the number of contacts expands. You will want to keep a current record of:
   - names
   - addresses
   - telephone and fax numbers and email addresses
   - places of employment
   - job titles
   - personal information that will assist your communications with your contacts

7. Be a giver and not just a taker. Business organizations attempt to hire candidates with a reputation for being contributors to the team, not people who are self-serving. Therefore, don't provide information to your network contacts only because you think you will get some in return.

College Placement Office

Most postsecondary institutions have a career centre to provide their graduates with a variety of job search assistance. At the beginning of your job campaign, contact the office to find out what resources you have, including access to online job-posting systems. Watch for announcements of employers hosting events on campus.

Sometimes the career centre personnel arrange for company representatives to conduct interviews on campus. These centres often maintain a list of job openings prepared from the requests of human resource managers, who contact the career centre in search of prospective employees.

Watch for the announcement of forthcoming campus employment fairs at your school, and arrange to attend.

Employment Fairs

Look for and attend job fairs. Job fairs are often hosted at community centres and colleges. This will be an opportunity for you to meet face-to-face with prospective employers. Many employers will conduct a brief interview during the fair, and this is your opportunity to shine. Be sure to bring several copies of your résumé, and dress as if you were going on an interview.

The job fair will help you to determine if you are a good fit for an organization, as many prospective employers provide information detailing what they have to offer and who would make a good candidate. Take time to read the information so that if you do get called for an interview you will have a good understanding of your potential employer.

Job fairs may also be specific to certain fields. For instance, some are intended only for legal administrative professionals job seekers; others may be for medical administrative professionals. This helps you to tailor your search.

The number of administrative professionals who move to another city when an organization relocates is small compared to the number of executives who transfer to the new location. Therefore, you can expect that any organization that has relocated its offices to another city will be hiring administrative professionals.

Direct Application

Often, the best opportunities are not advertised. Many organizations prefer to select their employees from applicants who have taken the initiative to come to them seeking employment.

Do not wait for a job to come to you; it probably will not. Take the initiative to search for a job and apply. Call the organization and arrange an appointment with the hiring manager if possible.

Be optimistic. Some of the organizations on your prospective list may not be seeking administrative professionals at this time, but an impressive application and interview may put you in line for a future opportunity.

Federal Government

The federal government of Canada makes employment information readily available to the public. Service Canada, a Canadian federal institution, is part of Employment and Social Development Canada. They support an online job bank searchable for employment opportunities. Service Canada supports Future Skills, which examines and determines what emerging technologies to prepare for in demand careers in the Canadian workplace. In addition, Future Skills offers innovative approaches and keen insights to the evolving technological advances.

Staffing Agencies

Staffing agencies are a good source for locating job opportunities. Employment agencies keep information regarding available employment confidential until a candidate is tested, interviewed, and determined as suitable for the position.

Private employment agencies usually provide excellent service. They administer tests, conduct thorough interviews, and carry out a complete job hunt in collaboration with each applicant. Private employment agencies make a sincere effort to refer applicants to jobs for which they are qualified and which they are likely to accept.

Most employment agencies do not charge the applicant a fee for the agency's services. They do, however, charge the employer a **markup**. Once the agency has tested, selected, and placed the applicant, the employer pays the agency a rate. When the work is temporary and the worker is being paid by the hour, the agency collects the markup from the employer and pays the employee a portion of this.

It is unethical for Canadian employment agencies to restrict the applicant's right to hold contracts with other employment agencies. More than one contract means you may work for more than one personnel agency at the same time. This should provide more opportunities for work.

Job Search Boards and Search Engines

The end game of a job search is to secure an opportunity. In the last several years, job search methodologies are inclusive of searching and conducting online campaigns for potential opportunities. A **job search board** is a website hosting opportunity supplied by employers. By contrast, a **job search engine** combs through the web looking for all job postings and amalgamates chosen postings under their search engine. Monster is an example of a job search board and in fact is one of the largest in the world at the time of publication. Companies have listed available positions and regularly accept job applications directly through the job board. Employers pay a fee to the job board in order to list their jobs on the site. Eluta is an example of a job search engine. A job seeker will find a wider scope of job opportunities on job search engines because of their multiple source listings. Review some key advantages of using online methodologies:

- **Convenience.** There is no way to discount the advantage of applying for several opportunities online. An applicant does not have to drive from business to business to apply.
- **Saves money.** Employment hunting has associated costs such as printing résumés and cover letters.
- **Security.** Leaving paper copies of personal information may unintentionally be shared with others. Applying online electronically can reduce this possibility.

Some disadvantages to consider:

- **Competition.** Anyone with web access can apply for a job, and this translates to many applicants for the same position.
- **Scams.** Personal information revealed can lead to potential identity theft incidents
- **Lower wage.** With the volume of applicants, employers will have a greater selection and may not offer as competitive of a wage.

It is interesting to note that recent studies have shown networking is still key in 60% of successful job hunts.

As mentioned, job search boards provide an avenue for an effective job search. Here is a selection of job search boards:

- Monster
- Indeed
- Workopolis
- Career Builder

Figure 16-2 depicts a typical online posting specific to job requirements.

Prospects in Another Geographic Area

The best way to locate job opportunities in a different city or country is to get proactive on the internet. Websites such as www.jobstreet.com, which lists jobs in Asia, or most job search engines and boards, assist in finding jobs worldwide. Another underestimated, overlooked source of employment is known as the **hidden job market**. This is a virtual market of unadvertised opportunities in which you have to find the employer rather than where employers find you through employment agencies. Finding opportunities in the hidden job market requires determination and a good network.

FIGURE 16-2 Sample job posting for administrative professional.

- Previous administrative experience in a responsible role.

- Demonstrated initiative, good judgment, discretion, and tact in dealing effectively with all levels of staff and management.

- Excellent organizational skills, proven ability to set priorities, and ability to work under pressure with minimal supervision are integral for this position.

- Effective communication skills to prepare clear and concise reports, briefing materials, and internal communications.

- Extensive knowledge and experience in using various software programs (i.e., MS Word, Excel, PowerPoint, Access, Outlook, MS Project, MS Visio and SharePoint) is required.

- The successful candidate must be eligible to work in Canada and will be subject to a criminal background check.

Source: Workopolis.

Once you've located employment opportunities that interest you, follow through with your résumé and application letter. Be assertive! The opportunity to work abroad or even in another Canadian city will make your résumé more powerful, increase your future potential, and bring you self-satisfaction and personal growth.

Other ways to locate job opportunities in other geographic locations are:

- Conduct research on the web by city name or by company name.

- Ask the career counsellor in your college to help you. The career counsellor will have useful information and tips on how to secure employment and where to look for it.

- Inquire at the local public library for the telephone directory and newspapers for the city where you want to work.

Your career counsellor may have the most recent copy of *Career Options*, a publication from the Canadian Association of Career Educators and Employers. This valuable publication can be found online at www.careeroptionsmagazine.com. It offers useful information regarding your career search and industry profiles, and it also provides a directory of employers interested in hiring college graduates. The website provides a wealth of information to assist with job searching.

THE REBOUND: BOUNCING BACK

As a result of organizational **downsizing** or **rightsizing**, being overqualified, being made **redundant**, **company merger**, or **company takeover**, you've been fired or laid off. Now what? Should you get depressed, angry, or emotional? Go ahead. Allow yourself to vent, but keep it short and keep it private. Most people who have been released from their employment go through various emotional stages, but how they handle it will make a difference as to when they are ready to jump back into the job market.

Becoming Eligible for Employment

These ideas, if applied, will help to move you back to gainful employment:

1. Learn from the experience. Ask yourself why you are in this position. What responsibility is yours? Did you do something to invoke this? What can you learn from this? What will you do differently next time?

2. Cut out the "If only I had," "I should have," "I could have," phrases. The truth is that you didn't. That was then. This is now. Develop the attitude of putting the past behind you and moving forward with a new experience under your belt.

3. Develop the attitude that when one door closes, others open.

4. Look at the job market as a challenge that you are ready to accept. Take the challenge and prepare yourself to win.

5. Draw up an action plan that includes actions and dates to accomplish them. Stick to the plan.

6. Consider other types of work. This is an opportunity to start fresh.

7. Dress and act the part. Don't run your job campaign at home in your pyjamas. Get up at the same time every day, and prepare yourself in the same way as you did when you were employed. Take care of yourself.

8. Consider joining a health club to keep fit. Having a healthy body makes it easier to have a healthy mind.

9. Build a budget. If you are without a regular cheque, you will need to fall back on your reserves, so you will need to spend them wisely.

10. Inquire through your provincial and federal government agencies to see what financial or training assistance is available during the time you are searching for work.

11. Use the time away from work to upgrade your employment skills. Secure certification for your upgrading so that you can present this to potential employers.

12. Most of all, don't become discouraged. Get a friend or mentor to help keep you focused and on track with your action plan.

Applying for Jobs

You have brushed off your pride, scouted job opportunities, updated your skills, put on a good shirt, and cleared the clutter off your desk. You are ready to apply for new jobs, and who knows what opportunities that might bring?

The résumé, the application or cover letter, and the job interview are the applicant's direct contacts with prospective employers. The following discussions will provide you with methods for making these more persuasive and effective.

RÉSUMÉS

A résumé is sometimes called a **curriculum vitae** or CV. It is a summary of an applicant's qualifications for the job being sought. Note that the proper way to spell *résumé* is with two accents.

Your résumé should answer questions concerning:

1. who you are
2. the type of opportunity you are seeking
3. the qualifications you have to offer
4. the experience you have to offer

A résumé is a tool that you use to promote your skills and expertise to the right employer. It is not a document that rambles on about your qualifications and experience. It must be:

- well written
- well presented
- well organized

An excellent résumé can be your passport to success.

When preparing to write a résumé, find out what skills, knowledge, and experience are needed to do the job. Your job is to construct your résumé by highlighting the transferrable skills you have that match the position. This section will outline each section of a résumé and provides some tips on how to make your résumé targeted to your industry.

Rules for Writing a Résumé

There are four rules for writing a résumé.

Rule #1—Your résumé should be esthetically pleasing

- Margins should be 2.5 cm on all sides; white space makes the résumé easier to read.
- Use 11- to 12-point font for content and 14- to 16-point for headings, your name can be slightly larger.
- Avoid using Times New Roman; instead, use Arial, Calibri, or Tahoma.
- Do not overbold your fonts; bold all headings for consistency.
- Use consistent line spacing between points, sections, and after section headings.
- Use consistent tab spacing if indenting points.

Rule #2—Your résumé must be free from spelling and grammar mistakes

- Proofread, proofread, proofread.
- Read your résumé out loud to make sure it flows well.

Rule #3—Your résumé must be tailored to the position

- Customize each résumé to the position to which you are applying.
- Choose experiences that highlight your skills and competencies.
- Do not use résumé templates.
- Fill your résumé with keywords from your industry.

Rule #4—Your résumé must demonstrate your accomplishments for jobs you have held

- Focus on your skills and accomplishments, not just what your job responsibilities were.
- Write skill statements to provide evidence of your accomplishments, using numbers for context (see the section of writing skill statements).

Select a résumé style that suits your education, experience, and skills. Refer to the Chronological, Functional, and Combination styles later in this chapter, but general résumé guidelines and tips follow here.

Competitive Résumés

According to Sheila Musgrove, Canadian recruiter and author of *Hired!*, 80% of résumés are rejected in less than 11 seconds.

When reviewing résumés, recruiters do the 11-Second Skim Test, glancing immediately at the following five areas for an initial match:

1. What are the current and last positions, company, and title?
2. What were the start and end dates?
3. What is the candidate's level of education?
4. Where is the candidate located?
5. Has the candidate included numbers and percentages?

In order to grab the attention of the employer, the top third of the résumé should include one or two of the following strategies. These strategies are placed on your résumé after your contact information.

Strategy #1: Objective

- Generally, objectives are redundant and should be used with caution.
- If you have work experience, it is unlikely that an objective will be necessary.

Example:

Career Objective: An entry-level administrative support role in automotive sales.

Strategy #2: Headline

- Capture the employer's attention.
- Show the "fit" between what you can offer and what the employer needs.

Example:

Administrative Professional
~ Adaptable ~ Organized ~ Tactful

Strategy #3: Profile or Highlights Section

- Highlight your core strengths and summarize your qualifications, experience, and education.
- A profile may be written in a short paragraph, bullet-point form, or a combination.
- Limit your strengths to four to six key skills that are relevant to the job.
- Use adjectives to describe how well you use the skills to highlight the value you bring to the role.
- Students can include "selected" program learning outcomes paraphrased to demonstrate skills.

Example:

Professional Office Administrator
A hardworking and dedicated office administrator with broad knowledge of how to perform efficiently in a variety of office settings and courses utilizing a variety of technology including Microsoft Office Suite. Results-focused with superior organizational and multitasking talents. Strong documentation, data entry and reporting abilities. A personable individual with outstanding communication, listening, and interpersonal skills.

The Education Section

If you are currently in school or about to graduate, you should include your education underneath your objective, headline, or highlights/profile section.

There are three options on how to include your education:

Option #1: Include the program name (make sure to include the formal name of your program)

Example:

Office Administration—Executive, insert dates
Dean's List (if applicable)

Name of college, city, province

Option #2: Include the program name plus three to four relevant courses

Example:

Office Administration—Executive, insert dates
Dean's List (if applicable)
Name of college, city, province
Completed courses in Social Media and Web Management, Bookkeeping, Executive Office Management, Administrative Support and Records Management

Option #3: Include the program name plus three to four relevant learning outcomes

Example:

Office Administration—Executive,
Dean's List (if applicable) insert dates
Name of college, city, province
Relevant skills: acquiring a broad-based foundation for applying a variety of technology and effectively performing in an office environment
- Adhering to relevant legislation, standards and codes of ethics while conducting office responsibilities in a professional manner
- Insert three or four that are relevant to the position

Work Experience

Always list your work experience in reverse chronological order (include most recent position first, then your previous positions in order).

- Include the name of the employer, your position, and dates of employment, including the month and year. Dates should always be on the right hand side of the page.
- Use present tense verbs when describing your skills statements and past tense verbs to describe your skills from past positions

Optional Sections

You might also want to list additional assets. These will be located at the end of your résumé.

Professional Associations

- List current or past involvement with associations to demonstrate your currency in the field.

Community Involvement or Volunteer Work

- Include your involvement outside of paid work experience.
- Describe what you did and how long you have been involved.

Specialized Training and Certification

- Include additional training or certification completed outside formal education.

Skill Statements

If you want to pass the 11-Second Skim Test, write skill statements, not a list of your duties and responsibilities. Skill statements provide specific examples of what you actually did and the impact of your efforts using numbers and percentages to add context.

Look at the following statements. Which statement follows the skill statement strategy better?

Sentence #1: Responsible for data entry.

Sentence #2: Created a computer database using Access, resulting in a savings of four hours per week from previous manual method.

The second sentence is correct. This example provides concrete evidence of how the applicant used technology to improve efficiency. The formula for writing a skill statements with examples is like this:

Action verb + Describe what you did and how you did it + Result or outcome. See Figure 16-3 for examples.

FIGURE 16-3 Sample action verbs and descriptions.

ACTION VERB	DESCRIPTION	RESULT	SKILL STATEMENT
Start with an action verb in the past tense. What did you do?	What skills or techniques did you use? How did you do it?	What was the outcome or result? Use numbers for context.	
Created	A computer database using Access	Which saved 4 hours per week from previous manual method	Created a computer database using Access, which saved 4 hours per week from previous manual method.
Completed	An online safety-training program through the Ministry of Labour	Received a grade of 93%, demonstrating knowledge of safety precautions in the workplace	Completed an online safety training program through the Ministry of Labour and received a grade of 93%, demonstrating knowledge of safety precautions in the workplace.
Provided	Excellent customer service using effective marketing strategies	Increased sales by 25% in a two-week period	Provided excellent customer service using effective marketing strategies and increased sales by 25% in a two-week period.

Pat Roberts

Think of as many small and large accomplishments as you can and practice writing skill statements. Transfer these skill statements to your résumé under your work experience or skills section.

Questions to Help Generate Your Accomplishments

Think about what you did particularly well and what may have resulted from your involvement. Have you ever?

- Completed something on time or ahead of time?
- Increased sales?
- Delivered excellent customer service?
- Created something?
- Excelled in a course or group project?
- Received awards, commendations, or promotions?
- Worked safely?
- Demonstrated leadership skills?
- Designed a new process, program, or product?
- Achieved more with fewer resources or money?
- Trained staff?

Résumé Styles

All résumés should be personalized; however, there are three recommended formats that offer an attractive and easy-to-read document to the potential employer. The styles and benefits of these résumés are listed next.

Chronological Résumé   Often the most popular style, the chronological format arranges your work experience, education, and personal history so that the most recent information is first. The chronological résumé has many advantages: it is the preferred résumé for employers because it is easy to follow and shows exactly what the applicant has done, not what the applicant thinks he or she can do. This is certainly the résumé format of choice, especially when the applicant has an impressive work or educational history. This résumé works well for recent graduates because it emphasizes their education and also identifies previous work experience responsibilities that relate to the job being sought. The chronological résumé is most often the style preferred by employers. It is featured in Figure 16-4.

Functional Résumé   The functional résumé is designed to point to the applicant's skills, abilities, and accomplishments. If you have never been employed, the functional résumé will work well. A functional résumé will give you an opportunity to point out leadership and organizational experience, indicating that you will be a productive employee. A person who has not been employed but has acquired comparable work experience through volunteering and day-to-day living can also prepare a functional résumé. In this style of résumé, the experience section is organized by functions, without reference to the time of the performance or to an organization. Refer to the example in Figure 16-5.

Combination Résumé   A combination résumé format, or a hybrid, blends aspects of the chronological and functional résumé formats, and some job hunters prefer the style. This résumé format shows an equal balance on transferable skills and a progressive work history. A combination résumé works for those who have made significant career changes, or for seekers re-entering the workforce, and new graduates with internship or professional work experience. Figure 16-6 shows a sample combination résumé.

Top Five Dos and Don'ts for Résumés

Résumés are marketing documents. Your job is to create a one- or two-page document that demonstrates you have the qualifications to do this work.

Do

1. Put your jobs in reverse chronological order.
2. Tell the employer what you can do for them.
3. If you are a recent graduate or about to graduate, put your education at the top of the page under your objective, headline, or profile/highlights section.
4. Write strong skill statements to describe your accomplishments using numbers and percentages to quantify them.
5. Identify your strengths at the top of the page; remember, you need to get the employer's attention in the top third of the résumé.

Don't

- Make your résumé too long; minimum one page to a maximum of two pages, depending on experience.
- Forget to proofread your résumé to make sure it is free from spelling and grammar mistakes.
- Crowd your résumé; instead, use white space so it is easy to read.
- Put important information that is directly relevant to the job at the end of your résumé.
- Lie. Do not ever lie on your résumé or copy the résumé of someone else.

FIGURE 16-4 Chronological résumé.

Dini Lawrence
101 Keele Street
Toronto, ON M3P 1K1
416.555.1329   dizi@z-wave.ca   www.linkedin.com/in/dinilawrence

PROFESSIONAL PROFILE

- Over 7 years' experience working in a variety of office environments
- Strong interpersonal skills and effective in team environments
- Excellent organizational skills with the ability to manage multiple tasks
- Keyboarding skills of 70 words per minute
- Efficient time management skills and works well under pressure
- Demonstrated leadership and cooperation with a reputation for being a dedicated and loyal employee with perfect attendance.

Software Training

- Word
- Excel
- Peoplesoft
- PowerPoint
- Simply Accounting
- Access
- Project
- Visio
- Publisher
- Email and Outlook/Calendar

EDUCATION

Office Administration Diploma, Dean's List   (insert dates)
Southern Alberta Institute of Technology, Calgary, AB
Completed courses including:

- Report Writing
- Project Management
- Office Procedures
- Records Management
- Business Law
- Office Supervision

Customer Service Specialist, Dean's List   (insert dates)
Career College, Saskatoon, SA
Completed courses including:

- Conflict Resolution
- Effective Customer Service Strategies
- Marketing, Research
- Event Planning
- Project Management

Pat Roberts

FIGURE 16-4 *(Continued)*

Résumé of Dini Lawrence   *Page 2*
416.555.1329

<u>**PROFESSIONAL**</u>   **Administrative Assistant**   (insert dates)
<u>**EXPERIENCE**</u>   Coron Industries, Calgary, AB

Reported directly to the Chief Executive Officer and was responsible for the efficient operation of an office and directly supervised a staff of 5.

- Coordinated ISO 9000 procedures and developed a creative internal monthly newsletter using Publisher that highlighted and communicated department results and successes to a staff of over 50 senior managers.
- Supervised staff and assigned work resulting in successfully meeting deadlines 100% of the time and under budget.
- Processed a variety of confidential business correspondence using Microsoft word within tight timelines.

Sales Assistant   (insert dates)
Image Plus, Calgary, AB

Reporting directly to the Marketing Manager and was responsible for providing excellent customer service in a retail store of 50 employees.

- Provided excellent customer service using effective upselling techniques resulting in an increase of sales on a weekly basis of over 25%.
- Processed financial transactions with accuracy and speed while encouraging customers to sign up for promotions online.

<u>**PROFESSIONAL**</u>   **Association of Administrative Professionals**   (insert dates)
<u>**ASSOCIATIONS**</u>   Active member

Pat Roberts

FIGURE 16-5 Functional résumé.

Dini Lawrence

Toronto, Ontario
Dini.Lawrence@wava.ca
Phone: 416-555-1329

QUALIFICATIONS

- Business professional with superior organizational skills
- Excellent academic credentials in Business Administration
- Superior communicator
- Proven leadership in managing office employees and conducting presentations

SELECTED ACCOMPLISHMENTS

- Exceeded quotas for four consecutive years
- Launched mega products
- Improved team performance by 25% in first year at Image Canada Inc.

PROFESSIONAL EXPERIENCE

Business Analysis

- Collect and organized account data from multiple sources
- Used database applications
- Presented findings and recommendations to senior staff

Management

- Guided the activities of front-line staff
- Resolved complaints and concerns from staff and customers
- Interacted with administrative staff and senior management

EMPLOYMENT HISTORY

Image One Ltd., Fredericton, NB
Supervisor of Accounts, 2010–2019

Canada First Inc., Toronto, ON
Office Manager, 2006–2010

EDUCATION

Northern Alberta Institute of Technology, Edmonton, AB, 2004
Bachelor of Applied Business Administration

Northern Lights College, Fort Nelson, BC, 2002
Diploma Office Administration

FIGURE 16-6 Sample Combination résumé.

Dini Lawrence

101 Keele Street
Toronto, ON M3P 1K1

416.555.1329   dizi@z-wave.ca   www.linkedin.com/in/dinilawrence

PROFESSIONAL PROFILE

- Over 7 years' experience working in a variety of office environments
- Strong interpersonal skills and effective in team environments
- Excellent organizational skills with the ability to manage multiple tasks
- Keyboarding skills of 70 words per minute
- Efficient time management skills and works well under pressure
- Demonstrated leadership and cooperation with a reputation for being a dedicated and loyal employee with perfect attendance.

Software Training

- Word
- Excel
- Peoplesoft
- PowerPoint
- Simply Accounting

- Access
- Project
- Visio
- Publisher
- Email and Outlook/Calendar

EDUCATION

Office Administration Diploma, Dean's List   (insert dates)
Southern Alberta Institute of Technology, Calgary, AB
Completed courses including:

- Report Writing
- Project Management
- Office Procedures
- Records Management
- Business Law
- Office Supervision

Customer Service Specialist, Dean's List   (insert dates)
Career College, Saskatoon, SA
Completed courses including:

- Conflict Resolution
- Effective Customer
- Service Strategies
- Marketing
- Research
- Event Planning
- Project Management

Pat Roberts

FIGURE 16-6 (*Continued*)

Résumé of Dini Lawrence   *Page 2*
416.555.1329

PROFESSIONAL EXPERIENCE

Sales and Marketing
- Exceeded sales quotas for four consecutive years in MSS Corporation
- Launched mega products for Canadian region of MSS Corporation
- Improved sales team performance by 25% in Image Canada Co.

Business Analysis
- Collected and organized account data from multiple sources
- Prepared financial reports using database applications and created charts in PowerPoint presentations for management
- Presented findings and recommendations to over 25 senior staff on a monthly basis

Management
- Supervised and guided the activities of the front-line reception staff of 10
- Resolved complaints from customers and escalated urgent issues to management within a standard 24 hour period; resolved 90% of issues under the standard time
- Interacted with administrative staff and senior management to ensure timely communication of updates on projects

EMPLOYMENT HISTORY

Administrative Assistant   (insert dates)
Coron Industries, Calgary, AB

Sales Assistant   (insert dates)
Image Plus, Calgary, AB

PROFESSIONAL ASSOCIATIONS

Association of Administrative Professionals   (insert dates)

Pat Roberts

References

The question of whether or not to include references is often raised. Employers know that applicants list as references those persons who will give the applicant favourable recommendations. Many employers check with the persons who are listed as references; some do not.

Some résumés say, "References available upon request." Others go ahead and include the references. The people you select for your references must be people who will give you very positive reports. They should provide the pulling power you need to get the job. So why not include your references directly on your résumé? This is a way of encouraging the prospective employer to contact these people. Employers are busy people; by including the references on the résumé, you save the employer the effort and time of having to contact you again in order to make your references available. The best advice, then, is to include references with the résumé. You may wish to include references with some résumés and not with others. In this case, key your references on a separate page and treat them as a separate section. This way, you can choose to include the references or not.

For references, give two or more former employers or instructors who can provide a specific evaluation of your competence, work habits, and attitude towards work. If you include a character reference, do not give the name of a relative. Prior to using the references on your résumé, ask permission of each person you want to include.

For each reference, give the full name, position held, and contact information. Also include the preferable way to contact the reference. Use a courtesy title before each name. The position held is significant because it will indicate the person's association with you. The person you want to use as a reference may now be retired or may have moved to a different company. If that person's former title is important to your résumé, write, for example:

> Mrs. Christine Blackwell
> (Former) Director of Finances

or

> Mrs. Christine Blackwell
> (Retired) Director of Finance

Some tips for references to consider:

- Do not indicate "References Available Upon Request"; employers will ask you during the interview process for your references.
- Prepare a separate page and list your references, providing their name, position, company, address, phone number, and email address.

- Use the same heading for the top page of your references that you used on your cover letter and résumé. This will give your documents a consistent presentation, style, and layout.
- Provide three to five references. Hint: Put the people who know will give you the most glowing, positive reference first.
- Bring a copy with you to the interview. When asked, you can provide a copy quickly and show that you are confident and prepared.
- References are those individuals who can verify your employment or academic performance.
- They should never be your personal friends or relatives. Some options include:
  - former employer (who you reported to directly)
  - colleague (who your worked closely with)
  - teacher (who can confirm your attendance, academic skills etc.)
  - advisor (a trusted advisor who knows you well)
  - supervisor (who you reported to directly)
  - coach (who can comment of your personality attributes, team work etc.)
- Always ask the person if he or she is willing to be a reference.
- If you attend an interview and are asked to provide your references, let your references know they may be contacted. You can also let your references know what the employer is looking for so they can highlight those skills on your behalf.
- Remember to always thank your references and keep in touch periodically throughout your job search. See Figure 16-7 for a sample of reference listings.

Appearance of the Résumé

Remember that the résumé is a specimen of your work. Use appropriate software features to ensure your résumé will be a higher-quality document.

Print your résumé with a quality printer, if you need to print it. High-quality white paper is very acceptable. Many applicants choose a high-quality lightly coloured paper in order to attract attention to the résumé.

The rule, however, is to be conservative. Never use a bright or pastel shade that will detract from the conservative appearance.

Give the résumé plenty of white space, using margins of approximately 2.5 cm. The size of margins will actually depend on the setup and on the usual requirement to fit the résumé on two pages. To avoid a crowded look, use ample white space before and after headings and between entries. Too much white space, however, will suggest inefficient planning.

FIGURE 16-7 Reference sample.

Frances Small

123 Somewhere Street, Barrie, ON L0L 1L0

705.555.5555   fsmal@gmail.com

<u>REFERENCES</u>

Joe Doe, Manager
A Good Company
16 Somewhere Street
Barrie, ON
L4M 3X9
555.555.5555
jdoe@agoodcompany.com

John Smith, Supervisor
The Bar & Grill
35 Somewhere Street
Barrie, ON
L4M 3X9
555.333.3333
John.smith@thebar.ca

Jane Zoe, Manager
Georgian Zone
1 Georgian Highlights Drive
Barrie, ON
L4M 3X9
555.123.4567
Jane.zoe@georgianzone.ca

Pat Roberts

Print the main heading at the top of the first page. It should be centred, and it should be highlighted in such a way that it is eye-catching and easy to read. Suggestions are to use bold, enlarged, or italic print. Boxes or lines used in this area will enhance the appearance.

Remember the "be conservative" rule. Using too many enhancements will detract from the qualifications your résumé is trying to present.

Emailed Résumés

Emailing your résumé and cover letter might be preferable. Emailing has the advantage of keeping the document relatively confidential. However, it does not guarantee that the document will look more attractive. Although the document may look perfect on your screen, it may not have exactly the same format on the recipient's screen or printer.

Although emailing your résumé is a good option, some employers may not want to receive your résumé as an email attachment. This is due to the **proliferation** of computer viruses spread by opening attachments. If the employer has not requested your résumé be sent as an email attachment and you choose to send it that way, know that the receiver may decide not to open it.

Electronically Submitted Résumés

Increasingly, employers are seeking electronic résumé submission. An electronic résumé is a document that has been stripped of all format and design, which could interfere with the applicant tracking system (ATS). The applicant uploads into a special repository hosted by the employer. These application documents are best provided as a PDF or in a plain text format.

Electronically Scanned Résumés

A growing number of companies are relying on the services of executive search firms who use electronic scanning systems to digitally scan, store, and track résumés and cover letters. In fact, with current scanning technology, hundreds of résumés can be scanned in only a few minutes. When recruiters wish to retrieve or **short list** a group of appropriate candidates, they supply key words that are essential for the right applicant. These key words will identify expertise, experience, and education. For example, they might include such words as *bilingual, entrepreneur, desktop publishing, total quality management, supervisor,* and *teams.* The computer software scans the database, and within minutes a list of applicants whose résumés match the stated criteria is flagged on the screen.

Refer to Figure 16-8 for an example of a partial résumé that has been prepared for electronic scanning.

Electronically scanned résumés save the recruiter a large amount of time. However, even a résumé with extensive credentials may go unnoticed if the scanner cannot identify them. Many scanning programs make mistakes when reading words or special characters. To ensure that all the information on your résumé is collected by the electronic system, follow these tips to make sure your résumé is scan friendly:

1. Do not use italics. Instead, use a standard typeface.
2. Do not bold any text.
3. Do not underline or use graphic lines.
4. Do not use indents or centering.
5. Describe your personal traits in nouns, not verbs.
6. Use the key words found in the job ad.
7. Use straightforward words to describe your experience.
8. Use multiple pages if necessary. Unlike humans, computers do not tire of reading.
9. Use common résumé headings such as Objective, Education, Experience, and Interests.
10. Do not print your résumé on coloured paper.
11. Increase your lists of key words. Include specific software names such as Microsoft Word.

One advantage of an electronic scanning system is that electronic storage takes so much less space than paper storage. This means that résumés may be kept on file for an extended period of time.

If applicants are not aware of the electronic scanning process and submit attractive yet traditionally formatted résumés, they may not be identified by the computer, no matter how outstanding. The best approach when you do not know whether electronic or human screening will be used is to submit two résumés. The résumé intended for human scrutiny should be printed on attractive paper, using highlighting features, graphic lines, and so on. Place a removable note on the nicely formatted résumé that states "Visual Résumé." Place another removable note on the résumé destined for electronic scanning that says "Scannable Résumé." The reason you have included two résumés should be briefly explained in your cover letter.

Résumé Reminders

Before submitting your résumé, use the following checklist to ensure that your document will work for you. Remember that any poor work may cause an employer to send your résumé to the do-not-call pile.

Appearance

- The spacing is attractive.
- You have plenty of white space.

FIGURE 16-8 Partial résumé prepared for electronic scanning.

Ms. Kimberly Wong
10507 53 Avenue NW
Edmonton AB T6H 0R6
Tel 403-478-1320
Fax 403-478-2398
E-mail: kimwong@netcom.ca

OBJECTIVE
To earn the position of administrative assistant with a company that has a progressive team spirit.

EDUCATION
September 1996 to April 1998
Southern Alberta Institute of Technology
Office Administration Program
Calgary
Honours Diploma
Keying 70 words per minute
Microsoft Word
PowerPoint
Excel
President Office Administration Society
Team Leader Graduation Planning Committee
Leader Charity Fundraising

EXPERIENCE
May 1999 to September 2002
Administrative Assistant
Coron Industries
Calgary
Supervisor of junior staff
Coordinator of budget
Coordinator of conferences and seminars
Designer of brochures and newsletters
Coordinator ISO 9001

May 1998 to May 1999
Administrative Assistant
Image Publishers
Calgary
Supervisor of reception desk
Coordinator of media

- You have used quality paper that is white or of a conservative colour.
- Excessive enhancements have been avoided.
- A proportional font has been used.
- Your format is consistent throughout.
- Your headings are emphasized.
- Your information is in point form and uses bullets.

- You have followed the format described in this textbook.
- Your résumé is free of creases or folds.

Accuracy

- There are absolutely no errors in your résumé. It has been proofread repeatedly by you and by someone else who gave you constructive feedback.

- You have used the spell-check function to ensure your résumé is free of spelling errors.
- You have checked your résumé for spelling errors that the spell-check function would not detect.
- Your lists are consistent in wording as well as in format.
- You have stated your expected date of graduation if you have not already graduated.

Other

- Your résumé has been delivered in an appropriate way.
- Your résumé has been delivered on time, sometimes referred to as the closing date.

Self-Check

1. What questions should your résumé answer?
2. Describe a résumé format.
3. Under what circumstances does the functional résumé work particularly well?
4. What are electronically scanned résumés?

APPLICATION/COVER LETTERS

An application letter is a marketing of your knowledge, skills, and abilities in a concise document. Write an application letter as a covering letter for your résumé. The main purpose of a cover letter is to introduce your résumé in the hope of obtaining an interview.

Application letters are either prospecting or solicited. A **prospecting letter** is written by an applicant who does not know if a job opening exists. It is written to express the applicant's interest in working for a particular organization, to call attention to the applicant's qualifications, and to inquire about the possibility of a job opening. A **solicited letter** is written in response to an announcement that a job opening exists. The announcement might be placed with a private employment agency, sent to the placement office of a school, or disseminated through other sources. As a college graduate write prospecting application letters; don't wait until you know that a specific job opening exists.

The Prospecting Letter

A prospecting letter represents your initial effort at locating an employer seeking the qualifications you have to offer and at convincing the employer to consider your qualifications. You increase your application letter's chances of gaining attention when you submit a résumé along with it. Let the reader know what qualifications you possess so that he or she can compare them with the requirements of the jobs available within the organization.

Organize your prospecting application letter around the steps of a sales presentation:

1. Use an opening that gets the reader's attention and arouses interest in knowing more about your qualifications.
2. Emphasize facts that will convince the prospective employer that you possess qualifications that match the requirements of a job he or she is trying to fill.
3. Make a brief reference to the résumé you are enclosing.
4. Use a closing that requests action, which in most application letters is a request for an interview.

The Solicited Letter

When you hear or read about a job opening, write a solicited (invited) letter.

A solicited application letter can be more specific than a prospecting letter because the applicant knows that a particular job opening exists. Use the first paragraph to refer to the job and to reveal how you found out about it. Include a reference to the source. Request in the opening paragraph that you be considered for the job. Write a persuasive letter in such a way that you discuss the requirements mentioned in the announcement and show how you meet these qualifications.

Enclose a résumé and refer to it in the letter. In the résumé, cover all the qualifications and key words mentioned in the announcement, and include others that may contribute to your getting the job.

Close the letter by requesting action, which usually is a request for an interview where you can discuss your qualifications for the position.

For example, to respond to a job advertisement that says the successful incumbent will need office technology skills, you could write:

> *Please consider the enclosed résumé as an application for the position of Administrative Professional as advertised in the May 14 issue of the Cape Breton Post. I recently earned an honours diploma for Office Technology. Through my studies I mastered numerous office skills, including the use of word-processing, desktop publishing, and database management software packages. Because I am an energetic graduate who is willing to learn, I am confident I could contribute to your team.*
>
> *I would welcome an opportunity to further discuss my qualifications for the position. Please contact me at your earliest convenience. I can be reached by telephone at 306-456-7890. I look forward to hearing your positive response.*

These points are illustrated in two cover letters in Figure 16-9.

FIGURE 16-9 Prospecting letter of application.

Dini Lawrence
101 Keele Street
Toronto, ON M3P 1K1
416.555.1329   dizi@z-wave.ca   www.linkedin.com/in/dinilawrence

(insert date)

Mr. Joel Reid, Research Director
Research Company Inc.
55555 Hayden Street
Toronto, ON M4Y 1V8

Dear Mr. Reid:

1 I am writing to express my strong interest in working at Research Company Inc. in the role of Administrative Assistant. In addition to my diploma in Office Administration and my work experience in similar administrative roles, I am effective in organizing and managing information using Microsoft Word and Excel. My ability to work well with others complements my strong work ethic. My academic program, computer skills, and administrative skills have prepared me well for this position. It is my goal to work in a research or data collection organization, building on my administrative experience and developing analysis skills gained during my education.

2 Some key qualifications that are relevant to this opportunity include:
- Final grade of over 80% in courses related to finance, marketing, research, and management.
- Creative in producing visually appealing graphs in Excel, monthly newsletters in Publisher, and PowerPoint presentations.
- Efficient organizer and detailed minute-taker for faculty meetings.
- Diligent in managing confidential student information while complying with Freedom of Information legislation.
- Praised by my co-op supervisor for my ability to grasp new concepts and technology with ease.

3 In addition to my academic, computer, and administrative skills, I am committed to a high level of customer service, making me a valuable employee. Thank you for your time and consideration in reviewing my application. I look forward to meeting with you. Please feel free to contact me at 416.555.1329, or by email: dizi@z-wave.ca.

Sincerely,

Dini Lawrence

Dini Lawrence

Pat Roberts

1 1st paragraph: Indicate the job you are applying for and why you should be interviewed. **2** 2nd paragraph: Highlight your skills that match the job. **3** 3rd paragraph: Thank the employer and request an interview.

FIGURE 16-9 *(Continued)*

Dini Lawrence
101 Keele Street
Toronto, ON M3P 1K1

416.555.1329   dizi@z-wave.ca   www.linkedin.com/in/dinilawrence

(insert date)

Mr. Joel Reid, Research Director
Research Company Inc.
55555 Hayden Street
Toronto, ON M4Y 1V8

Dear Mr. Reid:

1 I am writing to express my strong interest in working at Research Company Inc. in the role of Administrative Assistant. In addition to my diploma in Office Administration and my work experience in similar administrative roles, I am effective in organizing and managing information using Microsoft Word and Excel. My ability to work well with others complements my strong work ethic. My academic program, computer skills, and administrative skills have prepared me well for this position. It is my goal to work in a research or data collection organization, building on my administrative experience and developing analysis skills gained during my education.

2 In my coursework in finance, marketing, research and management, I achieved Dean's List recognition. My previous role included **administrative duties** where I used **Excel** to create visually appealing graphs, developed presentations in **PowerPoint** and used **Publisher** to produce monthly newsletters. I organized and attended faculty meetings and prepared **detailed** minutes using **Word**. My role in Student Services at Georgian College required **managing** confidential student **information** while complying with Freedom of Information legislation. I received compliments on my ability to grasp new concepts and technology with ease from my co-op supervisor. These experiences will allow me to learn this new role quickly and become a productive contributor to the team in a short time.

3 In addition to my academic, computer, and administrative skills, I am committed to a high level of customer service, making me a valuable employee. Thank you for your time and consideration in reviewing my application. I look forward to meeting with you. Please feel free to contact me at 416.555.1329, or by email: dizi@z-wave.ca.

Sincerely,

Dini Lawrence

Dini Lawrence

Enclosure

Pat Roberts

1 1st paragraph: Indicate the job you are applying for and why you should be interviewed. **2** 2nd paragraph: Highlight your skills that match the job. **3** 3rd paragraph: Thank the employer and request an interview.

Appearance of the Application Letter

Use plain paper that matches the quality and shade of the paper used for your résumé. Include your personalized letterhead above the date. Since your application letter could get separated from your résumé, put your complete mailing address on both the letter and the résumé.

Address the letter to a specific person, if possible. Make an effort to find out the name of the employer to whom the letter should be addressed. This information can be obtained with a single telephone call to the company.

Limit your letter to one page. Since you have organized all your facts in the accompanying résumé, you can limit your application letter to three or four well-written paragraphs. Most letter styles are acceptable. The key factors in appearance are:

- Keep the font and format conservative.
- Keep the appearance professional.
- Keep the information balanced on the page.

Application/Cover Letter Guidelines

A cover letter is the window to your résumé, so it's critical that your cover letter gives the best view of your skills. Consider your application letter as one of your marketing tools. The following checklist will help you create an application letter that works for you.

Appearance

- The letter is keyed.
- You have used high-quality paper.
- Your paper and font match those of the résumé.
- Your cover letter is stapled to the top of your résumé.
- The documents have been placed in an envelope large enough that they lie flat without folding.

Content

- You have opened with an attention-getting statement.
- You have demonstrated knowledge of the company.
- Your letter complimented the company.
- Key words have been included that were used in the job posting.
- You have described what would make you valuable to the company.
- Your background has been summarized.
- You closed with a call to action.
- The letter is short.
- The letter is simple.

- The letter sounds sincere.
- The letter sounds enthusiastic.

Accuracy

- You have proofread the letter several times for typos, grammar, spelling, punctuation, and content.
- Another reliable person has proofread it and given you feedback on it.
- The letterhead contains the correct information (full address, telephone and fax numbers, and email address).

Application Forms

During your job campaign, you might be asked to complete application forms. When a company requests that you complete an application form, do so. Your résumé does not substitute for a completed application form. Be sure to complete each section of the application. If a question on the application form does not apply to you, write "Not Applicable" or "Does Not Apply" in the blank. If a question calls for salary expected and you do not want to state a figure, write "Open to Negotiation," which means you would prefer to discuss salary once an offer of employment is made. If you leave the answer blank, the employer may assume:

- You were careless and missed the question.
- You did not understand the question.

Either of these assumptions will eliminate your form from the stack of successful applications.

Each organization designs its own form for employee recruitment in order to include the specific questions it wants applicants to answer. Nevertheless, most application forms are similar.

Supplying information on the application forms you are requested to complete is a significant part of your job campaign. Follow the instructions carefully, and supply the information exactly as it is called for. If the instruction reads, "Please print," do so. Your printing and handwriting must be legible. After all, you want it to stand out in the pile.

Prepare your answers before you write or key on the application form. When you do this, your form will appear neat and organized. A completed application form becomes a part of the permanent record of the applicant who is hired.

Be prepared to complete the application. Do you:

- have a pen?
- know the current date?
- have the names, titles, addresses, telephone and fax numbers, and email addresses for your references?

- have the dates of previous employment?
- have a list of your volunteer activities and the associations you belong to?
- have the dates you attended high school and postsecondary institutions?
- know your Social Insurance Number?
- know the exact title of the job you are applying for?

Complete the form as requested even if you have your cover letter and résumé with you. In this case, staple a copy of your résumé to the back of the application form.

JOB INTERVIEWS

A job interview gives you the opportunity to convince a prospective employer that you can make a real contribution to the organization. An interviewer can judge your basic qualifications by studying your transcript, application letter, résumé, test results, and completed application form. During the interview, the interviewer will evaluate your personality, attitudes, professional presentation and conduct, and the ability to communicate. An impressive college record and evidence that you possess the necessary office technology skills are pluses, but your success in landing the job you want will hinge on the way you project yourself during the interview. Figure 16-10 depicts an interview or employment discussion.

FIGURE 16-10 Interviewer and applicant.

Antonio Guillem/Shutterstock

Remember that the purpose of the job interview is twofold:

1. to give the interviewer an opportunity to evaluate the applicant
2. to give the applicant a chance to evaluate the job and the organization

The interview is not just for the benefit of the employer. It should be mutually beneficial.

Sometimes getting an interview is extremely difficult. If getting an interview seems impossible, don't get discouraged: this difficulty may reflect the competition for jobs in your area.

Preparing before the Job Interview

Try to schedule several interviews with organizations that you believe will offer the type of work you are seeking. Don't set your expectations on one particular job. Becoming overly anxious about getting a particular job can create unnecessary tension. Nevertheless, you should enter each interview with the attitude that the job you are applying for is precisely the one you want. As you learn more about the job, it may *become* the job you want.

Prepare thoroughly for each interview. Your preparation should include the following:

- Research the organization where you have scheduled the interview. Glassdoor is an online app whereby individuals post reviews on employers detailing the organizational climate. It can be helpful to review some content posted.
- Take a practice run to the location of the interview.
- Learn what the current salaries are for administrative professionals in the community.
- Summarize your own qualifications.
- Decide which qualifications to emphasize.
- Anticipate the interviewer's questions.
- Formulate your answers to the interviewer's questions.
- Choose clothes appropriate for the interview.
- Schedule ample time for personal grooming.

Research Researching the organization is crucial. The following are effective research methods:

- Use the web to study the organization.
- Explore the organization in the media.
- Read the organization's most recent annual report.

Learn all you can about the organization. Research:

- the organization's strategic plan and core values

- financial reports if accessible
- the number of employees the organization has
- how long the organization has been operating
- the extent of the company's operations
- any recent expansion the company may have experienced
- any mergers or name changes the company has undergone
- the company's competitive standing in the industry
- the organization's hiring practices

Many applicants do poorly during an interview because they lack knowledge about the organization. The interviewer will tell you about the organization and its employment opportunities, but you will be able to converse with more ease and ask pertinent questions if you have researched the organization. Lack of knowledge could be viewed by the interviewer as lack of interest in the organization. Prepare thoroughly; show your interest in the organization through your knowledge about it.

Anticipate Questions   Think about what you have to offer and the qualifications you want to emphasize. Review your résumé before you go to the interview. The interviewer will expect you to discuss your job objective and why you feel qualified for it. You should be prepared to talk about yourself in an organized way without hesitation.

Anticipate the questions the interviewer will ask, and know what your answers will be. In an attempt to determine if you can handle the job, the employer may ask:

1. What do you know about this company?
2. What do you know about the position you are applying for?
3. We are looking for someone with extensive experience. Your résumé indicates limited experience as an office professional. How do you expect to compensate for your lack of experience?
4. Why do you believe you are a good fit for our organization?
5. What do you expect to be doing five years from now?
6. Why did you choose a career as an administrative professional?
7. Relating to the responsibilities described in the posting for this position, what strengths will you bring to our organization?
8. Relating to the responsibilities described in the advertisement for this position, what responsibilities do you believe will be your greatest challenges? How do you expect to meet these challenges?
9. How do you rate the education you received? Why?
10. Throughout your training to be an administrative professional, what courses did you enjoy the most? the least? Why?

At the outset of the interview, you may be asked some general questions relating to your personal interests, or you may be asked to give your opinion about the latest current events. Some interviewers begin with questions that they think will put the applicant at ease. Answer all questions thoroughly but without rambling. Consider your answers to all questions seriously; the interviewer is searching for qualified employees who will stay with the organization if they are hired.

To gain insight into your personality and to check on your attitude, the interviewer may ask questions such as these:

1. Tell me about yourself.
2. If we asked your friends or colleagues to describe you with three words, what words would they use?
3. Give an example of how you have displayed initiative.
4. Do you prefer working within a team or by yourself? Explain.
5. How do you spend your leisure time?
6. What personality characteristics do you think are essential for the job you are seeking?
7. How do you accept criticism?
8. Provide an example of a time when you were criticized.
9. Describe the best/worst employer/teacher you have ever had.
10. Explain a stressful situation you encountered, and describe how you handled it.

Recognize Unethical Questions   Interviewers who want information on marital status, age, smoking habits, physical disabilities, race, ancestry, or place of origin must phrase their inquiries very carefully. Many questions relating to these topics are unethical. Basing employment decisions on these factors is usually illegal.

Although most organizations fall under provincial human rights jurisdiction, some are under federal human rights jurisdiction. Those that are federally governed include all federal government departments, federal Crown corporations, federally chartered banks, and national interest organizations (such as transportation and communication companies). Most other organizations fall under provincial human rights authority. Some businesses are subject to both federal and provincial human rights acts. Human rights legislation is subject to change.

If you have concerns about your human rights as they relate to your job search, your best course of action is to contact both the Human Rights Commission for your province and the Canadian Human Rights Commission.

The Canadian Human Rights Commission provides standards surrounding employment equity, harassment in the workplace, discrimination, and many other topics.

Be Prepared to Ask Intelligent Questions An interviewer will expect you to ask questions, too. Some interviews lend themselves to the applicant asking questions periodically throughout the interview, while other interviews give the applicant an opportunity at the end of the interview to ask questions. Your research prior to the interview should help you generate a list of appropriate questions. State that you have researched the company website and that you prepared a few questions. Choose a selection of questions, key them on your crib sheet, take the sheet to the interview, and refer to it. The following is a list of good questions to ask on an interview:

- To whom would I report? To how many people would I report?
- What personal qualities improve the likelihood for success in this position?
- Can you describe the organizational culture?
- I read in the . . . that you are expanding your . . . division. How would that affect the position I am applying for?
- Does the organization have a human resource development program?
- What is the organization's plan to increase revenues or capacities?

Preparing Portfolios

A portfolio is one of best marketing tools you can have on a job interview. It is a collection of samples of your best work and should include only perfect work; nothing less than perfect is acceptable.

A portfolio is often presented in electronic form. An **e-portfolio** should contain the same documents as a hardcopy portfolio; however, the documents will be stored on a personal website or arranged in an electronic folder. An advantage of the e-portfolio is the ease of sending it to or leaving it with an employer. Note that due to the spread of computer viruses, many employers may not want to open a folder of materials that is sent as an email attachment. In this case, storing an e-portfolio on a personal website and providing a **hyperlink** from the email to the website would be preferable.

When a hard-copy portfolio is used, no writing of any kind should appear on the documents.

Regardless of whether the portfolio is presented on paper or electronically, it should contain samples of your original work and be highly organized. One suggestion is to organize it into sections such as:

- correspondence
- spreadsheets
- tables
- graphics

- minutes of meetings
- reports
- promotional material
- website developments
- documents demonstrating knowledge of specialized areas, such as legal or medical office administration

It should also contain:

- your transcript of marks (but only if it is impressive)
- letter/s of reference
- certificates and diplomas earned

When using an e-portfolio, transcripts, letters of reference, certificates, and diplomas should be scanned and stored electronically.

All portfolios must be well organized. To give the hardcopy portfolio an organized appearance, use a table of contents, dividers, and title pages. Protect all documents by placing them in plastic sleeves. Then package all of the work into an attractive leather or simulated leather case with rings to hold the pages. Do not use a binder, since it doesn't have the professional appearance you need. Keep your e-portfolio organized by using webpage links or electronic folders with titles that accurately reflect the contents.

During the interview, find an appropriate opportunity to introduce the portfolio and discuss your work with the interviewer. Remember that the portfolio is not intended to be an information tool. It is a sales tool, and the product it is promoting is you!

An e-portfolio creates a narrative of your skills and qualifications. Some web-based tools to help with the development of this record include:

- Pathbrite
- WordPress
- Sway
- FolioSpaces

Self-Check

1. What are two purposes of the job interview?
2. List two topics you could research about the prospective employer before your interview.
3. List three questions the interviewer may ask in order to determine if you can handle the job.
4. How is a portfolio considered a marketing tool?

Preparing to Go to the Interview

Although first impressions rarely win jobs, your general appearance can certainly cost you the job before you ever open your mouth. The steps you take right before the interview can help ensure that you set the right tone from the very beginning of the interview.

Your Professional Presence   Your goal is to look the part of a business professional. Your appearance should make the statement that you are a professional and that you want to be taken seriously. This is true even in companies that have a dress-down policy. Companies that encourage their employees to dress casually still expect applicants to dress and act professionally on the interview. Once they are successful and join the staff, they may adopt the dress code parameters of the company.

Tips for Looking Well Groomed   Spend the extra time it takes to look well groomed. Dress conservatively since you want the interviewer to focus on your answers without being distracted by your appearance. By applying the following guidelines to your interview preparation, you may be able to convey the proper message:

---

pro-Link
Did I Say That?

Did you know that the Canadian Human Rights Commission (CHRC) advises employers how to conduct job interviews without violating the law? Their guidelines for screening and selection are comprehensive, but these few examples are for *your* record:

- **Gender:** CHRC positions against asking gender-based questioning, and asking about pregnancy or childbearing plans.
    You may ask the applicant if attendance requirements can be met.

- **Marital status or sexual orientation:** CHRC states positions against asking applicants whether they are married, single, divorced, or whether an applicant's spouse is employed or subject to transfer. No discussions surrounding sexual orientation should be touched upon during the interview.
    You may ask if there are any circumstances that might prevent minimum service commitment.

- **Race, ethnicity or colour:** CHRC states that the employer should avoid any inquiry into race, ethnicity, or colour, including colour of eyes, skin, or hair.

- **Height and weight:** CHRC says that the employer can make no inquiry unless there is evidence it is for genuine occupational requirements.

- **Photographs:** CHRC says to avoid asking for a photograph of the applicant before the interview. Photographs for security passes or company files can be taken after successful selection.

- Your hair should be neat and away from your face.
- If you wear cosmetics, apply them sparingly.
- Your nails should be well manicured and clean.
- Your jewellery should be simple, minimal, and complementary. Since you don't know the nature of the interviewer, it is best to play it safe and wear limited and conservative jewellery.
- Shoes should be clean, polished, and conventional.
- White blouses or shirts. Cuffs or collars that have a grey appearance are a sign that grooming is less than perfect.
- Ties should complement a suit.
- Fragrance should be avoided due to sensitivity. A fragrance that is attractive to you could be offensive to another person.

Whatever you decide will be your image for an interview, consider the strong nonverbal message that your image will send. Clearly, there are things to avoid wearing for an interview, including the following:

- extreme colours of nail polish
- capris, leggings, or jean pants
- strapless dresses
- a midriff baring top

Business Professional versus Business Casual
When attending an interview, business professional is always the right choice. This means attire coordinated to the interview. The focus should be on you, not your wardrobe. Business casual is more relaxed: you may choose to wear a nonmatching jacket and skirt or pants. Remember, though, that this business casual look is only appropriate on the job, after you have been hired, not during the interview itself. Some organizations have dress-down days, and it is important you understand the guidelines your company sets for these days.

Punctuality   Know the exact location of the interview. Plan to arrive 10 to 15 minutes early, so you can avoid rushing before the interview. You can undermine yourself before the interview by becoming stressed because you did not allow yourself enough time. A few days before the interview, travel to the office, and time yourself. On the actual day of the interview, allow more time than is needed to get there.

Never schedule two interviews for the same morning or afternoon. You have no control over the length of the interview, and you will not feel at ease if you are concerned about time.

Park in a location where you do not risk getting a ticket; the last thing you need to worry about is your car.

What to Take to the Interview For the interview, you will want to have important materials on hand; but you will not want to be encumbered with items you do not need.

You should avoid bringing the following items to an interview. (Although it seems like common sense not to bring them, many employers report that applicants often do.)

- Never bring packages. Avoid shopping immediately before an interview, unless you can leave all the packages in your car.

- Carrying a large purse. A small handbag with only necessary items will not distract from a professional appearance.

- Carrying a briefcase that is oversized or resembles a schoolbag. Keep everything neat and simple and nondistracting.

- Most important of all, never bring another person. Naturally you shouldn't bring another person into the interview; but a number of applicants make plans to meet friends or relatives immediately after the interview.

The applicant needs to concentrate on the interview, not on the friends or relatives waiting in the lobby or reception area. In particular, don't bring children, since their behaviour may cause you to worry. Also, do *not* involve your parents. Don't let them make calls for you and do not bring them to your interview. This should not have to be said, and yet employers are reporting that more than a few job candidates have shown up with a parent in tow. Demonstrate that you are an independent person; arrive alone and leave alone.

Here's what you *should* take to the interview:

- Bring your portfolio; if prepared to a professional standard, it will be one of the best sales tools you have. Bring it to the interview and look for the perfect opportunity to walk through it with the interviewer.

- Always bring along a pen and paper to write down important facts you learn during the interview. Your pen should be attractive and in good condition. One that has been chewed or runs out of ink will give a poor impression.

- Bring along extra copies of your résumé. Offer copies to the interviewers just as the interview is ready to start. This demonstrates your preparation. You will also need a copy for yourself to refer to throughout the interview.

- If references do not appear on your résumé, you should bring a list of three or more references that includes names, titles, company names, company addresses, company phone numbers, and email addresses. This should be attractively keyed on a single sheet. Be prepared to leave this sheet with the interviewer.

- It is very acceptable to prepare a note sheet and bring it along to the interview. On the note sheet, you can list the responsibilities of the job, and for each one, cite specific examples of how you have demonstrated competence. Also, on this note sheet, key any questions you have prepared. Don't be afraid to refer to this sheet during the interview. The sheet should appear neat and organized and, of course, should be keyed.

- With desktop publishing, you can prepare personal business cards that are professional-looking when printed on cardstock. Or, for a nominal charge, you can have a professional printer produce a small number of business cards. The applicant who leaves a business card leaves a professional statement.

Conducting Yourself During the Interview

Be courteous, confident, and composed. As you approach the interviewer, smile, greet the interviewer by name, and introduce yourself. Give the interviewer a firm handshake. This will express your confidence. Try to relax. You will probably feel a little nervous because the interview is important to you. If you feel nervous, don't call attention to your nervousness by twisting your hair, tapping your foot, thumping on the table, sitting on the edge of the chair, talking too rapidly, or showing other outward signs.

There may be one interviewer or a panel of interviewers. The interviewers have a job to perform; they must match an applicant to the requirements of the job to be filled.

The initial interview will probably last 30 minutes or more. A good interviewer will allow the interviewee to talk throughout most of the interview.

Some interviewers break the interview into the following segments:

- getting acquainted
- presenting the organization's opportunities
- evaluating the applicant
- answering the applicant's questions

When you are asked a question, give a full answer, not simply a yes or no. The interviewer will use a question or a comment to introduce a subject you are expected to discuss. Look the interviewer in the eye, and answer all questions frankly. Be deliberate; don't start talking before the interviewer completes the question. Avoid talking too much; keep to the point. Don't attempt to answer a question you do not understand. Either restate the question as you understand it or ask the interviewer to clarify it.

While you are talking, keep your goal in mind, which is to promote yourself. Use every opportunity to emphasize your good points and to relate them to what you can do for the organization. To sound sincere, present facts, not your opinion, about yourself. Don't criticize yourself, and never make derogatory remarks about an instructor or a former employer.

As you are talking, the interviewer will evaluate your mental and physical alertness, your ability to communicate, your attitude towards life and towards the organization, and your enthusiasm for work. Be prepared for pre-employment testing in order to evaluate your skill level. This could take the form of a documentation preparation using a variety of applications.

As discussed in the section "Before the Interview," you should prepare questions to ask at the interview.

What about Salary?

At the initial interview, your first questions should not concern salary or benefits. The questions of salary can be an issue that many find difficult to address, but it is a necessary part of the job-searching process. You may wish to address salary closer to the end of the interview or choose to reserve these questions until you are offered the job. Many employers appreciate knowing whether the salary they are offering is suitable to a candidate, thus avoiding the waste of valuable time and resources. If the interviewer asks you about your expected salary, be prepared to state a range. Remember that the figure the interviewer is likely to remember and focus on is the low end of your range.

If you have prepared a personal budget and have researched office salaries in your location, you will know what an appropriate starting salary is for this employment opportunity.

Remember that although salary is often a negotiable item, these negotiations must be handled with diplomacy. Although job satisfaction will be achieved mostly through obtaining a challenging and responsible position, don't sell yourself short when salary is discussed. If you have earned postsecondary credentials, you have gained bargaining power.

The Campus Interview

Many organizations actively recruit postsecondary graduates. Your career centre may host appointments for students nearing graduation interviewed by representatives from various companies. These interviews often occur right on the campus.

Stress your strong points; listen attentively; in response to the interviewer's questions, relate how you meet the qualifications for the job; project your personality; and ask relevant questions.

Don't expect that because the interview is held on campus that it means you should dress casually. Give the interviewer a chance to see you as a serious professional in your manner, attire, and conduct. You essentially want to provide the impression you are capable of accepting responsibility. The interviewer will be comparing your professional presence with that of administrative professionals who currently work for the organization, not with the presentation of other college students.

If, as a result of the campus interview, you are invited for a second interview or to take tests, be sure to get the address of the building where you are to go. Write down the date, time, address, and name of the person who will meet with you.

Testing

Either as part of the job interview or before the interview, you might be asked to take one or more tests. The placement director and your instructors may know which organizations in your area give tests. If you apply for a job with an organization that administers tests, be prepared to take a production test or a keying test. These tests could test your skill on any software application or your ability to compose correspondence, for example.

Many tests have time limits. Listen carefully to the instructions you receive. If you do not clearly understand what you are expected to do, ask questions. You will be expected to perform at speed levels determined by the organization administering the tests. Test papers are usually evaluated by degree of accuracy.

Personality tests and mental ability tests are also popular. It is not possible to prepare for these. The goal of these examinations is to determine which applicants will work well with existing staff members, which applicants will most likely share the company's goals, and which applicants have potential leadership skills.

Behavioural Descriptive Interviews

An applicant can prepare thoroughly for an interview; however, it is impossible to anticipate all possible interview scenarios. Recruiters use behavioural descriptive interview questions to sort facts from exaggerations. These interviews use a "domino" questioning technique, in which each question leads to the next and probes deeper into an experience or scenario described by the applicant. A typical set of behavioural interview questions is:

1. Describe a situation where you were a team leader in a professional environment and conflict arose within the team.
2. What did you do to resolve this conflict?
3. What did you learn from this experience?
4. Since the conflict, how have you applied what you learned?
5. Who has benefited from your ability to resolve conflict?

Some applicants feel threatened and almost interrogated by the probing nature of these questions. However, these questions, if presented in a diplomatic manner, are highly successful in determining the best candidate. Sometimes information expressed in the application documents does not identify the best candidate.

Behavioural descriptive questions are not difficult to answer if the candidate has the experience the recruiter is seeking. If you are asked a behavioural descriptive question and simply don't have the experience necessary to answer the question, be honest. The best policy is to tell the interviewer that you have no experience in this particular area. If you have related experience, ask the recruiter if you might refer to a similar situation in a different type of environment.

Closing the Interview   Watch for cues that the interview is coming to an end. The interviewer may thank you for coming, suggest that you schedule a time to take employment tests, invite you to arrange for a second interview, stand up, tell you that you will hear by a certain date if the organization is interested in your application, or offer you a job.

A good closure to an interview would include the following actions:

- Firmly shake hands.
- Restate your interest in the position. Example: "I hope you will consider me for the job. I feel confident I would make a positive contribution to your organization."
- Check the follow-up procedure that will be employed by the organization. Example: "When might I expect to hear from you? If I don't hear from you by that date, may I call you?"
- Leave a business card.

If you are offered a position, you are not expected to accept it on the spot. You are making a long-term commitment, and you should be sure that it is the job you want. The interviewer would prefer that you give it enough thought to be absolutely certain. You may accept at once if you have no doubts about it. Otherwise, tactfully say that you would like time to consider it. Ask if you can let the interviewer know in a day or two or at some definite time you can agree upon.

You cannot always accurately judge how you are being rated by an interviewer. Interviewers who rely on the second interview for making a decision are noncommittal during the initial interview. Appear interested and confident as the interview draws to a close. Always express appreciation to the interviewer before leaving.

Preparing for the Second Interview

You may be invited for more than one interview. During the initial interview, members of the interview team will screen the interviewees. If tests are part of the screening, it will probably be the human resource department that administers them and evaluates the results.

A procedure commonly used is this. When human resource staff members discover applicants they are willing to recommend as candidates for specific jobs, they arrange interviews for the applicants with the actual employers. When you are told that you will be interviewed by the person who will be your manager if you are hired, you will know that your chances of getting the job are increasing. The final selection will be made by the person for whom the administrative professional will work directly.

The second interview provides you with an opportunity to promote yourself to the person for whom you would work. Emphasize your strong points. Be as relaxed and natural as

possible, so that the interviewer can detect your true personality. Ask questions about the scope of the job and about the responsibilities that the person performing it would have. Listen carefully, and answer the questions you are asked. When you know you want the job, say so. The interviewer is not just searching for a qualified applicant; the interviewer is searching for a person who is definitely interested in working for the organization.

Self-Check

1. List three precautions you can take to ensure you are not late for an interview.
2. List three guidelines you should follow during an interview to leave a favourable impression.
3. What would be an acceptable response if you are offered a job at the end of the interview?

Following Up after the Interview

Make each interview a learning experience. Ask yourself the following questions to improve your self-promotion techniques:

- What points did I make that seemed to interest the interviewer?
- Did I present my qualifications well?
- Did I overlook any qualifications that are pertinent to the job?
- Did I learn all I need to know about the job, or did I forget or hesitate to ask about factors that are important to me?
- Did I talk too much? too little?
- Did I interview the employer rather than permit the employer to interview me?
- How can I improve my next interview?

Follow-Up Correspondence   The letters essential for continuing and finalizing a job campaign fall into five categories: thank-you, reminder, inquiry, job acceptance, and job refusal. Key follow-up letters on the same quality paper you used for the résumé; be sure to include your contact information. Check them carefully for accuracy. Be sure that the company's name and the interviewer's name are spelled correctly.

All of the letters can be sent as email messages, but your choice to use this method will depend on the formality of the situation. Most employers are interested in quick and to-the-point communication, so email is very appropriate. However, where the environment is very formal, a letter on bond paper may be necessary.

Thank-You Letters   Writing a thank-you letter following a job interview is not a requirement but a courtesy. Always write a thank-you letter and send it immediately

FIGURE 16-11 Thank-you letter.

Ms. Dini Lawrence
101 Keele Street
Toronto, ON M3P1K1
Tel: 416-555-1329   Fax: 416-555-2390   Email: dini@z-wave.ca

July 1, 20xx

Mr. Noah Wilson
Progressive Digital Solution PDI
Vice-President of Marketing
3431 Bloor Street
Toronto, ON M8X 1G4

Dear Mr. Wilson:

Speaking to you yesterday afternoon about the responsibilities of an administrative professional with PDI convinced me that this is exactly the position I am seeking.

The time and information you shared with me discussing the opportunity and management policies at PDI was certainly appreciated. Thank you.

I feel confident I can meet the requirements of the position and am looking forward to hearing a positive response from you.

Sincerely,

Dini Lawrence

Dini Lawrence

Pearson Education, Inc.

after the interview. If you want the job for which you were interviewed, you can use a thank-you letter to do far more than express appreciation to the interviewer. Not everyone writes thank-you letters; consequently, when your thank-you letter arrives at the interviewer's desk, it will single you out from other applicants and call attention once more to your application. See Figure 16-11 for a sample of a standard thank-you letter for mailing, faxing, or delivering in person.

Reminders   When you do not receive a response to an application or are told that your application has been placed on file, write a message after a few weeks have elapsed to remind the human resource manager that you still are interested. You will find reminder messages especially helpful when you plan to move from one region of Canada to another and make inquiries about jobs months in advance of your availability for employment.

Inquiries   Following a job interview, you can write a letter of inquiry or make a phone call if you have not heard anything by the time the human resource manager said you would receive a reply. Be patient. Wait a day or two beyond the time you are expecting a reply and, if you do not hear, telephone or write to inquire. If you are told that the job has not been filled, indicate that you definitely are interested.

Job Acceptance   Even when you accept a job offer during an interview or over the phone, follow up with an email or a letter. You will probably receive a letter offering you a job and suggesting that you call to accept. Respond by telephone, but also send a letter to leave no doubt about your acceptance. The letter offering you the job, plus your written response, should contain all the elements of a contract and, as such, constitutes a contract.

In the opening, accept the job enthusiastically. Mention the specific job being accepted. If you have received a form for supplying additional information, complete it, enclose it, and refer to it in your letter. Repeat the report-to-work instructions, giving the date, time, and place. In either the beginning or the closing, express appreciation. Keep a copy of the letter of offer and your reply. Please refer to Figure 16-12 for an example of a job acceptance letter.

Job Refusal   If you conduct a thorough job campaign, you may be offered more than one job. In this case, you will have to refuse all but one offer. What a good problem to have!

Be as prompt in refusing as possible. If you have already accepted a job, refuse the second offer at once. This is a courtesy you owe the person who must search elsewhere to fill the job offered to you. If you accept a job and then get a better offer from your dream job, do not neglect to inform the first company that you will not be joining that company. A practice called *ghosting* is becoming an increasing problem for employers, who think they have filled a position only to be disappointed when the new hire never shows up.

Since your letter will be disappointing to the reader, you should organize it in the same way you organize other letters of disappointment. Begin by making a favourable statement concerning your contact with the interviewer or about the organization. Express appreciation for the job offer at either the beginning or the end of the letter. Include at least one reason for refusing the job offer. State the refusal tactfully, but make it clear that you are refusing. By making a definite statement about already having accepted a job or about your

continuing to search for a particular job, you will be refusing the offer without making a negative statement. Close with a pleasant comment.

Close the Loop   You may want to work for the organization at some point in the future. Check your letter to make sure that the attitude reflected by your statements does not close the door for you. In Figure 16-13, the writer shows appreciation and says they would be interested in a more senior position.

Self-Check

1. List two categories of letters essential in continuing and finalizing your job campaign.
2. Suggest two factors to be considered when you prepare a job refusal letter.

ETHICAL ISSUES IN THE JOB SEARCH

As you know, many businesses adopt a formal document called a code of ethics that states the primary values and ethical rules they expect all employees to follow. Naturally, they expect prospective employees to hold similar values in terms of their job search as they would exhibit in the workplace.

Consider that you read an employment posting and you believe you are capable of assuming the role. However, the posting mentions the need for specific experience. Although you do not have experience in the area mentioned in the posting, you feel you can do the job. After all, you believe you are a quick learner. The action you choose will determine your success. Based on your values and beliefs, study the following options:

- Option 1: Move to the next employment posting. Because you don't have the required experience, you don't qualify for the position.

- Option 2: Create false experiences and apply for the position. You can just make something up. After all, the last company you worked for isn't in business anymore.

- Option 3: Take a chance and apply for the position. In the interview process, you can emphasize you have related skills and share how you can apply those skills to the position.

Let's consider the options above. In the first option, you may be missing a great opportunity. Although you lack the specified experience, you may have related skills that would be acceptable to the employer. You can proceed as Option 3 shows. The worst that can happen is that your résumé would be rejected. The best that can happen is the prospective employer will see your potential and decide experience is not as important as initiative.

FIGURE 16-12 Job acceptance letter.

Ms. Dini Lawrence
101 Keele Street
Toronto, ON M3P1K1
Tel: 416-555-1329   **Fax: 416-555-2390**   **Email: dini@z-wave.ca**

July 1, 20xx

Mr. Noah Wilson
Progressive Digital Solution PDI
Vice-President of Marketing
3431 Bloor Street
Toronto, ON M8X 1G4

Dear Mr. Wilson:

As I expressed over the phone, I am delighted to accept the position as an administrative professional at PDI.

Enclosed are the forms you requested I complete after our conference last week.

I appreciate the opportunity to join your team and am eager to commence work on Monday, August 1. Thank you for this opportunity.

Sincerely,

Dini Lawrence

Dini Lawrence

Pearson Education, Inc.

In Option 2, you are mishandling a situation that could have significant consequences. Adding false or misrepresenting information is never a good idea. Misrepresentation of information has a way of "snowballing." If you are hired and cannot perform the duties that your résumé indicated you could, you will lose the respect of your manager and co-workers—and possibly your job.

INTERNATIONAL EMPLOYMENT

Working overseas can be an exciting option. The potential benefits to working abroad are many, including lucrative salaries, tax exemptions, overseas service premiums, free housing, completion bonuses, 40 days or more of annual vacation time, international travel, and education allowances for dependents.

FIGURE 16-13 Job refusal letter.

Ms. Sabrina Tang

1010 Carlton Avenue, Toronto, ONM4W 1R1
Tel: 416-555-1111   Fax: 416-555-3333   E-mail: stang@home.com

05 September 20xx

Mr. Jeremy Davis
Public Relations Manager
Telus Corporation
1111 Bloor Street East
Toronto, ON M4W 3R3

Dear Mr. Davis:

Subject: Receptionist Position

Thank you for the job offer to become receptionist in the Public Relations Division of Telus Corporation. However, as I mentioned at the time of the interview, I am seeking a position as an administrative assistant. Another company in the city has offered me this level of employment and I have accepted it.

Mr. Davis, I appreciate the offer to work for your company and the interest you have shown in me. In the future, if a more senior position becomes available, I would be very interested in working for Telus Corporation.

Yours truly,

Sabrina Tang

Sabrina Tang

The range of international employment opportunities available is broader than most Canadians expect. Staffing requirements in the overseas job market are as diverse as in the domestic Canadian market. Highly skilled administrative professionals are in great demand, particularly if they communicate fluently in the English language, which is considered the international language of business.

The curriculum vitae (CV) or international-style résumé is used in overseas job hunting. The standard CV is between four and eight pages long and may contain a personal information section, references, detailed information on all former positions held, a list of memberships in professional organizations, overseas living and working experience, publication credits, and detailed education information. It should also include a recent picture. You will be required to present copies of all diplomas, certificates, transcripts, and a copy of your passport as the selection process progresses. Before hiring, countries may require results of medical examinations and chest X-rays, and proof of up-to-date immunizations as required by the host country. Many countries also require certificates of screening based on legal conduct, which you may request from your local court and police authorities. The certificate of good conduct certifies that you do not have a criminal record.

You should be aware that companies and organizations outside Canada do not fall under Canadian legal constraints as to what information they may require from a potential job candidate. Depending on the country in which you are seeking employment, you should be prepared to provide personal information such as pictures, marital status, date of birth, number of children, and other information that would be restricted by discrimination codes in Canada.

Research can be conducted easily on the internet by using a job search engine or a simple web-based search using a browser such as Google to search for *international résumé*, *international curriculum vitae*, or similar topics.

Interviews conducted for international employment may not follow the same process as in Canada. For example, you may find that you are asked questions of a personal nature—about family, marital status, and health. Restrictions on questions that can be asked will vary with the country's policies guarding personal information and human rights issues. Even within the same country, company interviewing policies may vary, within the guidelines set down by that country. Researching the web for information on the recruitment and interview process before the event will minimize the chances that you will be unprepared for differences from what you would encounter in Canada.

QUESTIONS FOR STUDY AND REVIEW

1. Explain the meaning of the term *networking*. State ways you could network to improve your opportunity for employment.

2. What services are generally available to the postsecondary graduate through the career success centres?

3. What is the advantage of searching for job openings that are not advertised?

4. Explain what a job search engine is. How does it support a job search campaign?

5. Provide three tips that would help you re-enter the workforce once you have been laid off from your employment.

6. What is the meaning of the term *curriculum vitae*?

7. What is the main purpose of a résumé?

8. Suggest why a prospective employer would be interested in information about an applicant's work experience unrelated to office work.

9. Should you include the names of references on your résumé? Explain.

10. What is the purpose of the cover letter?

11. How does the purpose of the solicited application letter differ from the purpose of the prospecting application letter?

12. Why would an organization request that an applicant fill out its application form when the applicant has already submitted a résumé?

13. If a question on an application form asks what salary you are expecting, how should you complete this question?

14. State three guidelines for being prepared to complete a job application form.

15. Describe the contents of a portfolio you would show on an interview. How would composing a portfolio support your employment search?

16. What information about an applicant can an interviewer glean from a personal interview that cannot be learned from the applicant's résumé or transcript?

17. List two items you should avoid bringing to the interview. List two items that *should* be taken to an interview.

18. Suggest three appropriate questions for the applicant to ask at the interview.

19. At what stage in an interview should salary range be discussed?

20. How will you know when the interview is over?

21. State four guidelines for effective closure to a job interview.

22. What is the purpose of behavioural descriptive interviews?

23. If you do not have the experience to answer a behavioural descriptive interview question, how should you respond?

24. Explain how the purpose of the second interview differs from the purpose of the initial interview.

25. List two advantages of writing a thank-you letter following a job interview.

26. Why should you write a job acceptance letter in addition to accepting a job by phone?

27. Give three reasons why companies might prefer electronically scanned résumés over the traditional method of screening résumés.

28. State three guidelines for preparing a résumé for electronic scanning.

Key Terms

company merger 340

company takeover 340

curriculum vitae 341

downsizing 340

e-portfolio 360

hidden job market 339

hyperlink 360

job search board 339

job search engine 339

markup 339

mentor 338

networking 336

proliferation 352

prospecting letter 354

redundant 340

rightsizing 340

short list 352

solicited letter 354

EVERYDAY ETHICS

The Job Offer

Sandy recently had an interview for an administrative professional position at a busy real estate office. This morning, she received a call from Ronn Edwards, the office manager of the real estate office, with a job offer. Sandy advised Ronn that she would need a day or two to think about the offer. Sandy didn't want to give an answer to Ronn because she had an interview later in the day at a municipal office in her town. She really wants the job with the municipality but doesn't want to ruin her chance at a job at the real estate office.

- In your opinion, did Sandy handle this situation correctly?
- If you knew Sandy, would you advise her to do anything differently? Why or why not?

Problem Solving

1. The interview has just begun, and you realize quickly that it is a behaviour descriptive interview. The interviewer has just asked you to describe a time when you were faced with a difficult situation and how you handled it. What example would you use in this case? What is the employer looking to find out about you through your answer?

2. A position posted on job board appeals to you. A variety of responsibilities are listed. You believe that you have the qualifications required for the job. The salary is excellent. The address of the company is local, but you have never heard of the company. You would like to know more about the company before you apply. What can you do next to become informed about the company?

3. You have just sent your résumé by email and quickly realized you made a mistake in the years you stated you worked at your last job. Should you resend this résumé? Is this anything else you can or should do?

Special Reports

1. Research the web for online career centres. Make a list of webpages, their addresses, and what they offer to the job seeker. Share this information with your fellow students through a class presentation.

2. Find a job posting through a job search engine you are interested in applying. Write the opening paragraph of the letter you would send in response to the posting. Submit the paragraph for feedback.

3. Assume that you have been offered a job that you do not want to accept. Write a job refusal letter. Submit the letter for feedback.

4. Consider that you are applying for the position posted in Figure 16-2. Write an introductory paragraph for your cover letter for this position.

5. Assume it has been one week since you had your interview for the job you applied for in question #4. The interviewer indicated she would be in touch within three to four days. Since you haven't heard back, you decide to write a follow-up email to determine the position status. Write the email message and submit it for evaluation.

6. Working with a team of three or four members, research behaviour descriptive interview questions. As a team, prepare a list of 20 questions. Then choose five of these questions to present to the class, and challenge your classmates to try to answer them through role-playing exercises. Hand in your group's list to your instructor.

PRODUCTION CHALLENGES

16-A Personal Inventory

Supplies needed:

- *Personal Inventory form, Form 16-A on Companion Website*

Completing a personal inventory is a useful step in developing a successful résumé. Attempt to make exhaustive lists when you work through the Personal Inventory form. Share the results of your form with a family member and again with a fellow student. These people will probably be able to help you add to your list. When your Personal Inventory form is complete, consider how you will infuse it into your employment search documentation.

16-B Visual Résumé and Scannable Résumé

Supplies needed:

- *Personal Inventory form, Form 16-A, completed in Production Challenge 16-A*

- *Plain bond paper*

Use the Personal Inventory form completed in Production Challenge 16-A and the information in this chapter to prepare an attractive résumé for human scanning. Then prepare one for electronic scanning.

16-C Your Job Campaign

Supplies needed:

- *Checklist for Your Job Campaign, Form 16-C-1, Companion Website*

- *Application for Employment, Form 16-C-2, Companion Website*

- *Plain bond paper*

All 13 activities in this challenge are real. They provide guidelines for conducting your own job campaign.

Planning and conducting your own job campaign should be an exciting part of your office procedures course. Possessing office administration skills, knowledge of the business world, and a desire to work in an office are assets in your favour. However, the job market is competitive. To land the job you have prepared for, you must conduct a successful job campaign.

Start your job campaign at the beginning of the semester in which you are seeking full-time employment. Continue your job campaign throughout the semester or until you land a job.

Your instructor will assist you in planning your job campaign and will suggest the dates on which you should complete many of the job campaign activities. Enter the due dates on Form 16-C-1.

Job-Campaign Activities

1. Using the suggestions given in this chapter, prepare a self-appraisal inventory. Use Form 16-A. It should be helpful to you in determining which qualifications to emphasize during an interview and in preparing your résumé.

2. Look up a local corporation. Prepare a concise report on the corporation, and submit the report for feedback.

3. Obtain literature that may be helpful to you in your job campaign from the career success office of your school. Read the literature, and then file it for ready reference in a job campaign file that you create.

4. Join a committee of peers to study employment opportunities for administrative professionals in your community. Separate committees should be organized on the basis of where the members of the class plan to seek employment—for instance, corporations, small companies, law firms, medical offices, hospitals, financial institutions, government offices, and other broad classifications. Consult several sources to study one organization. Obtain literature made available to prospective employees, ask corporations for annual reports and brochures, and confer with friends and former graduates who work in the various types of offices being studied. Share your findings with the members of your committee and other classmates.

5. Prepare for a job interview. Key a list of qualifications you plan to emphasize during the interview. Anticipate the questions you will be asked and list them. Also key a list of questions you may ask the interviewer. Submit a copy of your qualifications and of your questions.

6. Prepare a résumé for employment with a specific organization. Use the example and suggested outline for preparing a résumé presented in this chapter. Submit your résumé for feedback.

7. Write a prospecting job application letter (or a solicited one). Review the suggestions given in this chapter. Use the letter to promote your skills to a prospective employer.

8. Once you have the feedback on your résumé, incorporate the suggestions made and print copies of your résumé for use in your job campaign. Take your résumé with you to your job interviews.

9. Build an e-portfolio displaying samples of your work. Choose a platform host for your portfolio, arrange your content, and provide the link for feedback on the development.

10. For several weeks, study job posting in the community in which you are seeking employment. Select postings that reflect employment opportunities for administrative professionals. Analyze the postings to obtain information about job trends, qualifications sought, salary, and

so on. This will benefit you in your employment campaign portfolio.

11. Using the questions presented in this chapter, write an evaluation of your performance during an early job interview. Make suggestions that should be helpful to you during your next interview. List both what you think you did well and what you believe you should improve. Share what you have learned about job interviews with the members of your class.

12. To gain confidence in completing an application form neatly and accurately, complete the application form provided in Production Challenge 16-C, Form 16-C-2. Study the form carefully, and then write your answers in your most legible handwriting in the spaces provided. Key an application form when it is possible to do so.

13. When you accept a job, write a job acceptance letter. Submit a copy of your job acceptance letter (or your job refusal letter) for feedback.

Weblinks

Job Opportunities

www.monster.ca

This popular Canadian site includes job postings; career, résumé, and interview information; access to jobs around the world; and much more.

www.workopolis.com

Workopolis is a large Canadian job site that includes job postings, resources, hints for researching companies and industries, and much more.

www.careerowl.ca

This leading-edge e-recruiting service brings postsecondary students, recent graduates, and employers together, matching job seekers with employers.

www.jobstreet.com

This user-friendly site provides information on job opportunities throughout Asia.

www.jobsdb.com/

Here you will find numerous job opportunities in a number of international locations including Asia, Australia, and the United States.

Career Lab

www.careerlab.ca

This site offers information offers articles explaining how to manage challenges when job searching.

Employability Skills

www.conferenceboard.ca

The Conference Board of Canada site provides information on the skills that make Canadians employable.

Canadian Association of Career Educators and Employers (CACEE)

www.cacee.com

This association provides information, advice, professional development opportunities, and other services to employers, career services professionals, and students. The publication *Career Options* is also available on this site.

Employment and Social Development (ESDC)

www.canada.ca

This Government of Canada site provides employment-related information on services for individuals, businesses, and other organizations.

Canadian Human Rights Commission

www.chrc-ccdp.ca

This site deals with employment equity, workplace harassment, discrimination, and related topics.

Training and Careers (Job Bank)

https://www.jobbank.gc.ca/home

Services Canada's online resource centre on training and careers in Canada includes links to regional service centres in your area where you can get personal help with your job search.

How to Write an International Curriculum Vitae

www.cvtips.com

In addition to providing useful information on how to write an international résumé or curriculum vitae, this site provides tips on writing résumés for specific countries, since preferences among countries vary greatly.

Glassdoor

www.glassdoor.ca

This website or mobile app provides insights from past employees about working at a business or organization.

Chapter 17
Professional Development

Flamingo Images/Shutterstock

LEARNING OUTCOMES

After completion of this chapter, the student will be able to:

1 Describe components of a professional image.

2 Recognize the benefits of establishing mentor-based relationships.

3 Consider educational pathways and certification opportunities related to enhanced career growth.

4 Describe the benefits of cross-training to both the organization and the employee.

5 Explore the qualities of an effective office supervisor.

6 Explain how the position of administrative professional is excellent training for management.

7 Understand foundational strategies for professional development.

Professional behaviour and image, whether outwardly acknowledged or not, becomes a professional trademark or brand for each person. This stems from your appearance, demeanour, and the way you speak. It can be the distinguisher between an administrative professional with a superior skill set, attitude, team player, and experience matched up against another equally qualified candidate. The way you perform or present yourself will either diminish or enhance your perceived credibility. Many administrative professionals expect consideration as a professional with a serious focus on their career development and advancement. This chapter focuses on the outlook of the role of the administration professional, professional image, and development opportunities for career growth.

CHALLENGE TRADITIONAL STEREOTYPES

The attitude that someone is "just a secretary" has no relevance in the contemporary office. This **stereotype** developed at a time when the administrative professional had a limited skill set. This scenario is, of course, no longer accurate or valid. The stereotype of an office worker who typed, filed, took shorthand, and did only routine tasks, has been replaced by a bold and professional image.

Develop a Professional Image

A professional image reflects:

- an educated and skilled employee
- a team player who is expected to contribute valuable ideas
- a polished individual whose appearance and communication style are "professional"
- a person who can solve problems and integrate ideas
- a person who takes pride in each piece of work he or she produces
- an employee who works for the betterment of the organization and is not self-serving
- a person who takes pride in the career of administrative professional and who has aspirations for the future
- an employee who manages assignments by applying quality standards
- an employee who is willing to work hard and accept new and more challenging responsibilities

Prepare for Advancement and Demonstrate Value

Many opportunities for advancement are available in industry for those who are prepared to accept additional responsibilities. Often, administrative professionals aspire to move up the ladder with opportunities involving supervision and management. The challenge is planning a career pathway to transition from one position to another. Consider viewing your capabilities through the lens of an HR recruiter. Do you present as someone who is ready for promotion?

The administrative professional's role has evolved into a broader and more diversified role, requiring thorough knowledge of technology and personal management skills, as well as strong problem-solving and critical-thinking skills. This career requires people who have technical expertise as well as excellent human relations skills, it attracts diverse and competent people. Competence indicates a detailed scope of knowledge and skills that enable someone to act in a wide variety of situations. This demonstrates value to an employer. Value is not the same as the number of years on the job. It is the ability to delegate, offer solutions, and build a professional development plan.

During your first year of employment, set a professional goal for yourself. Do you want to become a team leader, a supervisor, or a manager? Once you have affirmed your goal, study and network to provide yourself with the background necessary to achieve that goal. Networking within your profession or organization will require you to join networking groups such as Business Network International Canada (BNI) or your local chamber of commerce. Many personal performance and altruistic clubs and associations such as Toastmasters, Rotary Clubs, and the Progress Clubs welcome new members and usually provide a significant membership of experienced businesspeople from whom you can learn.

To accomplish your goal, you may need support and resources from management. If so, select a person in management on whom you can rely for assistance and with whom you can develop a **mentor** relationship.

Learn from a Mentor

Mentors are people in your profession who are more senior than you are. They understand the organization's policies, procedures, politics, and history, and they are helpful for transference of knowledge. Often, you will find a willingness to share useful advice with more junior members. They help people who are new to the organization or the profession to become successful. The mentor relationship often involves a new team member and an office veteran. The new member may have strong state-of-the-art technical skills, but the veteran knows the organization or industry.

Meetings with mentors and the information they share is immensely valuable, since a mentor's advice as provided illustrates for a junior member pathways to success and helps with the onboarding process, which when deployed effectively

Daryan Coryat

Daryan Coryat

Unit Clerk
Southlake Regional Health Centre Office
Administration Diploma-Medical (Honours)
Georgian College
Barrie, Ontario 2015

"Attention to detail, time management, organization, and most importantly open-mindedness are just a few skills."

Daryan Coryat is an eager individual who could not wait to put her newly acquired skills to the test. She was quickly approaching her placement date and could not be more excited. During her first morning of her placement, she was extremely overwhelmed actually having to put these skills into play all at the same time. By day 2 and onward, Daryan was starting to get the hang of the job. She was required to manage up to six telephone lines, three different patient information systems, as well as take orders from three different physicians—all in a timely manner, without having the look of panic on her face. She was starting to doubt her ability to do the job. She then remembered her lessons around time management.

By the second week of her placement, she was starting to feel confident in herself and her abilities. Her time management had improved drastically; therefore, she was able to perform all of her clerical duties successfully. Knowing that this is the environment that she wanted to be in, Daryan started to apply to positions within the hospital hoping she would get recognized and provided the opportunity to demonstrate her new set of skills. Before her two-week placement was up she had already been called to interview for permanent positions within the hospital.

Skipping a few weeks into the future and a couple interviews later, Daryan was given a casual unit clerk position in the Emergency department (exactly where she always dreamed to be). Her new duties include answering up to eight telephone lines, taking verbal orders from the nursing staff, booking transportation for patients to their tests as well as home, and completing the orders for up to 10 physicians for 30-40 patients. Her shifts are a long 12 hours, days, evenings, and nights, but each day is a new challenge that she gladly accepts.

Wanting to expand her knowledge of the hospital, Daryan applied for and received a new part-time position on the Cancer Care and Palliative floor. Although it wasn't as exciting as the Emergency department, the life-saving procedures and treatments that were being done on that floor were incredible. The sense of urgency was much less than at her previous department, but the same techniques applied. Her responsibilities included putting orders in for the primary physicians as well as the consulted physicians, directing and managing calls from wpatients, their families, and their healthcare team, and booking tests for patients and transportation to get them there. She was grateful for the environmental change that Cancer Care had brought to her. However, she later returned to the Emergency department as she felt her specific set of skills learned from the Medical Office Administrative program were being challenged more frequently. Just the way she liked it.

Attention to detail, time management, organization, and most importantly, open-mindedness are just a few skills the program taught her to be successful in all aspects of life.

offers significant guidance for developing and planning career objectives.

People often consider their mentor as the most important person in their professional career.

Navigating your career and figuring out how to get ahead can be unnerving. When selecting a mentor, here are some general characteristics to consider:

- The mentor's strengths and weaknesses complement yours, especially as they relate to your style.
- Core values align with yours.

- A mentor is a person with whom you feel comfortable to asked targeted questions

As well, the mentor is someone who has the answers to your questions about:

- how the organization works
- how information flows in the organization
- with whom to align for development
- how to navigate challenging personalities within the organization

- how the organization selects people for promotion
- who holds power to make decisions
- how to get your ideas noticed and accepted

Self-Check

1. Identify three ways you can present and develop a professional image.
2. Why would you benefit by having a mentor?
3. List three ways a mentor would support growth and development.

ADVANCE BY EDUCATION

A college diploma and an undergraduate degree with progressive leadership experience are becoming more prevalent in industry. In fact, most additional education will prove helpful when seeking professional growth and advancement. When you have an efficient and effective performance record, additional education may provide the competitive edge you need to optimize opportunity.

Many organizations offer in-house training. These courses are usually of short duration and do not carry college or university credit but still carry relevance of skill set development. Continually explore these options within your organization. Express an interest in taking courses that will help you perform your job or advance in your career. When you successfully complete enough courses, they will become an impressive part of your employment record and will support your efforts towards promotion.

If you are interested in obtaining a university degree, you may be able to use credits from courses you have already taken. Many colleges in Canada today have established **articulation agreements** with universities. Under these agreements, universities will grant substantial transfer credit from recognized office administration programs. The key benefit of this arrangement is that it reduces the time needed to obtain a degree while recognizing your prior learning coupled with your industry experience. As well, you may be able take classes on a part-time basis while still staying employed—and thus continue to gain professional experience. Check with your college to find out what articulations may exist for your program.

Most large organizations have educational benefits. Some organizations will pay all or part of the tuition for job-related courses that are successfully completed. Ask your supervisor about educational benefits; express your interest in taking job-related courses. Consider courses in these areas:

- project management
- team building
- communication
- time management
- business administration
- software applications
- organizational behaviour
- office management
- social media and web development
- financial management
- supervision/management leadership

The emphasis in education today is on continuing education. By committing yourself to lifelong learning, you will be increasing your opportunities for promotion and enriching your personal life. Employees who believe in and practise continuous education are more likely to survive during periods of company **rightsizing** and **recession**.

As an administrative professional, you choose either to have a job or to have a professional career. If you have a strong desire to advance and to earn a reputation for being a professional who contributes to the organization, you will seek ways to achieve professional recognition.

Join a Professional Association

Becoming a member of a professional association is an excellent way of gaining educational skills and new credentials in your field. A number of associations that promote office professionalism are available. The following discussion will identify three associations that offer credentials to office professionals willing to study and take the challenge.

If you are interested in joining or establishing a branch of one of these professional associations in your community, write or call the head office for information.

Association of Administrative Professionals (AAP)

The Association of Administrative Professionals is a Canadian, chartered, nonprofit organization formed in 1951. The motto of the AAP is "Professionalism through Education." The association has the mandate of encouraging office professionals to upgrade skills and enhance professionalism. By helping members with skills, knowledge, and professional development, the AAP will meet its mission to enhance employment opportunities and contributions to the workplace and to the community.

It awards the designation of Qualified Administrative Assistant (QAA) to those who meet the criteria. In order to achieve the QAA, office professionals must complete a selection of courses at recognized institutions throughout Canada. The program consists of compulsory courses and electives. The courses range in subject matter such as:

- business administration
- organizational behaviour
- effective business english
- marketing
- economics
- human resource management
- financial accounting
- psychology
- commercial law
- principles and practices of supervision
- interpersonal communication
- computer technology

These courses assist participants to add value to their organizations, explore corporate initiatives, and develop greater core competencies. Earning this designation will foster a competitive edge when seeking additional responsibilities and career progression. For more detailed information, visit the AAP weblink provided at the end of the chapter.

International Association of Administrative Professionals® (IAAP®)

IAAP is an association committed to advancing office professionals by promoting high standards and enhancing the image of the profession. This association provides resources and information to help its members enhance their skills, so they may contribute to their organizations in an even more effective manner. Not only does it work to improve the professional skills of its members, it also works to educate the public about the value of the office professional.

The educational program of IAAP includes workshops, seminars, and study courses on administrative topics. This proactive organization holds an international conference each year and publishes a popular magazine called *OfficePro*.

IAAP has a professional certification where successful candidates earn their Certified Administrative Professional® (CAP®) designation. Specific educational and/or industry exposure is required to be eligible to write the exam for this certification. The current exam breakdown reflects the following key competencies:

- organizational communications
- business writing and document production
- technology and information distribution
- office and records management
- event and project management
- human resources
- financial functions

For more information about the IAAP and the CAP certifications, visit the association's weblink provided at the end of this chapter.

Canadian Association of Virtual Assistants (CAVA)

A **virtual assistant**, or VA, is a self-employed professional offering administrative support to a variety of clients through his or her home office. CAVA is a professional organization designed to bring together virtual assistants. Its goal is to provide a forum in which virtual assistants can network and share knowledge and skills. CAVA offers professional development opportunities, and it also helps to connect virtual assistants with potential employers. Visit the organization's website at www.cvac.ca.

NALS—The Association for Legal Professionals

NALS provides a testing program and professional certification for legal administrative professionals. Part of its mandate is to offer continuing legal education training programs and networking for its members. NALS is not an acronym (although it started as one), but an organization with a long history of serving legal assistants.

Office professionals who wish to demonstrate their commitment to and aptitude for the legal profession are encouraged to take the examination leading to the basic certification of the legal professional, ALP®, previously known as Accredited Legal Professional. Testing for the ALP certification covers the following topics:

- communications
- legal procedures and knowledge
- ethics and authority

NALS also offers an advanced certification for legal professionals, the Certified Legal Professional or CLP®. The CLP is a designation for legal administrative professionals who want to be identified as exceptional. A benchmark of work history is required to sit the exam, which covers

- written communication
- office procedures and technology
- ethics and judgment
- legal knowledge and skills

For more information visit the weblink provided for NALS.

Increase Technical Certification

Technical skills are some of the most highly valued skills of office professionals. By continuing to upgrade technical skills, office professionals can improve their résumés and increase their opportunities for employment and advancement. To validate technical skills, office professionals should earn certification from recognized programs.

One of the most recognized and popular types of technical certification is the Microsoft Office Specialist certification (MOS). Candidates begin by selecting the Microsoft Office track and then the product for which they want certification in a Microsoft Office Suite application program. Then they select the appropriate level of expertise. Two exam track levels exist: core and expert. Core is the first level and expert is the higher level. MOS exams are usually available in the current Microsoft Office Suite edition. When a new edition of Microsoft Suite is launched, the testing is developed to test the competencies in the most recent version. In order to sit for the certification exams, an authorized testing centre must be attended.

Here are some of the common application choices for exam certification:

- Word (core and expert)
- Excel (core and expert)
- PowerPoint
- Access

Various practice and training materials are available before taking an exam.

Cross-Train

Cross-training involves learning and performing the responsibilities of your co-workers. It is very valuable to the organization. When one employee is absent from work, other employees can simply fill in. However, it has even greater benefits to the person who has the initiative to learn how to perform other job functions. The more you know and the more you can do, the more valuable to the organization you will be. Consistently remember to demonstrate your value to the organization.

Cross-training gives the administrative professional the opportunity to:

- Take on new technical and communication challenges.
- Learn more about the organization and the flow of work.
- Get more exposure by working with new people.
- Get acknowledgment from management.

Cross-trained employees are more challenged and more knowledgeable, and generally experience more job satisfaction.

> ### Self-Check
> 1. Why should you take the MOS certification exams?
> 2. Why would an administrative professional want to cross-train?
> 3. What are two advantages of professional organizations?

BECOME A SUPERVISOR

Many administrative professionals migrate into a supervisory role. This acquired position is often the result of seniority, hard work, and success as an administrative professional. A supervisory job requires a different skill set from the administrative professional's job. Therefore, specialized training is a genuine asset. Knowledge, skills, and abilities are the critical areas for development. As a supervisor, you will need to manage yourself, others, and systems. On your route to becoming a supervisor, get as much supervisory training as possible.

Know What It Takes

One of the greatest assets of any good supervisor is effective human relations skills. Good human relations skills will enable you to direct the work of other employees and help them to derive personal satisfaction in their work. Experience in performing your own job, even when you perform it exceptionally well, is not enough to prepare you for leading others.

Being a good supervisor requires actual experience. You can *learn* to accept responsibility as a supervisor and to carry out your function effectively. You can learn from many sources that will be available to you, as well as from experience.

Through discussions with management, arrive at an understanding of what your supervisory responsibilities are and what authority you have for carrying them out. In addition, your new role should be announced outlining the scope of responsibilities and authority.

A human resource representative will discuss general policies surrounding the position. Nevertheless, one of your ongoing functions will be to interpret policies and provide context to personnel under your supervision or even departmentally. Study the organization's policies until you can answer questions accurately and clearly. Keep accurate records and update changes in policies and procedures.

You can learn from your manager. Observe and recall supervisory principles and techniques that your manager uses successfully. Decide if you can apply them in your situation.

Network and collaborate with other supervisors, and encourage them to share with you their best practices. Be a good listener; learn the "why" as well as the "what" of the problems and solutions being discussed.

Improve your ability to communicate. Much of your success as a supervisor will depend on effective communication.

As a supervisor, self-appraisal and reflection is important. Envision your total job, which could include staffing, planning, organizing, directing, coordinating, reporting, and budgeting. Frequently evaluate your own performance. Think in terms of what you did well and why. Recognize areas in which you need to improve. Concentrate on the skills that need improvement until you have accomplished greater expertise. As you improve, your confidence will increase.

Many reference sources are available related to supervision, personnel management, business psychology, personal relations in business, motivation, communications, and so on. College and university courses are available on these same topics. Read materials and enrol in courses that will help you.

Technical expertise is an asset for a supervisor. However, the supervisor's role is to lead and guide. A good supervisor supports *employees* to be better and become better technical experts and relies on their expertise and recommendations to improve and enhance current processes.

You will be directing the work of people who are producing products and services; thus, it is beneficial to learn about equipment, supplies, and methods that will enable employees to perform their jobs more economically and effectively. Keep current on the technical aspects of your job. Securing buy-in from your team is critical for success, and it can be supported by demonstrating respect, as is a broad knowledge base related to industry requirements. Additionally, empower employees to make recommendations and decisions on matters that directly affect their work.

Along with your staff, examine methods to improve the work you are managing. Brainstorm with your team to find the best solutions for new procedures and new products. Based on the solutions determined by your team, make reasonable adjustments. If the recommended changes are outside your realm of authority, you will need to get approval from management. The approval process from management is dependent on clearly identified objectives and benefits. Cost-effectiveness is another consideration in the approval cycle.

Prepare to Be an Office Manager

If you aspire to transition into management, remember that the competition for management roles is intense. Today, more management positions are available to administrative professionals who have educational credentials, regardless of length of service. An academic degree is not always required, but it is usually a requirement.

There is no prescribed method or guaranteed success strategy for becoming a manager. Much of your success will be based on your ability to refine your skills and to demonstrate competence in leadership. Volunteering to lead committees and projects is an excellent way to practise your leadership skills, demonstrate your commitment to the organization, learn more about the organization, and gain recognition as a prospective manager.

Immersing your interests and joining a management association are progressive steps towards movement into a managerial appointment.

The role of the administrative professional is excellent training for a managerial position. In fact, the administrative professional is constantly making decisions and managing projects, people, and time. The following are examples of management responsibilities that the administrative professional undertakes in a daily routine. Each of these functions is excellent preparation for advancement into a manager's position.

Manager of Communications   One of the most important functions of the administrative professional is to create and edit office documentation. As well, it is the administrative professional who is the expert in the functionality of communication equipment (computers, phone systems, photocopiers, etc.) in the office.

Manager of Crises   A skilled office professional will be able to remain calm, maintain office efficiency, and handle people with diplomacy even through an office crisis.

Manager of Records and Information Controlling paper and electronic files is usually the responsibility of the administrative professional. The administrative professional develops the structural framework for organizing, finding, retrieving, and storing information.

Manager of Public Relations The administrative professional is the first point of contact in an organization that the public sees and to whom the public speaks. The image that administrative professionals project will reflect on the organization they represent. Administrative professionals must manage the reception area and visitors.

Manager of Planning It is the administrative professional who keeps track of meetings, schedules, deadlines, and the whereabouts of the office staff.

Manager of Policies and Procedures Office policies and procedures need to be interpreted, updated, and organized. Of course, the administrative professional manages these responsibilities.

Manager of Inventory Maintaining control of inventory, ordering new stock, and selecting the best product for the best price are just some of the responsibilities of the administrative professional in the role of inventory manager.

> **Self-Check**
> 1. Identify ways in which you can evaluate your own performance as a supervisor.
> 2. How does an administrative professional's role prepare them for managerial roles?

CONTINUE TO DEVELOP PROFESSIONALLY

As you read this chapter, you may conclude that preparation for a successful career is endless. Your conclusion is correct.

Continue to increase both your general knowledge of foundational office management systems and processes and develop specialized skills. The ability to relate well to customers, clients, and co-workers is essential. As we also are aware, working knowledge of computer software—for word processing, spreadsheets, project management, graphics, desktop publishing, electronic messaging and calendaring, database management, and so on—is essential. Computer technology and software are changing at a rapid pace. Develop an affinity for new equipment and learn the new applications. Figure 17-1 highlights this importance visually.

FIGURE 17-1 The ability to relate to clients and co-workers is essential for professional growth.

Stockfour/Shutterstock

To advance in your career, you need a broad, general education. An understanding of how to navigate relationships and business and management concepts is a valuable asset. Organizations are looking for employees who are critical thinkers and problem solvers.

If you wish to advance professionally, make decisions and carry them out. Then take responsibility for both your successes and your failures. **Procrastination** and the inability to make decisions will be viewed as weaknesses and will hinder opportunities for promotion.

Contemporary Office Professional

In order to plan for your future professional development, you should understand what the **contemporary** office requires. Professionals in the contemporary office will do the following:

- Supervise people in nontraditional work styles that include flexible working hours in flexible locations.
- Use the most current office technology and high-tech communication.
- Harvest reliable information management strategies.
- Make productivity a primary focus.
- Work effectively with diverse groups.

Involvement in professional organizations and lifelong education are the keys to keeping current and continuing to develop professionally.

Get Started on Your Career Path

To begin your path of professional development, you should:

- Attend seminars, conventions, conferences, and workshops to keep abreast of new technology and procedures.

- Volunteer to be a committee member or chairperson for special events.
- Apply or offer to work on special task forces.
- Request that you be placed on the office circulation list for all informational and professional materials.
- Make a point of meeting new people and listening to their ideas.
- Follow local and foreign events.
- Travel to as many locations as possible.
- Visit libraries and make note of the many resources available to you.
- Learn about other organizations.
- Become aware of your company's policies.
- Watch documentaries and study new topics.
- Make learning a lifelong commitment.

Professional growth is stimulating. It has a motivating effect, and your reward will be a successful and enjoyable career.

Commit to Your Values and Ethics

Values and ethics are central to any organization. Throughout this book, **ethical** issues have been discussed. Let's take a closer look at values.

Values can be defined as those things that are important to or valued by someone. Values are what people judge to be right. They are more than words—they are the moral, ethical, and professional attributes of **character**. When values are shared by all members of an organization, they are extraordinarily important tools for making judgments, assessing probable outcomes of contemplated actions, and choosing among alternatives. Perhaps more importantly, they put all employees on the same level with regard to what all employees as an organization consider important.

Values are the embodiment of what an organization stands for and should be the basis for the behaviour of its employees. Additionally, an organization may publish one set of values, perhaps in an effort to present a positive image, while the values that really guide organizational behaviour are very different. Disconnects may occur and may create problems. However, the central purpose of values remains. They state either an actual or an idealized set of criteria for evaluating options and deciding what is appropriate, while also taking into account other factors such as experience.

How do values relate to ethics? *Values* can help to determine what is right and what is wrong, and doing what is right or wrong is what is meant by *ethics*. To behave ethically is to behave in a manner consistent with what is right or moral. Part of the difficulty in deciding whether or not behaviour is ethical is in determining *what* is right or wrong.

Consider the values illustrated in the following cases and how those values lead to ethical or unethical decisions.

CASE A   You unknowingly give a caller incorrect information by phone.

Ethical: You realize your error and immediately call the person to apologize and correct the error.

Unethical: You realize your error but, because you don't want to admit you made a mistake, you decide not to call with the correct information. You tell yourself that maybe it won't matter.

The caller phones to verify whether the information is correct because he or she is doubtful. You pretend you are unaware of the whole situation, including the previous call.

CASE B   Your manager is out of the office today, and your workload is light and not urgent. You realize your co-worker is rushing to meet a tight deadline.

Ethical: You know you can postpone your work until tomorrow, and you offer to help the co-worker.

Unethical: You consider offering help, but instead, you decide to leave work early because, after all, you deserve some free time—and your manager will never know. Besides, your co-worker's workload is not your responsibility.

CASE C   An administrative professional with a hearing impairment has just joined your organization. You work in an open-concept office, and her desk is across the room. You occasionally need to communicate informally to each other across the room.

Ethical: You suggest ideas that would make it easier to communicate (e.g., arrange the desks so you face each other), and you encourage her ideas, too.

Unethical: When you need to catch her attention, you simply call her name. You feel she is not making an effort to be cooperative when she fails to respond.

CASE D   Your manager asks you to alter expenses on her travel claim to include expenditures that did not really occur.

Ethical: You are apprehensive about upsetting your manager. However, you feel you cannot falsify the information. You tactfully advise your manager that the Finance department will need receipts to substantiate all spending and you cannot agree to complete the claim without receipts to support the amounts.

Unethical: Although you know it is wrong, you agree to make the changes because you are applying for a promotion and want your manager to give you a good recommendation.

Create an Ethical Climate

Actions based on strong personal values—integrity, honesty, loyalty, tolerance, respect, and accountability—are consistent with good business practices and will conform to your organization's code of ethics.

The organization, to an extent, is dealing with individuals whose value base has been established already. While the internalized values of individuals are important, the organization has a major impact on the behaviour of its members and can have a positive or negative influence on their values. Staying committed to your values increases your satisfaction with your decisions and results.

How can you help to create an ethical climate? Be certain your pattern of behaviour aligns with your own values as well as your organizations. Increase your awareness of how to apply your organization's code of conduct. Through additional training, learn how to deal with situations with an ethical dimension and how to anticipate situations that involve your values and, ultimately, ethical choices.

QUESTIONS FOR STUDY AND REVIEW

1. Identify and discuss three aspects of presenting a professional image.

2. Explain the purpose of having a mentor.

3. Describe three qualities you should look for when selecting a mentor.

4. Name an association providing professional certification for administrative professionals.

5. How can Microsoft Office Specialist certification position you for greater success?

6. Explain cross-training.

7. Describe the advantages to an employee of cross-training. Describe the advantages to the organization.

8. Suggest steps an administrative professional can take to transition to a supervisory role.

9. Describe two ways that the position of administrative professional is excellent training for being a manager.

10. Identify the expectations that have already and will continue to be placed on office professionals.

11. Suggest three ways to grow professionally once you are already employed.

Key Terms

articulation agreements 376

character 381

contemporary 380

ethical 381

mentor 374

procrastination 380

recession 376

rightsizing 376

stereotype 374

virtual assistant 377

EVERYDAY ETHICS

You have been working for Bellco, a corporate insurance company, for six months. You realize that you have much to learn in regard to office politics, policies, and procedures, and simply how to get ahead.

One of the senior managers, Ken O'Mallie, has welcomed your questions on several occasions. In fact, a mentor relationship is clearly starting to form. Your co-workers, who have no mentors, have noticed that Ken appears to be nurturing your career. They are jealous.

Rumours have started about the amount of time you spend in Ken's office with the door closed.

■ What should you do?

Problem Solving

1. You have been employed by a large organization as an administrative professional for six years. You would like to specialize in project management. You have just found out about a four-day workshop on project management taking place in your city later in the month. You really see a future for yourself in this area, and this is a wonderful professional development opportunity. In order to complete this course, you will need to take two days off work. How will you approach your employer to secure the days off you need and also receive support for your ambition? Draft a brief statement describing how you will secure support from your boss on this idea. What will you do if your boss turns you down?

2. You supervise a temporary employee, Karen, who assists you with your work. It is Friday afternoon, and she is keying a multipage report. Your manager is waiting for the report and intends to fax it to the head office as soon as it is finished. Karen volunteered to stay after 5 p.m. to finish the report; you leave. As soon as Karen finishes the report, she prints it, hands it to the manager, and leaves the office. Early Monday morning the manager calls you to her office to explain that she could not send the report because it contained errors. Could you have done something to prevent this?

3. You supervise two full-time office workers. One of them told you she was ill and asked to go home at noon. You insisted that deadlines had to be met and asked that she stay to finish her work if she possibly could. About 2 p.m. this employee passed out and had to be rushed to the hospital. You realize that you made a mistake. What can you do now? Suggest alternatives you could have pursued to get the employee's work finished.

4. You pride yourself on being very adept in your knowledge of many application software packages. In fact, many staff members, including your immediate supervisor, come to you for help when they are experiencing challenges with software. Recently, a supervisory opportunity has become available in your department. You have applied and have been interviewed by a panel for this opportunity. You hope to hear back from the hiring committee in a few days. You know your boss is evaluating your performance closely, and you also know you can handle this new opportunity. In the last few days, however, your supervisor has been asking for a lot of computer assistance, so much so that you are falling behind on your duties. If you fall behind, you may not get this new opportunity as your supervisor may not recommend you for the position. Is there anything you can do to keep harmony with your supervisor and at the same time not fall behind on your responsibilities?

Special Reports

1. Use the internet to locate articles and book reviews on either:
   - *cross-training as a supervisor's motivation tool, or*
   - *the qualities of a great mentor.*

   Write an abstract of your findings and document your sources.

2. Locate a university where an articulation agreement exists between an office administration program and a university. Read the articulation requirements for earning a degree and then create a list that includes the name of the degree, the number of degree credits needed, and the number of degree credits awarded with the office administration diploma. Share this list with your instructor.

3. Find articles and tips from current issues of *OfficePro* magazine that discuss professional growth. Summarize the tips into a brief report. Share this information with your instructor and other class members.

4. Use the internet to research two different professional organizations that you would like to join. Find the following information: how do you obtain a membership, what can the organization do to further your career, and is there any certification available? Determine which organization you would prefer to join, and be able to support your decision. Prepare a chart where you can compare the two organizations. Present your findings to your class.

5. Develop a strategy for your own professional development. To do so, design an electronic spreadsheet that will capture the following information:
   - *State your immediate career goal upon graduation.*
   - *State your career goal for the end of a five-year period.*
   - *Identify the gap between the two goals in terms of the experience, training, certification, human relations skills, and supervision/management leadership skills needed.*
   - *For each of the factors in the gap, describe your plan for achieving the necessary skills to close the gap.*

6. Interview an office professional (in person or by email) who began his or her career as an administrative professional and who has since moved into progressive levels of responsibility. Find out the career path this individual took to get where he or she is now. In a brief report to be submitted to your instructor, outline your questions and the responses you received.

Weblinks

Professional Associations

www.aaa.ca

This website provides information about the Association of Administrative Assistants, its mission, and its certification.

https://www.iaap-hq.org

The International Association of Administrative Professionals (IAAP) has an extensive website with information about the organization, certification, benefits of membership, and its publication.

www.nals.org

The NALS (Association for Legal Professionals) site offers information about the association, the benefits of membership, and certification.

Canadian Association of Virtual Assistants

https://canadianava.org/

The Canadian Association of Virtual Assistants (CAVA) site is designed to bring Canadian VAs and worldwide clients together to network, learn, and benefit.

Microsoft Office Specialist

www.microsoft.com

This Microsoft site gives detailed information about what is involved in earning Microsoft Office Specialist certification.

Psychometrics—Online Testing

http://www.psychometrics.com

Perform online tests to learn about your career values, competencies, interests, and personality.

Canadian HR Reporter

www.hrreporter.com

This guide to human resource management offers current news, information on the latest trends and practices, expert advice, experience, and insights from HR practitioners, research, and resources.

Peer Mentoring

https://www.mentors.ca/

This site discusses the benefits of a mentor relationship. Links to other mentoring sites are provided.

Appendix

Common Proofreaders' Marks

Meaning	Symbol	Example
Insert *(This could be used to indicate you want to insert words, punctuation, or a space.)*	$\wedge$ OR $\vee$	Justyne PDA to the CEO,
Insert Space	#	highschool
Close up the space	⌒	every day
Delete	ℓ	Benjamin Ross is the
Let it remain as is *(You may have deleted something and then changed your mind.)*	stet	Benjamin Ross is the stet
Start a new paragraph	¶	policies were accepted. ¶ The no-smoking policy stipulated that
Do not start a new paragraph	no ¶	policies were accepted. ¶ The no-smoking policy stipulated that
Move right	⌐	The judge insisted on the following penalties: • $5000 fine • 30 days in jail
Move left	⌐	The judge insisted on the following penalties: • $5000 fine • 30 days in jail

(continued)

Meaning	Symbol	Example
Transpose letters or words	⌐⌐	coloured red labels OR coloured
Lower	⊔	H₂O
Raise	⌐⌐	E = M C²2
Use lowercase	/c	Do (NOT) remove supplies. /c
Capitalize	☰	Do not remove supplies.
Use boldface	bf	Do (not) remove supplies. bf
Underline or use italics	—	Do not remove supplies.
Align *(This could be used to indicate the need to align right or left, top or bottom.)*	//	‖ You are invited to attend a business seminar.
Centre	] [	] You are invited to attend a business seminar. [
Spell the word/s out	SP	(C.N.I.B.) SP
Use parentheses	( )	Canadian National Institute for the Blind (C.N.I.B.)

Glossary

Abridged Shortened by using fewer words while maintaining the fundamental content.

Adjournment A temporary or indefinite halt to a meeting.

Administrative management A type of management style in which a leader displays conscientiousness, especially related to orderliness. The prime focus is on rules and processes over individual preferences.

Agenda A formal list of items to be achieved or discussed at a meeting.

Almanacs A yearly book or calendar of days, weeks or months.

Ambient lighting Illumination that surrounds us and is not directly focused on one area, as is task lighting.

Ambiguous Having more than one interpretation, thereby causing uncertainty or confusion.

Annotating The process of making notes on a document for comment or criticism.

Application program A program or software that performs a collection of related tasks, such as word processing, and that allows the user to specify the data input and output.

Archiving Transferring inactive electronic records into storage.

Area code A series of digits placed before the local number to indicate the area in which the call is to be delivered. Also known as a routing code.

Articulation agreement An agreement between two educational institutions through which transfer credits may be used towards an academic credential at either institution.

Artificial intelligence (AI) A term for simulated intelligence by computers, systems and machines.

Augmented reality (AR) Technology that imposes a computer-generated image on a user's viewpoint of the real world, thus providing a composite view.

Authoritarian management This type of management style is a leader who displays conscientiousness, especially related to orderliness.

Automated teller machine (ATM) A public electronic funds transfer machine for making bank deposits, withdrawals, and accessing information.

Backup A copy of data, often in a separate location from the original. The contents of the hard disk are backed up using CDs, external hard drives, or servers (computers dedicated solely for the backups).

Bandwidth The volume of information that can be transmitted in a period of time.

Bibliography A list of details about books, their authors and publishers, used or referred to by another author.

Bit A binary digit. The smallest possible piece of computer information. A 1 or 0 in the binary system represents each bit. A sequence of eight bits forms a byte (*see* **byte**).

Blog This term is short for weblog. A blog can best be described as a journal available on the web.

Brainstorming The unrestrained offering of ideas or suggestions by all members of a conference; the purpose is to find a solution to a problem.

Branding The business practice of creating a name, symbol, design, and logo that identifies and differentiates a product from other products.

Bridge A virtual facility where conference call participants meet for their exclusive conference.

Broadband Signals are transmitted digitally over a range of frequencies, allowing high-speed access to the internet.

Budget An estimate based on income and expenditures over a set period of time.

Business intelligence Analytics gained to help businesses decide how to improve marketing and customer service.

Buyout The purchase of one company by another company.

Byte A unit of data equivalent to one computer character (*see* **bit**).

Call management services A set of telephone-user options provided by the telephone company (e.g., display of incoming call information, call forwarding).

Cancelling mail A process where bars are printed over the stamps, and the envelope is stamped to indicate the date, time, and municipality where the mail was processed.

Carpal tunnel syndrome (CTS) Caused by inflammation of the tendons in the tunnel at the base of the hand, normally attributed to repetitive use of the hand and wrist.

Casual day A working day designated by management as a day when casual, but respectable, attire may be worn in the office.

Central processing unit (CPU) The part of a computer where the processing actually occurs.

Centralization Who makes the decisions in an organization. Decision-making power concentrated at a sole level.

Chain of command An uninterrupted line of authority that extends from the top of the organization down to the bottom.

Change management The management of change and development within an organization.

Character A pattern of behaviour built upon the basic values of life.

Charge-out A system of keeping track of materials that have been removed from the office paper files.

Chronological Time-ordered arrangement of events.

Cite To reference something or someone as an example to support what has been said or written.

Clarity Sharpness of image and or sound.

Code of ethics A formal document that states the organization's primary values and ethical rules of conduct.

Coding A system of symbols and numbers that convey meaning to the users of the system.

Coherence The quality of being consistent or intelligible.

Colloquialism A word or expression that is considered informal speech or writing.

Command An instruction that the operator gives to a computer to tell it what function to perform.

Commuter flight Short, direct flight between two neighbouring cities.

Company merger Joining together two or more companies to conduct business.

Company takeover An individual or organization takes control of another organization.

Compatible The ability of different hardware or software products to function together effectively.

Competitive advantage Implies a company does something better than other organizations and it can or cannot be sustained over time. Such as case an organization can secure an advantage with designed recruitment, selection, and performance management structure.

Composure The state of being calm in mind and manner.

Concise Brief and to the point.

Conference A meeting or discussion to exchange ideas.

Conference call A meeting or discussion conducted over the telephone between three or more participants.

Connecting flight A flight on which the passenger, at some point between departure and destination, changes to another flight of the same airline.

Conscientiousness The personality trait of being careful to do work right.

Consensus When every team member can support the team decision, the team has reached a consensus. The final decision may not be the choice of each team member; however, all members must agree that they can support it both inside and outside the confines of the meeting.

Contemporary Characteristically modern in style.

Convenience copier A small, inexpensive photocopier.

Copyright The legal right of publishers and artists to control their own work.

Correctness Free from error.

Courtesy title A respectful title to be used in formal address (e.g., Mr., Ms., Mrs., Miss, Mayor, Vice-President, Major).

Credenza A sideboard or cabinet used as an extension of a desk.

Cross-referencing A method of locating a single record from two or more file references.

Culture Refers to a system of shared values, beliefs, morals, and social standards embraced by a group of people.

Curriculum vitae A form of résumé, often referred to as a CV. The actual Latin words mean "course of life." The term describes a document that summarizes a person's history and professional qualifications.

Customer relationship management (CRM) A strategy for understanding your customers and their needs in order to optimize your interactions with them.

Cybersecurity The method to protect data from unauthorized interception or use.

Database a collection of information organized so that it can be easily accessed, managed, and updated.

Debrief To receive information or to recap a meeting or procedure that has concluded.

Deductive A writing technique that leads the reader from a general idea to a specific concept.

Demographics A structure of populations that recognizes groupings by age, gender, race, and other statistics.

Desktop computer A stand-alone computer used to perform personal or office applications.

Desktop publishing (DTP) A computer application that enables the user to design and create professional documents that integrate text and graphics.

Digital Age The place in time with the implementation of the personal computer and subsequent technology introduced providing the ability to transfer information freely and quickly.

Direct flight A flight on which, regardless of the number of stops en route, the passenger remains on the same plane from departure to arrival at destination.

Directory An electronic directory is a section of the computer system that identifies certain electronic files. It works much like a filing cabinet. (Also called a catalogue or folder.)

Discrimination Showing prejudice or being unfairly partial.

Display A screen or monitor.

Diversity The variety of experiences and perspectives that arise from differences in race, culture, religion, mental or physical abilities, heritage, age, gender, sexual orientation, and other characteristics.

Division of labour To separate work based on similar job tasks also known as work specialization.

Divisional structure Clusters organizational functions into product or regional divisions. Each division within this structure can align with each other concerning products or geographical location.

Domestic mail Mailable matter that is transmitted within Canada, which includes the 10 provinces, the Yukon, the Northwest Territories, and Nunavut.

Downsizing Reducing the size of an organization, often by laying off employees.

Duplex Printing on both sides of the paper.

Ecommerce A broad term that describes the environment in which commercial transactions are conducted over the internet.

E-file The electronic storage location and reference name for electronic documents.

E-portfolio An electronic version of a portfolio where documents are stored on a personal website or electronic folder.

Effectiveness The practical and productive effect of a procedure on a process.

Efficiency Producing the desired results with the least output of time, but in a capable and competent fashion.

Electronic calendar A computer-based personal calendar. When computers are networked, calendars may also be used to schedule and plan on behalf of the user.

Electronic data interchange (EDI) EDI provides a standard exchange of business data from one computer to another.

Electronic funds transfer (EFT) A method of transferring funds via computer and other forms of technology.

Electronic mail (email) A computer network–based message routing, storing, and retrieval system.

Electronic presentation software Application software that enables you to create individual electronic slides that can be displayed as a slide show. Graphs, charts, and other images created using this software add visual appeal to a presentation.

Empowered To be authorized and trusted to complete a job or task.

Encryption Process of taking information and translating into a code language to protect it.

Encryption software Security that encodes computer information into something beyond recognition with the use of a software "key."

Environmental sustainability A state in which the demands placed on the environment can be met without draining resources; its capacity to allow all people to live well.

ePassport (electronic passport) A passport with an electronic chip inserted in the back for scanning purposes, replacing the standard paper copy of the passport.

Ergonomics The study of efficiency, safety, and ease of action between people and their working environment.

Esthetically A way of viewing design that is in good taste and pleasant to look at.

Ethical Agreeing with principles of accepted moral conduct.

Ethnicity The cultural identity of a person.

Etiquette Customs and rules of social or corporate correct behaviour.

Event An occurrence, happening, or occasion such as an award presentation.

Facsimile A device that will copy and transmit, over telephone lines, graphical or textual documents to a corresponding remote facsimile. Also called a fax.

Fibre optic cable A technology using glass (or plastic) threads (fibres) to transmit data.

Field A field is an area or a location in a unit of data such as a record, message header, or computer instruction. A field can be subdivided into smaller fields.

File A file is a related collection of *records*.

Filing The act of storing files in a manual filing system.

Firewall A hardware and software computer security system designed to reduce the threat of unauthorized intrusion.

Flash drive A portable, miniaturized permanent memory device used with the USB ports of a computer. Sometimes called *pen drives* or memory keys.

Flextime A contraction of "flexible time." Readjusting working hours to accommodate both employee and employer.

Format The arrangement of text and graphics on a page.

Gazetteer An index of geographical names.

Gender identity is one's innermost concept of self as male, female, a blend of both, or neither—how individuals perceive themselves

Gigabyte Approximately 1 billion bytes.

GIGO An acronym for Garbage In, Garbage Out. The acronym means that poor-quality input to a computer will only result in poor-quality output.

Global marketplace The worldwide business environment. An international forum in which to conduct business.

Grammar check A word processing feature that compares the grammar of a keyed document with conventional rules.

Grapevine An informal channel of communication within an organization.

Hard skills Technical skills, including working with a variety of technologies, using technology to produce and manage information, and maintaining and troubleshooting problems.

Hardware The physical part(s) of a computer system.

Hidden job market The vibrant job market that exists without advertising. The potential employee must research and network to discover what opportunities are available.

Hierarchy The levels of management and reporting structure in any business, from highest to lowest.

Hotline A telephone line or special number that is reserved for critical calls such as technical support.

Hotspot This is a site that provides a wireless local area network through the use of a router connected to a link to an internet service provider.

Human capital The knowledge, skills, and abilities possessed by an individual or groups, regarded in terms of their value or cost to an organization.

Human resource management (HRM) The term used to describe formal systems devised for the management of people within an organization.

Hyperlink A link from a hypertext document to the same or another hypertext document.

Icon A picture used to represent a computer software function.

Immunization An inoculation that gives selective immunity to infections.

Indexing Classifying and providing an ordered list of items for easy retrieval.

Inductive A writing technique that introduces the reader to a concept and then leads the reader to a reasonable conclusion.

Informal organization An organization or group that develops naturally among personnel without direction from the management of the company within which it operates.

Information Data translated into a form that is more convenient to manipulate by computers.

Information management The skilful handling or use of information.

Input Data submitted to a computer for processing.

Integrating application software Seamlessly connecting data created in one software with different software to allow all the features of each software to remain. For example, if you integrate an Excel spreadsheet into a Word document, the spreadsheet will appear as a Word table. However, clicking on the table will open the Excel spreadsheet within Word and allow you to make changes to it. Clicking anywhere on the Word page outside the Excel spreadsheet will make the Word document active and display the spreadsheet once again as a Word table.

Interconnect equipment Telephone equipment that organizations purchase or lease from suppliers other than the telephone company.

Interface The software and/or hardware that connects one device or system to another, either electronically or physically.

International mail Canadian mail addressed to points of destination outside Canada and the United States of America.

Interpersonal communication Personal interaction between individuals or members of a group.

Interpersonal skills Qualities that determine a person's ability to get along with others. Examples are ability to work as a team player, negotiator, customer service provider, and teacher.

Intranet A company's private computer network.

Itinerary A detailed plan for a journey.

Jet lag The disruption of the body's natural rhythm that comes from changing time zones as a result of high-speed jet travel.

Job search board Companies post job opportunities through an employment host provider usually online.

Job search engine A search system containing posted employment opportunities from a variety of sources.

Keyboard An input device consisting of an arrangement of keys similar to that on a typewriter.

Kilobyte Approximately 1000 bytes.

Laptop computer (notebook) A small-scale personal computer. It has all the functionality of a desktop personal computer, but it weighs about three kilograms and is the approximate size of this textbook.

Life cycle The series of changes in the life span of a record from creation to disposal.

Line organization An organization structure based on authority. Line authority is hierarchical; the president has ultimate authority and reduced authority is given to others down the line to supervisor.

Line-and-staff organization An organizational structure where line managers have operational positions and staff managers have advisory or administrative positions. Line-and-staff organization structures are often found in large, diverse companies.

Linkage The connection and interactions between tasks, functions, and departments promoting information flow and productivity; can be horizontal or vertical in nature.

Local area network (LAN) Two or more local personal computers or terminals connected together by communication lines in order to share common programs and data.

Mail merge The process of combining text (letters/memos) from one file with names and addresses from another file.

Management by objectives (MBO) A management and operational strategy designed to improve performance. Employees and management come together to identify common goals, form action plans to secure participation, and foster commitment with employees.

Management process The series of steps taken in partnership with key management functions.

Management theory Encompasses how managers and leaders relate to their organizations in the knowledge of its objectives; it is also the implementation of effective methods to meet their objectives along with how to motivate employees to perform to a high standard.

Markup An additional monetary value added to the cost price.

Matrix Organizational structure is a structure in which the reporting relationships are set up as a grid, or matrix, rather than in the traditional hierarchy.

Meeting An assembly of people, usually for discussion.

Megabyte Approximately 1 million bytes.

Memory Temporary memory is the place in a computer where programs and data are stored while in use. For permanent memory, (*see* **hard disk drive**).

Mentor In a corporate setting, a mentor is a person who usually holds a position of a higher level than yours. This person can offer you career advice, guidance, and information about the organization.

Merger The unification of two or more companies.

Metric A system or standard of measurement.

Microprocessor chip A processing unit miniaturized to fit on a single integrated circuit (chip).

Minutes Records of meeting discussion or, informally, notes, are the instant written record of a meeting or hearing.

Mixed layout Combination of open spaces, with private meeting areas for discussions and closed offices for higher-ranking employees where privacy is essential in order to meet the organization's objectives.

Mobile banking Chartered banks offer customers with smartphones, tablets, and PDAs access to banking services similar to web-based banking.

Modular furniture Furniture designed to be used as separate modules or placed together to form larger units.

Monitor Screen output for a computer.

Motivation The inner reason that causes an individual to act.

Mouse Hand-operated input device. It is rolled across a surface to control the movement of a cursor.

Mousing The act of using the PC "mouse" to control software applications.

Negotiating The process of exchanging ideas, information, and opinions with others to work towards agreements; consequently, policies and programs are formulated, and decisions, conclusions, or solutions are the result of a joint effort.

Network Various processors or terminals connected within the same computer environment.

Networking Informal communications between people, departments, divisions, or organizations for the purpose of sharing information.

No-frills flight A flight on which regular services that travellers have come to expect are absent. For example, in-flight cabin services by flight attendants are not provided, and travellers are required to provide their own food and drink.

Nonstop flight A flight that is uninterrupted from point of departure to destination.

Notice of meeting A designed document to notify shareholders or directors of the time, date, and place of a corporate meeting.

Office politics The tactics and strategies used in an office to gain an occupational advantage.

Offset printing A printing process in which a rubber cylinder transfers an inked impression from an etched plate to a sheet of paper.

Online Describing a device connected directly to a computer.

Open ticket A booking arrangement for some forms of transportation where the scheduling details of the return journey are not specified.

Operating system A computer's fundamental internal commands or instructions needed to operate; the first program loaded upon starting the computer, the operating system enables the application programs to work.

Organization chart A guide to the formal internal structure of an organization.

Organizational behaviour (OB) The study of both group and individual performance and activity within an organization.

Organizational climate How the members of an organization experience their work and workplace on a daily basis.

Organizational culture An invisible but powerful entity that influences the behaviour of the members of that group.

Organizational structure A system used to outline order within an organization. It identifies job roles, functions, and reporting hierarchy within the organization.

Orientation Becoming familiar with a situation or environment.

Out folder A substitute folder that replaces an active folder, which has been removed from the filing cabinet.

Out guide A substitute document that replaces an original document temporarily taken from a folder. The out guide provides a description of the removed document.

Output Information resulting from computer processing.

Participatory management A management style that is both permissive and democratic. It involves employees in some aspects of decision making and emphasizes autonomy in work activities.

Passport A travel document, given to citizens by their own government, granting permission to leave the country and to travel in certain specified foreign countries.

Pen drive A portable, miniaturized permanent memory device used with the USB ports of a computer. Also called a *flash drive*.

Per diem rate A daily allowance for expenses. *Per diem* is Latin for *by the day*.

Peripheral An external device such as a printer, scanner, or disk drive that is connected to and controlled by the computer.

Personal preference A personal quality or like related to a person, not a group.

Personal qualities Qualities that determine a person's values and sense of what is important, such as attitude, dependability, integrity and honesty, and self-image.

Personal space The distance at which one person feels comfortable talking to another.

Personality The combination of characteristics or qualities that form an individual distinguishing character.

Petty cash A small amount of cash kept onsite and used for paying for small transactions.

Phone tag An occurrence in which two parties attempt to contact each other by phone, but neither is able to reach the other for a conversation.

Plagiarism Using the words or ideas of someone else as your own without permission or reference to the original source.

Poise Ease and dignity of manner.

Postal code A unique alphanumeric code used to identify the local destination of a mail item.

Primary sources Direct, firsthand accounts of a subject, from people who had an immediate connection with it.

Printer A device that produces copy on paper.

Priorities The assignment of precedence of tasks to be accomplished. Typically, the tasks will be ranked in order of importance.

Processing Computer manipulation of data.

Procrastination An unproductive behaviour pattern that causes you to delay working on your most important assignments and to focus on tasks that aren't priorities.

Professionalism Aspiring to meet the highest possible standards of your profession rather than a set of minimum requirements.

Project management The process of planning, organizing, securing, managing, leading, and controlling resources to achieve goals.

Proliferation The act of increasing greatly in number.

Prospecting letter An application letter that is written without knowing if a job opening exists.

Quality assurance The process of ensuring a project is produced in the right way. It is proactive and concerned about the processes and activities during the projects development.

Quality control Consists of the observation techniques and activities used to fulfill requirements for quality.

Race The physical characteristics of a person.

Random-access memory (RAM) A storage location within the computer, containing data or instructions that can be erased. This area of memory is a temporary storage location.

Raw data Source information in its original form.

Read-only memory (ROM) A storage location within the computer, containing data or instructions that cannot be erased by overwriting or loss of power.

Recession An economic decline in business activity.

Record A record consists of fields of individual data items, such as customer name, customer number, and customer address.

Redundant No longer needed; something that has been superseded and is now considered extra.

Reference A source of information such as a book or an author.

Relative index An alphabetic listing of all topics that appear in a filing system.

Removable storage Storage media that can be physically removed from the computer and transported elsewhere. This might include archived CD-ROMs, DVDs, pen drives and other external storage systems.

Repetitive strain injury Repetitive strain injury (RSI) and can affect anyone whose work calls for long periods of steady hand movement. RSIs tend to come with work that involves prolonged and repetitive movement, such as keying.

Reprographics Hard-copy reproduction process (copying) of text or graphics.

Request for proposal (RFP) A document that asks for a proposal, often made through a bidding process, by an agency or company interested in procurement of a service or potential supplier.

Rightsizing To adjust the size of the organization, up or down, to meet market and environmental demands. A way of optimizing company resources to achieve efficiency.

Routers Devices that route information from one network to another. Routers allow independent networks to function as a large so that users of any network can reach users of any other.

Satellite An object that orbits the earth transmitting a two-way digital signal to receptor dishes located on earth.

Screening A procedure used to selectively answer telephone calls.

Search engine Complex software tools that send out probes called bots into the internet to find, analyze, and index webpages and other forms of content, constantly growing their database of information.

Secondary sources One step removed from primary sources, they often quote or otherwise use primary sources. They can cover the same topic, but add a layer of interpretation and analysis.

Self-confidence The firm belief in one's own abilities.

Short list In an employment scenario, this is a list of applicants that has been reduced to the best possible choices.

Sign on A term used to describe the process of starting the computer, entering a password, and ultimately connecting to the application desired.

Smartphone A mobile phone that works on a mobile computing platform.

Social media A general term used to describe web-based tools that encourage exchange of information by users.

Soft skills Personal qualities and interpersonal skills that impact on success in the workplace.

Software The programs, data, or intangible part(s) of a computer system.

Solicited letter An application letter that is written in response to an advertisement.

Solicitors Visitors to business who are attempting to sell products or services.

Spam Unwanted commercial email usually sent out in volume; also called junk mail.

Spam-filtering software A software application designed to detect and reduce spam email.

Speculation An opinion based on incomplete information or evidence.

Spreadsheet A computerized representation of a paper spreadsheet in which data are organized in rows and columns.

Stereotype The oversimplified image held of one thing or person by another. It is also standardized and simplified conceptions of groups based on prior assumptions.

Stress A mental or physical state of tension.

Subscription database Published journals, magazines, reports, newspapers, books, image collections, encyclopedias, statistical data, and other documents not typically freely available to the public.

Supervisor A person who watches over or controls the work of others.

Supply chain The connection between a company and its suppliers to produce and distribute its products.

Synopsis A statement giving a brief, general review or summary.

Tablet computer A portable personal computer equipped with a touch screen with a virtual keyboard for data input in place of a traditional keyboard.

Task lighting Directed lighting (illumination) designed to increase visibility of a specific work area.

Technology The application of information utilizing methods, devices, and systems to produce goods and complete task-based objectives.

Teleconference A conference held between people in remote or distant places via telecommunication facilities.

Terabyte Approximately 1 trillion bytes.

Time distribution chart A chart designed to show the distribution of work and time for several workers performing related office tasks.

Time management A skill that enables you to manage time efficiently.

Time-sharing The simultaneous access of a computer by two or more users.

Total quality management (TQM) A management approach to long–term success through customer satisfaction.

Transmittal sheet Typically the first page of a fax transmission, which provides contact details of the originator and intended recipient.

Travel fund advance A cash advance paid to an employee prior to a business trip.

Unabridged Containing original information, not condensed.

USA mail Canadian mail addressed to points of destination within the United States of America.

Value chain A set of related processes a company uses to create its own competitive advantage.

Venue A place where events are held.

Verbatim Repeated or copied word for word.

Videoconference A conference between remote participants in which sound and images are transferred over telephone lines or satellite.

Virtual Something practically real in effect even though it may not be in reality.

Virtual assistant A virtual assistant, or VA, is a self-employed professional offering administrative support to a variety of clients through his or her home office.

Virtual network A communications connection that may involve routing through several locations and devices. However, it has the appearance and functionality of two computers directly connected with wires.

Virtual receptionist A software application that performs the routine tasks of a receptionist.

Virus A rogue computer program that affects computers with unpredictable and damaging results.

Visa A stamped permit to travel within a given country for a specified length of time. It is granted by the foreign country's government and is usually stamped or attached inside the passport.

Visible filing Paper filing: that which you can touch.

Visitor Management is the process of tracking everyone who enters your building or your office.

Voice mail A telephone network–based message routing, storing, and retrieval system.

Voice-recognition software Software that transcribes the dictator's words directly to the computer screen.

Web application A computer program or app designed to work on the web.

Web conferencing Meeting over the internet using web conferencing software much as you would meet via telephone to take part in a telephone conferencing call.

Web-banking Banking services provided online.

Web-enabled device A device that is accessible on the web.

Webcasting (or netcasting) Broadcasting live or recorded audio and/or video transmissions via computer.

Website An address on the World Wide Web, where information or links to other websites can be obtained.

Website Content Management System (WCMS) A software application or set of related programs used to create and manage digital content

White noise Also known as white sound. A continuous sound formed from many frequencies of equal volume; it has the effect of deadening surrounding sounds.

Wide area network (WAN) Two or more computers and/or local area networks connected together by communications media in order to share programs and data.

Wiki A collaborative website that allows its users to add, modify, or delete its content via a web browser.

Windows™ A trademarked name for a graphically interfaced operating system that operates on personal computers. Functions are represented through icons and menus.

Workspace A specific area set aside for individuals to work.

Workstation A personal workspace, often defined by freestanding partitions; a terminal or personal computer.

Yellow Pages A business directory accessible in print and online.

Zero-plus dialling A telephone number prefixed with "0" so that the caller can obtain assistance or special service from the operator.

Index

A

AAA. *See* Association of Administrative Assistants
abbreviations (Canada, US mail), 183
abbreviations, alphabetic filing rules for, 221–222
abridged dictionaries, 76
abusive customers, 120
Access to Information Act, 204, 205
accommodations for, conferences, 255
accounting, ethics in, 330
  See also office commerce
accusations, 24
acknowledgments, letters and, 294–295
acoustics, 93–94
ACTA. *See* Alliance of Canadian Travel Associations
action requested slip, 169, 170
addressing mail
  abbreviations for Canada and US, 183
  bilingual addressing for, 184
  change of address for, 185–186
  civic addresses and, 178
  country name for, 181–182
  delivery symbols for, 182
  format for, 177–178
  guidelines for, 177
  for international business letters, 310
  non-address data and, 178
  postal code for, 181
  return address for, 185
  street directions for, 178
  street types and symbols for, 179–181
  unit designators for, 178
  unit identifiers for, 178
adjournment of meetings, 262
admail, 172
administrative assistants
  business letters for signature of, 293–296
  expectations of, 14
administrative management, 89
Administrative Professionals Week, 376
advanced preparation, 60–61
Advice of Receipt, 174
age/generational diversity, 34
agenda for meetings, 254, 258–260, 266
airline services, 176
air travel, 238–241
Alectra Utilities, 279
algorithm, 152
Alliance of Canadian Travel Associations (ACTA), 237
almanacs, 76
alphabetic filing rules
  abbreviations for, 221–222
  alphabetizing in, 219–220
  basic names for, 220

  for business names, 220
  for government names, 225–226
  for identical names, 224–225
  indexing in, 219
  for institutions, 224
  for minor words, 220–221
  for numbers, 223
  order of filing units for, 219–220
  for organizations, 224
  for people names, 220
  for prefixes, 223
  for punctuation, 221
  single letters for, 221–222
  standardization of, 219
  for suffixes, 222
  for symbols, 220–221
  for titles, 222
  units in, 219
  variations in, 225–226
alphabetic filing system, 218–219
ambient lighting, 93
ambiguity, ethics and, 25
analytical reports, 298–299
annotating mail, 167
answering services, 139
antiviral programs, 154
APA style, 80
appearance, physical, 280–281,
  360–361
appendix, in formal reports, 306–307
application/cover letters, 354–357
application programs
  defined, 130
  DTP, 132, 136–137
  integrating, 137
  operating system and, 130
  presentation software, 137
  purpose of, 135
  spreadsheets, 132, 136
  word processing, 135–136
applied research, 73
appointment management, 112–116
  business letters concerning, 293–294
  calendar entries for, 115–116
  changing, 116
  with electronic calendars, 114–115
  by e-mail, 113
  with paper calendars, 115
  by phone, 113
  refusing, 118–119
  scheduling, 113
  visitors with, 117
  visitors without, 118

appreciation letters, 296
archiving electronic records, 217
area codes, 109
aresearchguide.com, 313
ARMA. *See* Association of Records Management and Administrators
articulation agreements, 376
artificial intelligence (AI), 132–133
Association of Administrative Assistants (AAA), 377, 384
Association of Records Management and Administrators (ARMA), 219, 233
associations, professional, 377–378, 384
atlases, 76–77
ATM. *See* automated teller machine
attitude
    composure, 23
    consideration of others, 21–22
    positive, 24
    self-esteem, 23
    sociability, 22
augmented reality (AR), 133
authoritarian management, 89
authority, classifications of, 87–89
automated inquiry system, CP, 174
automated mail services, 160–162
automated sorting system, 209
automated teller machine (ATM), 316, 317
automatic answering service, 106
automatic recording machines, 139

B

backstabbers, 19
backup, 135
Bala, Devika, 101
bandwidth, 147
bank drafts, 319
Bank of Montreal, 333
bank reconciliation, 323–325
banquet seating, 255
B2B, 152, 316
BBB. *See* Better Business Bureau
B2C, 152
behavioural descriptive interviews, 363
Better Business Bureau (BBB), 119
beverages
    for conference, 255
    for meeting, 260
bibliography, 305
bilingual addressing, 184
biographical information, 77
bitdefender.com, 157
bits, 133
blamers, 19
blank endorsements, 321
blogs, 150
Bluejacking, 154
Bluetooth, 131
body language, in meetings, 270
Bombardier, 72

bookingcalendar.com, 126
bouncing back to employment, 340–341
brainstorming, 51
    in team meetings, 268
branding, conferences, 254
broadband connectivity, 131
budget for, conferences, 254
budget preparation, 328, 330
buffer paragraph, 291
bulletin boards, 65
bullies, 18
bureaucratic organizations, 86
bus express, 176
businessballs.com, 202
business cards, 246
businessethics.ca, 32
business letters
    acknowledgments and, 294–295
    addressing international, 310
    for administrative assistants signature, 293–296
    application/cover letters, 354–357
    appointments and, 293–294
    appreciation, 296
    categories of, 289–296
    clarity of, 287–288
    coherence of, 286–287
    completeness of, 286, 297
    components of, 296–297
    conciseness of, 287
    correctness of, 286
    courtesy in, 288
    covering, 295
    direct requests with, 290–291
    of disappointment, 291–292
    document style guide, 296
    effective, 285–286
    ethics in, 310
    favourable, 290–291
    focus on reader in, 286
    follow-up, 295–296
    formats for, 296–298
    full-block style for, 297
    goodwill in, 291
    inquiries, 366
    international, 310–311
    job acceptance, 366, 367
    job refusal, 366, 368
    for manager's signature, 293
    modified-block style for, 298
    notices of delay and, 295
    persuasive, 292–293
    prospecting letter, 354–356
    purpose for, 286
    readability of, 289
    reminder, 365–366
    replies with, 290, 291, 294
    routine replies with, 294
    routine requests, inquiries, and orders with, 294
    solicited letter, 354

style in, 288–289
thank-you, 364–365
tone for, 288
websites for, 313
business lunch, 29–30
business meetings. *See* meetings
business messaging platforms, 162
business names, alphabetic filing rules for, 220
business organization, 14
business research
methods, 73–74
types, 73
business-to-business, 316
buyouts, 26
bytes, 133

C

cable modem, 148
CACEE. *See* Canadian Association of
Career Educators and Employers
cache, 155
calendars
electronic, 62, 114–115
entries in, 115–116
organization of, 64
paper, 115
websites for, 126
call management services, 138
campus area network (CAN), 131
Canada, 79, 84, 109, 126
Canada Business Network, 98, 277
canada.gc.ca, 84
canadainternational.gc.ca, 47
Canada Library Gateway, 84
Canada Pension Plan (CPP), 14, 328
Canada Post (CP)
automated inquiry system of, 174
business services of, 159, 173
change of address for, 185–186
e-commerce and, 170
efficiency improvements of, 170–171
Electronic Post Office, 165
electronic services of, 163–165
metered mail and, 185
outgoing mail services of, 172–185
Priority Courier service of, 173
refusing mail, 186
returning undelivered mail, 186
return to sender with, 175
sizes for, 173
website for, 159, 190
Xpresspost service of, 174
Canada Research Chairs Program (CRCP), 38
Canada Revenue Agency (CRA), 245, 315, 327–328, 333
Canada's Anti-Spam Legislation, 234
Canadian Air Transport Security Authority (CATSA), 243
Canadian Association of Career Educators and Employers
(CACEE), 372
Canadian Association of Professional Speakers (CAPS), 277

Canadian Association of Virtual Assistants (CAVA), 377, 384
Canadian Business, 46
Canadian Centre for Occupational Health and Safety
(CCOHS), 93, 98
Canadian Charter of Rights and Freedoms, 34
Canadian government publications, 78–79
Canadian Human Rights Act (CHRA), 34, 38
Canadian Human Rights Commission (CHRC), 361, 372
Canadian Library Gateway, 75
Canadian Marketing Association, 333
Canadian Medical Protective Association, 234
Canadian Multiculturalism Act of 1971, 34
Canadian Parliamentary Guide, 79
Canadian Postal Guide, 172
Canadian Society of Professional Event Planners (CanSPEP), 256
cancelled cheques, 325
cancelling mail, 185
CanSPEP.ca, 277
CAP. *See* Certified Administrative Professional
CAPM. *See* Certified Associate in Project Management
CAPS. *See* Canadian Association of Professional Speakers
careerlab.com, 372
careerowl.ca, 372
carpal tunnel syndrome (CTS), 92
car rental services, 241
carry-on luggage, 243
cash withdrawals, 321
casual days, 281
CATSA. *See* Canadian Air Transport Security Authority
cause-and-effect diagram, 267, 269–270
CCOHS. *See* Canadian Centre for Occupational Health and
Safety
Center for Internet Security (CIS), 157
centralization, 87
central processing unit (CPU), 130
Centre for Intercultural Learning, 47
Certified Administrative Professional (CAP), 377
Certified Associate in Project Management (CAPM), 196
certified cheques, 318–319
chain of command, 87
chamber of commerce directories, 79
change in workplace, 26
change of address, 185–186
character, 381
charge-out methods for filing, 209–210
chequebooks, 319
cheques
bank reconciliation and, 323–325
cancelled, 325
cash withdrawals and, 321
certified, 318–319
depositing, 321–323
endorsing, 321
keyed entries on, 320
stop-payment notification on, 320–321
voucher, 319
writing, 319–321
Chicago Manual of Style, 80
CHRC. *See* Canadian Human Rights Commission

chronological reports, 310
chronological resumes, 344–346
circulation slips, 170
CIS. *See* Center for Internet Security
Citizen and Immigration Canada, 46
city directories, 79
civic addresses, 178
classroom seating, 255
client servers, 198–199
closed office layout, 91
cloud/file sharing applications, 152–153
COD. *See* collect on delivery
code of ethics, 25
coding, 207
collect on delivery (COD), 175
college placement office, 338
colour coding, 218
combination résumés, 344, 348–349
common knowledge, 79–80
communication
    See also business letters; reports
    constructive criticism and, 20–21, 282–283
    effective, 279
    eye contact and, 281
    facial expressions and, 281–282
    image and, 280–281
    international business and interpersonal, 40–41
    interpersonal, 279
    listening and, 282
    nonverbal, 280–282
    online, 131
    personal space and, 281
    phone communication skills, 103–104
    posture and, 281
    public speaking and, 283–284
    verbal, 279–280
    websites for, 313
    written, 285
commuter flights, 239
company mergers, 26, 340
compatibility, 130
competitive advantage, 13
competitive résumés, 342
complaining customers, 119–120
completing tasks, 61
composure, 23
computerhope.com, 144
computerized postage machine, 185
computers
    See also application programs
    accuracy of input information for, 134
    backup for, 135
    desktop, 129
    flash drives for, 131
    functions of, 130–131
    hard disk drive for, 131
    input and output data of, 130, 134
    laptop, 129, 261–262
    memory of, 130–131

networking, 131–132
notebook, 129
online, 131
operating system of, 130
PCs, 129
pen drives for, 210
for processing, 130
productivity with, 137–138
proliferation of, 352
smartphones, 129
storage for, 131, 134–135
tablet, 129
terminology for, 133
troubleshooting for, 133
types of, 128–129
universal serial bus, 131
versatility of, 132
viruses and, 153
web-enabled devices, 131
The Conference Board of Canada, 336, 337
conferences
    See also meetings
    beverages for, 255
    branding, 254
    budget, 254
    calling, 108–109, 272, 273
    definition, 254
    food for, 255
    international, 274
    vs. meeting, 254
    request for proposals, 254–255
    room setup, 255
    seating plans, 255
    speakers and entertainment, 255
    teleconferences, 108–109, 272, 273
    travel and accommodations, 255
    video, 150–151
    videoconferences, 255, 257, 272–273
    web, 140, 150–151, 272–274
confidential information, 21
confidentiality request statement, 163
confidential mail, 166
connecting flight, 239
conscientiousness, 89
consensus, 269
consideration of others, 21–22
constructive criticism, 20–21, 282–283
contemporary office professional, 380
contemporary organization structures, 86
content management systems
    capabilities of, 146
    connection, 146–147
    connectivity method, 148
    network thpes, 148
    search engines, 148–149
convenience copiers, 140
cookies, 154

copiers
    classes of, 140
    convenience, 140
    functions of, 140
    needs survey for, 141
    prices for, 141
    selecting, 141
    service for, 141
    vendors for, 141
copyright violation, 80
Coryat, Daryan, 375
cost estimation, for conferences, 254
country name, for addressing mail, 181–182
courier services, 176
courtesy in telephone use, 106–107
courtesy titles, 293
covering letters, 295
cover letters, 354–357
CP. *See* Canada Post
CPP (Canada Pension Plan), 328
CPU. *See* central processing unit
CRA. *See* Canada Revenue Agency
creative thinking and planning, 54
credenza, 65
credit cards, 244
cross-cultural awareness, 39
cross-cultural competence, 39
cross-cultural encounters, 39–40
cross-referencing, 207–208
cross-training, 378
CTS. *See* carpal tunnel syndrome
cultural awareness, 39
cultural competence, 38
cultural diversity, 34–35
culture
    blunders with, 44
    defined, 45
    gender and, 45
    gift giving and, 45
    international travel arrangements and, 247–248
    system of, 38
    time management in, 40
currency conversion, 252, 333
currency exchange, international, 330
curriculum vitae (CV), 341, 368
    See also résumés
customer relationship management (CRM), 41, 162
customer service, 20
CV. *See* curriculum vitae
cvtips.com, 372
cybersecurity
    bluejacking, 154
    computer viruses, 153
    cookies, 154
    credential reuse, 153
    defined, 153
    denial of service, 153
    hacking, 153
    malware, 153
    mousetrapping, 154
    pagejacking, 154
    pharming, 154
    phishing, 153
    spam, 153
    worms and trojan horses, 153

D

daily plan, for time management, 62–63
dangerous goods, 175
databases
    defined, 74
    electronic, 214–215
    for frequently used phone, 65
    research, 74, 75
data collection, 73–74
data encryption software, 155
data security
    cybersecurity threats, 153–154
    general data security risks, 152–153
    maintaining internet security, 154–155
date stamp, 57
Daylight Saving Time (DST), 111
Day-Timer, 126
DDD. *See* direct-distance dialling
debriefing, in team meetings, 270
decor, 92
deductive arrangement, 309
delivery symbols, 182
democratic style leadership, 89
demographics, 34
Denial of Service (DoS), 153
dependability, 22
deposits, 321–323
deposit slips, 322
desktop applications, 198
desktop computers, 129
desktop publishing (DTP), 132, 136–137
detail management, 57–58
dictionaries, 76–77
difficult customers
    abusive customers, 120
    complaining customers, 119–120
    difficult callers, 119
    special needs visitors, 121–122
    tips for success with, 120
    unwanted visitors, 119
    visitors with language barriers, 120–121
difficult tasks, beginning with, 58
digital assistants, 102
digital devices
    computer basic functions, 130–131
    computers types, 128–129
    networking computers, 131–132
digital recording, 139
digital subscriber line (DSL), 148
digital travel services, 237
digression, 18
direct application for jobs, 338

direct-distance dialling (DDD), 110
direct flight, 238
direction, lack of, 18
directories, 133
  chamber of commerce, 79
  city, 79
  for electronic records, 210
  telephone, 79, 109
direct payroll deposit, 317
direct requests, letters, 290–291
disappointment letters, 291–292
discounting, 18
discrimination, 35
display, 130
distributing mail, 169–171
diversity
  age/generational, 34
  benefits of, 36–37
  consciousness, 38–40
  cultural diversity, 34–35
  defined, 34
  equity and, 34–37
  in international business, 40–43
  physical ability and disability, 35–36
  race/ethnic, 35
  religious, 35
  sexual orientation/gender identity, 35
  in workplace, 34–36
diversityintheworkplace.ca, 46
divisional organizational structure, 86
division of labour, 87
documentation, for formal reports, 304
domestic long-distance calls, 109–112
domestic mail, 172–175
dominating team members, 18
downsizing, 340
DSL. *See* digital subscriber line
DST. *See* Daylight Saving Time
DTP. *See* desktop publishing
Dun & Bradstreet, 77, 84
duplex, 140

E

Ebsco, 84
e-commerce
  CP and, 170
  legislative protection fo, 316–317
  privacy and, 316
  transactions in, 316
ecommerce-guide.com, 333
EDI. *See* electronic data interchange
education, for professional development, 376–378
effectiveness, 52
efficiency
  See also time management
  CP improving, 170–171
  effectiveness compared to, 52
  work area, 58, 63
  work habits and, 52–53

e-file, 211
EFT. *See* electronic funds transfer
EI (Employment Insurance), 328
electronically scanned résumés, 352, 353
electronically submitted résumés, 352
electronic calendars, 62, 114–115
electronic databases, storage of, 214–215
electronic data interchange (EDI), 316
electronic date and time, 57
electronic funds transfer (EFT), 315
electronic mail, 160
    See also e-mail
Electronic Medical Records (EMRs), 162, 217
electronic money transfer, 163
Electronic Postage Setting System (EPSS), 185
Electronic Post Office, 165
electronic presentation software, 137
electronic records
  archiving, 217
  directories for, 210
  filing, 210–211
  retention of, 217
  supplies for, 213
electronic services, from CP, 163–165
e-mail
  appointments by, 113
  automated mail services, 160–162
  defined, 160
  ethics with, 186–187
  etiquette for, 162
  hyperlinks with, 360
  message, 161
  privacy, 171–172, 186–187
  reports, 300–301
  résumés through, 352
  sending and receiving, 160–162
employability skills, 335–337
employer obligations, 38
Employment and Social Development Canada
    (ESDC), 339, 372
employment eligibility, 340–341
Employment Equity Act (EEA), 37, 38
employment fairs, 338
Employment Insurance (EI), 14, 328
employment strategies
    See also job applications; job interviews; job prospects
  bouncing back and, 340–341
  follow-up correspondence for, 364–366
  international, 367–369
  websites for, 372
empowerment, 18
EMRs. *See* Electronic Medical Records
encryption software, 153, 155
encyclopedias, 76–77
encyclopedic filing system, 227
endorsing cheques, 321
englishplus.com, 313
environmental management, 66
environmental sustainability, 66

ePassport, 242
e-portfolios, 360
EPSS. *See* Electronic Postage Setting System
equity
   diversity and, 34–37
   human rights and standards of, 37
ergonomics
   acoustics and, 93–94
   defined, 92
   furniture and, 93
   lighting and, 93
   position and posture and, 94–95
   websites for, 98
esthetics, 92
ethical, 381
ethics
   in accounting, 330
   ambiguity and, 25
   in business letters, 310
   climate, 382
   code of, 25
   committing to, 381
   confidential information, 21
   e-mail and, 186–187
   ethical practice, 25
   job interview questions and, 359
   job search and, 366, 367
   in meetings, 273–274
   office romance and, 31
   in public speaking, 285
   in records management, 229
   travel expenses and, 247–248
   with visitors, 122
   work, time, and resources, 25–26
ethnicity, 35
etiquette
   books on, 77–78
   for business lunch, 29–30
   for e-mail, 162
   in foreign countries, 42
   for Internet, 162
   for phone use, 126
   protocol, 32
   travel and, 252
event, 254
Eventbrite, 255
executives, learning names of, 54
exercises, 98
expandable folders, 212
expedia.ca, 252
external memory, computers, 131
extranet, 148
eye contact, communication and, 281

F

facial expressions, communication with, 281–282
facilitators, for team meetings, 267
facsimile, 162–163
favourable letters, 290–291

F&B for conference, 255
Federal Express, 190
federal government
   job prospect information from, 339
   website for, 84
fibre optic cable, 148
fields, 133
file folders, 211–212
files, 133
filing, 64–65
   administrative professional
      role in, 206
   alphabetic rules for, 219–226
   alphabetic system for, 218–219
   aspects of, 204
   cabinet, 213
   charge-out methods for, 209–210
   coding and, 207
   cross-referencing and, 207–208
   of electronic records, 210–211
   indexing and, 207, 219
   open-shelf, 211
   papers in folders for, 209
   preparation for, 206–209
   reviewing for, 206–207
   sorting for, 208–209
   storage for, 213–215
   visible, 206–209, 211–213
   websites for, 233–234
filing supplies
   electronic, 213
   folders for, 211–212, 218
   guides for, 211
   labels, 212–213
   ordering online, 211
filing systems
   alphabetic, 218–219
   encyclopedic, 227
   geographic, 218, 227
   numeric, 218, 227–229
   subject, 218, 226–227
filingsystems.com, 233
financial information, 77
Financial Post Data Group, 77
firewall, 155
flash drives, 131
flat organizational structure, 86
flexible planning, 56–57
flextime, 53, 65
flight reservations, 239–240
flights, types of, 238–239
Fluid Life, 49
folders for, 211–212, 218
follow-up letters, 295–296
food
   for conference, 255
   for meetings, 260–261
forecast at completion, 197
formal meetings, 259, 263, 265

formal reports
  appendix in, 306–307
  arranging, 309–310
  composing, 307–310
  documentation for, 304
  formatting guidelines for, 301–304
  introduction to, 307
  letter of transmittal for, 309
  list of tables in, 306
  margins in, 302
  organizing, 307–308
  page numbers in, 303
  paragraph indention for, 302
  preliminary sections of, 305–306
  preliminary steps for, 301–302
  quotations for, 304
  references in, 305–306
  spacing in, 302
  subject headings for, 302–303
  supplementary sections of, 305–307
  table of contents in, 305
  tables in, 303–304
  title page in, 305
  writing, 308–309
forms, 57
  job application, 357–358
fraud, 326
Freedom of Information and Protection of Privacy Act, 205
freight shipments, 176
frequently used phone, 65
front-line reception
  See also telephone use
  appointments, 112–116, 293–294
  difficult customers for, 119
  greeting visitors, 116–119
  receiving visitors at, 121–122
  reception design and layout, 100–101
  visitor management systems, 102–103
  VRs, 101–102
  workstation of, 116
full-block letter style, 297
full endorsements, 321
functional authority, 88–89
functional organizational structure, 86
functional resumes, 344, 347
Fusion Projects, 193

G

Gantt chart, 60–61, 197
Garbage in, garbage out (GIGO), 134
gazetteer, 77
gender, culture and, 45
gender identity, 35
geographic filing system, 218, 227
gift giving, culture and, 45
gigabytes, 133
GIGO. *See* Garbage in, garbage out
glassdoor.ca, 372
Global Affairs Canada, 252

global marketplace, 26
global positioning systems (GPSs), 129
goodwill letters, 291
Google, 128
Google Hangout Chats, 162
gossips, 18–19
government names, alphabetic filing rules for, 225–226
Government of Canada, 98
GPSs. *See* global positioning systems
grapevine, 90
Greenwich Mean Time, 111
greeting office visitors
  with appointments, 117
  ethics and, 122
  immediate attention for, 116–117
  interrupting meetings when, 118
  introductions with, 117–118
  with language barriers, 120–121
  refusing appointments with, 118–119
  with special needs, 121–122
  staff visitors, 117–118
  terminating meetings and, 118
  unwanted visitors and, 119
  visitors preparation, 117
  without appointments, 118
Greyhound shipping services, 190
ground transportation, 241
groups, forming, 24
guidance team, 267
guides for filing, 211

H

hacking, 153
Half, Robert, 335
hanging file folders, 212
hard disk drive, 131
hard skills, 14
hardware, 128
hashtag, 152
Herjavec Group, 147
hidden job market, 339
hierarchy, 86
high-tech office, 92
high-volume copiers, 141
HipChat, 162
honesty, 23
HootSuite, 152
hotel reservations, 241–242
hotspot, 148
hrreporter.com, 384
hrworld.com, 98
human capital, 13
human factors engineering. *See* ergonomics
human relations
  business organization types, 14
  confidential information and, 21
  consideration of others, 21–22
  constructive criticism embraced for, 20–21
  customer service and, 20

hard skills in, 14
HRM, 13–14
interpersonal skill development for, 16–22
manage people, personalities, 18–19
negotiating effectively for, 20
soft skills in, 15
teaching other for, 19
teamwork and, 16–18
Human Resources Management (HRM), 32
defined, 13
overview of, 13–14
human rights, equity standards, 37
H.W. Wilson (website), 84
hyperlinks, 360

I

IAAP. *See* International Association of Administrative
    Professionals
IATA. *See* International Air Transportation Association
icon format, 161
identical names, alphabetic filing rules for, 224–225
image, communication and, 280–281
immunization requirements, 243
important records, 216
income tax deduction, 328, 329
incoming mail
    action requested slip in, 169, 170
    advertising in, 169
    annotating, 167
    circulation slips in, 170, 171
    date-time stamping, 166–167
    distributing, 169–171
    inspecting, 166
    Mail-Expected record and, 169
    manager absence and answering, 171–172
    opening, 166
    packages in, 168–169
    presenting, 168
    publications mail, 169
    reading, 167
    responsibilities with, 165–168
    routing slips and, 169, 171
    sorting, 166
indexing, 207, 219
individual names folders, 218
inductive arrangement, 309
infobel.com, 126
informal meetings, 259–260, 263
informal organization structure, 90–91
informal reports, 299–301
information
    See also storage of information
    biographical, 77
    common knowledge, 79–80
    confidential, 21
    data and, 133
    defined, 133
    financial, 77
    privacy legislation and, 205
    protecting, 204–205
    sources of, 73–74
    withholding or selectively sharing, 24
informational reports, 298
information management
    See also filing; reference sources
    aspects of, 204
    retaining records for, 215–217
    transferring records for, 215–217
Innocation, Science and Economic Development Canada, Office
    of Consumer Affairs (OCA), 333
input and output data, computers, 130, 134
institutions, alphabetic filing rules for, 224
integrating application software, 137
integrity, 23
intelligentediting.com, 313
Intelligent Office, 126
Interactive Voice Response (IVR), 106
interconnect equipment, 138
interface, 200
internal commands, 130
internal memory, computers, 130–131
internal reports, short, 300
International Air Transportation Association (IATA), 237
International Association of Administrative Professionals
    (IAAP), 376, 377, 384
international business
    diversity in, 40–43
    hosting international visitors, 43–44
    interpersonal communication in, 40–41
    management of international client relations, 41–42
    time management perception, 40
    working in foreign country, 42–43
international calls, 112
international clients, 41–42
international conferences, 274
international currency exchange, 330
international employment, 367–369
international holidays, 187
international letters, 310–311
international mail, 172, 175
International Organization for Standardization (ISO), 229, 233
international teamwork, 42
international travel, culture and, 247–248
international visitors, hosting, 43–44
Internet
    See also e-mail
    airline reservations on, 240
    benefits, 146
    business messaging platforms, 162
    cable modem connection to, 148
    change with, 26
    computers connecting to, 131
    content management systems, 146–149
    DSL connection to, 148
    Electronic Post Office and, 165
    encryption software and, 155
    etiquette for, 162
    fibre optic cable for, 148

Internet (*Continued*)
  firewall and, 155
  job search boards and search engines, 339
  networking on, 139
  podcasting and, 151
  professional setting usage, 151–152
  for reference sources, 75, 84
  satellite connection to, 148
  search engines for, 148–149
  security on, 154–155, 157
  sign on to, 129
  terminology for, 152
  uses for, 139–140
  web, 272–274
  webcasting and, 140, 151
  web conferencing and, 140, 150–151
  webinar and, 151
  Wi-Fi connection to, 148
internet service provider (ISP), 147
interpersonal communication, 279
  in international business, 40–41
interpersonal skills, 16
  developing, 16–22
interruptions
  managing, 61
  of meetings, 118
interviews. *See* job interviews
intranet, 148, 160
introduction, for formal reports, 307
introductions, office visitors and, 117
ISO. *See* International Organization for Standardization
itinerary, 244–246
IVR. *See* Interactive Voice Response

J

jet lag, 238
job acceptance, 366, 367
job applications
  acceptance of, 366, 367
  application/cover letters for, 354–357
  follow-up correspondence for, 364–366
  forms for, 357–358
  interviews for, 358–366
  letter of inquiry and, 366
  preparing portfolios for, 360
  prospecting letter for, 354–356
  refusal of, 366, 368
  reminders for, 365–366
  résumés for, 341–354
  short list for, 352
  solicited letter for, 354
  thank-you letters for, 364–365
jobbank.gc.ca/home, 372
job fairs, 338
job interviews
  appearance for, 360–361
  approach to, 362–363
  attire for, 361
  behavioural descriptive, 363

on campus, 363
closing, 364
ethics and questions in, 359
follow-up correspondence for, 364–366
intelligent questions in, 360
items to bring to, 362
learning from, 364
opportunities of, 358
preparation for, 358–360
punctuality for, 361
purpose of, 358
questions anticipated for, 359
research for, 358–359
salary and, 363
second, 364
testing and, 363
job prospects
  college placement office and, 338
  direct application for, 338
  ethical issues in search for, 366, 367
  federal government information for, 339
  hidden, 339
  on Internet, 339
  job fairs for, 338
  job search boards, 339
  job search engine, 339
  networking and, 336, 338
  in other geographic areas, 339–340
  staffing agencies for, 339
job refusal, 366, 368
jobsdb.com, 372
job search boards, 339
job search engine, 339
job sharing, 65
jobstreet.com, 372

K

keyboard, 130
kilobyte, 133
know-it-alls, 19
KPMG Enterprise, 315

L

labels, 212–213
lack of direction, 18
landscaped office, 91
language barriers, visitors with, 120–121
LANs. *See* local area networks
laptop computers, 129, 261–262
Law Society of Upper Canada, 234
leadership, 20
  and management, 49–50
learning job, 53–54
lesbian, gay, bisexual, and transgender identified
      (LGBTQ), 35
lettermail, 172
letter of inquiry, 366
letter of transmittal, for formal reports, 309
letter reports, 299–300

letters. *See* business letters
libraries support and assistance
   research database, 75
   search engines, 75–76
   website content evaluation, 76
lighting, 93
line-and-staff organization, 88
line authority, 87
line organization, 87
listening, communication and, 282
list of tables, in formal reports, 306
Live Meeting, 150
local area networks (LANs), 131
local calls, 109
long-distance calls
   domestic, 109–112
   international, 112
long-distance directory assistance, 110–111
low-volume copiers, 140
lunch, business, 29–30

M

magazines, 47
mail
   See also addressing mail; incomingmail; mail services and
     delivery; outgoing mail
   cancelling, 185
   computerized postage machine for, 185
   international holidays and, 187
   merge, 135
   metered, 185
   refusing, 186
   returning undelivered, 186
   supplemental services for, 174–175
   unsolicited, 186
Mail-Expected record, 169
mail services and delivery
   See also addressing mail; e-mail; incoming mail; outgoing mail
   airline services for, 176
   bus express for, 176
   business messaging platforms, 162
   courier services for, 176
   CP electronic services, 163–165
   electronic money transfer, 163
   Electronic Post Office, 165
   freight shipments for, 176
   international holidays and, 187
   VM, 104–109, 139, 165
mainframe computer, 129
Major Projects Management Office, 202
makeuseof.com, 333
malware, 153
manage by example (MBE), 195
management
   See also project management; time management
   adapting to new, 26–27
   demands from, 54–55
   detail, 57–58
   environmental, 66

five functions, 50
   of international client relations, 41–42
   leadership and, 49–50
   process, 50
   styles, 89–90
   team problem-solving approach for, 51
   theory, 50
   total quality management, 50–51
management by objectives (MBO), 52
Management Help, 70
manage people, personalities, 18–19
managers
   absence of, explaining, 107
   absence of, incoming mail answered in, 171–172
   absence of, working during, 246–247
   business letters for signature of, 293
   office, 379–380
   one manager, advantages and disadvantages of, 56
   project, 194–195
   return of, 247
   special instructions by, 246
   supervisors, 91, 378–380
manual charge-out systems, 209
margins, in formal reports, 302
markups, 339
mashup, 152
matrix organizational structure, 86
maximum working area, 63
MBE. *See* manage by example
McAfee software, 157
McInnis, Vanessa, 160
medical records, electronic, 217
meetings
   See also team meetings
   action checklist for, 256–257
   adjournment of, 262
   agenda for, 254, 258–260, 266
   behavioural solutions for, 271–272
   beverages for, 260
   body language in, 270
   vs. conference, 254
   dynamics of, 270–272
   ethics in, 273–274
   executives scheduling, 257
   following up on, 262
   food for, 260–261
   formal, 259, 263, 265
   informal, 259–260, 263
   interrupting, 118
   materials assembled for, 261
   minutes for, 256, 262–265
   note-taking for, 262
   notices for, 258
   participation in, 271
   preparation for, 271
   punctuality for, 270–271
   recording, 261–262
   reserving room for, 257–258
   responsibilities with, 256

meetings (*Continued*)
Robert's Rules of Order for, 78
rudeness in, 271
scheduling, 257
seating plan, 255
supplies, equipment, software for, 260
terminating, 118
venue for, 254
virtual, 272–273
websites for, 277
meetingsmeanbusiness.ca, 277
megabytes, 133
memory, computers, 130–131
memory keys, 131
mental filter, 41
mentors, 338, 374–376, 384
mergers, 26, 340
metered mail, 185
metric, 55
microprocessor chip, 130
Microsoft Office Specialist Certification (MOS), 378, 384
Microsoft Office Tools, 144
Microsoft Outlook, 214
Microsoft Project, 198
microsoft teams, 162
Microsoft Word, 352
mid-volume copiers, 140–141
mind tools, 98
mindtools.com, 70
minor words, alphabetic filing rules for, 220–221
minutes, for meetings, 256, 262–265
miscellaneous folders, 218
mixed office layout, 92
MLA style, 80
MNP, 88
mobile apps, 199
mobile banking, 317
mobile devices, 129, 152
modem, 148
modified-block letter style, 298
modular furniture, 93
MoneyGram, 163
money orders, 319
monitors, 130
monster.ca, 372
Moody's services, 77
MOS. *See* Microsoft Office Specialist Certification
motivation, 196
mouse, 130
mousetrapping, 154
mousing, 95
MSDs. *See* musculoskeletal disorders
musculoskeletal disorders (MSDs), 94
Musgrove, Sheila, 342

N

NALS, 377–378, 384
names, filing
abbreviations, 221–222
basic alphabetic rules for, 220
government names, 225–226
identical names, 224–225
people, 220
punctuation of, 221
single letters, 221–222
suffixes, 222
titles, 222
negotiating, effective, 20
netcasting, 140, 151
networks, 148, 336, 338
computer, 131–132
newspaper indexes, 78
newspapers, 47
NGT. *See* Nominal Group Technique
no-frills flights, 240
Nominal Group Technique (NGT), 268–269
non-address data, 178
nonessential records, 216
nonstop flight, 238
nontraditional work arrangements, 65–66
nonverbal communication, 280–282
normal working area, 63
Norton antivirus software, 157
notebook computers, 129
note-taking, for meetings, 262
notices of delay, 295
notices of meeting, 258
numbers, alphabetic filing rules for, 223
numeric filing system, 218, 227–229

O

office commerce
ATM for, 316, 317
bank drafts for, 319
bank reconciliation for, 323–325
budget preparation for, 328, 330
cancelled cheques and, 325
cash withdrawals for, 321
certified cheques for, 318–319
cheques writing for, 319–321
departments for handling, 315
deposits and, 321–323
direct payroll deposit for, 317
e-commerce, 171, 316
EFT and, 315
endorsing cheques for, 321
ethics in accounting and, 330
fraud and, 326
international currency exchange and, 330
mobile banking for, 317
money orders for, 319
non-electronic transfers for, 318–319
payroll processing for, 327–328
petty cash and, 325–327
preauthorized payments for, 317–318
record keeping for, 325–328
stop-payment notification and, 320–321
supplies for, 328

web-banking for, 317
websites for, 333
office layout
closed office, 91
decor, 92
high-tech office, 92
mixed layout, 92
open office, 91–92
workspace, 91
workstation design, 92
office managers, 379–380
office manuals, 81–82
Office of the Privacy Commissioner of Canada, 333
office politics, 24, 32
office romance, 31
office supplies, organization of, 63–64
Office Team, 335
office technology
See also computers; Internet
application programs, 130, 135–138
business messaging platforms, 162
copiers, 140–141
CP electronic services, 163–165
phone, 138–139
purposes of, 128
reprographics, 140–141
telephone, 129
offset printing, 140
online, 131
open office layout, 91–92
open-shelf filing, 211
open tickets, 239
operating system, 130
operator-assisted dialling, 110
organization
of calendars, 64
of office supplies, 63–64
recycling program, 66
of workstation, 64–65
Organizational behaviour (OB), 14
organizational climate, 13
organizational culture, 13
organizational linkage, 90
organization chart, 89, 90
organizations, alphabetic filing rules, 224
organization structure
authority classifications for, 87–89
building blocks, 87–89
contemporary, 86
divisional structure, 86
flat, 86
functional, 86
functional authority for, 88–89
informal, 90–91
line authority for, 87
management styles, 89–90
matrix, 86
organization chart, 90
staff authority for, 87

traditional, 86
typical departmental, 87
orientation, 53
out folder, 209
outgoing mail
admail in, 172
Advice of Receipt for, 174
airline services for, 176
bus express for, 176
COD for, 175
courier services for, 176
CP automated inquiry system for, 174
CP services for, 172–185
dangerous goods and, 175
domestic mail and, 172–175
freight shipments for, 176
international mail and, 172, 175
lettermail in, 172
parcels in, 172–173
Priority Courier service for, 174
publications mail in, 172
registered mail in, 174
returning undelivered mail, 186
return to sender for, 175
sizes for, 173
supplemental services for, 174–175
USA mail and, 172, 175
Xpresspost service for, 174
out guide, 209
output, 130

P

PA. *See* project assistant
packages, 168–169
page-jacking, 154
page numbers, in formal reports, 303
paper calendars, 115
paper records retention, 215–216
paper records transfe, 216–217
paragraph indention, for formal reports, 302
parcels, 172–173
participatory management, 89
Passport Canada, 47
passports, 238, 242, 252
passwords, 154
payroll processing, 327–328
PC Magazine, 144
PCs. *See* personal computers
PC Webopedia, 144
pen drives, 131, 210
people, alphabetic filing rules
for names of, 220
per diem rate, 245
periodical indexes, 78
periodic transfer, 217
peripherals, 128
perpetual transfer, 217
personalbest.com, 32
personal computers (PCs), 129

Personal Information Protection and Electronic Documents Act (PIPEDA), 172, 190, 205, 316, 333
personality, 18
    tests, 363
personal mail, 166
personal preference, 89
personal qualities, 15, 22–24
personal space, communication and, 281
persuasive letters, 292–293
petty cash, 325–327
PgMP. *See* Program Management Professional
pharming, 154
phishing, 153
phone communication skills
    listen actively, 104
    speak clearly, 103
    use correct pronunciation and grammar, 103–104
phone messages, 139
phone tag, 105
physical appearance, 280–281, 360–361
Pilon, Stephanie, 15
PIPEDA. *See* Personal Information Protection and Electronic Documents Act
plagiarism
    common knowledge and, 79–80
    cut and paste and, 81
    defined, 79
    recognition and avoidance of, 79–80
    referencing styles and, 80
planning, 56–57
PMI. *See* Project Management Institute
PMI Agile Certified Practitioner (PMI-ACP), 197
PMI Professional in Business Analysis (PMIPBA), 197
PMI Risk Management Professional (PMI-RMP), 197
PMI Scheduling Professional (PMI-SP), 197–198
PMP. *See* Project Management Professional
podcasting, 151
poise, 23
political networks, 24
polycom.com, 157
Portfolio Management Professional (PfMP), 197
portfolios, 360
positioning of equipment, 94–95
postal codes, 181
posture
    communication and, 281
    ergonomics and, 94
preauthorized payments, 317–318
prefixes, alphabetic filing rules for, 223
preparation, advanced, 60–61
presentation software, 137
primary guides, 218
primary sources, 82
printer, 130
priorities, 54–56
Priority Courier service, 174
privacy
    e-commerce and, 316
    e-mail, 171–172, 186–187

legislation, 205, 233
    of personal relationships, 28–29
Privacy Act, 205
private libraries, 75
private mail, 166
processing, 130
procrastination, avoiding, 59, 380
professional associations, 377–378, 384
professional development
    advancement preparation for, 374
    contemporary office professional and, 380
    continuing, 380–381
    cross-training for, 378
    education for, 376–378
    ethics and, 381
    image for, 374
    mentors for, 338, 374–376, 384
    professional associations for, 377–378, 384
    starting, 380–381
    stereotypes, 374–375
    technical certification and, 378
professional image, 374
professionalism, 23
Program Management Professional (PgMP), 197
project assistant (PA), 192, 195
projectconnections.com, 202
project management
    certifications and credentials for, 196–198
    defining, 192
    PAs in, 195
    phases of, 192–194
    problem solving and decision making with, 199
    project managers for, 194–195
    software and apps for, 198–199
    team for, 194–198
    terms for, 197
    tools for, 198–199
    websites for, 202
Project Management Institute (PMI), 192, 196, 202
Project Management Professional (PMP), 197
project managers, 194–195
project team, 196
    members, 267
prospecting letter, 354–356
psychometrics.com, 384
publications mail, 169, 172
public libraries, 75
public speaking, 283–284
punctuality
    for job interviews, 361
    in meetings, 270–271
punctuation, alphabetic filing rules for, 221
Purolator, 190

Q

QAA. *See* Qualified Administrative Assistant
QR Code. *See* Quick Response Code
Qualified Administrative Assistant (QAA), 377
qualitative research, 73

quality assurance, 194
quality control, 194
quantitative research, 73
quarrelling, 18
Quebec Pension Plan, 328
Quick Response Code (QR Code), 150
Quill & Quire, 76
quotations, for formal reports, 304
quotation sources, 77–78

R

race, 35
random-access memory (RAM), 130
raw data, 135
RBC Financial Group, 333
Readers' Guide, 78
read-only memory (ROM), 130–131
reception. *See* front-line reception
recession, 376
record disposal, 217
recorder, for team meeting, 267
recording meetings, 261–262
record keeping, 325–328
record, life cycle of, 215
record retention, 215–217
records, 133
records management, 229
record transfer, 215–217
recycled or recyclable materials, 66
recycling program, 66
redundancy, 340
refdesk.com, 84
references, formal reports, 305–306
reference sources
    almanacs as, 76
    atlases as, 76–77
    biographical information as, 77
    books in print for, 76
    dictionaries as, 76–77
    directories for, 79
    encyclopedias as, 76–77
    etiquette books as, 77–78
    financial information for, 77
    gazetteer for, 77
    Internet for, 75, 84
    libraries support and assistance, 74–75
    newspaper indexes as, 78
    new technology for, 73
    office manuals as, 81–82
    periodical indexes as, 78
    placement of, 65
    quick, 76–79
    quotation sources as, quotation sources
    research database, 75
    yearbooks as, 76
references, résumés, 350–351
referencing styles, 80
refusing appointments, 118–119
refusing mail, 186

registered mail, 174
relative index, 227, 228
relaxation, 59–60
religious diversity, 35
reluctant team members, 18
reminder letters, 365–366
removable storage, 131, 210
repetitive strain injury (RSI), 92
replies, letters, 290, 291, 294
reports
    See also formal reports
    analytical, 298–299
    chronological, 310
    classification of, 298–299
    e-mail, 300–301
    informal, 299–301
    informational, 298
    letter, 299–300
    short internal, 300
    websites for, 313
reprographics, 140–141
Research and development (R&D), 72–73
research database, 75
resources, ethics and, 25–26
responsibility, 22
restrictive endorsements, 321
résumés
    appearance of, 350, 352
    checklist for, 352–354
    chronological, 344–346
    combination, 344, 348–349
    community involvement/volunteer work, 343
    competitive, 342
    dos and don'ts for, 344
    education section in, 342
    electronically scanned, 352, 353
    electronically submitted, 352
    e-mailing, 352
    functional, 344, 347
    keys to, 341
    professional associations, 343
    references for, 350–351
    rules for writing, 341
    skills in, 343–344
    styles of, 341, 344
    training and certification, 343
    work experience in, 343
retaining records, 215–217
return address, 185
returning undelivered mail, 186
return to sender, 175
rightsizing, 340, 376
Robert's Rules of Order, 78
ROM. *See* read-only memory
romance, office, 31
routers, 139
routine replies, 294
routine requests, 294
routing slips, 169, 171

RSI. *See* repetitive strain injury
RSS, 152
rudeness, in meetings, 271

S

salary, job interviews and, 363
satellite Internet connection, 148
Scannable Résumé, 352
scanner, 130
Scheewe, Nathan, 279
Scotiabank, 333
Scott's Directories, 79
screening calls, 108
search engines, 75–76, 148–149
secondary sources, 73
11-Second Skim Test, 342, 343
security
    data, 152–155
    Internet and, 157
    travel, 243–244
self-esteem, 23
self-management, 23
self-starters, 22, 52
sexual orientation/gender identity, 35
SharePoint, 150
short internal reports, 300
sign on, 129
similar tasks, grouping, 58–59
single letters, alphabetic filing rules for, 221–222
slack, 162
SlideShare, 150, 157
smartphones, 129
snap admail, 172
sociability, 22
socializing at work, 52
social media, 150
social networking, 139
social skills
    for business lunch, 29–30
    for personal relationship privacy, 28–29
soft skills, 15
software, 128
solicited letter, 354
solicitors, 118
sorting for filing, 208–209
spacing, in formal reports, 302
spam, 153, 205
spam filtering software, 153
span of control, 87
special guides, 218
special needs visitors, 121–122
speculation, 107
speculative transferring of calls, 107–108
speeches, 283–284
spreadsheets, 132, 136
staff authority, 87
staffing agencies, 339
staff visitors, 117–118

Standard & Poor's, 77
Staunton, Tracy, 204
stereotypes, 37, 374
stop-payment notification, 320–321
storage area network (SAN), 131
storage, computer, 131, 134–135
storage of information
    for business contacts, 214
    for electronic databases, 214–215
    for electronic media, 214
    filing cabinets, 213
    removable storage media for, 131, 210
    vertical filing cabinet for, 213
    for visible document, 213–214
    wire organizer for, 214
street directions, 178
street types and symbols, 179–181
stress management
    causes of stress, 27
    suggestions for, 27–28
    website for, 32
    wellness in workplace, 27
subject filing system, 218, 226–227
subject headings, for formal reports, 302–303
subject line, 299
subscription database, 74
suffixes, alphabetic filing rules for, 222
supercomputers, 128–129
supervisors, 91, 378–380
supplemental mail services, 174–175
supply chain, 90
suspension folders, 212
symbols, alphabetic filing rules for, 220–221
symmetric digital subscriber lines
    (SDSLs), 148
synopsis, 305

T

table of contents, in formal
    reports, 305
tables, in formal reports, 303–304
tablet computers, 129
task completion, 61
task lighting, 93
TD Canada Trust, 333
teaching other, 19
team leader, 267
team meetings, 265
    agenda for, 266
    brainstorming in, 268
    closure for, 269–270
    debriefing in, 270
    discussion and solution in, 269
    ground rules for, 268
    NGT for, 268–269
    participant roles in, 266–267
    preparing, 265–266
    productive start to, 267–268

team problem-solving approach, 51
teamwork
    ground rules for, 17
    human relations and, 16–18
    international, 42
    nonproductive team behaviours, 18
    productive behaviour for, 16–18
    total quality management, 50–51
technical certification, 196–198, 378
technical skills, 14
technology, 128
    See also office technology; telephone technology and equipment
telecommunications, 103
teleconferences, 108–109, 272, 273
telephone directories, 79, 109
telephone messages, 107
telephone technology and equipment, 112
    answering services, 139
    automatic recording machines, 139
    call management services, 138
    interconnect equipment, 138
    IVR, 106
    smartphones, 129
    VM, 139, 165
    wireless telephones, 138–139
telephone use
    additional reception tools, 103–112
    appointments by, 113
    automatic answering service and, 106
    conference calling in, 108–109, 272, 273
    courtesy in, 106–107
    distributing messages with, 108
    domestic long-distance calls and, 109–112
    etiquette for, 126
    international calls and, 112
    local calls and, 109
    mobile banking and, 317
    phone communication skills, 103–104
    screening calls and, 108
    taking messages in, 107, 139
    telephone directories for, 79, 109
    transferring calls for, 107–108
    VM and, 104–109
terabytes, 133
terminating meetings, 118
thank-you letters, 364–365
thebalancecareers.com, 313
thephonelady.com, 144
thinking time, 54
third-party providers, 153
tickets, checking, 244
time distribution chart, 55
time, ethics and, 25–26
time management, 52–63
    advanced preparation for, 60–61
    completing tasks for, 61
    daily plan for, 62–63
    defining, 52

detail management and, 57–58
difficult tasks first for, 58
doing it right on first try for, 60
elements of, 52
flexible planning for, 56–57
flextime and, 53, 65
grouping similar tasks for, 58–59
interruptions and, 61
learning job, 53–54
one task at a time for, 58
perception, 40
priorities assigned for, 54–56
procrastination avoided for, 59, 380
relaxation and, 59–60
thinking time for, 54
website for, 70
work area efficiency for, 58, 63
time-sharing, 131
time wasters, 52
time zones, 111–112
title page, in formal reports, 305
titles, alphabetic filing rules for, 222
to do list, 57
total quality management (TQM), 50–51
traffic (website), 152
transferring calls, 107–108
transferring records, 215–217
transmittal sheet for fax, 163, 164
travel agencies, 237
travel arrangements
    air travel for, 238–241
    business cards for, 246
    car rental services and, 241
    carry-on luggage and, 243
    credit cards and, 244
    culture and international, 247–248
    digital travel services, 237
    ePassport, 242
    ethics with expenses and, 247–248
    etiquette and, 252
    hotel reservations and, 241–242
    immunization requirements for, 243
    itinerary for, 244–246
    manager's absence and, 246–247
    manager's return and, 247
    passports and, 238, 242, 252
    per diem rate for, 245
    phases of, 236
    questions to ask for, 236–237
    security and, 243–244
    special instructions, 246
    tickets for, 244
    travel agencies for, 237
    travel consultants for, 237
    travel expense voucher and, 245
    travel fund advance for, 244
    trip information needed for, 236–238
    trip planning and, 236–238

travel arrangements (*Continued*)
  visas and, 238, 242–243
  websites for, 252
travel consultants, 237
travel expense voucher, 245
travel fund advance, 244
travel.gc.ca, 252
Travel Masters, 236
travelocity.ca, 252
Treasury Board of Canada Secretariat, 252
trending, 152
trip planning, 236–238
trojan horses, 153
trust, 18
24-hour clock, 240
Twitter, 255

U

UCG. *See* user generated content
UCLA ergonomics, 98
unabridged dictionaries, 76
uncluttered desks, 64
undelivered mail, 186
unethical behaviour, 247
unit designators, 178
unit identifiers, 178
units, in alphabetic filing rules, 219
universal serial bus (USB), 131
unsolicited mail, 186
unwanted visitors, 119
UPS, 190
USA mail, 172, 175
useful records, 216
user generated content (UCG), 150

V

value chain, 90
VDT. *See* video display terminal
venue for meetings, 254
verbal communication, 279–280
verbatim record, 261
versatile computer, 132
vertical filing cabinet, 213
video conferencing (VC), 150–151, 255, 257, 272–273
video display terminal (VDT), 130
viral, 152
virtual assistants, 377
virtual meetings, 132, 272–273
virtual network, 139
virtual offices, 95
virtual receptionists (VRs), 101–102
virtualreferencelibrary.ca, 84
viruses, computer, 153
visas, 238, 242–243
visible filing, 206–209, 211–213
visitor management systems, 102–103
visitors. *See* greeting office visitors
Visual Résumé, 352

vital records, 216
vitalrecordsprotection.org, 233
voice mail (VM), 104–109, 139, 165
voice over internet protocol (VoIP), 151
voice-recognition software, 135
voice recorders, 261
voucher cheques, 319
VRs. *See* virtual receptionists

W

WAN. *See* wide area network
Web 1.0, 2.0, and 3.0, 149–150
web applications, 149–152
web-banking, 317
web-based software, 199
webcasting, 140, 151
web conferencing, 140, 150–151, 272–274
web-enabled devices, 131
webinar, 151
website, 146
website content evaluation, 76
website content management system (WCMS), 146, 147
Website Site Advisor, 155
web tools, 150
wellness in workplace, 27
Western Union, 163, 190
Whitaker's Books in Print, 76
white noise, 94
WHO. *See* World Health Organization
wide area network (WAN), 131
Wi-Fi. *See* wireless fidelity
wikis, 150
Windows, 130
wireless fidelity (Wi-Fi), 148
wireless local area networks (WLAN), 131–132
wireless phones, 138–139
wire organizer, 214
word processing, 135–136
work area efficiency, 58, 63
work, ethics and, 25–26
working environment
  change in, 26
workopolis.com, 372
workplace ethics. *See* ethics
workplace protections, 38
workplaces, nontraditional, 65–66
workspaces, 91
work specialization, 87
workstation
  defined, 92
  ergonomic issues, 98
  for front-line reception, 116
  maximum working area, 63
  normal working area, 63
  organization of, 64–65
  organizing necessary items for, 64–65
  purging unnecessary items for, 64
  uncluttered desks in, 64

workstation computers (PCs), 129
workstation design office, 92
WorldCat, 75
World Catalogue Mobile App, 84
World Clock, 126
World Health Organization (WHO), 243, 252
World Organization, 70
World Time Server, 252
WorldWeb travel guide, 252
worms, 153
written communication, 285
    See also business letters

X
Xpresspost service, 174

Y
yearbooks, 76
Yellow Pages, 109

Z
zero-plus dialling, 110
zero zone, 111